Fodor's 94 New York City

Fodor's Travel Publications, Inc.
New York • Toronto • London • Sydney • Auckland

Copyright © 1993
by Fodor's Travel Publications, Inc.

ISBN 0-679-02533-2

Grateful acknowledgement is made to the following for permission to reprint previously published material: Sterling Lord Literistic, Inc.: Excerpt from *New York Proclaimed,* by V.S. Pritchett. Copyright © 1965 by V.S. Pritchett. Reprinted by permission of Sterling Lord Literistic, Inc.

"What Makes New Yorkers Tick," by Calvin Trillin. Copyright © 1990 by Calvin Trillin. Originally appeared in *Time.* Reprinted by permission.

Fodor's New York City

Editor: David Low
Contributors: Michael Adams, Laura Broadwell, Karen Cure, Peter Filichia, Theodore Fischer, Jane Hershey, Holly Hughes, Ann LaForge, John Mariani, Peter D. Meltzer, Denise Lewis Patrick, Marcy Pritchard, Linda K. Schmidt, Kate Sekules, Susan Spano Wells, Terry Trucco
Creative Director: Fabrizio La Rocca
Cartographer: David Lindroth
Illustrator: Karl Tanner
Cover Photograph: Francesco Ruggeri
Design: Vignelli Associates

Special Sales

MANUFACTURED IN THE UNITED STATES OF AMERICA
10 9 8 7 6 5 4 3 2 1

Contents

3 Exploring Manhattan 41

4 Exploring the Other Boroughs 138

5 Exploring New York City with Children 163

6 Sightseeing Checklists 175

7 Sports, Fitness, Beaches 184

8 Shopping 194

Maps and Charts

Foreword

While every care has been taken to ensure the accuracy of the information in this guide, the passage of time will always bring change, and consequently, the publisher cannot accept responsibility for errors that may occur.

All prices and opening times quoted here are based on information supplied to us at press time. Hours and admission fees may change, however, and the prudent traveler will avoid inconvenience by calling ahead.

Fodor's wants to hear about your travel experiences, both pleasant and unpleasant. When a hotel or restaurant fails to live up to its billing, let us know and we will investigate the complaint and revise our entries where the facts warrant it.

Send your letters to the editors of Fodor's Travel Publications, 201 E. 50th Street, New York, NY 10022.

Highlights'94 and Fodor's Choice

Highlights '94

For New Yorkers, 1993 began on a somber note with the February bombing of the **World Trade Center,** attributed to terrorists. The bombing proved fatal to six people, injured some 1,000, and caused considerable damage to the immediate area. However, many New Yorkers watching the news coverage of the incident were amazed that the evacuation of citizens from the building didn't turn into chaos. Most of these citizens had to endure hours of descending smoky, badly lit stairs to get out of the complex, and they handled the situation with courage and patience, as did the people who rushed to their aid. As this edition went to press, operations at the World Trade Center had returned to normal, and most of the tenants had moved in again. Of course, security at the complex has been tightened since the incident, and police are highly visible in the area. The **New York Vista Hotel** part of the Trade Center complex, planned to reopen by October 1993, with the completion of major renovations that were begun before the bombing.

On the museum front, the **Liberty Science Center,** the first world-class science museum in the New York metropolitan area, opened its doors in January 1993 at Liberty State Park, New Jersey, a short drive from downtown Manhattan. The impressive four-floor center encompasses more than 60,000 square feet of exhibition space, with more than 250 interactive exhibits concentrating on three themes—environment, health, and invention. The museum also claims the world largest OMNIMAX theater, featuring an eight-story domed screen and the largest film format in motion-picture history.

In Soho the **Museum for African Art** opened on lower Broadway in February 1993. The museum displays traditional and contemporary African art in a handsome, two-story space designed by Maya Lin, architect of Washington, D.C.'s Vietnam Veterans Memorial. On Soho's Spring Street the **Children's Museum of the Arts** has found a new loftlike home, where kids ages 18 months to 10 years experience the visual and performing arts.

Uptown, in April 1993, the **American Museum of Natural History** (Central Park West at 79th St.) unveiled its Hall of Human Biology and Evolution, which explores the workings of the human body and features a computerized archaeological dig and an electronic newspaper about human evolution. In June 1993 the **Jewish Museum** (Fifth Ave. at 92nd St.) opened in expanded and renovated facilities. The 1908 mansion's facade was extended, so the museum front now resembles a late–French Gothic château. Inside, where museum space has been doubled, the permanent two-floor exhibition traces the development of Jewish culture and identity over 4,000 years. On a sadder note, in early 1993 the **New-York Historical Society** closed its galleries due to lack of funding.

Takashimaya New York, a branch of Japan's largest department-store chain, finally opened its doors on Fifth Avenue (between 54th and 55th Sts.) in April 1993. The pristine store carries clothes for women and men and household items that incorporate design styles from East and West. A garden atrium and a two-floor art gallery contribute to the store's elegant ambience.

The city's most popular new dance spot is **Club USA,** owned by Peter Gatien, who also controls Limelight, the Palladium, and the Tunnel; the new club is a five-story wonder housed in a former burlesque theater, with room for 2,000 frenetic dancers.

On the restaurant scene the hot new arrivals continue to be moderately priced bistros and their equivalent. **Vong** is an exotic Thai-French restaurant spawned by talented chef Jean-Georges Vongerichten, whose uptown bistro, Jojo, remains a tough reservation to snare. **Becco,** an appealing Italian trattoria owned by Lidia Bastianich (of Felidia fame) and her son Joseph, and **Brasserie des Théâtres** (the latest spin-off of the Park Bistro and Les Halles group) breathe new life into the Theater District. Meanwhile, crowd-pleasing scenes such as **Steak Frites** and **West Broadway** have made downtown dining an even more popular pastime. For fun food with a live beat, consider two fashionable entrants, **Banana Café** and **Lola Belle.** See Chapter 9 for more on these restaurants.

You may still find a good **lunch deal** at some of the city's most posh restaurants. Several high-price establishments that offered $19.92 lunch specials during the 1992 Democratic convention found that business increased so much that they kept a low daytime price in 1993, so it pays to watch for special lunch menus at those great restaurants you might have thought you could never afford.

Several Manhattan hotels have changed their names or owners (for more on New York City lodging, *see* Chapter 10). The former Regent of New York (on 57th Street between Park and Madison avenues) became **The Four Seasons New York.** This I.M. Pei–designed lodging with 367 rooms (in the Very Expensive price category) was due, at press time, to open in spring 1993. Among the outstanding claims made by the owners was that the hotel's bathtubs would fill completely in 60 seconds. The property features a semiformal restaurant, a bar, a lobby lounge, and a spa, along with a business center and ample meeting areas.

Another fancy newcomer is **The Michelangelo** (on the corner of 51st Street and Seventh Avenue), a former Grand Bay and Parc Fifty-One property that has now been taken over by the Italian Starhotels group. The 178-room lodging (in the Very Expensive price category) features elegant guest rooms, a fitness room, and a close relationship with the Bellini by Cipriani restaurant.

The Hotel Maria (on Lafayette and Howard streets, near Canal Street) has become the **Holiday Inn Downtown.** This moderately priced, 220-room hotel will continue to have an Asian accent, in keeping with its Hong Kong–style restaurant. Soho's other eagerly awaited lodging, the 78-room **Mercer Hotel** at Mercer and Prince streets, should open during 1994. At press time the hotel had plans for a restaurant managed by Karen and David Waltuck of Chanterelle fame. A welcome addition to Lower Manhattan is the **Best Western Seaport Inn,** steps from South Street Seaport.

Another name change comes to the Times Square area as the **Ramada Renaissance** drops the parent company's name from its logo. This 315-room hotel (in the Expensive price category) is attractive but perhaps not as well run as it should be, given its room prices. Rooms with their own fax machines and baths have sophisticated decor. At press time the fitness center was still rather bare-bones, and meeting space seemed limited for a business-oriented lodging. Still, the hotel's outside neon is a welcome addition, and the management seems anxious to improve any lags in its service.

The **Fitzpatrick** (at Lexington Avenue and 56th Street) is a bustling Irish newcomer whose highly affordable suites and friendly service make it a popular celebrity-and-business stop. The 92-room hotel has rooms whose amenities equal or surpass those of far more expensive places.

The **Hotel Tudor** (at 42nd Street and Second Avenue), a once-popular budget property, has been completely refurbished with attractive room decor and luxurious baths; it now fits in the lower end of the Expensive price category. The new owners, Sarova Hotels, have added a fitness center and an appealing restaurant-bar complex in the lobby.

Finally, the **Sutton** (on East 56th Street near First Avenue) is a relatively new high-price hotel aimed at the long-term visitor; the minimum booking is 30 days. Full-service studios and apartments are done in elegant English-country style; there's also a restaurant and a 55-foot-long pool.

Fodor's Choice

No two people will agree on what makes a perfect vacation, but it's fun and helpful to know what others think. We hope you'll have a chance to experience some of Fodor's Choices yourself while visiting New York City. For detailed information about each entry, refer to the appropriate chapters within this guidebook.

Views

The lower Manhattan skyline, seen from the Brooklyn Heights Promenade

The vista of skyscrapers ringing Central Park, best viewed from the reservoir's northwest corner

A moonlit look at the harbor from the Staten Island Ferry

The sun setting over New Jersey and the lights of Manhattan snapping on one by one, from the World Trade Center's observation deck, 107 stories up

Architecture

The Woolworth Building, the Flatiron Building, the Empire State Building, and the World Trade Center's twin towers—each, in its time, the world's tallest building

The Chrysler Building, with its Art Deco chrome spire

The Dakota, grande dame of apartment buildings

The unbroken front of cast-iron beauties along Greene Street in SoHo

The graceful town houses along St. Luke's Place in the West Village

The Cathedral of St. John the Divine, an immense Gothic cathedral still abuilding

Museums

The Pierpont Morgan Library, and Morgan's personal library within

The newly restored dinosaur dioramas at the American Museum of Natural History

The American Wing's garden courtyard, among other delights at the Metropolitan Museum of Art

The restored and expanded Guggenheim Museum

The medieval Cloisters, especially its unicorn tapestries

Holidays and Seasonal Events

The lighting of the Christmas tree in Rockefeller Plaza

Cherry blossoms in bloom at the Brooklyn Botanical Garden

Late August when the Mets play at Shea and nearby the U. S. Open is held at Flushing Meadows

The Halloween parade in Greenwich Village

Giant balloons bobbing through the air in Macy's Thanksgiving Day Parade, on West 77th Street

Entertainment

The first preview of any new play—before the critics' verdict

Jazz into the wee hours at the Blue Note

Standing-room tickets for the Metropolitan Opera

Cabaret at the Algonquin, the Carlyle, or Rainbow & Stars

Viewing any movie at the Film Forum, the Angelika, the Walter Reade, or MoMA

Standing in line at the TKTS booth

Restaurants

The Four Seasons (*Very Expensive*)

Lutèce (*Very Expensive*)

La Caravelle (*Expensive*)

Smith & Wollensky (*Expensive*)

Jo Jo (*Moderate*)

Mesa Grill (*Moderate*)

Park Bistro (*Moderate*)

Union Square Café (*Moderate*)

E.J.'s Luncheonette (*Inexpensive*)

Mandarin Court (*Inexpensive*)

Shopping

Ralph Lauren's Polo store on the East Side

Zabar's, an outstanding food store and cultural institution

Barneys New York for men's and women's clothing

F.A.O. Schwarz, the ultimate toy store

Annex Antiques Fair and Flea Market, for everything from earrings to end tables

Hunting for used books at secondhand shops

The Margo Feiden Gallery, for a theatrical caricature by Al Hirschfeld

Hotels

The Carlyle (*Very Expensive*)

The Essex House (*Very Expensive*)

The Pierre (*Very Expensive*)

Holiday Inn Crowne Plaza (*Expensive*)

The United Nations Plaza (*Expensive*)

The Fitzpatrick (*Moderate–Expensive*)

Embassy Suites (*Moderate*)

The Paramount (*Inexpensive*)

Street Life

Crowds surging through Grand Central Terminal at rush hours, viewed from a balcony above the fray

The steps of the New York Public Library, weekdays at lunchtime

Lincoln Center's central plaza, just before an 8 PM concert.

Central Park's Mall, Bethesda Terrace, and Conservatory Water on weekend afternoons

Walking east to west on Bleeker Street on a weekend

Quintessentially New York

Browsing among the melon-squeezers on a Saturday morning at the Union Square Greenmarket.

Watching the frenzy on the floor of the New York Stock Exchange

Going to a deli restaurant for a pastrami-on-rye, garlic pickles, and an egg cream

Spotting celebrities—anywhere and everywhere

Buying the Sunday *New York Times* on Saturday night

Walking out of Shubert Alley onto 44th or 45th Street to gaze at the marquees

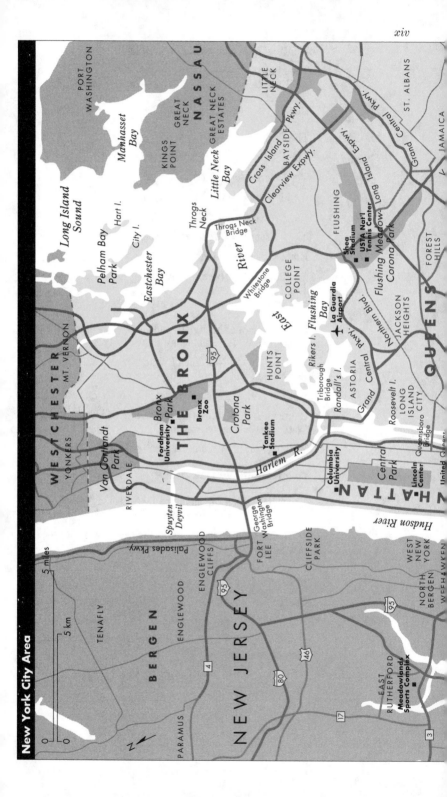

New York City Area

World Time Zones

Numbers below vertical bands relate each zone to Greenwich Mean Time (0 hrs.).
Local times frequently differ from these general indications,
as indicated by light-face numbers on map.

Algiers, **29**

Anchorage, **3**

Athens, **41**

Auckland, **1**

Baghdad, **46**

Bangkok, **50**

Beijing, **54**

Berlin, **34**

Bogotá, **19**

Budapest, **37**

Buenos Aires, **24**

Caracas, **22**

Chicago, **9**

Copenhagen, **33**

Dallas, **10**

Delhi, **48**

Denver, **8**

Djakarta, **53**

Dublin, **26**

Edmonton, **7**

Hong Kong, **56**

Honolulu, **2**

Istanbul, **40**

Jerusalem, **42**

Johannesburg, **44**

Lima, **20**

Lisbon, **28**

London (Greenwich), **27**

Los Angeles, **6**

Madrid, **38**

Manila, **57**

Introduction

*By Michael
Adams*

*Senior writer for
the business
travel magazine*
Successful
Meetings,
*Michael Adams
finally moved to
his hometown,
New York City,
12 years ago.*

In 1925, the youthful songwriting team of Richard Rodgers and Larry Hart wrote "Manhattan," arguably the loveliest city anthem ever. "We'll have Manhattan, the Bronx, and Staten Island, too," it promises, drawing its images from the merry scramble that was the city more than 60 years ago: "sweet pushcarts," "baloney on a roll," a subway that "charms," Brighton Beach, Coney Island, and the popular comedy *Abie's Irish Rose.* "We'll turn Manhattan into an isle of joy," coos the refrain.

Several decades later, in 1989, an album called simply *New York,* by aging enfant terrible rocker Lou Reed, views the same city with glasses fogged by despair and cynicism: Drugs, crime, racism, and promiscuity reign in what Reed considers to be a sinkhole of "crudity, cruelty of thought and sound." His voice brittle with weary irony, he sings, "This is no time for celebration." Manhattan's "sweet pushcarts" now apparently overflow with deadly vials of crack.

So, whom to believe—Lou or Larry?

The truth of the matter is slippery, for New York has long been a mosaic of grand contradictions, a city for which there has never been—nor ever will be—a clear consensus. Hart himself took the city to task in another song, "Give It Back to the Indians," whose lyrics count off a litany of problems that still exist: crime, dirt, high prices, traffic jams, and all-around urban chaos. Yet for all that, millions live here, grumbling but happy, and millions more visit, curious as cats to find out what the magnificent fuss is all about.

I was in eighth grade in suburban Detroit when I first really became aware of New York. A friend's Manhattan-born mother still subscribed to the Sunday *New York Times,* and at their house I'd pore over the "Arts and Leisure" section, as rapt as an archaeologist with a cave painting. The details of what I read there have blurred, but I remember vividly the sensation I felt while reading: a combined anticipation and nostalgia so keen it bordered on pain. Although I had never been there, I was homesick for New York.

It's my home now, yet I can still understand and appreciate the impulse that draws visitors here. In a city so ripe with possibilities, we are all more or less visitors.

I think of this on an uncharacteristically warm day in late March, as I and fellow New Yorkers escape from the hives of offices and homes to celebrate spring's first preview. We unbutton our jackets, leave buses a stop or two before our usual destinations, quicken our resolve to visit that new exhibit at the Met or jog around the Central Park Reservoir. A jubilant sense of renewal infects us all, and I overhear one happy fellow saying to a friend, "I felt just like a tourist yesterday."

Whenever I get the New York blues, the best tonic for me is to glimpse the city through the eyes of a visitor. One day, after subway construction had rerouted me well out of my usual path, I found myself in the grimy Times Square station—hardly the place for a spiritual conversion. As usual I had that armor of body language that we New Yorkers reflexively assume to protect ourselves from strangers bent on (1) ripping us off, (2) doing us bodily harm, (3) converting us, (4) making sexual advances, or (5) being general pains-in-the-butt just for the hell of it. But that day, tucked away in a corner, was a group of musicians—not an uncommon sight in New York—playing the guitar, organ, and accordion with gusto and good spirits behind a homemade sign that dubbed them the "Argentinian Tango Company." Like many street musicians in Manhattan, they were *good*, but I was only half listening, too intent on cursing the city. Just as I passed the band, however, I noticed four teenagers drawn to the music—visitors surely, they were far too open and trusting to be anything else. Grinning as widely as the Argentinians, they began to perform a spontaneous imitation of flamenco dancing—clapping hands above their heads, raising their heels, laughing at themselves, and only slightly self-conscious. Passersby, myself included, broke into smiles. As I made my way to the subway platform, buoyed by the impromptu show, I once again forgave New York. This minor piece of magic was apology enough.

I wonder whether that was the moment one of those teenagers happened to fall in love with the city. It *can* happen in a single moment, to a visitor or to a longtime resident. Perhaps it hits during a stroll through Riverside Park after a blanketing snowfall, when trees have turned to crystal and the city feels a hush it knows at no other time; or when you turn a corner and spy, beyond a phalanx of RVs and a tangle of cables and high-beam lights, the filming of a new movie.

That moment could also come when the house lights begin to dim at the Metropolitan Opera, and the gaudily sparkling chandeliers make their magisterial ascent to the ceiling; or when you first glimpse the magnificently bright Prometheus statue in Rockefeller Center, gleaming like a giant present under the annual Christmas tree as dozens of skaters cut swirls of seasonal colors on the ice below. You may even be smitten in that instant when, walking along the streets in the haze of a summer afternoon, you look up above the sea of anonymous faces to see—and be astonished by—the lofty rows of skyscrapers, splendid in their arrogance and power. At times like these it is perfectly permissible to stop for a moment, take a breath, and think, "Wow! *This is New York!*" We who live here do it every so often ourselves.

For some, of course, that special moment comes with a happy shock of recognition when they spot a street or building made familiar by movies or television, anything from *I Love Lucy* to *On the Waterfront*. At the Empire State Building, who can help but remember King Kong's pathetically courageous swing from its pinnacle? Or at the brooding Dakota, the chilling destiny created for Rosemary's baby within those fortresslike walls? In the mind's eye, Audrey Hepburn is eternally pairing diamonds and a doughnut as she wends her swank way down Fifth Avenue to have breakfast at Tiffany's. And the miniature park on Sutton Place will always be where Woody Allen and Diane Keaton began their angst-ridden *Manhattan* love affair, with the 59th Street bridge gleaming beyond and Gershwin music swelling in the background.

There's a moment of sudden magic when a New York stereotype, seen so often on screen that it seems a joke, suddenly comes to life: when a gum-cracking waitress calls you "hon," or a stogie-sucking cabbie asks, "How 'bout them Yankees, Mac?" There's also the thrill of discovering one of New York's cities-within-the-city: Mulberry Street in Little Italy; Mott Street in Chinatown; Park Avenue's enclave of wealth and privilege; SoHo and TriBeCa, with their artistic types dressed in black from head to toe; or Sheridan Square, the nexus of the city's prominent lesbian and gay communities. The first glimpse of a landmark could begin the visitor's infatuation, too: frenetic Grand Central Station, abustle with suburban commuters; the concrete caverns of Wall Street, throbbing with power and ambition; or the Statue of Liberty, which neither cliché nor cheap souvenir can render common.

As you ready yourself to take on New York's contradictions, prepare to wonder and to exult. Here, on a single day, you might catch a glimpse of Jacqueline Onassis—she's been known to stop at Burger Heaven and have lunch at the counter—or Rollerena, the gloriously tacky drag-queen-cum-fairy-godmother on roller skates, who waves her magic wand to bestow blessings on select public events. Here you can eat sumptuously at a hot dog stand or at a world-celebrated gourmet shrine.

Excess and deprivation mingle here: As a limousine crawls lazily to take its pampered passengers to their luxe destination, it rolls past a threadbare beggar seeking the warmth that steams from the city's belly through an iron grate. It's a ludicrously bright cartoon and a sobering documentary, New York—almost too much for one city to be. It's maddening and it's thrilling; monstrous, yet beautiful beyond parallel.

And I envy anyone their first taste of it.

1 Essential Information

Before You Go

Visitor Information

The **New York Convention and Visitors Bureau** (2 Columbus Circle, New York, NY 10019, tel. 212/397–8222) provides brochures, subway and bus maps, an up-to-date calendar of events, listings of hotels and weekend hotel packages, and discount coupons for Broadway shows. **The New York Division of Tourism** (1 Commerce Plaza, Albany, NY 12245, tel. 518/474–4116 or 800/225–5697) offers a free series of "I Love New York" booklets listing New York City attractions and tour packages.

Tours and Packages

Should you buy your travel arrangements to New York packaged or do it yourself? There are advantages either way. Buying packaged arrangements saves you money, particularly if you can find a program that includes exactly the features you want. You also get a pretty good idea of what your trip will cost from the outset. You have two options: fully escorted tours and independent packages. Escorted tours mean having limited free time and traveling with strangers. Escorted tours are most often via motorcoach, with a tour director in charge. Your baggage is handled, your time rigorously scheduled, and most meals planned. Escorted tours are therefore the most hassle-free way to see New York, as well as generally the least expensive. Independent packages allow plenty of flexibility. They generally include airline travel and hotels, with certain options available, such as sightseeing, car rental, and excursions. Independent packages are usually more expensive than escorted tours, but your time is your own.

Travel agents are your best source of recommendations for both tours and packages. They will have the largest selection, and the cost to you is the same as buying direct. Whatever program you ultimately choose, be sure to find out exactly what is included: taxes, tips, transfers, meals, baggage handling, ground transportation, entertainment, excursions, sports or recreation (and rental equipment if necessary). Ask about the level of hotel used, its location, the size of its rooms, the kind of beds, and its amenities, such as pool, room service, or programs for children, if they're important to you. Find out the operator's cancellation penalties. Nearly everyone charges them, and the only way to avoid them is to buy trip-cancellation insurance. Also ask about the single supplement, a surcharge assessed to solo travelers. Some operators do not make you pay it if you agree to be matched up with a roommate of the same sex, even if one is not found by departure time.

Fully Escorted Tours Escorted tours are usually sold in three categories: deluxe, first-class, and tourist or budget class. The most important differences are the price and the level of accommodations. Some operators specialize in one category, while others offer a range. **Bixler Tours** (Box 37, Hiram, OH 44234, tel. 216/569–3222 or 800/325–5087) has four-night programs that include accommodations at the Waldorf-Astoria and Broadway show tickets. **Mayflower Tours** (1225 Warren Ave., Downers Grove, IL 60515, tel. 708/960–3430 or 800/323–7604) has two New York City packages. **Maupintour** (Box 807, Lawrence, KS 66044, tel. 913/

843–1211 or 800/255–4266) has one program, offered at Thanksgiving, to view the Macy's Thanksgiving Day parade.

Most itineraries are jam-packed with sightseeing, so you see a lot in a short amount of time (usually one place per day). To judge just how fast-paced the tour is, review the itinerary carefully. If you are in a different hotel each night, you will be getting up early each day to head out, travel to your next destination, do some sightseeing, have dinner, and go to bed, then you'll start all over again. If you want some free time, make sure it's mentioned in the tour brochure; if you want to be escorted to every meal, confirm that any tour you consider does that. Also, when comparing programs, be sure to find out if the motorcoach is air-conditioned and has a rest room on board. Make your selection based on price and stops on the itinerary.

Independent Packages Independent packages are offered by airlines, tour operators who may also do escorted programs, and any number of other companies from large, established firms to small, new entrepreneurs. **Bixler Tours** (*see above*) also does independent programs. Among the other operators are **Amtrak** (tel. 800/USA–RAIL) and **SuperCities** (tel. 800/333–1234). Among the major airlines offering packages to New York are **American Airlines Fly AAway Vacations** (tel. 800/321–2121), **Continental's Grand Destinations** (tel. 800/634–5555), **Delta Dream Vacations** (tel. 800/872–7786), and **United Airlines' Vacation Planning Center** (tel. 800/328–6877).

Independent programs come in a wide range of prices based on levels of luxury and options—in addition to hotel and airfare, sightseeing, car rental, transfers, admission to local attractions, theater tickets, and other extras. Note that when pricing different packages, it sometimes pays to purchase the same arrangements separately, as when a rock-bottom promotional airfare is being offered, for example. Again, base your choice on what's available at your budget for the destinations you want to visit.

Special-Interest Travel Special-interest programs may be fully escorted or independent. Some require a certain amount of expertise, but most are for the average traveler with an interest and are usually hosted by experts in the subject matter. When the program is escorted, it enjoys the advantages and disadvantages of all escorted programs; because your fellow travelers are apt to be passionate or knowledgeable about the subject, they can prove as enjoyable a part of your travel experience as the destination itself. The price range is wide, but the cost is usually higher—sometimes a lot higher—than for ordinary escorted tours and packages, because of the expert guiding and special activities.

Music **Dailey-Thorp Travel** (330 W. 58th St., New York, NY 10019 tel. 212/307–1555; book through travel agents), a performing arts specialist, has lively New York City programs.

Special Events **Gadabout Tours** (700 E. Tahquitz Way, Palm Springs, CA 92262, tel. 619/325–5556 or 800/952–5068) does packages at Christmas, with tickets to the Radio City holiday pageant; at Thanksgiving, with a stay at a hotel with a good vantage point on the parade; and at Easter, with a special dinner.

Theater **Broadway Theatours, Inc.** (71 Broadway, New York, NY 10006, tel. 212/425–6410 or 800/843–7469) does Broadway, as does

Sutherland "Hit Show" Tours (370 Lexington Ave., New York, NY 10017, tel. 212/532–7732 or 800/221–2442).

Tips for British Travelers

Government Tourist Office Contact the **State of New York Division of Tourism** (2 Cinnamon Row, Plantation Wharf, York Place, London SW11 3TW, tel. 071/978–5275) for brochures and tourist information.

Passports and Visas British citizens need a valid 10-year passport. A visa is not necessary unless 1) you are planning to stay more than 90 days; 2) your trip is for purposes other than vacation; 3) you have at some time been refused a visa or refused admission to the United States, or have been required to leave by the U.S. Immigration and Naturalization Service; or 4) you do not have a return or onward ticket. You will need to fill out the Visa Waiver Form, 1–94W supplied by the airline. To apply for a visa or for more information, call the U.S. Embassy's Visa Information Line (tel. 0891/200–290; calls cost 48p per minute or 36p per minute cheap rate).

Customs British visitors age 21 or over may import the following into the United States: 200 cigarettes or 50 cigars or 2 kilograms of tobacco; one U.S. liter of alcohol; gifts to the value of $100. Restricted items include meat products, seeds, plants, and fruits. Never carry illegal drugs.

Returning to the United Kingdom, you may import duty-free 200 cigarettes, 100 cigarillos, 50 cigars or 250 grams of tobacco; 1 liter of spirits or 2 liters of fortified or sparkling wine; 2 liters of still table wine; 60 millileters of perfume; 250 millileters of toilet water; plus £36 worth of other goods, including gifts and souvenirs.

Insurance Most tour operators, travel agents, and insurance agents sell specialized policies covering accident, medical expenses, personal liability, trip cancellation, and loss or theft of personal property. Some policies include coverage for delayed departure and legal expenses, winter-sports, accidents, or motoring abroad. You can also purchase an annual travel-insurance policy valid for every trip you make during the year in which it's purchased (usually only trips of less than 90 days). Before you leave, make sure you will be covered if you have a preexisting medical condition or are pregnant; your insurers may not pay for routine or continuing treatment, or may require a note from your doctor certifying your fitness to travel.

The **Association of British Insurers,** a trade association representing 450 insurance companies, advises extra medical coverage for visitors to the United States.

For advice by phone or a free booklet, "Holiday Insurance," which sets out what to expect from a holiday-insurance policy and gives price guidelines, contact the Association of British Insurers (51 Gresham St., London EC2V 7HQ, tel. 071/600–3333; 30 Gordon St., Glasgow G1 3PU, tel. 041/226–3905; Scottish Provincial Bldg., Donegall Sq. W, Belfast BT1 6JE, tel. 0232/249176; call for other locations).

Tour Operators Tour operators offering packages to New York City include the following **Albany Travel (Manchester) Ltd.** (Central Buildings, 211 Deansgate, Manchester M2 5QR, tel. 061/833–0202), **American Airplan** (Airplan House, Churchfield Rd., Walton-on-

Thames, Surrey KT12 2TJ, tel. 0932/231422 for information, 0932/246347 for brochures), **American Travel Centre** (77 Victoria St., Windsor, Berkshire SL4 1EH, tel. 0753/831300), **Jetsave** (Sussex House, London Rd., East Grinstead, Sussex RH19 1LD, tel. 0342/312033), **Speedbird Holidays** (Pacific House, Hazelwick Ave., Crawley, W. Sussex RH10 1NP, tel. 0293/611611), and **Thomas Cook Ltd.** (Box 36, Thorpe Wood, Peterborough PE3 6SB, tel. 0733/332333).

Airfares Fares vary enormously. Fares from consolidators are usually the cheapest, followed by promotional fares such as APEX (advance purchase excursion). A few phone calls should reveal the current picture. When comparing fares, don't forget to figure airport taxes and weekend supplements. Once you know which airline is going your way at the right time for the least money, book immediately, since seats at the lowest prices often sell out quickly. Travel agents will generally hold a reservation for up to 5 days, especially if you give a credit card number.

Seven airlines fly direct from Heathrow to New York, JFK, or Newark: **British Airways** (tel. 081/897–4000), **American Airlines** (tel. 0800/010151), **Virgin Atlantic** (tel. 0293/747747), **United Airlines** (tel. 0426/915500), **Air India** (081/759-1818), **Kuwait Airways** (081/745–7772), and **El Al** (081/759–9771); BA and Virgin also serve Gatwick, as does **Continental Airlines** (tel. 0293/567977), and Virgin and AA both fly direct to Manchester, too. Flight time is approximately seven hours on all routes.

Some travel agencies that offer cheap fares to New York City include **Trailfinders** (42–50 Earl's Court Rd., London W8 6EJ, tel. 071/937–5400), specialists in Round-The-World fares and independent travel: **Travel Cuts** (295a Regent St., London W1R 7YA, tel, 071/637–3161), the Canadian Students' travel service; **Flightfile** (49 Tottenham Court Rd., London W1P 9RE, tel. 071/700–2722), a flight-only agency.

Travelers with Main information sources include the **Royal Association for Dis-**
Disabilities **ability and Rehabilitation** (RADAR, 25 Mortimer St., London W1N 8AB, tel. 071/637–5400), which publishes travel information for the disabled in Britain, and **Mobility International** (228 Borough High St., London SE1 1JX, tel. 071/403–5688), the headquarters of an international membership organization that serves as a clearinghouse of travel information for people with disabilities.

When to Go

At one time, it seemed New York's cultural life was limited to the months between October and May, when new Broadway shows opened, museums mounted major exhibitions, and formal seasons for opera, ballet, and concerts held sway. Today, however, there are Broadway openings even in mid-July, and a number of touring orchestras and opera and ballet companies visit the city in summer. In late spring and summer, the streets and parks are filled with ethnic parades, impromptu sidewalk concerts, and free performances under the stars. Except for regular closing days and a few holidays (such as Christmas, New Year's Day, and Thanksgiving), the city's museums are open year-round. The parks are always free, so in winter you can cross-country ski, in summer you can swim or sunbathe, and in summer and fall you can watch migrating birds make their semiannual New York visits.

Climate Although there's an occasional bone-chilling winter day, with winds blasting in off the Hudson, snow is hardly ever a problem in the city (the skyscrapers trap enough heat to melt most snowfalls). Summer is the only unpleasant time of year, especially the humid, hot days of August, when many Manhattanites vacate the island for summer homes. Most hotels are air-conditioned, but if you're traveling in the summer and choosing budget accommodations, it's a good idea to ask whether your room has an air conditioner. Air-conditioned stores, restaurants, theaters, and museums provide respite from the heat; so do the many green expanses of parks. Subways and buses are usually air-conditioned, but subway stations can be as hot as saunas (and considerably dirtier).

Because the metropolitan area's water needs are so enormous, occasional summer droughts may entail strict conservation, with the result that air-conditioning is cut back, grass goes unwatered, fountains stand dry, and restaurants serve water only upon request.

The following table shows each month's average temperatures for New York City—the daily highs and lows, expressed in both Fahrenheit and centigrade:

Jan.	41F	5C	May	70F	21C	Sept.	76F	24C
	29	− 2		54	12		61	16
Feb.	43F	6C	June	81F	27C	Oct.	67F	19C
	29	− 2		63	17		52	11
Mar.	47F	8C	July	85F	29C	Nov.	56F	13C
	34	1		70	21		43	6
Apr.	61F	16C	Aug.	83F	28C	Dec.	43F	6C
	45	7		68	20		31	− 1

Information For current weather conditions for cities in the United States
Sources and abroad, plus the local time and helpful travel tips, call the **Weather Channel Connection** (tel. 900/WEATHER; 95¢ per minute) from a touch-tone phone.

Festivals and Seasonal Events

When it comes to special events, New York is indeed, as one classic song puts it, "the city that doesn't sleep." Here is a list of some of the more important or unusual events projected to take place throughout the year; for more up-to-date information, pick up a copy of *New York* magazine, the *Village Voice*, or the Friday edition of The *New York Times* upon your arrival in the city; contact the New York Convention and Visitors Bureau (*see* Visitor Information, *above*); or contact the event sponsor noted at the end of some listings.

Dec. 31–Jan. 1: New Year's Eve is marked by the famous countdown in Times Square; expect throngs of somewhat unruly revelers waiting for the ball to drop. Fireworks and a midnight run are held in Central Park.
Jan.: Ice Capades makes its regular winter appearance at Madison Square Garden. Tel. 212/465–6000.
Jan. 7–18: The National Boat Show, at the Jacob K. Javits Convention Center, gives the public a look at all sorts of seaworthy vessels and related equipment. Tel. 212/922–1212.
Jan.: The Winter Antiques Show, an exhibition of 17th- and 18th-century furniture, paintings, and statues, is held at the

Seventh Regiment Armory, Park Avenue at 67th Street. Tel. 212/439–0300.

Feb.: The Chinese New Year crackles with fireworks and energy as the Chinatown community prepares for and celebrates the lunar New Year.

Feb.: The Westminster Kennel Club Dog Show showcases top-of-the-line pooches at Madison Square Garden. Tel. 212/465–6000.

Feb.: The Millrose Games, an international track-and-field competition, is held at Madison Square Garden. Tel. 212/465–6000.

Early Mar.: The International Cat Show, at Madison Square Garden, displays favorite breeds along with varieties you've never heard of. Tel. 212/465–6000.

Mar.: Big East Basketball Championships at Madison Square Garden provide some exciting basketball action. Tel. 212/465–6000.

Mar. 5–7: Artexpo NY displays artworks in all media to the public at the Jacob K. Javits Convention Center. Tel. 800/331–5706.

Mar. 17: St. Patrick's Day Parade, a classic parade down Fifth Avenue, reflects the vitality of the Irish and Irish-American sector of the city's population.

Mid-Mar.–Apr.: Ringling Bros. Barnum & Bailey Circus brings its three-ring act to Madison Square Garden. Tel. 212/465–6000.

Mar.–Apr.: Radio City Easter Extravaganza fills last couple of weeks before Easter with dancers, spectacle, and other nonreligious pageantry. Tel. 212/247–4777.

Apr.–June: The New York City Ballet (tel. 212/870–5570) and **American Ballet Theatre** (tel. 212/362–6000) launch the spring season with performances at Lincoln Center.

Apr.–Oct.: The major-league baseball season sees the Yankees play their home games at Yankee Stadium in the Bronx, while the Mets hold court at Shea Stadium, Queens.

Apr. 3: Easter Parade, with all its finery, takes place along Fifth Avenue from 49th to 59th streets.

Late Apr.: The Cherry Blossom Festival is in full bloom at the Brooklyn Botanic Garden. Tel. 718/622–4433.

May: Ukrainian Festival, held on 7th Street between Second and Third avenues, is a refreshingly homespun event with what is probably the best food of any of the street fairs. Tel. 212/228–6840.

May: Martin Luther King, Jr., Parade marches down Fifth Avenue in memory of the civil rights leader.

Mid-May: The Ninth Avenue International Food Festival features food and merchandise from 32 countries. Tel. 212/581–7217.

Late May–early June: Washington Square Art Show (also held in early Sept.) displays artists' current work around the Greenwich Village central square for two weekends, starting Memorial Day weekend. Tel. 212/982–6255.

June–July: Metropolitan Opera performs free on weekday evenings in parks throughout the five boroughs.

June 2–11: Feast of St. Anthony, a 10-day festival, spills over from SoHo to Little Italy. Tel. 212/777–2755.

June 12: Welcome Back to Brooklyn Day is a gala celebration from noon to 5 along Eastern Parkway from Grand Army Plaza to Washington Avenue. Tel. 718/855–7882.

June 26: Lesbian and Gay Pride Day Parade runs down Fifth Avenue to Washington Square.

Late June: JVC Jazz Festival features vintage stars and newcomers at venues all around town.

July 4: Independence Day is celebrated with fireworks and street fairs at various locations.

July–Aug.: Shakespeare in the Park presents free productions at the Delacorte Theater in Central Park. Tel. 212/598–7100.

July–Aug.: The New York Philharmonic chips in with free concerts in various city parks. Tel. 212/360–1333.

Mid-July–Aug.: Mostly Mozart Festival presents a distinguished series of classical concerts at Avery Fisher Hall in Lincoln Center. Tel. 212/875–5030.

July–Nov.: New York City Opera performs at the New York State Theater in Lincoln Center. Tel. 212/870–5570.

Aug. 1–14: Harlem Week presents a series of workshops, street fairs, gospel festivals, and cultural events. Tel. 212/427–7200.

Late Aug.–Sept.: Lincoln Center Out-of-Doors hosts a variety of cultural events on the complex's plazas.

Late Aug.–early Sept.: U.S. Open Tennis Championships bring world-class excitement to the National Tennis Center in Flushing Meadows, Queens. Tel. 718/271–5100.

Late Aug.–Dec.: New York Giants and **New York Jets** play NFL football at Giants Stadium in East Rutherford, New Jersey. Tel. 201/935–3900.

Mid-Sept.: New York Is Book Country transforms Fifth Avenue into a reader's paradise.

Mid-Sept.: Feast of San Gennaro, a popular, somewhat overcrowded 10-day extravaganza in Little Italy, features games, vendors, and fabulous food. Tel. 212/226–9546.

Sept.–June: New York Philharmonic plays at Lincoln Center's Avery Fisher Hall. Tel. 212/875–5030.

Late Sept.–early Oct.: New York Film Festival features an eclectic mix of new and notable international films at Lincoln Center's Alice Tully Hall. Tel. 212/875–5050.

Oct. 2: Feast of St. Francis at the Cathedral of St. John the Divine draws a crowd of thousands to watch the Blessing of the Animals, which includes everything from pet hamsters to circus elephants.

Oct. 10: Columbus Day Parade gives New York's Italian-Americans a chance to strut their stuff.

Oct.: The International Antique Dealers Show, a vetted exhibition of antique furniture, porcelain, and other decorative objets d'art, is held at the Seventh Regiment Armory, Park Avenue at 67th Street. Tel. 212/439–0300.

Oct.–Apr.: Metropolitan Opera commands center stage at Lincoln Center. Tel. 212/362–6000.

Oct.–Apr.: New York Knicks Basketball and **New York Rangers Hockey** get underway at Madison Square Garden. Tel. 212/465–6000.

Oct. 31: Halloween Parade, New York's most outrageous parade, is held in Greenwich Village.

Early Nov.: New York City Marathon starts at the Verrazano Bridge in Staten Island and proceeds through all five boroughs. Tel. 212/860–4455.

Mid-Nov.: Virginia Slims Tennis Tournament brings top women pros to Madison Square Garden. Tel. 212/465–6000.

Nov. 24: Macy's Thanksgiving Day Parade sends giant balloons and a sleigh-borne Santa from Central Park West at 77th Street to Broadway and 34th Street.

Mid-Nov.–Jan.: Christmas Spectacular, a musical performance featuring the high-kicking Rockettes, hits the Radio City **Music Hall** stage. Tel. 212/247–4777.

Late Nov.–early Jan.: Lord & Taylor and **Saks Fifth Avenue** present animated window displays.

Dec.–early Jan.: The New York City Ballet's *Nutcracker* performances are a seasonal fixture at Lincoln Center. Tel. 212/870–5570.

What to Pack

Clothing Jackets and ties are required for men in a number of restaurants. For sightseeing and casual dining, jeans and sneakers are acceptable just about anywhere in the city. Sneakers or other flat-heeled walking shoes are highly recommended for pounding the New York pavements; you may even see businesspeople in button-down office attire lacing them on for the sprint from one appointment to another.

Miscellaneous An extra pair of glasses, contact lenses, or prescription sunglasses is always a good idea. If you take any prescription medicines, pack enough to last the duration of your trip.

Pack light, because porters and luggage trolleys can be hard to find at New York airports. You may need a fistful of quarters to rent a trolley, if no personnel are on duty by the coin-operated trolley racks.

Luggage
Regulations Free baggage allowances on an airline depend on the airline, the route, and the class of your ticket. In general, you are entitled to check two bags—neither exceeding 62 inches, or 158 centimeters (length + width + height), or weighing more than 70 pounds (32 kilograms). A third piece may be brought aboard as a carryon; its total dimensions are generally limited to less than 45 inches (114 centimeters), so it will fit easily under the seat in front of you or in the overhead compartment. There are variations, so ask in advance. The only rule, a Federal Aviation Administration safety regulation that pertains to carry-on baggage on U.S. airlines, requires only that carryons be properly stowed and allows the airline to limit allowances and tailor them to different aircraft and operational conditions. Charges for excess, oversize, or overweight pieces vary, so inquire before you pack.

Safeguarding Your
Luggage Before leaving home, itemize your bags' contents and their worth; this list will help you estimate the extent of your loss if your bags go astray. To minimize that risk, tag them inside and out with your name, address, and phone number. (If you use your home address, cover it so that potential thieves can't see it.) At check-in, make sure that the tag attached by baggage handlers bears the correct three-letter code for your destination. If your bags do not arrive with you, or if you detect damage, do not leave the airport until you've filed a written report with the airline.

Insurance In the event of loss, damage, or theft on international flights, airlines limit their liability to $20 per kilogram for checked baggage (roughly about $640 per 70-pound bag) and $400 per passenger for unchecked baggage. On domestic flights, the ceiling is $1,250 per passenger. Excess-valuation insurance can be bought directly from the airline at check-in but leaves your bags vulnerable on the ground.

Sources include **The Travelers Companies** (1 Tower Sq., Hartford, CT 06183, tel. 203/277–0111 or 800/243–3174) and **Wallach and Company, Inc.** (107 W. Federal St., Box 480, Middleburg, VA 22117, tel. 703/687–3166 or 800/237–6615), underwritten by Lloyds, London.

What It Will Cost

There's no doubt that New York is an expensive city to visit. Hotel rooms with views of Central Park can easily run as high as $250 a night; dinner for two at a moderate restaurant, plus orchestra seats at a Broadway show, can set you back $150–$200 (*see* Chapters 8, 9, and 10). If you're on a budget, don't despair. New Yorkers themselves know how to find bargains; they comb discount clothing outlets, grab food at corner delis, walk just about everywhere, and attend free concerts and plays in the parks. You, too, can moderate the cost of your visit if you do as they do (*see* Manhattan for Free in Chapter 3 and Discount Tickets in Chapter 10).

Hotel taxes add up to 21¼% once you get past the $100-a-night rate level (which covers most New York hotels!). The customary tipping rate is 15%–20% for taxi drivers and waiters (see Chapter 8 for further tipping advice), and bellhops are usually given $2 in luxury hotels, $1 elsewhere. Hotel maids should be tipped around $1 per day of your stay.

Getting Money from Home

Cash Machines Automated-teller machines (ATMs) are proliferating; many are tied to international networks such as **Cirrus** and **Plus.** You can use your bank card at ATMs away from home to withdraw money from your checking account and get cash advances on a credit-card account (providing your card has been programmed with a personal identification number, or PIN). Check in advance on limits on withdrawals and cash advances within specified periods. Remember that finance charges apply on credit-card cash advances from ATMs as well as on those from tellers. And note that transaction fees for ATM withdrawals outside your home turf will probably be higher than for withdrawals at home. For specific Cirrus locations in the United States and Canada, call 800/424–7787 (for U.S. Plus locations, 800/843–7587), and press the area code and first three digits of the number you're calling from (or the calling area where you want an ATM).

American Express Cardholder Services The company's **Express Cash** system lets you withdraw cash and/or traveler's checks from a worldwide network of 57,000 American Express dispensers and participating bank ATMs. You must *enroll first* (call 800/CASH–NOW for a form and allow two weeks for processing). Withdrawals are charged not to your card but to a designated bank account. You can withdraw up to $1,000 per seven-day period on the basic card, more if your card is gold or platinum. There is a 2% fee (minimum $2.50, maximum $10) for each cash transaction, and a 1% fee for traveler's checks (except for the platinum card), which are available only from American Express dispensers.

At AmEx offices, cardholders can also cash personal checks for up to $1,000 in any seven-day period; of this, $200 can be in cash, more if available, with the balance paid in traveler's checks, for which all but platinum cardholders pay a 1% fee. Higher limits apply to the gold and platinum cards.

Traveling with Cameras, Camcorders, and Laptops

About Film and Cameras If your camera is new or if you haven't used it for a while, shoot and develop a few rolls of film before leaving home. Pack some lens tissue and an extra battery for your built-in light meter, and invest in an inexpensive skylight filter, to both protect your lens and provide some definition in hazy shots. Store film in a cool, dry place—never in the car's glove compartment or on the shelf under the rear window.

Films above ISO 400 are more sensitive to damage from airport security X-rays than others; very high speed films, ISO 1,000 and above, are exceedingly vulnerable. To protect your film, don't put it in checked luggage; carry it with you in a plastic bag and ask for a hand inspection. Such requests are honored at American airports. Don't depend on a lead-lined bag to protect film in checked luggage—the airline may very well turn up the dosage of radiation to see what you've got in there. Airport metal detectors do not harm film, although you'll set off the alarm if you walk through one with a roll in your pocket. Call the Kodak Information Center (tel. 800/242–2424) for details.

About Camcorders Before your trip, put new or long-unused camcorders through their paces, and practice panning and zooming. Invest in a skylight filter to protect the lens, and check the lithium battery that lights up the LCD (liquid crystal display) modes. As for the rechargeable nickel-cadmium batteries that are the camera's power source, take along an extra pair, so while you're using your camcorder you'll have one battery ready and another recharging.

About Videotape Unlike still-camera film, videotape is not damaged by X-rays. However, it may well be harmed by the magnetic field of a walk-through metal detector. Airport security personnel may want you to turn the camcorder on to prove that that's what it is, so make sure the battery is charged when you get to the airport.

About Laptops Security X-rays do not harm hard-disk or floppy-disk storage. Most airlines allow you to use your laptop aloft but request that you turn it off during takeoff and landing so as not to interfere with navigation equipment. Make sure the battery is charged when you arrive at the airport, because you may be asked to turn on the computer at security checkpoints to prove that it is what it appears to be. If you're a heavy computer user, consider traveling with a backup battery.

Traveling with Children

See Chapter 5 for the many free and exciting activities for children in the Big Apple.

Publications Newsletter *Family Travel Times,* published 10 times a year by Travel With Your Children (TWYCH, 45 W. 18th St., 7th Floor Tower, New York, NY 10011, tel. 212/206–0688; annual subscription $55), covers destinations, types of vacations, and modes of travel; an airline issue comes out every other year (the last one, February/March 1993, is sold to nonsubscribers for $10). On Wednesday, the staff answers subscribers' questions on specific destinations.

General-Interest Books	*Great Vacations with Your Kids*, by Dorothy Jordan and Marjorie Cohen ($13; Penguin USA, 120 Woodbine St., Bergenfield, NJ 07621, tel. 800/253–6476), and *Traveling with Children—And Enjoying It*, by Arlene K. Butler ($11.95 plus $3 shipping per book; Globe Pequot Press, Box 833, Old Saybrook, CT 06475, tel. 800/243–0495; in CT, 800/962–0973), help plan your trip with children, from toddlers to teens.
Getting There *Air Fares*	On domestic flights, children under 2 not occupying a seat travel free, and older children currently travel on the "lowest applicable" adult fare.
Baggage	The adult baggage allowance applies for children paying half or more of the adult fare. Check with the airline for particulars.
Safety Seats	The FAA recommends the use of safety seats aloft and details approved models in the free leaflet "**Child/Infant Safety Seats Recommended for Use in Aircraft**" (available from the Federal Aviation Administration, APA–200, 800 Independence Ave. SW, Washington, DC 20591, tel. 202/267–3479). Airline policy varies. U.S. carriers must allow FAA-approved models, but because these seats are strapped into a regular passenger seat, they may require that parents buy a ticket even for an infant under 2 who would otherwise ride free.
Facilities Aloft	Airlines do provide other facilities and services for children, such as children's meals and freestanding bassinets (to those sitting in seats on the bulkhead, where there's enough legroom to accommodate them). Make your request when reserving. The annual February/March issue of *Family Travel Times* gives details of the children's services of dozens of airlines (*see above*). "Kids and Teens in Flight" (free from the U.S. Department of Transportation, tel. 202/366–2220) offers tips for children flying alone.
Tour Operators	**GrandTravel** (6900 Wisconsin Ave., Suite 706, Chevy Chase, MD 20815, tel. 301/986–0790 or 800/247–7651) offers international and domestic tours for grandparents traveling with their grandchildren. **Rascals in Paradise** (650 5th St., Suite 505, San Francisco, CA 94107, tel. 415/978–9800 or 800/872–7225) specializes in programs for families.
Baby-Sitting Services	You can usually make child-care arrangements through your hotel's concierge or housekeeper. For New York City agencies, *see* Chapter 5.
Around Town	Children under age 6 travel free on subways and buses; children age 6 and older must pay full fare. Clean rest rooms are often difficult to find; your best bet is to use the washrooms at museums, department stores, hotels, and restaurants while you are there.
	If you find you need a stroller once you get here, ask your hotel concierge to find one for you, or contact **AAA-U-Rent** (861 Eagle Ave., Bronx, NY 10456, tel. 718/665–6633).

Hints for Travelers with Disabilities

Many buildings in New York City are now wheelchair-accessible. The subway is still hard to navigate, however; people in wheelchairs do better on public buses, most of which "kneel" to facilitate getting on and off. For brochures and further information, contact the **Mayor's Office for People with Disabilities** (52 Chambers St., Office 206, New York, NY 10007, tel. 212/788–2830). Blind or visually impaired visitors may appreciate a visit to the **Andrew Heiskell Library for the Blind and Physically Handicapped** (40 W. 20th St., tel. 212/206–5400), a public library branch with a large collection of Braille, large-print, and recorded books, housed in a layout specially designed for easy access by the visually impaired.

Organizations Several organizations provide travel information for people with disabilities, usually for a membership fee, and some publish newsletters and bulletins. Among them are the **Information Center for Individuals with Disabilities** (Fort Point Pl., 27–43 Wormwood St., Boston, MA 02210, tel. 617/727–5540; in MA, 800/462–5015 between 11 and 4, or leave message; TDD/TTY, 617/345–9743); **Mobility International USA** (Box 3551, Eugene, OR 97403, voice and TDD tel. 503/343–1284), the U.S. branch of an international organization based in Britain (*see* Tips for British Travelers, *above*); **MossRehab Hospital Travel Information Service** (1200 W. Tabor Rd., Philadelphia, PA 19141, tel. 215/456–9603; TDD, 215/456–9602); the **Society for the Advancement of Travel for the Handicapped** (SATH, 347 5th Ave., Suite 610, New York, NY 10016, tel. 212/447–7284, fax 212/725–8253); the **Travel Industry and Disabled Exchange** (TIDE, 5435 Donna Ave., Tarzana, CA 91356, tel. 818/368–5648); and **Travelin' Talk** (Box 3534, Clarksville, TN 37043, tel. 615/552–6670).

Travel Agencies **Directions Unlimited** (720 N. Bedford Rd., Bedford Hills, NY
and Tour Operators 10507, tel. 914/241–1700), a travel agency, has expertise in tours and cruises for the disabled. **Evergreen Travel Service** (4114 198th St. SW, Suite 13, Lynnwood, WA 98036, tel. 206/776–1184 or 800/435–2288) operates Wings on Wheels Tours for those in wheelchairs, White Cane Tours for the blind, and tours for the deaf and makes group and independent arrangements for travelers with any disability. **Flying Wheels Travel** (143 W. Bridge St., Box 382, Owatonna, MN 55060, tel. 800/535–6790; in MN, 800/722–9351), a tour operator and travel agency, arranges international tours, cruises, and independent travel itineraries for people with mobility disabilities. **Nautilus**, at the same address as TIDE (*see above*), packages tours for the disabled internationally.

Publications The New York Division of Tourism (1 Commerce Plaza, Albany,
Local Resources NY 12245, tel. 518/474–4116 or 800/225–5697) offers the *I Love New York Travel and Adventure Guide,* which includes ratings of various facilities' accessibility. The New York State Parks Department (Empire State Plaza, Albany, NY 12238, tel. 518/474–0456) provides information on handicapped facilities in the *Guide to New York State Parks, Historic Sites and Programs.*

General In addition to the fact sheets, newsletters, and books men-
Information tioned above are several free publications available from the Consumer Information Center (Pueblo, CO 81009): "New Horizons for the Air Traveler with a Disability," a U.S. Department of Transportation booklet describing changes resulting from the 1986 Air Carrier Access Act and those still to come from the 1990 Americans with Disabilities Act (include Department 608Y in the address), and the Airport Operators Council's *Access Travel: Airports* (Dept. 5804), which describes

facilities and services for the disabled at more than 500 airports worldwide.

Twin Peaks Press (Box 129, Vancouver, WA 98666, tel. 206/694–2462 or 800/637–2256) publishes the *Directory of Travel Agencies for the Disabled* ($19.95), listing more than 370 agencies worldwide; *Travel for the Disabled* ($19.95), listing some 500 access guides and accessible places worldwide; the *Directory of Accessible Van Rentals* ($9.95) for campers and RV travelers worldwide; and *Wheelchair Vagabond* ($14.95), a collection of personal travel tips. Add $2 per book for shipping.

Hints for Older Travelers

Organizations The **American Association of Retired Persons** (AARP, 601 E St. NW, Washington, DC 20049, tel. 202/434–2277) provides independent travelers the Purchase Privilege Program, which offers discounts on hotels, car rentals, and sightseeing, and the AARP Motoring Plan, provided by Amoco, which furnishes domestic trip-routing information and emergency road-service aid for an annual fee of $39.95 per person or couple ($59.95 for a premium version). AARP also arranges group tours, cruises, and apartment living through AARP Travel Experience from American Express (400 Pinnacle Way, Suite 450, Norcross, GA 30071, tel. 800/927–0111); these can be booked through travel agents, except for the cruises, which must be booked directly (tel. 800/745–4567). AARP membership is open to those 50 and over; annual dues are $8 per person or couple.

Two other membership organizations offer discounts on lodgings, car rentals, and other travel products, along with such nontravel perks as magazines and newsletters. The **National Council of Senior Citizens** (1331 F St. NW, Washington, DC 20004, tel. 202/347–8800) is a nonprofit advocacy group with some 5,000 local clubs across the United States; membership costs $12 per person or couple annually. **Mature Outlook** (6001 N. Clark St., Chicago, IL 60660, tel. 800/336–6330), a Sears Roebuck & Co. subsidiary with 800,000 members, charges $9.95 for an annual membership.

Note: When using any senior-citizen identification card for reduced hotel rates, mention it when booking, not when checking out. At restaurants, show your card before you're seated; discounts may be limited to certain menus, days, or hours. If you are renting a car, ask about promotional rates that might improve on your senior-citizen discount.

Tour Operators **Saga International Holidays** (222 Berkeley St., Boston, MA 02116, tel. 800/343–0273), which specializes in group travel for people over 60, offers a selection of variously priced tours and cruises.

Further Reading

Many a famous writer has set down his or her impressions of this fascinating city. Some of the best full-length accounts are *Christopher Morley's New York*, a mid-1920s essay; *Walker in the City*, by Alfred Kazin; and *Apple of My Eye*, a 1978 account of writing a New York guidebook, by Helene Hanff. *New York Style*, by Suzanne Slesin, Stafford Cliff, and Daniel Rozensztroch, has several sections devoted to the city. Dan Wakefield recalls his early literary days in *New York in the 50s*. Perhaps the best of all is E. B. White's 1949 essay "Here Is New York."

The early history of New York is wittily told in the classic *Knickerbocker's History of New York*, by Washington Irving. For a fine historical introduction to the city, find the heavily illustrated *Columbia Historical Portrait of New York*, by John Kouwenhoven. *New York, New York*, by Oliver E. Allen is a well-rounded, up-to-date history of the city. *You Must Remember This*, by Jeff Kisseloff, is an oral history of ordinary New Yorkers early in this century. *The Park and its People*, by Roy Rosenzweig and Elizabeth Blackmar, tells how Central Park evolved.

Fiorello H. La Guardia and the Making of Modern New York, by Thomas Kessner, is a biography of the charismatic Depression-era mayor. *The Power Broker* by Robert Caro is a fascinating biography of Robert Moses, one of the city's most influential parks commissioners. Robert Daley's *Prince of the City* is a true-life drama of New York police corruption. Highly critical accounts of the city's recent politics can be found in *The Streets Were Paved with Gold*, by Ken Auletta; *The Rise and Fall of New York City*, by Roger Starr; *Imperial City*, by Geoffrey Moorhouse; and *City for Sale*, by Jack Newfield and Wayne Barrett. *A License to Steal*, by Benjamin J. Stein, concerns Wall Street's notorious Michael Milken, as does *Den of Thieves*, by James B. Stewart.

Theater lovers may want to read *Act One*, the autobiography of playwright Moss Hart; for more up-to-date essays on the city's theater scene, try David Mamet's *The Cabin*. *The Kingdom and the Power*, by Gay Talese offers a behind-the-scenes look at the *New York Times;* life at one of the city's most venerable magazines is recounted in *Here at the New Yorker*, by Brendan Gill. Speaking of that august publication, *Up in the Old Hotel* brings together Joseph Mitchell's *New Yorker* stories, which deal with colorful New York characters. *From Manet to Manhattan*, by Peter Watson, explores the city's art world. *Literary New York*, by Susan Edmiston and Linda D. Cirino, traces the haunts of famous writers, neighborhood by neighborhood. *The Heart of the World*, by Nik Cohn, is a block-by-block history of Manhattan's most famous street, Broadway.

AIA Guide to New York City, by Elliot Willensky and Norval White, is the definitive guide to the city's many building styles; Paul Goldberger's *The City Observed* describes Manhattan building by building. John Kieran's *A Natural History of New York* explores the wildlife of the city's parks, while Eugene Kinkead concentrates on the most famous park in *Central Park: The Birth, Decline, and Renewal of a National Treasure*.

Perhaps because so many writers have lived in New York City, there is a wealth of fiction set here. Jack Finney's *Time and Again* is a delightful time-travel story illustrated with 19th-century photos; *Winter's Tale*, by Mark Helprin, uses surreal fantasy to create a portrait of New York's past. Novels set in 19th-century New York include Henry James's *Washington Square*, Edith Wharton's *The Age of Innocence*, and Stephen Crane's *Maggie, A Girl of the Streets*. O. Henry's short stories depict the early years of this century, while Damon Runyon's are set in the raffish underworld of the 1930s and 1940s. F.

Scott Fitzgerald (*The Beautiful and Damned*, 1922), John Dos Passos (*Manhattan Transfer*, 1925), John O'Hara (*Butterfield 8*, 1935), and Mary McCarthy (*The Group*, 1938) also wrote about this city. J. D. Salinger's *Catcher in the Rye* (1951) partly takes place here, as does Thomas Pynchon's *V* (1965). Truman Capote's 1958 novella *Breakfast at Tiffany's* is a special favorite of many New Yorkers.

More current New York novels include *Bonfire of the Vanities*, by Tom Wolfe; *The Mambo Kings Play Songs of Love*, by Oscar Hijuelos; *The New York Trilogy*, by Paul Auster; and *People Like Us*, by Dominick Dunne. For portraits of gay life, try Larry Kramer's *Faggots*, David Leavitt's *The Lost Language of Cranes*, Sarah Schulman's *After Delores* and *People in Trouble*, and John Weir's *The Irreversible Decline of Eddy Socket*. The downtown scene is depicted in Tama Janowitz's *Slaves of New York* and Jay McInerney's *Bright Lights, Big City*.

The black experience in Harlem has been chronicled in Ralph Ellison's *Invisible Man*, James Baldwin's *Go Tell It on the Mountain*, and Claude Brown's *Manchild in the Promised Land*. For a portrait of Harlem during the 1920s, there's *When Harlem Was in Vogue*, by David Levering Lewis. The history of New York's Jewish population can be traced through such books as *World of Our Fathers*, by Irving Howe; *Call It Sleep*, by Henry Roth; *The Promise*, by Chaim Potok; *Enemies, A Love Story*, by Isaac Bashevis Singer; and *Our Crowd*, by Stephen Birmingham.

Greenwich Village and How It Got That Way is a fascinating study of that fascinating neighborhood by Terry Miller. Francine Prose's *Household Saints* is a fictional portrait of life in Little Italy. *The New Chinatown*, by Peter Kwong, is a recent study of the community across Canal Street. Kate Simon's *Bronx Primitive*, Laura Cunningham's autobiographical *Sleeping Arrangements*, and E. L. Doctorow's novel *World's Fair* are set in the Bronx. Brooklyn's history is beautifully illustrated in *Brooklyn: People and Places, Past and Present*, by Grace Glueck and Paul Gardner.

Mysteries set in New York City range from Dashiell Hammett's urbane 1933 novel *The Thin Man*, to Rex Stout's series of Nero Wolfe mysteries (continued by Robert Goldsborough) to more recent picks: *While My Pretty One Sleeps*, by Mary Higgins Clark; *Greenwich Killing Time* by Kinky Friedman; *Dead Air*, by Mike Lupica; and *Unorthodox Practices*, by Marissa Piesman.

Arriving and Departing

By Plane

Flights are either nonstop, direct, or connecting. A **nonstop** flight requires no change of plane and makes no stops. A **direct** flight stops at least once and can involve a change of plane, although the flight number remains the same; if the first leg is late, the second waits. This is not the case with a **connecting** flight, which involves a different plane and a different flight number.

Airports   Virtually every major U.S. and foreign airline serves one or more of New York's three airports: **La Guardia Airport** and **John F. Kennedy International Airport,** both in the borough of Queens, and **Newark International Airport** in New Jersey.

Airlines   U.S. carriers serving the New York area include **America West** (tel. 800/247–5692); **American** (tel. 800/433–7300); **Continental** (tel. 800/525–0280); **Delta** (tel. 800/221–1212); **Northwest** (tel. 800/225–2525); **TWA** (tel. 800/221–2000); **United** (tel. 800/241–6522); and **USAir** (tel. 800/428–4322).

Smoking   Since February 1990, smoking has been banned on all domestic flights of less than six hours duration; the ban also applies to domestic segments of international flights aboard U.S. and foreign carriers. On U.S. carriers flying overseas, a seat in a no-smoking section must be provided for every passenger who requests one, and the section must be enlarged to accommodate such passengers if necessary as long as they have complied with the airline's deadline for check-in and seat assignment. If smoking bothers you, request a seat far from the smoking section.

Between the Airports and Manhattan
La Guardia Airport   **Taxis** cost $18–$23 plus tolls (which may be as high as $4) and take 20–40 minutes. Group taxi rides to Manhattan are available at taxi dispatch lines just outside the baggage-claim areas during most travel hours (except on Saturdays and holidays). Group fares run $8–$9 per person (plus a share of tolls) depending on your destination.

Carey Airport Express buses (tel. 718/632–0500, 800/456–1012, or 800/284–0909) depart for Manhattan every 20 minutes from 6 AM to midnight. It's a 20- to 30-minute ride to 42nd Street and Park Avenue, directly opposite Grand Central Terminal. The bus continues from there to the Port Authority Bus Terminal, the New York Hilton, Sheraton Manhattan, Holiday Inn Crowne Plaza, and Marriott Marquis hotels. Other midtown hotels are a short cab ride away. The bus fare is $8.50 ($10 to the hotels); pay the driver. **The Gray Line Air Shuttle Minibus** (tel. 212/315–3006 or 800/622–3427) serves major Manhattan hotels directly to and from the airport. The fare is $12 per person; make arrangements at the airport's ground transportation center or use the courtesy phone.

The most economical way to reach Manhattan is to ride the Q-33 bus (there are no luggage facilities on this bus) to either the Roosevelt Avenue–Jackson Heights station, where you can catch the E or F subway, or the 74th Street–Broadway station (it's the same station), where you can catch the No. 7 subway. Allow 90 minutes for the entire trip to midtown; the total cost is two tokens ($2.50 at press time). You can use exact change for your bus fare but will have to purchase a token to enter the subway.

JFK International Airport   **Taxis** cost $25–$30 plus tolls (which may be as much as $4) and take 35–60 minutes.

Carey Airport Express buses (tel. 718/632–0500, 800/456–1012, or 800/284–0909) depart for Manhattan every 30 minutes from 6 AM to midnight, from all JFK terminals. The ride to 42nd Street and Park Avenue (Grand Central Terminal) takes about one hour. The bus continues from there to the Port Authority Bus Terminal, the New York Hilton, Sheraton Manhattan, Holiday Inn Crowne Plaza, and Marriott Marquis hotels; it's a short cab ride to other midtown hotels. The bus fare is $11 ($12.50 to the hotels); pay the driver.

The Gray Line Air Shuttle Minibus (tel. 212/315–3006 or 800/622–3427) serves major Manhattan hotels directly from the airport; the cost is $15 per person. Make arrangements at the airport's ground transportation counter or use the courtesy phone.

New York Helicopter (tel. 800/645–3494) offers daily flights between the airport and the heliport at East 34th Street and the East River. Planes leave from International Terminal 3 beginning at 8:50 AM, running roughly every 45 minutes in the morning and every half hour from 2:30 to 7:15 PM. Many passengers who use helicopter transport do so because it has been included in their long-distance airfare (check with your airline, especially if you are traveling first or business class); for other passengers the one-way fare is $65 plus tax. Reservations are recommended.

The cheapest but slowest means of getting to Manhattan is to take the Port Authority's free shuttle bus, which stops at all terminals, to the Howard Beach subway station, where you can catch the A train into Manhattan. Alternatively, you can take the Q-10 bus (there are no luggage facilities on this bus) to the Union Turnpike–Kew Gardens station, where you can catch the E or F subway, or to the Lefferts Boulevard station, where you can catch the A subway. Allow at least two hours for the trip; the total cost is one token ($1.25 at press time) if you use the shuttle or two tokens ($2.50) if you use the Q-10. You can use exact change for your fare on the Q-10, but you will need to purchase a token to enter the subway.

Newark Airport **Taxis** cost $28–$30 plus tolls ($4) and take 20–45 minutes. "Share and Save" group rates are available for up to four passengers between 8 AM and midnight; make arrangements with the airport's taxi dispatcher.

NJ Transit Airport Express buses (tel. 201/762–5100) depart every 15–30 minutes for the Port Authority Bus Terminal, at Eighth Avenue and 42nd Street. From there it's a short cab ride to midtown hotels. The ride takes 30–45 minutes. The fare is $7; buy your ticket inside the airport terminal.

Olympia Airport Express buses (tel. 212/964–6233) leave for Grand Central Terminal, Penn Station, and 1 World Trade Center (next to the Vista hotel) about every 30 minutes from around 6 AM to midnight. The trip takes 35–45 minutes to Grand Central and Penn Station, 20 minutes to WTC. The fare is $7.

The Gray Line Air Shuttle Minibus (tel. 212/315–3006 or 800/622–3427) serves major Manhattan hotels directly to and from the airport. You pay $17 per passenger; make arrangements at the airport's ground transportation center or use the courtesy phone.

Passengers arriving in Newark can also take New Jersey Transit's **Airlink buses,** leaving every 20 minutes from 6:15 AM to 2 AM, to Penn Station in Newark. The ride takes about 20 minutes; the fare is $4. From there they can catch **PATH Trains** (tel. 800/234–7284), which run to Manhattan 24 hours a day. The trains run every 10 minutes on weekdays, every 15–30 minutes on weeknights, every 20–30 minutes on weekends, and stop at the World Trade Center and at five stops along Sixth Avenue—

Christopher Street, 9th Street, 14th Street, 23rd Street, and 33rd Street. The fare is $1.

Car Services Car services are a great deal, because the driver will often meet you on the concourse or in the baggage-claim area and help you with your luggage. You ride in late-model American-made cars that are comfortable, if usually a bit worn. New York City Taxi and Limousine Commission rules required that all be licensed and pick up riders only by prior arrangement. Call 24 hours in advance for reservations, or at least a half-day before your flight's departure. Try **All State Car and Limo** (tel. 212/741–7440), **Carey Limousines** (tel. 212/599–1122), **Carmel Car and Limousine Service** (tel. 212/662–2222), **Eastside Limo Service** (tel. 212/744–9700), **La Limousine** (tel. 212/736–0484), **London Towncars** (tel. 212/988–9700), **Sherwood Silver Bay Limousine Service** (tel. 718/472–0183), and **Wheels of New York** (tel. 212/465–1630).

Airline Ticket Many airlines have ticket offices in convenient midtown and
Offices lower-Manhattan locations. American, Continental, Delta, Northwest, TWA, United, USAir, and Virgin Atlantic, for example, all have offices at the **Airlines Building** (100 E. 42nd St.). Offices are generally open weekdays 8–7, weekends 9–5, but hours vary among carriers.

Ticket offices are also clustered in three other Manhattan locations: the New York Hilton Hotel at 1335 Sixth Avenue (American, Continental, and Delta); the Sherry Netherland Hotel at 1 East 59th Street (American, Continental, Delta, TWA, United, and USAir); and 1 World Trade Center (American, British Airways, Continental, Delta, Lufthansa, Northwest, TWA, United, and USAir). Many foreign carriers have ticket offices along Fifth Avenue north of 50th Street.

By Car

If you plan to drive into Manhattan, try to time your arrival in late morning or early afternoon. That way you'll avoid the morning and evening rush hours (a problem at the crossings into Manhattan) and lunch hour (when traffic slows to a slower crawl than usual in Manhattan).

The **Lincoln Tunnel** (I–495), **Holland Tunnel,** and **George Washington Bridge** (I–95) connect Manhattan with the New Jersey Turnpike system and points west. The Lincoln Tunnel comes into midtown Manhattan; the Holland Tunnel into lower Manhattan; and the George Washington Bridge into northern Manhattan. Each of the three arteries requires a toll ($4 for cars) eastbound into New York, but no toll westbound.

The **Bayonne Bridge** connects Route 440 in Staten Island with Route 440 in New Jersey; a $4 toll for cars is collected southbound into New York. The **Outerbridge Crossing** and **Goethals Bridge** connect Staten Island with the New Jersey Turnpike and points west. The Outerbridge Crossing, which also feeds into the Garden State Parkway, comes into southern Staten Island, and the Goethals Bridge into the northern part of the borough. Both bridges are linked through Route 278 to the Verrazano-Narrows Bridge into southern Brooklyn. The Goethals and Outerbridge require a toll ($4 for cars) eastbound into New York, but no toll westbound. The Verrazano requires a toll of $5 for cars westbound only.

From Long Island, the **Midtown Tunnel** (I–495) and **Triborough Bridge** (I–278) are the most direct links to Manhattan. Both require tolls ($2.50 for cars) in both directions.

From upstate New York, the city is accessible via the **New York (Dewey) Thruway** (I–87) (toll) to the **Major Deegan Expressway** (I–87) through the Bronx and across the **Triborough Bridge** ($2.50 toll), or via the **Taconic State Parkway** to the **Saw Mill River Parkway** ($1.25 toll bridge) into upper Manhattan.

From New England, the **Connecticut Turnpike** (I–95) connects with the **New England Thruway** (I–95) (toll) and then the **Bruckner Expressway** (I–278). Take the Bruckner to the **Triborough Bridge** ($2.50 toll) or to the **Cross Bronx Expressway,** which enters upper Manhattan on the west side ($1.25 toll bridge).

Manhattan has two major north–south arteries that run the length of the island. The **West Side Highway** skirts the Hudson River from Battery Park (where it's known as West Street) through midtown (it then becomes the Henry Hudson Parkway north of 72nd Street) and past the George Washington Bridge. Both the Holland and Lincoln tunnels enter Manhattan just a few blocks east of this route; the Cross Bronx Expressway connects with the Henry Hudson Parkway in northern Manhattan at the George Washington Bridge. **Franklin D. Roosevelt Drive** (FDR Drive) runs along the East River from Battery Park into upper Manhattan, where it becomes Harlem River Drive north of 125th Street. Both the Queens Midtown Tunnel (East 36th Street) and the Queensboro Bridge (East 59th Street) can be entered a few blocks west of FDR Drive, which connects with the Triborough Bridge at East 125th Street.

Be forewarned: The deterioration of the bridges linking Manhattan, especially those spanning the East River, is a serious problem, and repairs will be ongoing for the next few years. Don't be surprised if a bridge is all or partially closed.

Driving within Manhattan can be a nightmare of gridlocked streets and predatory motorists. Free parking is difficult to find in midtown, and violators may be towed away literally within minutes. All over town, parking lots charge exorbitant rates—as much as $15 for two hours in some neighborhoods. If you do drive, don't plan to use your car much for traveling within Manhattan.

Car Rentals

If you find you absolutely need a car—perhaps for a weekend escape or because Manhattan is part of a longer trip—you'll have to sort out Manhattan's confusing array of car-rental possibilities. Although rates were once cheaper out of Newark airport, that is no longer the case; prices charged by national firms are the same at Newark, Kennedy, and La Guardia, as well as at Manhattan rental locations. For a subcompact, expect to pay $50–$80 per day, with unlimited mileage. Companies with multiple Manhattan and airport locations include **Avis** (tel. 800/331–1212), **Budget** (tel. 800/527–0700), **Dollar** (tel. 800/800–4000), **Hertz** (tel. 800/654–3131), **National** (tel. 800/328–4567), and **Thrifty** (tel. 800/367–2277). Some regional budget companies, such as **Rent-A-Wreck** (tel. 212/721–0080), offer lower rates. If you are flying into La Guardia or Kennedy, you might look into some local Queens agencies with lower rates, such as **Universal** (tel. 718/786–0786). **Sunshine Rent-A-Car** (tel. 212/989–7260) is good for budget rentals in Greenwich Village.

Extra Charges Picking up the car in one city or country and leaving it in another may entail drop-off charges or one-way service fees, which can be substantial. New York has outlawed the sale of collision damage waiver.

One last tip: Remember to fill the tank when you turn in the vehicle, to avoid being charged for refueling at what you'll swear is the most expensive pump in town.

By Train

Amtrak (tel. 800/USA–RAIL) offers frequent service within the Northeast Corridor, between Boston and Washington, DC. Trains arrive at and depart from **Pennsylvania Station** (31st–33rd Sts., between 7th and 8th Aves.). Amtrak trains serve Penn Station from upstate New York, Montréal, the Southeast, Midwest, and Far West. Penn Station also handles **Long Island Railroad** trains (tel. 718/217–5477), with service to and from all over Long Island, and **New Jersey Transit** trains (tel. 201/762–5100), with frequent service from the northern and central regions of New Jersey.

Metro-North Commuter Railroad (tel. 212/532–4900) serves the northern suburbs and Connecticut from Grand Central Terminal as far east as New Haven. The other Metro-North Manhattan stop is at 125th Street and Park Avenue in East Harlem—not a good place to get off the train unless you are visiting this neighborhood.

PATH Trains (tel. 800/234–7284) run 24 hours a day to New York City from terminals in Hoboken, Jersey City, Harrison, and Newark, New Jersey; they connect with seven major New Jersey Transit commuter lines at Hoboken Station, Broad Street Station (Newark), and Penn Station (Newark). PATH trains stop in Manhattan at the World Trade Center and along Sixth Avenue at Christopher Street, 9th Street, 14th Street, 23rd Street, and 33rd Street. They run every 10 minutes on weekdays, every 15–30 minutes on weeknights, and every 20–30 minutes on weekends. The fare is $1.

By Bus

All long-haul and commuter bus lines feed into the **Port Authority Terminal,** a mammoth multilevel structure that occupies a nearly 2-square-block area between 40th and 42nd streets and Eighth and Ninth avenues. Though it was recently modernized and is fairly clean, large numbers of vagrants make the terminal an uncomfortable place to spend much time. Especially with night arrivals, plan to move through the terminal swiftly. Beware of hustlers trying to help you hail a cab on Eighth Avenue—they will demand a tip for performing this unnecessary service and can be hostile and aggressive if crossed.

For information on any service into or out of the Port Authority Terminal, call 212/564–8484. Some of the individual bus lines serving New York include **Greyhound** (consult local information for a number in your area); **Adirondack Pine Hill Trailways** from upstate New York (tel. 800/225–6815); **Bonanza Bus Lines** from New England (tel. 800/556–3815); **Martz Trailways** from northeastern Pennsylvania (tel. 800/233–8604); **New Jersey Transit** from around New Jersey (tel. 201/762–5100); **Peter Pan Bus Lines** from New England (tel. 413/781–2900); and **Vermont Transit** from New England (tel. 802/862–9671).

The **George Washington Bridge Bus Station** is located at Fort Washington Avenue and Broadway between 178th and 179th streets in the Washington Heights section of Manhattan. Six bus lines, serving northern New Jersey and Rockland County, New York, make daily stops there from 5 AM to 1 AM. The terminal connects with the 175th Street station on the A subway, making it slightly more convenient for travelers going to and from the West Side.

Staying in New York

Important Addresses and Numbers

Tourist Information
New York Convention and Visitors Bureau. The main office is at 2 Columbus Circle (tel. 212/397–8222) and is open weekdays 9–6, weekends 10–6.

Emergencies
Dial 911 for **police, fire,** or **ambulance** in an emergency.

Deaf Emergency Teletypewriter (tel. 800/342–4357), for medical, fire, and ambulance emergencies.

Doctor
Doctors On Call, 24-hour house-call service (tel. 212/737–2333). Near midtown, 24-hour emergency rooms are open at **St. Luke's-Roosevelt Hospital** (58th St. at 9th Ave., tel. 212/523–6800) and **St. Vincent's Hospital** (7th Ave. and 11th St., tel. 212/790–7997).

Dentist
The **Dental Emergency Service** (tel. 212/679–3966; after 8 PM, tel. 212/679–4172) will make a referral.

24-Hour Pharmacy
Kaufman's Pharmacy (Lexington Ave. and 50th St., tel. 212/755–2266) is the only one. However, prices are exorbitant; before 10 or 11 PM, look for a pharmacy in a neighborhood that keeps late hours, such as Greenwich Village or the Upper West Side.

Hotlines
The New York Telephone Company lists important emergency and community services numbers in the front of its white-pages directory. Here are some numbers that may come in handy:

Better Business Bureau of Metropolitan New York (tel. 212/533–6200).

Crime Victims' Hotline (tel. 212/577–7777).

Mental Health (tel. 212/566–4766).

NYC On Stage (tel. 212/768–1818) provides up-to-the-minute information on tickets for theater, music, and dance performances.

Sex Crimes Report Line (tel. 212/267–7273).

Telephones

There are more than 58,000 public telephones in New York City, nearly 25,000 of which are in Manhattan. A visitor should never have to hunt more than three or four blocks before finding a coin-operated phone. If you're making a brief call—and don't mind the cacophonous sound of traffic or subways rumbling in the background—street phones are probably your best bet. If you want to consult a directory or make a more leisurely call, pay phones in the lobbies of office buildings or hotels (some of which take credit cards) are a better choice.

The area code for Manhattan is 212; for Brooklyn, Queens, the Bronx, and Staten Island, it's 718. Pay telephones cost 25¢ for the first three minutes of a local call (this includes calls between 212 and 718 area codes); an extra deposit is required for each additional minute.

Rest Rooms

Public rest rooms in New York run the gamut when it comes to cleanliness. Facilities in Penn Station, Grand Central Terminal, and the Port Authority bus terminal are often quite dirty and are inhabited by homeless people. Rest rooms in subway stations are even more filthy and are often downright unsafe.

As a rule, the cleanest bathrooms are in midtown department stores such as Macy's, Lord & Taylor, and Bloomingdale's, in museums, or in the lobbies of large hotels. Public atriums, such as the Citicorp Center and Trump Tower, also provide good public facilities. Restaurants, too, have rest rooms, but usually just for patrons. If you're dressed well and look as if you belong, you can often just sail right on in. Be aware that cinemas, Broadway theaters, and concert halls have limited amenities, and there are often long lines before performances, as well as during intermissions.

Precautions

Despite New York's bad reputation in the area of crime, most people live here for years without being robbed or assaulted. Nevertheless, as in any large city, travelers make particularly easy marks for pickpockets and hustlers, so caution is advised.

Ignore the panhandlers on the streets (some agressive, many homeless); people who offer to hail you a cab (they often appear at Penn Station, Port Authority, and Grand Central Station); and limousine and gypsy cab drivers who offer you a ride. Someone who appears to have had an accident at the exit door of a bus may flee with your wallet or purse if you attempt to give aid; the individual who approaches you with a complicated story is probably playing a confidence game and hopes to get something from you. Beware of strangers jostling you in crowds, or someone tapping your shoulder from behind.

Keep jewelry and valuables out of sight on the street; better yet, leave them at home. Don't wear gold chains, or gaudy jewelry, even if it's fake. Women should never hang their purse on a chair in a restaurant or on a hook in a rest-room stall. Men are advised to carry wallets in their front pants pockets rather than in their hip pockets.

Avoid deserted blocks in out-of-the-way neighborhoods. If you end up in an empty area or a side street that feels unsafe, it probably is. Go to the nearest avenue and hail a cab. A brisk, purposeful pace helps deter trouble wherever you go.

The subway is usually most safe to ride during the day and early evening; after the theater or a concert, travel by bus or taxi. You can also ride the subway in relative safety; just ride in the center car of the subway train, with the conductor, and wait among the crowds on the center of the platform. Watch out for unsavory characters lurking around the inside or outside of stations, particularly at night. When you're waiting for a train, stand away from the edge of the subway platform, especially when trains are entering or leaving the station, so you can avoid being pushed on to the tracks, either accidentally or intentionally. Once the train pulls into the station, avoid empty cars. When disembarking from a train, stick with the crowd until you reach the comparative safety of the street.

If you aren't in a hurry, buses are often more pleasant than subways to ride, particularly when you sit next to a window and can view the passing street life. Buses are usually safer than the subways because they carry fewer passengers than the average subway car, and each bus has a driver who can stop the vehicle at a moment's notice. Also, panhandlers who often appear in subway cars are rarely found on buses.

Opening and Closing Times

New York is very much a 24-hour city. Its subways and buses run around the clock, and plenty of services are available at all hours and on all days of the week. To compensate for being open at odd times, however, many businesses close during what one would expect to be their normal workweek, so it's always a good idea to check ahead.

Banks are open weekdays 9–3 or 9–3:30, although a few branches in certain neighborhoods may stay open late on Friday or open on Saturday morning.

Post offices are generally open weekdays 10–5 or 10–6. The main post office on Eighth Avenue between 31st and 33rd streets is open daily 24 hours.

Museum hours vary greatly, but most of the major ones are open Tuesday–Sunday and keep later hours on Tuesday or Thursday evenings.

Stores are normally open Monday–Saturday 10–5 or 10–6. Major department stores usually have late hours at least one evening a week. In business districts, stores may open earlier, while in neighborhoods such as the Village and SoHo, they open later and close later. Many stores in residential neighborhoods are open on Sundays.

Changing Money

Foreign travelers visiting New York can exchange foreign currency and traveler's checks at a number of offices around Manhattan. Large banks—Bank Leumi, Chase Manhattan, Chemical, and Citibank, for example—accommodate travelers during weekday business hours. Other companies provide exchange services up to seven days a week and often quote rates over the phone. They include:

American Express Travel Service, with nine Manhattan locations including: 822 Lexington Avenue, tel. 212/758–6510; Bloomingdale's, 59th Street and Lexington Avenue, tel. 212/

705–3171; 150 E. 42nd Street, tel. 212/687–3700; 374 Park Avenue, tel. 212/421–8240; American Express Tower, 200 Vesey Street, tel. 212/640–5130; and Macy's Herald Square, 151 W. 34th Street, tel. 212/695–8075. Hours vary among locations.

Chequepoint USA, 551 Madison Avenue at 55th Street, tel. 212/980–6443. Open weekdays 8–7, weekends 10–6.

Freeport Currencies, 132 W. 45th Street, tel. 212/730–8339. Open weekdays 8:30–6, weekends 9:30–5. At 49 W. 57th Street. Open weekdays 8:30–7, weekends 9:30–6.

Harold Reuter & Co., Metropolitan Life Building, 200 Park Avenue, Room 332 East, 3rd floor, tel. 212/661–0826. Open weekdays 8–5. At Abraham & Straus, 32nd Street and Sixth Avenue, 6th floor, tel. 212/268–8517. Open Mon.–Sat., 10–6, Sun. 11–6.

New York Foreign Exchange, 61 Broadway, Suite 805, tel. 212/248–4700. Open weekdays 9–5.

People's Foreign Exchange, 500 Fifth Avenue (at 42nd Street), Suite 200, tel. 212/983–4727. Open daily 9–6.

Thomas Cook Currency Service (tel. 212/757–6915) has branches at 630 Fifth Avenue in Rockefeller Center; 1 Herald Center at 33rd Street and Sixth Avenue; 41 E. 42nd Street; and 29 Broadway. Open weekdays 9–5, Saturdays 10–3.

Getting Around

On Foot The cheapest, sometimes the fastest, and usually the most interesting way to explore this city is by walking. Because New Yorkers by and large live in apartments rather than in houses, and travel by cab, bus, or subway rather than by private car, they end up walking quite a lot. As a result, street life is a vital part of the local culture. On crowded sidewalks, people gossip, snack, sunbathe, browse, buy drugs, cement business deals, make romantic rendezvous, encounter long-lost friends, and fly into irrational quarrels with strangers. It's a wonderfully democratic hubbub. Also sharing the streets, however, are increasing numbers of panhandlers, some aggressive, others more or less insane.

The typical New Yorker, if there is such an animal, walks quickly, dodging around cars, buses, bicycle messengers, construction sites, and other pedestrians. Although the natives seem hurried and rude, they will often cheerfully come to the aid of a lost pedestrian, so don't hesitate to ask passersby for directions.

Before you start out, keep a few simple rules in mind: Above 14th Street, the city is planned along a grid, with Fifth Avenue marking the dividing line between east and west. The streets, numbered from 1 to 220, are straight lines running east to west. The avenues—from First to Twelfth—run north to south. Below 14th Street, however, chaos reigns (*see* Orientation in Chapter 3).

By Subway The 230-mile subway system operates 24 hours a day and, especially within Manhattan, serves most of the places you'll want to visit. It's cheaper than a cab and, during the workweek, often faster than either cabs or buses. The trains have finally been rid of their graffiti (some New Yorkers, of course, perversely miss the colorful old trains), and sleek new air-conditioned cars predominate on many lines. The New York subway deserves much of its negative image, however. Many trains are

Manhattan Subways

crowded, dirty, and noisy, and even occasionally unsafe. Although trains are scheduled to run frequently, especially during rush hours, you never know when some incident somewhere on the line may stall traffic indefinitely. Unsavory characters lurk around certain stations, and panhandlers frequently work their way through the cars. Don't write off the subway—some 3.5 million passengers ride it every day without incident—but stay alert at all times (*see* Precautions, *above*).

The subway fare at press time was $1.25, but transit authority officials were already predicting that it should be raised to $1.50, which may have occurred by the time you visit New York. Reduced fares are available for handicapped people and senior citizens during nonrush hours. You must use a token to enter; they are sold at token booths that are *usually* open at each station. It's advisable to buy several tokens at one time to prevent waiting in line later (it always seems the lines are longest just as your train is roaring into the station). A token permits unlimited transfers within the system.

This book's subway map covers the most-visited parts of Manhattan. Maps of the full subway system are posted on many trains and at some stations, but don't rely on finding one when you need it. You may be able to pick up free maps at token booths, too, but they are often out of stock. Make sure the map you refer to is up-to-date—lengthy repair programs can cause reroutings that last long enough for new "temporary" maps to be printed.

For route information, ask the token clerk or a transit policeman. Call 718/330–1234 (a local call, 25¢ from pay phones) for information from 6 AM to 9 PM daily. And don't hesitate to ask a fellow rider for directions: Once New Yorkers realize you're harmless, most bend over backward to be helpful.

By Bus Most buses follow easy-to-understand routes along the Manhattan grid. Routes go up or down the north–south avenues, or east and west on the major two-way crosstown streets. Most bus routes operate 24 hours, but service is infrequent late at night. Buses are great for sightseeing, but traffic jams—a potential threat at any time or place in Manhattan—can make rides maddeningly slow. Certain bus routes now offer "Limited-Stop Service"; buses on these routes stop only at major cross streets and transfer points and can save traveling time. The "Limited-Stop" buses usually run on weekdays and during rush hours. For information about routes, bus stops, and hours of operation, call 718/330–1234 daily 6–9.

Bus fare is the same as subway fare: $1.25 at press time, in coins (no pennies; no change is given) or a subway token. When you get on the bus you can ask the driver for a free transfer coupon, good for one change to an intersecting route. Legal transfer points are listed on the back of the slip. Transfers have time limits of at least two hours, often longer. You cannot use the transfer to enter the subway system.

Guide-A-Rides, which consist of route maps and schedules, are posted at many bus stops in Manhattan and at major stops throughout the other boroughs. Each of the five boroughs of New York has a separate bus map, and they are scarcer than hens' teeth. They are occasionally available in subway token booths, but never on buses. The best places to obtain them are the Convention and Visitors Bureau at Columbus Circle or the information kiosks in Grand Central Terminal and Penn Station.

By Taxi Taxis are usually easy to hail on the street or from a taxi rank in front of major hotels. You can tell if a cab is available by checking its rooftop light; if the center panel is lit, the driver is ready to take passengers. Taxis cost $1.50 for the first ⅕ mile, 25¢ for each ⅕ mile thereafter, and 25¢ for each 75 seconds not in motion. A 50¢ surcharge is added to rides begun between 8 PM and 6 AM. There is no charge for extra passengers, but you must pay any bridge or tunnel tolls incurred during your trip (sometimes a driver will personally pay a toll to keep moving quickly, but that amount will be added to the fare when the ride is over). Taxi drivers also expect a 15% tip. Barring performance above and beyond the call of duty, don't feel obliged to give them more.

To avoid unhappy taxi experiences, try to have a general idea of where you want to go. A few cab drivers are dishonest; some are ignorant; some can barely understand English. If you have no idea of the proper route, you may be taken for a long and costly ride.

By Trolley The **Manhattan Neighborhood Trolley** (180 Eldridge St., New York, NY 10002, tel. 212/677–7268), a 1900 vintage red-and-green car seating 30 passengers, runs weekends and holidays, noon–6 PM, April through October, making stops every hour at South Street Seaport, Battery Park, the World Trade Center, the World Financial Center, City Hall Park, Chatham Square in Chinatown, Grand Street in Little Italy, and Orchard Street on the Lower East Side. Tickets, which are valid for boarding and reboarding all day, cost $4 for adults, $3 for senior citizens and children under age 12, and may be purchased from a tour guide on board, who provides a running narration.

By Limousine If you want to ride around Manhattan in style, you can rent a chauffeur-driven car from one of many limousine services. Companies usually charge by the hour or offer a flat fee for sightseeing excursions. The Manhattan yellow pages provides a full listing of limousine operators, but here are several recommended companies: **All State Car and Limo** (tel. 212/741–7440); **Bermuda Limousine International** (tel. 212/249–8400); **Carey Limousines** (tel. 212/599–1122); **Carmel Car and Limousine Service** (tel. 212/662–2222); **Chris Limousines** (tel. 718/356–3232); **Concord Luxury Limousine** (tel. 212/230–1600); **Eastside Limo Service** (tel. 212/744–9700); **Gordon's Limousine Service** (tel. 212/921–0081); **La Limousine** (tel. 212/736–0484); **London Towncars** (tel. 212/988–9700); **Sherwood Silver Bay Limousine Service** (tel. 718/472–0183).

Guided Tours

Orientation Tours
Boat Tours The most pleasant way to get a crash orientation to Manhattan is aboard a **Circle Line Cruise.** Once you've finished the three-hour, 35-mile circumnavigation of Manhattan, you'll have a good idea of where things are and what you want to see next. Narrations are as interesting and individualized as the guides who deliver them. *Pier 83, west end of 42nd St., tel. 212/563–3200. Fare: $16 adults, $8 children under 12. Operates early Mar.–Dec., daily.*

For a shorter excursion, the **TNT Express,** a hydroliner, will show you the island of Manhattan in 75 minutes. *Pier 11, 2* *blocks south of South Street Seaport, tel. 800/342–5868. Fare: $15 adults, $13 senior citizens, $8 children under 12, children under 5 free. Boats depart Apr.–Sept, weekdays and Sat. at noon and 2 PM.*

World Yacht Cruises (Pier 81, W. 42nd St. at Hudson River, tel. 212/630–8100) serve lunch ($27.50) and Sunday brunch ($39.95) on two-hour cruises, and dinner (Sun.–Thurs. $62; Fri.–Sat. $69.50; drinks extra) on three-hour cruises. The Continental cuisine is restaurant quality, and there's even music and dancing on board. The cruises run daily year-round.

The Spirit of New York (Pier 9, three blocks south of South Street Seaport on East River, tel. 212/742–7278) sails on lunch ($22.95), brunch ($29.95), dinner ($42.95–$48.95), and moonlight cocktail ($18) cruises.

At South Street Seaport's Pier 16 you can take two- or three-hour voyages to New York's past aboard the iron cargo schooner *Pioneer* (tel. 212/669–9400) or 90-minute tours of New York Harbor aboard the sidewheeler *Andrew Fletcher* or the *DeWitt Clinton,* a re-created steamboat (tel. 212/269–3200).

Bus Tours **Gray Line** (254 W. 54th St., tel. 212/397–2620) offers a number of standard city bus tours, plus cruises and day trips to Brooklyn and Atlantic City. **Short Line Tours** (166 W. 46th St., tel. 212/354–5122) offers some 20 different tour options.

Helicopter Tours **Island Helicopter** (heliport at E. 34th St. and East River, tel. 212/683–4575) offers four fly-over options, from $47 (for 7 miles) to $119 (for 35 miles). From the West Side, **Liberty Helicopter Tours** (heliport at W. 30th St. and Hudson River, tel. 212/465–8905) has three tours ranging from $55 to $119.

Special-Interest Tours **Backstage on Broadway** (tel. 212/575–8065) is a talk about the Broadway theater held in an actual theater, given by a theater professional. Reservations are mandatory; groups of 25 or more only. **Stardom Tours** (tel. 800/STARDOM) offers a tour around the city emphasizing celebrity homes and memorable movie locations. **Art Tours of Manhattan** (tel. 609/921–2647) custom-designs tours of museum and gallery exhibits as well as artists' studios and lofts. **Gallery Passports** (tel. 212/288–3578) takes you to galleries and museums in Manhattan. **Doorway to Design** (tel. 212/221–1111) tours fashion and interior design showrooms as well as artists' private studios. **Harlem Your Way!** (tel. 212/690–1687), **Harlem Spirituals, Inc.** (tel. 212/757–0425), and **Penny Sightseeing Co., Inc.** (tel. 212/410–0080) offer bus and walking tours and Sunday gospel trips to Harlem. **The Lower East Side Tenement Museum** (tel. 212/431–0233) offers Sunday tours through former immigrant communities. **River to River Downtown Tours** (tel 212/321–2823) specializes in lower Manhattan for two-hour walking tours. **Fulton Fish Market** tours give an insider's view of the early morning seafood market (tour guide Richard Lord, tel. 201/798–3901). **Louis Singer** (tel. 718/875–9084), an encyclopedia of New York trivia, provides tours of Brooklyn and Manhattan.

Walking Tours **Sidewalks of New York** (tel. 212/517–0201 or 212/662–6300) hits the streets from various thematic angles—Ye Old Tavern tours, Celebrity Home tours, Famous Murder Sites, Chelsea Saints and Sinners, and so forth. These walks are offered on weekends year-round; weekday tours are available by appointment. **Adventure on a Shoestring** (tel. 212/265–2663) is an organization dating from 1963 that explores New York neighborhoods. Tours are scheduled periodically for $5 per person. **Citywalks** (tel. 212/989–2456) offers two-hour walking tours exploring various neighborhoods in depth, weekends at 1 PM for $12. **Urban Explorations** (tel. 718/721–5254) runs Thursday, Friday, and weekend tours with an emphasis on architecture and urban planning; Chinatown is a specialty. The **Municipal Art Society** (tel. 212/935–3960) operates a series of bus and walking tours. The **Museum of the City of New York** (tel. 212/534–1672) sponsors Sunday afternoon walking tours. The **Urban Park Rangers** (tel. 212/427–4040) offer weekend walks and workshops, most of them free, in city parks. The **92nd Street Y** (tel. 212/996–1100) often has something special to offer on weekends and some weekdays. Other knowledgeable walking-tour guides include **Arthur Gelfand** (tel. 212/222–5343), **Joyce Gold** (tel. 212/242–5762), and **Arthur Marks** (tel. 212/673–0477).

The most comprehensive listing of tours offered during a particular week is published in the "Other Events" section of *New York* magazine's "Cue" listings.

Self-Guided Walking Tours The **New York Convention and Visitors Bureau's** "I Love New York Visitors Guide and Map" is available at the bureau's information center (2 Columbus Circle, tel. 212/397–8222). Walkers in Brooklyn can pick up two maps—"Brooklyn on Tour" and "Downtown Brooklyn Walking Tours"—as well as a handy "Brooklyn Neighborhood Book," all free of charge, at the public affairs desk of the **Brooklyn Borough President's** office (209 Joralemon St., 3rd floor). All three are available by mail, at $5 each, from the **Fund for the Borough of Brooklyn** (16 Court St., Suite 1400 W, Brooklyn, NY 11241, tel. 718/855–7882).

The **Municipal Art Society of New York** has prepared a comprehensive "Juror's Guide to Lower Manhattan: Five Walking Tours" for the benefit of jurors who are often required to kill time while serving in downtown courthouses. Along with an explanation of the New York jury system, the pamphlet includes tours of lower Manhattan and Wall Street, the City Hall district, Chinatown and Little Italy, South Street Seaport, and TriBeCa. Nonjurors can purchase copies for $5 at **Urban Center Books** (457 Madison Ave. at 51st St., inside the courtyard of the New York Palace hotel, tel. 212/935–3592).

A free "Walking Tour of Rockefeller Center" pamphlet is available from the information desk in the lobby of the GE building (30 Rockefeller Plaza).

2 Portraits of New York City

The New York Babel

By V. S.
Pritchett

*One of the great
living masters of
English prose,
V. S. Pritchett
expounds
delightfully on
his impressions
of the city in* New
York Proclaimed.
*Here are some
choice passages
from the book.*

If Paris suggests Intelligence, if London suggests Experience, then the word for New York is Activity. York itself is an almost intolerably famous name, but adding New to it was one of the lucky prophetic insights of nomenclature, for newness, from day to day, was to be the moral essence of the place. There is no place where newness is so continuously pursued.

What is not naturally active in New York soon has to turn to and become so. There is not an inactive man, woman, or child in the place. It might be thought that a contemplative, passive New Yorker, one who is inhabited by his feelings and his imaginings, who lives in an inner world, or was born torpid, must be immune to the active spirit. This is not so in New York, where states like passivity, contemplation, vegetativeness, and often sleep itself are active by prescription. Pragmatism sees to that. The prime example is the bum or derelict. There he lies asleep or drunk on the doorstep or props himself against a wall in the Bowery, an exposed, accepted, but above all an established figure of a 51st state. In a city where all activity is specialized, he has his specialty: he must act in protest against activity, which leads him from time to time on a chase for alcohol, a smoke, or a coin as persistent as a salesman's, but in solitude. Virginia Woolf used to ask where Society was; the notion was metaphysical to her. But Skid Row exists as a recognized place. You go there when the thing comes over you. You graduate in dereliction. You put in a 20-hour day of internal fantasy-making in your studied rejection of the New York norm. The Spanish mendicant has his rights and takes his charity with condescension; the bum grabs with resentment. He is busy. You have upset his dream. The supremely passive man in theory, he will stop in the middle of the street as he crosses the Bowery, holding up his dirty hand at the traffic, and scream in the manner of madness at the oncoming driver. Screaming like that—and New York is dotted with screamers on a scale I have seen in no other city in the world, though Naples has its share—reveals the incessant pressure of the active spirit.

For ourselves who are trying to settle first what we see before our eyes, this active, practical spirit has curious manifestations. New York City is large, but Manhattan is small in extent, so small that a large part of its population has to be pumped out of it every night by bridges and tunnels. Despite the groans about the congestion of its traffic, it is easy to dash from one end to the other of the island and to drive fast all around it. And most people do dash. The only real difficulty is in the downtown tangle of named streets in old New York; the grid has settled the rest. The grid is an unlovely system. It is not originally American: Stuttgart and Berlin hit upon this method of automatically extending cities in the 17th century. By the 18th century Europe had discovered that cities must be designed before they are extended: mere pragmatism and planning will not do. It absolutely will not do if left to engineers, soldiers, or what are called developers. The makers of the New York grid confused the idea that parallel lines can be projected into infinity without meeting, with the idea of design. The boredom this has inflicted upon the horizontal life of Manhattan has turned out to be endurable to the primarily active man who is impatient of the whole idea of having neighbors. The striping, unheeding avenues of the grid have given one superb benefit. They cut through long distances, they provide long vistas that excite the eye, and these are fine where the buildings are high, if they are featureless where the buildings are low. No other city I can think of has anything like the undulating miles that fly down Park Avenue from 96th Street to Grand Central, blocked now though it is by the brutal mass of the Pan Am Building—a British affront to the city and spoken of as a revenge for Suez—or the longer streak of Madison. These two avenues impress most as a whole, other avenues in part, by their assurance as they cleave their way through the cliffs.

Of course, being a stranger, you have been living it up, for if you want a night city, this is preeminently the one. There is a large fluorescent population of pale faces—who is that old man sitting alone in the Automat at this late hour? Where are all those taxis streaking to endlessly through the night? You have been listening to the jazz in Birdland perhaps, listening to the long drumming that says "Encroach, encroach, encroach, encroach, overcome, come!" or to that woman with the skirling voice which is shoving, pushing, and struggling cheerfully to get all her energy out of her body and into her mouth as she sings what is really the theme song of the city: "And it's good. It's all good, good, good." She was wired in to some dynamo.

Those words never fade from the mind. In sleep you still hear them. You are a receiving station for every message Babel sends out day and night. The sirens of the police cars, the ambulances and fire engines, mark the hours, carrying the mind out to fantasies of disaster. I say "fantasies," for surely all these speeding crews are studiously keeping alive the ideal of some ultimate dementia while the rest of us sleep. New York demands more than anything else that one should never fail to maintain one's sense of its drama; even its social manners, at their most ceremonious, have this quality. Where the crowds of other cities are consolidating all day long, filling up the safes and cellars of the mind, the New York crowd is set on the pure function of self-dispersal. A couple of cops idling through the night in a police car will issue their noise as if it were part of the uniform and to keep up their belief in their own reality and in the sacred notion of the Great Slaying or the Great Burglarization. Then there is light traffic on the highways, with its high, whipping, cat-gut whine. On 104th Street on the West Side I used to have the sensation of being flayed alive all night by knives whipping down Riverside Drive; it was not disagreeable. City life is for masochists. On many other avenues the trucks bulldozed the brain. There were bursts of noctambulist shouting off Madison and 60th at 3 or 4; followed by the crowning row of the city, the clamor of the garbage disposers, successors to Dickens's gentlemanly swine, that fling the New York garbage cans across the pavement and grind the stuff to bits on the spot. Often I have sat at my window to watch these night brutes chew up the refuse. The men have to rush to keep up with its appetite. As a single producer of shindy this municipal creature is a triumph.

T he only way of pinning some sort of identity onto the people is to think of them as once being strangers like yourself and trace them to their districts. The man who used to bring my breakfast, saying, every morning, "Lousy day," was a 115th Street Puerto Rican, of five years' standing. You learn to distinguish. You know where the Ukrainians, the Sephardic Jews, early and late Italians, degrees of Irish, live. You build up a map of the black and Puerto Rican pockets. You note the Germans are at 86th Street and yet the Irish are there, too; that, at the bottom, on East End Avenue, the neighborhood has become suddenly fashionable. The Greenwich Village Italians are pretty fixed; the several Harlems have established their character, for they have stuck to their district for 60 years, which must be a record for New York. You know the Greeks are on Ninth Avenue. The Lower East Side, now largely transformed, is Jewish and Puerto Rican. But large groups break away; poor give place to poorer. Sometimes poor give place to rich. In Sutton Place they cleared the poor away from that pleasant little cliff on the East River. But one must not understand these quarters as being the old parishes or the ancient swallowed-up villages of European cities, though they were sometimes the sites of farms. Topographically they are snippings of certain avenues and cross streets. For the avenues stripe the city and the groups live on a block or two along or across the stripe. One would have to analyze New York street by street, from year to year, to know the nuances of racial contact.

Statistics deceive, but it is clear that the oldest American stock of Dutch, British, and German, though dominant in wealth and traditional influence, is a small minority in New York. The question no one can answer is how far the contents of the melting pot have really melted and whether a new race has yet been created. For a long time the minorities resist, huddle into corners. Some foreign groups of New Yorkers melt slowly or not at all. O. Henry in his time called Lower Manhattan "Bagdad-on-the-Subway," thinking then of the unchanging Syrians and Armenians around Rector Street, but they have almost vanished. The Ukrainians still have their shops and churches near Avenue A. The Russian Orthodox priest walks down the street. The Poles shout from their windows or sit on the cagelike fire escapes east of Greenwich Village. Slowly these people, no doubt, merge; but the tendency for social classes to be determined by race is marked. Many groups of Orthodox Jews remain untouched. Over in Williamsburg you see a sect wearing beards, the men in black hats and long black coats, their hair often long, with curls at the ears, walking with a long loping shuffle as if they traveled with knees bent. They look like a priesthood, and the boys, curled in the same way, might be their acolytes. You will meet them with their black cases of treasure between their feet, standing on the pavement outside the diamond markets of 47th Street.

The foreign are tenacious of their religions—there must be more Greek Orthodox and Russian Orthodox churches than in any other city outside of Europe—and of their racial pride. The old Romanian who cleans your suit has never seen Romania, but he speaks with his old accent; as one looks at his settled, impersonal, American face, one sees the ghost person of another nation within its outlines, a face lost, often sad and puzzled. The Italian cop stands operatically in the full sun at the corner of Union Square; the nimble Greek with his four pairs of hands in the grocer's has the avidity of Athens under that slick, standard air of city prosperity. It occasionally happens that you go to restaurants in New York kept by the brother-in-law or uncle, say, of the man who has the founding place in London, Naples, or Paris; you fall into family gossip, especially with Italians, who are possibly more recent but who are still entangled in the power politics of the European family system. I once talked to an Irish waiter who rushed away into the bar crying, "D'ye see that bloody Englishman? He knows me father." I didn't, but I did know that his father was a notorious leader of one of those "columns" of the I.R.A. in the Irish Civil War.

In this quality of being lost and found there is the mixture of the guilt, the sadness, the fading mind of exile with the excited wonder at life which is an essential New York note. New York tolerance allows the latitude to civilization. People are left alone and are less brutally standardized than in other cities. "Clearly"—these foreigners tell you with resignation—"this is not Europe. But"—they suddenly brighten, tense up, and get that look of celebration in their eyes—"it is New York." That is to say, the miracle. Although New Yorkers of all kinds curse the city for its expense and its pressures, and though all foreigners think it is the other foreigners who make it impossible, they are mad about the place. There is no place like it in the world. And although a Londoner or a Parisian will think the same about their cities, here the feeling has a special quality: that of a triumphant personal discovery of some new thing that is getting bigger, richer, higher, more various as every minute of the day goes by. They have come to a ball. And this is felt not only by the New Yorker with the foreign strain, but also by the men and women who come in from the other states, drawn by its wealth but even more by the chances, the freedom, and the privacy that a metropolis offers to human beings. Its very loneliness and ruthlessness are exciting. It is a preemptive if not a literal capital. Scott Fitzgerald speaks of his wife Zelda coming up because she wanted "luxury and largeness beyond anything her world provided," and that precisely describes the general feeling of many a newcomer.

What Makes New Yorkers Tick

By Calvin Trillin

Calvin Trillin, who considers himself a "resident out-of-towner" in Manhattan for 30 years, writes regularly for The New Yorker and The Nation. His most recent book is Enough's Enough (and Other Rules of Life).

In the first place, we have more weird-looking people in New York City than can be found in any other American city. Also, more rich people. We have so many rich people that I once came to the conclusion that other cities were sending us the rich people they wanted to get rid of ("Listen, if Frank down at the bank doesn't quit talking about how much his Jaguar cost, we're just going to have to put him in the next shipment to New York"). Some of the weird-looking people and some of the rich people are the same people. Why would a rich person want to look weird? As we New Yorkers like to say: Go know.

When I moved to New York, back in 1961, I remember saying that 90% of the people walking along the street in Manhattan would be interviewed in any other town, and the other 10% would be arrested. It's got a lot weirder since then.

Of course, it's got weirder everywhere since then. But someone in a silly getup in Houston or Cleveland or Denver has to be aware that everyone is looking at him. If a 300-lb. man costumed as Eleanor of Aquitaine walks onto a crosstown bus in New York carrying both an attaché case and a rib roast, the other passengers might glance up for a second, but then they'd go back to their tabloids. If you asked the driver why he didn't seem to be registering such a sight, he'd say, "Hey whadaya—kidding? I seen a million guys like that. You think I'm some kinda farmer or something?"

So if you're making a list of how New Yorkers differ from other Americans—even other city dwellers—write "funny looking" near the top. Also write "jaded" or maybe "blasé": New Yorkers have seen a million guys like that no matter what the guy is like. We've seen everything. We've seen everybody. We are not impressed. The common response of New Yorkers to the presence of the President in their city is not excitement but irritation: His motorcade is going to tie up traffic. He may think he's in town to address the United Nations or raise money at one of those fat-cat banquets at the Waldorf, but as far as New Yorkers are concerned, he is there to cause them aggravation. And why, as a matter of fact, is the United Nations in New York? Also to cause aggravation, this time by taking up a lot of curb space with diplomatic-plate-only parking zones. In the minds of true New Yorkers, an awful lot that happens in the world happens to cause them aggravation. In fact, "aggravation," in that particular usage, is basically a New York word. I know there are people who think it's a Yiddish word—nobody thinks it's an English word—but a Yiddish word and a New York word are the same thing. It's true that you can detect an Italian bounce to some New York phrases, and it's true that white students at expensive Manhattan private schools are as likely as Harlem teenagers to shout "Yo!" when they come across a friend, but I think the basic structure and inflection of the language New Yorkers speak owe their greatest debt to Yiddish. The only purely New York word I can think of—cockamamie—sounds Yiddish, even though it isn't. It means ridiculous or harebrained and is commonly used in such phrases as "another one of the mayor's cockamamie schemes."

A scheme thus classified was launched some years ago by the then mayor, Edward Koch, who had come back from China smitten with the idea of bicycle transportation. He had protective strips of concrete installed to create a bicycle lane up Sixth Avenue. As someone who schlepps around (as we say here) on an old Raleigh three-speed, I was pathetically grateful for the bike lane myself: I suppose that shows that no matter how long I live in New York, I am, at heart, an out-of-towner. The cabdrivers, of course, hated it ("He likes China so much, he shoulda stood in China"). Some storekeepers hated it. But who complained most bitterly about the bike lanes? The bicyclers. The true New York bicyclers complained that the bike lane was full of pedestrians and garment-center pushcarts and people who schlepped around on Raleigh three-speeds. And slush. "It's October," I said to the bicycler who made that complaint: "there's no slush in October." "When there's slush," he said, "the bike lane will have slush."

The bike-lane episode reminds me that you'd better put "contentious" near the top of that list, right under "funny looking." (Not just "funny looking" come to think of it, but also "funny": New York is the only city I've ever been in where almost everyone you meet on the street considers himself a comedian—a fact brought home to me a couple of years ago when a panhandler near my subway stop said to me, "Can you spare some change? I'd like to buy a few junk bonds.") In the matter of contentiousness, I once tried to indicate the difference between New York and the Midwest, where I grew up, by saying that in the Midwest if you approach someone who is operating a retail business and ask him if he has change for a quarter, he is not likely to call you a fascist. He is certainly not going to say, "G'wan—get lost." He would never say, "Ya jerky bastard, ya."

New Yorkers are not polite. If you asked a New York cabdriver why he wasn't more polite, he might say something like "Polite! Where do you think you are—Iowa or Indiana or one of them?" New York cabdrivers do not usually bother to distinguish among states that begin with *I*.

Earlier this year, some booster organization in New York got the idea of launching a campaign to make New Yorkers more polite. Talk about cockamamie ideas! What are they—crazy? Do they think this is Illinois or Idaho or someplace? In the first place, the whole idea of a booster organization is as foreign to New York as Girl Scout cookies. (Yes, I know that thousands of Girl Scout cookies are sold every year in places like Queens and Staten Island. You think I'm a farmer or something?) I have never heard of a New York Chamber of Commerce. If it exists, I suspect it spends most of its time putting out press releases about aggravations. Also, telling New Yorkers not to be rude is the equivalent of telling Neapolitans not to talk with their hands: it could render us speechless.

I don't think there's anything particularly surprising about the level of rudeness in New York. A lot of it is just show. New York has been portrayed in so many books and movies and stand-up acts that the stock characters know how to behave badly. They've all read their press clippings. The Jewish deli waiter knows what to say to an out-of-towner who asks if he could get a pastrami sandwich ("When I'm ready, I'll get" or "Listen, the pastrami here I wouldn't wish on Arafat"). The Irish cop knows how to act like an Irish cop who does not go overboard in showing respect to the citizenry. Some of the newer stock characters, like the Korean greengrocer and the Indian news dealer, aren't certain how to act yet—there haven't been enough movies about them—but when they do get it all hardened into a New York shtick, I rather doubt that they're going to sound like the flight attendant of the month.

Also, I believe rudeness tends to vary in direct proportion to the size of the city, so it's only natural that the largest city is the rudest. It isn't just that the little daily irritations tend to build up in a large city faster than they do in a small town; it's the anonymity. In a small town, what you shout at someone who makes a sudden turn in front of you without a signal is limited in nastiness by the realization that you might find yourself sitting beside that person the next day at the Kiwanis lunch or the PTA meeting. If the town is small enough, the chance that you'll never see the offending party again is nonexistent. That puts a sort of governor on your behavior. In New York, the odds are almost the opposite; you are almost certainly not going to see that person again. The governor is removed. Knowing that, you might do a lot worse than "Ya jerky bastard, ya."

Not you? Yes, you. Right at the top of the list you should write down that there's nothing genetic about any of this. New Yorkers weren't born that way. A lot of New Yorkers weren't even born in New York. Some of them were born on farms. I was born in Kansas City. If you moved to New York, you'd be a New Yorker, and you'd act like a New Yorker. You'd only glance for a moment at the guy costumed as Eleanor of Aquitaine. You'd scheme to get the last seat on the subway car. You'd become a comedian. You might even use harsh language with taxi drivers. You wouldn't behave that way? Well, how about Mother Teresa?

Mother Teresa! Right. In Calcutta, Mother Teresa is probably an absolute pussycat, but if she moved to New York, she'd be a New Yorker. A couple of years ago, I started to use a true story about Mother Teresa to illustrate how all New Yorkers, living in what I believe could be considered a rather challenging environment, find themselves trying to get a little edge. Around 1987, Mayor Koch was briefly hospitalized with a slight stroke, and a few days later he got a surprise visit from Mother Teresa, who happened to be in town to establish a hospice. She told him he had been in her prayers, and he took the occasion to say that New York was grateful for her presence and that she should let him know if there was any way he could be of assistance. She said that as a matter of fact, there was one thing he might do. It would be helpful at the hospice to have a reserved parking spot. So envision this scene: here is Mother Teresa, perhaps a saint, making a sick call on a man who has just had a stroke—and she's trying to hustle him for a parking spot. You've got to say it's a tough town.

3 Exploring Manhattan

Manhattan is, above all, a walker's city. Along its busy streets there's something else to look at every few yards. Attractions, many of them world-famous, are crowded close together on this narrow island, and because it has to grow up, not out, new layers are simply piled on top of the old. The city's character changes every few blocks, with quaint town houses shouldering sleek glass towers, gleaming gourmet supermarkets sitting around the corner from dusty thrift shops, and soot-smudged warehouses inhabited at street level by trendy neon-lit bistros. Many a visitor has been beguiled into walking a little farther, then a little farther still—"Let's just see what that copper dome and steeple belongs to . . ."—and ending up with a severe case of blisters. So be warned: Wear your most comfortable shoes, preferably sneakers, and take time along the way to stop and rest.

Our walking tours cover a great deal of ground, yet they only scratch the surface. If you plod dutifully from point to point, nose buried in this book, you'll miss half the fun. Look up at the tops of skyscrapers and you'll see a riot of mosaics, carvings, and ornaments. Go inside an intriguing office building and study its lobby decor; read the directory to find out what sorts of firms have their offices there. Peep around corners, even in crowded midtown, and you may find fountains, greenery, and sudden bursts of flowers. Find a bench or ledge to perch on, and take time just to watch the street life. New York has so many faces that every visitor can discover a different one.

Orientation

The map of Manhattan bears a Jekyll-and-Hyde aspect. The rational, Dr. Jekyll part prevails above 14th Street, where the streets form a regular grid pattern, imposed in 1811. Consecutively numbered streets run east and west (crosstown), while broad avenues, most of them also numbered, run north (uptown) or south (downtown). The chief exceptions are Broadway (which runs on a diagonal from East 14th to West 79th streets) and the thoroughfares that hug the shores of the Hudson and East rivers.

Fifth Avenue is the east–west dividing line for street addresses: in both directions, they increase in regular increments from there. For example, on 55th Street, the addresses 1–99 East 55th Street run from Fifth, past Madison, to Park (the equivalent of Fourth) avenues, 100–199 East 55th would be between Park and Third avenues, and so on; the addresses 1–99 West 55th Street are between Fifth and Sixth avenues, 100–199 West 55th would be between Sixth and Seventh avenues, and so forth. Above 59th Street, where Central Park interrupts the grid, West Side addresses start numbering at Central Park West, an extension of Eighth Avenue. Avenue addresses are much less regular, for the numbers begin wherever each avenue begins and increase at different increments. An address at 552 Third Avenue, for example, will not necessarily be anywhere near 552 Second Avenue. New Yorkers themselves cannot master the complexities of this system, so in their daily dealings they usually include cross-street references along with avenue addresses (as far as possible, we follow that custom in this book). New Yorkers also rely on the handy Manhattan Address Locator found in the front of the local phone book.

Manhattan Neighborhoods

HARLEM

Marcus Garvey Park

Randall's Island

Columbia University

W.116th St.

E.116th St.

Morningside Park

E.110th St.

Ward's Island

Henry Hudson Pkwy.

Riverside Dr.

Broadway

Amsterdam Ave.

UPPER WEST SIDE

Central Park West

Central Park

UPPER EAST SIDE

W.86th St.

E.86th St.

Metropolitan Museum of Art

E.79th St.

Columbus Ave.

Museum of Natural History

West End Ave.

Park Ave.

E.72nd St.

Lexington Ave.

W.72nd St.

E.65th St.

Broadway

FDR Dr.

Roosevelt Island

QUEENS

Lincoln Center

E.59th St.

Queensboro Bridge

W.57th St.

E.57th St.

11th Ave.

10th Ave.

9th Ave.

8th Ave.

Rockefeller Center

5th Ave.

Times Square

Grand Central Terminal

1st Ave.

W.42nd St.

E.42nd St.

Lincoln Tunnel

Port Authority Bus Terminal

MIDTOWN

Madison Ave.

3rd Ave.

Queens-Midtown Tunnel

W.34th St.

Javits Convention Center

Madison Square Garden

Empire State Building

2nd Ave.

East River

W.23rd St.

Ave. of the Americas

Broadway

E.23rd St.

CHELSEA

7th Ave.

GRAMERCY

W.14th St.

Union Sq.

E.14th St.

GREENWICH VILLAGE

EAST VILLAGE

West Side Hwy.

W. Houston St.

E. Houston St.

Williamsburg Bridge

SOHO

LITTLE ITALY

Canal St.

Holland Tunnel

TRI-BECA

CHINA-TOWN

Manhattan Bridge

W. Broadway

Chambers St.

Brooklyn Bridge

NEW JERSEY

Hudson River

World Trade Center

South Street Seaport

BROOKLYN

LOWER MANHATTAN

0   440 yards

0   400 meters

Battery Park

Brooklyn-Battery Tunnel

Below 14th Street—the area that was already settled before the 1811 grid was decreed—Manhattan streets reflect the disordered personality of Mr. Hyde. They may be aligned with the shoreline or they may twist along the route of an ancient cow path. Below 14th Street you'll find West 4th Street intersecting West 11th Street, Greenwich Street running roughly parallel to Greenwich Avenue, Leroy Street turning into St. Luke's Place for one block and then becoming Leroy again. There's an East Broadway and a West Broadway, both of which run north–south and neither of which is an extension of plain old Broadway. Logic won't help you below 14th Street; only a good street map and good directions will.

You may also be confused by the way New Yorkers use "uptown" and "downtown." These terms refer both to locations and to directions. Uptown means north of wherever you are at the moment; downtown means to the south. But Uptown and Downtown are also specific parts of the city (and, some would add, two very distinct states of mind). Unfortunately, there is no consensus about where these areas are: Downtown may mean anyplace from the tip of Lower Manhattan through Chelsea; it depends on the orientation of the speaker.

A similar situation exists with "East Side" and "West Side." Someone may refer to a location as "on the east side," meaning somewhere east of Fifth Avenue. A hotel described as being "on the west side" may be on West 42nd Street. But when New Yorkers speak of the East Side or the West Side, they usually mean the respective areas above 59th Street, on either side of Central Park. Be prepared for misunderstandings.

Exploring

Highlights for First-Time Visitors

Rockefeller Center, Tour 1
Times Square, Tour 3
The United Nations, Tour 3
The Metropolitan Museum of Art, Tour 5
Central Park, Tour 7
The American Museum of Natural History, Tour 8
The Statue of Liberty, Tour 17
The World Trade Center, Tour 17
South Street Seaport, Tour 18
The Brooklyn Bridge, Tour 18

Tour 1: Rockefeller Center and Midtown Skyscrapers

Numbers in the margin correspond to points of interest on the Tours 1–3: Midtown map.

When movies and TV shows are set in Manhattan, they often start with a panning shot of Rockefeller Center, for no other city scene—except perhaps the downtown skyline—so clearly says "New York." Begun during the Great Depression of the 1930s by John D. Rockefeller, this 19-building complex occupies nearly 22 acres of prime real estate between Fifth and Seventh avenues and 47th and 52nd streets. Its central cluster of buildings are smooth shafts of warm-hued limestone, streamlined with glistening aluminum, but the real genius of the complex's design was its intelligent use of public space: plazas, concourses, and street-level shops that create a sense of community for the nearly quarter of a million human beings who use it daily. Restaurants, shoe-repair shops, doctors' offices, barbershops, banks, a post office, bookstores, clothing shops, ·variety stores—all are accommodated within the center, and all parts of the complex are linked by underground passageways.

Rockefeller Center helped turn midtown into New York City's second "downtown" area, which now rivals the Wall Street area in the number of its prestigious tenants. The center itself is a capital of the communications industry, containing the headquarters of a TV network (NBC), several major publishing companies (Time-Warner, McGraw-Hill, and Simon & Schuster), and the world's largest news-gathering organization, the Associated Press.

Let's begin the tour with a proud symbol of the center's might: the huge statue of Atlas supporting the world that stands sentry before the **International Building** (5th Ave. between 50th and 51st Sts.). The building, with a lobby inspired by ancient Greece and fitted with Grecian marble, houses many foreign consulates, international airlines, and a U.S. passport office.

One block south on Fifth Avenue, between 49th and 50th streets, you'll come to the head of the **Channel Gardens,** a promenade with six pools surrounded by flowerbeds filled with seasonal plantings, conceived by artists, floral designers, and sculptors—10 shows a season. They are called the Channel Gardens because they separate the British building to the north from the French building to the south (above each building's entrance is a coat of arms bearing that country's national symbols). The French building contains among other shops the **Librairie de France,** which sells French-language books, periodicals, and records; its surprisingly large basement contains a Spanish bookstore and a foreign-dictionary store.

At the foot of the Channel Gardens is perhaps the most famous sight in Rockefeller Center (if not all of New York): the great gold-leaf statue of the fire-stealing Greek hero **Prometheus,** sprawled on his ledge above the **Lower Plaza.** A quotation from Aeschylus is carved into the red granite wall behind, and 50 jets of water spray around the statue. The plaza's trademark ice-skating rink is open from October through April; the rest of the year, it becomes an open-air café. In December the plaza is decorated with an enormous live Christmas tree. On the Esplanade above the Lower Plaza, flags of the United Nations' members alternate with flags of the states.

The backdrop to the Lower Plaza is the center's tallest tower, the 70-story **GE Building** (formerly the RCA Building until GE acquired RCA in 1986), occupying the block bounded by Rockefeller Plaza, Avenue of the Americas (which New Yorkers call Sixth Avenue), and 49th and 50th streets. The block-long street called Rockefeller Plaza, officially a private street (to maintain that status, it closes to all traffic on one day a year), is often choked with celebrities' black limousines, for this is the headquarters of the NBC television network. From this building emanated some of the first TV programs ever; the *Today* show has been broadcast from here since 1952, and a shot of this

Tours 1-3: Midtown

Algonquin Hotel, **23**
American Craft Museum, **7**
Bryant Park, **21**
Carnegie Hall, **18**
Chrysler Building, **26**
Citicorp Center, **10**
Duffy Square, **20**

Ford Foundation Building, **27**
GE Building, **3**
General Motors Building, **17**
Grand Central Terminal, **25**
IBM Building, **15**
International Building, **1**
ICP Mid-Town, **22**

Lever House, **8**
Lower Plaza, **2**
Museum of Modern Art, **6**
Museum of Television and Radio, **5**
New York Public Library, **24**

The Plaza, **16**
Radio City Music Hall, **4**
St. Bartholomew's Church, **11**
St. Patrick's Cathedral, **13**
Saks Fifth Avenue, **12**
Seagram Building, **9**
Times Square, **19**
Trump Tower, **14**
United Nations Headquarters, **28**

4,5,6 M

E. 58th St.

E. 57th St.

E. 56th St.

E. 55th St.

E. 54th St.

E,F

E. 53rd St.

TURTLE BAY

E. 52nd St.

E. 51st St.

E. 50th St.

E. 49th St.

E. 48th St.

E. 47th St.

E. 46th St.

E. 45th St.

E. 44th St.

E. 45th St.

E. 44th St.

E. 43rd St.

**Grand
Central
Terminal**

E. 42nd St.

4,5,6,7,S

E. 41st St.

E. 40th St.

E. 39th St.

E. 38th St.

Madison Ave.

Park Ave.

Vanderbilt Ave.

Lexington Ave.

Third Ave.

Second Ave.

First Ave.

Sutton Pl.

FDR Drive

Tudor City Pl.

Park Ave.

Queens-
Midtown
Tunnel

East River

building is included in the opening credit sequences of *Saturday Night Live* and *Late Night with David Letterman*, both of which have been taped here.

One way to see what goes on inside is to spend $7.75 to take a tour of the NBC studios: One leaves from the street level of the GE Building every 15 minutes, 9:30–4:30, Monday–Saturday, and on Sundays during the summer. You can also buy a T-shirt, Frisbee, and other items with the logos of your favorite NBC programs at a boutique in the black granite lobby.

As you enter the GE Building from Rockefeller Plaza, look up at the striking sculpture of Zeus above the entrance doors, executed in limestone cast in glass by Lee Lawrie, the same artist who sculpted the big Atlas on Fifth Avenue. Inside, crane your neck to see the dramatic ceiling mural by Jose Maria Sert: Wherever you stand, the figure seems to be facing you. From the lobby information desk, go down the escalator in the right-hand corner and turn right to find a detailed exhibit on the history of the center (admission free; open weekdays 9–5). Then wander around the marble catacombs that connect the various components of Rockefeller Center. There's a lot to see: restaurants in all price ranges, from the chic American Festival Café to McDonald's; a post office and clean public rest rooms (scarce in midtown); and just about every kind of store. To find your way around, consult the strategically placed directories or obtain the free "Shops and Services Guide" at the GE Building information desk.

Returning to the GE Building lobby, you can take an elevator to the 65th floor to enjoy the spectacular view with drinks or a meal at the **Rainbow Room** (*see* Chapter 8). Exit the GE Building on Sixth Avenue to see the allegorical mosaics above that entrance.

Across 50th Street from the GE Building is America's largest ❹ indoor theater, the 6,000-seat **Radio City Music Hall.** Home of the fabled Rockettes chorus line (which actually started out in St. Louis in 1925), Radio City was built as a movie theater with a stage suitable for live shows as well. Its days as a first-run movie house are long over, but after an announced closing in 1978 Radio City has had an amazing comeback, producing concerts, awards presentations, and special events, along with its own Christmas and Easter extravaganzas. On most days you can take a one-hour tour of the premises. *Tel. 212/247–4777; tour information, 212/632–4041. Tour admission: $7 adults, $3.50 children under 6. Tours usually leave from main lobby every 30–45 min, Mon.–Sat. 10:15–4:45, Sun. 11:15–4:45.*

Later additions to Rockefeller Center include Sixth Avenue's skyscraper triplets—the first between 47th and 48th streets, the second (the **McGraw-Hill Building**) between 48th and 49th streets, and the third between 49th and 50th streets—and their cousin immediately to the north, the **Time & Life Building,** between 50th and 51st streets. All have street-level plazas, but the most interesting is McGraw-Hill's, where a 50-foot steel sun triangle points to the seasonal positions of the sun at noon and a pool demonstrates the relative size of the planets.

Time Out   For supercasual eating when the weather is good, the **Sixth Avenue food vendors** near Rockefeller Center offer the best selection in the city. These "à la cart" diners offer far more than trite hot dogs—there's a truly international menu of tacos, falafel, souvlaki, tempura, Indian curry, Afghani kofta kebabs, and Caribbean beef jerky.

NBC isn't the only network headquartered in Manhattan. The **CBS Building** is a black monolith popularly called Black Rock, on Sixth Avenue between 52nd and 53rd streets. (ABC, once a close neighbor, has now moved its main office to 66th Street on the West Side.) From here, you can choose among a cluster of museums: the Museum of Television and Radio, the American Craft Museum, or the major collection at the Museum of Modern Art. Go east on 52nd Street to the **Museum of Television and Radio,** housed in a new limestone building by Philip Johnson and John Burgee that reminds everyone of a 1930s-vintage radio. Three galleries exhibit photographs and artifacts relating to the history of broadcasting, but most visitors to this museum come to sit at a console and sample its stupendous collection of more than 32,000 TV shows, 13,000 commercials, and 16,000 radio programs. *25 W. 52nd St., tel. 212/621–6800 for daily events or 212/621–6600 for other information. Suggested donation: $5 adults, $4 students, $3 senior citizens and under 13. Open Tues.–Wed. and Fri.–Sun. noon–6, Thurs. noon–8.*

Just east of the Museum of Television and Radio, you'll pass the famous restaurant **The "21" Club,** with its trademark row of jockey statuettes parading along the wrought-iron balcony. Now wonderfully restored after an extensive renovation, it still has a burnished men's-club atmosphere and a great downstairs bar. In the movie *The Sweet Smell of Success,* Burt Lancaster as a powerful Broadway columnist held court at his regular table here, besieged by Tony Curtis as a pushy young publicist.

To reach the other museums, on 53rd Street, walk toward Fifth Avenue and turn left to cut through the shopping arcade of 666 Fifth Avenue. On the north side of 53rd is the **Museum of Modern Art** (MOMA), in a bright and airy six-story structure built around a secluded sculpture garden. In the second- and third-floor galleries of painting and sculpture, some of the world's most famous modern paintings are displayed: Van Gogh's *Starry Night,* Picasso's *Les Demoiselles d'Avignon,* Matisse's *Dance.* The collection also includes photography, architecture, decorative arts, drawings, prints, illustrated books, and films. Afternoon and evening film shows, mostly foreign films and classics, are free with the price of admission; tickets are distributed in the lobby on the day of the performance, and often they go fast. Programs change daily; call 212/708–9480 for a schedule. There's a good bookstore just off the lobby, and the even more interesting MOMA Design Store across the street. And leave time to sit outside in that wonderful Sculpture Garden. *11 W. 53rd St., tel. 212/708–9500. Admission: $7.50 adults, $4.50 students and senior citizens. Pay what you wish Thurs. 5–9. Open Fri.–Tues. 11–6, Thurs. 11–9.*

On the south side of 53rd, the **American Craft Museum** spotlights the work of contemporary American and international craftspersons working in clay, glass, fabric, wood, metal, paper, or even chocolate. Distinctions between "craft" and "high art" become irrelevant here, for much of this work is provocative and fun to look at. *40 W. 53rd St., tel. 212/956–3535. Admission: $4.50 adults, $2 students and senior citizens. Open Tues. 10–8, Wed.–Sun. 10–5.*

For a look at some of the city's landmark skyscrapers, head east on 53rd Street across Fifth Avenue. At Madison Avenue, you may want to detour left (north) to 55th Street to see the **American Telephone & Telegraph Co. Building,** designed by architect Philip Johnson. Unlike the sterile ice-cube-tray buildings of Sixth Avenue, AT&T's rose granite columns, its regilded statue of the winged *Golden Boy* in the lobby, and its peculiar "Chippendale" roof have made it an instant landmark for New Yorkers, who consider it the first postmodern skyscraper. There's also a pleasant open-air atrium on the street level where you can sit.

East of Madison Avenue, the next street is broad Park Avenue, with its planted median. On the west side of Park Avenue between 53rd and 54th streets is **Lever House,** a 1952 creation by Gordon Bunshaft, of Skidmore, Owings, & Merrill. It's basically a sheer, slim glass box, resting on one end of a one-story-thick shelf that seems to float above the street, balanced on square chrome columns. Because the tower occupies only half of the space above the lower floors, a great deal of air space is left open, and the tower's side wall displays a reflection of its neighbors.

On the other side of Park Avenue, one block south between 52nd and 53rd streets, the **Seagram Building** is the only New York building by German architect Mies van der Rohe, a leading interpreter of the International style. This, too, is a simple boxlike tower, although the black metal and bronze glass exterior looks more severe than Lever House's cool blue-green. Built in 1958, it created a sense of spaciousness with its ground-level plaza, an innovation at the time that has since become a common element in urban skyscraper design. Inside is one of New York's most venerated restaurants, **The Four Seasons** (*see* Chapter 9).

Go one block east to Lexington Avenue, between 53rd and 54th streets, to see the soaring, luminescent white shaft of the **Citicorp Center** (1977), designed by Hugh Stubbins & Associates. Its most striking feature is the angled top, originally intended to carry an immense solar-energy collector that was never installed. At street level, the Citicorp Center has a pleasant mall of restaurants and shops. Attached to the Center, on the corner of 54th Street and Lexington Avenue, is **St. Peter's Church** (tel. 212/935–2200), which offers jazz vespers on late Sunday afternoon; below the church is a theater where various acting troupes perform.

For a pleasing contrast, return to Park Avenue and walk down to 51st Street, where you'll see **St. Bartholomew's Church** nestled amid the skyscrapers. Built in 1919, it has rounded arches, while its intricate tiled dome is Byzantine. Church fathers have been eager to sell the air space over St. Bart's, to take advantage of the stratospheric property values in this part of town, but landmark preservation forces have so far prevented any such move.

Tour 2: Fifth Avenue and 57th Street

The stretch of Fifth Avenue upward from Rockefeller Center glitters with elegant shops, but the rents are even higher along East 57th Street, a parade of very exclusive smaller shops and upmarket art galleries. This is one of the world's great shopping districts, and every year more and more international fashion firms try to muscle in on this turf. The list of designer boutiques reads like a roll call of haute couture—Dior, Gucci, Vuitton, Ferragamo, Fendi, Chanel—and we have space here to point out only a few major stores. If your goal here is to spend a lot of money, *see* Chapter 8 for more details.

The string of stores begins right across the street from Rockefeller Center's Channel Gardens (*see* Tour 1, *above*), with **Saks Fifth Avenue** (5th Ave. and 50th St.), the flagship of the national department store chain. On the next block is Gothic-style **St. Patrick's,** the Roman Catholic Cathedral of New York. Dedicated to the patron saint of the Irish—then and now one of New York's principal ethnic groups—the white marble and stone structure was begun in 1858, consecrated in 1879, and completed in 1906. Among the statues in the alcoves around the nave is a striking modern interpretation of the first American-born saint, Mother Elizabeth Seton. From outside, catch one of the city's most photographed views: the ornate white spires of St. Pat's against the black glass curtain of **Olympic Tower,** a multiuse building of shops, offices, and luxury apartments.

Cartier, Inc., displays its wares in a jewel box of a turn-of-the-century mansion on the southeast corner of 52nd Street and Fifth Avenue; similar houses used to line this street, and many of their occupants were parishioners of **St. Thomas Church** (5th Ave. at 53rd St.), an Episcopal institution that has occupied the site since 1911. The impressive huge stone reredos behind the altar holds the statues of more than 50 apostles, saints, martyrs, missionaries, and church figures. The Christmas Eve services here have become one of the season's highlights.

On the northwest corner of Fifth Avenue and 54th Street, you'll see the imposing bulk of the **University Club,** a granite palace built by New York's leading turn-of-the-century architects, McKim, Mead & White, for this exclusive midtown men's club, one of several that only recently have begun accepting women members. Pick out the crests of various prestigious universities above its windows. Across the street is **Takashimaya New York** (683 5th Ave.), a branch of Japan's largest department-store chain. The elegant store features a garden atrium, a two-floor gallery, and three floors of men's and women's clothing and household items that combine Eastern and Western styles.

Fifth Avenue Presbyterian Church, a grand brownstone church (1875), sits on the northwest corner of Fifth Avenue and 55th Street. On the same block is **Henri Bendel** (712–716 5th Ave.), a fashion store organized like a little tower of intimate boutiques; the facade's René Lalique art-glass windows from 1912 can be viewed at close range from balconies ringing the four-story atrium. Next door is **Harry Winston** (718 5th Ave.), with a spectacular selection of fine jewelry.

Trump Tower, on Fifth Avenue between 56th and 57th streets, is an exclusive 68-story apartment and office building named for its developer, Donald Trump. The grand Fifth Avenue entrance leads into a glitzy six-story shopping atrium paneled in pinkish-orange marble and trimmed with lustrous brass. A fountain cascades against one wall, drowning out the clamor of the city.

Just north of Trump Tower, the intersection of Fifth Avenue and 57th Street is ground zero for high-class shopping. And what more fitting resident for this spot than **Tiffany & Co.** (727 5th Ave. at 57th St.), the renowned jewelers, with its Fort Knox–like Art Deco entrance. One quintessential New York movie, *Breakfast at Tiffany's*, opens with Audrey Hepburn, dressed in an evening gown, emerging from a yellow cab at dawn to stand here window-shopping with a coffee and Danish.

Around the corner on East 57th Street, anchoring the north side of Trump Tower, is the new French contender for most glamorous New York department store, **Galeries Lafayette,** a branch of the Paris fashion emporium. Its stylish salons occupy the six-story space that was formerly Bonwit Teller. Both English and French are spoken here, and you can convert your French francs to American dollars on premises.

⓯ At Madison Avenue and 57th Street, look up at the **IBM Building,** a five-sided sheath of dark gray-green granite and glass by Edward Larrabee Barnes. On the ground level there's the entrance to the subterranean **IBM Gallery of Science and Art,** which presents a variety of temporary art shows and the permanent science exhibition *Think,* including lasers, magnets, and superconductors. *Tel. 212/745–6100. Admission free. Open Tues.–Sat. 11–6.*

Time Out | At the 56th Street corner, step into IBM's high, cool atrium, one of the most inviting public spaces in town. Small marble-topped tables and wrought-iron chairs are provided, live music plays at noontime most weekdays, and a small café serves lunch. The atrium closes at 10 PM.

Cross 57th Street and head back toward Fifth Avenue on the north side of the street, with its stellar lineup of boutiques: the French shop **Hermès** (11 E. 57th St.), the English shop **Burberrys Ltd.** (9 E. 57th St.), the new German shop **Escada** (7 E. 57th St.), and the French classic **Chanel** (appropriately located at 5 E. 57th St.). Back at Fifth Avenue (at 754, to be exact), you can visit **Bergdorf Goodman:** The women's boutiques are on the west side of the avenue and the men's store on the east side, both between 57th and 58th streets. **Van Cleef & Arpels** jewelers is located within Bergdorf's 57th Street corner.

Cross 58th Street to **Grand Army Plaza,** the open space along Fifth Avenue between 58th and 60th streets. The southern block features the Pulitzer Fountain, donated by publisher Joseph Pulitzer of Pulitzer Prize fame. Appropriately enough for this ritzy area, the fountain is crowned by a female figure representing Abundance. The block to the north holds a gilded (some say *too* gilded) equestrian statue of Civil War general William Tecumseh Sherman; beyond it is a grand entrance to Central Park (*see* Tour 7, *below*).

⓰ Appropriately named **The Plaza,** the famous hotel (*see* Chapter 9) at the western edge of this square is a registered historical landmark built in 1907. Its architect, Henry Hardenbergh, was the same man who designed the rather dour Dakota apartment building (*see* Tour 8, *below*), but here he achieved a sprightly birthday-cake effect with white-glazed brick busily decorated and topped off with a copper-and-slate mansard roof. The hotel has been featured in many movies, from Alfred Hitchcock's *North by Northwest* to more recent films such as *Arthur, Croc-*

odile Dundee, Home Alone 2, and of course, *Plaza Suite.* Among the many upper-crust parties that have taken place in the Plaza's ballroom was Truman Capote's Black and White Ball of 1966, attended by everyone who was anyone—all dressed, naturally, in black and white.

⑰ Adjacent to Grand Army Plaza stands the **General Motors Building,** a 50-story tower of Georgia marble. One section of the main floor is the flagship of the legendary **F.A.O. Schwarz** toy store, with its fantastic mechanical clock right inside the front doors. Bigger than it looks from outside, the toy-o-rama offers a vast, wondrously fun selection, although it definitely tends toward expensive imports. Browsing here should bring out the child in everyone, as it did in the movie *Big,* when Tom Hanks and his boss got caught up in tap-dancing on a giant keyboard.

Now return to 57th Street and head west, where the glamour eases off a bit (but not much). You'll pass the excellent **Rizzoli** bookstore at 31 West 57th (Robert DeNiro and Meryl Streep trysted here in their bomb movie *Falling In Love*), and beyond that is arguably the handsomest McDonald's in the land, with an elegant blue-neon decorating scheme that's definitely not standard-issue for the burger chain. Across Sixth Avenue (remember, New Yorkers *don't* call it Avenue of the Americas, despite the street signs), you'll know you're in classical-music territory when you peer through the showroom windows at **Steinway** (109 W. 57th St.). But before you get to Carnegie Hall, you may want to cross the street to grab a bite (or at least steal a peek) at **Planet Hollywood** (140 W. 57th St., tel. 212/333-7827), where, behind the pink-and-green striped awnings and plastic palm trees, you'll find a trendy restaurant stuffed with movie memorabilia—everything from Humphrey Bogart's Maltese Falcon to *Star Wars*' R2D2 and C3PO robots. To assemble such a cache, you'd need good Tinseltown connections, but since the restaurant's owners include actors Arnold Schwarzenegger, Bruce Willis, and Sylvester Stallone, as well as producer-director John Hughes, apparently it was a cinch. A few doors down from Planet Hollywood is the more staid, but no less celebrity-studded, **Russian Tea Room** restaurant (150 W. 57th St., tel. 212/265-0947) in its bright turquoise town house.

An old joke says it all: A tourist asks an old guy with a violin case, "How do you get to Carnegie Hall?" His reply: "Practice, practice, practice." Presiding over the southeast corner of Seventh Avenue and 57th Street, **Carnegie Hall** has been hosting **⑱** musical headliners since 1891, when its first concert was conducted by no less than Tchaikovsky. Outside it's a stout, square brown building with a few Moorish-style arches added, almost as an afterthought, to the facade. Inside, however, is a simply decorated, 2,804-seat auditorium that is considered one of the finest in the world. It was extensively restored before its gala 1990–1991 centennial season, although critics still debate whether the main auditorium's acoustics will ever be as perfect as they were before. The lobby is bigger now, though, and a museum has been added just east of the main auditorium, displaying memorabilia from the hall's illustrious history. Hour-long guided tours of Carnegie Hall are also available. *Carnegie Hall Museum: 881 7th Ave., tel. 212/903–9629. Admission free. Open daily 11–4:30. Guided tours (tel. 212/247–7800) offered Mon., Tues., and Thurs. 11:30, 2, and 3 (performance schedule* *permitting); admission: $6 adults, $5 students and seniors, $3 children.*

Devotees of classical music may want to head from here up to nearby Lincoln Center (*see* Tour 8, *below*). If rock-and-roll music is more to your liking, head west one more block to the **Hard Rock Cafe** (221 W. 57th St., tel. 212/459–9320), New York City's outpost of the restaurant chain. Since the opening of Planet Hollywood, which was inspired by the Hard Rock's success, the sidewalk lines behind the velvet rope here are a little shorter, but it's still a popular scene. If you don't want to eat, you can always drop into the adjacent shop to buy one of those ubiquitous T-shirts.

Tour 3: Across 42nd Street

As midtown Manhattan's central axis, 42nd Street ties together several major points of interest, from the United Nations on the East River, past the Grand Central railroad terminal, to Times Square. While it's never less than a busy commercial thoroughfare, a few blocks of 42nd Street are downright disreputable, living up to the often-held image of New York as a den of pickpockets, porno houses, prostitutes, and destitutes. An ambitious plan to redevelop Times Square is currently under way, but in the meantime try to imagine West 42nd Street as a scene out of the movie *Taxi Driver*, lyrical in its squalor.

19 While it may not exactly be the Crossroads of the World, as it is often called, **Times Square** is one of New York's principal energy centers. It's one of many New York City "squares" that are actually triangles formed by the angle of Broadway slashing across a major avenue—in this case, crossing Seventh Avenue at 42nd Street. The square itself is occupied by the former Times Tower, now resheathed in white marble and called **One Times Square Plaza**. When the *New York Times* moved into its new headquarters on December 31, 1904, it publicized the event with a fireworks show at midnight, thus starting a New Year's Eve tradition. Each December 31, workmen on this roof lower a 200-pound ball down the flagpole by hand, just as they have since 1908. The huge intersection below is mobbed with revelers, and when the ball hits bottom on the stroke of midnight, pandemonium ensues.

The present headquarters of the *New York Times* (229 W. 43rd St.) occupies much of the block between Seventh and Eighth avenues; look for the blue delivery vans lined up along 43rd Street. From 44th to 51st streets, the cross streets west of Broadway are lined with some 30 major theaters (*see* Chapter 11). This has been the city's main theater district since the turn of the century; movie theaters joined the fray beginning in the 1920s. As the theaters drew crowds of people in the evenings, advertisers began to mount huge electric signs here, which gave the intersection its distinctive nighttime glitter. Even the developers who want to change this area intend to preserve the signs, making them bigger and brighter with new technology. One of the newest features a 42-foot-tall bottle of Coca-Cola hanging over Broadway and 47th Street, and a steaming Eight O'Clock Bean Coffee cup now warms up 46th Street.

20 The northern triangle of the intersection, which reaches up to 47th Street, is named **Duffy Square** after World War I hero Father Francis P. Duffy, the "Fighting Chaplain," who later was pastor of a theater district church on West 42nd Street. Besides the suitably military statue of Father Duffy, there's also one of George M. Cohan, the indomitable trouper who wrote "Yankee Doodle Dandy." Today Duffy Square is an important place to visit for the **TKTS discount ticket booth,** which sells half-price and 25%-off tickets to Broadway and some Off-Broadway shows (*see* Chapter 11). Some days it seems that almost every show in town is up for grabs; at other times there may be nothing available but a few long-running hits and some sleepers. The lines may look long, but they move surprisingly fast.

The main live theater on 42nd Street is provided by a group of thriving Off-Broadway playhouses, called **Theatre Row** (*see* Chapter 11), between Ninth and Tenth avenues. As you walk east, peek into No. 330, between Eighth and Ninth avenues, behind the Port Authority Bus Terminal. Originally the Mc-Graw-Hill Building, it was designed in 1931 by Raymond Hood, who later worked on Rockefeller Center. The lobby is an Art Deco wonder of opaque glass and stainless steel. The block between Seventh and Eighth avenues that was once the heart of the theater district is now a sleazy strip of X-rated bookstores, peep shows, and movie theaters; the sidewalks are full of loiterers and panhandlers who drift between here and the Port Authority bus station at 42nd Street and Eighth Avenue. The most prominent vestige of the old 42nd Street is the **New Amsterdam** (214 W. 42nd St.), a designated landmark that opened in 1903. Today the New Amsterdam is "dark"—lying fallow in anticipation of the area's redevelopment—but in its prime it was an opulent theater facility that showcased the likes of Eddie Cantor, Will Rogers, Fanny Brice, and the Ziegfeld Girls.

Heading east on 42nd Street, you'll pass **Hotaling's News** (142 W. 42nd St., tel. 212/840–1868), a bustling little shop that carries more than 220 daily newspapers from throughout the United States, most issues only a day or two old. The rear section stocks current newspapers, magazines, and foreign-language books from more than 40 countries.

At the intersection of 42nd Street and Sixth Avenue, look north to see, on the side of a low 43rd Street building, the **National Debt Clock,** an electronic display established by real-estate developer Seymour Durst to remind passersby of how much deeper in debt the United States gets every second. Across Sixth Avenue you'll see steps rising into the shrubbery and trees of ㉑ the handsomely renovated **Bryant Park,** named for the poet and editor William Cullen Bryant (1794–1878). This was the site of America's first World's Fair, the Crystal Palace Exhibition of 1853–54; today it's the backyard of the New York Public Library's central research branch. One reason to enter the park is to visit the **Bryant Park Dance and Music Tickets Booth,** which, in a setup similar to that of TKTS, sells tickets for music and dance performances throughout the city (*see* Chapter 11).

On the northwest corner of Sixth Avenue and 43rd Street, you can visit a branch of the International Center of Photography ㉒ (*see* Tour 5, *below*), **ICP Mid-Town,** which presents several photography shows a year in an ultracontemporary, multilevel space. *Tel. 212/768–4680. Admission: $4 adults, $2.50 students and senior citizens, $1 children under 12. Open Tues. 11–8, Wed.–Sun. 11–6.*

㉓ A block north, you'll see the **Algonquin Hotel** (59 W. 44th St.; *see* Chapter 10), which is surprisingly unpretentious considering its history as a haunt of well-known writers and actors. Its most famous association is with a witty group of literary Manhattanites who gathered in its lobby and dining rooms in the 1920s—a clique that included short-story writer Dorothy Parker, humorist Robert Benchley, playwright George S. Kaufman, and actress Tallulah Bankhead. One reason they met here was the hotel's proximity to the former offices of *The New Yorker* magazine at 28 West 44th (it finally moved in 1991, all the way to 20 West 43rd Street).

Next door to the Algonquin is the more humble (and cheaper) **Iroquois Hotel** (49 W. 44th St.; *see* Chapter 10), where struggling actor James Dean lived in the early 1950s. Across the street is the **Royalton Hotel** (44 W. 44th St.; *see* Chapter 10), chicly redone by French designer Philippe Starck. You might want to step into its lobby for a peek, but unless your clothes are suitably trendy, you may be hustled along by the staff. The hotel restaurant, 44 (*see* Chapter 9), has become a popular meeting place for the publishing industry. Next door, at 42 West 44th Street, is the **Association of the Bar of the City of New York,** with a neoclassical facade resembling the courthouses where its members spend so much of their time.

Back on the north side of the street, at 37 West 44th Street is the **New York Yacht Club,** former longtime home of the America's Cup trophy. Notice its swelling windowfronts, looking just like the sterns of ships, complete with stone-carved water splashing over the sill. The redbrick **Harvard Club** (27 W. 44th St.) echoes the Harvard campus with its modest Georgian-style architecture. Even if you're not a Harvard graduate who belongs to the Club, you may stay here if recommended by a member. At 20 West 44th, the **Mechanics' and Tradesmen's Institute Building,** in a turn-of-the-century prep school building, has a wonderful library in a three-story-high hall; here you'll also find the intriguing **Mossman Collection of Locks,** open free to the public (tel. 212/840–1840; open weekdays 10–3, except the first Wed. of every month).

At the corner of Fifth Avenue, look left to notice the large clock on a pedestal set in the Fifth Avenue sidewalk, a relic of an era when only rich people could afford watches. Then turn right and walk south. Between 40th and 42nd streets on Fifth Avenue, you'll find the central research building of the **New York Public Library.** This 1911 masterpiece of Beaux Arts design was financed largely by John Jacob Astor, whose previous library building downtown has since been turned into the Public Theater (*see* Tour 13, *below*). Its grand front steps are guarded by two crouching marble lions—dubbed "Patience" and "Fortitude" by Mayor Fiorello La Guardia, who said he visited the facility to "read between the lions." After admiring the white marble neoclassical facade (crammed with statues, as is typical of Beaux Arts buildings), walk through the bronze front doors into the grand marble lobby with its sweeping double staircase. Turn left and peek into the Periodicals Room, decorated with trompe l'oeil paintings by Richard Haas commemorating New York's importance as a publishing center. Then take a (quiet) look upstairs at the huge, high-ceilinged main reading room, a haven of scholarly calm, or visit the current exhibition in the art gallery. Among the treasures you might see are Gilbert Stuart's portrait of George Washington, Charles Dickens's desk, and Thomas Jefferson's own handwritten copy of the Declaration of Independence. Free one-hour tours, each as individual as the library volunteer who leads it, are given Tuesday–Saturday at 11 AM and 2 PM. *Tel. 212/930–0800. Open Tues.–Wed. 11–7:30, Thurs.–Sat. 10–6.*

25 Continue east on 42nd Street to **Grand Central Terminal** (not a "station," as many people call it, since all runs begin or end here). Constructed between 1903 and 1913, this Manhattan landmark was originally designed by a Minnesota architectural firm and later gussied up with Beaux Arts ornamentation. Stop on the south side of 42nd Street to admire the three huge windows separated by columns, and the Beaux Arts clock and sculpture crowning the facade above the elevated roadway (Park Avenue is routed around Grand Central's upper story). Go in the side doors on Vanderbilt Avenue to enter the cavernous main concourse, with its 12-story-high ceiling displaying the constellations of the zodiac. If you can handle it, the best time to visit is at rush hour, when this immense room crackles with the frenzy of scurrying commuters, dashing every which way. (You may have seen Barbra Streisand and Nick Nolte battling just such crowds in the film *The Prince of Tides*.) *Free tours Wed. at 12:30 PM (meet in front of Chemical Bank inside terminal on main level), tel. 212/935–3960.*

On the southwest corner of Park Avenue and 42nd Street, directly opposite Grand Central, the **Whitney Museum of American Art at Philip Morris** (120 Park Ave.) occupies the ground floor of the Philip Morris Building. Each year this free branch of the Whitney Museum (*see* Tour 5, *below*) presents five successive exhibitions of 20th-century painting and sculpture. An espresso bar and seating areas make it a much more agreeable place to rest than anywhere in Grand Central. *Tel. 212/878–2453. Admission free. Sculpture court open Mon.–Sat. 7:30 AM–9:30 PM, Sun. 11–7; gallery open Mon.–Wed. 11–6, Thurs. 11–7:30, Fri.–Sat. 11–6. Lectures on Mon., Wed., Fri. at 1 PM.*

The southeast corner of 42nd and Park is a major departure point for buses to the three New York area airports, and upstairs at 100 East 42nd Street you'll find ticket counters for most major U.S. airlines. Next door is the **Home Bank for Savings,** better known as **Bowery Savings Bank** (110 E. 42nd St.), whose massive arches and 70-foot-high marble columns give it a commanding presence. At the end of the block is the **Chanin Building** (122 E. 42nd St.), notable for the geometric Art Deco patterns that adorn its facade. Across the street you'll see the **Grand Hyatt** (Park Ave. at Grand Central Terminal), which was created by wrapping a new black glass exterior around the former Commodore Hotel.

Ask New Yorkers to name their favorite skyscraper and most
26 will choose the Art Deco **Chrysler Building** at 42nd Street and Lexington Avenue. Although the Chrysler Corporation itself moved out a long time ago, this graceful shaft culminating in a stainless-steel spire still captivates the eye and the imagination. The building has no observation deck, but you can go inside its elegant dark lobby, which is faced with African marble and covered with a ceiling mural that salutes transportation and human endeavor.

Although its future seems in question since its purchase by publisher Mortimer Zuckerman, who laid off many staff members, the *Daily News* was at this writing still being produced in the **Daily News Building** (220 E. 42nd St.), an Art Deco tower designed with brown-brick spandrels and windows to make it seem loftier than its 37 stories. Step into the lobby for a look at its revolving illuminated globe, 12 feet in diameter; the floor is laid out as a gigantic compass, with bronze lines indicating air mileage from principal world cities to New York. A small gallery displays *News* photos.

㉗ The **Ford Foundation Building** (320 E. 43rd St., with an entrance on 42nd St.) encloses a 12-story, ⅓-acre greenhouse. With a terraced garden, a still pool, and a couple of dozen full-grown trees, the Ford atrium is open to the public—for tranquil strolling, not for picnics—weekdays from 9 to 5.

Climb the steps along 42nd Street between First and Second avenues to enter **Tudor City,** a self-contained complex of a dozen buildings featuring half-timbering and lots of stained glass. Constructed between 1925 and 1928, two of the apartment buildings of this residential enclave originally had no east-side windows, lest the tenants be forced to gaze at the slaughter-houses, breweries, and glue factories then located along the East River. Today, however, they're missing a wonderful view of the United Nations Headquarters; you'll have to walk to the terrace at the end of 43rd Street to overlook the UN. This will place you at the head of the **Sharansky Steps** (named for Natan—formerly Anatoly—Sharansky, the Soviet dissident), which run along the **Isaiah Wall** (inscribed "They Shall Beat Their Swords Into Plowshares"); you'll also look down into **Ralph J. Bunche Park** (named for the black American UN undersecretary) and **Raoul Wallenberg Walk** (named for the Swedish diplomat and World War II hero who saved many children from the Nazis).

㉘ The **United Nations Headquarters** complex occupies a lushly landscaped 18-acre riverside tract just east of 1st Avenue between 42nd and 48th streets. Its rose garden is especially pleasant to stroll in, although picnicking is strictly forbidden. A line of flagpoles with banners representing the current roster of 159 member nations stands before the striking 550-foot-high slab of the Secretariat Building, with the domed General Assembly Building nestled at its side. The headquarters were designed in 1947–53 by an international team of architects led by Wallace Harrison. You can enter the General Assembly Building at the 46th Street door; the interior corridors overflow with imaginatively diverse artwork donated by member nations. Free tickets to most sessions are available on a first-come, first-served basis 15 minutes before sessions begin; pick them up in the General Assembly lobby. (The full General Assembly is in session from the third Tuesday in September to the end of December.) Visitors can take early luncheon in the Delegates Dining Room (jacket required for men) or eat anytime in the public coffee shop. *Tel. 212/963–7713. Tours offered daily 9:15–4:45. 1-hr tours leave the General Assembly lobby every 15–30 min. Tour admission: $6.50 adults, $4.50 students and senior citizens, $3.50 students in 8th grade and under. Children under 5 not permitted.*

Tour 4: Murray Hill to Gramercy Park

Numbers in the margin correspond to points of interest on the Tour 4: Murray Hill to Gramercy Park map.

As the city grew progressively north throughout the 19th century, one neighborhood after another had its fashionable heyday, only to fade from glory. But three neighborhoods, east of Fifth Avenue roughly between 20th and 40th streets, have preserved much of their historic charm, in Murray Hill's brownstone mansions and town houses, Madison Square's classic turn-of-the-century skyscrapers, and Gramercy Park's London-like leafy square. The only "must-see" along this route is the Empire State Building, but the walk as a whole is worth taking for the many moments en route when you may feel as if you've stepped back in time.

❶ Begin on East 36th Street, between Madison and Park avenues, at the **Pierpont Morgan Library.** The core of this small, patrician museum is the famous banker's own study and library, completed in 1906 by McKim, Mead & White. If you walk east past the museum's main entrance on 36th Street, you'll see the original library's neoclassical facade, with what is believed to be McKim's face on the sphinx in the right-hand sculptured panel. Around the corner, at 37th Street and Madison Avenue, is the latest addition to the library, an 1852 Italianate brownstone that was once the home of Morgan's son, J. P. Morgan, Jr. The elder Morgan's own house stood at 36th Street and Madison Avenue; it was torn down after his death and replaced with the simple neoclassical annex that today holds the library's main exhibition space. On your left as you enter are handsome benches, but don't be fooled into thinking that you can sit and rest on them; the guards will shoo you off them. But you can go inside and visit the galleries for rotating exhibitions; go straight to see items from the permanent collection, principally drawings, prints, manuscripts, and rare books, and to pass through the new glass-roofed garden court to the fine bookstore. Turn right just past the entrance and go down a long cloister corridor for the library's most impressive rooms: the elder Morgan's personal study, its red-damask-lined walls hung with first-rate paintings, and his majestic personal library with its dizzying tiers of handsomely bound rare books, letters, and illuminated manuscripts. *29 E. 36th St., tel. 212/ 685–0008. Suggested donation: $5 adults, $3 students and senior citizens. Open Tues.–Sat. 10:30–5, Sun. 1–5.*

❷ As you proceed south on Madison Avenue, at 35th Street you'll pass the **Church of the Incarnation,** a broodingly dark brownstone version of a Gothic chapel. Inside, however, there's enough jewellike stained glass to counteract the dour effect. Look especially for the north aisle's 23rd Psalm Window, by the Tiffany Glass works, or the south aisle's two Angel windows dedicated to infants, which are by the 19th-century English writer-designer William Morris.

At 35th Street and Madison Avenue, veteran globe-trotters will enjoy a stop at **The Complete Traveller Bookstore** (199 Madison Ave., tel. 212/679–4339), a comprehensive shop for travel literature and a charming old-world bookstore in its own right.

Occupying the block between 35th and 34th streets from Madison to Fifth avenues is a landmark building that from 1906 to

60

Tour 4: Murray Hill to Gramercy Park

E. 38th St.

Queens-Midtown Tunnel

E. 37th St.

E. 36th St. **❶**

MURRAY HILL

❷

E. 35th St.

Park Ave.

Fifth Ave.

E. 34th St.

E. 33rd St.

Ⓜ **6**

❸

Madison Ave.

E. 32nd St.

E. 31st St.

Third Ave.

Second Ave.

First Ave.

FDR Drive

E. 30th St.

E. 29th St.

❹ **❺**

Ⓜ **N,R**

E. 28th St.

Ⓜ **6**

Broadway

E. 27th St.

❼

❽

Park Ave. S.

E. 26th St.

Lexington Ave.

E. 25th St.

E. 24th St.

6

❾

Ⓜ **N,R**

Madison Square

Ⓜ **6**

E. 23rd St.

❿

E. 22nd St.

E. 21st St.

⓫

Gramercy Park **⓭**

E. 20th St.

E. 19th St.

N

Irving Pl.

E. 18th St.

E. 17th St.

Union Square

Stuyvesant Square

E. 16th St.

0   440 yards

0   400 meters

⓬

E. 15th St.

L,N,R,4,5,6 Ⓜ

Ⓜ **L**

E. 14th St.

Ⓜ **L**

Appellate Division of
the State Supreme
Court, **8**
Church of the
Incarnation, **2**
Church of the
Transfiguration, **5**
Empire State
Building, **3**
Flatiron Building, **10**
Gramercy Park, **13**
Madison Square, **6**
Marble Collegiate
Church, **4**

Metropolitan Life
Insurance Tower, **9**
New York Life
Insurance Building, **7**
Pierpont Morgan
Library, **1**
Theodore Roosevelt
Birthplace, **11**
Union Square, **12**

1989 was the home of **B. Altman,** one of New York's grand old department stores, which was speedily driven into bankruptcy by its last owner, the Australian conglomerate the Hooker Corporation.

❸ At Fifth Avenue and 34th Street, you can't miss the **Empire State Building.** It may no longer be the world's tallest building, but it is certainly one of the world's best-loved skyscrapers. The Art Deco playground for King Kong opened in 1931 after only about a year of construction. The crowning spire was originally designed as a mooring mast for dirigibles, but none ever docked here; in 1951, a TV transmittal tower was added to the top, raising the total height to 1,472 feet. Today more than 16,000 people work in the building, and more than 2½ million people a year visit the 86th- and 102nd-floor observatories. At night the top 30 stories are illuminated with colors appropriate to the season (red and green around Christmas; orange and brown for Halloween). In 1956, revolving beacons named the Freedom Lights were installed. These lights are illuminated from dusk to midnight.

Pass beneath the stainless-steel canopy on 34th Street to enter the three-story-high marbled lobby, where illuminated panels depicting the Seven Wonders of the World brazenly add the Empire State as the Eighth Wonder. Go to the concourse level to buy a ticket for the observation decks. The 102nd-floor observation spot is glassed in; the 86th floor is open to the air. In the movie *An Affair to Remember,* Cary Grant waited here impatiently for his rendezvous with Deborah Kerr. *5th Ave. and 34th St., tel. 212/736–3100. Admission: $3.50 adults, $1.75 children 5–11. Open daily 9:30 AM–midnight; the last elevator up leaves at 11:30 PM.*

Also on the concourse level of the Empire State Building, you'll find the **Guinness World of Records Exhibition,** where clever displays tell the story of various unusual record-holders. *Tel. 212/947–2335. Admission: $7 adults, $3.25 children under 12. Open Mon.–Thurs. 9–9, Fri.–Sun. 9 AM–9:30 PM.*

❹ Continue south on Fifth Avenue to 29th Street and the **Marble Collegiate Church** (1854), a marble-fronted structure built for the Reformed Protestant Dutch Congregation first organized in 1628 by Peter Minuit, the canny Dutchman who bought Manhattan from the native Indians for $24. Its pulpit was once occupied by Dr. Norman Vincent Peale *(The Power of Positive Thinking)*, Marble Collegiate's pastor from 1932 to 1984.

❺ Go east on 29th Street to the **Church of the Transfiguration** (1 E. 29th St.), which is better known as the Little Church Around the Corner. Set back in a shrub-filled New York version of an old English churchyard, it won its memorable appellation in 1870 when other area churches refused to bury actor George Holland, a colleague of well-known thespian Joseph Jefferson. Jefferson was directed to the "little church around the corner," which did that sort of thing, and the Episcopal institution has welcomed literary and show-biz types ever since. Go inside to see the south transept's stained-glass window, by John LaFarge, depicting 19th-century superstar actor Edwin Booth in his most famous role, Hamlet.

Bordered by Fifth Avenue, Broadway, Madison Avenue, 23rd and 26th streets, **Madison Square** was the site (circa 1845) of New York's first baseball games. On the north end, an imposing

1881 statue by Augustus Saint-Gaudens memorializes Civil War naval hero Admiral Farragut.

The block at 26th Street and Madison Avenue is occupied by the
❼ ornate **New York Life Insurance Building,** designed in 1928 by Cass Gilbert, who also did the Woolworth Building (*see* Tour 17, *below*). Its birthday-cake top is capped by a gilded pyramid that is stunning when lit at night. Go inside to admire the soaring lobby's coffered ceilings and ornate bronze doors. This was formerly the site of the second (1890–1925) Madison Square Garden, designed by architect and playboy Stanford White, who was shot in the Garden's roof garden by Harry K. Thaw, the jealous husband of actress Evelyn Nesbit—a lurid episode more or less accurately depicted in the movie *Ragtime*.

Coincidentally, other scenes in *Ragtime* were filmed in front of
❽ the **Appellate Division of the State Supreme Court,** which is at Madison Avenue and 25th Street. The roof balustrade of this imposing white marble Corinthian structure depicts great lawmakers of the past: Moses, Justinian, Confucius, and others, although a statue of Muhammed had to be removed because it offended the Islamic religion.

❾ The **Metropolitan Life Insurance Tower** (Madison Ave. between 23rd and 24th Sts.) made this building the world's tallest when it was added in 1909. The 700-foot tower re-creates the campanile of St. Mark's in Venice. The four dials of its clock are each three stories high; wait for the quarter hour to hear it chime. Met Life's North Building, between 24th and 25th streets, is connected by a skywalk. Its Art Deco loggias have attracted many film crews—it appeared in such films as *After Hours*, *Radio Days*, and *The Fisher King*. Step into the lobby of the South Building during weekday business hours to see a fine set of Wyeth murals; the guard may stop you, but if you explain what you want to see, you should be issued a pass.

❿ The Renaissance-style **Flatiron Building,** by architect Daniel Burnham, occupies the triangular lot formed by Broadway, Fifth Avenue, and 23rd Street. This, too, was the tallest building in the world when it opened (1902). Its rounded front point is only 6 feet wide, but gentle waves built into the molded limestone-and-terra-cotta side walls soften the wedge effect. Winds invariably swooped down its 20-story, 286-foot height, billowing up the skirts of women pedestrians on 23rd Street, and local traffic cops had to shoo away male gawkers—coining the phrase "23 Skiddoo." Originally named the Fuller Building, it was instantly rechristened by the public because of its resemblance to a flatiron, and eventually the nickname became official.

The Flatiron Building has lent its name to the once seedy, now trendy Flatiron District that lies to the south between Fifth Avenue and Park Avenue South. The neighborhood's massive buildings, the last of the preskyscraper era, have had their ornate Romanesque facades gleamingly restored; hip boutiques and restaurants occupy their street levels, while advertising agencies, publishing houses, architects' offices, graphic design firms, and residential lofts fill the upper stories.

Time Out A good stop for hearty soups, salads, or wonderful sandwiches on thick, crusty bread is **La Boulangère** (49 E. 21st St., tel. 212/ 475–8582). You can either sit at one of the tiny tables or order take-out (enjoy a picnic on a bench in either Madison Square or Union Square to the south).

Continue south on Broadway and turn east on 20th Street to ⑪ the **Theodore Roosevelt Birthplace,** a reconstruction of the Victorian brownstone where Teddy lived until he was 15 years old. Before becoming president, Roosevelt was New York City's police commissioner and the governor of New York State. The house contains Victorian period rooms and Roosevelt memorabilia; a selection of videos about the namesake of the teddy bear can be seen on request. Saturday-afternoon chamber-music concerts are offered each fall, winter, and spring. *28 E. 20th St., tel. 212/260–1616. Admission: $2 adults, free to senior citizens and children under 17. Open Wed.–Sun. 9–5; guided tours 9–3:30.*

If you pass by **890 Broadway** (between 19th and 20th St.), you may see actors and actresses leaving and entering the building. At this address is the Lawrence A. Wein Center for Dance and Theater, a honeycomb of rehearsal halls for upcoming plays and musicals. The space was founded by the late Broadway director-choreographer Michael Bennett, and it was here that he developed the award-winning musical *Dreamgirls.*

⑫ **Union Square** lies between Park Avenue South and Broadway and 14th and 17th streets. Its name, originally signifying the fact that two main roads merged here, proved doubly apt in the early 20th century when the square became a rallying spot for labor protests and mass demonstrations; many unions, as well as fringe political parties, moved their headquarters nearby. Over the years the area deteriorated into a habitat of drug dealers and kindred undesirables, until a massive renewal program in the 1980s transformed it. If possible, visit on Greenmarket day (Monday, Wednesday, Friday, and Saturday), when farmers from all over the Northeast, including some Pennsylvania Dutch and latter-day hippies, bring their goods to the big town: fresh produce, homemade bakery goods, cheeses, cider, New York State wines, even fish and meat.

At 5 Union Square West, the trendy gossip magazine *Spy* has its offices, where its staff produces its controversial issues that poke fun at political and popular-culture figures.

Just east of Union Square on rather disreputable 14th Street is the **Palladium** (126 E. 14th St.), a former movie palace turned into a cavernous, innovative disco—now well past its brief "in" moment—by Ian Schrager and the late Steve Rubell, of Studio 54 fame, and designed by Arata Isozaki. The Palladium is now owned by Peter Gatien, who also controls three other New York nightclubs: Limelight, the Tunnel, and Club USA. The Palladium stands at the foot of Irving Place, named after the writer Washington Irving (1783–1859), author of *The Legend of Sleepy Hollow*. Walk north to 40 Irving Place, where you'll see a huge bust of the writer outside **Washington Irving High School,** alma mater of Claudette Colbert and Whoopi Goldberg. A plaque on the redbrick house at 17th Street and Irving Place proclaims it as the home of Washington Irving, but it was his nephew's house, though the famous writer did visit there often.

More than a century later another famous chronicler of New York life, O. Henry, whose real name was William Sidney Porter, lived at 55 Irving Place, in a building long ago demolished.

But his legend lives on at **Pete's Tavern** (18th St. and Irving Pl., tel. 212/473–7676), which claims that O. Henry wrote "The Gift of the Magi" while sitting in the second booth to the right. Pete's Tavern also claims to be the oldest saloon in New York (1864); both facts are disputed, but stop here anyway for a casual drink and absorb the atmosphere of the Gaslight Era. Across the street is **Fresh Art** (71 Irving Pl., tel. 212/955–5044), an attractive plant store, and **Friend of a Farmer** (77 Irving Pl., tel. 212/477–2188), a popular country-style café.

At the top of Irving Place, between 20th and 21st streets, lies **⑬ Gramercy Park,** a picture-perfect city park complete with flower beds, bird feeders, sundials, and cozy benches. It stays nice largely because it's surrounded by a locked cast-iron fence, and, alas, only residents of the property around the park can obtain keys. Laid out in 1831 according to a design inspired by London's residential squares, Gramercy Park is surrounded by interesting buildings.

On the south side of the square, peek inside the park and you'll see a statue of actor Edwin Booth playing Hamlet. Booth lived at No. 16, which he remodeled in the early 1880s to serve as an actors' club, **The Players Club.** Stanford White, the architect for the renovation, was a member of the club, as were many other nonactors. Members over the years have included Mark Twain, Booth Tarkington, John and Lionel Barrymore, Irving Berlin, Winston Churchill, Lord Laurence Olivier, Frank Sinatra, Walter Cronkite, Jack Lemmon, and Richard Gere.

The **National Arts Club** (15 Gramercy Park S) was once the home of Samuel Tilden, a governor of New York and the Democratic presidential candidate who, in 1876, received more popular votes than Rutherford B. Hayes, who won more electoral college votes—and the election. Calvert Vaux, codesigner of Central Park, remodeled this building in 1874, conjoining two houses. Among its Victorian Gothic decorations are medallions portraying Goethe, Dante, Milton, and Benjamin Franklin. The Club now houses the Poetry Society of America, which sponsors poetry readings (*see* Readings and Lectures in Chapter 11).

On the west end of the square, note the row of redbrick Greek Revival town houses, with their fanciful cast-iron verandas looking like something out of New Orleans's French Quarter. Mayor James Harper (elected in 1888) lived at No. 4, behind the pair of street lanterns. The actor John Garfield died in 1952 while staying at No. 3.

At the northeast corner, the white terra-cotta apartment building at **36 Gramercy Park East** is guarded by concrete knights in silver-paint armor. The turreted redbrick building at **34 Gramercy Park East** was one of the city's first cooperative apartment houses; its tenants have included actors James Cagney, John Carradine, and Margaret Hamilton, who played the Wicked Witch in *The Wizard of Oz*. The austere gray-brown Friends Meeting House at 28 Gramercy Park South became **The Brotherhood Synagogue** in 1974, and a narrow plaza just east of the synagogue contains a Holocaust memorial. **19 Gramercy Park South** was the home in the 1880s of society doyenne Mrs. Stuyvesant Fish, a fearless iconoclast who shocked Mrs. Astor and Mrs. Vanderbilt when she reduced the time of formal dinner parties from several hours to 50 minutes, thus ushering in the modern social era.

If you're still energetic, wander over to Lexington Avenue in the high 20s, a neighborhood affectionately known as Little India, where Indian restaurants, spice shops, imported-video stores, and clothing stores abound. The area also plays host to Middle Eastern, Indonesian, and Vietnamese restaurants. In this multicultural part of town, better seen during the day, don't be surprised to find a Spanish-language playhouse across the street from an Islamic bookstore.

Tour 5: Museum Mile

Numbers in the margin correspond to points of interest on the Tours 5 and 6: Museum Mile, Upper East Side map.

Once known as Millionaire's Row, the stretch of Fifth Avenue between 79th and 104th streets has been fittingly renamed Museum Mile, for it now contains an impressive cluster of cultural institutions. The connection is more than coincidental: Many museums are housed in what used to be the great mansions of merchant princes and wealthy industrialists. In 1979 a group of 10 Fifth Avenue institutions formed a consortium that, among other activities, sponsors a Museum Mile Festival each June. The Frick Collection and the Whitney Museum of American Art are not officially part of the Museum Mile Consortium, but they're located close enough to be added to this tour.

It would be impossible to do justice to all these collections in one outing; the Metropolitan Museum alone contains too much to see in a day. You may want to select one or two museums to linger in and simply walk past the others, appreciating their exteriors (this in itself constitutes a minicourse in modern architecture). Save the rest for another day—or for your next trip to New York.

Be sure to pick the right day of the week for this tour: Most of these museums are closed on Mondays, but some have free admission during extended hours on Tuesday evenings.

❶ Begin at Fifth Avenue and 70th Street with **The Frick Collection,** housed in an ornate, imposing Beaux Arts mansion built in 1914 for coke-and-steel baron Henry Clay Frick, who wanted the superb art collection he was amassing to be kept far from the soot and smoke of Pittsburgh, where he'd made his fortune. The mansion was designed by architects Carrère and Hastings (also responsible for the Public Library on Fifth Avenue at 40th Street); opened as a public museum in 1935 and expanded in 1977, it still resembles a gracious private home, albeit one with a bona fide masterpiece in almost every room. Strolling through the mansion, one can imagine how it felt to live with Vermeers by the front stairs, Gainsborough and Reynolds portraits in the dining room, canvases by Constable and Turner in the library, and Titians, Holbeins, a Giovanni Bellini, and an El Greco in the living room. Some of the collection's best pieces include Rembrandt's *The Polish Rider* and Jean-Honoré Fragonard's series *The Progress of Love.* You can rest in the tranquil indoor court with a fountain and glass ceiling. *1 E. 70th St., tel. 212/288-0700. Admission: $3 adults, $1.50 students and senior citizens. Children under 10 not admitted. Open Tues.–Sat. 10–6, Sun. 1–6, closed holidays.*

Americas Society, **15**
Asia Society, **16**
Bloomingdale's, **12**
Carl Schurz Park, **19**
Conservatory
Garden, **11**
Cooper-Hewitt
Museum, **6**
El Museo Del
Barrio, **10**
Frick Collection, **1**
Gracie Mansion, **20**
Guggenheim
Museum, **4**
Henderson Place
Historic District, **18**
International Center
of Photography, **8**
Jewish Museum, **7**
Metropolitan Museum
of Art, **3**
Museum of the City of
New York, **9**
National Academy of
Design, **5**
Ralph Lauren, **17**
Seventh Regiment
Armory, **14**
Temple Emanu-El, **13**
Whitney Museum of
American Art, **2**

Tours 5 and 6: Museum Mile, Upper East Side

KEY

AE American Express Office

Walk one block east to Madison Avenue and head up to 75th
❷ Street to **The Whitney Museum of American Art.** This museum
grew out of a gallery in the studio of the sculptor and collector
Gertrude Vanderbilt Whitney, whose talent and taste were for-
tuitously accompanied by the wealth of two prominent families.
The current building, opened in 1966, is a minimalist gray
granite vault, separated from Madison Avenue by a dry moat;
it was designed by Marcel Breuer, a member of the Bauhaus
school, which prized functionality in architecture. The mono-
lithic exterior is much more forbidding than the interior, where
changing exhibitions offer an intelligent survey of 20th-century
American works; the second floor offers, among other exhibits,
daring new work from American video artists and filmmakers,
and the third-floor gallery features a sample of the permanent
collection, including Edward Hopper's haunting *Early Sunday
Morning* (1930), Georgia O'Keeffe's *White Calico Flower*
(1931), and Jasper Johns's *Three Flags* (1958). Alexander
Calder's *Circus*, a playful construction he tinkered with
throughout his life (1898–1976), stands near the front entrance. The Whitney also has a branch across from Grand Central Terminal (*see* Tour 3). *945 Madison Ave. at 75th St., tel.
212/570–3676. Admission: $6 adults, $4 students and senior
citizens. Open Wed. and Fri.–Sun. 11–6, Thurs. 1–8.*

Cut back to Fifth Avenue and walk north to **The American Irish
Historical Society,** in a town house once owned by U.S. Steel
president William Ellis Corey, who scandalized his social class
by marrying musical comedy star Mabelle Gilman. With its ornamentation and mansard roof, this is another fine example of
the French-influenced Beaux Arts style that was so popular at
the turn of the century. The society's library holdings chronicle
people of Irish descent who became successful in the United
States. *991 5th Ave. at 81st St., tel. 212/288–2263. Admission
free by appointment. Open Tues.–Sat. 11–4:30.*

❸ **The Metropolitan Museum of Art** offers valid evidence for billing itself as "New York's number one tourist attraction"; certainly the quality and range of its holdings make it one of the
world's greatest museums. It's the largest art museum in the
Western Hemisphere (1.6 million square feet), and its permanent collection of more than 3 million works of art from all over
the world includes objects from prehistoric to modern times.
The museum, founded in 1870, moved to this location in 1880,
but the original redbrick building by Calvert Vaux has since
been encased in other architecture. The majestic Fifth Avenue
facade, designed by Richard Morris Hunt, was built in 1902 of
gray Indiana limestone; later additions eventually surrounded
the original building on the sides and back. (On a side wall of
the new ground-floor European Sculpture Court, you can
glimpse the museum's original redbrick facade.)

The Fifth Avenue entrance leads into the Great Hall, a soaring
neoclassical chamber that has been designated a landmark.
Past the admission booths, a vast marble staircase leads up to
the European painting galleries, whose highlights include
Botticelli's *The Last Communion of St. Jerome*, Pieter
Brueghel's *The Harvesters*, El Greco's *View of Toledo*, Johan-
nes Vermeer's *Young Woman with a Water Jug*, and Rembrandt's *Aristotle with a Bust of Homer*. At press time, the
galleries housing the Met's fine Impressionist collection were
being remodeled into graceful neoclassical rooms, with the fo-

cal point of an oval gallery displaying 15 large Manets. During
the remodeling, all of the important pictures of this era were on
view in the European painting galleries, but if all goes according to schedule, the refurbished rooms for the Impressionist
paintings should be open by early 1994. The arcaded European
Sculpture Court includes Auguste Rodin's massive bronze *The
Burghers of Calais*.

American art has its own wing, back in the northwest corner;
the best approach is on the first floor, where you enter through
a refreshingly light and airy garden court graced with Tiffany
stained-glass windows, cast-iron staircases by Louis Sullivan,
and a marble Federal-style facade taken from the Wall Street
branch of the United States Bank. Take the elevator to the
third floor and begin working your way down through the
rooms decorated in period furniture—everything from a Shaker retiring room to a Federal-era ballroom to the living room of
a Frank Lloyd Wright house—and excellent galleries of American painting.

In the realm of 20th-century art, the Met was a latecomer, allowing the Museum of Modern Art and the Whitney to build
their collections with little competition until the Metropolitan's contemporary art department was finally established in
1967. The big museum has been trying to make up for lost time,
however, and in 1987 it opened the three-story Lila Acheson
Wallace Wing, in the southwest corner. Pablo Picasso's 1906
portrait of Gertrude Stein is the centerpiece of this collection.

There is much more to the Met than paintings, however. Visitors with a taste for classical art should go immediately to the
left of the Great Hall on the first floor to see the Greek and Roman statuary, not to mention a large collection of rare Roman
wall paintings excavated from the lava of Mount Vesuvius. Directly above these galleries, on the second floor, you'll find
room after room of Grecian urns and other classical vases. The
Met's awesome Egyptian collection, spanning some 3,000
years, lies on the first floor directly to the right of the Great
Hall. Its centerpiece is the Temple of Dendur, an entire Ro-
man-period temple (circa 15 BC) donated by the Egyptian government in thanks for U.S. help in saving ancient monuments.
Placed in a specially built gallery with views of Central Park to
refresh the eye, the temple faces east, as it did in its original
location, and a pool of water has been installed at the same distance from it as the river Nile once stood. Another spot suitable
for contemplation is directly above the Egyptian treasures, in
the Asian galleries: The Astor Court Chinese garden repro-
duces a Ming Dynasty (1368–1644) scholar's courtyard, complete with water splashing over artfully positioned rocks.

There's also a fine arms and armor exhibit on the first floor (go
through the medieval tapestries, just behind the main staircase, and turn right). The Met's medieval collection here is
lovely, but to see the real medieval treasures, don't miss a trip
to **The Cloisters**, the Met's annex in Washington Heights (*see*
Chapter 6). Keep going straight from the medieval galleries
until you enter the cool skylit white space of the Lehman Pavilion, where the small but exquisite personal collection of the late
donor, investment banker Robert Lehman, is displayed in
rooms resembling those of his West 54th Street town house.
This is one of the lesser-known wings of the Met (perhaps be-

cause it's tucked away behind so many other galleries), so it's a good place to go when the other galleries begin to feel crowded.

Although it exhibits only a portion of its vast holdings, the Met offers more than can reasonably be seen in one visit. Be aware also that cuts in cultural funding have forced the museum to close certain galleries either mornings or afternoons Tuesday–Thursday; in the course of a day, you can still see anything you want, but ask at the desk for an alternating-gallery schedule to avoid frustration. Choose what you want to see, find a map, and plan your tour accordingly. Walking tours and lectures are free with your admission contribution. Tours covering various sections of the museum begin about every 15 minutes on weekdays, less frequently on weekends; they depart from the Tour Board in the Great Hall. Self-guided audio tours can also be rented at a desk in the Great Hall. Lectures, often related to temporary exhibitions, are given frequently. *5th Ave. at 82nd St., tel. 212/535–7710. Suggested contribution: $6 adults, $3 students and senior citizens. Open Tues.–Thurs. and Sun. 9:30–5:15, Fri. and Sat. 9:30–8:45.*

Time Out While the Metropolitan has a good museum café, only a block away is a friendly, sparkling-clean coffee shop: **Nectar of 82nd** (1090 Madison Ave. at 82nd St., tel. 212/772–0916). Omelets, salads, soups, burgers—the portions are generous and the prices quite reasonable.

Across from the Met, between 82nd and 83rd streets on Fifth Avenue, one Beaux Arts town house stands its ground amid newer apartment blocks. It now belongs to the Federal Republic of Germany, which has installed a branch of the Goethe Institute here. **Goethe House** (tel. 212/439–8700; closed Sun.–Mon.) offers a changing series of art exhibitions as well as lectures, films, and chamber-music concerts; its extensive library (closed in the summer) includes current issues of German newspapers and periodicals. Up at 86th and Fifth, a brightly embellished limestone-and-redbrick mansion, designed by Carrère and Hastings to echo the buildings on the Place des Vosges in Paris, was once the home of Mrs. Cornelius Vanderbilt III. It now houses the **Yivo Institute for Jewish Research** (tel. 212/535–6700; open Mon. 9:30–8:30, Tues. and Thurs.–Fri. 9:30–5:30), with occasional exhibitions focusing on Eastern European and American Jewish history.

❹ Frank Lloyd Wright's **Guggenheim Museum** (opened in 1959) is a controversial work of architecture—even many of those who like its assertive six-story spiral rotunda will admit that it does not result in the best space in which to view art. Inside, under a 92-foot-high glass dome, a quarter-mile-long ramp spirals down past changing exhibitions of modern art. The museum has especially strong holdings in Wassily Kandinsky, Paul Klee, and Pablo Picasso; the oldest pieces are by the French Impressionists. A new annex called the Tower Galleries opened in June 1992, creating additional gallery space to display the newly acquired Panza Collection of Minimalist art, among other works. The 10-story annex designed by Gwathmey Siegel and based on Wright's original designs offers four spacious galleries that can accommodate the extraordinarily large art pieces that the Guggenheim owns but previously had no room to display. *1071 5th Ave. at 89th St., tel. 212/423–3500. Admis-*

*sion: $10 adults, $8 students and senior citizens. Open Fri.–
Wed. 10–8.*

❺ A block north is **The National Academy of Design,** housed in a
stately 19th-century mansion and a pair of town houses on 89th
Street. The academy itself, which was founded in 1825, required each elected member to donate a representative work of
art, which has resulted in a strong collection of 19th- and 20th-
century American art. (Members have included Samuel F. B.
Morse, Winslow Homer, John Singer Sargent, Frank Lloyd
Wright, and Robert Rauschenberg.) *1083 5th Ave. at 89th St.,
tel. 212/369–4880. Admission: $3.50 adults, $2 senior citizens
and children under 16; free Tues. 5–8. Open Tues. noon–8,
Wed.–Sun. noon–5.*

At 91st Street you'll find the former residence of industrialist
❻ Andrew Carnegie, now the home of the **Cooper-Hewitt Museum**
(officially the Smithsonian Institution's National Museum of
Design). Carnegie sought comfort more than show when he
built this 64-room house on what were the outskirts of town in
1901; he administered his extensive philanthropic projects
from the first-floor study. (Note the low doorways—Carnegie
was only 5 feet 2 inches tall.) The core of the museum's collection was begun in 1897 by the three Hewitt sisters, grand-
daughters of inventor and industrialist Peter Cooper; major
holdings include drawings, prints, textiles, furniture, metal-
work, ceramics, glass, woodwork, and wall coverings. The
Smithsonian rescued their museum from financial ruin in 1963,
and the Carnegie Corporation donated the mansion in 1972.
The changing exhibitions, which focus on various aspects of
contemporary or historical design, are invariably well re-
searched, enlightening, and often amusing. *2 E. 91st St., tel.
212/860–6868. Admission: $3 adults, $1.50 students and senior
citizens; free Tues. 5–9. Open Tues. 10–9, Wed.–Sat. 10–5,
Sun. noon–5.*

Across 91st Street from the Cooper-Hewitt, the **Convent of the
Sacred Heart** is in a huge Italianate mansion originally built in
1918 for financier Otto Kahn, a noted patron of the arts.

Time Out **Jackson Hole** (Madison Ave. and 91st St., tel. 212/427–2820) is
a cheerful spot that serves the great American hamburger plus
other sandwiches, omelets, chicken, and salads. Ski posters
evoke the mood of the eponymous Wyoming resort.

❼ **The Jewish Museum** opened its expanded and renovated facilities in June 1993. The expansion preserved the gray stone
Gothic-style 1908 mansion occupied by the museum since 1947
and enlarged the 1963 addition. At the same time, the mansion
facade was extended, giving the museum the appearance of a
late–French Gothic château. The permanent two-floor exhibition, presented alongside temporary shows, traces the development of Jewish culture and identity over 4,000 years. The
exhibition draws on the museum's enormous collection of art
works, ceremonial objects, and electronic media. *1109 5th Ave.
at 92nd St., tel. 212/423–3200. Admission: $6 adults, $4 students and senior citizens, children under 12 free (pay-as you-
wish Tues. after 5). Open Sun., Mon., Wed., Thurs. 11–5:45;
Tues. 11–8. Closed national and Jewish holidays.*

The handsome, well-proportioned Georgian-style mansion on
the corner of Fifth Avenue and 94th Street was built in 1914 for

Willard Straight, founder of *The New Republic* magazine. Today it is the home of **The International Center of Photography** (ICP), a relatively young institution—founded in 1974—building a strong collection of 20th-century photography. Its changing exhibitions often focus on the work of a single prominent photographer or one photographic genre (portraits, architecture, etc.). The bookstore carries an impressive array of photography-oriented books, prints, and postcards. *1130 5th Ave. at 94th St., tel. 212/860–1777. Admission: $4 adults, $2.50 students and senior citizens, $1 children under 12. Open Tues. 11–8, Wed.–Sun. 11–6.*

As you proceed north on Fifth Avenue, you may want to walk a few paces east on 97th Street to see the onion-domed tower of the **Russian Orthodox Cathedral of St. Nicholas,** built in 1902. Between 98th and 101st streets, Fifth Avenue is dominated by the various buildings of **Mount Sinai Hospital,** which was founded in 1852 by a group of wealthy Jewish citizens and moved here in 1904. The 1976 addition, the Annenberg Building, is a looming tower of Cor-Ten steel, which has deliberately been allowed to develop a patina of rust.

The Museum of the City of New York traces the course of Big Apple history, from the Dutch settlers of Nieuw Amsterdam to the present day, with period rooms, dioramas, slide shows, and clever displays of memorabilia. An exhibit on the Port of New York illuminates the role of the harbor in New York's rise to greatness; the noteworthy Toy Gallery has several meticulously detailed dollhouses. Weekend programs appeal especially to children. *5th Ave. at 103rd St., tel. 212/534–1672. Suggested contribution: $5 adults; $3 students, senior citizens, and children; $8 family. Open Wed.–Sat. 10–5, Sun. and all legal holidays (not Mon.) 1–5.*

El Museo Del Barrio, founded in 1969, concentrates on Latin culture in general, with a particular emphasis on Puerto Rican art. ("El Barrio" means "the neighborhood," and the museum is positioned on the edge of Spanish Harlem.) The permanent collection includes numerous pre-Columbian artifacts. *1230 5th Ave. at 104th St., tel. 212/831–7272. Suggested contribution: $2. Open Wed.–Sun. 11–5.*

Having completed this long walk, you may want to reward yourself by crossing the street to Central Park's **Conservatory Garden.** The entrance, at 105th Street, is through elaborate wrought-iron gates that once graced the mansion of Cornelius Vanderbilt II. In contrast to the deliberately rustic effect of the rest of the park, this is a symmetrical, formal garden. The central lawn is bordered by yew hedges and flowering crab apple trees, leading to a reflecting pool flanked by a large wisteria arbor. To the south is a high-hedged flower garden named after Frances Hodgson Burnett, author of the children's classic *The Secret Garden.* To the north is the Untermeyer Fountain, with its three spirited girls dancing at the heart of a huge circular bed where 20,000 tulips bloom in the spring, and 5,000 chrysanthemums in the fall.

Tour 6: The Upper East Side

The Upper East Side epitomizes the high-style, high-society way of life most people associate with the Big Apple. Between Fifth and Lexington avenues, up to about 86th Street, is an elegant enclave of wealth. Luxury co-ops and condominiums, exquisite town houses, private schools, posh galleries, and international shops line streets where even the sidewalks seem more sparkling clean than any others in Manhattan. You may find the people who live and work in this neighborhood a bit snobbish compared with other New Yorkers, but take it in stride—they treat everybody that way.

A fitting place to begin your exploration of the moneyed Upper East Side is that infamous shrine to conspicuous consumption, **⑫ Bloomingdale's** (59th St. between Lexington and 3rd Aves., tel. 212/705–2000). This block-long behemoth is noisy, trendy, and crowded; you'll find everything from designer clothes to high-tech teakettles in slick, sophisticated displays. Not one to shrink from the spotlight, Bloomie's has appeared in more than a few Manhattan movies. Diane Keaton and Michael Murphy shared a perfume-counter encounter here in Woody Allen's *Manhattan*; Robin Williams, playing a Russian musician, defected to the West in *Moscow on the Hudson*; and mermaid Darryl Hannah, in *Splash*, took a crash course in human culture in front of a bank of TVs in the electronics department.

Time Out On Bloomingdale's sixth floor, frazzled shoppers can take a break at **Le Train Bleu** restaurant (tel. 212/705–2100), decorated like a snappy railroad car and overlooking the 59th Street Bridge. Besides à la carte snacks, it offers one of the best bargains in town for afternoon tea (3–4:30 PM).

Leaving Bloomingdale's, head west on 60th Street toward Fifth Avenue. As you cross Park Avenue, stop for a moment on the wide, neatly planted median strip. Look south toward midtown and you'll see the Pan Am Building, towering over the gilded peaked roof of the Helmsley Building at the foot of the avenue. Then turn to look uptown, and you'll see a thoroughfare lined with massive buildings that are more like mansions stacked atop one another than apartment complexes. As you proceed into the Upper East Side, observe the trappings of wealth: well-kept buildings, children in private school uniforms, nannies wheeling grand baby carriages, dog-walkers, limousines, doormen in braided livery. This is the territory where Sherman McCoy, protagonist of Tom Wolfe's *Bonfire of the Vanities*, lived in pride before his fall, and where the heroine of Woody Allen's movie *Alice* felt suffocated amidst the trappings of wealth.

On the northwest corner of 60th Street and Park Avenue is **Christ Church United Methodist Church** (520 Park Ave., tel. 212/838–3036), built during the Depression but designed to look centuries old, with its random pattern of limestone blocks. Inside, the Byzantine-style sanctuary (open Sundays and holidays) glitters with golden handmade mosaics.

Continue west on 60th Street to pass a grouping of very different kinds of clubs. Ornate grillwork curls over the doorway of the scholarly **Grolier Club** (47 E. 60th St., tel. 212/838–6690), founded in 1884 and named after the 16th-century French bibliophile Jean Grolier. Its members are devoted to the bookmaking crafts; one of them, Bertram Grosvenor Goodhue, designed this neatly proportioned redbrick building in 1917. The club presents public exhibitions and has a specialized reference library open by appointment only. On the next block over, at 10

East 60th Street, a red canopy shelters the entrance to the **Copacabana** (tel. 212/755-6010), the once swanky nightclub; in a memorable scene in the movie *Goodfellas*, mobster Henry Hill wows a new girlfriend by nonchalantly slipping in the back door to swing a front-row table here. From the time it opened in 1940 until well into the 1950s, the Copa was one of Manhattan's most glamorous night spots, featuring such performers as Ella Fitzgerald, Sid Caesar, Frank Sinatra, Tony Bennett, Sammy Davis, Jr., Nat King Cole, Jimmy Durante, and Lena Horne. The club closed in 1973, although it has since had various comebacks, currently keeping a low profile as a disco and group-function space. Right next door is the **Harmonie Club** (4 E. 60th St.), one of several private men's clubs (many of which now admit women) in this area. Built in 1905 by McKim, Mead & White, this pseudo-Renaissance palace, awkwardly stretched to high-rise proportions, is closely guarded by a doorman, so it's best to admire it from afar. Across the street is the **Metropolitan Club** (1 E. 60th St.), an even more lordly neoclassical edifice built in 1893, also by McKim, Mead & White. J. P. Morgan established this club when a friend of his was refused membership in the Union League Club; its members today include rulers of foreign countries and presidents of major corporations.

Take a right at Fifth Avenue. On the next block you'll pass **The Pierre** (*see* Chapter 10), a hotel that opened in 1930; notice its lovely mansard roof and tower. As you cross 62nd Street, take a look at the brick-and-limestone mansion at 2 East 62nd, the home of the **Knickerbocker Club,** a private social club founded in 1871. Across the street is the **Fifth Avenue Synagogue** (5 E. 62nd St., tel. 212/838-2122), a limestone temple built in 1959. Its pointed oval windows are filled with stained glass in striking abstract designs. You may want to detour down this elegant block of town houses; take special note of No. 11, which has elaborate Corinthian pilasters and an impressive wrought-iron entryway.

⑬ Continue up Fifth Avenue to 65th Street, where you'll see **Temple Emanu-El,** the world's largest Reform Jewish synagogue (it has seats for 2,500 worshipers). Built in 1929 of limestone, it is covered with mosaics and designed in the Romanesque style with Byzantine influences; the building features Moorish and Art Deco ornamentation. *Tel. 212/744-1400. Services Fri. 5 PM, Sat. 10:30 AM. Weekday services Sun.-Thurs. 5:30 PM held around corner at community house, 1 E. 65th St. Guided group tours of synagogue by appointment.*

Head east on 66th Street, past the site of the house (3 E. 66th St.) where Ulysses S. Grant spent his final months, before moving permanently up to Grant's Tomb (*see* Tour 9). (If you are interested in presidential homes, you may want to detour over to 65th Street between Madison and Park avenues to Nos. 45 and 47 East 65th Street, a pair of town houses built in 1910 for Sara Delano Roosevelt and her son, Franklin; FDR once lay recovering from polio at No. 47.) Next door, at 5 East 66th Street, is the **Lotos Club,** a private club founded in 1870. Its current home is a handsomely ornate French Renaissance mansion originally designed as a private residence by Richard Howland Hunt.

Continue east to Park Avenue. Railroad tracks once ran down the middle of Park Avenue; they were covered with a roadway just after World War I, and the grand sweeping street that resulted became a distinguished residential address. The red Victorian castle-fortress at 66th Street and Park Avenue is the

⑭ Seventh Regiment Armory (643 Park Ave.). This huge structure is still used as a military headquarters (you can see soldiers in camouflage uniforms manning the driveway on Lexington Avenue), but it has plenty of meeting and social space as well, which is used for a tennis arena, a restaurant, a shelter for homeless people, and an exhibit hall that hosts, among other events, two posh annual antiques shows. Both Louis Comfort Tiffany and Stanford White helped design its surprisingly residential interior; go up the front stairs into the wood-paneled lobby and take a look around. Tours are available by appointment (tel. 212/744–2968).

On the west side of Park Avenue, a pair of grand mansions face each other across 68th Street. Though houses have generally been replaced by apartment buildings along Park Avenue, these survivors give you an idea of how the neighborhood once looked. The grandly simple silvery limestone palace on the southwest corner, built in 1920, now houses the prestigious **Council on Foreign Relations** (58 E. 68th St.). The dark-red brick town house on the northwest corner was built in 1909–1911 by McKim, Mead & White for Percy Pyne, the grandson of noted financier Moses Taylor. From 1948 to 1963, this mansion was the Soviet Mission to the United Nations; when the Russians moved out, developers wanted to raze the town house, but in 1965 the marquesa de Cuevas acquired the property and presented it to the Center for Inter-American Relations. Now

⑮ called the **Americas Society,** it has an art gallery that's open to the public. *680 Park Ave., tel. 212/249–8950. Suggested donation: $3. Open Tues.–Sun. noon–6.*

Note how the three houses to the north—built during the following decade, and designed by three different architects—carried on the Pyne mansion's Georgian design to create a unified block. Today these buildings hold the **Spanish Institute** (684 Park Ave.), the **Instituto Italiano di Cultura** (Italian Cultural Institute, 686 Park Ave.), and the **Italian Consulate** (690 Park Ave.).

⑯ Two blocks north, on the east side of Park Avenue, is the **Asia Society,** a museum and educational center in an eight-story red granite building in striking contrast to the older, more traditional architecture of the street. While this is the headquarters of a nonprofit educational society, not technically a museum, it does offer public exhibitions of Asian art, including South Asian stone and bronze sculptures; art from India, Nepal, Pakistan, and Afghanistan; bronze vessels, ceramics, sculpture, and paintings from China; Korean ceramics; and paintings, wood sculptures, and ceramics from Japan. *725 Park Ave. at 70th St., tel. 212/288–6400. Admission: $2 adults, $1 students and senior citizens; free Fri. 6–8. Open Tues.–Thurs. and Sat. 11–6, Fri. 11–8, Sun. noon–5.*

At this point, shoppers may want to double back to Madison Avenue and get down to shopping business (*see* Chapter 8). The catchphrase "Madison Avenue" no longer refers to the midtown advertising district (most major agencies have moved away from there anyway) but instead to Uptown's fashion district: Madison Mile, between 59th and 79th streets, an exclusive area of haute couture designer boutiques, patrician art galleries, and unique specialty stores. For the most part, these shops are small, intimate, expensive—and almost invariably closed on Sundays. Even if you're just window-shopping, it's **⑰** fun to step inside the tony digs of **Ralph Lauren** (867 Madison Ave. at 72nd St., tel. 212/606–2100), which hardly seems like a store at all. In fact, it's in the landmark Rhinelander Mansion and has preserved the grand house's walnut fittings, oriental carpets, and family portraits as an aristocratic setting in which to display high-style preppy clothing (it's draped about casually, as though waiting to be put away). Be sure to visit the fourth-floor home-furnishings section, where merchandise is arrayed in to-the-manor-born dream suites.

At Madison Avenue and 76th Street is the **Carlyle Hotel,** one of the city's most elite and discreet properties (*see* Chapter 10). In the early 1960s President John F. Kennedy frequently stayed here; rumor has it that he entertained Marilyn Monroe in his rooms when Mrs. Kennedy was not around. The hotel's current roster of rich-and-famous guests includes Elizabeth Taylor, George C. Scott, Steve Martin, Paul Newman, and Warren Beatty and Annette Bening.

West of Madison is the so-called **Gucci Town House** (16 E. 76th St.), the former Gucci family mansion, which in 1988 sold for $7 million, at the time the most ever paid for a New York town house.

The final leg of this tour is several blocks away, so walk up Lexington or Third avenues, where there are plenty of shops and restaurants at street level to entertain you. This is the part of the East Side where more ordinary mortals can manage to live.

Time Out   Among the many restaurants clustered along Third Avenue in the 70s and 80s, one of the least pretentious is **Luke's Bar and Grill** (1394 3rd Ave. between 79th and 80th Sts., tel. 212/249–7070), with its friendly staff, cozy wood paneling, and red-checkered tablecloths. Reasonably priced burgers, salads, sandwiches, and pasta fill the lunch menu.

As you get closer to 86th Street, the neighborhood becomes more modest and ethnic. Until the 1830s, when the New York & Harlem Railroad and a stagecoach line began racing through the area, this neighborhood was the quiet, remote hamlet of **Yorkville,** a predominantly German community. Over the years it has also welcomed waves of immigrants from Austria, Hungary, and Czechoslovakia, and local shops and restaurants still bear reminders of this European heritage.

⑱ On 86th at York Avenue, the **Henderson Place Historic District** includes 24 small-scale town houses built in the 1880s in the Queen Anne style, which was developed in England by Richard Norman Shaw. Designed to be comfortable yet romantic dwellings, they combine elements of the Elizabethan manor house with classic Flemish details. Note, especially, the lovely bay windows, the turrets marking the corner of each block, and the symmetrical roof gables, pediments, parapets, chimneys, and dormer windows.

⑲ When you reach East End Avenue, you'll be facing **Carl Schurz Park,** overlooking the East River. Stand by the railings and look out at the Triborough and Hell's Gate bridges, Ward's and Randall's islands, and, on the other side of the river, Astoria,

Queens. During the American Revolution, a house on this promontory was used as a fortification by the Continental army, then was taken over as a British outpost. In more peaceful times, the land became known as East End Park. It was renamed in 1911 to honor Carl Schurz (1829–1906), a famous 19th-century German immigrant who eventually served the United States as a minister to Spain, a major general in the Union Army, and a senator of Missouri. During the Hayes administration, Schurz was Secretary of the Interior; he later moved back to Yorkville and worked as editor of the *New York Evening Post* and *Harper's Weekly*.

⓴ Stroll up Carl Schurz Park to reach one of the city's most famous residences, **Gracie Mansion,** the official home of the mayor of New York. Surrounded by a small lawn and flowerbeds, this Federal-style yellow frame house still feels like a country manor house, which is what it was built as in 1779 by wealthy merchant Archibald Gracie. The Gracie family entertained many notable guests at the mansion, including Louis Philippe (later king of France), President John Quincy Adams, the marquis de Lafayette, Alexander Hamilton, James Fenimore Cooper, Washington Irving, and John Jacob Astor. The city purchased Gracie Mansion in 1887, and, after a period of use as the Museum of the City of New York (now at Fifth Ave. and 103rd St.—*see* Tour 5, *above*), Mayor Fiorello H. La Guardia made it the official mayor's residence. *Admission: $3 adults, $2 senior citizens. Guided tours mid-Mar.–mid-Nov., Wed. at 10, 11, 1, and 2, by reservation only. Tel. 212/570–4751.*

Tour 7: Central Park

Numbers in the margin correspond to points of interest on the Tour 7: Central Park map.

It's amazing that 843 acres of the world's most valuable real estate should be set aside as a park, yet the city's 1856 decision to do so has proved to be marvelous wisdom, for Central Park contributes mightily toward helping New Yorkers maintain their sanity. It provides space large enough to get lost in (the entire principality of Monaco would fit within its borders), space where you can escape from the rumble of traffic to hear a bird sing or watch an earthworm tumble through the soil.

Although it appears to be simply a swath of rolling countryside exempted from urban development, Central Park is in fact one of the most cunningly planned artificial landscapes ever built. When they began in 1858, designers Frederick Law Olmsted and Calvert Vaux were presented with a swampy neighborhood of a few farms, houses, and a church. It took them 16 years, $14 million, and 5 million cubic yards of moved earth to create this playground of lush lawns, thick forests, and quiet ponds. Hills and tunnels artfully conceal transverse roads (65th, 79th, 86th, and 97th streets) so crosstown traffic will not disturb park goers, and a meandering circular drive carries vehicular traffic in the park (the drive is closed to auto traffic on weekends year-round).

Today Central Park hosts just about any activity that a city dweller might engage in outdoors: jogging, cycling, horseback riding, softball, ice skating, roller skating, croquet, tennis, bird-watching, boating, chess, checkers, theater, concerts, skateboarding, and folk dancing. If you're traveling with children, you'll especially appreciate how much there is to do and see. Try to come on a weekend, when local residents gratefully flock here to play—free entertainment is on tap, and the entire social microcosm is on parade.

Weekend crowds also make it safe to go into virtually any area of the park, although even on weekdays you should be safe anywhere along this tour. Despite its bad reputation, Central Park has the lowest crime rate of any precinct in the city—though the spectacularly ugly and frightening attack on a jogger in 1989 has reminded New Yorkers that the wisest course is to stay out of it at night (unless you are attending a free concert along with thousands of others).

Our route covers a lot of territory, but Olmsted and Vaux scattered their attractions so generously that there's something to see or do at almost every turn. One caveat, however: Although there are cafés connected with several attractions, as well as food stands near many entrances, the range of food is limited and predictable. Do as most New Yorkers do and stop beforehand at a deli or gourmet food shop for a picnic to carry in with you. *Tel. 212/794–6565 for general information, 212/794–6564 for a recorded message on city park events, 212/427–4040 for information on weekend walks and talks led by Urban Park Rangers.*

At Grand Army Plaza, or most intersections of Central Park South (59th Street's name between Fifth and Eighth avenues), you can hire a ride in a horse-drawn carriage through the park. Carriages operate all year, except in extremely hot or cold weather, and blankets are provided when it's cool. The official rates are $34 for the first 30 minutes and $10 for each additional 15 minutes, although drivers may try to get more, so agree on a price in advance. By the way: You can charge the ride to an American Express card.

To explore the park on foot, begin at Grand Army Plaza. Enter the park along the main road (East Drive), turning down the ❶ first path to your left to the **Pond.** Walk along the shore to the Gapstow Bridge (each of the park's 30 bridges has its own name and individual design), where you can look back at the often-photographed view of midtown skyscrapers reflected in the pond. From left to right, you'll see the peak-roofed brown Sherry-Netherland hotel, the black-and-white General Motors building, the rose-colored "Chippendale" top of the AT&T building, the black glass shaft of Trump Tower, and in front the green gables of the white Plaza Hotel.

❷ Return to the main path and continue north to **Wollman Memorial Rink,** a skating rink that was once a symbol of municipal inefficiency to New Yorkers. Fruitless and costly attempts by the city to repair the deteriorated facility had kept it closed for years, until real-estate mogul Donald Trump adopted the project and quickly completed it. Even if you don't want to join in, you can stand on the terrace here to watch the skaters—ice-skating throughout the winter, roller-skating and playing miniature golf April through October. The blaring loudspeaker system in this otherwise quiet park makes the rink hard to ignore. *Tel. 212/517–4800. Admission: $6 adults, $3 children under 13. Skate rental: $3.25. Open Mon. 10–5, Tues.–Thurs. 10–9:30, Fri. and Sat. 10 AM–11 PM, Sun. 10–9:30.*

78

Tour 7: Central Park

From April through October part of the rink becomes the **Gotham Miniature Golf** course, where putters maneuver around scale models of various city landmarks. *Tel. 212/517–4800. Admission: $6.50 adults, $3.50 children under 13. Open Mon. 10–5, Tues.–Thurs. 10–9:30, Fri. and Sat. 10 AM–11 PM, Sun. 10–9:30.*

Turn your back to the rink and you'll see the painted, pointed ❸ eaves, steeple, and high-pitched slate roof of the **Dairy,** originally an actual dairy built in the 19th century when cows grazed here. Today it's the park's visitor center, offering maps, souvenirs, videos, children's programs, and some very interesting hands-on exhibits. *Tel. 212/794–6565. Open Tues.–Sun. 11–4, Fri. 1–4.*

As you leave the Dairy, follow the path to your right (west) and under the Playmates Arch—aptly named, because it leads to a large area of ballfields and playgrounds. Coming through the ❹ arch, you'll hear the jaunty music of the **Carousel.** Although this isn't the park's original one, it was built in 1908 and later moved here from Coney Island. Its 58 ornately hand-carved steeds are three-quarters the size of real horses, and the organ plays a variety of tunes, new and old. *Tel. 212/879–0244. Admission: 90¢. Open summer, weekdays 10:30–5:30, weekends 10:30–6:30; winter, weekends only 10:30–4:30, weather permitting.*

Climb the slope to the left of the Playmates Arch and walk beside the Center Drive. From here you can choose between two parallel routes: Turn left onto the paved path that runs along-❺ side the chain-link fence of the **Sheep Meadow,** or go all the way ❻ to the circular garden at the foot of the **Mall.** The broad formal walkway of the Mall called **"The Literary Walk"** is a peaceful spot, lined with the largest group of American elms in the Northeast and statues of famous men, including Shakespeare, Robert Burns, and Sir Walter Scott. The other path, however, buzzes on weekends with human activity: volleyball games, roller-skating, impromptu music fests. Watch out for speeding in-line skaters. By contrast, the 15 grassy acres of the Sheep Meadow make an ideal spot for picnicking or sunbathing. It's an officially designated quiet zone, where the most vigorous sports allowed are kite-flying and Frisbee-tossing. This lawn was actually used for grazing sheep until 1934; the nearby sheepfold was turned into the Tavern on the Green restaurant (*see* Tour 8, *below*).

The gravel path that borders the Sheep Meadow on the north is ❼ heady with the scent of lilacs in spring; it leads to the **Mineral Springs Pavilion,** where there's a snack bar. Behind it are the ❽ beautifully manicured **Croquet Grounds** and **Lawn Bowling Greens.** During the season (May–November), you can peer through gaps in the high hedges to watch the players, usually dressed in crisp white. To play, you must have a season permit (tel. 212/360–8133).

The 72nd Street transverse—the only crosstown street that connects with the East, Center, and West drives—cuts across the park just north of here, but you can cross it or pass beneath ❾ it through a lovely tiled arcade to reach **Bethesda Fountain,** set on an elaborately patterned paved terrace on the edge of the **Lake** and featured in the film *Home Alone 2.* This ornate, three-tiered fountain is named after the biblical Bethesda pool in Jerusalem, which was supposedly given healing powers by an angel (hence the angel rising from the center). Perch on the low terrace wall or the edge of the fountain and watch the rowboaters stroke past on the lake. If you want to get out on the water yourself, take the path east from the terrace to **Loeb Boathouse,** where in season you can rent a rowboat. The boathouse also operates a bike-rental facility and a better-than-average restaurant, where the characters in the movie *Three Men and a Little Lady* dined. *Boat rental $7 per hr, $20 deposit; tel. 212/517–4723. Bicycle rental $6 per hr, tandems $12 per hr; tel. 212/861–4137. Open May–Oct., daily 11–6.*

The path to the west of the terrace leads to **Bow Bridge,** a splendid cast-iron bridge arching over a neck of the lake. The view from either side is postcard-perfect, with the water reflecting a quintessentially New York image of vintage apartment buildings peeping above the treetops. If you continue across the bridge, you'll enter the **Ramble,** a heavily wooded 37-acre area laced with twisting, climbing paths. This is prime bird-watching territory; a rest stop along a major migratory route, it shelters many of the 269 species of birds that have been sighted in the park. Because it is so dense and isolated, however, it may not be a good place to wander alone.

If you don't venture into the Ramble, recross Bow Bridge and continue west on the lakeside path to **Cherry Hill,** where a circular plaza sets off a wrought-iron-and-gilt fountain that is smaller, but no less lovely, than Bethesda Fountain. This area was originally a carriage turnaround and watering area for horses. The path ahead leads back to the 72nd Street transverse; on the rocky outcrop directly across the road, you'll see a statue of a falconer gracefully lofting his bird. Turn to the right and you'll see a more prosaic statue, a pompous bronze figure of Daniel Webster with his hand thrust into his coat. Cross the drive behind Webster, being careful to watch for bikes hurtling around the curve.

You've now come to **Strawberry Fields,** the "international peace garden" memorializing singer John Lennon. Climbing up a hill, its curving paths, shrubs, trees, and flower beds create a deliberately informal pastoral landscape, reminiscent of the English parks Lennon may have been thinking of when he wrote the Beatles song "Strawberry Fields Forever" in 1967. A black-and-white mosaic set into one of the sidewalks contains simply the word "Imagine," another Lennon song title. Just beyond the trees, at 72nd Street and Central Park West, is the Dakota (*see* Tour 8, *below*), where Lennon and his wife, Yoko Ono, lived at the time of his death in 1980.

Cross the road at the top of Strawberry Fields' hill, turn right through a rustic wood arbor thickly hung with wisteria vines, then head back on the path down the hill and follow the West Drive north (cross the drive as soon as possible so you can walk along the lake). Shortly past the lake, you'll see on your right a dark-wood chalet that looks like something straight out of Germany's Black Forest. This is the **Swedish Cottage,** where marionette shows are staged. *Tel. 212/988–9093. Shows Sat. noon and 3, call for reservations.*

Turn right and walk past the cottage to the **Shakespeare Garden,** one of the park's few formal flower plantings, tucked onto terraces on the side of a relatively steep hill. In the garden,

you'll find plants that William Shakespeare mentioned in his
⑰ writings. The open-air **Delacorte Theater,** where the Joseph
Papp Shakespeare Theater Company performs each summer
(*see* Chapter 11), is just around the corner. But for the best
view of the Delacorte, head for the top of the hill, aptly called
Vista Rock.

⑱ Vista Rock is dominated by **Belvedere Castle,** built in 1872 of the
same gray Manhattan schist that thrusts out of the soil in dramatic outcrops throughout the park. If you step through the
pavilion out onto the lip of the rock, you can examine some of
this schist, polished and striated by Ice Age glaciers. From
here you can look down directly upon the stage of the Dela-
⑲ corte; you can also see the **Great Lawn** stretching beyond, a series of softball fields that hum with action on weekends and
most summer evenings. In summer, should you see a few hundred people picnicking in a row around the oval edge of the
lawn, you'll know they're waiting to pick up free tickets to a
Shakespeare performance at the Delacorte.

The castle itself, a typically 19th-century mishmash of styles—
Norman, Gothic, Moorish—was deliberately kept small so that
when it was viewed from across the lake, the lake would seem
bigger. (The Ramble's forest now obscures the lake's castle
view.) Since 1919 it has been a measurement station of the U.S.
Weather Bureau; look up to see the twirling meteorological instruments atop the tower. Climb out onto its balconies for a
dramatic view, or get a minilesson in geology from the exhibits
within. If you've got children with you, visit the ground-floor
learning center. *Tel. 212/772–0210. Admission free. Open mid-
Feb.–mid-Oct., Tues.–Thurs. and weekends 11–5, Fri. 1–5;
winter hours (mid-Oct.–mid-Feb.), closes at 4 PM.*

From the castle's plaza, follow the downhill path east along
⑳ **Turtle Pond,** populated by fish, ducks, and dragonflies, as well
as turtles. At the east end of the pond you'll pass a statue of
King Jagiello of Poland; groups gather here for folk-dancing on
㉑ weekends. Follow the path north to nearby **Cleopatra's Needle,**
a pollution-worn obelisk covered with hieroglyphics; it was a
gift to the city in 1881 from the khedive of Egypt. The copper
crabs supporting the huge stone at each corner almost seem
squashed by its weight. If you look just past the trees, you can
see the glass-enclosed wing of the Metropolitan Museum (*see*
Tour 5, *above*) that holds the Egyptian Temple of Dendur.

Vigorous walkers may want to continue north to the **Reservoir,**
popular with New Yorkers for the running track that sur-
rounds it, and, in springtime, for its fragrant flowering trees.
The city's main reservoirs are upstate; this one is more or less a
holding tank.

Others can return south from Cleopatra's Needle, following the
path to the left under Greywacke Arch, which leads around the
back corner of the Metropolitan Museum. This side of the park,
perhaps in keeping with its proximity to the East Side, has a
tamer landscape than the west side, and here you'll see more
uniformed nannies and fussy little dogs on leashes. A few minutes' walk will take you to one of the park's most formal areas:
㉒ the symmetrical stone basin of the **Conservatory Water,** where
you can watch some very sophisticated model boats being raced
each Saturday morning at 10. (Unfortunately, model boats are
not for rent here.) At the north end of the pond is one of the

park's most beloved statues, José de Creeft's 1960 bronze sculpture of **Alice in Wonderland,** sitting on a giant mushroom with the Mad Hatter, White Rabbit, and leering Cheshire Cat in attendance. Children are encouraged to clamber all over it. On the west side of the pond, a bronze statue of **Hans Christian Andersen,** the Ugly Duckling at his feet, is the site of storytelling hours on summer weekends.

Climb the hill at the far end of the Conservatory Water, cross the 72nd Street transverse, and follow the path south to the Children's Zoo, oft-threatened by city budget cuts and currently closed pending reconstruction. Pass under the Denesmouth Arch to the **Delacorte Clock,** a delightful glockenspiel set above a redbrick arch. Every hour its six-animal band circles around and plays a tune while monkeys on the top hammer their bells. A path to the left will take you around to the front ❷❸ entrance of the **Arsenal,** the Parks Department's headquarters, occupying what was a pre–Civil War arsenal. Since the city acquired it in 1857, it has served as, among other things, the first home of the American Museum of Natural History, now on Central Park West at 79th Street (*see* Tour 8, *below*). The downstairs lobby has some WPA-era great murals; an upstairs gallery features changing exhibitions, often of great interest to kids. *Tel. 212/360–8163. Open weekdays 9:30–4:30.*

❷❹ Just past the clock is the **Central Park Zoo,** recently renamed the **Central Park Wildlife Conservation Center,** a small but delightful menagerie. Clustered around the central Sea Lion Pool are separate exhibits for each of the earth's major environments; the Polar Circle features a huge penguin tank and polarbear floe; the open-air Temperate Territory is highlighted by a pit of chattering monkeys; and the Tropic Zone contains the flora and fauna of a miniature rain forest. This is a good zoo for children and adults who like to take time to watch the animals; even a leisurely visit will take only about an hour, for there are only about 100 species on display. Go to the Bronx Zoo (*see* Chapter 4) if you need tigers, giraffes, and elephants—the biggest specimens here are the polar bears. *Tel. 212/439–6500. Admission: $2.50 adults, $1.25 senior citizens, 50¢ children 3–12. No children under 16 allowed in without adult. Open Apr.–Oct., Mon. and Wed.–Fri. 10–4:30, Tues. 10–7, weekends and holidays 10–5; Nov.–Mar., daily 10–4.*

Tour 8: The Upper West Side

Numbers in the margin correspond to points of interest on the Tours 8 and 9: Upper West Side, Columbia map.

The Upper West Side has never been as fashionable as the East Side, despite the fact that it has a similar mix of real estate— large apartment buildings along Central Park West, West End Avenue, and Riverside Drive, and town houses on the shady, quiet cross streets. Once a haven for the Jewish intelligentsia, by the 1960s the West Side had become a rather grungy multiethnic community. In the 1970s gentrification began slowly, with actors, writers, and gays as the earliest settlers. Today, however, this area is quite desirable, with lots of restored brownstones and high-priced co-op apartments. Young families have gravitated to its large apartments; on weekends, the sidewalks are crowded with couples pushing babies around in their imported strollers. Columbus Avenue is a trendy boutique-

and-restaurant strip, somewhat hipper and more dynamic than Madison Avenue; Amsterdam Avenue is slowly following suit, although its architecture is still largely tenement-style, its shopfronts a mix of bodegas and boutiques. Along upper Broadway, new luxury apartment towers are slowly blocking in the horizon. Many longtime West Siders decry the "Yuppification" of their neighborhoods, but the good news is that small businesses now thrive on blocks that a few years ago were not safe to walk on.

❶ The West Side story begins at **Columbus Circle,** where a statue of Christopher himself crowns a stately pillar at the intersection of Broadway, Eighth Avenue, Central Park West, and Central Park South. Columbus Circle is a good place to begin any tour of New York, for it is the headquarters of the **New York Convention and Visitors Bureau,** located in a weird pseudo-Byzantine structure, ostensibly modeled after the Doge's Palace in Venice but locally nicknamed the Lollipop Building. Count on the bureau for brochures; bus and subway maps; hotel, restaurant, and shopping guides; a seasonal calendar of events; free TV-show tickets (sometimes) and discounts on Broadway theater; and sound advice. *2 Columbus Circle, tel. 212/397–8222. Open weekdays 9–6, weekends 10–6.*

On the southwest quadrant of the circle, the **New York Coliseum,** a blank functional-looking white brick building, was the city's chief convention and trade-show venue before the opening of the Jacob Javits Center. A soaring multiuse complex proposed for the site was bitterly opposed by New Yorkers determined not to let its huge shadow be cast across Central Park; the site continues to be embroiled in suits and countersuits. On the northeast corner of the circle, an entrance to Central Park is presided over by the Maine Monument, with its florid bronze figures atop a stocky limestone pedestal. The pie-shape wedge of land between Central Park West and Broadway holds the **Paramount Communications Building,** headquarters of a media empire. The box office of the subterranean Paramount movie theater juts above the ground on the Broadway side of the plaza.

At the world headquarters of the **American Bible Society** (1865 Broadway at 61st St., tel. 212/408–1200), ascend red-carpeted stairs to a little-known second-floor library (open weekdays 9–4:30), which displays, among other things, Helen Keller's massive 10-volume braille Bible, a replica of the original Gutenberg press, and a Torah (Jewish scriptures) from China.

When you pass **The Ballet Shop** (1887 Broadway between 61st and 62nd Sts.), a mecca for balletomanes searching for books, prints, and recordings, you'll know you're getting close to New ❷ York's major site for the performing arts: **Lincoln Center,** covering an eight-block area west of Broadway between 62nd and 66th streets. This unified complex of pale travertine marble was built during the 1960s to supplant an urban ghetto (*West Side Story* was filmed on the slum's gritty, deserted streets just before the demolition crews moved in). Lincoln Center can seat nearly 18,000 spectators at one time in its various halls (*see* Chapter 11).

Stand on Broadway, facing the central court with its huge fountain. The three concert halls on this plaza clearly relate to one another architecturally, with their symmetrical bilevel fa-

American Museum of
Natural History
and Hayden
Planetarium, **5**
Barnard College, **10**
Cathedral of St. John
the Divine, **8**
Columbia
University, **9**
Columbus Circle, **1**
The Dakota, **4**
Grant's Tomb, **14**
Jewish Theological
Seminary, **13**
Lincoln Center, **2**
Museum of American
Folk Art, **3**
Riverside Church, **15**
Riverside Park, **7**
Teachers College, **11**
Union Theological
Seminary, **12**
Verdi Square, **6**

Tours 8 and 9: Upper West Side, Columbia

cades, yet each has slightly different lines and different details. To your left, huge honeycomb lights hang on the portico of the **New York State Theater,** home to the New York City Ballet and the New York City Opera. Straight ahead, at the rear of the plaza, is the **Metropolitan Opera House,** its brilliant-colored Chagall tapestries visible through the arched lobby windows; the Metropolitan Opera and American Ballet Theatre perform here. To your right, abstract bronze sculptures distinguish **Avery Fisher Hall,** host to the New York Philharmonic Orchestra.

Wander through the plaza, then angle to your left between the New York State Theater and the Metropolitan Opera House into **Damrosch Park,** where summer open-air festivals are often accompanied by free concerts at the **Guggenheim Bandshell.** Angle to your right from the plaza, between the Metropolitan and Avery Fisher, and you'll come to the North Plaza, with a massive Henry Moore sculpture reclining in a reflecting pool. To the rear is the **Library and Museum of the Performing Arts,** a branch of the New York Public Library with an extensive collection of books, records, and scores on music, theater, and dance; visitors can listen to any of 50,000 records and tapes, or check out its four galleries. Next to the library is the wide glass-walled lobby of the **Vivian Beaumont Theater,** officially considered a Broadway house although it is far removed from the theater district. Below it is the smaller **Mitzi E. Newhouse Theater,** where many award-winning plays have originated.

An overpass leads from this plaza across 65th Street to the world-renowned **Juilliard School** (for music and theater). Check here to see if there's a concert or a play going on; actors Kevin Kline and Patti LuPone once performed here. Turn right for an elevator down to street level and **Alice Tully Hall,** home of the Chamber Music Society of Lincoln Center and the New York Film Festival. Or turn left from the overpass and follow the walkway west to Lincoln Center's newest arts venue, the **Walter Reade Theater,** opened in the fall of 1991, showing several unusual American and foreign films a day, seven days a week (*see* Chapter 11).

Visitors can wander freely through the lobbies of all these buildings. A one-hour guided "Introduction to Lincoln Center" tour covers the center's history and wealth of artworks and usually visits the three principal theaters, performance schedules permitting. *Tel. 212/875–5351 for schedule and reservations. Admission: $7.75 adults, $6.75 students and senior citizens, $4.50 children 6–12.*

Conveniently close to Lincoln Center, at the northwest corner of Broadway and 66th Street, is **Tower Records,** the uptown branch of that vast emporium of tapes and CDs—and, less than a block north, **Tower Video,** a haven of videotapes and laser discs.

❸ Across the busy intersection, the **Museum of American Folk Art** has found a new home at Columbus Avenue and 66th Street. Its collection includes naïve paintings, quilts, carvings, dolls, trade signs, painted wood carousel horses, and a giant Indian-chief copper weathervane. *2 Lincoln Sq., tel. 212/977–7298. Suggested donation: $2. Open Tues.–Sun. 11:30–7:30.*

Around the corner on 66th Street is the headquarters of the ABC television network; ABC owns several buildings along Columbus Avenue as well, including some studios where news shows and soap operas are filmed, so keep an eye out for your favorite daytime doctors, tycoons, and temptresses.

Turn onto West 67th Street and head toward Central Park along one of the city's most handsome blocks. Many of the apartment buildings here were designed as "studio buildings," with immense windows that make them ideal for artists; look up at the facades and imagine the high-ceilinged spaces within. Also notice the Gothic motifs, carved in white stone or wrought in iron, that decorate several of these buildings at street level. Perhaps the finest apartment building on the block is the **Hotel des Artistes** (1 W. 67th St.), built in 1918, with its elaborate mock-Elizabethan lobby. Its tenants have included Isadora Duncan, Rudolph Valentino, Norman Rockwell, Noël Coward, Fannie Hurst, and contemporary actors Joel Grey and Richard Thomas and artist Leroy Neiman; another tenant, Howard Chandler Christy, designed the lush, soft-toned murals in the excellent ground-floor restaurant, **Café des Artistes** (*see* Chapter 9), where Louis Malle's *My Dinner with André* was filmed.

Another dining landmark is just inside Central Park at 66th Street, **Tavern on the Green** (*see* Chapter 9). Originally built as a sheepfold, in the days when sheep grazed on the meadows of the park, it was converted into a restaurant in the 1930s. True, the high tone is not what it once was, but many of its dining rooms have fine park views; at night white lights strung through the surrounding trees create a magical effect.

Movie buffs may want to detour down to 65th Street, where you'll find the Art Deco building that was supposedly "Spook Central" in the movie *Ghostbusters* (55 Central Park West).

Continue up Central Park West to 72nd Street, where the ❹ stately **Dakota** presides over the northwest corner. Its tenants have included Boris Karloff, Judy Holliday, José Ferrer and Rosemary Clooney, Lauren Bacall, Rex Reed, and Gilda Radner. Resembling a buff-colored castle, with copper turrets, its slightly spooky appearance was played up in the movie *Rosemary's Baby*, which was filmed here. Stop by the gate on 72nd Street; this is the spot where, in December 1980, a deranged fan shot John Lennon as he came home from a recording session. Lennon is memorialized in Central Park's Strawberry Fields, across the street (*see* Tour 7, *above*).

Proceed up Central Park West and you'll see several other famous apartment buildings, including **The Langham** (135 Central Park West), where Mia Farrow's apartment was featured in Woody Allen's film *Hannah and Her Sisters;* the twin-towered **San Remo** (145–146 Central Park West), over the years home to Rita Hayworth, Dustin Hoffman, Raquel Welch, Paul Simon, Tony Randall, and Diane Keaton—but not to Madonna, whose application was rejected because of her flamboyant lifestyle; and **The Kenilworth** (151 Central Park), with its immense pair of ornate front columns, once home to Basil Rathbone, film's quintessential Sherlock Holmes.

❺ The **American Museum of Natural History,** the attached **Hayden Planetarium,** and their surrounding grounds occupy a four-block tract bounded by Central Park West, Columbus Avenue, and 77th and 81st streets. As you approach at 77th Street, you can see the original architecture in the pink granite corner towers, with their beehive crowns. A more classical facade was added along Central Park West, with its centerpiece an enormous equestrian statue of President Theodore Roosevelt, naturalist and explorer.

With a collection of more than 30 million artifacts, the museum displays something for every taste, from a 94-foot blue whale to the 563-carat Star of India sapphire. Among the most enduringly popular exhibits are the wondrously detailed dioramas of animal habitat groups, on the first and second floors just behind the rotunda, and the fourth-floor halls full of dinosaur skeletons. A five-story-tall cast of *Barosaurus* rears on its hind legs in the Roosevelt Rotunda, protecting its fossilized baby from a fossil allosaur. The Hall of Human Biology and Evolution, which opened in April 1993, investigates the workings of the human body and features a computerized archaeological dig and an electronic newspaper about human evolution. The Naturemax Theater projects films on a giant screen; the Hayden Planetarium (on 81st Street) has two stories of exhibits, plus several different Sky Shows projected on 22 wraparound screens; its rock-music laser shows draw crowds of teenagers on Friday and Saturday nights. *Museum: tel. 212/769–5100. Suggested contribution: $5 adults, $2.50 children. Open Sun.–Thurs. 10–5:45; Fri.–Sat. 10–8:45. Planetarium: tel. 212/769–5920. Admission: $5 adults, $3.75 senior citizens and students; $2.50 children 2–12; $7 for laser show. Open weekdays 12:30–4:45, Sat. 10–5:45, Sun. noon–5:45. Naturemax Theater film admission: $5 adults, $3.75 senior citizens and students, $2.50 children. Call 212/769–5650 for show times.*

Directly behind the museum is Columbus Avenue, where shoppers may want to forsake this tour for boutique-shopping. If you do, work your way up one side of the street and back down the other, going north to 86th Street and south to 67th Street (*see* Chapter 8).

Time Out For a delicious lunch of pizza or pasta, stop by **Presto's** (434 Amsterdam Ave. at 81st St., tel. 212/721–9141), a casual neighborhood restaurant where kids are welcome. Or try the homey, brick-walled **Phoebe's** (380 Columbus Ave. near 78th St., tel. 212/724–5145), which serves unpretentious American fare, such as chicken pot pie, in a country-style ambience.

Return to Broadway to join New Yorkers in a pilgrimage to some of the city's greatest food shrines, all on the west side of the street. **Zabar's** (between 80th and 81st Sts.) offers exquisite delicatessen items, prepared foods, gourmet groceries, coffee, and cheeses; a mezzanine level features cookware, dishes, and small appliances. Be prepared to muscle a lot of pushy strangers for elbow room, for Zabar's prides itself on carrying a vast range of hard-to-get foods, and at prices that are reasonable. **H & H Bagels** (at 80th St., southwest corner) sells several varieties of huge, chewy bagels hot from the oven, along with juices, cream cheese, and lox (but they will not dress your bagel in any way). **Citarella's** fish store (at 75th St., southwest corner) features intricate, often absurd arrangements of seafood on shaved ice in the front window. The fresh produce in the bountiful but unpretentious **Fairway Market** (2127 Broadway at 74th St.) practically bursts onto the street. Have a look at the handmade signs describing the produce and cheeses; they can be as fresh as the merchandise itself.

At 73rd Street and Broadway, look up at the white facade and fairy-castle turrets of the **Ansonia Hotel,** a turn-of-the-century luxury building whose thick, soundproof walls made it attractive to musicians; once home to Enrico Caruso, Igor Stravinsky, Arturo Toscanini, Florenz Ziegfeld, Theodore Dreiser, and Babe Ruth, today it consists of condominiums. The Ansonia served as the facade for the building in which Jennifer Jason Leigh terrorized Bridget Fonda in the film *Single White Female.* Here, where Broadway cuts across Amsterdam Avenue, the triangle north of 72nd is **Verdi Square** (for Italian opera composer Giuseppe Verdi). In the '70s, however, Verdi Square was better known as Needle Park because of the drug addicts who hung out there. The neighborhood has vastly improved, and elderly West Siders schmooze on the wood benches, but there are those who fear the area is returning to its inglorious past. The triangle south of 72nd Street is **Sherman Square** (named for Union Civil War general William Tecumseh Sherman); the **subway kiosk** here is an official city landmark, a structure with rounded neo-Dutch moldings that was the first express station north of 42nd Street.

Having bought your picnic lunch, you may now want to head west to **Riverside Park,** a long, slender green space along the Hudson River landscaped by Central Park architects Olmsted and Vaux. Beginning at about 80th Street is the **Promenade,** a broad formal walkway with a stone parapet looking out over the river. Descend the steps here and go through the underpass beneath Riverside Drive, to reach the **79th Street Boat Basin,** a rare spot in Manhattan where you can walk right along the river's edge, smell the salt air, and watch a flotilla of houseboats bob in the water.

If you walk to the end of the Promenade, you'll see a patch of its median strip exploding with flowers tended by nearby residents. Look up to your right, where the Civil War **Soldiers' and Sailors' Monument,** a tight circle of white marble columns, crests a hill along Riverside Drive. (The monument appeared in the PBS TV mini-series *The Civil War.*) Climb to the monument for a refreshing view of Riverside Park, the Hudson River, and the New Jersey waterfront.

Tour 9: Columbia University and Environs

On the high ridge just north and west of Central Park, a cultural outpost grew up at the end of the 19th century, spearheaded by a triad of institutions: Columbia University, which developed the mind; St. Luke's Hospital, which cared for the body; and the Cathedral of St. John the Divine, which tended the soul. Idealistically conceived of as an American Acropolis, the cluster of academic and religious institutions that developed here managed to keep these blocks stable during years when neighborhoods on all sides were collapsing into decay. In the past decade, West Side gentrification has reclaimed the area to the south, while the Harlem areas north and east of here haven't changed as much. Yet within the gates of the Columbia or Barnard campus, or inside the hush of the cathedral or Riverside Church, the pace of life seems slower, more contemplative. Being a student neighborhood, the area has a casual atmosphere that is hip, friendly, and fun.

❽ Our first stop will be at the **Cathedral of St. John the Divine,** New York's major Episcopal church. When it is completed, it will be the largest cathedral in the world (St. Peter's of Rome is larger, but it's technically a basilica). Here you can have a rare, fascinating look at a Gothic cathedral in progress. Before you go in the main entrance on Amsterdam Avenue at 112th Street, peer into the side lot just to the north—the cathedral's **stone-cutting yard,** one of the few such operations in the United States. This immense limestone-and-granite church has been built in spurts. Its first cornerstone was laid in 1892 and a second in 1925, but with the U.S. entry into World War II, construction came to a "temporary" halt that lasted until 1982. St. John's follows traditional Gothic engineering—it is supported by stonemasonry rather than by a steel skeleton—so new stonecutters, many of them youngsters from nearby Harlem neighborhoods, had to be trained before the current work could proceed on the two front towers, the transept, and, finally, the great central tower. The proposed south transept is a radical conception: a "bioshelter" with branching columns, a glass roof, and an upper-level arboretum where sunlight will filter down through lush greenery, echoing the effect of stained glass. A model in the superb gift shop inside shows what the cathedral might look like when completed, probably quite a few years into the future. The shop (open daily 9–5) is known for its fine selection of international crafts, jewelry, religious artifacts, and ecological literature.

On the wide steps climbing to the Amsterdam Avenue entrance, you'll see five portals arching over the entrance doors; the central one shows St. John having his vision of the Lord in glory. Statuary is still being slowly added to the portals. Before you go inside, take a closer look at the facade's huge blocks of limestone: Each one carries a pattern of rough chisel marks called "boasting," the individual mason's distinctive signature.

Inside is a vast nave, the length of two football fields, which can seat 5,000 worshipers. The small chapels that border the nave have a surprisingly contemporary outlook. The second chapel to your left is the only **Poet's Corner** in the United States; the right-hand aisle's chapels movingly mourn tragedies such as the Holocaust and the spread of AIDS.

Beneath the 155-foot-high central dome, which could comfortably contain the Statue of Liberty, you can see another quirk of the cathedral: Its original Romanesque-Byzantine design was scrapped in 1907, when architect Ralph Adams Cram took over and instated a Gothic style. Here, where the transept will someday cross the nave, note the rough granite walls of the original scheme (they will eventually be covered with limestone); note also that the side nearer the entrance has a pointed Gothic arch, while the arch near the altar is still rounded Romanesque. The altar area itself expresses the cathedral's interfaith tradition with menorahs, Shinto vases, and golden chests presented by the king of Siam; the church's international mission is represented in the ring of chapels behind the altar, dedicated to various ethnic groups. The **Baptistry,** to the left of the altar, is an exquisite octagonal chapel with a 15-foot-high marble font and a polychrome sculpted frieze commemorating New York's Dutch heritage.

To the south of the cathedral itself is the **cathedral close,** a peaceful precinct of Gothic-style châteaus that includes the

Bishop's House, the Deanery, and the Cathedral School. A circular plaza just off Amsterdam at 111th Street features the Peace Fountain, which is not for all tastes.

Along with Sunday services (8, 9, 9:30 [in Spanish], 10 and 11 AM, and 7 PM), the cathedral operates a score of community outreach programs and presents a full calendar of nonreligious (classical, folk, winter solstice) concerts. *Amsterdam Ave. and 112th St., tel. 212/316-7540, box office tel. 212/662-2133. Suggested donation: $2. Tours Mon.–Sat. 11, Sun. 12:45. Open daily 7–5.*

Time Out On the other side of Amsterdam Avenue, between 110th and 111th streets, you'll find two casual restaurants: **V & T Restaurant** (1024 Amsterdam, tel. 212/663-1708) for spicy pizza and Italian cooking; and the **Hungarian Pastry Shop** (1030 Amsterdam Ave., tel. 212/866-4230) for luscious desserts and coffees.

From here you have two options: go north on Amsterdam to Columbia University, or take a swing east on 113th Street to secluded **Morningside Drive.** On 113th Street you can still see the baroque 1896 core of **St. Luke's Hospital,** which has grown rather awkwardly into a jumble of newer buildings. On Morningside Drive at 114th Street you'll find **Eglise de Notre Dame,** a Roman Catholic church that features, behind the altar, a replica of the French grotto of Lourdes; stop in, if possible, during one of the frequent daily services. At 116th Street you may want to pause on the overlook on the right to gaze into **Morningside Park,** tumbling steeply into a wooded gorge. Designed by Central Park's Olmsted and Vaux, it's a lovely landscape, but bordered as it is by some rough blocks of Harlem, it may not be a safe place to take a stroll.

At 116th Street and Amsterdam, you can pass through the campus gates of **Columbia University,** a wealthy, private, coed institution that is New York City's only Ivy League school. The gilded crowns on the black wrought-iron gates serve as a reminder that this was originally King's College when it was founded in 1754, before American independence. Walk along the herringbone-patterned brick paths of College Walk into the refreshingly green main quadrangle, dominated by massive neoclassical **Butler Library** to your left (south) and the rotunda-topped **Low Memorial Library** to your right (north). Butler, built in 1934, holds the bulk of the university's 5 million books; Low, built in 1895–97 by McKim, Mead & White (who laid out the general campus plan when the college moved here in 1897), is now mostly offices, but on weekdays you can go inside to see its domed, templelike former Reading Room. The steps of Low Library, presided over by Daniel Chester French's statue Alma Mater, have been a focal point for campus life, not least during the student riots of 1968. Here Dan Aykroyd and Bill Murray, playing recently fired Columbia research scientists, hit upon the idea of going into business as Ghostbusters.

Before Columbia moved here, this land was occupied by the Bloomingdale Insane Asylum; the sole survivor of those days is **Buell Hall,** the gabled orange-red brick house just east of Low Library. Just north is **St. Paul's Chapel** (1907), an exquisite little Byzantine-style domed church laid out in the shape of a cross. Step inside to admire the tiled vaulting. *Tel. 212/854-6625. Open Sept.–May, weekdays 11–8; Sat. 11–2; Sun. for services, 7:30–1 and 5–9. Greatly reduced hours June–Aug.,*

*so call ahead for Sun. schedule. Free organ recitals Thurs.
noon.*

A student-run art gallery has been opened downstairs in the
chapel's Postcrypt. *Tel. 212/854–1953. Admission free. Open
Tues.–Fri. 2–6 and Sat. 9 PM–1 AM as a coffee house, offering
poetry readings and folk music.*

The university's renowned Journalism School, founded by Joseph Pulitzer (and the reason why Columbia bestows those Pulitzer Prizes each spring), holds classes in the building just
south of the campus's west gates. Go through the gates and
onto Broadway to find the official college bookstore at 115th
Street and Broadway.

⑩ Across Broadway from Columbia is its sister institution,
Barnard College, established in 1889. One of the former Seven
Sisters of women's colleges, Barnard has steadfastly remained
a single-sex institution and has maintained its independence
from Columbia, although its students can take classes there
(and vice versa). Note the bear (the college's mascot) on the
shield above the main gates at 117th Street. Through the gates
is **Barnard Hall,** its brick-and-limestone design echoing Columbia's buildings. Turn right to follow the path north through the
narrow but neatly landscaped campus; turn left from the main
gate to peek into a quiet residential quadrangle.

Follow Broadway north to 120th Street, where on your right
you'll see the redbrick Victorian buildings of Columbia Univer-
⑪ sity's **Teachers College,** founded in 1887 and today still the
world's largest graduate school in the field of education. Notice
the band of stone along the Broadway facade, inscribed with
the names of famous teachers throughout history. On your left
⑫ is the interdenominational **Union Theological Seminary** in its
rough gray collegiate Gothic quadrangle. Founded in 1836, the
seminary moved here in 1910; it has one of the world's finest
theological libraries. Step inside the main entrance, on Broadway at 121st Street, and ask to look around the pleasant central
quadrangle. At the corner of 122nd Street and Broadway, behind a large blank-walled redbrick tower that fronts the inter-
⑬ section at an angle, is the **Jewish Theological Seminary,**
founded in 1887 as a training ground for rabbis, cantors, and
scholars of Conservative Judaism. This complex was built in
1930, although the tower, which housed part of the seminary's
excellent library, was extensively renovated after a fire in
1966. Walk west on 122nd Street; at Claremont Avenue, you'll
see the prestigious **Manhattan School of Music** on your right,
with musical instruments carved into the stone beneath its up-
per-story windows. Between Claremont and Riverside Drive,
you may want to sit for a moment in **Sakura Park,** a quiet formal
garden.

⑭ Across Riverside Drive, in Riverside Park, stands **Grant's
Tomb,** where Civil War general and two-term president Ulysses S. Grant rests beside his wife, Julia Dent Grant. The white
granite mausoleum, with its imposing columns and classical
pediment, is modeled after Les Invalides in Paris, where Napoleon is buried. Under a small white dome, the Grants' twin
black marble sarcophagi are sunk into a deep circular chamber,
which you view from above; minigalleries to the sides display
photographs and Grant memorabilia. In contrast to this
austere monument, the surrounding plaza features fanciful

1960s-era mosaic benches, designed by local schoolchildren. *Riverside Dr. and 122nd St., tel. 212/666–1640. Admission free. Open Wed.–Sun. 9–4:30.*

Just south of Grant's Tomb, on Riverside Drive at 120th Street, ⑮ **Riverside Church** is a modern (1930) Gothic-style edifice whose smooth, pale limestone walls seem the antithesis of St. John the Divine's rough gray hulk; in fact, it feels more akin to Rockefeller Center, not least because John D. Rockefeller was a major benefactor of the church. While most of the building is refined and restrained, the main entrance, on Riverside Drive, explodes with elaborate stone carving (modeled after the French cathedral of Chartres, as are many other decorative details here). Inside, look at the handsomely ornamented main sanctuary, which seats only half as many people as St. John the Divine does; take the elevator to the top of the 22-story, 356-foot tower (admission: $1), with its 74-bell carillon, the largest in the world. Although affiliated with the Baptist church and the United Church of Christ, Riverside is basically nondenominational, interracial, international, extremely political, and socially conscious. Its calendar includes political and community events, dance and theater programs, and concerts, along with regular Sunday services at 10:45 AM. *Tel. 212/222–5900. Open Mon.–Sat. 9–5, Sun. noon–4; service each Sun. 10:45.*

Time Out   Returning to Broadway, eat with the Columbia and Barnard students at **Ollie's Noodle Shop** (2957 Broadway at 116th St., tel. 212/932–3300). The eclectic menu includes everything from eggplant parmesan to Mexican chili to grilled shrimp kebabs, but the main attraction is the savory Cantonese and Mandarin Chinese food. The dumplings and the noodle dishes are divine.

Tour 10: Harlem

Numbers in the margin correspond to points of interest on the Tour 10: Harlem map.

Harlem has been the mecca for black American culture and life for nearly a century. Originally called Nieuw Haarlem and settled by Dutch farmers, Harlem was a well-to-do suburb in the 19th century; black New Yorkers began settling here in large numbers in about 1900, moving into a surplus of fine apartment buildings and town houses built by real-estate developers for a middle-class white market that never materialized. By the 1920s, Harlem (with one "a") had become the most famous black community in the United States, perhaps in the world. In an astonishing confluence of talent known as the Harlem Renaissance, black novelists, playwrights, musicians, and artists gathered here. Black performers starred in chic Harlem jazz clubs—which, ironically, only whites could attend. Throughout the Roaring Twenties, while whites flocked here for the infamous parties and nightlife, blacks settled in for the opportunity this self-sustaining community represented. But the Depression hit Harlem hard. By the late 1930s, it was no longer a popular social spot for downtown New Yorkers, and many successful black families began moving out to homes in the suburbs of Queens and New Jersey.

By the 1960s, Harlem's population had dropped dramatically, and many of those who remained were disillusioned enough to join in civil rights riots. A vicious cycle of crowded housing, poverty, and crime was choking the neighborhood, turning it into a simmering ghetto. Today, however, Harlem is well on its way to restoring itself. Mixed in with some of the seedy remains of the past are old jewels such as the refurbished Apollo Theatre and such new attractions as the Studio Museum. A great number of Harlem's classic brownstone and limestone homes are being restored and lived in by young families, bringing new life to the community.

Deserted buildings, burned-out shopfronts, and yards of rubble still scar certain parts; although a few whites have begun to move in here, some white visitors may feel conspicuous in what is still a largely black neighborhood. But Harlemites are accustomed to seeing tourists on their streets; only common traveler's caution is necessary during daytime excursions to any of the places highlighted, although for nighttime outings it's smart to take a taxi. Bus tours may be a good alternative way to see Harlem, because they cover more areas than the central Harlem walk outlined below (*see* Special-Interest Tours in Chapter 1).

Sunday is a good time to tour Harlem, because that's when you can listen to gospel music at one of the area's many churches. Soulful, moving, often joyous, gospel music blends elements from African songs and chants, American spirituals, and rhythm and blues. Gospel fans and visitors are welcome at the **Canaan Baptist Church of Christ,** where Wyatt Tee Walker is pastor. *132 W. 116th St., tel. 212/866–0301; Sun. services 10:45 AM.*

As you head east from the church, notice on the southwest corner of 116th Street and Lenox Avenue the aluminum onion dome of the **Malcolm Shabazz Mosque** (102 W. 116th St.), a former casino that was converted in the mid-1960s to a black Muslim temple (Malcolm X once preached here). Several Muslim stores are located nearby.

On weekdays you may want to begin your tour at the next stop, **Marcus Garvey Park,** which interrupts Fifth Avenue between 120th and 124th streets. Renamed after Marcus Garvey (1887–1940), who led the back-to-Africa movement, this rocky plot of land is interesting less for itself than for the handsome buildings of the surrounding Mount Morris Historic District (Mount Morris Square was the park's original name). Walk up the west side of the park to admire the fine town houses facing the park or on the side streets.

Time Out At the other end of Marcus Garvey Park is **La Famille** (2017 5th Ave. between 124th and 125th Sts., tel. 212/722–9806), a bar and restaurant that serves great food upstairs and a changing nighttime menu of jazz downstairs (Wed.–Sun.). La Famille offers standard soul-food fare plus a more Continental menu.

Harlem's main street is **125th Street,** the chief artery of its cultural, retail, and economic life. Real-estate values here have never come close to those downtown along Fifth Avenue or even Broadway, and many of the commercial buildings rise only a few stories. New businesses have moved in of late, however, bringing smart new shopfronts along a retail row that used to see many "For Rent" signs. Above the street-level stores is the home of the **National Black Theater** (2033 Fifth Ave. between

Tour 10: Harlem

125th and 126th Sts., tel. 212/722–3800), which produces new works by contemporary black writers. As you walk west on 125th Street, notice a peculiarity of Harlem addresses: The city's numbered north–south avenues acquire different names up here, commemorating heroes of black history. Sixth Avenue becomes Lenox Avenue or Malcolm X Boulevard, 7th Avenue is Adam Clayton Powell Boulevard, and 8th Avenue is Frederick Douglass Boulevard. Even 125th Street has an alias: Martin Luther King Jr. Boulevard. However, just about everybody still uses the streets' former names.

On Lenox Avenue between 126th and 127th streets is **Sylvia's Soul Food Restaurant** (*see* Chapter 9), owned by Sylvia Woods, the self-proclaimed "Queen of Soul Food" in New York who remains most nights until 10 chatting with her customers.

❸ **The Studio Museum in Harlem,** one of the community's showplaces, is a small art museum that houses a large collection of paintings, sculpture, and photographs (including historic photographs of Harlem by James Van DerZee, popular in the 1930s). The museum often offers special lectures and programs, and its gift shop is full of black American and African-inspired books, posters, and jewelry. *144 W. 125th St., tel. 212/ 864–4500. Admission: $5 adults, $3 students and senior citizens, $1 children under 12. Open Wed.–Fri. 10–5, weekends 1–6.*

❹ A fantastic restoration brought the **Apollo Theatre,** one of Harlem's greatest landmarks, back to life in 1986. When it opened in 1913 it was a burlesque hall for white audiences only, but after 1934, music greats such as Billie Holiday, Ella Fitzgerald, Duke Ellington, Count Basie, and Aretha Franklin performed here. The theater fell on hard times and closed for a while in the early 1970s. The current Apollo's roster of stars isn't as consistent as it was in the past, but its regular Wednesday-night amateur performances at 7:30 PM are as wild and raucous as they were in the theater's heyday. *253 W. 125th St., tel. 212/749–5838. Call for performance schedules.*

❺ Return to Seventh Avenue and head north to 126th Street, where the **Black Fashion Museum** is housed in a brownstone. Costumes from black theater and films are displayed, and the work of black fashion designers of the past century is highlighted. *155 W. 126th St., tel. 212/666–1320. Suggested donation: $1.50 adults, $1 students and senior citizens, 50¢ children under 12. Open weekdays 12:30–7:30 by appointment.*

As you head up Seventh Avenue, between 131st and 132nd streets you'll pass what is today the Williams Institutional (Christian Methodist Episcopal) Church. Once this was the **Lafayette Theater,** which presented black revues in the 1920s and housed the WPA's Federal Negro Theater in the 1930s. A tree outside the theater was considered a lucky charm for black actors; having fallen victim to exhaust fumes, it has been replaced by the abstract metal "tree" on the traffic island in the center of Seventh Avenue.

❻ At 135th Street, cross back to Lenox Avenue, where you'll find the **Schomburg Center for Research in Black Culture.** In 1926 the New York Public Library's Division of Negro History acquired the vast collection of Arthur Schomburg, a scholar of black and Puerto Rican descent. In 1940, after Schomburg died, this collection, which includes more than 100,000 books, documents, and photographs recording black history, was named after him. In 1972, the ever-growing collection was designated a research library, and in 1980 it moved into this modern redbrick building from the handsome Victorian one next door (designed by McKim, Mead & White), which is now a branch library. The expansion and renovation of the original Schomburg building was completed in 1991 and includes the new **American Negro Theater,** with seating for 380, and increased gallery space. The center's resources include rare manuscripts, art and artifacts, motion pictures, records, and videotapes. Regular exhibits, performing-arts programs, and lectures continue to contribute to Harlem culture. *515 Lenox Ave. at 135th St., tel. 212/491–2200. Admission free. Open Mon.–Wed. noon–8, Thurs.–Sat. 10–6. Open Sun. noon–5 to view exhibits only.*

7 Founded downtown in 1808, the **Abyssinian Baptist Church** was one of the first black institutions to settle in Harlem when it moved here in the 1920s. The Gothic-style bluestone church was further distinguished by its famous family of ministers— Adam Clayton Powell, Sr., and his son, Adam Clayton Powell, Jr., the first black U.S. congressman. Stop in on Sunday to hear the gospel choir and the fiery sermon of its present minister, Rev. Calvin Butts. *132 W. 138th St., tel. 212/862–7474. Sun. services 9 and 11 AM.*

Across Seventh Avenue from the church is a handsome set of **8** town houses known as **Striver's Row** (W. 138th and W. 139th Sts. between 7th and 8th Aves.). Since 1919, black doctors, lawyers, and other middle-class professionals have owned these elegant homes, designed by famous period architects such as Stanford White (his contributions are on the north side of 139th Street). Musicians W. C. Handy ("The St. Louis Blues") and Eubie Blake ("I'm Just Wild About Harry") were among the residents here. The area became known as Striver's Row because less affluent Harlemites felt its residents were "striving" to become well-to-do. These quiet, tree-lined streets are a remarkable reminder of the Harlem that used to be.

Tour 11: Chelsea

Numbers in the margin correspond to points of interest on the Tour 11: Chelsea map.

Like the London district of the same name, New York's Chelsea has preserved its villagelike personality. Both have their quiet nooks where the 19th century seems to live on; both have been havens for artists, writers, and bohemians. Although London's Chelsea is a much more upscale chunk of real estate, New York's Chelsea is catching up, with town-house renovations reclaiming block after block of the side streets. Seventh, Eighth, and Ninth avenues may never be the shopping mecca that King's Road in London's Chelsea has been, but they have plenty of hip, one-of-a-kind boutiques sprinkled among the grubby grocery stores and other remnants of the neighborhood's immigrant tenement past.

Precisely speaking, the New York neighborhood was named not after Chelsea itself but after London's Chelsea Royal Hospital, an old soldiers' home. Running from 14th to 24th streets, from Eighth Avenue west, it was one family's country estate until the 1830s, when Clement Clarke Moore saw the city moving north and decided to divide his land into lots. With an instinctive gift for urban planning, he dictated a pattern of development that ensured street after street of graceful row houses. A clergyman and classics professor, Moore is probably best known for his 1822 poem "A Visit from St. Nicholas," which he composed while bringing a sleigh full of Christmas treats from lower Manhattan to his Chelsea home.

❶ Begin your tour of Chelsea at the corner of Seventh Avenue and 17th Street, in front of **Barneys New York** (tel. 212/929–9000), a fashionable department store that grew out of an outstanding menswear store. If nothing else, stroll past its store windows, where fashion is displayed with a quirky wit. Across Seventh Avenue are branches of **Williams-Sonoma** (gourmet cookware) and **Pottery Barn** (trendy home furnishings); a block uptown, at 18th Street, you'll find one of the city's best children's bookstores, **Books of Wonder** (132 7th Ave., tel. 212/989–3270).

It's appropriate to begin the Chelsea tour with a spate of shopping, because nearby Sixth Avenue was once known as Ladies Mile for its concentration of major department stores. After the stores moved uptown in the early 1900s, the neighborhood declined and the grand old store buildings stood empty and dilapidated. The 1990s, however, brought the renaissance of the Flatiron District to the east (*see* Tour 4, *above*), and now renovations are in progress all along Sixth Avenue. Stand at Sixth Avenue and 18th Street and imagine it in the latter part of the 19th century, when the elevated tracks of the Sixth Avenue El train still cast their shadow along this street. From the west side of the avenue, you can look across at the elaborately embellished, glazed terra-cotta building just north of 18th Street.
❷ Originally the **Siegel-Cooper Dry Goods Store**, built in 1895, it contains 15½ acres of space, yet it was built in only five months. In its retail heyday, the store's main floor featured an immense fountain—a circular marble terrace with an enormous white-marble-and-brass replica of "The Republic," the statue Daniel Chester French displayed at the 1883 Chicago World's Fair—which became a favorite rendezvous point for New Yorkers. During World War II, the building was a military hospital. Today its main tenant is **Bed, Bath & Beyond** (tel. 212/255–3550), an impressive emporium with 11 sections of household items at discounted prices. Look up at the building's splendid ornamentation: round wreathed windows, Corinthian and Doric pilasters, Romanesque rounded arches, lion heads, and more.

❸ Now cross Sixth Avenue and take a look at the building on the west side: the original **B. Altman Dry Goods Store,** built in 1876 with additions in 1887 and 1910. Look closely at the exposed columns at the base of the building—it's constructed of cast iron. B. Altman moved out of this giant in 1906 to set up shop in imposing quarters at Fifth Avenue and 34th Street. The latter store closed in 1990.

Time Out About a half-block east on 18th Street you can take a restful lunch, tea, or coffee break at the **Book Friends Cafe** (16 W. 18th St., tel. 212/255–7407), a literary hangout and bookstore in this newly artsy neighborhood. On the same block, bibliophiles will also enjoy perusing the shelves of **Academy Bookstore** (10 W. 18th St., tel. 212/242–4848), **Skyline Books and Records** (13 W. 18th St., tel. 212/759–5463), and **Barnes and Noble Sale Annex**

(18th St. and 5th Ave., tel. 212/633–3500), with its main store across the street (105 5th Ave., tel. 212/807–0099).

4 On the east side of Sixth Avenue at 20th Street is the Gothic-style **Church of the Holy Communion,** an Episcopal house of worship built in 1846 and designed by architect Richard Upjohn. To the horror of some preservationists, it was converted a few years ago into **Limelight,** a nightclub with state-of-the-art sound and video systems.

5 On the west side of Sixth Avenue between 20th and 21st streets stands another former retail palace, the **Hugh O'Neill Dry Goods Store.** Constructed in 1875, this cast-iron building features Corinthian columns and pilasters; its corner towers were once topped off with huge bulbous domes. The recently renovated structure now houses the Elsevier Science Publishing Company. Look up at the pediment and you'll see the name of the original tenant proudly displayed.

6 Turn left on 21st Street for a look at **The Third Cemetery of the Spanish & Portuguese Synagogue, Shearith Israel,** a private green oasis with a hardy old ailanthus tree. In use from 1829 to 1851, it is one of three graveyards created in Manhattan by this congregation (*see* Tours 12 and 16, *below*).

Continue west on 21st Street to Eighth Avenue, where the **Chelsea Historic District** officially begins. Between 20th and 23rd streets, from Eighth to Tenth avenues, you'll find examples of all of Chelsea's architectural periods: Greek and Gothic Revival, Italianate, and 1890s apartment buildings. But before

❼ you start prowling around there, you may want to head down to 19th Street and Eighth Avenue to see the Art Deco **Joyce Theater** (175 8th Ave., tel. 212/242–0800). The former Elgin movie house was gutted and transformed in 1982 into this sleek modern theater; if you have any interest in modern dance (*see* Chapter 11), it's well worth checking out who is performing at the Joyce during your stay. Its presence, which helped revitalize the area, has attracted several good, moderately priced restaurants along Eighth Avenue.

Time Out A pair of restaurants on Eighth Avenue between 20th and 21st streets are busily competing to see which can offer the best deal for a stylish nouvelle lunch. Take your pick—**Intermezzo** (202 8th Ave., tel. 212/929–3433) or **Chelsea Foods** (198 8th Ave., tel. 212/691–3948)—you can hardly go wrong.

❽ At 344 West 20th Street, between Eighth and Ninth avenues, you'll find **St. Peter's Church,** built between 1836 and 1838. The Greek Revival–style **rectory** (1832), to the right of the main church, originally served as the sanctuary. Four years after it was built, the congregation had already laid foundations for a bigger church when, it is said, a vestryman returned from England bursting with excitement over the Gothic Revival that had just taken hold there. The fieldstone **church** that resulted ranks as one of New York's earliest examples of Gothic Revival architecture. To the left of the church, the brick **parish hall** is an example of the so-called Victorian Gothic style; its churchlike front was added in 1871. The wrought-iron fence framing the three buildings once enclosed St. Paul's Chapel downtown (*see* Tour 17, *below*).

❾ When Clement Clarke Moore divided up his estate, he began by deeding a large section to the **General Theological Seminary,** where he taught Hebrew and Greek. At Ninth Avenue and 20th Street, the Episcopal seminary still occupies a block-long stretch. The stoutly fenced campus is accessible through the modern building on Ninth Avenue; during off hours you can view the grounds from West 20th Street. The **West Building** (1836) is another early example of Gothic Revival architecture in the city. Most of the rest of the complex was completed in 1883–1902, when Eugene Augustus Hoffman, the school's third dean, hired architect Charles Coolidge Haight to design a campus that would rival those of most other American colleges of the day, in the style known as English Collegiate Gothic, which Haight had pioneered. The general campus plan is in an "E" shape, with the spine facing 21st Street. In the center is the **Chapel of the Good Shepherd,** with its 161-foot-high bell tower. **Sherred Hall,** a three-story classroom building flanked by dormitories, expresses beautifully the simple quality and uniform look Haight strove for. **Hoffman Hall,** the refectory-gymnasium, has an enormous dining hall that resembles a medieval knight's council chamber. A 1960s-era building facing Ninth Avenue houses administrative offices, a bookstore, and the 210,000-volume **St. Mark's Library,** generally considered the nation's greatest ecclesiastical library; it has the world's largest collection of Latin Bibles. *Tel. 212/243–5150. Open weekdays noon–3, Sat. 11–4, Sun. 2–4 (no admission after 1 hour before closing), and by appointment.*

Across the street from the seminary, at **404 West 20th Street,** is the oldest house in the historic district. Built between 1829 and

1830 in the Federal style, it still has one clapboard side wall, although over the years it acquired a Greek Revival doorway and Italianate windows on the parlor floor, and the roof was raised one story. The houses next door, from 406 to 418 West 20th, are **Cushman Row,** some of the country's most perfect examples of Greek Revival town houses. Built by dry-goods merchant Don Alonzo Cushman, a friend of Clement Clarke Moore who became a millionaire by developing Chelsea, the houses retain such details as the tiny wreath-encircled attic windows, deeply recessed doorways with brownstone frames, and handsome iron balustrades, newels, and fences. Notice the pineapples, a traditional symbol of welcome, atop the newels in front of Nos. 416 and 418.

Farther down West 20th Street, at **Nos. 446 to 450,** you'll find some exceptional examples of Italianate houses. The arched windows and doorways are hallmarks of this style, which prized circular forms—not least because, being expensive to build, they showed off the owner's wealth.

When you reach Tenth Avenue, turn right and walk north (uptown). Movie buffs might make a quick detour right onto 21st Street to take a peek at **467 West 21st Street,** where, in the 1960s and '70s, Anthony Perkins of *Psycho* was the live-in landlord.

West 22nd Street also has a string of handsome old row houses just east of Tenth Avenue. **No. 435** was the longtime residence of actors Geraldine Page and Rip Torn; they nicknamed this Chelsea town house the Torn Page. In 1987, a year after winning an Oscar for *The Trip to Bountiful,* Page suffered a fatal heart attack here.

On the block spanning 23rd and 24th streets, between Tenth and Ninth avenues on the north side of the block, you can't miss the **London Terrace Apartments,** a huge complex containing 1,670 apartments. When it first opened in 1930, the doormen dressed as London bobbies. It's actually made up of two rows of interconnected apartment buildings, which enclose a block-long private garden. As you walk along 23rd Street, notice the lions on the arched entryways: From the side they look as though they're snarling, but from the front they display wide grins.

The site of the Clarke family manor (where Clement Clarke Moore was born in 1779) was just across 23rd Street here, on what was then a high bluff overlooking the Hudson.

During the 1880s and Gay '90s, 23rd Street was the heart of the entertainment district, lined with theaters, music halls, and beer gardens. Today it is an undistinguished, even run-down, commercial thoroughfare, but there is one relic of its once-proud past: the **Chelsea Hotel** (tel. 212/243–3700) at 222 West 23rd Street, between Eighth and Seventh avenues. Built of red brick with lacy wrought-iron balconies and a mansard roof, it opened in 1884 as a cooperative apartment house and became a hotel in 1905, although it has always catered to long-term tenants, with a tradition of broad-mindedness that has attracted many creative types. Its literary roll call of former tenants includes Mark Twain, Eugene O'Neill, O. Henry, Thomas Wolfe, Tennessee Williams, Vladimir Nabokov, Mary McCarthy, Brendan Behan, Arthur Miller, Dylan Thomas, William S. Burroughs, and Arthur C. Clarke (who wrote the script for *2001: A Space Odyssey* while living here). In 1966, Andy

Warhol filmed artist Brigid Polk in her Chelsea hotel room, which eventually became *The Chelsea Girls*, considered by many to be Warhol's best film. More recently, the hotel was seen on screen in *Sid and Nancy* (1986), a dramatization of a true-life Chelsea Hotel murder, when drugged punk rocker Sid Vicious accidentally stabbed to death his girlfriend Nancy Spungeon. The shabby, seedy aura of the Chelsea Hotel is part of its allure. Read the commemorative plaques outside and then step into the lobby to look at the unusual artwork, some of it donated in lieu of rent by residents down on their luck.

Tour 12: Greenwich Village

Numbers in the margin correspond to points of interest on the Tours 12 and 13: Greenwich Village and the East Village map.

Greenwich Village, which New Yorkers almost invariably speak of simply as "the Village," enjoyed a raffish reputation for years. Originally a rural outpost of the city—a haven for New Yorkers during early 19th-century smallpox and yellow fever epidemics—many of its blocks still look somewhat pastoral, with brick town houses and low-rises, tiny green parks and hidden courtyards, and a crazy-quilt pattern of narrow, tree-lined streets. In the mid-19th century, however, as the city spread north of 14th Street, the Village became the province of immigrants, bohemians, and students (New York University, today the nation's largest private university, was planted next to Washington Square in 1831). Its politics were radical and its attitudes tolerant, which is one reason it is now home to such a large gay community.

Today Village apartments and town houses go for high rents, and several posh restaurants have put down roots. Except for the isolated western fringe, where a string of tough gay bars along West Street attracts some drug traffic and prostitution, the Village is about as safe and clean as the Upper East Side. Nevertheless, something about the tangled street plan and the small buildings encourages anarchy. Shabby shopfronts, hole-in-the-wall restaurants, and nonmainstream arts groups persist and thrive here. There's still a large student population, and several longtime residents remain, paying cheap rents thanks to rent-control laws. The Village is no longer dangerous, but it still feels bohemian.

Several generations of writers and artists have lived and worked here: in the 19th century, Henry James, Edgar Allan Poe, Mark Twain, Walt Whitman, and Stephen Crane; at the turn of the century, O. Henry, Edith Wharton, Theodore Dreiser, and Hart Crane; and during the 1920s and '30s, John Dos Passos, Norman Rockwell, Sinclair Lewis, John Reed, Eugene O'Neill, Edward Hopper, and Edna St. Vincent Millay. In the late 1940s and early 1950s, the Abstract Expressionist painters Franz Kline, Jackson Pollock, Mark Rothko, and Willem de Kooning congregated here, as did the Beat writers Jack Kerouac, Allen Ginsberg, and Lawrence Ferlinghetti. The 1960s brought folk musicians and poets, notably Bob Dylan and Peter, Paul, and Mary.

Begin a tour of Greenwich Village at Washington Arch in **❶ Washington Square** at the foot of Fifth Avenue. Designed by Stanford White, a wood version of Washington Arch was built in 1889 to commemorate the 100th anniversary of George Wash-

Tours 12 and 13: Greenwich Village and the East Village

Balducci's, **4**
Colonnade Row, **19**
Cooper Union Foundation Building, **17**
Father Demo Square, **12**
Forbes Magazine Galleries, **3**

Grey Art Gallery, **2**
Grove Court, **9**
Jefferson Market Library, **5**
Joseph Papp Public Theater, **20**
Milligan Place, **7**
Old Merchant's House, **18**

Patchin Place, **6**
St. Luke's-in-the-Fields, **10**
St. Luke's Place, **11**
St. Mark's-in-the-Bowery, **14**
St. Marks Place, **13**
Sheridan Square, **8**

Tompkins Square, **16**
Ukrainian Museum, **15**
Washington Square, **1**

ington's presidential inauguration and was originally placed about half a block north of its present location. The arch was reproduced in stone in 1892, and the statues—*Washington at War* on the left, *Washington at Peace* on the right—were added in 1913. Bodybuilder Charles Atlas modeled for *Peace*.

Washington Square started out as a cemetery, principally for yellow-fever victims, and an estimated 10,000–22,000 bodies lie below. In the early 1800s it was a parade ground and the site of public executions; bodies dangled from a conspicuous Hanging Elm that still stands at the northwest corner of the square. Later Washington Square became the focus of a fashionable residential neighborhood and a center of outdoor activity.

By the early 1980s, Washington Square had deteriorated into a tawdry place only a drug dealer could love. Then community activism motivated a police crackdown that sent the drug traffic elsewhere and made Washington Square comfortable again for Frisbee players, street musicians, skateboarders, jugglers, stand-up comics, sitters, strollers, and a huge outdoor art fair each spring and fall.

Most of the buildings bordering Washington Square belong to New York University. **The Row,** a series of Federal-style town houses along Washington Square North between Fifth Avenue and University Place, now serves as university offices and faculty housing. At 7–12 Washington Square North, in fact, only the fronts were preserved, with a Fifth Avenue apartment building taking over the space behind. Developers were not so tactful when they demolished 18 Washington Square, once the home of Henry James's grandmother, which he later used as the setting for his novel *Washington Square* (Henry himself was born just off the square, in a long-gone house on Washington Place). The house at 20 Washington Square North is the oldest building (1820) on the block. Notice its Flemish bond brickwork—alternate bricks inserted with the smaller surface (headers) facing out—which before 1830 was considered the best way to build stable walls.

On the east side of the square, NYU's main building contains ❷ the **Grey Art Gallery,** whose changing exhibitions usually focus on contemporary art. *33 Washington Pl., tel. 212/998–6780. Suggested donation: $2.50. Open Sept.–July, Tues., Thurs. and Fri. 11–6:30, Wed. 11–8:30, Sat. 11–5.*

On the south side of the square, a trio of red sandstone hulks represents an abortive 1960s attempt to create a unified campus look for NYU, as envisioned by architects Philip Johnson and Richard Foster. At one time, plans called for all of the Washington Square buildings to be refaced in this red stone; fortunately, the cost proved prohibitive. On La Guardia Place, the undistinguished modern **Loeb Student Center** stands on the site of a famous boardinghouse, nicknamed the House of Genius for the talented writers who had lived there over the years: Theodore Dreiser, Stephen Crane, Willa Cather, O. Henry, and Eugene O'Neill, among others. A block west of the Student Center, at the corner of Washington Square South and Thompson Street, is the square-towered **Judson Memorial Church** (the tower is now an NYU dormitory), designed by McKim, Mead & White.

Go up Fifth Avenue half a block to **Washington Mews,** a cobblestoned private street lined on one side with the former stables of the houses on the Row. Writer Walter Lippmann and artist-patron Gertrude Vanderbilt Whitney (founder of the Whitney Museum) once had homes in the mews; today it's mostly owned by NYU. A similar Village mews, **MacDougal Alley,** can be found between Eighth Street and the square just off MacDougal Street, one block west.

Walk up Fifth Avenue, past the **Church of the Ascension** (Fifth Ave. and West 10th St.), a Gothic-style brownstone designed by Richard Upjohn. Inside, you can admire a mural depicting the Ascension of Jesus and stained-glass windows by John LaFarge and a marble altar sculpture by Louis Saint-Gaudens. In 1844, President John Tyler married Julia Gardiner here. ❸ Just past 12th Street, you can stop in the **Forbes Magazine Galleries,** where the late publisher Malcolm Forbes's idiosyncratic personal collection is on display. Exhibits change in the large gallery while permanent highlights include U.S. presidential papers, more than 500 intricate model boats, jeweled Faberge eggs, and some 12,000 toy soldiers. *62 Fifth Ave. at 12th St., tel. 212/206–5548. Admission free. Open Tues.–Wed. and Fri.– Sat. 10–4.*

Time Out If you walk a block east of the Forbes galleries to University Place, you'll find several dining spots located between 8th and 12th streets. At the corner of University Place and 12th Street, **Japonica** (tel. 212/243–7752) serves reasonably priced Japanese lunches, including fresh sushi and excellent sukiyaki. The owners change the restaurant decorations to coincide with the changing seasons and Japanese holidays.

Backtrack on Fifth Avenue to **West 11th Street** and turn right to see one of the best examples of a Village town-house block. One exception to the general 19th-century redbrick look is the modern, angled front window of 18 West 11th Street, usually occupied by a stuffed bear whose outfit changes from day to day. This house was built after the original was destroyed in a 1970 explosion; members of the radical Weathermen faction had started a bomb factory in the basement. At the time, actor Dustin Hoffman lived next door at No. 16; he was seen on TV news trying to rescue his personal possessions. Hoffman's costar in *The Graduate*, Anne Bancroft, later lived down at 52 West 11th Street with her husband, director Mel Brooks. At the end of the block, behind a low gray stone wall on the south side of the street, is the **Second Shearith Israel graveyard,** used by the country's oldest Jewish congregation after the cemetery in Chinatown (*see* Tour 16, *below*) and before the one in Chelsea (*see* Tour 11, *above*).

On Avenue of the Americas (Sixth Avenue), turn left to sample ❹ the wares at **Balducci's** (6th Ave. and 9th St., tel. 212/673–2600), a full-service gourmet food store that sprouted from the vegetable stand of the late Louis Balducci, Sr. Along with more than 80 Italian cheeses and 50 kinds of bread, this family-owned enterprise features imported Italian specialties and a prodigious selection of fresh seafood.

Directly opposite, the triangle formed by West 10th Street, Sixth Avenue, and Greenwich Avenue originally held a greenmarket, a jail, and the magnificent towered courthouse ❺ that is now the **Jefferson Market Library** (tel. 212/243–4334). Critics variously termed the courthouse's hodgepodge of styles Venetian, Victorian, or Italian; Villagers, noting the alternating wide bands of red brick and narrow strips of granite, dubbed it the Lean Bacon Style. Over the years, the structure has housed a number of government agencies (public works, civil defense, census bureau, police academy); it was on the verge of demolition when public-spirited citizens saved it and turned it into a public library in 1967. Note the fountain at the corner of West 10th Street and Sixth Avenue, and the seal of the City of New York on the east front; inside, look at the handsome interior doorways and climb the graceful circular stairway. If the gate is open, visit the flower garden behind the library, a project run by local green thumbs.

Just west of Sixth Avenue on 10th Street is the wrought-iron **⑥** gateway to a tiny courtyard called **Patchin Place**; around the corner, on Sixth Avenue just north of 10th Street, is a similar **⑦** cul-de-sac, **Milligan Place,** which few New Yorkers even know is there. Both were built around 1850 for the waiters (mostly Basques) who worked at the high-society Brevoort Hotel, long ago demolished, on Fifth Avenue. Patchin Place later became home to several writers, including Theodore Dreiser, e.e. cummings, Eugene O'Neill, and Djuna Barnes.

Take Christopher Street, which veers off from the southern end of the library triangle, a few steps to **Gay Street.** A curved lane lined with small row houses circa 1810, Gay Street was originally a black neighborhood and later a strip of speakeasies. Ruth McKinney lived and wrote *My Sister Eileen* in the basement of No. 14, and Howdy Doody was designed in the basement of No. 12. At the end of Gay Street go west on Waverly Place to Christopher Street.

If you continue west on Christopher Street, you'll pass steps leading down to the **Lion's Head** (59 Christopher St.), a longtime hangout for literary types. Before she found stardom, Jessica Lange was a waitress here. The restaurant faces a green triangle that's technically called **Christopher Park,** but it contains a statue of Civil War general Philip Sheridan; this confuses New Yorkers, because there's another triangle to the south (between Washington Place, Barrow Street, and Seventh **⑧** Avenue) called **Sheridan Square.** Formerly covered with asphalt, Sheridan Square was recently landscaped following an extensive dig by urban archaeologists, who unearthed artifacts dating back to the Dutch and Native American eras.

Sheridan Square was the site of a nasty 1863 riot in which a group of freed slaves were nearly lynched; in 1969, gays and police clashed nearby during a protest march that galvanized the gay-rights movement. Across the busy intersection of Seventh Avenue, **Christopher Street** comes into its own as the symbolic heart of New York's gay community. Many bars and stores along here cater to that clientele, although the street is by no means off-limits to other people. Two shops worth a visit are **McNulty's Tea and Coffee Co.** (109 Christopher St., tel. 212/ 242–5351), with a large variety of tea and coffee blends, and **Li-Lac Chocolate Shop** (120 Christopher St., tel. 212/242–7374), a longtime favorite in the area for its homemade chocolate and buttercrunch.

West of Seventh Avenue, the Village turns into a picture-book town of twisting, tree-lined streets, quaint houses, and tiny restaurants. Follow Grove Street from Sheridan Square past the house where Thomas Paine died (59 Grove St.) and the boyhood home of poet Hart Crane (45 Grove St.).

Time Out   **The Pink Tea Cup** (42 Grove St., tel. 212/807–6755) is a typical Village restaurant only insofar as it is quirky and one-of-a-kind. Stop here if you have a hankering for down-home hamhocks, chitterlings, or fried pork chops; more standard fare is featured on the menu as well.

At this point, you'll be close to the intersection of Grove and Bleecker streets. You may now choose to take a leisurely stroll along the portion of Bleecker Street that extends west of 7th Avenue from Grove to Bank Street, heading in the direction of Abington Square. This section of Bleecker Street is full of crafts and antiques shops, coffeehouses, and small restaurants. Some shopping highlights along the way include **An American Craftsman** (317 Bleecker St., tel. 212/727–0841) for handcrafted gifts; **Pierre Deux** (367–369 Bleecker St., tel. 212/243–7740) and **Susan Parrish** (tel. 212/645–5020) for antiques; **Simon Pearce** (385 Bleecker St., tel. 212/924–1142) for fine glass and pottery; **Biography Bookstore** (400 Bleecker St., tel. 212/807–8655); and **Bird Jungle** (401 Bleecker St., tel. 212/242–1757), with unusual, often colorful species of birds on display in the windows.

If you choose to forego Bleecker Street, continue your walk west on Grove Street. The secluded intersection of Grove and Bedford streets seems to have fallen through a time warp into the 19th century. On the northeast corner stands one of the few remaining clapboard structures in the city (17 Grove St.); wood construction was banned as a fire hazard in 1822, the year it was built. The house has since served many functions; it housed a brothel during the Civil War. Behind it, at 102 Bedford Street, is **Twin Peaks,** an 1835 house that was rather whimsically altered in the 1920s, with stucco, half-timbers, and a pair of steep roof peaks added on.

9   Grove Street curves in front of the iron gate of **Grove Court,** an enclave of brick-fronted town houses from the mid-1800s. Built originally as apartments for employees at neighborhood hotels, Grove Court used to be called Mixed Ale Alley because of the residents' propensity to pool beverages brought from work. It now houses a more affluent crowd: A town house there recently sold for $3 million.

Walk down Bedford Street a couple of blocks to 77 Bedford Street, the oldest house in the Village (1799). The place next door, 75½ Bedford Street, has an even greater claim to fame: Not only was it the residence (at different times) of both Edna St. Vincent Millay and John Barrymore, it is also, at 9½ feet wide, New York's narrowest house. The lot was an alley until rising real-estate prices inspired construction in 1873.

Heading west on Commerce Street, you soon reach the **Cherry Lane Theater** (tel. 212/989–2020), one of the original Off-Broadway houses and the site of American premieres of works by O'Neill, Beckett, Ionesco, and Albee. Across the street stand two nearly identical brick houses separated by a garden. Popularly known as the **Twin Sisters,** the houses were said to have been built by a sea captain for two daughters who loathed each other. Historical record insists that they were built by a milkman who needed the two houses and an open courtyard for his work.

Follow Barrow Street to Hudson Street, so named because this was originally the bank of the Hudson River. The block to the northwest is owned by **St. Luke's-in-the-Fields,** built in 1822 as a country chapel for downtown's Trinity Church; its first warden was Clement ("'Twas the Night Before Christmas") Clarke Moore, who figured so largely in Chelsea's history (*see* Tour 11, *above*). An unadorned structure of soft-colored brick, St. Luke's was nearly destroyed by fire in 1981, but a flood of donations, many quite small, from residents of the West Village financed restoration of the square central tower. Bret Harte once lived at 487 Hudson Street, at the end of the row.

Time Out   At the corner of Hudson Street and St. Luke's Place, the **Anglers and Writers Cafe** (420 Hudson St., tel. 212/675–0810) lives up to its name with bookshelves, fishing tackle, and pictures of Door County, Wisconsin, hung on the walls. A meal here can be pretty pricey, but weary wanderers may linger over a pot of tea and a slice of cake for an hour or so, absorbing the place's restful charm.

East of Hudson Street, for the length of a block, Leroy Street becomes **St. Luke's Place,** a row of classic 1860s town houses shaded by graceful gingko trees. Novelist Theodore Dreiser wrote *An American Tragedy* at No. 16; poet Marianne Moore lived at No. 14, playwright Sherwood Anderson at No. 12. Mayor Jimmy Walker (first elected in 1926) lived at No. 6; the lampposts in front are "mayor's lamps," which were sometimes placed in front of the residences of New York mayors. This block is often used as a film location, too: No. 12 was shown as the Huxtables' home on *The Cosby Show* (although the family supposedly lived in Brooklyn), and No. 4 was the setting of the Audrey Hepburn movie *Wait Until Dark*. Before 1890 the playground on the south side of the street was a graveyard where, according to legend, the dauphin of France—the lost son of Louis XVI and Marie Antoinette—is buried.

Across Seventh Avenue, St. Luke's Place becomes Leroy Street again, which terminates in an old Italian neighborhood at Bleecker Street. Amazingly unchanged amid all the Village gentrification, Bleecker between Sixth and Seventh avenues seems more vital these days than Little Italy does. Right at the corner of Leroy and Bleecker, **Grandpa's** restaurant (252 Bleecker St., tel. 212/627–9119) isn't particularly atmospheric, but it has celebrity value: It's owned by actor Al Lewis, best known as the vampire Grandpa on the old TV show *The Munsters*, and he is often there greeting patrons. For more authentic Italian ambience, stop into one of the fragrant Italian bakeries (**A. Zito & Sons,** 259 Bleecker St., and **Rocco's,** 243 Bleecker St.), or look inside the old-style butcher shops (**Ottomanelli & Sons,** 285 Bleecker St., and **Faicco's,** 260 Bleecker St.). **John's Pizzeria** (278 Bleecker St., tel. 212/243–1680) is one of those places that locals swear by. Be forewarned, however: no slices; whole pies only. You may also be tempted to stop in at the **Lafayette Bakery** (298 Bleecker St.); it's French rather than Italian, but the treats are luscious all the same. The activity here focuses on **Father Demo Square** (Bleecker St. and 6th Ave.). Across Bleecker Street you'll see the **Church of Our**

Lady of Pompeii, where Mother Cabrini, a naturalized Italian immigrant who became the first American saint, often prayed.

Head up Sixth Avenue to Third Street and check out the playground caged there within a chain-link fence. NBA stars of tomorrow learn their moves on this patch of asphalt, where city-style basketball is played all afternoon and evening in all but the very coldest weather.

Return along Washington Square South to MacDougal Street and turn right. The **Provincetown Playhouse** (133 MacDougal St., tel. 212/477–5048) premiered many of Eugene O'Neill's plays. Louisa May Alcott wrote *Little Women* while living at 130–132 MacDougal Street. The two houses at 127 and 129 MacDougal Street were built for Aaron Burr in 1829; notice the pineapple newel posts, a symbol of hospitality.

Time Out The neighborhood's oldest coffeehouse is **Caffe Reggio** (119 MacDougal St., tel. 212/475–9557), where an antique machine steams forth espresso and cappuccino. The tiny tables are close together, but the crowd usually makes for interesting eavesdropping.

At **Minetta Tavern** (113 MacDougal St., tel. 212/475–3850), a venerable Village watering hole, turn right onto **Minetta Lane,** which leads to narrow **Minetta Street,** another former speakeasy alley. Both streets follow the course of Minetta Brook, which once flowed through this neighborhood and still bubbles deep beneath the pavement.

The foot of Minetta Street returns you to the corner of Sixth Avenue and Bleecker Street, where you reach the stomping grounds of 1960s-era folksingers (many of them performed at the now-defunct Folk City one block north on West 3rd Street). This area still attracts a young crowd—partly because of the proximity of NYU—to its cafés, bars, jazz clubs, coffeehouses, theaters, and cabarets (*see* Chapter 12), not to mention its long row of unpretentious ethnic restaurants.

Tour 13: The East Village

The gritty tenements of the East Village—an area bounded by 14th Street on the north, Fourth Avenue or the Bowery on the west, Houston Street on the south, and the East River—provided inexpensive living places for artists, writers, and actors after real estate prices in SoHo (*see* Tour 14, *below*) zoomed sky-high. New residents brought in their wake new restaurants, shops, and somewhat cleaner streets, while the old East Villagers maintained the trappings of the counterculture. Longtime bastions of the arts, such as the theaters CSC and LaMaMa, St. Mark's-in-the-Bowery Church, and the repertory movie house Theater 80 St. Marks, were joined by newer institutions such as P.S. 122, and several "hot" art galleries opened in narrow East Village storefronts. But the East Village scene lasted only a couple of years—just long enough to drive up rents substantially on some blocks, but not long enough to drive out all of the neighborhood's original residents. Today, an interesting mix has survived: artistic types in black leather, some homeless people and drug addicts (more so as you head deeper east into the slums of so-called Alphabet City along Avenues A, B, C, and D), and longtime members of various immigrant enclaves, principally Polish, Ukrainian, and Slovene.

To explore the East Village, begin at the intersection of East 8th Street, Fourth Avenue, and Astor Place. Sculpture adorns two traffic islands here: One island contains *Alamo*, a massive black cube sculpted by Bernard Rosenthal; another bears an ornate cast-iron replica of a Beaux Arts subway entrance, providing access to the uptown No. 6 line. Go down into the station to see the authentically reproduced wall tiles.

⓭ Go straight east to **St. Marks Place** (the name given to 8th Street in the East Village), the longtime hub of the "hip" East Village. During the 1950s, beatniks such as Allen Ginsberg and Jack Kerouac lived and wrote in the area; the 1960s brought Bill Graham's Fillmore East concerts, the Electric Circus, and hallucinogenic drugs. The black-clad, pink-haired or shaven-headed punks followed, and some of them remain today. St. Marks Place between Second and Third avenues is lined with vegetarian restaurants, jewelry stalls, leather shops, and stores selling books, posters, and weird clothing, although the recent arrival of a branch of The Gap seems to signal that this street has lost its countercultural relevance. Late in the evening, this stretch of St. Marks Place sometimes attracts unpleasant characters you may wish to avoid.

Time Out Restaurants along St. Marks Place may come and go, but **DoJo** (24 St. Marks Pl., tel. 212/674–9821) lives on. The menu is heavy on brown rice, tofu, vegetables, and legumes, all tastily cooked. The atmosphere is casual, and prices are so low even impoverished students are happy.

Second Avenue, which St. Marks crosses after one block, was known in the early part of this century as the Yiddish Rialto. Between Houston and 14th streets, eight theaters presented Yiddish-language productions of musicals, revues, and heart-wrenching melodramas. Today the theaters are gone; all that remains are Hollywood-style stars that have been embedded in the sidewalk in front of the **Second Avenue Deli** (2nd Ave. and 10th St., tel. 212/677–0606) to commemorate Yiddish stage luminaries.

Catercorner to the Second Avenue Deli is another East Village
⓮ landmark, **St. Mark's-in-the-Bowery Church,** a 1799 fieldstone country church to which a Greek Revival steeple and a cast-iron front porch have been added. This, the city's oldest continually used church building (the old Dutch governor Peter Stuyvesant and Commodore Perry are buried here), had to be completely restored after a disastrous fire in 1978. Over the years, St. Mark's has hosted much countercultural activity. In the 1920s a forward-thinking pastor injected the Episcopalian ritual with Native American chants, Greek folk dancing, and Eastern mantras. During the hippie era, St. Mark's welcomed avant-garde poets and playwrights. Today dancers, poets, and performance artists cavort in the main sanctuary, where pews have been removed to accommodate them.

From in front of the church, you can investigate **Stuyvesant Street,** which angles southwest back to Astor Place. This area was once Governor Stuyvesant's "bouwerie," or farm; among the handsome redbrick row houses is one at 21 Stuyvesant

Street that was built in 1804 as a wedding gift for a great-great-granddaughter of the governor.

 Continue up Second Avenue to the **Ukrainian Museum,** a small upstairs gallery celebrating the cultural heritage of the Ukraine. Now that this country has become independent again, there's something especially poignant about this collection, nurtured in exile throughout the years of Soviet domination: ceramics, jewelry, hundreds of brilliantly colored Easter eggs, and an extensive collection of Ukrainian costumes and textiles. *203 2nd Ave. between 12th and 13th Sts., tel. 212/228–0110. Admission: $1 adults, 50¢ students and senior citizens. Open Wed.–Sun. 1–5.*

Time Out   For some of the best Italian pastries in the city, try **De Robertis Pasticceria** (176 1st Ave., tel. 212/674–7137) or the more famous **Veniero Pasticerria** (342 E. 11th St. near 1st Ave., tel. 212/674–7264), both with rows and rows of incredibly fresh cannolis, fruit tarts, cheesecakes, and other desserts on display.

As you continue down First Avenue, you'll pass at 9th Street **P.S. 122** (150 1st Ave., tel. 212/477–5288), a former public school building transformed into a complex of spaces for avant-garde entertainment (*see* Chapter 11), and, just west of the avenue on St. Marks Place, **Theater 80 St. Marks** (80 St. Marks Pl., tel. 212/254–7400), one of New York's few remaining revival movie houses. Check out the posters in front to see what today's vintage double bill may be. Also, be sure to look down at the sidewalk, where you'll find the handprints, footprints, and autographs of such past screen luminaries as Joan Crawford, Ruby Keeler, Alexis Smith, and Gloria Swanson.

Turn left on St. Marks Place and head east, to where the avenues are labeled with letters, not numbers. Until relatively recently, this area's nickname, Alphabet City, meant a burned-out territory of slums and drug haunts, but some blocks and buildings were gentrified during the height of the East Village art scene a few years ago. The old and new East Villagers sev-
 eral times clashed around **Tompkins Square,** the leafy park bordered by Avenues A and B and 7th and 10th streets. The square's well-established tent city of homeless people provided the spark in the summers of 1988 and 1989, as police moved to rid the park of vagrants, and neighborhood residents vociferously took up sides. Riots broke out, and tempers ran high. The homeless people have since moved on, and the park has received a much-needed renovation, making it a pleasant place to sit on a bench on a sunny afternoon.

To head back west, follow 7th Street away from the southwest corner of Tompkins Square, studying the mix of small stores and restaurants to get a reading on the neighborhood's culture-in-flux. After crossing First and Second avenues, note **McSorley's Old Ale House** (15 E. 7th St., tel. 212/473–9138), one of several claimants to the distinction of being New York's oldest bar, often crammed with collegiate types enticed by McSorley's own brands of ale. McSorley's opened in 1854 but didn't admit women until 1970. Just past McSorley's is **Surma, The Ukrainian Shop** (11 E. 7th St., tel. 212/477–0729), with its exotic stock of Ukrainian books, magazines, cassettes, and greeting cards, as well as musical instruments, painted eggs, and an exhaustive collection of peasant blouses. Across the street is **St. George's Ukrainian Catholic Church** with its mosaic dome.

17 Across Third Avenue, the massive brownstone **Cooper Union Foundation Building** dominates **Cooper Square,** the large open space created where Fourth and Third avenues merge into the Bowery. A statue of industrialist Peter Cooper, by Augustus Saint-Gaudens, presides over the square. Cooper founded this college in 1859 to provide a forum for public opinion and free technical education for the working class; it still offers tuition-free education in architecture, art, and engineering. Cooper Union was the first structure to be supported by steel railroad rails—rolled in Cooper's own plant. Three galleries present changing exhibitions during the academic year (admission free; open weekdays noon–7, Sat. noon–5).

Musicians may want to stop in at the **Carl Fischer Music Store** (62 Cooper Sq., tel. 212/677–1148) to select from the infinitude of sheet music, confer with the knowledgeable staff, and hang out with the musicians here.

If you're here on a Sunday, go down to the foot of Cooper
18 Square and head a half-block east on 4th Street to the **Old Merchant's House.** Built in 1830, this Federal-style house was home to the Tredwell family from 1835 to 1933, when the last of the elderly Tredwell sisters died. The original furnishings and architectural features remain intact, offering a rare glimpse of family life in the mid-19th century. *29 E. 4th St., tel. 212/777–1089. Admission: $3 adults, $2 students and senior citizens. Open Sun. 1–4; other times by appointment ($60 charge for private tour).*

One block west of Cooper Square, turn right up Lafayette Street. The long block between East 4th Street and Astor Place
19 contains on the west side **Colonnade Row** (1833), a grand sweep of four houses (originally nine) fronted by marble Corinthian columns. Although sadly run-down today, in their time these houses were home to millionaires John Jacob Astor and Cornelius Vanderbilt; writers Washington Irving, William Makepeace Thackeray, and Charles Dickens all stayed here at one time or another.

In 1854 Astor opened the city's first free library in the imposing Italian Renaissance–style structure directly across the street, which was renovated in 1967 to serve as the New York Shake-
20 speare Festival's **Joseph Papp Public Theater** (425 Lafayette St., tel. 212/598–7150). Under the leadership of the late Joseph Papp, the Public's five playhouses and one cinema built a fine reputation for bold and innovative performances (*see* Chapter 11); the long-running hit *A Chorus Line* had its first performances here, but so have many less commercial plays.

West of Astor Place, turn left on Broadway to hit a trendy downtown shopping strip, especially strong in funky secondhand and surplus clothing stores. Above street level, the old warehouses here have mostly been converted into residential lofts. Walk south to 4th Street, where you'll see **Tower Records** (692 Broadway, tel. 212/505–1500), a very big and very good tape-and-CD store that also serves as a mingling place for young hipsters (or would-be hipsters).

Time Out For splendid soups, juicy burgers, large salads, omelets, and great french fries, sample **NoHo Star** (333 Lafayette St. at Bleecker St., tel. 212/925–0070), a sleek, friendly place that attracts an artsy crowd. After 6, dishes with an Asian accent are added to the menu.

Tour 14: SoHo and TriBeCa

Numbers in the margin correspond to points of interest on the Tours 14–16: SoHo, TriBeCa, Little Italy, Chinatown map.

Today the names of these two downtown neighborhoods are virtually synonymous with a certain postmodern chic—an amalgam of black-clad artists, hip young Wall Streeters, track-lit loft apartments, hip art galleries, and restaurants with a minimalist approach to both food and decor. It's all very urban, very cool, very now. But 25 years ago, they were virtual wastelands. SoHo (so named because it is the district *S*outh of *Ho*uston Street, bounded by Broadway, Canal Street, and Sixth Avenue) was described in a 1962 City Club of New York study as "commercial slum number one." It was saved by two factors: (1) preservationists discovered here the world's greatest concentration of cast-iron architecture and fought to prevent demolition, and (2) artists discovered the large, cheap, well-lit spaces that cast-iron buildings provide. At first it was technically illegal for artists to live in their loft studios, but so many did that eventually the zoning laws were changed to permit residence.

By 1980, the tide of loft dwellers, galleries, and trendy shops and cafés had made SoHo so desirable a residential area, despite the still-gritty look of the neighborhood, that none but the most successful artists could afford it anymore. Seeking similar space, artists moved downtown to another half-abandoned commercial district, for which a new SoHo-like name was invented: TriBeCa (the *Tri*angle *Be*low *Ca*nal Street, although in effect it goes no farther south than Murray Street and no farther east than West Broadway). The same scenario played itself out again, and TriBeCa's rising rents are already beyond the means of most artists, who have moved instead to Long Island City (*see* Queens in Chapter 4) or areas of Brooklyn or New Jersey. But just because the artists have left doesn't mean that SoHo and TriBeCa aren't still a vital scene.

Perhaps the best introduction to these areas is a walk up Greene Street, where the block between Canal and Grand streets contains the longest continuous row of cast-iron buildings anywhere (Nos. 8–34 Greene St.). The architectural rage between 1860 and 1890, cast-iron buildings were popular because they did not require massive walls to bear the weight of the upper stories. With no need for load-bearing walls, they were able to have more interior space and larger windows. They were also versatile, with various architectural elements produced from standardized molds to mimic any style—Italianate, Victorian Gothic, neo-Grecian, to name but a few visible in SoHo. Look, for example, at 28–30 Greene Street, an 1873 building nicknamed the **Queen of Greene Street.** Besides its pale paint job, notice how many decorative features have been applied: dormers, columns, window arches, and projecting central bays. Handsome as they are, these buildings were always commercial, containing stores and light manufacturing, principally textiles. Along this street notice the iron loading docks and the sidewalk vault covers studded with glass disks to let light into basement storage areas. In front of 62–64 Greene Street there's one of the few remaining turn-of-the-century bishop's-crook lampposts, with various cast-iron curlicues from the base to the curved top.

❷ At 72–76 Greene Street is the so-called **King of Greene Street,** a five-story Renaissance-style building with a magnificent projecting porch of Corinthian columns. Today the King (now painted yellow) houses the **M-13** art gallery (tel. 212/925–3007) and **The Second Coming,** which sells vintage clothing, furniture, and other curiosities.

At the northeast corner of Prince and Greene streets, turn to look at the corner diagonally opposite for a rare glimpse of the side of an iron-front building. You'll see the same window pattern and decoration continued, with one window open and a cat sitting on the sill—where it has sat since 1973, when artist Richard Haas first painted this meticulously realistic **mural** on the blank side wall.

Take Prince Street west to Wooster Street, which, like a few other SoHo streets, still has its 19th-century pavement of Belgian blocks, a smoother successor to traditional cobblestones.
❸ Start at the **Paula Cooper Gallery** (149–155 Wooster St., tel. 674–0766), one of SoHo's oldest galleries. At 141 Wooster Street, one of several outposts of the DIA Art Foundation, you
❹ can visit the **New York Earth Room,** Walter de Maria's avant-garde 1977 artwork that consists of 140 tons of gently sculpted soil filling a second-floor gallery. *Tel. 212/473–8072. Admission free. Open Wed.–Sat. noon–6. Closed Memorial Day–Labor Day.*

At 131 Wooster Street, a store named **Home Town** (tel. 212/674–5770) has the serendipitous quality of an upscale flea market, an eclectic stock of "found objects" and country-style antiques for making trendy lofts feel homey. Across the street is a SoHo newcomer, the **Gagosian Gallery** (136 Wooster St., tel. 212/228–2828), operated by prominent uptown dealer Larry Gagosian. The gallery's silver-and-glass front resembles a very wide garage door. Below Prince Street is a defiantly untrendy
❺ museum, the **Museum of Colored Glass and Light,** where illuminated stained-glass pictures are mounted in a sort of dimly lit wooden maze. The artist, Russian immigrant Raphael Nemeth, runs the museum himself but isn't very talkative. *72 Wooster St., tel. 212/226–7258. Admission: $1. Open daily 1–5.*

West Broadway (which, somewhat confusingly, runs parallel to and four blocks west of regular Broadway) is SoHo's main drag, and on Saturday it can be crowded with smartly dressed uptowners and suburbanites who've come down for a little store- and gallery-hopping (*see* Chapter 8). In the block between Prince and Spring streets alone there are three major art stops: **420 West Broadway,** with six separate galleries including two of the biggest SoHo names, Leo Castelli (tel. 212/431–5160) and the Sonnabend Gallery (tel. 212/966–6160); the **Mary Boone Gallery** (417 West Broadway tel. 212/431–1818); and another excellent cluster of galleries at **415 West Broadway,** including the Witkin Gallery (tel. 212/925–5510) for photog-

Tours 14-16: SoHo, TriBeCa, Little Italy, Chinatown

raphy. One block south, at **383 West Broadway,** OK Harris (tel. 212/431–3600) has its digs.

Time Out The crowded, lively **Cupping Room Cafe** (359 West Broadway, tel. 212/925–2898) specializes in comforting soups, muffins, and daily specials, as well as substantial Bloody Marys.

Go east to Broome Street and Broadway, where, on the northeast corner, you'll see the sadly unrestored classic of the cast-iron genre, the **Haughwout Building** (488 Broadway), nicknamed the Parthenon of Cast Iron. Built in 1857 to house Eder Haughwout's china and glassware business, the exterior was inspired by a Venetian palazzo. Inside, it contained the world's first commercial passenger elevator, a steam-powered device invented by Elisha Graves Otis.

Head north up Broadway, which temporarily loses its SoHo ambience in the midst of discount clothing stores. Just below Prince Street, the 1907 **Singer Building** (561 Broadway) shows the final flower of the cast-iron style, with wrought-iron balconies, terra-cotta panels, and broad expanses of windows. Across the street is one of New York's gourmet shrines, the gleaming **Dean & DeLuca** food market (560 Broadway, tel. 212/431–1691), whose bread and produce arrangements often are worthy of still-life paintings. The smartly restored **560 Broadway** building also houses a respected multigallery exhibit space; another such space is just up the street at **568 Broadway.** On the ground floor at 568 Broadway is the **Armani Exchange** store (tel. 212/431–6000), featuring a new line by the famous Italian designer—casual, basic clothes like those sold at The Gap, just right for fashion in a recession.

On the west side of Broadway, the Guggenheim Museum opened a SoHo branch in 1992: the **Guggenheim Museum SoHo,** which displays a revolving series of exhibitions, both contemporary work and pieces from the Guggenheim's permanent collection. The museum occupies space in a landmark 19th-century redbrick structure with its original cast-iron storefronts and detailed cornice. Arata Isozaki designed the two floors of stark, loftlike galleries as well as the museum store facing West Broadway. Scheduled exhibitions for 1994 plan to concentrate on the work of Robert Morris and Claes Oldenburg. *575 Broadway, tel. 212/423–3500. Admission: $5 adults, $3 senior citizens and students. Open Sun., Mon., Wed. 11–6; Thurs.–Sat. 11–10. Admission higher for special exhibitions.*

A few doors up the street, the **New Museum of Contemporary Art** shows experimental, often radically innovative work by unrecognized artists, none of it more than 10 years old. *583 Broadway, tel. 212/219–1222. Admission: $3.50 adults, $2.50 students, senior citizens, and artists. Open Wed., Thurs., Fri., and Sun. noon–6; Sat. noon–8.*

A few doors up the street (north) from the New Museum is the **Museum for African Art,** dedicated to contemporary and traditional African art. This fascinating addition to the SoHo scene is housed in a handsome, two-story space designed by Maya Lin, who also designed Washington, D.C.'s Vietnam Veterans Memorial. Exhibits may include contemporary sculpture, ceremonial masks, architectural details, costumes, and textiles. The museum store features African crafts, clothing, and jewelry. *593 Broadway, tel. 212/966–1313. Admission: $3 adults;*

$1.50 students, senior citizens, and children under 12. Open Wed., Thurs., Sun. 11–6; Fri. and Sat. 11–8

 Across Broadway, the **Alternative Museum,** a gallery that exhibits art with a political or sociopolitical twist, has moved up to SoHo from its former TriBeCa home. *594 Broadway, tel. 212/966–4444. Suggested donation: $3. Open Tues.–Sat. 11–6.*

Go one block west to Mercer Street, where the sidewalks may be cluttered with cartons of cloth or leather remnants discarded by the sweatshops upstairs (artists find a lot of good collage material here).

Time Out | Amid all the artful minimalism of SoHo restaurants, **Fanelli's Cafe** (corner of Mercer and Prince Sts., tel. 212/226–9412) is a breath of fresh air. It's been in operation since 1872 and it looks it, with its etched-glass front door, carved mahogany bar, and pressed-tin walls. Order some standard bar food—burgers, omelets, or pizza with a thin, crisp crust.

Next to Fanelli's is **A Photographer's Place** (133 Mercer St., tel. 212/966–2356), which features photography books, calendars, postcards, and antique cameras and pictures.

Between Broome and Spring streets is **Enchanted Forest** (85 Mercer St., tel. 212/925–6677), with a fanciful selection of stuffed animals, books, and handmade toys that almost deserves to be considered an art gallery. Both kids and adults have a great time here.

At the foot of Mercer Street, bustling Canal Street leads east to Chinatown (*see* Tour 16, *below*); across the street, TriBeCa officially begins. To avoid Canal Street's commercial chaos, cross as soon as you can and then turn south down West Broadway. A life-size iron Statue of Liberty crown rises above the blue-tiled entrance to **El Teddy's** (219 West Broadway, tel. 212/941–7070), a gourmet Mexican restaurant. Stop in for a drink, if only to see the kitschy decor.

In the mid-19th century, Worth Street was the equivalent of Seventh Avenue today, the center of the garment trade; the area to the west, near the Hudson River docks, became the heart of the wholesale food business. Turn right onto Duane Street to reach **Duane Park,** preserved since 1800 as a calm, shady triangle; it is still surrounded by cheese, butter, and egg warehouses (note the Land O'Lakes sign facing the south tip of the park).

One block north on Hudson Street, on your right, you'll see the Art Deco **Western Union Building** (60 Hudson St.), where 19 subtly shaded colors of brick are laid in undulating patterns. Turn up quiet Jay Street and pause at narrow Staple Street, little more than an alley, where a green pedestrian walkway overhead links two warehouses. The street is named for the staple products unloaded here by ships in transit that didn't want to pay duty on any extra cargo. Framed at the end of the alley is the redbrick **New York Mercantile Exchange,** its square corner tower topped by a bulbous roof. On the ground floor is an acclaimed restaurant, **Chanterelle** (*see* Chapter 9).

If you continue west on Jay Street, you'll pass the loading docks of a very active food wholesaler, **Bazzini's Nuts and Confections.** Tucked into a corner of its extensive warehouse is its upscale retail shop (corner of Jay and Greenwich Sts., tel. 212/ 334–1280), where you can buy nuts, coffee beans, candies, cookies, and various other delicacies.

On Greenwich Street near Harrison Street, the **TriBeCa Grill** (*see* Chapter 9) is located on the first floor of the old Martinson Coffee Building, which now houses actor Robert De Niro's **Tribeca Film Center,** a movie production complex. Movie fans may want to continue north to Moore Street, where a right turn will take you two blocks to 14 Moore Street, the firehouse (still in use) that was filmed as the **Ghostbusters' headquarters** in the movies *Ghostbusters* and *Ghostbusters II*.

As you walk back down Greenwich Street, notice on your right a surprising row of early 19th-century town houses nestled in the side of a huge high-rise apartment complex. These three-story redbrick houses were moved here to Harrison Street from various sites in the neighborhood when, in the early 1970s, the food-wholesalers' central market nearby was razed and moved to the Bronx. Walk around the houses to peer into the green yard they enclose.

⑫ The high-rise towers belong to **Independence Plaza,** a pleasant, if somewhat utilitarian, project of the mid-1970s that was supposed to be part of a wave of demolition and construction— until the preservationists stepped in. For several years Independence Plaza remained a middle-class island stranded downtown, far from stores, schools, and neighbors; with TriBeCa's growing chic, however, plus the development of Battery Park City to the south, it has become a much more desirable address.

Continuing south on Greenwich Street, you'll soon come to the ⑬ 2½-acre **Washington Market Park,** a much-needed recreation space for this neighborhood. Named after the great food market that once sprawled over this area, it is a green, landscaped oasis with tennis courts, a playground, and even a gazebo. Just across Chambers Street, P.S. 234, a public elementary school, has opened to serve TriBeCa's younger generation. At the corner, a stout little red tower resembles a lighthouse, and iron ship figures are worked into the playground fence—reminders of the neighborhood's long-gone dockside past.

Tour 15: Little Italy

Mulberry Street is the heart of Little Italy; in fact, at this point it's virtually the entire body. In 1932 an estimated 98% of the inhabitants of this area were of Italian birth or heritage, but since then the growth and expansion of neighboring Chinatown have encroached on the Italian neighborhood to such an extent that merchants and community leaders of the Little Italy Restoration Association (LIRA) negotiated a truce in which the Chinese agreed to let at least Mulberry remain an all-Italian street. If you want the flavor of a whole Italian neighborhood, you'd do better visiting Carroll Gardens in Brooklyn or Arthur Avenue in the Bronx (*see* Chapter 4); or rent a video of the Martin Scorsese movie *Mean Streets*, which was filmed in Little Italy back in the very early 1970s.

 Start at the intersection of Spring and Mulberry streets, which still has a residential feel to it. The **D & G Bakery** (45 Spring St., tel. 212/226–6688) is one of the last coal-oven bakeries in the United States. Buy a loaf of savory prosciutto bread, a meal in itself, with the Italian ham baked right into the bread.

Walk down Mulberry Street to Broome Street, where the classic Little Italy really begins, crowded with restaurants, cafés, bakeries, imported-food shops, and souvenir stores. Especially on weekends, when suburbanites flock here, this is a street for strolling, gawking, and inhaling the aroma of garlic and olive oil. Some restaurants and cafés display high-tech Eurodesign; others seem dedicated to staying exactly as their old customers remember them. At the southwest corner of Broome and Mulberry streets, stairs lead down through a glass entrance to what seems to be a blue-tiled cave—and, appropriately

⑮ enough, it is the **Grotta Azzurra** (Blue Grotto) restaurant (387 Broome St., tel. 212/925–8775), a longtime favorite for both the hearty food and the very Italian ambience. Across Mulberry Street is **Caffe Roma** (385 Broome St., 212/226–8413), a traditional pastry shop where you can eat cannoli at postage-stamp-size wrought-iron tables.

At the corner of Mulberry and Grand streets, stop to get the lay of the land. Facing north (uptown), on your right you'll see a series of wide, four-story houses from the early 19th century, built long before the great flood of immigration hit this neighborhood between 1890 and 1924. Turn and look south along the east side of Mulberry Street to see Little Italy's predominant architecture today: tenement buildings with fire escapes projecting over the sidewalks. Most of these are of the late-19th-century New York style known as railroad flats: six-story buildings on 25-by-90-foot lots, with all the rooms in each apartment placed in a straight line like railroad cars. This style was common in the densely populated immigrant neighborhoods of lower Manhattan until 1901, when the city passed an ordinance requiring air shafts in the interior of buildings. On the southeast corner, **E. Rossi & Co.** (191 Grand St., tel. 212/966–6640; established in 1902) is an antiquated little shop that sells housewares, espresso makers, embroidered religious postcards, and jocular Italian T-shirts. Down Grand Street is **Ferrara's** (195 Grand St., tel. 212/226–6150), a 100-year-old pastry shop that ships its creations—cannoli, peasant pie, Italian rum cake—all over the world. Another survivor of the pretenement era is at 149 Mulberry Street, formerly the Van Rensselaer House (built in 1816); notice its dormer windows. Today it houses **Paolucci's Restaurant** (tel. 212/226–9653).

⑯ **Umberto's Clam House** (129 Mulberry St., tel. 212/431–7545) is perhaps best known as the place where mobster Joey Gallo was munching scungili in 1973 when he was fatally surprised by a task force of mob hit men. Quite peaceful now, Umberto's specializes in fresh shellfish in a spicy tomato sauce. Turn onto Hester Street to visit yet another Little Italy institution,

⑰ **Puglia** (189 Hester St., tel. 212/966–6006), a restaurant where guests sit at long communal tables, sing along with house entertainers, and enjoy moderately priced southern Italian specialties with quantities of homemade wine. (For other Little Italy restaurants, *see* Chapter 9.)

One street west, on Baxter Street toward Canal Street, stands

⑱ the **San Gennaro Church** (officially, Most Precious Blood Church, National Shrine of San Gennaro), which each year around September 19 sponsors Little Italy's keynote event, the annual Feast of San Gennaro. (The community's other big festival celebrates St. Anthony of Padua, in June; that church is at Houston and Sullivan streets, in what is now SoHo.) During the feasts, Little Italy's streets are closed to traffic, arches of tinsel span the thoroughfares, the sidewalks are lined with booths offering games and food, and the whole scene is one noisy, crowded, kitschy, delightful party.

Tour 16: Chinatown

Visibly exotic, Chinatown is a popular tourist attraction, but it is also a real, vital community, where about half of the city's population of 300,000 Chinese still live. Its main businesses are restaurants and garment factories; some 55% of its residents speak little or no English. Theoretically, Chinatown is divided from Little Italy by Canal Street, the bustling artery that links the Holland Tunnel (to New Jersey) and the Manhattan Bridge (to Brooklyn). However, in recent years, an influx of immigrants from the People's Republic of China, Taiwan, and especially Hong Kong has swelled Manhattan's Chinese population, and Hong Kong residents, anticipating the return of the British colony to PRC domination in 1997, have been investing their capital in Chinatown real estate. Consequently, Chinatown now spills over its traditional borders into Little Italy to the north and the formerly Jewish Lower East Side to the east.

Originally Canal Street was a tree-lined road with a canal running its length. Today the Chinatown stretch of Canal Street is almost overwhelmed with sidewalk markets bursting with stacks of fresh seafood and strange-shaped vegetables in extraterrestrial shades of green. Food shops proudly display their wares: If America's motto is "a chicken in every pot," then Chinatown's must be "a roast duck in every window."

⑲ The slightly less frantic **Kam Man** (200 Canal St., tel. 212/571–0330), a duplex supermarket, sells an amazing assortment of fresh and canned imported groceries, herbs, and the sort of dinnerware and furniture familiar to patrons of Chinese restaurants. Choose from dozens of varieties of noodles or such delicacies as dried starch and fresh chicken feet.

⑳ The **Chinatown History Museum,** at the corner of Bayard and Mulberry streets, shows interactive photographic exhibitions on Asian-American labor history. It also has a resource library and bookstore and offers a walking tour of Chinatown. *70 Mulberry St., 2nd floor, tel. 212/619–4785. Admission: $1. Open weekdays and Sun. noon–5.*

Mott Street, the principal business street of the neighborhood, looks the way you might expect Chinatown to look: narrow and twisting, crammed with souvenir shops and restaurants in funky pagoda-style buildings, crowded with pedestrians at all hours of the day or night. Within the few dense blocks of Chinatown, hundreds of restaurants serve every imaginable type of Chinese cuisine, from fast-food noodles or dumplings to sumptuous Hunan, Szechuan, Cantonese, Mandarin, and Shanghai feasts (*see* Chapter 9). Every New Yorker thinks he or she knows the absolute, flat-out best, but whichever one you try, at 8 PM on Saturday, don't be surprised if you have to wait in line to get in.

As you proceed down Mott Street, take a peek down Pell Street, a narrow lane of wall-to-wall restaurants whose neon signs stretch halfway across the thoroughfare. At 35 Pell Street is **May May Chinese Gourmet Bakery** (tel. 212/267–6733), a good place to stop for Chinese pastries, rice dumplings, and vegetarian specialties, such as yam cakes and vegetarian spring rolls.

Time Out A few steps down Pell Street, turn onto Doyers Street to find the **Viet-Nam Restaurant** (11 Doyers St., tel. 212/693–0725), an informal, inexpensive little basement restaurant that serves spicy, exotic Vietnamese dishes.

At the corner of Mott and Mosco streets stands the **Church of the Transfiguration.** Built in 1801 as the Zion Episcopal Church, this imposing Georgian structure with Gothic windows is now a Chinese Catholic church where mass is said in Cantonese, Mandarin, and English. Directly across the street from the church is **Quong Yuen Shing & Co.** (32 Mott St., tel. 212/962–6280), one of Chinatown's oldest curio shops, with porcelain bowls, teapots, and cups for sale.

㉑ At the end of Mott Street is **Chatham Square,** which is really more of a labyrinth than a square: 10 streets converge here, creating pandemonium for cars and a nightmare for pedestrians. A Chinese arch honoring Chinese casualties in American wars stands on an island in the eye of the storm. On the far end of the square, at the corner of Catherine Street and East Broadway, you'll see a branch of the Manhattan Savings Bank, built to resemble a pagoda (in this neighborhood, even some public phone booths have been styled as pagodas).

Skirting Chatham Square, head back to the right to go down Worth Street. The corner of Worth, Baxter, and Park streets was once known as Five Points, the central intersection of a tough 19th-century slum of Irish and German immigrants. To-
㉒ day it has been replaced by **Columbus Park,** a shady, paved urban space where children play and elderly Chinese gather to reminisce about their homelands.

Return to Chatham Square, cross Park Row (on your right) and take a sharp right turn on St. James Place to find two remnants of this neighborhood's pre-Chinatown past. On St. James Place
㉓ is the **First Shearith Israel graveyard** (predecessor of the cemeteries in Greenwich Village and Chelsea; *see* Tours 11 and 12, *above*). The first Jewish cemetery in the United States, this site was consecrated in 1656, when it was considered to be well outside of town. Walk a half block farther, turn left on James Street, and you'll see **St. James Church,** a stately 1837 Greek Revival edifice where Al Smith, who rose from this poor Irish neighborhood to become New York's governor and a 1928 Democratic presidential candidate, once served as altar boy.

㉔ Go back past Chatham Square and up the Bowery to **Confucius Plaza,** the open area monitored by a statue of Confucius and the sweeping curve of a redbrick high-rise apartment complex named for him. At 18 Bowery, at the corner of Pell Street, stands one of Manhattan's oldest homes, a Federal and Georgian structure built in 1785 by meat wholesaler Edward Moon-
㉕ ey. A younger side of Chinatown is shown at the **Asian American Arts Centre,** which displays current work by Asian American artists. *26 Bowery, tel. 212/233–2154. Admission free. Open weekdays 10–6.*

For some exotic shopping, duck into the **Canal Arcade,** a passage linking the Bowery and Elizabeth Street. A few doors down, at 50 Bowery, you'll see the **Silver Palace** restaurant (*see* Chapter 9), worth a peek inside for its Chinese rococo interior, complete with dragons whose eyes are blinking lights.

At the intersection of the Bowery and Canal Street, a grand arch and colonnade mark the entrance to the Manhattan Bridge, which leads to Brooklyn. This corner was once the center of New York's diamond district. Many jewelry dealers have moved uptown to 47th Street between Fifth and Sixth avenues (*see* Off the Beaten Track, *below*), but a substantial number still occupy shops on the Bowery and the north side of Canal. The selection is pretty good, but don't pay the first price quoted.

Tour 17: Wall Street and the Battery

Numbers in the margin correspond to points of interest on the Tours 17 and 18: Lower Manhattan map.

Lower Manhattan doesn't cover many acres, but it is packed with attractions, for it has always been central to the city's networks of power and wealth. It was here that the New Amsterdam colony was established by the Dutch in 1625; in 1789, the first capital building of the United States was located here. The city did not really expand beyond these precincts until the middle of the 19th century. Today Lower Manhattan is in many ways dominated by Wall Street, which is both an actual street and a shorthand name for the vast, powerful financial community that clusters around the New York and American stock exchanges. Visit on a weekday to catch the district's true vitality—but expect to be jostled on the crowded sidewalks if you stand too long, peering at the great buildings that surge skyward on every corner. A different but equally awe-inspiring sight can be found on the tip of the island, as you look out across the great silvery harbor and see enduring symbols of America: the Statue of Liberty and Ellis Island, port of entry for countless immigrants to a new land.

Our tour begins at the southernmost point of Manhattan, at the **Staten Island Ferry Terminal** (for subway riders, that's just
❶ outside the South Ferry station on the No. 1 line). The **Staten Island Ferry** is still the best deal in town: The 20- to 30-minute ride across New York Harbor provides great views of the Manhattan skyline, the Statue of Liberty, the Verrazano Narrows Bridge, and the New Jersey coast—and it costs only 50¢ roundtrip (you must use quarters in the turnstiles). Boats embark on various schedules: every 15 minutes during rush hours, every 20–30 minutes most other times, and every hour after 11 PM and on weekend mornings. A word of advice, however: While commuters love the ferry service's swift, new low-slung craft, the boats ride low in the water and have no outside deck space. Wait for one of the higher, more open old-timers. Once you're on Staten Island, you can, of course, stay as long as you like.

❷ To the west of South Ferry lies **Battery Park,** a verdant landfill, loaded with monuments and sculpture, at Manhattan's green toe. The park's name refers to a line of cannons once mounted here to defend the shoreline (which ran along what is currently State Street). Head north along the water's edge to the **East Coast Memorial,** a statue of a fierce eagle that presides over eight granite slabs inscribed with the names of U.S. servicemen who died in the Western Atlantic during World War II. Climb the steps of the East Coast Memorial for a fine view of the main features of **New York Harbor;** from left to right: **Governors Island,** a Coast Guard installation; hilly **Staten Island** in the distance; the **Statue of Liberty** on Liberty Island; **Ellis Island,** gateway to the New World for generations of immigrants; and the old railway terminal in **Liberty State Park,** on the mainland in Jersey City, New Jersey.

Continue north past a romantic **statue of Giovanni da Verrazano,** the Florentine merchant who piloted the ship that first sighted New York and its harbor in 1524. The Verrazano Narrows Bridge between Brooklyn and Staten Island—the world's longest suspension bridge—is visible from here, just beyond Governors Island.

❸ Built in 1811 as a defense for New York Harbor, the circular brick fortress now called **Castle Clinton** was, when first built, on an island 200 feet from shore. In 1824 it became Castle Garden, an entertainment and concert facility that reached its zenith in 1850 when more than 6,000 people (the capacity of Radio City Music Hall) attended the U.S. debut of the "Swedish Nightingale," Jenny Lind. After landfill connected it to the city, Castle Clinton became, in succession, an immigrant processing center, an aquarium, and now a restored fort, museum, and ticket office for ferries to the **Statue of Liberty** and **Ellis Island.** The ferry ride is one loop; you can get off at Liberty Island, visit the statue, then reboard any ferry and continue on to Ellis Island, boarding another boat once you have finished exploring the historic immigration facility there. *Ferry information: tel. 212/269–5755. Round-trip fare: $6 adults, $5 senior citizens, $3 children 3–17. Daily departures every 30 min 9:30–3:30; more frequent departures and extended hours in summer.*

❹ After arriving on Liberty Island, you have two choices from the ground-floor entrance to the **Statue of Liberty** monument: you can take an elevator 10 stories to the top of the 89-foot-high pedestal, or if you're strong of heart and limb, you can climb 354 steps (the equivalent of a 22-story building) to the crown. (Visitors cannot go up into the torch.) It usually takes two to three hours to walk up to the crown because of the wait beforehand. Erected in 1886 and refurbished for its centennial, the Statue of Liberty weighs 225 tons and stands 151 feet from her feet to her torch. Exhibits inside illustrate the statue's history, including videos of the view from the crown for those who don't make the climb. There is also a model of the statue's face for the blind to feel. *Tel. 212/363–3200. Admission free.*

❺ The ferry's other stop, **Ellis Island,** opened in September 1990 to record crowds after a $140 million restoration. Now a national monument, Ellis Island was once a federal immigration facility that processed 17 million men, women, and children between 1892 and 1954—the ancestors of more than 40% of Americans living today. The island's main building contains the **Ellis Island Immigration Museum,** with exhibits detailing not only the island's history but the whole history of immigration to America. Perhaps the most moving exhibit is the American Immigrant Wall of Honor, where the names of nearly 400,000 immigrant Americans are inscribed along an outdoor promenade overlooking the Statue of Liberty and the Manhattan skyline. *Tel. 212/363–3200. Admission free.*

Tours 17 and 18: Lower Manhattan

KEY

AE American Express Office

--- Ferry

440 yards

400 meters

Alexander Hamilton
Customs House, **6**
Battery Park, **2**
Brooklyn Bridge, **22**
Castle Clinton, **3**
City Hall, **18**

Criminal Courts
Building, **25**
Ellis Island, **5**
Federal Hall National
Memorial, **9**
Federal Reserve
Bank, **12**
Fraunces Tavern, **8**
Municipal Building, **21**

New York County
Courthouse, **24**
New York Stock
Exchange, **10**
St. Paul's Chapel, **13**
South Street Seaport
Historic District, **17**

Staten Island Ferry, **1**
Statue of Liberty, **4**
Surrogate's Court, **20**
Trinity Church, **11**
Tweed Courthouse, **19**
U.S. Courthouse, **23**
Vietnam Veterans
Memorial, **7**

Woolworth
Building, **14**
World Financial
Center, **16**
World Trade
Center, **15**

A broad mall that begins at the landward entrance to Castle Clinton leads back across the park to the **Netherlands Memorial,** a quaint flagpole depicting the bead exchange that bought from the Native Americans the land to establish Fort Amsterdam in 1626. Inscriptions describe the event in English and Dutch.

❻ As you leave the park, across State Street you'll see the imposing **Alexander Hamilton Customs House,** built in 1907 in the ornate Beaux Arts style fashionable at the time. Above the base, the facade features massive columns rising to a pediment topped by a double row of statuary. Daniel Chester French, better known for the statue of Lincoln in the Lincoln Memorial in Washington, DC, sculpted the lower statues, which symbolize various continents (left to right: Asia, the Americas, Europe, Africa); the upper row represents the major trading cities of the world. The Customs House facade appeared in the movie *Ghostbusters II* as the fictional New York Museum of Art. Federal bankruptcy courts are currently housed in the Customs House; in fall 1994, the National Museum of the American Indian (*see* Chapter 6) will move here and be renamed the George Gustav Heye Center.

The Customs House faces onto **Bowling Green,** an oval greensward at the foot of Broadway that became New York's first public park in 1733. On July 9, 1776, a few hours after citizens learned about the signing of the Declaration of Independence, rioters toppled a statue of British King George III that had occupied the spot for 11 years; much of the statue's lead was melted down into bullets. In 1783, when the occupying British forces fled the city, they defiantly hoisted a Union Jack on a greased, uncleated flagpole so it couldn't be lowered; patriot John Van Arsdale drove his own cleats into the pole to replace the flag with the Stars and Stripes.

From Bowling Green, head south on State Street. A stunning semicircular office tower in reflective glass hugs the bend of the street at 17 State Street. Next door is the **Shrine of St. Elizabeth Ann Seton** (7–8 State St.). What is now the rectory of the shrine is a redbrick Federal-style town house with a distinctive wood portico shaped to fit the curving street. This house was built in 1793 as the home of the wealthy Watson family; Mother Seton and her family lived here from 1801 to 1803. She joined the Catholic Church in 1805, after the death of her husband, and went on to found the Sisters of Charity, the first American order of nuns. In 1975 she became the first American-born saint. Masses are held here daily.

❼ Continue around onto Water Street, passing on your right **New York Plaza,** a complex of high-tech office towers linked by an underground concourse. Just beyond it is the **Vietnam Veterans Memorial,** where letters from servicemen and servicewomen have been etched into a wall of greenish glass.

❽ Return to Broad Street and go one block inland to **Fraunces Tavern,** a complex of five largely 19th-century buildings housing a museum, restaurant, and bar (*see* Chapter 9). The main building is a Colonial home (brick exterior, cream-colored marble portico and balcony) built in 1719 and converted to a tavern in 1762. This was the site where, in 1783, George Washington delivered a farewell address to his officers celebrating the British evacuation of New York; later, the building housed some offices of the fledgling U.S. government. Today Fraunces Tavern contains two fully furnished period rooms and other displays of 18th- and 19th-century American history. *Broad and Pearl Sts., tel. 212/425-1778. Admission: $2.50 adults, $1 students, senior citizens, and children under 12. Museum open weekdays and some Sats. 10-4:45.*

Walk through the lobby of the office building at **85 Broad Street,** which, paying due homage to urban archaeology, traces the course of the old Dutch Stone Street with a line of brown paving stones. At the side of the building, on Pearl Street, peer through the transparent panel in the sidewalk to see the excavated foundations of the 17th-century Stadt Huis, the old Dutch City Hall.

Time Out   The brick plaza behind 85 Broad Street is flanked by a variety of small restaurants. Order a take-out meal or snack and eat it out here on the benches, where you can watch busy office workers milling past and enjoy not being one of them.

Head up Pearl Street to **Hanover Square,** a quiet tree-lined plaza that stood on the waterfront when the East River reached Pearl Street. This was the city's original printing-house square; on the site of 81 Pearl Street, William Bradford established the first printing press in the colonies. The pirate Captain Kidd lived in the neighborhood, and the brownstone **India House** (1837) used to house the New York Cotton Exchange. Today it holds Harry's at Hanover Square, a vintage Wall Street bar.

Walk inland up Hanover Square to the rounded corner of South William and Beaver streets, where a graceful columned porch marks the entrance to **Delmonico's** restaurant, opened in 1888 on the site of an earlier Delmonico's founded in 1827. A pioneer in serving Continental cuisine, it was *the* place to go at the turn of the century; under different ownership, it is still a restaurant today.

Two blocks farther north, William Street crosses **Wall Street,** so called because it traces the course of a wood wall built across the island in 1653 to defend the Dutch colony against the native Indians. Arguably the most famous thoroughfare in the world, though only a third of a mile long, Wall Street began its financial career with stock traders conducting business along the sidewalks or at tables beneath a sheltering buttonwood tree. Today it's a dizzyingly narrow canyon—look to the right and you'll glimpse a sliver of East River waterfront; look to the left and you'll see the spire of Trinity Church, tightly framed by skyscrapers at the head of the street.

To learn the difference between Ionic and Corinthian columns, look at the **Citibank Building** to your right (55 Wall St.). The lower stories were part of an earlier U.S. Customs House, built in 1863, and it was literally a bullish day on Wall Street when oxen hauled its 16 granite Ionic columns up to the site. When the National City Bank took over the building in 1907, the architects McKim, Mead & White added a second tier of columns but made them Corinthian.

One block west on Wall Street, where Broad Street becomes Nassau Street, you'll find on your right a regal statue of George Washington on the steps of the **Federal Hall National Memorial.**

This 1883 statue by noted sculptor and presidential relative John Quincy Adams Ward marks the spot where Washington was sworn in as the first U.S. president in 1789. After the capital moved to Philadelphia in 1790, the original Federal Hall became New York's City Hall, then was demolished in 1812 when the present City Hall (*see* Tour 18, *below*) was completed. The clean and simple lines of the current structure, built as (yet another) U.S. Customs House in 1842, were modeled after the Parthenon, a potent symbol for a young nation striving to emulate classical Greek democracy. It's now a museum featuring exhibits on New York and Wall Street. *26 Wall St., tel. 212/264-8711. Admission free. Open weekdays 9–5.*

In building a two-story investment bank at the corner of Wall and Broad streets, J. P. Morgan was in effect declaring himself above the pressures of Wall Street real-estate values. Now **Morgan Guaranty Trust,** the building bears pockmarks near the fourth window on the Wall Street side, created when a bomb that had been placed in a pushcart exploded in 1920.

⑩ Perhaps the heart of Wall Street is the **New York Stock Exchange,** which has its august Corinthian main entrance around the corner at 20 Broad Street. Compared with the Federal Hall memorial, this neoclassical building is much more elaborately decorated, as befitted the more grandiose national image of 1901, when it was designed. Inside, after what may be a lengthy wait, you can take an elevator to the third-floor visitor center. A self-guided tour, informative slide shows, video displays, and guides may help you interpret the seeming chaos you'll see from the visitors' gallery overlooking the immense (50-foot-high) trading hall. *Tickets available at 20 Broad St., tel. 212/656–5168. Free tickets are distributed beginning at 9:05; come before 1 PM to assure getting in. Open weekdays 9:15–3:15.*

⑪ **Trinity Church** (Broadway and Wall St.) was established as an Anglican parish in 1697. The present structure (1846), by Richard Upjohn, ranked as the city's tallest building for most of the second half of the 19th century. Its three huge bronze doors were designed by Richard Morris Hunt to recall Ghiberti's doors for the Baptistry in Florence, Italy. After the exterior sandstone was restored in 1991, New Yorkers were amazed to discover that a church they had always thought of as black was actually a rosy pink. The church's Gothic Revival interior is surprisingly light and elegant, although you may see derelicts napping in the pews. On the church's south side is a 2½-acre graveyard: Alexander Hamilton is buried beneath a white stone pyramid; and a monument commemorates Robert Fulton, the inventor of the steamboat (he's actually buried in the Livingstone family vault, with his wife).

Just north of the church is tiny Thames Street, where a pair of skyscrapers playfully called the **Thames Twins**—the Trinity and U.S. Realty buildings—display early 20th-century attempts to apply Gothic decoration to skyscrapers. Across the street at 120 Broadway, the 1915 **Equitable Building** rises 30 stories straight from its base with no setback; its overpowering shadow on the street convinced the city government to pass the nation's first zoning law. Large public plazas around the bases of skyscrapers have helped to alleviate this problem, and a good example is between Cedar and Liberty streets, where the black-glass **Marine Midland Bank** (1971) features in its street-level plaza a red-and-silver Noguchi sculpture, *Cube*. Two blocks east at William and Pine streets, the plaza surrounding the 65-story **Chase Manhattan Bank Building** holds a striking black-and-white sculpture, *Group of Four Trees*, by Jean Dubuffet.

Liberty Street converges with William Street and Maiden Lane at triangular **Louise Nevelson Plaza,** which contains four black welded-steel abstract Nevelson sculptures, three middle-size pieces and one huge 70-footer. Sit in the plaza and contemplate the **Federal Reserve Bank** directly across the street, which looks the way a bank ought to look: gray, solid, imposing, absolutely impregnable—and it had better be, for its vaults reputedly contain a third of the world's gold reserves. *33 Liberty St., tel. 212/720-6130. Admission free. 1-hr tour by advance (at least one month) reservation, weekdays at 10, 11, 1, and 2.*

Proceed one block north to John Street, where you'll see the **John Street Methodist Church** (44 John St.), on the site of the first Methodist Church in America. Then return to Broadway and head north to **St. Paul's Chapel** (Broadway and Fulton St.), the oldest (1766) surviving church in Manhattan and the site of the prayer service following George Washington's inauguration as president. Built of rough Manhattan stone, it was modeled after London's St. Martin-in-the-Fields. It's open until 4 (Sundays until 3) for prayer and meditation; look in the north aisle for Washington's pew.

Two blocks up Broadway is the so-called Cathedral of Commerce, the ornate white terra-cotta **Woolworth Building** (Park Pl. and Broadway). When it opened in 1913 it was, at 792 feet, the world's tallest building; it still houses the Woolworth corporate offices. Among its extravagant Gothic-style details are sculptures set into arches in the lobby ceiling; one of them represents an elderly F. W. Woolworth pinching his pennies, while another depicts the architect, Cass Gilbert, cradling in his arms a model of his creation.

Go west on Park Place and turn down Church Street to the **World Trade Center,** a 16-acre, 12-million-square-foot complex that contains New York's two tallest buildings (1,350 feet high). To reach the observation deck on the 107th floor of 2 World Trade Center, elevators glide a quarter of a mile into the sky—in only 58 seconds. The view potentially extends 55 miles, although signs at the ticket window disclose how far you can see that day and whether the outdoor deck is open. In late February 1993, the Center was the site of a bombing, attributed to terrorists, that killed six people and caused extensive damage to the area. However, at press time the Center had, for the most part, returned to normal operations; many former tenants had moved back in. Of course, security has been tightened considerably within the complex. *Tel. 212/435-7397. Admission: $4 adults, $2.25 senior citizens, $2 children. Open June–Sept., daily 9:30 AM–11:30 PM; Oct.–May, daily 9:30 AM–9:30 PM.*

You can get the same view with a meal at **Windows on the World** (*see* Chapter 9) atop 1 World Trade Center; lighter meals or drinks are available at its **Hors d'Oeuvrey** (jacket required).

Some 50,000 people work in this seven-building complex, and at street level and underground it contains more than 60 stores, services, and restaurants, as well as the adjacent New York Vista hotel (*see* Chapter 11). There's a TKTS booth selling discount tickets to Broadway and Off-Broadway shows (*see* Chapter 11) in the mezzanine of 2 World Trade Center (open weekdays 11–5:30, Sat. 11–1), and on the ninth floor of 4 World Trade Center, a visitors' gallery overlooks the trading floor of the Commodities Exchange (tel. 212/938–2025; open weekdays 9:30–3).

More than a million cubic yards of rock and soil were excavated for the World Trade Center—and then moved across West Street to help beget the 100-acre Battery Park City development, a complete neighborhood built from scratch. Take the pedestrian overpass north of 1 World Trade Center to Battery Park City's centerpiece, the **World Financial Center,** a four-tower complex designed by Cesar Pelli, with some heavy-duty corporate tenants, including Merrill Lynch, American Express, and Dow Jones. You'll come out into the soaring **Winter Garden Atrium,** its mauve marble cascade of steps spilling down into a vaulted plaza with 16 giant palm trees, framed by a vast arched window overlooking the Hudson. This stunning space has become a popular venue for free performances by top-flight musicians and dancers (tel. 212/945–0505). Surrounding the atrium are several upscale shops—Godiva chocolatiers, Rizzoli bookshop, Ann Taylor for women's clothing, Mark Cross for leather goods—plus a skylit food court.

Time Out   While the courtyard also offers several full-service restaurants, for a quick bite head for **Minters** (tel. 212/945–4455)—and be sure to leave room for great ice-cream cones.

Of the few spots in Manhattan that directly overlook the rivers, **Battery Park City** just may be the best. The outdoor plaza right behind the atrium curls around a tidy little yacht basin; take in the view of the Statue of Liberty and read the stirring quotations worked into the iron railings. Just north of the basin is the terminal for ferry service to Hoboken, New Jersey (tel. 908/463–3779; fare: $2), on the other side of the Hudson River. It's an eight-minute ride to Frank Sinatra's hometown, with a spectacular view of lower Manhattan.

To the south, a longer riverside promenade that eventually will extend to Battery Park accompanies the residential part of Battery Park City, a mix of high rises, town houses, shops, and green squares that does a surprisingly good job of duplicating the rhythms of the rest of the city. Especially noteworthy among the art works populating the esplanade are Ned Smyth's columned plaza with chessboards; and the South Cove, a collaborative effort, a romantic curved stage set of wood piers and a steel-frame lookout. Slated to open in early 1995 behind South Cove is the **Living Memorial to the Holocaust–Museum of Jewish Heritage** (Battery Pl. between 1st and 2nd Pl., tel. 212/687–9141).

Tour 18: The Seaport and the Courts

New York's role as a great seaport is easiest to understand downtown, with both the Hudson River and East River waterfronts within walking distance. While the deeper Hudson River came into its own in the steamship era, the more sheltered waters of the East River saw most of the action in the 19th century, during the age of clipper ships. This era is preserved in the South Street Seaport restoration, centered on Fulton

Street between Water Street and the East River. Only a few blocks away, you can visit another seat of New York history: the City Hall neighborhood, which includes Manhattan's magisterial collection of court buildings.

Walk down Fulton Street, named after the ferry to Brooklyn that once docked at its foot (the ferry itself was named after its inventor, Robert Fulton), to Water Street, which was once the shoreline. On the 19th-century landfill across the street is the **17** 11-block **South Street Seaport Historic District,** which was created in 1967 to save this area from being overtaken by skyscrapers. The Rouse Corporation, which had already created slick so-called "festival marketplaces" in Boston (Quincy Market) and Baltimore (Harborplace), was later hired to restore and adapt the existing historic buildings.

The little white lighthouse at Water and Fulton streets is the **Titanic Memorial,** commemorating the sinking of the RMS *Titanic* in 1912. Beyond it, Fulton Street, cobbled in blocks of Belgian granite, is a pedestrian mall that swarms with visitors, especially on fine-weather weekends. Immediately to your left is the **Cannon's Walk Block,** which contains 15 restored buildings.

At 211 Water Street is **Bowne & Co.,** a reconstructed working 19th-century print shop. Around the corner, a narrow court called Cannon's Walk, lined with shops, opens onto Fulton Street; follow it around to Front Street. Directly across Front Street is the **Fulton Market Building,** a modern building, full of shops and restaurants, that re-creates the bustling commercial atmosphere of the old victual markets that were on this site from 1822 on. On the south side of Fulton Street is the seaport's architectural centerpiece, **Schermerhorn Row,** a redbrick terrace of Georgian- and Federal-style warehouses and countinghouses built in 1811–12. Today the ground floors are occupied by upscale shops, bars, and restaurants, and the **South Street Seaport Museum.** *Tel. 212/669–9400. Admission to ships, galleries, walking tours, Maritime Crafts Center, films, and other seaport events: $6 adults, $5 senior citizens, $4 students, $3 children. Open fall–spring, daily 10–5; summer, daily 10–6.*

Cross South Street under an elevated stretch of the FDR Drive to **Pier 16,** where the historic ships are docked, including the *Peking,* the second-largest sailing ship in existence; the full-rigged *Wavertree;* and the lightship *Ambrose.* A restored **Pilothouse** is the pierside information center. Pier 16 is also the departure point for the 90-minute **Seaport Line Harbor Cruise.** *Tel. 212/233–4800. Fare: $12 adults, $11 senior citizens, $10 students, $6 children. Combination fares—for the cruise and the other attractions—run $15.25, $13.50, $12, and $7.50.*

To the north is **Pier 17,** a multilevel dockside shopping mall. Its weathered-wood rear decks make a splendid spot from which to sit and contemplate the river; look north to see the Brooklyn, Manhattan, and Williamsburg bridges, and look across to see Brooklyn Heights.

Time Out   If you're hungry, head for the fast-food stalls on Pier 17's third-floor **Promenade Food Court.** The cuisine is nonchain eclectic: Seaport Fries, Pizza on the Pier, Wok & Roll, the Yorkville Packing House, and the Salad Bowl. What's really spectacular is the view from the tables in a glass-walled atrium.

As your nose may already have surmised, the blocks along South Street north of the museum complex still house a working fish market, which has been in operation since the 1770s. Although the city has tried to relocate the hundreds of fishmongers of the **Fulton Fish Market** to the South Bronx, the area remains a beehive of activity. Get up early (or stay up late) if you want to see it: The action begins around midnight and ends by 8 AM. To arrange an early morning, behind-the-scenes tour of the market, call tour guide Richard Lord (tel. 201/798–3801) as far in advance as possible.

Return to Fulton Street and walk away from the river to Broadway, where St. Paul's Chapel is (*see* Tour 17, *above*). As you turn right, forking off to your right is **Park Row,** which was known as Newspaper Row from the mid-19th to early 20th century, when most of the city's 20 or so daily newspapers had offices there. In tribute to that past, however, a statue of Benjamin Franklin (who was, after all, a printer) stands in front of Pace University farther up on Park Row.

To the left of Park Row is triangular **City Hall Park,** originally the town common. A bronze statue of patriot Nathan Hale, who was hanged as a spy by the British troops occupying New York City, stands on the Broadway side of the park. In its day this green spot has hosted hangings, riots, and demonstrations; it is also the finish line for ticker-tape parades up lower Broadway (though ticker-tape is nowadays replaced with perforated margin strips torn off from tractor-feed computer paper).

⓲ **City Hall,** built between 1803 and 1812, is unexpectedly sedate, small-scale, and charming. Its exterior columns reflect the classical influence of Greece and Rome, and the handsome cast-iron cupola is crowned with a statue of Lady Justice. Originally its front and sides were clad in white marble while the back was faced in cheap brownstone, because the city fathers assumed New York would never grow farther north than this. (Limestone now covers all four sides.) The major interior feature is a domed rotunda from which a sweeping marble double staircase leads to the second-floor public rooms. The wood-paneled City Council Chamber in the east wing is small and clubby; the Board of Estimate chamber to the west has colonial paintings and church-pew-style seating; and the Governor's Room at the head of the stairs, used for ceremonial events, is filled with historic portraits and furniture. The mayor's office is on the ground floor.

⓳ Looming directly behind City Hall is the **Tweed Courthouse,** named after notorious politician "Boss" William Marcy Tweed, under whose corrupt management this building took some $12 million and nine years to build (it was finally finished in 1872, but the ensuing public outrage drove Tweed from office). Although it is imposing, with its columned classical pediment outside and seven-story rotunda inside, almost none of the boatloads of marble that Tweed had shipped from Europe made their way into this building. Today it houses municipal offices; it has also served as a location for several films, most notably *The Verdict.*

⓴ Across Chambers Street the **Surrogate's Court,** also called the **Hall of Records** (31 Chambers St.), is the most ornate of this City Hall trio. In true Beaux Arts fashion, sculpture and ornament seem to have been added wherever possible to the basic neoclassical structure, yet the overall effect is graceful rather than cluttered. A courtroom here was the venue for *Johnson* v. *Johnson*, where the heirs to the Johnson & Johnson fortune waged their bitter battle.

㉑ On the east side of Centre Street is the city government's first skyscraper, the **Municipal Building,** built in 1914 by McKim, Mead & White. The "roof" section alone is 10 stories high, bristling with towers and peaks and topped by a gilt statue of Civic Fame. This is where New Yorkers come to pay parking fines and get marriage licenses. An immense arch straddles Chambers Street (traffic used to flow through here); the vaulted plaza in front was the site of a scene in the movie *Crocodile Dundee*, in which the Aussie hunter coolly scares off would-be muggers with his bowie knife.

㉒ Just south of the Municipal Building, a ramp curves up into the pedestrian walkway over the **Brooklyn Bridge.** The Great Bridge promenade takes a half-hour to walk and is a New York experience on a par with the Statue of Liberty trip or the Empire State Building ascent. Before this bridge was built, Brooklynites had to rely on the Fulton Street ferry to get to Brooklyn—a charming way to travel, surely, but unreliable in the fog and ice of winter. After some 50 years of talk about a bridge, John Augustus Roebling, a respected engineer, was handed a bridge construction assignment in 1867. As the project to build the first steel suspension bridge slowly took shape over the next 15 years, it captured the imagination of the city; on its completion in 1883, it was called the Eighth Wonder of the World. Its twin Gothic-arched towers rise 268 feet from the river below. The roadway is supported by a web of steel cables, hung from the towers and attached to block-long anchorages on either shore. It is hardly the longest suspension bridge in the world anymore, but it remains a symbol of what man can accomplish. As you look south from the walkway, the pinnacles of downtown Manhattan loom on your right, Brooklyn Heights stands sentinel on your left, and before you yawns the harbor, with Lady Liberty showing herself in profile. Turn about for a fine view up the East River, spanned within sight by the Manhattan and Williamsburg bridges. You don't need binoculars to enjoy the vistas, but you'd do well to bring a hat or scarf, because the wind whips through the cables like a dervish.

㉓ Head north up Centre Street to **Foley Square,** a name that has become synonymous with the New York court system; the district attorneys on the TV series *Law and Order* frequently hold their on-screen colloquies in this vicinity. The **U.S. Courthouse** at 40 Centre Street, designed by Cass Gilbert, has marble steps climbing to a massive columned portico; above this rises a 32-story tower topped by a gilded pyramid, not unlike that with which Gilbert crowned the New York Life building uptown. This courthouse has been the site of such famous cases as the tax evasion trial of hotel queen Leona Helmsley.

㉔ With its stately columns, pediments, and 100-foot-wide flight of marble steps, the **New York County Courthouse,** built in 1926, set the precedent here for neoclassical grandeur. It's actually more eccentric than it looks, having been built in a hexagonal shape to fit an irregular plot of land. That quintessential courtroom drama *Twelve Angry Men* was filmed here, as was the more recent *Legal Eagles*.

Turn to look across Foley Square at **Federal Plaza,** which sprawls in front of the gridlike skyscraper of the **Javits Federal Building.** The black glass box to the left houses the **U.S. Court of International Trade.**

㉕ Continue up Centre Street past neoclassical civic office buildings to 100 Centre Street, the **Criminal Courts Building,** a rather grim Art Deco tower connected by a skywalk to the detention center known as The Tombs. In *The Bonfire of the Vanities*, Tom Wolfe wrote a chilling description of this court's menacing atmosphere.

In contrast, the **Civil and Municipal Courthouse** across the way at 111 Centre Street is an uninspired modern cube, although it, too, has held sensational trials, including that of subway vigilante Bernhard Goetz. On the west side of this small square is the slick blank granite **Family Court** (60 Lafayette St.), with its off-putting angular facade.

As you walk up Leonard Street, which runs just south of the Family Court, take a look at the ornate Victorian building that runs the length of the block on your left. This is the old New York Life Insurance Company headquarters (346 Broadway), an 1870 building that was remodeled and enlarged in 1896 by McKim, Mead & White. The ornate clocktower facing Broadway is now occupied by the avant-garde **Clocktower Gallery,** an outpost of P.S. 1 in Long Island City, Queens (*see* Tour 21 in Chapter 4). The gallery showcases the work of contemporary sculptors, photographers, painters, and other artists. After looking at the art on the 13th floor, the adventurous will want to climb a narrow spiral stairway inside the clocktower to see the huge clock's mechanism or step outside on the balcony for a dramatic view of New York City. *108 Leonard St., tel. 212/233–1096. Suggested donation: $1. Open Thurs.–Sun. noon–6.*

Manhattan for Free

One of the best, and least expensive, places to be in New York is out on the streets, soaking up the city. That's where you're likely to stumble upon the many free performances—both scheduled and impromptu—given by professionals and amateurs year-round. Music, dance, mime, acting, magic tricks, and more are offered for free or at pass-the-hat prices in parks and plazas all around town (*see* Chapter 11).

Parks and Public Places Another free-but-fascinating New York pastime is people-watching, and one of the best places to go for that is **Central Park** (*see* Tour 7, *above*), where the Mall and the areas around Bethesda Fountain and the Conservatory Water buzz with activity on weekends and holidays from about noon to dusk. Stroll over to Wollman Rink and watch the skaters, or head up to the Great Lawn to find groups of folk dancers. In the summer, take a picnic, a blanket, and a Frisbee to the Great Lawn in the early afternoon (before noon on weekends) to stake out a spot in line for free tickets to that evening's performance (usually a Shakespeare play) at the Delacorte Theater. While you're waiting, settle back to watch the strollers, joggers, softball teams, soccer players, and even snake charmers who congregate in this area. It makes for a long day—tickets aren't handed out until around 6:15 PM, and the plays begin at 8—but the experience is unforgettable.

Another lovely way to spend a day in Central Park is on a walking tour given by **Urban Park Rangers** (tel. 212/427–4040), who are knowledgeable about the history, design, geology, wildlife, and botany of the park. Call the park's **Events Hotline** (tel. 212/794–6565) for an up-to-date list of events.

Rockefeller Center (*see* Tour 1, *above*) is another good place to enjoy New York for free. In summer, there are various outdoor entertainment programs; in winter, you can watch ice skaters swirl about beneath the giant Christmas tree (should you care to ice-skate here, that's another costly story). **Lincoln Center** (*see* Tour 8, *above*) hosts crafts fairs and outdoor performances frequently throughout the summer. The **World Financial Center** (*see* Tour 17, *above*) often has free concerts at lunchtime and on weekends in its Winter Garden Atrium. **South Street Seaport** (*see* Tour 18, *above*) offers an assortment of fun free activities year-round: concerts on the pier during summer, a jazz festival in winter, and daily street entertainment.

Free Tours Volunteers lead free guided tours daily of the **New York Public Library's Central Research Branch.** For a free guided tour of **Grand Central Terminal,** meet in front of the terminal's Chemical Bank branch at 12:30 PM on Wednesdays (*see* Tour 3, *above*). Admission to official meetings of the General Assembly at the **United Nations** is free (pick up tickets at the information desk in the General Assembly lobby, at 46th St. and 1st Ave.). The mayor's residence, **Gracie Mansion,** in the Upper East Side's Carl Schurz Park, can be toured for free on Wednesdays by advance appointment (*see* Tour 6, *above*).

The **New York Stock Exchange** on Wall Street offers free tours that include a multimedia presentation and a stop in the visitors' gallery overlooking the trading floor. You can also arrange in advance for a free tour of the **Federal Reserve Bank** (33 Liberty St., tel. 212/720–6130).

Museums On Tuesday evenings, the **National Academy of Design** (1083 5th Ave. at 89th St.) and the **Cooper-Hewitt Museum** (2 E. 91st St.) charge no admission.

The **Metropolitan Museum of Art** (5th Ave. at 82nd St.), the **Museum of the City of New York** (1220 5th Ave. at 103rd St.), **El Museo Del Barrio** (1230 5th Ave. at 104th St.), the **Cloisters** (Fort Tryon Park, at the northern tip of Manhattan), the **American Museum of Natural History** (Central Park West at 79th St.), the **Museum of American Folk Art** (Columbus Ave. and 66th St.), the **Grey Art Gallery** (33 Washington Pl.), the **Pierpont Morgan Library** (29 E. 36th St.), and the **Museum of Television and Radio** (1 E. 53rd St.) all have pay-what-you-wish or suggested-donation policies. If all you can spare is a penny, they may not look too happy, but they'll still let you in. You can also pay what you wish to get into the **Jewish Museum** (5th Ave. at 92nd St.) on Tuesday evenings and the **Museum of Modern Art** (11 W. 53rd St.) on Thursday evenings.

Off the Beaten Track

Public Spaces Under the city's zoning laws, new office buildings can receive a variance—to add extra stories, for example—by designing and maintaining a portion of interior or exterior space for public use. Such spaces are a boon for city dwellers and visitors: They provide clean, safe, attractive areas where you can sit, relax, read a newspaper, and people-watch (although you may see some people you'd rather avoid). Most are planted with greenery, from potted plants to towering trees, or have some form of falling water to muffle the sounds of the city. Many have snack bars, working telephones, and—what can be very difficult to find elsewhere in Manhattan—clean public rest rooms. The following public spaces are listed from lower Manhattan up.

In the modernistic atrium of the **Continental Insurance Building** (180 Maiden La. at Front St.) just two blocks south of the South Street Seaport Museum, benches surround copious foliage amid an ultramodern structure that looks as if it's made out of Tinker Toys. *Near Tours 17 and 18.*

ChemCourt (272 Park Ave. between 47th and 48th Sts.) in the Chemical Bank Building provides benches around plantings of exotic shrubs, all informatively labeled in English and Latin. A glass roof lets the sunshine into the ground floor of the 50-story silver-gray tower. *Near Tour 1.*

On the mezzanine and basement floors of 875 **Third Avenue** (between 52nd and 53rd Sts.), tables and chairs are set in a lobby surrounded by an array of fast-food establishments selling pizza, bagels, muffins, Chinese food, sandwiches, and salads. The basement also connects with the 53rd Street subway station (E, F lines). *Near Tour 2.*

A boon to midtown's weary, **Paley Park** (3 E. 53rd St.), named for the former CBS executive William Paley, was the first of New York's "pocket parks" to be inserted among the high-rise behemoths, placed on the site of the former society night spot the Stork Club. A waterfall blocks out traffic noise, and feathery honey locust trees provide shade. There's a snack bar that opens when weather permits. *Near Tour 1.*

Another pocket park, **McGraw-Hill Park** (6th Ave. between 48th and 49th Sts.), behind the McGraw-Hill Building, has a stunning walk-through wall of water during most fair-weather days. *Near Tour 1.*

Nice Places to Live Many of the loveliest residential areas of the city remain so precisely because they *are* off the beaten track, and hence out of the commercial flow. Here, from south to north, is an utterly subjective sampling, uptown and down.

The city's longest stretch of redbrick town houses preserved from the 1820s and 1830s runs along the north side of **Charlton Street** (west of 6th Ave.), with high stoops, paneled front doors, leaded-glass windows, and narrow dormer windows all intact. While you're here, stroll along parallel King and Vandam streets for more fine Federal houses. This quiet enclave was once an estate called Richmond Hill, whose various residents included George Washington, John and Abigail Adams, and Aaron Burr. *Near Tours 12 and 14.*

Sniffen Court (off 36th St. between Lexington and 3rd Aves.) is an easily overlooked cul-de-sac of 19th-century brick stables converted into town houses, with an atmosphere that's equal parts old London and New Orleans. Sniffen Court was for many years the home of sculptor Malvina Hoffman. *Near Tour 4.*

In the exclusive East Side neighborhood known as Turtle Bay, the secluded two-block-long **Beekman Place** (east of 1st Ave. between 49th and 51st Sts.) has an aura of unperturbably elegant calm. Residents of its refined town houses have included the Rockefellers, Alfred Lunt and Lynn Fontanne, Ethel Barrymore, Irving Berlin, and of course, Auntie Mame, a character in the well-known Patrick Dennis play of the same name. Go down the steps at 51st Street to reach a walkway along the East River. *Near Tour 2.*

Roosevelt Island (East River, 48th to 85th Sts.) is a 2½-mile-long East River island that was taken over by a residential complex in the 1970s, although only half of the high-rise buildings originally planned have been built. Some fragments remain of the asylums and hospitals once clustered here, when it was known as Welfare Island. Walkways along the edge of the island provide fine river views, and it's surprisingly quiet, compared with the city so near. The real treat, however, is the 3½-minute ride over on an aerial tram. The one-way fare is $1.40. *Near Tour 6.*

Built at the turn of the century, the white Beaux Arts town houses lining **West 105th Street** (between West End Ave. and Riverside Dr.) are like a vision of Paris. The apartment building at the northeast corner of Riverside Drive now belongs to the American Buddhist Academy; go around the corner to see its immense bronze Buddha. Marion Davies, mistress of William Randolph Hearst, once lived in the house at 331 Riverside Drive. *Near Tours 8 and 9.*

Commercial Districts The tendency in New York is for merchants in similar trades to cluster together in certain neighborhoods, where their customers can hop from one office to another. As you walk about the streets, you'll come upon sudden thickets of fur dealers, hat makers, button sellers, or flower suppliers, to name just a few. These three districts are particularly large and vibrant:

Gansevoort Market (around Gansevoort and Greenwich Sts.) features otherwise undistinguished warehouse buildings that each morning become the meat market for the city's retailers and restaurants. Racks of carcasses make a fascinating if not very pretty sight. Action peaks on weekdays from 5 to 9 AM. *Near Tours 11 and 12.*

The **Garment District** (7th Ave. between 31st and 41st Sts., also called Fashion Avenue) teems with warehouses, workshops, and showrooms that manufacture and finish mostly women's and children's clothing. On weekdays the streets are crowded with trucks and the sidewalks swarm with daredevil deliverymen wheeling garment racks between factories and specialized subcontractors. *Near Tour 3.*

The relatively unglitzy jewelry shops at street level in the **Diamond District** (47th St. between 5th and 6th Aves.) are just the tip of the iceberg; upstairs, millions of dollars' worth of gems are traded, and skilled craftsmen cut precious stones. Wheeling and dealing goes on at fever pitch, all rendered strangely exotic by the presence of a host of Hasidic Jews in severe black dress, beards, and curled sidelocks. If you're in a hurry, avoid this street during the day, when it becomes one of the slowest streets to navigate by foot in Manhattan. *Near Tour 1.*

4 Exploring the Other Boroughs

Many visitors to Manhattan notice the four outer boroughs—Brooklyn, Queens, the Bronx, and Staten Island—only from a Circle Line cruise, leaving those areas to remain ciphers, part of the city yet not. *Don't fall asleep on the subway*, the unschooled tourist tells himself, *or you may end up in the Bronx!*

Manhattanites themselves, many driven over the river by astronomical rents, discovered the outer boroughs some years back. They found sky, trees, and living space among the 19th-century brownstones, and converted industrial lofts, Art Deco apartment palaces, and tidy bungalows. They also found fascinating ethnic enclaves and a host of museums and parks.

The reality is that Manhattan is only a small part of New York City. Its population of 1.509 million is smaller than that of either Brooklyn (2.3 million) or Queens (1.95 million), and only slightly larger than that of the Bronx (1.223 million). Staten Island may be less populous (380,000), but it's 2½ times the size of Manhattan.

There are things to see and do in the outer boroughs that you simply won't find in Manhattan, and most are just a subway ride away from midtown. Manhattanites may try to put you off such a journey, but don't be daunted. After a couple of beers, those same people may rave about their favorite place for cheesecake (Junior's on Flatbush Avenue in Brooklyn), or a great outdoor barbecue they had at their sister-in-law's suburban-style house (in Forest Hills Gardens, Queens); you may even have to listen to a story about their life's peak experience—found in the bleachers of Yankee Stadium in . . . the Bronx!

Brooklyn

Tour 19: Brooklyn Heights, Cobble Hill, and Carroll Gardens

Numbers in the margin correspond to points of interest on the Tour 19: Brooklyn Heights, Cobble Hill, and Carroll Gardens map.

"All the advantages of the country, with most of the conveniences of the city." So ran the ads for a real-estate development that sprang up in the 1820s just across the East River from downtown Manhattan. Brooklyn Heights—named for its enviable hilltop position—was New York's first suburb, linked to the city first by ferry and later by the Brooklyn Bridge. Feverish construction quickly transformed the airy heights into a fashionable upper-middle-class community. Happily, some 600 buildings more than 100 years old remain intact today, making Brooklyn Heights a kind of picture book of 19th-century American architecture.

Take the No. 2 or 3 subway from Manhattan to Clark Street. Exit the subway station and turn left on Henry Street toward Pineapple Street. (Street names in the Heights are an eccentric collection, reportedly created by a certain Miss Middagh, who despised the practice of naming streets for the town fathers and preferred instead various fruits.) Above the rooftops, look up to see the blue towers of the Manhattan Bridge linking Brooklyn to Manhattan; you'll have a view of the Brook-

The Five Boroughs

5 miles

5 km

PORT WASHINGTON

Manhasset Bay

KINGS POINT

GREAT NECK

NASSAU

GREAT NECK ESTATES

LITTLE NECK

LITTLE NECK

ST. ALBANS

Grand Central Pkwy.

Cross Island Pkwy.

BAYSIDE Pkwy.

Long Island Sound

Clearview Expwy.

JAMAICA

Hart I.

City I.

Pelham Bay Park

Eastchester Bay

Throgs Neck

Throgs Neck Bridge

Whitestone Bridge

River

COLLEGE POINT

FLUSHING

Long Island Expwy.

Shea Stadium

USTA Nat'l Tennis Center

Flushing Meadow Corona Park

FOREST HILLS

WESTCHESTER

MT. VERNON

East

La Guardia Airport

Northern Blvd.

JACKSON HEIGHTS

YONKERS

95

THE BRONX

HUNTS POINT

Riker I.

ASTORIA

Grand Central Pkwy.

QUEENS

Bronx Zoo

Fordham University

Bronx Park

Crotona Park

Yankee Stadium

Triborough Bridge

LONG ISLAND CITY

Van Cortlandt Park

Harlem R.

Central Park

Queensboro Bridge

RIVERDALE

MANHATTAN

Spuyten Deyvil

Fort George Washington Bridge

Hudson River

Palisades Pkwy.

FORT LEE

CLIFFSIDE PARK

WEST NEW YORK

ENGLEWOOD CLIFFS

TENAFLY

BERGEN

ENGLEWOOD

NORTH BERGEN

95

NEW JERSEY

PARAMUS

4

46

80

EAST RUTHERFORD

Meadowlands Sports Complex

17

3

N

lyn Bridge itself in a few minutes. Turn left onto Orange Street. On the north side of the block between Henry and Hicks streets is a formidable institution: the **Plymouth Church of the Pilgrims,** which was the vortex of abolitionist sentiment in the years before the Civil War, thanks to the stirring oratory of Brooklyn's most eminent theologian, Henry Ward Beecher. In the Underground Railroad that smuggled slaves to freedom, Plymouth Church was more or less "Grand Central Station." Beside the church is a courtyard (locked, alas) with a statue of Beecher. Walk on to Willow Street and turn right to see Beecher's house, a prim Greek Revival brownstone, at **22 Willow Street.** At the corner of Willow and Middagh (pronounced *mid*-awe) streets, **No. 24** is the oldest home in the neighborhood—an 1824 Federal-style wood residence with a mansard roof. Peer through a door in the wall on the Willow Street side for a glimpse of the cottage garden and carriage house in the rear. Now turn around and catch a glimpse between the buildings of the **Brooklyn Bridge,** the historic steel suspension bridge designed by John Augustus Roebling and completed in 1883 (*see* Tour 18 in Chapter 3). In the foreground you can also spot the world headquarters of the **Jehovah's Witnesses,** located in the Heights since 1909. Venture a few steps west on Middagh to watch neighborhood children and their parents playing at the **Harry Chapin Playground,** a pleasant neighborhood park named after the late singer-songwriter.

Backtrack on **Willow Street,** which between Clark and Pierrepont streets is one of the prettiest and most architecturally varied blocks in the Heights. Note Nos. 108–112, built in the blend of terra-cotta reliefs, bay windows, and towers known as the Shingle or Queen Anne style. Farther down the block, on the other side, stand three distinguished brick Federal row houses allegedly part of the Underground Railroad.

As you turn right onto Pierrepont Street, heading toward the river, glance down Columbia Heights to your right, where Nos. 210–220 comprise a brownstone grouping often cited as the most graceful in New York. Norman Mailer lives on this street—lucky Mr. Mailer—and from a rear window in No. 111, John Roebling's son Washington (who in 1869 succeeded his father as chief engineer for the Brooklyn Bridge) directed the building of the bridge from his sickbed.

Pierrepont Street ends at the **Brooklyn Heights Promenade,** a sliver of park one-third of a mile long, hanging over the ferry district like one of Babylon's fabled gardens. Cantilevered over two lanes of the Brooklyn–Queens Expressway and a service road, this quiet esplanade area has benches offering views of the Manhattan skyline. Circling gulls squawk, tugboats honk, and the city seems like a vision from another planet.

As you leave the Promenade (via Montague Street), look left to see Nos. **2** and **3 Pierrepont Place,** two brownstone palaces built in the 1850s by a China trader and philanthropist, and used as a location for John Huston's film *Prizzi's Honor* (the frightful Mafia chieftain Don Corrado lived here). On your right lies **Montague Terrace,** where Thomas Wolfe lived when he finished *You Can't Go Home Again.* In the 1940s and 1950s, the neighborhood was said to be home to the city's largest number of writers outside Greenwich Village, among them Carson McCullers, W. H. Auden, Arthur Miller, and Truman Capote.

Brooklyn Heights
Promenade, **3**
Brooklyn Historical
Society, **5**
Christ Church, **9**
Church of St. Ann and
the Holy Trinity, **4**
Cobble Hill Park, **8**
Guido Funeral
Home, **10**
197 Amity St., **7**
Our Lady of Lebanon
Maronite Cathedral, **6**
Plymouth Church of
the Pilgrims, **1**
24 Middagh Street, **2**

Tour 19: Brooklyn Hgts., Cobble Hill, Carroll Gdns.

As you head east, Montague Street turns into a commercial district often disparaged for its homogeneous Yuppie character. Still, restaurants here feature everything from Greek to Mexican to Japanese food, and window shopping can be fun. The **4** **Church of St. Ann and the Holy Trinity** lies at the northwest corner of Montague and Clinton streets. Its historic stained-glass windows—the first made in the United States—are currently being restored. In recent years, the church has become a performing arts center frequented by downtown Manhattan types. *157 Montague St., tel. 718/858-2424. Box office open Tues.–Sat. noon–6.*

Beyond Clinton on the north side of Montague Street, note an interesting row of banks: **Chemical** (No. 177), a copy of the Palazzo della Gran Guardia in Verona, Italy; a **Citibank** (No. 183) that looks like a latter-day Roman temple; and the Art Deco **Municipal Credit Union** (No. 185).

A block north of Montague, at the corner of Clinton and **5** Pierrepont, is the **Brooklyn Historical Society,** with its 1989 Shellens Gallery. The collection includes Brooklyn Dodgers' bats and balls, trick mirrors from Coney Island, and a 300-pound cast-zinc eagle saved from the offices of the *Brooklyn Eagle*. The society's library on the second floor—with its rich carved-wood bookcases and lustrous stained-glass windows—is a showcase for late-19th-century interior design; it also holds 12,000 rare photographs and 110,000 books. *128 Pierrepont St., tel. 718/624–0890. Library research fee: $5. Open Tues.– Sat. 10–4:45. Shellens Gallery admission: $2.50 adults, $1 children under 12; Wed. free. Open Wed.–Sat. noon–5.*

Return south along Clinton Street, then turn right onto Remsen Street. At the corner of Remsen and Henry streets, stop to **6** take in the Romanesque Revival **Our Lady of Lebanon Maronite Cathedral** (113 Remsen St.), designed by prolific architect Richard Upjohn. It features the Shrine of St. Sharbel Makhlouf and doors salvaged from the 1943 wreck of the ocean liner *Normandie*.

If you want to see more of Brooklyn Heights, turn left onto Hicks Street to visit another Upjohn creation, the Gothic Revival **Grace Church** (254 Hicks St.). Across Hicks Street is **Grace Court Alley,** a traditional mews with a score of restored carriage houses, where the stables used to be. Then stroll west on Joralemon Street, where a row of **Greek Revival brownstones** (nos. 29–75) delicately sidestep their way down the hill toward the river and the piers. Follow **Willow Place** south along the peaceful block between Joralemon and State streets; in late afternoon, the houses take on the colors of a faded quilt.

To reach Cobble Hill and Carroll Gardens, return to Clinton Street and go south across Atlantic Avenue, a busy thoroughfare crowded with Middle Eastern restaurants and downscale antiques shops.

Time Out Between Henry and Clinton streets on Atlantic Avenue is **Waterfront Ale House** (136 Atlantic Ave., tel. 718/522–3794), a homey pub serving up delicious burgers and salads to accompany the nearly 50 kinds of beer in bottle and 12 on tap here.

Atlantic Avenue is the official dividing line between the neighborhoods of Brooklyn Heights and **Cobble Hill,** the latter a peaceful residential area of leafy streets lined with notable town houses of varying architectural styles. The neighborhood is popular with young families, and on most days you can see an assortment of people pushing strollers, walking dogs, or returning home with grocery-laden bags. Go south down Clinton Street to Amity, two blocks south of Atlantic. Turn left and **❼** make your way to **197 Amity,** where Jennie Jerome, the mother of Winston Churchill, was born in 1854. (Perversely, a plaque at 426 Henry Street, southwest of here, identifies *that* building as the famous woman's birthplace. The Henry Street address is actually where Jennie's parents lived before she was born.)

Return to Clinton and go one more block south, where on the **❽** west side of the street you'll find **Cobble Hill Park,** a small oasis of green encircled by pavement, with a playground at one end. Rest on one of the benches here and drink in the sounds of children playing and neighbors chatting. Bordering the park's south side between Clinton and Henry streets is **Verandah Place,** a charming row of converted stable buildings where Thomas Wolfe once lived.

Proceed south down Clinton Street to observe the block after block of distinguished row houses, ranging from Romanesque Revival to neoclassical to Italianate brownstone. Three blocks south of the park, at the southwest corner of Kane and Clinton **❾** streets, is the Episcopal **Christ Church** (320 Clinton St.), a sandstone structure that is yet another creation of Richard Upjohn, who lived near here at 296 Clinton Street. Interior furnishings in the church, including the pulpit, lecturn, and altar, were designed by Louis Comfort Tiffany. The church's setting, on a tree-embowered patch of green enclosed by a wrought-iron fence, has the tranquil air of an English churchyard.

As you approach President Street, Cobble Hill gives way to the largely Italian neighborhood of **Carroll Gardens,** an area distinguished by unusually deep blocks that allow for large—by New York standards—front yards. Wander down President, Carroll, 1st, and 2nd places to see the lovingly tended gardens; notice the abundance of religious statuary that attests to the largely Catholic makeup of the neighborhood.

On the northwest corner of Carroll and Clinton streets is the **❿** **Guido Funeral Home** (440 Clinton St.), once the John Rankin Residence. Built in 1840, this freestanding redbrick building may be the finest example of a Greek Revival town house in the city.

Go east on Carroll Street to reach Court Street, the main commercial thoroughfare of the neighborhood, where you can gather a few edible mementos of your visit here. Fresh pasta, cheeses, sausages, olives, and prepared Italian dishes are available at a number of shops, including **Pastosa Ravioli** (347 Court St.), where the gnocchi is particularly good, and **Caputo's Dairy** (460 Court St.), with a wide selection of homemade pasta sauces. Bakeries also abound here, but movie buffs will want to cut over to Henry Street to the **Cammareri Brothers Bakery** (502 Henry St.), where Nicholas Cage worked in the 1987 film, *Moonstruck.* Buy a loaf of the pepperoni-studded lard bread here and remind yourself that not all cholesterol is bad.

Time Out **Mola Pizzeria** (404 Court St., tel. 718/852–0240) and **Leonardo's Brick Oven Pizza** (383 Court St., tel. 718/624–9620), across the street from each other, both serve delectable pizza baked in brick ovens.

To return to the city, catch the F train at the corner of 2nd Place and Smith Street, two blocks northwest of Leornardo's. Note also that although cruising cabs are rare in Brooklyn, a number of them do travel north on Clinton Street en route to Manhattan; you may be able to catch one there.

Tour 20: Park Slope

Numbers in the margin correspond to points of interest on the Tour 20: Park Slope map.

This neighborhood, which grew up in the late 1800s on the west side of Prospect Park, is today one of Brooklyn's most sought-after sections. Many families have moved in to renovate the handsome brownstones that line its blocks—beware the heavy traffic in baby strollers!

Begin on **Seventh Avenue,** the area's main commercial street, accessible by the D, Q, 2, or 3 subway trains. Here, among other interesting shops, you'll find a wine store of real distinction, **Leon Paley Ltd.** (88 7th Ave.), as well as three diet-defying bakeries: **Cousin John's** (70 7th Ave.); **Faith's** (around the corner at 169 Lincoln Pl.); and the **New Prospect At Home** (52 7th Ave.). The corner of Seventh Avenue and Sterling Place was the site of a horrendous plane crash in 1960, which leveled several buildings around the intersection; down the street, the **Brownstone Gallery** (76 7th Ave.) keeps a photograph of the grounded plane on display.

Turn east on Lincoln Place to find the Slope's most venerable
❶ edifice, the **Montauk Club** (25 8th Ave.), an 1891 mansion modeled on Venice's Ca' d'Oro. Notice the friezes of Montauk Indians and the private side entrance, built especially for members' wives in the 19th century.

Make your way south along Eighth Avenue, sampling the brownstones on various streets along the way (President and Carroll streets are especially handsome), until you reach
❷ **Montgomery Place,** a block-long street between Eighth Avenue and Prospect Park West. This is considered by many to be the neighborhood's finest block, lined by a picturesque variety of town houses designed by the Romanesque Revival genius C.P.H. Gilbert.

❸ Return along Prospect Park West to **Grand Army Plaza,** a geographic star from which radiate Prospect Park West, Eastern Parkway, and Flatbush and Vanderbilt avenues. At its center stands the **Soldiers' and Sailors' Memorial Arch,** honoring Civil War veterans and patterned on the Arc de Triomphe in Paris. Three heroic sculptural groupings adorn the arch: atop, a four-horsed chariot by Frederick MacMonnies, so dynamic that it almost seems on the verge of catapulting off the arch; to the sides, the victorious Union Army and Navy of the Civil War. Inside are bas-reliefs of Presidents Abraham Lincoln and Ulysses S. Grant, sculpted by Thomas Eakins and William O'Donovan, respectively. To the northwest, Neptune and a passel of debauched tritons leer over the edges of the **Bailey**

Tour 20: Park Slope

Fountain, where tulle-drenched brides and grooms in technicolor tuxes come to pose after exchanging vows.

To the southeast of the plaza is the main entrance to **Prospect Park,** a 536-acre urban playground designed in 1866 by Frederick Law Olmsted and Calvert Vaux, who considered it superior to their earlier creation, Central Park, because no streets divided it and no bordering skyscrapers would break its rural illusion. Woods, water, and meadows remain the park's three basic thematic elements. Inside the entrance is the 90-acre **Long Meadow,** full of picnickers and kite-fliers on weekends, and the site of free New York Philharmonic and Metropolitan Opera performances in the summer. Follow the circular drive to the right, and at the entrance at Prospect Park West and 3rd Street you'll see the **Litchfield Villa,** an Italianate mansion built in 1857 for a wealthy lawyer. It now holds the park's administrative offices, but visitors are welcome to step inside and view the interior. Across the main drive is the **Picnic House** (tel. 718/965–6516), stage for a year-round schedule of drama, dance, music, and puppetry, as well as yoga and t'ai chi.

If you follow the drive to the left of the main entrance, you'll come to the **zoo,** recently renamed the **Prospect Park Wildlife Conservation Center.** Reopened in 1993, the Center offers a state-of-the-art children's zoo, with such exhibits as "World of Animals" and "Animal Lifestyles." (Admission prices and hours of operation were unavailable at press time.) Just beyond the zoo is a restored 1912 **carousel** (50¢ a ride; closed winter months) and the **Lefferts Homestead,** a gambrel-roofed Dutch colonial farmhouse (1783) that was moved here in 1918 and now holds a museum of period home furnishings and changing exhibitions. *Tel. 718/965-6505. Admission free. Open mid-Apr.– mid-Dec., weekends noon–4.*

The middle of the park is a forested ravine, cut by a stream and dotted with bridges. Follow the circular drive. A smaller central drive that branches off to your right leads to the **Quaker Cemetery,** not open to the public (the Urban Park Rangers lead periodic tours through here, tel. 718/287-3400). Montgomery Clift is among the people buried in this quiet cemetery. If you stay on the circular drive, you'll soon pass the terra-cotta ❼ **Boathouse** (tel. 718/287-3474; closed winter months), styled after the Library of St. Marks in Venice; today the 1905 structure houses a visitor center, art exhibitions, and a café. Farther down the path is the giant, gnarled **Camperdown Elm,** which Marianne Moore immortalized in a poem in the 1960s. Moore became one of the park's chief advocates, a labor she termed ❽ "my only mortal entanglement." South of here is **Concert Grove,** site of outdoor summer performances, near the shore of a 60-acre **lake** inhabited by ducks and swans.

If you return to Grand Army Plaza, to the east of the park's ❾ main entrance, you will find the main branch of the **Brooklyn Public Library.** Built in 1941, it applies Art Deco streamlining to the grand neoclassical look of Beaux Arts public buildings. Notice the bas-relief carvings and the inscription picked out in gold above the entrance. Step inside to admire the murals in the lobby. *Tel. 718/780-7700. Open Tues.–Thurs. 9–8, Fri. and Sat. 10–6, Sun. 1–5.*

Eastern Parkway, which runs from Grand Army Plaza past the library, mimics the grand sweep of the boulevards of Paris and Vienna. Every Labor Day weekend the parkway hosts the biggest and liveliest carnival outside the Caribbean—a cacophony of calypso, steel band, and reggae music, with plenty of conch curry, spice bread, and meat patties to go around.

A couple of hundred yards along the parkway is an entrance to ❿ the **Brooklyn Botanic Garden,** which occupies 52 acres across Flatbush Avenue from Prospect Park. The garden exudes a beguiling Oriental atmosphere, due to the presence of a **Japanese Garden,** complete with a blazing red torii gate and a pond laid out in the shape of the Chinese character for "heart." The Japanese cherry arbor turns into a heart-stopping cloud of pink every May. Wander through the **Cranford Rose Garden** (5,000 bushes, 1,200 varieties); the **Fragrance Garden,** designed especially for the blind; the **Shakespeare Garden,** featuring 80 plants immortalized by the bard (including roses of many names); and **Celebrity Path,** Brooklyn's answer to Hollywood's famous sidewalk, with the names of homegrown stars—including Mel Brooks, Woody Allen, Zero Mostel, Barbara Stanwyck, and Mae West—inscribed on stepping-stones. A complex of handsome greenhouses called the **Steinhardt Conservatory** holds thriving desert, tropical, temperate, and aquatic vegetation, as well as a display charting the evolution of plants over the past 140 million years. The **C.V. Starr Bonsai Museum** in the Conservatory grows about 75 miniature Japanese plants. The Botanic Garden Shop is a fine place to stop, particularly if you're a gardener yourself. *1000 Washington Ave. near Empire Blvd., tel. 718/622-4433. Admission to garden free. Admission to Steinhardt Conservatory Nov.–Mar. free; Apr.–Oct., $2 adults, $1 senior citizens and children 3–12. Garden open*

Tues.–Fri. 8–4:30, weekends and holidays 10–4:30. Closed Thanksgiving, Dec. 25, and Jan. 1. Conservatory open Apr.– Sept., Tues.–Sun. 10–5; Oct.–Mar., Tues.–Sun. 10–4.

⑪ **The Brooklyn Museum,** designed by the McKim, Mead & White team in 1897, sports huge Daniel Chester French statues of Brooklyn and Manhattan (as classical ladies) on its Eastern Parkway front. With more than 2 million objects, the Brooklyn collection is the seventh largest in the country. The museum's renovation and expansion project by Japanese architect Arata Isozaki and New York firm James Stewart Polshek includes a new auditorium with a wavelike ceiling, and new galleries in the oldest part of the building, adding 30,000 square feet of exhibition space. Look especially for its **Egyptian Art** collection (third floor), considered the best of its kind anywhere outside London or Cairo, or the **African and Pre-Columbian Art** (first floor), another collection recognized worldwide. In the gallery of **American painting and sculpture** (fifth floor) you'll find *Brooklyn Bridge* by Georgia O'Keeffe, as well as striking works by Winslow Homer, John Singer Sargent, and Gilbert Stuart. The **Period Rooms** (fourth floor) include the complete interior of the Jan Martense Schenck House, built in the Brooklyn Flatlands section in 1675, as well as a suite of rooms decorated in Moorish style from the 54th Street mansion of John D. Rockefeller. Outdoors, the **Frieda Schiff Warburg Memorial Sculpture Garden** features relics from "lost New York," such as a lion's head from Coney Island's Steeplechase Park. The museum also offers excellent special exhibitions, a treasure chest of a gift shop, and dramatic views of Manhattan from its Eastern Parkway–Washington Avenue corner. *200 Eastern Pkwy., tel. 718/638–5000. Suggested contribution: $4 adults, $1.50 senior citizens, $2 students with valid ID. Open Wed.–Sun. 10–5.*

Queens

Tour 21: Long Island City

Numbers in the margin correspond to points of interest on the Tours 21 and 22: Long Island City and Astoria map.

In the 1800s, along the East River in Queens, a string of neighborhoods thrived due to their ferry links with Manhattan. One of the busiest ferries connected a finger of land called Hunters Point with East 34th Street, Manhattan. Here, a business district known as Long Island City burgeoned. (Queens is, after all, on the western end of Long Island, as is Brooklyn.) Factories, boardinghouses, municipal buildings, and restaurants clustered around the intersection of Vernon Boulevard and Jackson Avenue, while north along Vernon Boulevard tycoons built summer homes, with boathouses and lawns that reached gracefully to the banks of the river. Today the community has found new life as a mecca for artists, who've migrated with their paint pots and welding tools to airy, low-rent studios.

A 10-minute ride on the No. 7 subway from Times Square or Grand Central Terminal will take you to the 45th Road Court House Square station. This noisy intersection is a fine introduction to this part of Queens, where the dark, clanking hulk of the El keeps the sunlight from penetrating to the street.

Long Island City's streets puzzle cartographers and visitors alike; you'll find numbered streets running north and south, and numbered avenues, roads, and drives going east–west. Consider 45th Avenue: To its south lies 45th Road, and to its north is 44th Road, 44th Avenue, and 44th Drive. But bear with this confusion and turn east onto 45th Avenue, where you'll find the **Hunters Point Historic District**, full of immaculate row houses, dating from 1870, with their original stoops and cornices. Their fine condition is due partly to their having been faced in resilient Westchester stone. At 21st Street, a small park offers benches (for pigeons and people) and a setting for a large metal sculpture called *Bigger Bird* by Daniel Sinclair. The warehouses surrounding the park are a warren of artists' studios; above their low roofs there's an unimpeded view of Manhattan.

On 21st Street, between 46th Road and 46th Avenue, is **P.S.1 Museum,** a contemporary art museum housed in what was originally a Ward 1 school. The founders of P.S.1 were the first of the art-conscious to see the possibilities in the area; back in 1976 they turned the old school into lecture rooms, studio space for artists, and galleries. On display are special exhibitions and a number of permanent works, including James Turrell's sky piece *Meeting* and Alan Saret's *Fifth Colar Chthonic Wall Temple. 46–01 21st St., tel. 718/784–2084. Admission: $2. Open Wed.–Sun. noon–6 when a show is on display.*

The intersection of **Jackson Avenue** and **Vernon Boulevard** is still the commercial center of the neighborhood, as it was when the ferry operated from the foot of Borden Avenue. Modest shingled homes, butcher shops, diners, and the Vernon–Jackson subway stop crowd together beneath the huge, four-barreled stacks of the old Pennsylvania Railroad generating plant. (Schwartz Chemicals, as the structure is identified on its eastern face, was a later occupant; today the behemoth contains an assortment of smaller manufacturing firms and some indoor tennis courts.) At 49th Avenue and Vernon Boulevard, the steeple of **St. Mary's Roman Catholic Church** rises more spiritually into the sky than the stacks of old Schwartz.

Vernon Boulevard, originally called the Williamsburg Turnpike Road, was Queens's first true highway, leading to the mansions along the river, all now demolished. The area to the west of Vernon is slated to change dramatically, when the Hunters Point Development plan turns 90 acres of riverfront and landfill between the Midtown Tunnel and Queensboro Bridge into an apartment complex.

Time Out   Only locals know about **Café Vernon** (46–18 Vernon Blvd., tel. 718/472–9694), a tiny, unassuming Italian restaurant at Vernon Boulevard and 46th Road. Don't let its modesty fool you, though, because it offers splendid, filling repasts of Italian sandwiches, soups, and pastas. Prices are moderate; the atmosphere is homey.

A white concrete block of a building rises at the foot of 44th Drive. Another warehouse? Hardly. This is the **Water's Edge Restaurant** (44th Dr. and East River, tel. 718/482–0033), a Queens dining spot where in summertime umbrellas sprout up on the dock, and boaters check in for quick drinks. Inside is an elegant restaurant that charges Manhattan prices, bringing in

American Museum of
the Moving Image, **8**

Court House Square, **5**

Hunters Point Historic
District, **1**

International Design
Center, **6**

Isamu Noguchi Garden
Museum, **12**

LaGuardia Community
College, **7**

P.S. 1 Museum, **2**

St. Demetrios
Cathedral, **9**

St. Irene
Chrysovalanto
Cathedral, **10**

Silvercup Studios, **4**

Socrates Sculpture
Park, **11**

Water's Edge
Restaurant, **3**

Tours 21 and 22: Long Island City and Astoria

its sophisticated clientele via a complimentary ferry service from the city's 34th Street Marina Tuesday–Saturday in summer, weekends in winter. From the pier outside you can survey the **Queensboro Bridge,** which extends 7,000 feet, from Manhattan's East 60th Street to Crescent Street, Queens. Finished in 1909, its construction claimed the lives of 50 workers. A detour north on Vernon Boulevard will take you to the bridge's base at Queens Plaza, where there's a riverfront park and a lonely remnant of the past century, the old **New York Architectural Terra Cotta Company,** complete with Tudor Revival adornments and chimney pots.

It's ironically appropriate that the sometimes tatty western section of Queens should have become an outpost for America's glitziest industry, the motion pictures. In Long Island City, filmmakers began to gather in 1983 to make movies and commercials at a three-block-long complex, converted from a bakery into 14 soundstages. **Silvercup Studios** (42–25 21st St., tel. 718/784–3390) can be reached by walking east from Vernon to the intersection of 21st Street and 43rd Avenue. Such movies as *Godfather III, Sea of Love,* and *When Harry Met Sally* were shot within the walls of old Silvercup.

Now hike back down 21st Street to 45th Avenue, which will bring you back to **Court House Square.** Notice first—you probably couldn't fail to—the towering green **Citicorp Building.** When it was built, Manhattan office space ran at $40–$95 per square foot, while in Queens you could rent at a cool $17–$27. I. M. Pei is responsible for the building's basic design, which carries over some general themes from the Citicorp Building Manhattan's.

Much more modest is the **New York State Supreme Courthouse** (25–10 Court House Sq.) across from Citicorp. Built in 1909 in a jumbled Beaux Arts architectural style, the courthouse is being restored through the 1990s, but depending on where the work is being done, you may be able to step inside the four-story-high lobby to see the mosaic tile floors, elaborate iron banisters, and stained-glass ceiling. The courthouse's orginal construction entailed so much graft and corruption that the Queens borough president, Joseph Bermel, resigned and the architect, Peter M. Coco, was tried for grand larceny in one of the very courtrooms he had designed. Today it's frequently used as a location by neighborhood movie studios.

Thomson Avenue will lead you—perilously, due to roaring traffic alongside—over the mind-boggling mesh of the Long Island Railroad tracks. Just past here, Thomson Avenue merges into **Queens Boulevard,** one of the borough's chief transverses.

To your right lie the shells of several once-thriving industries: the **Sunshine Biscuit Company** (Skillman between 29th St. and 30th St.), **American Eveready Building** (29–10 Thomson Ave.), **Adams Chewing Gum Factory** (30–30 Thomson Ave.), and **White Motor Company Factory** (31–10 Thomson Ave.), all built between 1914 and 1920 in a delightful mix of the practical and the ornamental. The **International Design Center** (tel. 718/937–7474), completed in 1985, now occupies the former three structures. This vast marketplace (1 million square feet) for the products of interior designers was built at a cost of more than $125 million. Peek inside to see the ballooning central atrium, surrounded by showrooms ad infinitum. Gigantic elevators for unloading train cars occupied those central spaces back in the days when these buildings still turned out crackers, bubble gum, and auto parts.

❼ Next door, in the old White Motor Company factory, is **La Guardia Community College,** whose **Archives** (31–10 Thomson Ave., Room E-238; open Mon.–Fri. 9–5, but call 718/482–5065 for appointment to view documents) contain the papers of the city's most colorful mayor, Fiorello H. La Guardia. New York's "Little Flower," as La Guardia came to be called, presided over the metropolis during the Depression.

Tour 22: Astoria

One of New York's most vital ethnic neighborhoods, Astoria was originally German, then Italian, but today you're likely to hear more Greek spoken. It has been said that Astoria is home to more Greeks than anyplace in the world except Athens; whether that was ever true is disputable, but now that the tide of Greek immigration has ebbed somewhat and many second-generation Greek-Americans have moved to the suburbs, a safe guess would put Astoria's Greek population at around 35,000. There are also lots of Asians, Eastern Europeans, Irish, and Hispanic immigrants in Astoria, not to mention a healthy contingent of young people born in the United States who can't afford Manhattan rents and appreciate Astoria's proximity to the city and safe, friendly atmosphere. Our tour emphasizes the Greek population of Astoria only because it is so established— and because their food is so good.

From Manhattan, take the N train to the Broadway stop in Queens. Here, at the intersection of Broadway and 31st Street, you'll be at the epicenter of the Greek community, where Greek *xaxaroplasteion* (pastry shops) and *kaffenion* (coffeehouses) shoot heady smells onto the avenue. On the northeast corner is one of the neighborhood's few architectural landmarks, a four-story building from the early 1860s that now houses Interbank. During the 1920s, it contained a bar owned by the same family that runs the **Oyster Bay Restaurant and Crystal Palace** caterers at 31–01 and 31–11 Broadway; the Crystal Palace part was originally a movie theater. Late into the night the **Grecian Cave** nightclub next door resounds with Greek crooners and bouzouki music. The **Omonia Cafe,** one block east at 32–20 Broadway, is another temptation; if you don't want to sit at a table, you can still stop by the bakery counter to buy such pastries as cream-filled *ekmek* or flaky layered *pontikaki*.

Time Out Two blocks east, the **Roumeli Taverna** (33–04 Broadway, tel. 718/278–7533) is a standout among the many Greek rstaurants here; try the house specialty, *mezedakia,* or Greek hors d'oeuvres.

Farther east on Broadway, the **K & T Deli** (37–11 Broadway, tel., 718/545–2890) sends 500 whole lambs to city kitchens every week.

Go south on 36th Street for one of the neighborhood's main attractions, though it has nothing to do with the Greeks. In the 1920s, such stars as Gloria Swanson, Rudolph Valentino, and the Marx Brothers came to this neighborhood to work at "the Big House," Paramount's movie-making center in the east. Today the 13-acre **Kaufman Astoria Studios** (34–12 36th St., tel., 718/392–5600), with its monumentally columned entrance, remains a principal player in the movie biz. Since 1977, scores of pictures have been produced here, including *The Cotton Club*, *The Verdict*, *Arthur*, *The Wiz*, and *Scent of a Woman*.

❽ A visit to the **American Museum of the Moving Image** next door should satisfy almost any film fan's cravings. Opened in September 1988, the museum houses a 195-seat theater and a 60-seat screening room where fascinating film series flicker by— among them a John Ford program and tributes to leading Hollywood cinematographers. Galleries feature exhibitions such as "Behind the Screen: Producing, Promoting Motion Pictures and Television" and hands-on displays that allow visitors to try their skills at film editing. Commissioned artworks are on display, such as the Red Grooms and Lysiane Luong theater; *Tut's Fever Movie Palace*, a metaphorical recapitulation of Egyptian-style picture palaces of the 1930s (you'll find lifelike figures of Theda Bara at the ticket booth and Mae West serving up popcorn); and Korean Nam June Paik's video installation, "The Getaway Car," a commentary on movies. The museum's collection of movie memorabilia includes 83,000 items; in the costume display you might find outfits worn by Rudolph Valentino or Bette Davis. *35th Ave. at 36th St., tel. 718/784–0077. Admission: $5 adults, $4 senior citizens, $2.50 students and children. Open Tues.–Fri. noon–4, weekends noon–6.*

Return to Broadway and 31st Street to explore the Greek community in more depth. Two blocks up 31st Street, you'll see

❾ Astoria's heart, the Greek Orthodox **St. Demetrios Cathedral** (30–11 30th Dr., tel. 718/728–1718), a brick building with a red-tile roof and the largest Orthodox congregation outside Greece. Directly behind the cathedral, in an empty schoolyard at 30th Avenue and 30th Street, plans were still afoot at press time to open an amphitheater, with statues of Greeks gods and philosophers guarding the entrance.

Continue up 31st Street to 31st Avenue, where you may want to turn right three blocks to visit **Zenon Taverna Meze House** (34–10 31st Ave., tel. 718/956–0133), a restaurant run by immigrants not from Greece but from Greek Cyprus, a group that keeps growing as Greek and Turkish forces continue to dispute ownership of the island. The **Pan Cypriot Community Center** is eight blocks north on 31st Street, above **Taverna Vraka** (23–15 31st St.). Continue north on 31st Street to reach 23rd Avenue, where Greek-owned businesses bustle. Among the popular spots here is, one block north of 23rd Avenue, **Elias Corner** (24–01 31st St., tel. 718/932–1510). It isn't open for lunch, but if you love seafood, you should think seriously about hanging around for an early dinner here. There are no menus, so just go to the fish case and point.

❿ Five blocks east of 31st Steet on 23rd Avenue is **St. Irene Chrysovalantou Cathedral,** an independent Greek church where worshipers can pray to an icon that reportedly wept real tears at the outbreak of the Persian Gulf war in 1991. There was an outcry when the icon was stolen several months later; it was mysteriously returned through the regular mail, wrapped in brown paper, minus its jewel-encrusted frame. While the congregation rejoiced, the mainstream Greek Orthodox priests down at St. Demetrios took the opportunity to denounce the apostates once again and to deny that the icon ever wept at all.

Such local dramas are the stuff of immigrant communities, making New York seem like not such a big city after all.

The ancient Greeks excelled in the art of sculpture, so it is appropriate that Astoria should contain two sculpture parks. If you're up for a hike, return to Broadway and head eight blocks west until you reach the East River, at Vernon Boulevard. Before you is **Socrates Sculpture Park** (Vernon Blvd. at Broadway, tel. 718/956–1819), 4.2 acres of large, abstract artworks that first appear almost as an urban hallucination. You can get a fine view of Manhattan across the water here. Three blocks south is **The Isamu Noguchi Garden Museum,** where Japanese sculptor Isamu Noguchi took studio space in a photo-engraver's factory some 30 years ago. Part of it now holds 12 galleries that offer Noguchi devotees a concentration of the sculptor's evocative work in stone, and garden and stage-set design, along with videos documenting his long career. A small sculpture garden adjoins the museum. *32–37 Vernon Blvd., tel. 718/204–7088. Suggested contribution: $2. Museum open Apr.–Nov., Wed. and Sat. 11–6. Saturday bus service to Noguchi Museum leaves every hour on the half-hour, 11:30–3:30, from the Asia Society, Park Ave. and 70th St. in Manhattan. Fare: $5.*

The Bronx

Tour 23: Fordham and the Zoo

Numbers in the margin correspond to points of interest on the Tour 23: Fordham and the Bronx Zoo map.

The only borough attached to the North American mainland, the Bronx was first settled by Dutch, French, English, and Swedish country squires, who established manorial holdings there while fighting off Indians. The Village of Fordham was founded by John Archer in the mid-1600s, although little now remains from the Colonial era. But the area does dramatically illustrate another aspect of Bronx history—the influx of immigrant groups from the 1840s onward: first the Irish, then Germans, Italians, and Jews. Later waves included blacks and Hispanics, and today there are new infusions of Albanian and Cambodian immigrants.

To reach the old Village of Fordham, ride the D subway to the Kingsbridge Road station (or take a Metro North train to the Fordham stop and pick up the tour just past bullet number 3 below). From the Kingsbridge Road subway station, you'll alight alongside a fine stretch of that Bronx Champs Elysées, the **Grand Concourse.** Here you get a sense of the roadway as engineer Louis Riis envisioned it—a 4-mile-long "speedway," facilitating excursions into the country—as well as a view to the west of the **Kingsbridge Armory,** built in 1912, one of the largest such structures in the world.

Poe Park, at East Kingsbridge Road and the Grand Concourse, is so named because it contains the **Edgar Allan Poe Cottage,** whose white wood siding and green shutters recall earlier, more idyllic days. Here Poe and his sickly wife, Virginia, sought refuge from Manhattan and from the vicissitudes of the writerly life between 1846 and 1849. He wandered the countryside on foot and listened to the tintinnabulation of the church bells at nearby St. John's College Church (now Fordham

Tour 23: Fordham and the Bronx Zoo

University). Among the works he completed during this period are the poems "Ulalume," "The Bells," "Eureka," and "Annabel Lee." *Tel. 718/881–8900. Admission: $2. Hours of operation unavailable at press time.*

A couple of blocks south is the intersection of Fordham Road and the Grand Concourse, the Times Square of the Bronx. Venture south on the Grand Concourse to **Loew's Paradise Theatre** (2413 Grand Concourse, tel. 718/367–1288), which many claim is the best remaining 1930s-style movie house. The exterior ornamentation looks like a claymation fantasy; inside, a sloping, tiled entryway leads to a gorgeously garish Baroque-style lobby. Tell the ticket-taker that you're an architecture student and you may be able to get in without paying for the latest kung fu movie. John Eberson, the dean of bijou-builders, designed this gem in 1929; it was converted to a quadplex in 1981.

Don't stroll farther south on the Grand Concourse from the Paradise—the neighborhood swiftly declines. Instead, turn west on East 188th Street to peek at the **Creston Avenue Baptist Church** (114 E. 188th St.), built in 1905 and looking like it belongs not among the commercial chaos of Fordham Road, but in Merry Old England.

The Bx 12 bus will take you east along Fordham Road to Arthur Avenue; if you prefer the hike, you'll pass myriad coffee shops and discount stores, the Metro North train's Fordham stop, 1 Fordham Plaza (a modern green-and-white birthday-cake-like construction), and the looming Theodore Roosevelt High School.

Belmont, the neighborhood surrounding the intersection of Arthur Avenue and East 187th Street, has come to be called the Bronx's Little Italy—although actually it's a bigger Little Italy than the one in Manhattan. It really lights up after the sun sets, but it's also a daytime place, where some 14,500 families socialize, shop, work, and eat fabulously. Along Arthur Avenue you'll pass **Ciccarone Playground,** sporting a huge painted Italian flag. Indeed, as you study the surrounding two-story frame homes and tenements, the neighborhood begins to seem tinted exclusively in shades of white, red, and green: Italy's colors. A left turn onto East 187th Street takes you into an Italian commercial panoply; on one stellar block between Hughes and Belmont avenues you'll find **Egidio's Pastry Shop** (622 E. 187th St.), **Danny's Pork Store** (626 E. 187th St.), **Catholic Goods** (630 E. 187th St.), which sells Italian greeting cards, **Borgatti's Ravioli & Egg Noodles** (632 E. 187th St.), and the **Roma Luncheonette** (636 E. 187th St.). Across the street, residents' spiritual lives are tended to at **Our Lady of Mt. Carmel Roman Catholic Church** (627 E. 187th St.). The church, built in 1907, is an imposing brick structure with columned arches and four jutting flagpoles; inside, amid the marble columns and the intricate stained-glass windows, there is an indescribable smell of old religion, as well as many more saints.

A block south is the **Enrico Fermi Cultural Center/Belmont Branch New York Public Library** (610 E. 186th St., tel. 718/933–6410), where the Heritage Collection contains several volumes outlining the contributions of Italians and Italian-Americans. Nearby the **Arthur Avenue Retail Market** (2344 Arthur Ave.), a skylit shopping mart, offers 70 stalls, where Italian sausages and cheeses hang from on high.

Time Out   **Dominick's** (2335 Arthur Ave., tel. 718/733–2807) enjoys a reputation as Belmont's best restaurant. Here there are no menus, no wine lists—just hearty Italian food, savored at congested common tables, and cooked by members of a family that's been at Dominick's for 30 years. Finish off your meal with an espresso laced with sambuco.

Return to Fordham Road to explore the 85-acre campus of **Fordham University,** built around the site of the old Rose Hill Manor House (1838). Begun in 1841 as a Jesuit college, Fordham now has an undergraduate enrollment of 7,500, and an auxiliary campus near Lincoln Center.

Enter the grounds via Bathgate Avenue and you'll find yourself in an enclave of Collegiate Gothic architecture, shady trees, and green turf. Maps are posted around the campus or are available in the admissions office at Dealy Hall; use them to locate such highlights as the **Old Rose Hill Manor Dig;** the **University Church,** with its stained glass donated by King Louis Philippe of France (1773–1850); the pleasant **Edward's Parade;** and **Keating Hall,** sitting like a Gothic fortress in the center of things. After meandering through Fordham, make your way to the university's main entrance, fronting on Bronx (or, properly, New York Zoological) Park.

One of the best reasons to make a trip to the Bronx, is the **New York Botanical Garden.** The Fordham entrance leads into this serene but extraordinarily varied treasury, the dream of a husband-and-wife botanical team, Dr. Nathaniel Lord and

Elizabeth Britton. After visiting England's Kew Gardens in 1889, they returned full of fervor to create a similar haven in New York. In 1991, the New York Botanical Garden celebrated its centennial.

The garden stretches for 250 acres around the dramatic gorge of the Bronx River. It holds the historic **Lorillard Snuff Mill,** built by two French Huguenot manufacturers in 1840 to power the grinding of tobacco for snuff. Nearby, the Lorillards grew roses to supply fragrance for their blend. The snuff mill now houses a café, open daily 10–5. A walk along the Bronx River from the mill leads the visitor to the botanical garden's 40-acre **Forest,** the only uncut woodland in New York City. Outdoor plant collections include the **Erpf Compass Garden,** where cobblestones denoting the points of a compass are surrounded by flowers. Inside the luminous **Enid A. Haupt Conservatory** are displays of ferns, tropical flora, and Old and New World deserts. At the **Museum Building,** there's a gardening shop, a library, and a world-renowned herbarium holding 5.5 million dried plant specimens. *Bronx Park, tel. 718/220–8700. Conservatory admission: $3 adults, $2 senior citizens and students; free Sat. 10–noon. Last admission 1 hr before closing. Open Nov.–Mar., Tues.–Sun. and Mon. holidays 10–4; Apr.–Oct., Tues.–Sun. and Mon. holidays 10–6. Parking: $4.*

9 Also in Bronx Park is the **Bronx Zoo,** the nation's largest urban zoo and recently renamed the **International Wildlife Conservation Park.** It deserves nearly an entire day's visit on its own; if you want to return on another day, you can take the Liberty Lines BxM11 bus that runs up Madison Avenue ($3.50).

At the zoo you'll see two different historical methods of wild-animal keeping. The turn-of-the-century zoological garden houses monkeys, sea lions, and elephants (among many others) in fancy Beaux Arts–style edifices at **Astor Court.** It's being gradually replaced by the animal-in-habitat approach used in the **World of Birds,** with its capacious walk-through indoor natural habitats; in **Jungleworld,** an indoor tropical rain forest complete with five waterfalls, millipedes, flowering orchids, and pythons; and in the new **Baboon Reserve.** The **Children's Zoo** ($1.50 admission; open Apr.–Oct.) features many hands-on learning activities, as well as a large petting zoo. At the **Zoo Center,** visitors will find a rare Sumatran rhino. The zoo as a whole has more than 4,000 animals representing 667 species. *Bronx Park, tel. 718/367–1010. Admission: Thurs.–Tues. $5.75 adults, $2 senior citizens and children 2–12 (Nov.–Feb. $2.50 adults, $1 senior citizens and children); Wed. voluntary contribution. Open Mar.–Oct., weekdays 10–5, weekends and holidays 10–5:30; Nov.–Feb., daily 10–4:30.*

Staten Island

Tour 24: Snug Harbor and Richmondtown

Numbers in the margin correspond to points of interest on the Tour 24: Staten Island map.

Even though Staten Island is officially a borough of New York City, many Staten Islanders (as do the rest of the bridge and tunnel crowd) refer to Manhattan as "the City." Perhaps that's because farms and vast woodlands have distinguished it from the more crowded and developed Manhattan since 1661, when Staten Island was permanently settled as a farming community by the Dutch (after several fatal battles with the Native American tribes who already inhabited the area). When oystering became a thriving industry in the early 1800s, farmers brought free blacks up from Maryland to help plant new oyster beds. The black community on the south shore became known as Sandy Ground; descendants of the first black oystermen still live there. Factories came later, as did shipbuilding. Today Staten Island still feels more residential than the other boroughs. Getting around can be somewhat difficult for visitors because the various attractions are so spread out, but bus service is convenient.

The greatest way to introduce yourself to Staten Island is by taking the 20-minute ride across New York Harbor on the **Staten Island Ferry,** which leaves regularly from the southern tip of Manhattan (*see* Tour 17 in Chapter 3). On the boats with outer decks, passengers can get a better look at the spectacular views of lower Manhattan's skyscrapers and the splendidly restored Ellis Island and Statue of Liberty.

From the ferry terminal, a seven-minute ride on the S40 bus or on a special trolley will take you to the **Snug Harbor Cultural Center,** which on a warm summer afternoon might be hosting a New York Philharmonic concert, an art show, or an old-fashioned flea market. Once part of a sprawling farm, then a home for "aged and decrepit sailors," the 80-acre center is based around a row of five columned Greek Revival temples, built between 1831 and 1880, facing onto the Kill Van Kull, a wide stream that flows into Upper New York Bay. The former chapel is now the 210-seat **Veterans Memorial Hall,** site of many indoor concerts and gatherings. *1000 Richmond Terr., tel. 718/448–2500. Admission free; various charges for special events. Open 8 AM–dusk. Free guided tours Sat.–Sun. 2 PM.*

On the Snug Harbor grounds, the **Newhouse Center for Contemporary Art** features changing exhibitions (open Wed.–Sun. noon–5; $1 voluntary contribution).

The **Staten Island Botanical Gardens,** also on the Snug Harbor grounds, feature a perennial garden, a greenhouse, 10 acres of natural marsh habitat, a fragrance garden for the blind, and a bonsai collection. *1000 Richmond Terr., tel. 718/273–8200. Admission free. Open 9 AM–dusk.*

The **Staten Island Children's Museum,** also in Snug Harbor, offers four revolving hands-on exhibitions to introduce children to such diverse topics as news and media, storytelling, and insects. *1000 Richmond Terr., tel. 718/273–2060. Admission: $3. Open Tues.–Sun. noon–5.*

Return to the ferry terminal and catch the S52–Bay Street bus for the 2-mile ride to Hylan Boulevard and the **Alice Austen House.** Photographer Alice Austen (1866–1952) defied tradition when, as a girl of 10, she received her first camera as a gift from an uncle and promptly began taking pictures of everything around her. Austen went on to make photography her lifetime avocation, recording on film a vivid "social history" of Staten Island in the early part of the century; one of the local ferries is actually named for her. The cozy, ivy-covered Dutch-style cottage known as Clear Comfort, where she lived almost all her life, has been restored, and many of her photographs are

Tour 24: Staten Island

NEW JERSEY

Kill Van Kull

Bayonne Bridge

Staten Island Ferry ❶

❷ Richmond Ter.

Snug Harbor Cultural Center

Richmond Ter.

Broadway

Richmond

Forest Ave.

South Ave.

Forest Ave.

Richmond Ave.

Willow Brook Expwy. Ter.

Castleton Ave.

Forest Ave.

Clove Rd.

Victory Blvd.

Bay St.

Tompkins Ave.

Hylan Blvd.

Upper New York Bay

B R O O K L Y N

Clove Lakes Park

Jewett Ave.

440

440

Blvd.

Victory

Staten Island Expwy.

278

❸ **Alice Austen House**

Verrazano Narrows Bridge

Willow Brook Park

Brielle Ave.

Ave.

Rockland Ave.

Richmond Rd.

Hylan Blvd.

Capodanno Blvd.

Lower New York Bay

William T. Davis Wildlife Refuge

Richmond Hill Rd.

La Tourette Park

❹ **Richmondtown Restoration**

Richmond Rd.

Father

Hylan Blvd.

Arthur Kill Rd.

Richmond Cr.

N

0 ____ 2 miles

0 ____ 3 km

on exhibit. *2 Hylan Blvd., tel. 718/816–4506. Suggested donation: $2 adults. Open Thurs.–Sun. noon–5.*

Take the S74–Richmond Road bus from the ferry terminal to ❹ the **Richmondtown Restoration,** a unique museum village on the site of Staten Island's first permanent settlement, founded in 1685. The 26 historic buildings on this 96-acre complex have been restored inside and out; some were here originally, while others were relocated from other spots on the island. Many of the buildings, such as the Greek Revival courthouse that serves as the **visitor center,** date from the 19th century; other architectural styles on site range from Dutch Colonial to Victorian Gothic Revival. The **Voorlezer's House,** built in 1695, is the oldest elementary schoolhouse in the United States; it looks like the mold from which all little red schoolhouses were cast.

During the warmer months, costumed interpreters demonstrate Early American crafts and trades such as printing, tinsmithing, and baking. The **Staten Island Historical Society Museum,** built in 1848 as the second county clerk's and surrogate's office, now has in its archives American china, furniture, toys, and tools, plus a collection of Staten Island photographs.

During a summer visit, you might want to make reservations for the 19th-century dinner, cooked outdoors and served with utensils of the period. The Autumn Celebration shows off craftspeople demonstrating their skills; the annual Encampment in June is a re-creation of a Civil War battle; December brings a month-long Christmas celebration. Richmondtown regularly hosts other fairs, flea markets, and tours of the historic buildings. There is a tavern where folk music is played. *Tel. 718/351–1611. Admission: $4 adults, $2.50 senior citizens and children 6–18. Open Jan.–Mar., Wed.–Fri. 1–5; Apr.–Dec., Wed.–Sun. 1–5.*

Off the Beaten Track

Brooklyn **Coney Island.** It's the home of the hot dog, "the king of roller coasters" (the Cyclone), the Wonder Wheel, suntan lotion, crowds, fried clams, girls and boys necking under the boardwalk, and old men staring vacantly out to sea. While it may have declined from its glory days early in this century—when visitors lunched at an ocean-side hotel built in the shape of an elephant, glided across the nation's biggest dance floor at Dreamland, or toured a replica of old Baghdad called Luna Park—Coney Island still has a boardwalk, a 2.7-mile-long beach, and a huge amusement park. The **Aquarium for Wildlife Conservation** (tel. 718/265–3474) keeps watery beasts—sharks, black-footed penguins, octopuses, piranhas, and Beluga whales, —on view nearby. Coney Island memorabilia is on view at the nearby **Sideshows By the Seashore** museum (W. 12th St. and Boardwalk, tel. 718/372–5159; admission: 99¢; open Memorial Day–Labor Day, Wed.–Sun.; rest of year, weekends only), which also has a theater presenting a circus sideshow. Two blocks away is **Brighton Beach Avenue,** the main street of a community of some 30,000 Soviet émigrés, where inexpensive restaurants serving up Soviet Georgian cuisine abound. D, Q, N, B, and F subways serve the Coney Island–Brighton Beach area.

Green-Wood Cemetery (25th St. and 5th Ave.). Built in the 1840s, the cemetery features a stately Gothic Revival gatehouse, designed by Richard Upjohn, that still moves visitors to a sublime pitch of melancholy. The 478 acres contain 5 lakes, 22 miles of lanes, and 209 paths named for bushes, flowers, and trees. Among the illustrious—or infamous—citizens interred there are Samuel F.B. Morse, Boss Tweed, and Peter Cooper. It's open daily 8–4; call the superintendent (tel. 718/768–7300) for permission to tour. The closest subway stop is 25th Street and 4th Avenue (R train).

Queens **Flushing.** This Queens neighborhood, which played a role in the fight for religious freedom in America, is surrounded by a multiethnic community that is increasingly dominated by people of Asian descent; it's a bubbling melting pot rarely visited by New Yorkers themselves. Take the No. 7 subway to its final stop, the Main Street–Flushing station. Main Street and its two parallel neighbors, Prince and Union streets, serve up a banquet for Korean, Chinese, and Indian gourmands. Go north on Main Street to Northern Boulevard, where the wood-shingled, tiny-windowed **Friends Meeting House** (137–16 Northern Blvd.) is New York City's oldest place of worship. Built in 1694, it's still used for the Quakers' 11 AM Sunday services. Turn right on Bowne Street to see **Bowne House** (37–01 Bowne St., tel. 718/359–0528; admission: $2 adults, $1 senior citizens and children under 12; open Tues. and weekends 2:30–4:30), occupied from 1661 to 1945 by the same family, descendants of John Bowne, a Quaker leader who led an historic fight for religious tolerance. The Bowne House displays household furnishings used by nine generations of the family and is the oldest house in Queens.

Across Bowne Street you can see the **Fox Oaks Rock,** marking the site of an impassioned sermon delivered in 1672 by George Fox, founder of the Quaker sect. North of Bowne House, inside the **Kingsland Homestead** (143–35 37th Ave., tel. 718/939–0647; admission: $2 adults, $1 students, senior citizens, and children; open Tues., Sat., and Sun. 2:30–4:30), a gambrel-roofed wood farmhouse built circa 1785, the Queens Historical Society mounts exhibits about local history. In the park beside the Kingsland Homestead is the **Weeping Beech,** a huge beech tree with trailing branches, planted from a cutting brought by Samuel Parsons from Belgium in 1847.

Bronx   **Riverdale.** This is perhaps the Bronx's most attractive neighborhood; wide-open territory for outer-borough explorers, it's best visited by car, taking the Kappock Street exit from the Henry Hudson Parkway. If you don't have a car, take the Metro North train to the Riverdale stop. Manhattan millionaires built summer homes here, with stirring views of the New Jersey Palisades across the Hudson River, in the early part of this century. A drive along Palisade Avenue, picturesque Sycamore Avenue above West 252nd Street, and Independence Avenue between West 248th and 254th streets will take you past some of Riverdale's handsomest mansions. Only **Wave Hill** (675 W. 252nd St., tel. 718/549–2055) is open to the public, but a visit to this 28-acre estate will conjure up the image of Riverdale's wealthy past. Built in 1844, then lavishly added onto by J. P. Morgan's partner George Perkins, the estate offers two mansions and splendid views of the Hudson. *Admission: weekends, $4 adults, $2 senior citizens and students; weekdays, free. Open mid-May–mid-Oct., Sun.–Tues. and Thurs.–Fri., 10–5:30, Sat. and Wed. 10–7; mid-Oct.–mid-May, Tues.–Sun. 9:30–4:30.*

City Island. At the extreme west end of the Bronx is a bona fide island measuring 230 acres wide. Back in 1761, a group of the area's residents planned a port to rival New York's, but when that scheme hit the shoals, they returned to perennial maritime pursuits such as fishing and boatbuilding. City Island–produced yachts have included a number of America's Cup contenders. Connected to Pelham Bay Park by bridge, City Island offers visitors a maritime atmosphere and good seafood restaurants. To reach City Island, take the No. 6 subway to Pelham Bay Parkway and then catch the No. 29 bus. While you're there, be sure to stop by the **North Wind Undersea Museum,** with its displays devoted to marine mammal rescue and deep-sea diving. *610 City Island Ave., Bronx, tel. 718/885–0701. Admission: $3 adults, $2 children under 12. Open weekdays 10–5, weekends noon–5.*

Staten Island   **Staten Island Train.** There's no subway on Staten Island, but there is one above-ground train line, and it accepts New York City subway tokens. For a leisurely look at Staten Island's topography, ride the train its full length, from the Staten Island ferry terminal to Tottenville, about a 40-minute trip. You'll get a stunning view of the Verrazano Bridge and then ramble through residential neighborhoods, woods, and wetlands.

5 Exploring New York City with Children

New York is as magical a place for children as it is for adults. Although hotels and restaurants tend to be geared firmly to the grown-ups, when provision has been made for children, it is usually accomplished in a grand way. The world's best and largest toy shop, the biggest dinosaur skeletons, the biggest and best park, the nicest city seaport, the best burgers, and of course, some of the world's tallest buildings are here. Besides such sights, there are rare ambient treats to stumble upon— from brightly colored pictograms in Chinatown to exotic-looking Hasidim in the Diamond District, from Central Park squirrels to Greenwich Village street musicians good enough to appear on television (and sometimes they do).

For calendars of children's events, consult *New York* magazine and the weekly *Village Voice* newspaper, available at newsstands. The Friday *New York Times* "Weekend" section and the Friday edition of *New York Newsday* also provide a good listing of children's activities.

Two other good sources of information on happenings for kids are **New York Family** (141 Halstead Ave., Mamaroneck, NY 10543, tel. 914/381–7474), published eleven times a year, and the monthly **Big Apple Parents' Paper** (36 E. 12th St., New York, NY 10003, tel. 212/533–2277), which is available free at toy stores, children's museums and clothing stores, and other places around town where parents and children are found.

To get children psyched up for a New York trip, give them *Eloise*, by Kay Thompson, *Harriet the Spy*, by Louise Fitzhugh, or *Stuart Little*, by E.B. White.

Sightseeing

As far as outdoors sights are concerned, there is plenty to please; surprising pockets of street sculpture, graffiti art, strange building facades, and quirky shop windows may be found on almost every block. In no other city are you more likely to entertain offspring simply by wandering. Children get a kick from the sheer size of the buildings, and from riding cabs, or even buses and subways (especially the first or last car, with a view of the track and tunnels). For more exotic transportation, try the **horse-drawn carriages** around Central Park (at Grand Army Plaza or intersections of Central Park S between 5th and 7th Aves.; $34 for the first 30 minutes); summer sailboats, named *The Pioneer* (South St. Seaport, tel. 212/669–9417; $15 adults, $5 children under 12, for 2 hours) or *The Petrel* (Battery Park, tel. 212/825–1976; $14–$25 adults, $10 children under 13, for 45 mins.–2 hours); or an **Island Helicopter** tour (34th St. and East River, tel. 212/683–4575; $41–$94).

For little more than the price of a subway token, the **Roosevelt Island Aerial Tramway** across the East River is a sure hit. Trams board at Second Avenue and 60th Street and run every 15 minutes during regular hours, and every 7½ minutes during rush hours, which you might wish to avoid.

Don't miss the **Statue of Liberty, Ellis Island,** (*see* Tour 17 in Chapter 3) or the **South Street Seaport** (*see* Tour 18 in Chapter 3), all appreciated by children. Ferry rides are always fun; try the bargain 50¢ ride on the **Staten Island Ferry** (terminal in Battery Park), or a cruise on the beautiful sidewheeler and steamboat of the **Seaport Line** (*see* Tour 18 in Chapter 3).

While in lower Manhattan, visit **Fraunces Tavern,** whose museum holds kids' workshops; the fairy-tale palacelike lobby of the **Woolworth Building** (*see* Tour 17 in Chapter 3); the indoor jungle at Battery Park City's **Winter Garden Atrium;** and the great sweep of **Brooklyn Bridge** (*see* Tour 18 in Chapter 3). Of course, the **World Trade Center**'s 107th-floor panorama is another popular downtown sight (*see* Tour 17 in Chapter 3). The favorite midtown high-level view is from the **Empire State Building,** (*see* Tour 4 in Chapter 3). Hop uptown to **Grand Central Terminal** (*see* Tour 3 in Chapter 3) for the whispering gallery, star-bedecked ceiling, and amazing bustle.

Museums

Although just about every major museum in New York City has something to interest children, certain ones hold special appeal. At the top of the list is the **American Museum of Natural History** (Central Park at 79th St., tel. 212/769–5100), with its lifelike dioramas and giant dinosaurs (partially off-limits until 1995, when restoration of the entire collection will be completed). Also intriguing are the Discovery Room, with hands-on exhibits for children, and the Naturemax Theater, which shows awesome nature films on a gigantic screen. The adjacent **Hayden Planetarium** offers astronomical exhibits and sky shows; there is also a preschool show (reservations required; tel. 212/769–5920) (*see* Tour 8 in Chapter 3).

The **Children's Museum of Manhattan,** is a kind of indoor playground for kids 2–12, with interactive exhibits organized around common childhood experiences. Children can paint, make collages, and try on costumes. *212 W. 83rd St., tel. 212/ 721–1234. Admission: $4. Open Mon., Wed., and Thurs. 1:30–5; Fri.–Sun. 10–5.*

The **Children's Museum of the Arts,** in a loftlike space in Soho, allows children ages 18 months to 10 to become actively involved in visual and performing arts. Highlights include the Monet Ball Pond, where children can play with brightly colored balls near a water-lily mural; the Lines and Shapes alcove, where kids have access to computer drawing; and the Creative Play area, which provides a large playpen, a reading corner, art activities, and cushions and futons for relaxation. Weekend workshops are included in the admission price. *72–78 Spring St., tel. 212/941–9198. Admission: $4 adults under 65 and children 18 months and older. Admission free, Thurs., 4–7. Open Tues.–Sun. 11–5; Thurs. 11–7.*

Another favorite with the younger generation is the ***Intrepid Sea-Air-Space Museum,*** an immense World War II aircraft carrier. On deck is a startling array of aircraft; inside there are aviation and military exhibits, as well as skinny hallways, winding staircases, and dozens of knobs, buttons, and wheels to manipulate. *Pier 86 at 12th Ave. and W. 46th St., tel. 212/ 245–0072. Admission: $7 adults, $6 senior citizens and veterans, $4 children 6–12. Open Wed.–Sun. 10–5.*

Kids tend to like the **Forbes Magazine Galleries** (62 5th Ave. at 12th St., tel. 212/206–5548) for the collections of toy soldiers and boats, and rooms with the bejeweled Fabergé eggs (*see* Tour 12 in Chapter 3). Another good bet is the **New York City Fire Museum** (278 Spring St., tel. 212/691–1303), with displays of fire-fighting equipment and tours given by real firefighters (*see* Chapter 6).

Other museums offer special programs for kids or families. Among these are the **Museum of Modern Art,** the Junior Museum at the **Metropolitan Museum of Art,** the **Jewish Museum,** the **Museum of the City of New York,** with wonderful collections of dollhouses and antique toys, the **El Museo del Barrio** (*see* Tour 5 in Chapter 3), and the **Lower East Side Tenement Museum** (*see* Chapter 6). At the **Whitney Museum of American Art** (*see* Tour 5 in Chapter 3), children like the Calder circus.

The **Brooklyn Museum** (*see* Tour 20 in Chapter 4) has special programs for kids and families. For children who like hands-on involvement, the place to go is the **Brooklyn Children's Museum,** full of tunnels, bubbles, animals, and neon lights. Exhibits cover the environment, nature, science, and more. *145 Brooklyn Ave., tel. 718/735-4432. Suggested donation: $3. Open. June–Aug., Wed.–Sun. noon–5; Sept.–May, Wed.–Fri. 2–5; weekends and holidays noon–5.*

In Queens, the **New York Hall of Science** in Flushing Meadows–Corona Park allows budding researchers access to 150 exhibits (many of them touchable) on such topics as color and illusion, the atom, self-sensory machines, and microorganisms. *111th St. at 40th Ave., tel. 718/699-0005. Admission: $3.50 adults, $2.50 senior citizens and children; free Wed. and Thur. 2–5. Open Wed.–Sun. 10–5.*

Astoria, Queens has the **American Museum of the Moving Image** (*see* Tour 22 in Chapter 4), the only museum in the United States devoted to both film and television.

The **Staten Island Institute of Arts and Sciences** offers kids' programs and wonderful exhibits covering natural history and the arts from nearly all angles. *75 Stuyvesant Pl., tel. 718/727-1135. Suggested donation: $2.50 adults, $1.50 senior citizens and children. Open Mon.–Sat. 9–5, Sun. 1–5.*

Also on Staten Island are the hands-on exhibits of the **Staten Island Children's Museum** (*see* Tour 24 in Chapter 4). Children may also enjoy **Richmondtown Restoration's Staten Island Historical Society** (*see* Tour 24 in Chapter 4), which has a Museum of Childhood with displays of antique dolls, toys, and children's furniture.

The **Liberty Science Center,** the largest science museum in the New York metropolitan area, opened in 1993 in Liberty State Park, New Jersey. This impressive four-floor center is guaranteed to keep kids busy for hours with more than 250 interactive exhibits that concentrate on three themes—environment, health, and invention. Highlights include laser light and sound displays, an insect zoo, a 100-foot touch tunnel, an amazing 700-pound geodesic globe, and the Kodak OMNI Theater, for viewing OMNIMAX movies on a gigantic screen. *Liberty State Park, 251 Philip St., Jersey City, NJ, tel. 201/200-1000. Admission: $8 adults, $7 students and senior citizens, $5 children 5–12. OMNI Theater Admission: $7 adults, $6 students and senior citizens, $5 children 5–12. Combined admission to exhibits and OMNI Theater: $12 adults, $10 students and senior citizens, $8 children 5–12. Admission "pay-as-you-wish" on first Wed. of every month 1 PM–closing. Open Tues.–Thurs. 9:30–5:30, Fri.–Sun. and holidays 9:30–6:30.*

The Center is reached from Manhattan by car by taking the Holland Tunnel to Exit 14B on the New Jersey Turnpike (about a 10-minute drive without heavy traffic).

To reach the center by train from Manhattan, take the PATH train (tel. 800/234-7284) in the direction of Jersey City to Exchange Place, Journal Square, or Grove Street stops and then take a Central Avenue bus to the Center. Visitors can also take a Port Imperial ferry (tel. 800/53-FERRY) from the World Financial Center in downtown Manhattan to Liberty State Park.

Parks and Playgrounds

New York's great outdoors sounds like a contradiction in terms, especially when you add children to the equation. But, in addition to the wide open spaces of Central Park, pockets of green all over town provide relief from concrete.

In Central Park, children can ride bicycles, play tennis, row boats, go horseback riding, ice-skate, roller-skate, rollerblade, skateboard, fly kites, feed ducks, throw Frisbees, and much more (*see* Tour 7 in Chapter 3; *see also* Chapter 7). Favorite destinations include the **Zoo** (*see below*) and the **Conservatory Water,** which attracts owners of large, remote-controlled model boats and is located near the statues of Alice in Wonderland and Hans Christian Andersen. Younger children enjoy the hands-on activities at the **Dairy** and **Belvedere Castle** (tel. 212/772–0210), as well as an antique **Carousel** (midpark at 65th St., tel. 212/879–0244), complete with painted horses that prance to jaunty organ music; it costs only 90¢ a ride. The **Wollman Rink** (tel. 212/517–4800) has rollerblading and roller-skating classes and sessions—ice-skating in winter—and a **Miniature Golf** course, with obstacles of city buildings (*see* Chapter 7).

At Brooklyn's 536-acre **Prospect Park,** enjoy kite flying and picnicking on the 90-acre Long Meadow (*see* Tour 20 in Chapter 4). Near the park, bring the family for a stroll at the **Brooklyn Botanic Garden** (*see* Tour 20 in Chapter 4).

In the Bronx, adjacent to the Bronx Zoo, the **New York Botanical Garden** (*see* Tour 23 in Chapter 4) is one of the world's largest botanical gardens, with a large conservatory, 12 outdoor gardens, walking trails, and 40 acres of forest.

Off the beaten track, there are short marked nature trails suitable for young hikers at the **Alley Pond Environmental Center** (228–06 Northern Blvd., Douglastown, tel. 718/229–4000) and **Jamaica Bay Wildlife Refuge** (tel. 718/474–0613) in Queens, and at **Van Cortlandt Park** (tel. 212/430–1890) in the Bronx. (For more park listings, *see* Chapter 6.)

Manhattan has wonderful state-of-the-art playgrounds. **Central Park**'s adventure playgrounds are full of slides, bridges, bars, swings, towers and tunnels; they're carpeted with sand or soft rubber matting and often cooled in summer by sprinklers, fountains, or running water. Good ones can be found along Fifth Avenue at 67th Street near the Zoo, at 71st and 77th Streets, and at 85th Street near the Metropolitan Museum. Along Central Park West, the best ones are at 68th, 85th, 93rd (with a Wild West theme), and 96th streets. The large **Hecksher Playground,** midpark at 62nd Street, for toddlers, has good water features.

Also top-rated by Manhattan kids are the playgrounds at **Battery Park City** (West St. south of Vesey St.), **Washington Square Park** (at foot of 5th Ave. between Waverly Pl. and W. 4th St.), **Abingdon Square Park** (at the triangular junction of Bleecker, Bank, and Hudson Streets in the West Village), **Carl Schurz Park** (84th St. near East End Ave.), **John Jay Park** (off York Ave. near 77th St., within sight of the East River), and the **Pearl Street Playground** (Fulton, Water, and Pearl Sts.). In **Riverside Park,** west of Riverside Drive, the best playgrounds are at 77th and 91st Streets; the one at 77th Street has a circle of spouting elephant fountains. The **Playground for All Children** (Flushing Meadows–Corona Park, Corona Ave. and 111th St., Queens, tel. 718/699–8283) enables children to play together regardless of their disabilities, with Braille nature trails, tracks for wheelchair racing, and so on.

Zoos

Central Park Zoo, recently renamed the **Central Park Wildlife Conservation Center,** is of a very manageable size, even for toddlers (*see* Tour 7 in Chapter 3). With only 100 or so mostly small species on display, it may disappoint older children, but everyone loves the penguins on display.

On the more impressive side is the largest zoo of any city in the United States: the **Bronx Zoo,** recently renamed the **International Wildlife Conservation Park** (*see* Tour 23 in Chapter 4). Most of the animals here live in replicas of their natural habitats. Don't miss the Children's Zoo area (open Apr.–Oct.), with fishes, reptiles, and small animals behind glass, as well as a petting farm.

Brooklyn's **Prospect Park Zoo,** recently renamed the **Prospect Park Wildlife Conservation Center,** (*see* Tour 20 in Chapter 4) was scheduled at press time to reopen in 1993.

The **Queens Zoo,** recently renamed the **Queens Wildlife Conservation Center,** shows North American animals in approximations of their natural habitat. The inhabitants include black bears, mountain lions, sea lions, bobcats, coyotes, bison, and elk. *53–51 111th St., Flushing Meadows Park, tel. 718/271–7761. Admission: $2.50 adults, $1.25 seniors, 50¢ children 3–12. Open Apr.–Oct., Mon.–Fri. 10–5, weekends and holidays 10–5:30; Nov.–Mar., daily 10–4:30.*

The **Staten Island Zoo** is small but of high quality and features one of the world's finest collections of reptiles, as well as a separate Children's Zoo. *Barrett Park, 614 Broadway, Staten Island, tel. 718/442–3100. Admission: $3 adults, $2 children 3–11. Suggested donation Wed. 2–4:45. Open daily 10–4:45.*

Nearly 300 different varieties of fish are on display in Brooklyn at the **Aquarium for Wildlife Conservation.** You'll marvel at the dolphins, sea lions, and electric eels; be sure to catch the penguin and shark feedings. *Surf Ave. at W. 8th St., Coney Island, tel. 718/265–3474. Admission: $5.75 adults, $2 senior citizens and children 2–12. Open June–Aug., weekdays 10–5:45, weekends and holidays 10–8; Sept.–May., daily 10–5:45.*

Shopping

Adults and children alike find shopping nirvana in New York. One of the world's best toy stores, **F.A.O. Schwarz** (where Tom Hanks danced on the giant piano in the movie *Big*), is probably highlight number one (*see* Toys in Chapter 8), but even shopping for clothes, often resented by children, can be fun here.

In addition to the stores listed under Children's Clothing in Chapter 8, try, on the Upper West Side, **Morris Brothers** (2322 Broadway between 84th and 85th Sts., tel. 212/724–9000) and **Monkeys & Bears** (506 Amsterdam Ave., tel. 212/873–2673) for hip, all-age clothes; and **Shoofly** (465 Amsterdam Ave., tel. 212/580–4390) for designer footwear. The Upper East Side's boutiques of choice are **Magic Windows** (infant–sixth grade: 1046 Lexington at 75th St., tel. 212/517–7271; infant–preteen, 1186 Madison Ave. at 87th St., tel. 212/289–0028), and **Chocolate Soup** (946 Madison Ave. between 74th and 75th Sts., tel. 212/861–2210) for handsewn and imported clothes for kids. Downtown boys like **Boy Oh Boy!** (18 E. 17th St., tel. 212/463–8250) for sizes 2–20. SoHo's **Too Cute** (113 Prince St. between Greene and Wooster Sts., tel. 212/777–5974), stocks casual clothes embroidered with cartoon characters.

Also visit the clothing and toy departments at **Macy's** for the thrill of size and **A&S** for the cool atrium plaza. Go to Macy's during the holiday season between Thanksgiving and Christmas, and enjoy the enchanting Christmas window displays for free. Don't miss the animated windows at **Lord & Taylor**, either; the elegant ones at **Bergdorf Goodman**, **Bloomingdale's**, **Saks Fifth Avenue** and, especially, at **Barneys New York** tend to be aimed squarely at adults, but kids usually enjoy them, too (*see* Department Stores in Chapter 8).

For stores featuring toys, games, magic, and general gizmos, *see* Fun and Games in Chapter 8. **Think Big!** (390 W. Broadway, tel. 212/925–7300) and **Dollhouse Antics** (1343 Madison Ave. at 94th St., tel. 212/876–2288), at opposite ends of town, make intriguing partners—one stocks giant replicas of common objects while the other features miniature furnishings at 1″ scale. Children should also enjoy the **Big City Kite Co.** (1201 Lexington Ave. between 81st and 82nd Sts., tel. 212/472–2623), which has one of the best kite selections anywhere. For older kids, there's **Forbidden Planet** (821 Broadway at 12th St., tel. 212/473–1576), stocking everything relating to science fiction and fantasy, such as comic books, fiction, and monster masks; **Sabado Bazaar** (54 Greene St. between Broome and Grand Sts., tel. 212/941–6152) for its colorful carnival of Mexican toys and ceramics; and **Pull Cart** (31 W. 21st St., 7th floor, tel. 212/727–7089), a ceramics studio where you paint your own tablewares. For small consumer monsters, **Toys R Us** (1293 Broadway in Herald Center, tel. 212/594–8697) may be of interest.

The most pleasant sources for children's reading materials are **Bank Street Bookstore, Books of Wonder,** and **Eeyore's Books for Children** (*see* Children's Books in Chapter 8), but you can also find kids' books at a discount at **Barnes and Noble** and **Tower Books** (*see* Books in Chapter 8).

For comics, besides **Forbidden Planet** (*see above*), try **Village Comics** (163 Bleecker St., 2nd floor, tel. 212/777–2770) and

Funny Business Comics (656 Amsterdam Ave., tel. 212/799–9477), which both carry a delightful stock of old and new issues.

Babies have their own shopping needs, though they don't know it. Their parents may be interested in, on the Upper West Side, the comprehensively stocked **Albee's** (715 Amsterdam Ave. at 95th St., tel. 212/662–5740) and the very upscale **Bellini** (473 Columbus Ave. at 83rd St., tel. 212/362–3700), which also has a branch for East Siders (1305 2nd Ave. at 68th St., tel. 212/517–9233). **Hush-A-Bye** (1459 1st Ave. at 76th St., tel. 212/988–3540) also caters to Upper East Siders, and **Schneider's** (20 Ave. A at 2nd St., tel. 212/228–3540) is a very well-stocked store for downtown infants and discount hunters.

Dining

The following is a diverse selection of places, both for everyday refueling and for special family-dining occasions.

In lower Manhattan, the younger ones should enjoy **Minter's Fun Food and Drink** (4 World Financial Ctr., tel. 212/945–4455) for chocolate beverages, and **Minter's Ice Cream Kitchen** (Pier 17, 3rd floor, South St. Seaport, tel. 212/608–2037). At South Street Seaport, Pier 17's **Promenade Food Court** has a variety of quick foods. The surprising charms of the only **McDonald's** branch with doorman, pianist, and table service (160 Broadway between Maiden La. and Liberty St., tel. 212/385–2063) are obvious. In TriBeCa, **Bubby's** (120 Hudson St. at N. Moore, tel. 212/219–0666) has casual dining and great baked goods; and **Hows Bayou Café** (355 Greenwich St. at Harrison St., tel. 212/925–5405) feeds kids gumbo and gives them Mardi Gras beads. In Chinatown, don't miss the green-tea and red-bean ice cream at the **Chinatown Ice Cream Factory** (65 Bayard St., tel. 212/608–4170). Chinatown is also a good place to take the whole family for lunch or dinner at reasonable prices, whether it be for noodles and dumplings at **Noodle Town** or **Wong Kee** or for dim sum at **Mandarin Court** (*see* Chapter 9). Don't be surprised if you see a lot of families from the neighborhood bringing their own children out to dine!

Delis are great for kids; on the Lower East Side, **Katz's** (205 E. Houston St. at Ludlow St., tel. 212/254–2246), **Ratner's** (138 Delancey St. between Norfolk and Suffolk Sts., tel. 212/677–5588) and the kosher-Chinese **Bernstein-on-Essex** (135 Essex St. between Delancey and Houston Sts., tel. 212/473–3900) are best, and in the East Village, there's the **Second Avenue Delicatessen** (at 10th St., tel. 212/677–0606). Also in the East Village, any of the Polish cafés provide good, filling very inexpensive fare—try **Teresa's** (103 1st Ave. near 6th St., tel. 212/228–0604), the Ukrainian **Veselka** (144 2nd Ave. at 9th St., tel. 212/228–9682), or **Odessa** (117 Ave. A between 7th and 8th Sts., tel. 212/473–8916). For pasta, visit **Brunetta's** (190 1st Ave., near 11th St., tel. 212/228–4030).

In SoHo, **5&10 No Exaggeration** (77 Greene St., between Spring and Broome Sts., tel. 212/925–7414) is fun for the piles of antique knickknacks, all for sale, and vintage movies; **Fanelli's Café** (corner of Mercer and Prince Sts., tel. 212/226–9412) serves good burgers, fries, and pizza; **Tennessee Mountain** (143 Spring St. at Wooster St., tel. 212/431–3993) serves BBQ; and the **Cupping Room Café** (359 W. Broadway, near

Broome St., tel. 212/925–2898) provides waffles and other light meals throughout the day. In the West Village, try **Arturo's** (106 W. Houston St. at Thompson St., tel. 212/475–9828) and its pizza; **Aggie's** (146 W. Houston St. at MacDougal St., tel. 212/673–8994), a funky coffee shop with sprightly soups and sandwiches; **Elephant and Castle** (68 Greenwich Ave. near 11th St., tel. 212/243–1400) for burgers and great french fries; and **Benny's Burritos** (113 Greenwich Ave. at Jane St., tel. 212/727–0584) for huge Cal-Tex servings at low prices. Also take time out for **Tea and Sympathy** (108 Greenwich Ave., tel. 212/807–3329), offering an authentic British afternoon tea, and the **Cowgirl Hall of Fame** (519 Hudson St. at W. 10th St., tel. 212/633–1133) for Cajun cooking and cowgirl memorabilia.

As you head uptown, just off Union Square, **America** (9 E. 18th St., tel. 212/505–2110) has huge everything—menu, portions, spaces—except checks. Chelsea offers the hip, all-rounder **Empire Diner** (210 10th Ave. at 22nd St., tel. 212/243–2736) and the fun, bustling, neon-decorated **Lox Around the Clock** (676 6th Ave. at 21st St., tel. 212/691–3535). Higher up, near the Flatiron Building, teens go for the scene at **Live Bait** (14 E. 23rd St., tel. 212/243–7969), which bears some resemblance to the **Coffee Shop** (129 Union Sq. W, tel. 212/243–7969), at least in the model-photographer-trendy-pretty clientele. Near Gramercy Park, the **Maryland Crab House** (237 3rd Ave. between 19th and 20th Sts., tel. 212/598–4890) serves hard-shells with a mallet and bib.

Midtown, the **American Festival Café** (Rockefeller Center, 20 W. 50th St., tel. 212/246–6699) is the essential N.Y.C. family dining experience. Other midtown choices include the casual **Hamburger Harry's** (145 W. 45th St., tel. 212/840–2756), **Stage Delicatessen** (834 7th Ave. at 54th St., tel. 212/245–7850), and **Au Café** (7th Ave. at 53rd St., tel. 212/757–2233). On the East Side, **The Brasserie** (100 E. 53rd St., tel. 212/751–4840) is always open, and the French bistro food's popular all 'round. The **Royal Canadian Pancake House** (1004 2nd Ave. at 53rd St., tel. 212/980–4131) is bound to serve your favorite kind of pancake.

As you go farther north, **Serendipity 3** (225 E. 60th St., tel. 212/838–3531), "the ice cream parlor to the stars," is perfect for a light meal or dessert. **Jackson Hole** (232 E. 64th St., tel. 212/371–7187) is a reliable, pleasant burger joint with branches around town, and the **7th Regiment Mess** (643 Park Ave. between 66th and 67th Sts., tel. 212/744–4107) serves wonderful American fare for families. Central Park's **Boathouse Café** (near 72nd St., tel. 212/517–2233) is somewhat overpriced for the average food, but it's pretty on a spring day.

As you move west, the two highlights are the inevitable **Hard Rock Café** (326 W. 57th St., tel. 212/459–9320) and its rival, **Planet Hollywood** (140 W. 57th St., tel. 212/333–7827). **Mickey Mantle's** (42 Central Park S near 6th Ave., tel. 212/688–7777) also excites, because you never know if the Mick will drop in. The upscale ice cream parlor **Rumpelmayer's** (50 Central Park S near 5th Ave., tel. 212/755–5800) is always popular.

Good bets near Lincoln Center are **The Saloon** (1920 Broadway at 64th St., tel. 212/874–1500), with a long menu and an occasional skating waiter; **Fiorello's Roman Café** (1900 Broadway near 63rd St., tel. 212/595–5330) for individual pizzas and outside seating; and **Vince & Eddie's** (70 W. 68th St., tel. 212/721–

0068). Farther north, try **Sidewalkers** (12 W. 72nd St., tel. 212/799–6070) for buckets of spiced blue crabs; **EJ's Luncheonette** (433 Amsterdam Ave. near 80th St., tel. 212/873–3444); **Amsterdam's** (428 Amsterdam Ave. between 80th and 81st Sts., tel. 212/874–1377), a good-value rotisserie joint; **Presto's** (434 Amsterdam at 81st St., tel. 212/721–9141) for pasta and pizza; **Phoebe's** (380 Columbus Ave. near 78th St., tel. 212/724–5145) for its homey atmosphere; **Lucy's** (503 Columbus Ave. at 84th St., tel. 212/787–3009); and the brasserie-style **Boulevard** (2398 Broadway at 88th St., tel. 212/874–7400), where kids can draw on the tablecloths.

And don't forget the **Steve's Ice Cream** (286 Columbus Ave. at 74th St., tel. 212/496–1325), where Oreo cookies, sprinkles, and other tidbits can be blended into your favorite flavor.

Lodging

Since the vast majority of hotels are in midtown Manhattan, your choice of which neighborhood to pick for a family stay is limited. If anything, it may be best to avoid the environs of seedy Times Square, just in case your offspring escapes alone or gets lost. That said, **Embassy Suites** (*see* Chapter 10), a few blocks from Times Square, is among the best places for families because it has "child-proof" suites available and a complete day-care center. Generally speaking, as in any other big city, most Manhattan hotels will provide an extra bed, baby-sitting, and stroller rental—all the common requirements of families traveling with young children—but calling ahead before you make reservations is a good idea to ascertain how child-friendly your chosen base will turn out to be.

If you prefer to make your own baby-sitting arrangements, rather than leave it to the hotel concierge or housekeeper, the **Babysitters' Guild** (60 E. 42nd St., Suite 912, tel. 212/682–0227), in business for more than 40 years, has a multilingual staff that can take your children on sightseeing tours. Rates start at $10 an hour for one or two children over age two; $12.50 an hour for an infant, plus a $4.50 transportation charge ($7 after midnight); minimum booking is for four hours. Two other reliable agencies, though they cater more to long-term child care than to baby-sitting, are the **Gilbert Child Care Agency** (25 W. 39th St., Suite 700, tel. 212/921–4848) and the **Avalon Registry** (250 W. 57th St., Suite 723, tel. 212/245–0250). If you need a stroller, ask your hotel concierge to find one for you, or contact **AAA-U-Rent** (861 Eagle Ave., Bronx, tel. 718/665–6633).

Good bets for families include, at the top end of the scale, the aforementioned **Embassy Suites** and—largely for their child-pleasing swimming pools, which are rare in Manhattan—the **Holiday Inn Crowne Plaza**, the **Sheraton Manhattan**, the **Vista** and the **UN Plaza–Park Hyatt**. Less costly, any of the **Manhattan Suites East** properties would make an excellent choice, since they resemble tiny apartments. **The San Carlos**'s larger suites likewise have kitchen facilities that enable families to save on restaurant bills, and the hotel is secure. **The Wyndham** large rooms are suitable for families; the **Iroquois**, long the bargain alternative to the Algonquin, is worth considering for its large suites, also with kitchenettes. The **Vanderbilt Y** has some family rooms with two bunk beds apiece for a rock-bottom $88 per night. (*See* Chapter 10 for detailed information about all the hotels mentioned above.)

Or plan ahead for a **bed-and-breakfast** stay (*see* Chapter 10) or a **home exchange** (*see* Traveling with Children in Chapter 1).

The Arts and Entertainment

In New York, theater groups exist just for children, art museums organize special programs, and kids can choose among art classes, summer courses, the circus, music concerts, storytelling, parades, and puppet shows.

Madison Square Garden (7th Ave. between 31st and 33rd Sts., tel. 212/465–6000) offers, besides sports events (*see* Chapter 7), some Disney and *Sesame Street* extravaganzas that appeal especially to children. There are major ice shows in winter, and each spring brings the **Ringling Bros. Barnum & Bailey Circus** (check local newspapers for dates, times, and ticket information) Meanwhile, the **Big Apple Circus** (35 W. 35th St., tel. 212/268–0055) charms the toughest New Yorkers in locations all over the five boroughs during spring and summer and in residence at Lincoln Center from October through January.

Music

The **Little Orchestra Society** (220 W. 42nd St., tel. 212/704–2100) organizes concert series that introduce classical music to children ages 3–5 at Florence Gould Hall (55 E. 59th St.) and ages 6–12 at Lincoln Center; the **Metropolitan Opera** offers its **Growing Up with Opera** program (tel. 212/769–7022). Lincoln Center (tel. 212/875–5400) also sponsors an **Out-of-Doors** summer arts program, with plenty in it for children. The **92nd Street Y** (1395 Lexington Ave., tel. 212/415–5440) and **Brooklyn Academy of Music** (30 Lafayette Ave., tel. 718/636–4100) both organize musical entertainment for young people.

Theater

Hartley House Theater (413 W. 46th St. tel. 212/666–1716) stages classic fairy tales; **Henry Street Settlement** (466 Grand St. between Pitt and Willett Sts., tel. 212/598–0400) has an Arts for Family weekend program; **Little People's Theater** (The Courtyard Playhouse, 39 Grove St. between W. 4th St. and 7th Ave., tel. 212/765–9540) brings fairy tales and nursery rhymes to life on Sunday afternoons; **New York Children's Theater** (Lincoln Sq. Theater, 250 W. 65th St., tel. 212/496–8009) is determinedly realistic in style and explores topics such as literacy and aging; **The Open Eye: New Stagings for Youth** (270 W. 89th St., tel. 212/769–4143) presents both classic and new plays; **Paper Bag Players** (tel. 212/362–0431) performs amusing productions for children ages four through nine, with a winter season at Symphony Space (Broadway at 95th St., tel. 212/864–6400); **Tada!** (120 W. 28th St., tel. 212/627–1732) is a popular children's group with a multiethnic perspective; **Theaterworks/USA** (Promenade Theater, Broadway at 76th St., tel. 212/677–5959) mounts classic stories and original productions about historical figures; **13th Street Theater** (50 W. 13th St., tel. 212/

675–6677) presents its children's offerings on weekends; **Vineyard Theater** (108 E. 15th St. and 309 E. 26th St., tel. 212/353–3366) offers kids' events in December.

Puppet Shows

The International Festival of Puppet Theater, sponsored by the Jim Henson Foundation, takes place in September at the Joseph Papp Public Theater (425 Lafayette St., tel. 212/598–7107); **Marionette Theater** (Swedish Cottage, Central Park at 81st St., tel. 212/988–9093) features Saturday programs; **Puppet Playhouse** (Asphalt Green, 555 E. 90th St., tel. 212/369–8890) offers weekend shows with puppets and marionettes; **Puppetworks** (338 6th Ave., Park Slope, Brooklyn, tel. 718/965–3391) presents marionettes performing classic children's stories on weekends.

Storytelling

Eeyore's Books for Children (2212 Broadway at 79th St., tel. 212/362–0634; 25 E. 83rd St., tel. 212/988–3404) has storytelling hours on weekends, except July–August. **Storyland** (1369 3rd Ave. at 78th St., tel. 212/517–6952) offers weekly story hours on Wednesday, Saturday and Sunday; call ahead for locations.

Film

Several museums sponsor special film programs aimed at families and children, including the **Museum of Modern Art,** the **Museum of Television and Radio** (*see* Tour 1 in Chapter 3), and the **American Museum of the Moving Image** (*see* Tour 22 in Chapter 4). Kids thrill at the amazing nature films shown on the huge screen at the Naturemax Theater (tel. 212/769–5650) at the **American Museum of Natural History** (*see* Tour 8 in Chapter 3). The immaculate **Walter Reade Theater** (70 Lincoln Center Plaza, Broadway at W. 65th St., tel. 212/875–5600) shows films for children on Saturday and sponsors children's film festivals.

6 Sightseeing Checklists

The following checklists organize New York City's attractions by category, so you can supplement sights from the walking tours with related places of interest throughout the five boroughs. They may also help you choose walking tours by showing you which routes include sites that may be related to your own special interests. Attractions that have already been covered in Chapters 3 or 4 include nothing more than a reference to the walking tour in which they appear. Attractions that appear here only are followed by a brief description and useful information.

Museums and Galleries

Abigail Adams Smith Museum. Once the converted carriage house of the home of President John Adams's daughter Abigail and her husband, Colonel William Stephen Smith, this 18th-century treasure is now owned by the Colonial Dames of America. Nine rooms display furniture and articles of the Federal and Empire periods, and an adjoining garden is designed in 18th-century style. *421 E. 61st St., tel. 212/838–6878. Admission: $3 adults, $2 senior citizens and students. Open Mon. and Wed.–Fri. noon–4, Tues. noon–8. Closed Aug.*

Afro Arts Cultural Centre. Artifacts from East, West, North, and Central Africa are on exhibit. *2191 Adam Clayton Powell, Jr., Blvd. (7th Ave.), tel. 212/996–3333. Suggested contribution: $3.75 adults, $2.75 children. Open daily 9–5.*

American Craft Museum. *See* Tour 1 in Chapter 3.

American Museum of the Moving Image. *See* Tour 22 in Chapter 4.

American Museum of Natural History. *See* Tour 8 in Chapter 3.

American Numismatic Society. The society, founded in 1858, displays its vast collection of coins and medals, including many that date back to ancient civilizations, in one of several museums in the Audubon Terrace complex. *Broadway at 155th St., tel. 212/234–3130. Admission free. Open Tues.–Sat. 9–4:30, Sun. 1–4.*

Americas Society. *See* Tour 6 in Chapter 3.

Asia Society. *See* Tour 6 in Chapter 3.

Asian American Arts Center. *See* Tour 16 in Chapter 3.

Black Fashion Museum. *See* Tour 10 in Chapter 3.

Brooklyn Children's Museum. *See* Museums in Chapter 5.

Brooklyn Historical Society. *See* Tour 19 in Chapter 4.

Brooklyn Museum. *See* Tour 20 in Chapter 4.

Children's Museum of Manhattan. *See* Museums in Chapter 5.

China House Gallery (China Institute). A pair of fierce, fat stone lions guards the doorway of this pleasant redbrick town house, where changing public exhibitions of Chinese art are held. *125 E. 65th St., tel. 212/744–8181. Admission: $3. Open Mon.–Sat. 10–5.*

Clocktower Gallery (Institute for Contemporary Art). *See* Tour 18 in Chapter 3.

The Cloisters. Perched atop a wooded hilltop near Manhattan's northernmost tip, the Cloisters houses the Metropolitan Museum of Art's medieval collection in the style of a medieval monastery. Colonnaded walks connect authentic French and Spanish monastic cloisters, a French Romanesque chapel, a 12th-century chapter house, and a Romanesque apse. An entire room is devoted to a superb set of 15th- and 16th-century tapestries depicting a unicorn hunt. The view of the Hudson River and the

New Jersey Palisades (an undeveloped Rockefeller family preserve) enhances the experience. The M–4 "Cloisters–Fort Tryon Park" bus provides a lengthy but scenic ride; catch it along Madison Avenue below 110th Street, or Broadway above; or take the A subway to 190th Street. *Fort Tryon Park, tel. 212/923–3700. Suggested donation: $6 adults, $3 senior citizens and students. Open Tues.–Sun. 9:30–5:15. Closes at 4:45 Nov.–Feb.*

Cooper-Hewitt Museum (Smithsonian Institution's National Museum of Design). *See* Tour 5 in Chapter 3.

Federal Hall National Memorial. *See* Tour 17 in Chapter 3.

Forbes Magazine Galleries. *See* Tour 12 in Chapter 3.

Fraunces Tavern Museum. *See* Tour 17 in Chapter 3.

Frick Collection. *See* Tour 5 in Chapter 3.

Garibaldi-Meucci Museum. Housed in an altered Federal farmhouse, this museum offers letters and photographs describing the life of fiery Italian patriot Giuseppe Garibaldi; it also documents Antonio Meucci's indisputable claim to having invented the telephone before Alexander Graham Bell did. *420 Tompkins Ave., Staten Island, tel. 718/442–1608. Admission free. Open Tues.–Fri. 10–5, weekends 1–5.*

Grolier Club. *See* Tour 6 in Chapter 3.

Guggenheim Museum. *See* Tour 5 in Chapter 3.

Guggenheim Museum SoHo. *See* Tour 14 in Chapter 3.

Guinness World of Records Exhibition. *See* Tour 4 in Chapter 3.

Harbor Defense Museum of New York City. Located at the Brooklyn end of the Verrazano-Narrows Bridge in Fort Hamilton, an active military base, this museum features small arms, uniforms, artillery equipment dating to the 18th century, and an array of military miniatures. *Bldg. 230, Fort Hamilton, Brooklyn, tel. 718/630–4349. Admission free. Open Mon.–Fri. 1–4.*

Hayden Planetarium. *See* Tour 8 in Chapter 3.

Hispanic Society of America. An extensive collection of ancient and modern Hispanic paintings, sculpture, and decorative arts is housed in a richly appointed building. *Broadway at 155th St., tel. 212/926–2234. Admission free. Open Tues.–Sat. 10–4:30, Sun. 1–4. Closed holidays.*

IBM Gallery of Science and Art. *See* Tour 2 in Chapter 3.

ICP Mid-Town. *See* Tour 3 in Chapter 3.

International Center of Photography. *See* Tour 5 in Chapter 3.

***Intrepid* Sea-Air-Space Museum.** *See* Museums in Chapter 5.

Isamu Noguchi Garden Museum. *See* Tour 22 in Chapter 4.

Japan Society Gallery. This wonderfully serene setting holds exhibitions from well-known Japanese and American museums, as well as private collections. Also offered are movies, lectures, classes, concerts, and dramatic performances. *333 E. 47th St., tel. 212/832–1155. Suggested donation: $2.50. Open Tues.–Sun. 11–5, but only when shows are installed.*

Jewish Museum. *See* Tour 5 in Chapter 3.

Library and Museum of the Performing Arts (New York Public Library at Lincoln Center). *See* Tour 8 in Chapter 3.

Lower East Side Tenement Museum. America's first urban "living-history" museum preserves and interprets the life of immigrants and migrants in New York's Lower East Side. Models of Hester Street, Little Italy, and Chinatown are featured. Gallery exhibits, walking tours, and dramatic performances are offered. *97 Orchard St., tel. 212/431–0233. Suggested donation: $2. Tours: $12 adults, $10 students and senior citizens. Open Tues.–Fri. 11–4.*

Marchais Center of Tibetan Art. One of the largest private, non-profit collections of Tibetan sculpture, scrolls, and paintings outside of Tibet is displayed in a museum resembling a Tibetan temple. Try to visit on a day when the monks bless the temple—and you. *338 Lighthouse Ave., Staten Island, tel. 718/987–3478. Admission: $3 adults, $2.50 senior citizens, $1 children; occasionally, an additional $2 charge for special Sun. programs. Open Apr.–Nov., Wed.–Sun. 1–5; Dec.–Mar., by appointment.*

Metropolitan Museum of Art. *See* Tour 5 in Chapter 3.

Municipal Art Society. A revolving series of exhibitions at this midtown gallery illuminates the art and architecture of the city. *457 Madison Ave. at 50th St., tel. 212/935–3960. Admission free. Open Mon.–Wed., Fri.–Sat. 11–5.*

Museo del Barrio. *See* Tour 5 in Chapter 3.

Museum for African Art. *See* Tour 14 in Chapter 3.

Museum of American Financial History. On the site of Alexander Hamilton's law office (today the Standard Oil Building), this one-room museum displays artifacts of the financial markets' history, including a vintage ticker-tape machine. *24 Broadway, tel. 212/908–4519. Admission free. Open weekdays 11:30–2:30 or by appointment.*

Museum of American Folk Art. *See* Tour 8 in Chapter 3.

Museum of Colored Glass and Light. *See* Tour 14 in Chapter 3.

Museum of Television and Radio. *See* Tour 1 in Chapter 3.

Museum of the City of New York. *See* Tour 5 in Chapter 3.

Museum of Modern Art. *See* Tour 1 in Chapter 3.

National Academy of Design. *See* Tour 5 in Chapter 3.

National Museum of the American Indian (Smithsonian Institution). What began as the private collection of George Gustav Heye has grown into the largest grouping of Native American materials in the world. Various exhibits are devoted to North, Central, and South American Indians. Its artifact collection, spanning more than 10,000 years, covers the entire Western Hemisphere. In the fall of 1994, the museum will move downtown to the Alexander Hamilton Customs House (*see* Tour 17 in Chapter 3), where it will be called the George Gustav Heye Center. *3753 Broadway at 155th St., tel. 212/283–2420. Admission: $3 adults, $2 students and senior citizens, children under 7 free. Open Tues.–Sat. 10–5, Sun. 1–5.*

New Museum of Contemporary Art. *See* Tour 14 in Chapter 3.

New York City Fire Museum. Hand-pulled and horse-drawn apparatus, engines, sliding poles, uniforms, and fireboat equipment are featured in this comprehensive collection of authentic fire-fighting tools from the 18th, 19th, and 20th centuries. *278 Spring St., tel. 212/691–1303. Suggested donation: $3 adults, 50¢ children. Open Tues.–Sat. 10–4. Closed Sun., Mon., and holidays.*

New York City Transit Museum. A converted 1930s subway station displays 18 restored classic subway cars and has an operating signal tower. *Boerum Pl. at Schermerhorn St., Brooklyn Heights, tel. 718/330–3060. Admission: $3 adults, $1.50 senior citizens and children. Open Tues.–Fri. 10–4, Sat.–Sun. 11–4.*

New York Hall of Science. *See* Museums in Chapter 5.

Nicholas Roerich Museum. Housed in an Upper West Side town house (built in 1898), this small, eccentric museum displays the work of the Russian artist who, among many other things, designed sets for Diaghilev ballets. Vast paintings of the Himalayas are a focal point of the collection. *319 W. 107th St., tel. 212/864–7752. Admission free. Open Tues.–Sun. 2–5.*

North Wind Undersea Museum. *See* Off the Beaten Track in Chapter 4.

Pierpont Morgan Library. *See* Tour 4 in Chapter 3.

Police Academy Museum. The second floor of the city's police academy is full of law-enforcement memorabilia—uniforms, firearms, batons, badges, even counterfeit money—dating back to the time of the Dutch. *235 E. 20th St., tel. 212/477–9753. Admission free. Open weekdays 9–3, large groups by appointment.*

P.S. 1 Museum. *See* Tour 21 in Chapter 4.

Queens Historical Society (Kingsland Homestead). *See* Off the Beaten Track in Chapter 4.

Queens Museum. In Flushing Meadows–Corona Park, at the end of the World's Fair mall, this museum is housed in what was the New York City Pavilion for the 1939 fair. Its most notable exhibit is the recently restored Panorama, a 9,355-square-foot architectural model of New York City's five boroughs. *Tel. 718/592–2405. Suggested donation: $3 adults, $1.50 senior citizens, students, and children over 5. Open Tues.–Fri. 10–5, weekends noon–5.*

Schomburg Center for Research in Black Culture (New York Public Library). *See* Tour 10 in Chapter 3.

Snug Harbor Cultural Center. *See* Tour 24 in Chapter 4.

Society of Illustrators Museum of American Illustration. A 1,000-piece collection features contemporary and historical works. Solo, group, and themed shows are exhibited. *128 E. 63rd St., tel. 212/838–2560. Admission free. Open weekdays 10–5, Tues. 10–8.*

South Street Seaport Museum. *See* Tour 18 in Chapter 3.

Staten Island Children's Museum. *See* Tour 24 in Chapter 4.

Staten Island Historical Society Museum. *See* Tour 24 in Chapter 4.

Studio Museum in Harlem. *See* Tour 10 in Chapter 3.

Ukrainian Museum. *See* Tour 13 in Chapter 3.

Urban Center. Exhibits on architecture, urban design, and historic preservation are housed in the north wing of the Villard Houses, at the foot of the New York Palace Hotel. *457 Madison Ave. between 50th and 51st Sts., tel. 212/935–3960. Admission free. Open Mon.–Wed., Fri. and Sat. 11–5.*

Whitney Museum of American Art. *See* Tour 5 in Chapter 3.

Whitney Museum of American Art at Philip Morris. *See* Tour 3 in Chapter 3.

Architectural Landmarks

Alexander Hamilton Customs House (1907, Cass Gilbert). *See* Tour 17 in Chapter 3.

American Telephone & Telegraph Building (1983, Philip Johnson and John Burgee). Now occupied by the Sony Corporation, this rose granite postmodern skyscraper is distinguished on the skyline by its pediment roofline, shaped like a Chippendale cabinet top. *Madison Ave. at 55th St.*

Bayard Building (1898, Louis Sullivan). Built in 1898 as the Condict Building, this is the only structure in New York City designed by Louis Sullivan, one of the Chicago School's leading architects. Its simplicity and emphatic vertical lines made it radically different from the then-prevailing Beaux Arts style in New York. *65–69 Bleecker St. near Lafayette St.*

Carnegie Hall (1891, William B. Tuthill). *See* Tour 2 in Chapter 3.

Chrysler Building (1929, William Van Alen). *See* Tour 3 in Chapter 3.

Citicorp Center (1977, H. Stubbins & E. Roth). *See* Tour 1 in Chapter 3.

City Hall (1812, Mangin, McComb). *See* Tour 18 in Chapter 3.

Dakota Apartments (1884, Henry J. Hardenbergh). *See* Tour 8 in Chapter 3.

Empire State Building (1931, Shreve, Lamb, Harmon). *See* Tour 4 in Chapter 3.

Flatiron Building (1902, Daniel H. Burnham). *See* Tour 4 in Chapter 3.

GE Building, formerly the **RCA Building** (1933, Raymond Hood). *See* Tour 1 in Chapter 3.

Grand Central Terminal (1913, Warren & Wetmore, Reed & Stem). *See* Tour 3 in Chapter 3.

Guggenheim Museum (1959, Frank Lloyd Wright). *See* Tour 5 in Chapter 3.

Haughwout Building (1857, John P. Gaynor). *See* Tour 14 in Chapter 3.

Jacob K. Javits Convention Center (1986, I. M. Pei). The largest of its kind in the Western Hemisphere, the center contains 1.8 million gross square feet set on a 22-acre, five-block site. The glassed-in entry lets in lots of sky, earning it the nickname the Crystal Palace. *11th Ave. at 35th St.*

Lever House (1952, Skidmore, Owings & Merrill). *See* Tour 1 in Chapter 3.

Metropolitan Life Building (1963, Emery Roth & Sons, Pietro Belluschi, and Walter Gropius). What began as the notorious Pan Am Building—detested not only for its faceted walls of precast concrete but also for the fact it shuts off the light from much of Park Avenue—is now considered a stately-looking 59-story monolith. (Its construction was largely responsible for Grand Central Terminal's receiving its protected landmark status in 1965.) *200 Park Ave. at 45th St.*

New York Public Library (1911, Carrere & Hastings). *See* Tour 3 in Chapter 3.

Plaza Hotel (1907, Henry J. Hardenbergh). *See* Tour 2 in Chapter 3.

Seagram Building (1958, Mies van der Rohe with Philip Johnson). *See* Tour 1 in Chapter 3.

United Nations (1953, Wallace K. Harrison and international committee). *See* Tour 3 in Chapter 3.

Villard Houses (1886, McKim, Mead & White). Now part of the New York Palace hotel, these three brownstone mansions, conceived by newspaper publisher Henry Villard, form an early Italian Renaissance–style courtyard set off by elaborate ironwork. Many of the original interior spaces remain in prime condition. *Madison Ave. at 50th St.*

Woolworth Building (1913, Cass Gilbert). *See* Tour 17 in Chapter 3.

World Financial Center (1989, Cesar Pelli). *See* Tour 17 in Chapter 3.

World Trade Center (1977, Yamasaki & Roth). *See* Tour 17 in Chapter 3.

Worldwide Plaza (1989, Skidmore, Owings, & Merrill and Frank Williams). This massive, rose-colored multiuse complex sits on the border between Hell's Kitchen and midtown, on the former site of the second Madison Square Garden. An impressive office tower on Eighth Avenue is followed by a pleasing midblock plaza with a fountain; lower-scaled residential units and movie theaters fill the block through to Ninth Avenue. *50th–51st Sts. between 8th and 9th Aves.*

Historical Sites

Bartow-Pell Mansion. This Federal-style building with a Greek Revival interior restoration—and sunken gardens, period furnishings, paintings, and a 200-volume library—was built in 1842. *895 Shore Rd. N, Pelham Bay Park, Bronx, tel. 718/885–1461. Admission: $2 adults, $1 senior citizens. Open Wed. and weekends noon–4.*

Bowne House. *See* Off the Beaten Track in Chapter 4.

Castle Clinton. *See* Tour 17 in Chapter 3.

Edgar Allan Poe Cottage. *See* Tour 23 in Chapter 4.

Ellis Island. *See* Tour 17 in Chapter 3.

Fraunces Tavern. *See* Tour 17 in Chapter 3.

Gracie Mansion. *See* Tour 6 in Chapter 3.

Kingsland Homestead. See Off the Beaten Track in Chapter 4.

Morris-Jumel Mansion. In 1776 George Washington spent six weeks at this hilltop house, built in 1765. His office can still be seen in what is Manhattan's oldest residence. *1765 Jumel Terr., 160th St. west of Edgecombe Ave., tel. 212/923–8008. Admission: $3 adults, $2 senior citizens and students. Open Tues.–Sun. 10–4.*

New York Stock Exchange. *See* Tour 17 in Chapter 3.

Old Merchant's House. *See* Tour 13 in Chapter 3.

Radio City Music Hall. *See* Tour 1 in Chapter 3.

Richmondtown Restoration. *See* Tour 24 in Chapter 4.

South Street Seaport. *See* Tour 18 in Chapter 3.

Theodore Roosevelt Birthplace. *See* Tour 4 in Chapter 3.

Van Cortlandt Museum. This 1748 house is full of furnishings and household goods that reflect both its Dutch and British owners. It's now run by the National Society of Colonial Dames. *Broadway at 246th St., Bronx, tel. 718/543–3344. Admission: $2 adults, $1.50 senior citizens and students. Open Tues.–Fri. 10–3, Sat.–Sun. 11–4.*

Wave Hill. *See* Off the Beaten Track in Chapter 4.

Churches and Temples

Abyssinian Baptist Church (Baptist). *See* Tour 10 in Chapter 3.

Brotherhood Synagogue (Conservative Jewish). *See* Tour 4 in Chapter 3.

Cathedral of St. John the Divine (Episcopal). *See* Tour 9 in Chapter 3.

Central Synagogue (Reform Jewish). Built in 1872, this Moorish-style temple is the oldest continually used synagogue building in the city. Note its onion-domed exterior and colorfully stenciled interior. *652 Lexington Ave. at 55th St.*

Church of Our Lady of Pompeii (Roman Catholic). *See* Tour 12 in Chapter 3.

Fifth Avenue Synagogue (Orthodox Jewish). *See* Tour 6 in Chapter 3.

Friends Meeting House (Quaker). *See* Off the Beaten Track in Chapter 4.

Grace Church (Episcopal). This fine mid-19th-century example of an English Gothic Revival church, the site of many society weddings (including that of the P.T. Barnum show member Tom Thumb), is set in a small green yard in Greenwich Village. Topped by a finely ornamented octagonal marble spire, this design by James Renwick, Jr., has some excellent pre-Raphaelite stained-glass windows inside. *802 Broadway at E. 10th St.*

Islamic Cultural Center of New York (Islamic). This stunning gray granite mosque looks sleek and contemporary under its vast copper dome, a slender minaret rising to the side. *1711 3rd Ave. at 97th St.*

John Street Methodist (United Methodist). *See* Tour 17 in Chapter 3.

Little Church Around the Corner (Church of the Transfiguration) (Episcopal). *See* Tour 4 in Chapter 3.

Marble Collegiate (Reformed). *See* Tour 4 in Chapter 3.

Riverside Church (Interdenominational). *See* Tour 9 in Chapter 3.

Spanish & Portuguese Synagogue, Shearith Israel (Orthodox Jewish). Built in 1897, this is the fifth home of the oldest Jewish congregation in the United States, founded in 1654. The adjoining "Little Synagogue" is a replica of Shearith Israel's Georgian-style first synagogue. *8 W. 70th St.*

St. Bartholomew's (Episcopal). *See* Tour 1 in Chapter 3.

St. Luke's-in-the-Fields (Episcopal). *See* Tour 12 in Chapter 3.

St. Mark's-in-the-Bowery (Episcopal). *See* Tour 13 in Chapter 3.

St. Patrick's Cathedral (Roman Catholic). *See* Tour 2 in Chapter 3.

St. Paul's Chapel (Episcopal). *See* Tour 17 in Chapter 3.

St. Paul's Chapel at Columbia University (Nondenominational). *See* Tour 9 in Chapter 3.

Temple Emanu-El (Reform Jewish). *See* Tour 6 in Chapter 3.

Trinity Church (Episcopal). *See* Tour 17 in Chapter 3.

Parks and Gardens

Battery Park. *See* Tour 17 in Chapter 3.
Brooklyn Botanic Gardens. *See* Tour 20 in Chapter 4.
Carl Schurz Park. *See* Tour 6 in Chapter 3.
Central Park. *See* Tour 7 in Chapter 3.
Flushing Meadows–Corona Park. Running from Flushing Bay to the Grand Central Parkway, this large Queens park offers a marina, boats, a carousel, bicycling paths, an indoor ice-skating rink, picnic grounds, a swimming pool, a zoo, and theaters and museums, not to mention **Shea Stadium,** home of the New York Mets, and the U. S. **Tennis Association National Tennis Center** (*see* Chapter 7). The park was the site of both the 1939 and 1964 World's Fair, and several structures from those expositions remain, including the **Unisphere,** a 380-ton steel globe, and the 1939 New York Pavilion (now home to the **Queens Museum**).

Fort Tryon Park. At the northern tip of Manhattan, high over the Hudson, this park offers stunning views of the Palisades, plus an attractive though somewhat wild garden. It also contains the Cloisters (*see* Museums and Galleries, *above*).

Jamaica Bay Wildlife Refuge. Part of the National Gateway Recreation Area, a series of parks sprawling across Brooklyn and Staten Island around the mouth of New York Harbor, this large refuge offers temporary accommodations for migrating birds, plus nature trails around ponds and wooded uplands and through marshes. Stop in the visitor center (Crossbay Blvd.,

Broad Channel, Queens, tel. 718/474–0613; open daily 8–5) for a free permit to explore the refuge.

Kissena Park. Located in southwest Flushing, Queens, this park protects precious acres of original Long Island forests and marshland, demonstrating to visitors what the area looked like 100,000 years ago. Visitors can enjoy the new walking trails. *Tel. 718/353–1047.*

New York Botanical Garden. *See* Tour 23 in Chapter 4.

Pelham Bay Park. With more than 2,000 acres, this Bronx park is the largest in the city. Purchased by Thomas Pell from the Indians in 1654, its facilities include a mile-long beach, nature paths, a canoe launch, bridle path and riding academy, fishing, picnic grounds, and tennis courts.

Prospect Park. *See* Tour 20 in Chapter 4.

Riverside Park. *See* Tours 8 and 9 in Chapter 3.

Staten Island Botanical Gardens. *See* Tour 24 in Chapter 4.

United Nations Rose Garden. *See* Tour 3 in Chapter 3.

Van Cortlandt Park. Located on 2 square miles of the north-central Bronx, this park includes facilities for tennis, swimming, running, baseball, soccer, cricket, and rugby. The nation's oldest municipal golf course is here, as is Van Cortlandt Museum (*see* Historical Sites, *above*).

Washington Market Park. *See* Tour 14 in Chapter 3.

Zoos

Aquarium for Wildlife Conservation. *See* Zoos in Chapter 5.

Bronx Zoo (International Wildlife Conservation Park) & Children's Zoo. *See* Tour 23 in Chapter 4.

Central Park Zoo (Central Park Wildlife Conservation Center) & Children's Zoo. *See* Tour 7 in Chapter 3.

Prospect Park Zoo (Prospect Park Wildlife Conservation Center). *See* Tour 20 in Chapter 4.

Queens Zoo (Queens Wildlife Conservation Center). *See* Zoos in Chapter 5.

Staten Island Zoo. *See* Zoos in Chapter 5.

7   Sports, Fitness, Beaches

By Karen Cure

Updated by Peter Filichia

New Yorkers think the out-of-doors is a wonderful place, and they are stopped by nothing in their passion for their sports: You can see them jogging in the park when it's sleeting, or heading for the tennis bubble on the most blustery of Sunday winter afternoons. From boccie to croquet, no matter how esoteric the sport, there's a place to pursue it in New York. You'll find oases of greenery you'd never imagine here (13% of the city, in fact, is parkland). And if you strike up a conversation while waiting to rent a boat or a bike at the Loeb Boathouse, or while stretching before a jog around the Reservoir in Central Park, you'll discover a friendly, relaxed side of New Yorkers that you might not otherwise get the chance to see.

Just one word before you set out: Weekends are very busy. If you need to rent equipment or secure specific space—for instance, a tennis court—go very early or be prepared to wait.

Spectator Sports

Many events described below take place at **Madison Square Garden** (7th Ave. between 31st and 33rd Sts.); tickets can be ordered by phone through the box office (tel. 212/465–6000) or Ticketmaster (tel. 212/307–7171). The area's other major sports venue is across the Hudson River at the **Meadowlands** (Rte. 3, East Rutherford, NJ; for box office and information, tel. 201/935–3900). Even when events are sold out, you can often pick up a pair of tickets on the day of the game outside the venue, either from a scalper or from a fellow sports fan whose guests couldn't make it at the last minute. Ticket agencies, listed in the Manhattan yellow-pages phone directory and the sports pages of *The Daily News* and *New York Newsday*, can be helpful—for a price.

Baseball

The **New York Mets** play at Shea Stadium (tel. 718/507–8499, or call Ticketmaster at 212/307–6387), at the penultimate stop on the No. 7 subway in Flushing, Queens. Yankee Stadium (tel. 718/293–6000), accessible by the No. 4, D, or C subway to the 161st Street station in the Bronx, is the home of the **New York Yankees.** Baseball season runs from April through October.

Basketball

Only recently have the **New York Knickerbockers** (the "Knicks") aroused any hometown passion, but the team turnaround has made tickets for home games at Madison Square Garden hard to come by. For up-to-date game roundups, phone the New York Knickerbockers Hot Line (tel. 212/465–5867). Another NBA team, the **New Jersey Nets,** plays at the Meadowlands in the Brendan Byrne Arena. Basketball season is late October–April.

Boxing and Wrestling

The *Daily News*'s annual Golden Gloves **boxing** bout and other major competitions are staged in Madison Square Garden. **Wrestling,** a more frequent Garden presence since the days of "Gorgeous" George and "Haystack" Calhoun in the late '50s, is stagy and outrageous, drawing a rowdy but enthusiastic crowd.

Football

The **New York Giants** and the **New York Jets** play September–December at Giants Stadium in East Rutherford, New Jersey (tel. 201/935–8111 for the Giants; 516/538–6600 for the Jets). All seats for Giants games and most for Jets games are sold on a season-ticket basis, and there's a waiting list for those; remaining Jets tickets for scattered singles are snapped up almost as soon as they go on sale in August. The **Columbia Lions** (tel. 212/854–1754) of Columbia University may traditionally be college football's least successful team (losing streaks have been known to hit 40-plus games), but a fan can still revel in the charms of Ivy League tradition some Saturday afternoons at Columbia's Wein Stadium each September through November.

Hockey

The **New York Rangers** play at Madison Square Garden (tel. 212/465–6741); the **New York Islanders** at Nassau Veterans Memorial Coliseum in Uniondale, Long Island (for tickets call 516/888–9000); and the **New Jersey Devils** at the Brendan Byrne Arena at the Meadowlands. Tickets for the Islanders and Devils are usually available at game time; Rangers tickets are a more difficult ducat. The hockey season runs from October through April.

Horse Racing

Thoroughbreds Modern **Aqueduct Racetrack** (Rockaway Blvd., Ozone Park, Queens), with its spate of new lawns and gardens, holds races late October–early May. The action moves in May to **Belmont Park** (Hempstead Turnpike, Elmont, Long Island), home of the third jewel in horse racing's triple crown, the Belmont Stakes. Horses run here May–July; then after a few weeks upstate at Saratoga, they return to Belmont from late August through October. Races are held Wednesday–Monday. For information on the New York tracks, call 718/641–4700.

The **Meadowlands** (East Rutherford, NJ, tel. 201/935–8500), generally a trotting venue, also has a flat track season from Labor Day through December.

Standardbreds **Yonkers Raceway** (Central Ave., Yonkers, NY, tel. 718/562–9500) features harness racing daily year-round.

The **Meadowlands** (East Rutherford, NJ, tel. 201/935–8500) runs both trotters and pacers January–mid-August.

Running

The **New York City Marathon** has taken place annually on a Sunday in early November since 1970, and New Yorkers love to cheer on the pack of 25,000 (some 16,000 of them finish). Racewalkers, "jogglers," oldsters, youngsters, and disabled competitors help to make this what former Olympic Organizing Committee president Peter V. Ueberroth called "the best sporting event in the country." Spectators line rooftops and sidewalks, promenades, and terraces all along the route—but don't go near the finishing line in Central Park around 2 PM unless you relish mob scenes.

Tennis

The annual **U.S. Open,** held from late August through early September at the U.S.T.A. National Tennis Center, is one of the high points of the tennis buff's year, and tickets to watch the late rounds are some of the hottest in town. Early-round matches are entertaining, too, and with a stadium court ticket you can also view matches in outlying courts—where the bleachers are so close you can almost count the sweat beads on the players' foreheads—and in the grandstand, where bleacher seating is first-come, first-served. During early rounds, ushers may help you move down to better seats in the stadium court or the grandstand (you may wish to consider giving a gratuity of $5 or $10). Wherever you sit, the attractive crowd of casual visitors, tennis groupies, and celebrities makes for terrific people-watching. The U.S. Tennis Association (Flushing Meadows–Corona Park, Flushing, NY 11368, tel. 718/271–5100) sells tickets by mail beginning in May.

The tennis year winds up in Madison Square Garden with the **Virginia Slims Tournament,** a major women's pro event in mid-November (tel. 212/465–6500), with tickets on sale beginning in September.

Participant Sports

Bicycling

Although it's a problem to keep a bicycle in most Manhattan apartments, that doesn't affect the popularity of the sport here. A sleek pack of dedicated racers zooms around Central Park at dawn and at dusk daily, and on weekends, parks swarm with recreational cyclists. **Central Park**'s circular drive is closed to traffic from 10 AM to 3 PM and 7 to 10 PM on weekdays, and from 7 PM Friday to 6 AM Monday. On holidays, it's closed from 8 PM the night before until 6 AM the day after. In **Riverside Park,** the promenade between 72nd and 110th streets, with its Hudson River view, gets a more easygoing crowd. Other good bets: the **Wall Street** area, deserted on weekends; the Hudson-view **Battery Park Esplanade;** or the winding roads in Brooklyn's **Prospect Park,** also closed to cars.

Bike Rentals Expect to leave a deposit or a credit card at the following: **AAA Bikes in Central Park** (Loeb Boathouse, mid-park near East 74th St., tel. 212/861–4137); **85th Street Bicycles** (204 E. 85th St., tel. 212/722–2201); **Gene's Bicycles** (242 E. 79th St., tel. 212/249–9218); **Metro Bicycles** (1311 Lexington Ave. at 88th St., tel. 212/427–4450); or **Pedal Pusher** (1306 2nd Ave. between 68th and 69th Sts., tel. 212/288–5592). Some rent only 3-speeds; others have 10-speeds as well.

Group Trips For organized rides with other cyclists, call or write these organizations a few weeks before you come to New York: **Country Cycling Tours** (140 W. 83rd St., 10024, tel. 212/874–5151) and **Staten Island Bicycling Association** (1/5 Stuyvesant St., tel. 718/273–0805). Support vans are almost always offered in case you get tired.

Billiards

It used to be that pool halls were dusty, grimy, sticky places—
and there are still a few of those around. But they've been
joined by a group of oh-so-chic spots with deluxe decor, high
prices, and even classical music or jazz in the background. The
halls listed below are usually open late into the night, but it's
best to call ahead for closin յ hours.

Amsterdam Billiard Club, (344 Amsterdam Ave., between 76th
and 77th Sts., tel. 212/496–8180).
Billiard Club (220 W. 19th St., tel. 212/206–7665).
Chelsea Billiards (54 W. 21st St., tel. 212/989–0096).
Julian's Billiards (138 E. 14th St., tel. 212/475–9338).
Klipper Klub (636 6th Ave. at 19th St., tel. 212/924–5151).
Sharky's Billiards (10 E. 21st St., tel. 212/529–8600).
SoHo Billiards Sports Center (298 Mulberry St. at Mott and
Houston Sts., tel. 212/925–3753).
West Side Billiards Center (601 W. 50th St., tel. 212/246–1060).

Bird-Watching

Manhattan's green parks and woodlands provide habitat for
thousands of birds, everything from summer tanagers and
fork-tailed flycatchers to Kentucky warblers and common
nighthawks. Since the city is on the Atlantic flyway, a major
migratory route, you can see birds that nest as far north as the
High Arctic. May is the best season, since the songbirds are in
their freshest colors—and so many are singing at once that you
can hardly distinguish their songs. To find out what's been seen
where, call the Rare Bird Alert (tel. 212/979–3070). For information on best bird-watching spots in various parks, call the
Urban Park Rangers, a uniformed division of the Parks Department: Manhattan (tel. 212/427–4040); the Bronx (tel. 718/548–
7070); Brooklyn (tel. 718/287–3400); Queens (tel. 718/699–
4204); and Staten Island (tel. 718/667–6042).

Good bets include 1,146-acre **Van Cortlandt Park** in the Bronx,
with its freshwater marshes and upland woods. In Brooklyn
there are 526-acre **Prospect Park** and **Green-Wood Cemetery**
(call superintendent at 718/768–7300 for permission to enter
grounds). The Ramble in Manhattan's **Central Park** is another
prime spot. In Queens, try **Jamaica Bay Wildlife Refuge,** 9,155
acres of salt marshes, fresh and brackish ponds, and open water (stop by visitor center, Crossbay Blvd., Broad Channel,
Queens, tel. 718/474–0613, to get permit). In Staten Island,
head for the fairly undeveloped 317-acre **Wolfe's Pond Park,**
where the pond and the nearby shore can be dense with geese
and ducks during the annual migrations.

Guided Walks The **New York City Audubon Society** (71 W. 23rd, tel. 212/691–
7483) has occasional bird-watching outings; call 1–4 PM for
information. Also check with the **Urban Park Rangers** at the
numbers listed above.

Boating

The boating available on New York City's ponds and lakes con-
jures up 19th-century images of a parasol-twirling lady being
rowed by her swain. But there's a huge demand for it, and on
weekends you'd better go early or be prepared to wait.

In **Central Park,** the boats are rowboats (plus one Venetian gondola for nighttime glides in the moonlight) and the rowing terrain is the 18-acre Central Park Lake. Rent your boat at **Loeb Boathouse** (tel. 212/517–4723), near 74th Street, from spring through fall.

Boccie

This pinless Italian version of bowling thrives in New York, with 100 city courts in the five boroughs. The easiest to get to from midtown are at 96th Street and First Avenue; at East River Drive and 42nd Street; and at the Thompson Street Playground (at Houston St.) in Greenwich Village. There's also a boccie court at **Il Vagabondo,** (351 E. 62nd St., tel. 212/832–9221), a vintage Italian restaurant east of Bloomingdale's, and at **Villa LuLu** (235 Park Ave. S at 19th St., tel. 212/529–4770), a lively Italian restaurant fairly new to the downtown area.

Bowling

Standard American-style bowling refuses to flourish in Manhattan, so your options are more limited. The **Leisure Time Bowling Recreation Center** (625 8th Ave. at 42nd St., tel. 212/268–6909) offers 30 lanes on the second floor of the Port Authority Bus Terminal. **Bowlmor** (110 University Pl., tel. 212/255–8188) is a funky 44-lane operation frequented by a colorful Village crowd.

Chess and Checkers

Central Park's Chess & Checkers House is picturesquely situated atop a massive stone outcrop. Ten tables are available for indoor play on weekends, 11:30–4:30, and 24 outdoor tables are available during all daylight hours. Pick up playing pieces at the **Dairy** (mid-park at 64th St., tel. 212/794–6565) 11–4 daily; there is no charge, but a deposit is required.

Downtown in Greenwich Village, the **Village Chess Shop** (230 Thompson St., tel. 212/475–9580) is always an active spot. Uptown, the **Manhattan Chess Club** (353 W. 46th St., tel. 212/333–5888) sponsors tournaments and exhibitions; instruction is available on both beginning and intermediate levels.

Golf

Many New Yorkers are avid golfers, and on weekends they jam the handful of verdant, well-kept city courses.

Bethpage State Park (tel. 516/249–8917), in the Long Island town of Bethpage, about one hour and 20 minutes from Manhattan, is home to five golf courses, including its 7,065-yard par-71 Black, generally ranked among the nation's top 25 public courses. Reservations for tee times are not accepted; on weekends and Monday, the line starts forming at midnight for the Black course's tee-time tickets to go on sale at 4 AM. It's not so congested on other days, or on the other four courses on the property.

Of the 13 city courses, the 6,585-yard Split Rock in **Pelham Bay Park,** the Bronx, is considered the most challenging (tel. 718/885–1258). Slightly easier is its sister course, the 6,405-yard

Pelham, which has fewer trees to contend with. **Van Cortlandt Park** has the nation's first municipal golf course, established in 1895—the hilly 6,052-yard Van Cortlandt (tel. 718/543–4595). Queens has a 5,431-yard course at **Forest Park** in Woodhaven (Park La. S and Forest Pkwy., tel. 718/296–0999); Staten Island has the 5,891-yard **Silver Lake** (915 Victory Blvd. one block south of Forest Ave., tel. 718/447–5686).

Driving Range In midtown Manhattan you can practice your swing in netted cages, with bull's-eye backdrops, at the **Richard Metz Golf Studio** (425 Madison Ave. at 49th St., 3rd floor, tel. 212/759–6940). **Midtown Golf Club** (7 W. 45th St., tel. 212/869–3636) offers netted cages, golf simulators, and putting greens.

Miniature Golf Putting courses are at **Gotham Miniature Golf** (at Wollman Rink, Central Park near 64th St., tel. 212/517–4800), where, from late April through early October, putters maneuver outdoors around scale models of city landmarks.

Horseback Riding

A trot on the bridle path around Central Park's Reservoir, renovated in 1987, provides a pleasant look at New York. The carefully run **Claremont Riding Academy** (175 W. 89th St., tel. 212/724–5100) is the city's oldest riding academy and the only riding stable left in Manhattan. Private lessons, including dressage, are available at beginner through advanced levels, for $35 per half hour. Experienced riders can rent horses, at $33 per hour, for a walk, trot, or canter (but not a gallop) in nearby Central Park; call ahead to reserve.

Hotel Health Clubs

Although space is tight in Manhattan hotels, most of them offer some kind of fitness facility, even if it's just an arrangement enabling guests to use a nearby health club (*see* Chapter 10). These hotels have some of the better on-premises workout centers for their guests:

Doral Fitness Center (90 Park Ave., tel. 212/370–9692), available to guests of the **Doral Park Avenue, Doral Court,** and **Doral Tuscany.** This serious health club offers a number of workout programs, including one-on-one training, aerobic equipment, and Nautilus and Eagle equipment.

Holiday Inn Crowne Plaza (1605 Broadway at 49th St., tel. 212/977–4000) has a facility operated by the New York Sports Club. Features include a lap pool, fitness and cardiovascular equipment, and an aerobics studio.

The Peninsula (700 5th Ave., tel. 212/247–2200) reserves floors 21–23 for its health club, with a pool on the 22nd floor, plus exercise machines and a poolside dining terrace.

Sheraton Manhattan (790 7th Ave. at 51st St., tel. 212/581–3300) has a health club with a large pool, aerobic and aquatic exercise equipment, swimming lessons, and a sun deck.

U.N. Plaza (1 United Nations Plaza, tel. 212/355–3400; health club tel. 212/702–5016) combines a handsome pool with a roomful of exercise machines.

Vanderbilt YMCA (224 E. 47th St., tel. 212/755–2410) offers guests access to the Y's athletic facilities—pools, gym, running track, weight room, machines, and exercise classes.

New York Vista (3 World Trade Ctr., tel. 212/938–9100) has a pool, an exercise area, and a running track.

The Waldorf-Astoria (301 Park Ave., tel. 212/355–3000) provides one-on-one training, aerobics and resistance equipment, massage therapy, and a steam room.

Ice Skating

Each of the city's rinks has its own character, but all have scheduled skating sessions, with the surfaces tended between times. Lockers, skate rentals, music, and snack bars complete the picture. Major rinks include the one in **Rockefeller Center** (50th St. at 5th Ave., lower plaza, tel. 212/757–5730), postage-stamp size and utterly romantic, especially when the enormous Christmas tree towers above it; **Sky Rink** (450 W. 33rd St., 16th floor, tel. 212/239–8385), the city's biggest indoor skating spot and its only year-round rink; and the beautifully situated **Wollman Memorial Rink** (6th Ave. at 59th St., tel. 212/517–4800). Be prepared for crowds on weekends.

Jogging and Racewalking

Jogging   In New York, lawyers jog, doctors jog, investment bankers jog, antiques dealers jog, and mothers jog (sometimes pushing their toddlers ahead of them in speedy Baby Jogger strollers). Publicity notwithstanding, crime is not a problem as long as you jog when and where everybody else does.

In Manhattan, **Central Park** is the busiest spot, specifically along the 1.58-mile track circling the **Reservoir.** A runners' lane has been designated along the park roads, which are closed to traffic weekdays 10–3 and 7–10, and from 7 PM Fridays to 6 AM Mondays. A good 1.72-mile route starts at Tavern on the Green along the West Drive, heads south around the bottom of the park to the East Drive, and circles back west on the 72nd Street park road to your starting point. **Riverside Park,** along the Hudson River bank in Manhattan, is glorious at sunset. You can cover 4½ miles by running from 72nd to 116th streets and back. There are eight laps to a mile on the park's outdoor track near 74th Street. On Manhattan streets, figure 20 north–south blocks per mile.

Other favorite Manhattan circuits are around **Gramercy Park** (⅕ mile), **Washington Square Park** (½ mile), and the **Battery Park City Esplanade** (about 2 miles). In Brooklyn, try the **Brooklyn Heights Esplanade,** facing the Manhattan skyline, or the roads in **Prospect Park.**

Races and   A full, year-round schedule is organized by the **New York Road**
Group Runs   **Runners Club** (9 E. 89th St., tel. 212/860–4455), including group runs at 6:30 PM and 7:15 PM on weekdays, starting at the club headquarters, and at 10 AM Saturdays at 90th Street and Fifth Avenue in Central Park. One of the most popular events is the 5-mile Runner's World Midnight Run, held on New Year's Eve with many of the runners wearing inventive costumes.

Racewalking   Elbows pumping vigorously at their sides, racewalkers can move as fast as some joggers, the great difference being that their heels are planted firmly with every stride. A number of competitive racewalking events are held regularly in Central Park and around the metropolitan area; you can also join in Wednesday-evening and Sunday-morning group racewalks in Central Park. For information, contact the **Park Walker's Club** (320 E. 33rd St., tel. 212/628–1317).

Roller Skating

With the advent of in-line skates, or Rollerblades—high-quality boot skates with a single row of smooth-rolling wheels—roller skating is once again very popular in New York, with speed the prime objective. The premier skate shop, **Peck & Goodie** (917 8th Ave. at 54th St., tel. 212/246–6123; 1414 2nd Ave. at 73rd St., tel. 212/249–3178), sells and rents skates and also gives in-line skating lessons in Central Park's Wollman Rink and in Brooklyn's Prospect Park.

Those who think roller skates should be used for disco dancing can be found, whirling and twirling and wearing headphones, weekends in Central Park between the Mall and Bethesda Fountain. **Wollman Rink** (6th Ave. at 59th St., tel. 212/517–4800) converts to a roller rink during warm months, and rentals are available. You can also rent at **Blades West** (105 W. 72nd St., tel. 212/787–3911) and **Blades East** (160 E. 86th St., tel. 212/996–1644).

Swimming

With the wave of city budget cuts, many municipal pools have been closed; among the few that remain is the **Carmine Street Pool** (7th Ave. S and Clarkson St., tel. 212/242–5228). The **U.N. Plaza** (1 United Nations Plaza, tel. 212/702–5016) and **Parker Meridien** (119 W. 56th St., tel. 212/245–5000) hotels have lovely rooftop swimming pools that can be used by nonguests for a $30-a-day fee. The **YWCA** has a sparkling 75-foot lap pool available at $6 per half hour to members of all YWCAs (610 Lexington Ave. at 53rd St., tel. 212/755–4500).

Tennis

The New York City Parks Department maintains scores of tennis courts. The most scenic are the 26 clay courts and four hard courts in **Central Park** (mid-park near 94th St., tel. 212/280–0205), set in a thicket of trees with the skyline beyond. Modestly priced, same-day, single-play admissions are available at the Tennis House adjoining the courts.

You can also play where John McEnroe and Ivan Lendl do: at the **U.S.T.A. National Tennis Center** (tel. 718/592–8000) in Flushing Meadows–Corona Park, Queens, site of the U.S. Open tournament. The center has 29 outdoor and 9 indoor courts, all Deco Turf II. Reservations are accepted up to an hour in advance, though a call two days in advance is suggested. A $150 million expansion of the center added 15 new courts open to the public and three new stadiums.

Local clubs that will book courts to nonmembers include:

Crosstown Tennis (14 W. 31st St., tel. 212/947–5780), with four indoor hard courts that are air-conditioned in summer.

HRC Tennis (Piers 13 and 14, East River at Wall St., tel. 212/422–9300), with eight Har-Tru courts under two bubbles, which are air-conditioned in summer. HRC Tennis is also affiliated with **Village Tennis Courts** (10 University Pl., tel. 212/989–2300), with two courts that are air-conditioned in summer.

Manhattan Plaza Racquet Club (450 W. 43rd St., tel. 212/594–0554), on whose five courts Virginia Slims and U.S. Open players have been known to practice—not to mention a soap opera star or two, since many actors live in special housing near the club.

Beaches

Fine weather brings sun-worshiping New Yorkers out in force. Early in the season, the nearest park or even a rooftop is just fine for catching rays, but later on everyone heads for New York City beaches. Before you go, call to check on swimming conditions.

Long Island

New Yorkers' favorite strand may be **Jones Beach** (tel. 516/785–1600), one of the great man-made beaches of the world, built during the era of the famous parks commissioner Robert Moses. Up the shore is another good beach at **Robert Moses State Park** on Fire Island (tel. 516/669–0449). The Long Island Railroad (tel. 718/217–5477) runs regular transportation in the summer from Penn Station to Jones Beach, Robert Moses State Park, and Long Beach.

City Beaches

The most popular spot is just a subway ride away: Take the A train to the 7½-mile Atlantic strand in Queens's **Rockaways** (tel. 718/318–4000), site of some of the city's best surf, with 4- to 5-foot waves occasionally in view.

Jacob Riis Park (tel. 718/474–4600), part of the Gateway National Recreation Area in Brooklyn, has a boardwalk stretching a full mile along the surfy Atlantic. On Staten Island, there's a good Atlantic-surf beach at **Wolfe's Pond Park** (tel. 718/984–8266).

8 Shopping

By Karen Cure

Updated by Peter Filichia

Shopping in New York is theater, architecture, and people-watching all rolled into one. Big stores and small ones, one-of-a-kinds and chains together present an overwhelming array of "Things." There are fabulous department stores, with something for everyone, and tiny specialists: You can find a store full of balloons (**Toy Balloon**, 204 E. 38th St., tel. 212/682–3803), and others offering paper products (**Kate's Paperie,** 561 Broadway, tel. 212/941–9816), personal and business security equipment (**Counter Spy Shop,** 630 3rd Ave., tel. 212/557–3040; by appointment only), and skeletons and fossils (**Maxilla & Mandible,** 410 Columbus Ave. at 80th St., tel. 212/724–6173).

Another big Manhattan shopping lure is the bargain. Major intersections are instant markets as street peddlers hawk fake Gucci and Cartier watches at $15–$25 each. (These may just possibly last a year or two.) There are thrift shops and resale shops where, it's whispered, Jackie O sends her castoffs and Catherine Deneuve snaps up antique lace. At off-price and discount stores, mark-offs are, as locals say, "to die for," and the sales are even better. Designers' showroom sales allow you to buy cheap at the source; auctions promise good prices as well.

Shopping Hours Stores are generally open Monday–Saturday from 10 AM to 5 or 6 PM, but neighborhood peculiarities do exist. In midtown and lower Manhattan, shops are often closed all weekend. Most stores on the Lower East Side and in the Jewelry District on 47th Street close on Friday afternoon and all day Saturday for the Jewish Sabbath while keeping normal hours on Sunday. Sunday hours, also common on the West Side and in the Village, are the exception on the Upper East Side.

Sales Sales take place in August (for summer merchandise) and in December and January (for winter wares); these sales are announced in the papers. Sales of special merit may end up in *New York* magazine's "Sales and Bargains" column. These often include sales in manufacturers' showrooms that are otherwise never promoted to the public. If your visit is planned for April or October, when most take place, you might phone your favorite designer and ask whether one is in the offing. Find out before you go whether the seller requires cash or accepts credit card or checks (whether local or out-of-state).

Shopping Neighborhoods

New York shops are collected in neighborhoods rather than in malls, so there's nothing more pleasant than shop-crawling when the weather is fine. Locations, if not included here, can be found in store listings below.

South Street Seaport The Seaport's shops are located along the cobbled, pedestrians-only extension to Fulton Street; in the Fulton Market building, the original home of the city's fish market; and on the three levels of Pier 17. You'll find some of the best of the country's upscale retailers: **Ann Taylor** and **Laura Ashley** for women's clothing, **Brookstone** for fancy gadgets and hardware, **Caswell-Massey** for fragrances, and **Sharper Image** for high-tech gimmickry. The big catalogue house **J. Crew** chose the Seaport as the location for its first retail outlet. There are also few-of-a-kind shops, notably the **Strand** bookstore, where second-hand volumes overflow into sidewalk bins; **Mariposa** for butterflies; and **Hats in the Belfry** for inexpensive hats. Business is brisk, especially on fine summer days and on weekends.

A & S Plaza, **12**

Annex Antiques Fair
and Flea Market, **13**

Barneys New York, **14**

Bergdorf Goodman, **4**

Bloomingdale's, **2**

Century 21, **16**

Henri Bendel, **5**

Lord & Taylor, **10**

Lower East Side
(Orchard Street), **15**

Macy's, **11**

Manhattan Art and
Antiques Center, **7**

Place des
Antiquaires, **3**

Rockefeller Center, **8**

Saks Fifth Avenue, **9**

South Street
Seaport, **17**

Trump Tower, **6**

Zabar's, **1**

Manhattan Shopping Highlights

57th Street / 5th Avenue Shopping

A La Vieille Russie, **1**
André Emmerich
Gallery, **16**
Ann Taylor, **9**
Bergdorf
Goodman, **4, 5**
Blum Helman, **29**
Buccellati, **33**
Bulgari, **28**
Burberry's, **11**
Cartier, **42**
Chanel, **10**
Charivari 57, **30**
Ciro, **38**
David Webb, **23**

Dempsey & Carroll, **22**
F.A.O. Schwarz, **3**
Fortunoff, **41**
Galeries Lafayette, **26**
Gazebo, **20**
Geoffrey Beene, **2**
Godiva, **39, 45**
H. Stern, **43**
Hammacher
Schlemmer, **21**
Harry Winston, **35**
Henri Bendel, **36**
Hermès, **12**
Hoya Crystal
Gallery, **24**

Israel Sack, **13**
J.N. Bartfield
Books, **31**
James Robinson, **13**
Kenneth Jay Lane, **33**
Laura Ashley, **14**
Manolo Blahnik, **37**
Martha, **17**
Matsuda, **18**
Pace Gallery, **25**
Place des
Antiquaires, **19**
Rizzoli, **7**
Saks Fifth Avenue, **44**

Salvatore
Ferragamo, **32**
Sheridan, **15**
Steuben, **34**
Susan Bennis Warren
Edwards, **6**
Takashimaya, **40**
Tiffany & Co., **27**
Van Cleef & Arpels, **8**

Aberbach Fine Art, **9**
America Hurrah, **43**
Baccarat, **54**
Barry Friedman, **3**
Books & Co., **16**
Bottega Veneta, **53**
Caviarteria, **52**
Cerutti, **32**
Charivari, **7**
Colnaghi, **36**
D.F. Sanders, **13**
D. Porthault, **29**
David Schorsch, **15**
DeLorenzo, **10**
Descamps, **44**
Didier Aaron, **42**
E. Braun, **45**
Eeyore's Books, **2**
Emanuel Ungaro, **33**
Encore, **1**
Erica Wilson, **46**
Florian Papp, **11**
Floris, **48**
Frette, **35**
Gagosian, **9**
Galo, **47**
Giorgio Armani, **31**
Givenchy, **12**
Godiva, **34**
Isselbacher, **6**
Jean Laporte, **23**
Koos van den
Akker, **37**
Lederer, **55**
Leigh Keno, **18**
Leo Kaplan Ltd., **14**
The Limited, **49**
Mabel's, **22**
Madison Avenue
Bookshop, **25**
Maud Frizon, **26**
Michael's Resale, **4**
Mishon, Mishon, **19**
Missoni, **28**
Montenapoleone, **41**
North Beach
Leather, **40**
Polo/Ralph Lauren, **20**
Pratesi, **27**
Second Act, **5**
Sherry Lehmann, **50**
Sonia Rykiel, **39**
Stair & Company, **17**
Teuscher, **51**
Thomas Woodard, **35**
Valentino, **30**
Vera Wang, **8**
Ximenes, **24**
Ylang Ylang, **38**
Yves St. Laurent, **21**

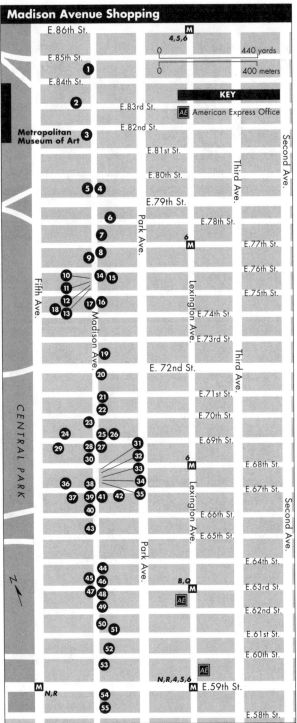

Madison Avenue Shopping

Acker Merrall &
Condit, **30**

Adriana's Bazaar, **20**

Ann Taylor, **35**

Aris Mixon &
Company, **17**

Avventura, **4**

The Ballet Shop, **37**

Betsey Johnson, **33**

Charivari, **3, 9,
14, 32**

Conran's Habitat, **13**

Ecco, **24**

Eeyore's Books for
Children, **18**

Endicott
Booksellers, **5**

Frank Stella Ltd., **6**

Greenstones and Cie, **7**

Gryphon Record
Shop, **26**

HMV, **27**

Laura Ashley, **15**

Maxilla and
Mandible, **10**

Murder Ink, **1**

Only Hearts, **16**

P.S. 44 Market, **21**

Penny Whistle
Toys, **8**

Peter Fox, **19**

Petrossian, **38**

Pottery Barn, **25**

Putumayo, **22**

Sensuous Bean, **34**

Shakespeare &
Company, **11**

Star Magic, **28**

Tip Top, **29**

To Boot, **31**

Tower Records, **36**

West Side Kids, **2**

Ylang Ylang, **24**

Zabar's, **12**

West Side Shopping

SoHo Shopping

Ad Hoc Softwares, **16**

Agnes B., **10**

Back Pages Antiques, **4**

Bébé Thompson, **14**

Betsey Johnson, **2**

Canal Jean, **26**

Comme des Garçons, **18**

Dean & DeLuca, **7**

Ecco, **12**

Enchanted Forest, **25**

Gallery 121, **22**

Harriet Love, **11**

Irish Books, **5**

Joovay, **15**

Kate's Paperie, **8**

La Rue des Rêves, **6**

Leo Castelli, **21**

Mary Boone, **17**

Multiple Impressions, **24**

O.K. Harris, **27**

Paula Cooper, **1**

Penny Whistle Toys, **23**

Peter Fox, **13**

Think Big!, **28**

Tootsie Plohound, **9**

Untitled, **3**

Wolfman-Gold & Good Company, **20**

Yohji Yamamoto, **29**

Zona, **19**

World Financial Center Although the nearby World Trade Center bills its concourse as the city's busiest shopping center, the World Financial Center in Battery Park City is a shopping destination to reckon with, thanks to stores such as **Barneys New York** for clothing, **Godiva Chocolatier** for chocolates, **Mark Cross** for leather goods, **Ann Taylor**, and **Caswell-Massey**. **Il Papiro** offers hand-marbled Italian paper products; **Rizzoli** has books and magazines, stocked on handsome wooden shelves; and **CD Street** strives to be the ultimate compact-disc store. Most are open on Sundays.

Lower East Side Once home to millions of Jewish immigrants from Russia and Eastern Europe, this area is New Yorkers' bargain beat. The center of it all is narrow, unprepossessing Orchard Street, which is crammed with tiny, no-nonsense clothing and shoe stores ranging from kitschy to elegant. Don't expect to schmooze with salespeople, especially on Sunday, the busiest day of the week. Start at Houston Street, walk down one side as far as Canal Street, then walk back up. Essential stops include **Fine & Klein** for handbags; **Forman's** for women's clothing; and **Lace-Up Shoes.** Grand Street (off Orchard Street, south of Delancey Street) is chockablock with linens, towels, and other items for the home; the Bowery (between Grand Street and Delancey Street), with lamps and light fixtures.

SoHo On West Broadway, SoHo's main drag, and on Broadway and Wooster, Greene, Mercer, Prince, Spring, Broome, and Grand streets, major art galleries keep company with chic clothing stores such as **La Rue des Rêves** and **Agnès B.** Well-known stops include decorative-items specialist **Wolfman-Gold & Good Company** and Southwest- and Italian-themed **Zona;** gourmet food emporium **Dean & DeLuca;** and the remarkable **Enchanted Forest** toy store. Many stores in SoHo close on Mondays.

Lower Fifth Avenue Fifth Avenue south of 20th Street along with the avenues fanning east and west are home to some of New York's hippest shops and a lively downtown crowd. Many of the locals sport clothes from the neighborhood—a mix of **Emporio Armani, Paul Smith,** and **Matsuda** (for Japanese clothing), sometimes finished off with big black shades from **Alain Mikli.** Book lovers head for the enormous outposts of **Barnes & Noble** and its **Sale Annex** on the southeast and southwest corners of 18th Street. **Barneys, Williams-Sonoma,** and **Pottery Barn** are within walking distance on nearby Seventh Avenue.

Herald Square Reasonable prices prevail at this intersection of 34th Street and Avenue of the Americas (Sixth Avenue). Giant **Macy's** has traditionally been the linchpin. Opposite, in glittering Herald Center, the chief draw is Manhattan's first **Toys "Я" Us.** Next door on Sixth Avenue, the **A&S Plaza** atrium mall is anchored by the Manhattan outlet of the Brooklyn-based A&S department store, which makes for wonderful browsing, as do **Lechter's,** for home furnishings, and **Mouse N' Around,** for cartoon-emblazoned merchandise. The concentration of shops in a small area makes it a good bet in nasty weather.

Midtown Near Grand Central The biggest men's clothiers are here on and just off the stretch of Madison Avenue nicknamed Trad Avenue: **J. Press, Brooks Brothers, Paul Stuart, F. R. Tripler,** and **Wallachs.** Most also handle women's clothing in dress-for-success styles.

Fifth Avenue The boulevard that was once home to some of the biggest names in New York retailing is not what it once was, that role having been usurped by Madison Avenue north of 57th Street. But Fifth Avenue from Central Park South to Rockefeller Center still shines with **F.A.O. Schwarz** and **Bergdorf Goodman** (both the main store and **Bergdorf Goodman Men** are at 58th St.), **Tiffany** and **Bulgari** jewelers (at 57th St.), the various luxury stores in **Trump Tower** (at 56th St.), **Henri Bendel,** across the street, **Steuben** glassware and **Ferragamo** shoes (at 55th St.), **Takashimaya** (at 54th St.), **Cartier** jewelers (at 52nd St.), and so on down to **Saks Fifth Avenue** (at 50th St.). **Rockefeller Center** itself provides a plethora of shops. To the south (at 47th St.) is the shiny 575 atrium mall, named for its Fifth Avenue address.

57th Street The thoroughfare of Carnegie Hall, the Russian Tea Room, and the Hard Rock Café supports stores that sell everything from remaindered books to $50,000 diamond-and-platinum bracelets. Begin at the **Compleat Strategist** game store (between 8th and 9th Aves.) and head eastward, via the **Pottery Barn, Coliseum Books,** and **Jerry Brown** and **Paron** fabric stores. As you approach Fifth Avenue, you're in the creamiest New York retail territory, with **Bergdorf Goodman**'s flagship store. East of Fifth you'll find the new **Galeries Lafayette New York,** a branch of the famous French department store, and such exclusive stores as **Chanel, Burberrys, Escada, Hermès,** and the **Place des Antiquaires** antiques shop complex. Above and alongside these stores are top art galleries such as **André Emmerich** and **Pace.**

Columbus Avenue Between 66th and 86th streets, this former tenement district is now home to some of the city's glitziest stores. Shops are mostly modern in design, upscale but not top-of-the-line. Clothing runs the gamut from preppy for men and women (**Frank Stella Ltd.**) to high funk (**Betsey Johnson**) and high style (**Charivari**). It's a good source for fine costume jewelry (**Ylang Ylang**).

Upper East Side On Madison and Lexington avenues, roughly between 57th and 79th streets, New York branches of world-renowned designer emporiums are joined by spirited retailers who fill their stores with the unique and stylish. Domestic and imported items for the home, fine antiques, and wonderful clothing predominate—and the prices aren't always sky-high.

Blitz Tours

Get your subway tokens ready, and save enough cash for cab fare to lug all your packages home from these shopping itineraries. They're arranged by special interest; addresses, if not included here, can be found in the store listings below.

Antiques Spend two hours at the **Manhattan Art & Antiques Center** (1050 2nd Ave. at 55th St.), then swing over to 57th Street to the more posh **Place des Antiquaires** and spend two hours there. Both have European, American, and Asian treasures. Stroll westward across 57th Street, stopping at **James Robinson** of silver-jewelry fame and **Israel Sack** with American antique furniture. Then head up Madison to **America Hurrah** (at 65th St.), **Didier Aaron** (on 67th St.), **Thomas K. Woodard** (near 69th St.), **Hirschl & Adler Folk** (at 70th St.), **Leigh Keno** (on 74th St.), **Stair & Company** (near 74th St.), **DeLorenzo** and **Leo Kaplan** (near 75th St.), **David A. Schorsch** (on 76th St.), **Florian Papp** (at 76th St.), and **Barry Friedman** (at 83rd St.).

Bargains Start early at **Century 21** or **Syms** in lower Manhattan. Take a cab to Hester and Orchard streets and shop along Orchard to Houston Street. (Prowl along Grand Street if you're more interested in soft goods for your home than in clothing.) Leave at 2:30 and take a cab to **S&W** in Chelsea; then take the subway uptown to **Loehmann's** (open until 9 PM) in the Bronx. But remember: On Saturdays, shops are closed on the Lower East Side.

Cook's Tour Browse in **Zabar's** (2245 Broadway at W. 80th St., tel. 212/787–2000) for a couple of hours beginning at 8 AM; then go across town to **Kitchen Arts & Letters** bookstore (1435 Lexington Ave., between 93rd and 94th Sts., tel. 212/876–5550) and proceed down to **Bridge Kitchenware** (214 E. 52nd St., tel. 212/688–4220). Head downtown to hit **Balducci's** in the Village, **Dean & DeLuca** and **Broadway Panhandler** (520 Broadway, tel. 212/966–3434) in SoHo, and, if there's time before 6, **Kam-Man** (200 Canal St., tel. 212/571–0330) in Chinatown. If not, head up to

Macy's Cellar area. If you live in an inland state, make your last stop in New York **Citarella** (2135 Broadway at 75th St., tel. 212/874–0383), and have some great fish packed in ice to go.

Luxury Spend 90 minutes at **Saks Fifth Avenue,** then stroll up Fifth. Leave **Trump Tower** by 2:30. Visit **Tiffany** and **Bergdorf Goodman** before closing time. On Thursday, windowshop your way across 57th Street and north on Lexington Avenue to **Bloomingdale's,** which closes at 9 PM. On other nights, clothes fanatics can take a cab downtown to **Barneys New York** for a finale.

Home Furnishings Start at **Barneys New York,** which opens at 10, and visit its Chelsea Passage. Then take a cab to SoHo and stroll around, making sure not to miss **Wolfman-Gold & Good Company** and **Zona.** When things there close—at 6 or 7—take the No. 6 subway to **Bloomingdale's,** if it's Thursday, or the Q, N, or R train to **Macy's,** open late Mondays, Thursdays, and Fridays.

Department Stores

Most of these stores keep regular hours on weekdays and are open until 8 at least one night a week. Many have personal shoppers who can walk you through the store at no charge.

A&S (33rd St. and 6th Ave., tel. 212/594–8500). What was the old Gimbel's, a block south of Macy's, lives again as home to A&S Plaza, whose nine floors are anchored by Abraham & Straus, working hard to become as well established here as in the outer boroughs.

Barneys New York (106 7th Ave. at 17th St., tel. 212/929–9000; Bldg. 2, World Financial Center, tel. 212/945–1600). Founded as a menswear discounter some 60 years ago, Barneys is still the place to see what's hot. The still-extensive selection of menswear ranges from made-to-measure and European and American couture to mass-market natural-shouldered suits; the women's store, in an adjacent group of brownstones, is a showcase of current women's fashion. The Chelsea Passage area can be counted on for distinctive home accessories.

Bergdorf Goodman (754 5th Ave., between 57th and 58th Sts., tel. 212/753–7300). Good taste reigns in an elegant and understated setting. The Home Department is room after exquisite room of wonderful linens, tabletop items, and gifts. The expanded men's store, across the street, occupies the former home of the giant F.A.O. Schwarz toy store.

Bloomingdale's (1000 3rd Ave. at 59th St., tel. 212/355–5900). Only a handful of department stores occupy an entire city block; Macy's is one, and this New York institution is another. The main floor is a stupefying maze of mirrors and black walls; elsewhere the racks are overfull, salespeople overworked, and the departments constantly on the move. Still, selections are dazzling at all but the lowest price points, and the markdowns on top-of-the-line designer goods can be extremely rewarding. Exotic special promotions regularly fill the store.

Galleries Lafayette New York (4–10 E. 57th St., tel. 212/355–0022). This branch of the French fashion store, occupying the former site of Bonwit Teller, carries mostly French labels in an upscale assortment of better and designer apparel. Styles here tend more toward youthful than classic.

Henri Bendel (712 5th Ave., between 55th and 56th Sts., tel. 212/247–1100). Now firmly established under its beautiful new roof (having moved from West 57th Street), Bendel's continues to delight with its stylish displays and sophisticated boutiques.

Lord & Taylor (424 5th Ave., between 38th and 39th Sts., tel. 212/391–3344). This store can be relied upon for the wearable, the fashionable, and the classic in clothes and accessories for women. It's refined, well stocked, and never overwhelming.

Macy's (Herald Sq., Broadway at 34th St., tel. 212/695–4400). No less than a miracle on 34th Street, Macy's main store is the largest retail store in America. Over the past two decades, it has grown chic enough to rival Bloomingdale's in the style department, but its main floor is reassuringly traditional. The latest trends are represented in almost every area the store covers. Estate Jewelry offers fine antique pieces. And for cooking gear and housewares, the Cellar nearly outdoes Zabar's.

Saks Fifth Avenue (611 5th Ave., between 49th and 50th Sts., tel. 212/753–4000). This wonderful store still embodies the spirit of service and style with which it opened in 1926. Saks believes in good manners, the ceremonies of life, and dressing for the part; the selection for men, women, and children—doubled by recent expansion—affirms this quality.

Takashimaya New York (693 5th Ave. near 54th and 55th Sts., tel. 212/350–0100). This pristine branch of Japan's largest department store carries stylish clothes for women and men and fine household items, all of which reflect a combination of Eastern and Western designs. The garden atrium and two-floor gallery contribute to the elegant ambience.

Specialty Shops

Antiques   Antiquing is fine sport in Manhattan. Goods run the gamut from rarefied museum-quality to wacky and eminently affordable. Premier shopping areas are on Madison Avenue north of 57th Street, and on 57th Street east of Fifth Avenue. Around 11th and 12th streets, between University Place and Broadway, a tantalizing array of settees, tables, bedsteads, and rocking chairs overflows onto the sidewalks in front of wholesalers with "To The Trade" signs on their doors; however, a card from your hometown architect or decorator may get you inside. Most dealers are open on Saturdays.

Many small dealers cluster in two antiques "malls":

Manhattan Art & Antiques Center (1050 2nd Ave., between 55th and 56th Sts., tel. 212/355–4400). More than 100 dealers stocking everything from paisley and Judaica to satsuma, scientifica, and samovars jumble the three floors here. The level of quality is not, as a rule, up to that of Madison Avenue, but then neither are the prices.

Place des Antiquaires (125 E. 57th St., tel. 212/758–2900). From its 30-foot-high marble-paved entrance to its glittering glass-walled shops, this is a lavish place. Its dealers offer such high-end goods as 17th-century tapestries, export porcelain, American folk art, and Chinese textiles.

American and   **America Hurrah** (766 Madison Ave., between 65th and 66th
English   Sts., 3rd floor, tel. 212/535–1930). Superb American patchwork quilts and other Americana can be found here.

David A. Schorsch (30 E. 76th St., No. 11A, tel. 212/439–6100). New York's Shaker specialist works by appointment only.

Florian Papp (962 Madison Ave., between 75th and 76th Sts., tel. 212/288–6770). This store has an unassailed reputation among knowledgeable collectors.

Hirschl & Adler Folk (21 E. 70th St., tel. 212/535–8810). This offshoot of the Hirschl & Adler Modern gallery around the corner is devoted to the best in Americana.

Hyde Park Antiques (836 Broadway, between 12th and 13th Sts., tel. 212/477–0033). This store features English decorative arts from the 18th and 19th centuries.

Israel Sack (15 E. 57th St., tel. 212/753–6562). This is widely considered one of the very best places in the country for 18th-century American furniture.

Leigh Keno American Furniture (19 E. 74th St., 1st floor, tel. 212/734–2381). Before he was 30, Leigh Keno set a new auction record in the American antiques field by paying $2.75 million for a hairy-paw-foot Philadelphia wing chair. He has a good eye and an interesting inventory.

Steve Miller American Folk Art (17 E. 96th St., tel. 212/348–5219). This gallery is run by one of the country's premier folk art dealers, the author of *The Art of the Weathervane*.

Thomas K. Woodard (799 Madison Ave., between 67th and 68th Sts., 2nd floor, tel. 212/794–9404). Americana and antique quilts are among the specialties of this prestigious dealer.

Eclectic **Newel Art Galleries** (425 E. 53rd St., tel. 212/758–1970). Located in the heart of the East Side's interior design district, this gallery, the city's biggest antiques store, has a huge collection that roams from the Renaissance to the 20th century.

European **Artisan Antiques** (81 University Pl. at 11th St., tel. 212/751–5214). Art-deco chandeliers come in merry profusion, along with lamps, sconces, and other lighting fixtures from France.

Barry Friedman (1117 Madison Ave., between 83rd and 84th Sts., tel. 212/794–8950). Wiener Werkstätte, Bauhaus, De Stijl, Russian Constructivist, and other European avant-gardists star.

Brass Antique Shop (32 Allen St., tel. 212/925–6660). Candlesticks, chandeliers, andirons, teapots, and other objects in brass, sterling, and copper fill the shelves and teeter on the tables in this old Lower East Side shop.

DeLorenzo (958 Madison Ave., between 75th and 76th Sts., tel. 212/249–7575). Come here to explore the sinuous curves, strongly articulated shapes, and highly polished surfaces of French art-deco furniture and accessories at their best.

Didier Aaron (32 E. 67th St., tel. 212/988–5248). This highly esteemed gallery specializes in superb 18th- and 19th-century furniture and paintings.

Leo Kaplan Ltd. (967 Madison Ave., between 75th and 76th Sts., tel. 212/249–6766). The impeccable items here include art-nouveau glass, pottery, and porcelain from 18th-century England, stunning antique and modern paperweights, and Russian artworks, including creations by Fabergé.

Malmaison Antiques (253 E. 74th St., tel. 212/288–7569). This gallery has the country's largest selection of Empire furniture and decorative arts.

Pierre Deux Antiques (369 Bleecker St., tel. 212/243–7740). The company that brought French provincial to a provincial America still offers an excellent selection.

Stair & Company (942 Madison Ave., between 74th and 75th

Sts., tel. 212/517–4400). Period rooms stylishly show off fine 18th- and 19th-century English mahogany here.

Fun Stuff **Back Pages Antiques** (125 Greene St., tel. 212/460–5998). To acquire an antique jukebox or slot machine, just drop in.

Darrow's Fun Antiques (309 E. 61st St., tel. 212/838–0730). The first of the city's nostalgia shops, the store is full of whimsy.

John T. Johnston's Jukebox Classics (6742 5th Ave., near 68th St., Brooklyn, tel. 718/833–8455). You'll find oodles of vintage jukeboxes, pinball machines, gumball machines, and other arcade goodies, all expertly restored.

Apothecary and **Aveda Aromatherapy Esthetique** (509 Madison Ave. between **Fragrance Shops** 52nd and 53rd Sts., tel. 212/832–2416). Concoct your own perfumes from the impressive selection of essential oils.

The Body Shop (773 Lexington Ave. at 61st St., tel. 212/755–7851). Stop here for clean, green goodies for skin and hair.

Caswell-Massey (518 Lexington Ave. at 48th St., tel. 212/755–2254). The original store displays its fragrant toiletries in polished old cases; branches are in the World Financial Center and South Street Seaport.

Essential Products Company (90 Water St., tel. 212/344–4288). This company, established in 1895, sells knockoffs of famous fragrances at a fraction of the original price tags.

Floris (703 Madison Ave., between 62nd and 63rd Sts., tel. 212/935–9100). Floral English toiletries beloved of such beauties as Cher, Sophia Loren, and Catherine Deneuve fill this re-creation of the cozy London original.

Jean Laporte L'Artisan Perfumeur (870 Madison Ave., between 70th and 71st Sts., tel. 212/517–8665.) Exquisite French scents and antique perfume bottles make a splendid array.

Kiehl Pharmacy (109 3rd Ave., near 13th St., tel. 212/475–3400). A favored haunt of top models and hairstylists, it's been a purveyor of quality skin and hair products since 1851.

Art Galleries America's art capital, New York has numerous wealthy collectors, so many galleries are minimuseums (*see also* Auctions, *below*).

Aberbach Fine Art (980 Madison Ave., between 76th and 77th Sts., tel. 212/988–1100). Exhibits here include paintings and sculpture by various modern and contemporary artists.

André Emmerich Gallery (41 E. 57th St., tel. 212/752–0124). Located in the Art Deco Fuller Building, this gallery displays major works by major modern artists.

Art in General (79 Walker St., tel. 212/219–0473). Come here for works in a variety of mediums (including painting, sculpture, and photography), by emerging contemporary artists.

Blum Helman (20 W. 57th St., tel. 212/245–2888). Contemporary art by Brian Hunt, Robert Moskowitz, Jack Barths, and Ellsworth Kelly, among others, is displayed here.

A Clean, Well-Lighted Place (363 Bleecker St., tel. 212/255–3656). Prints by well-known artists, including Sean Scully, Susan Rothenberg, Robert Motherwell, and David Hockney, are displayed here.

Colnaghi (21 E. 67th St., tel. 212/772–2266). This is the New York outpost of one of London's preeminent fine art galleries, offering European and English paintings and objets d'art.

Fred Dorfman, Inc. (123 Watts St., tel. 212/966–4611). This gallery has a reputation for being a place where dealers and collectors go to discover new pieces. You'll find paintings and graphics by Keith Haring, Roy Lichtenstein, Andy Warhol, and Mark Kostabi.

Gagosian (980 Madison Ave., between 76th and 77th Sts., tel. 212/744–2313). Works on display are by such artists as Richard Serra, Willem De Kooning, Jasper Johns, Frank Stella, Warhol, David Salle, and Philip Taaffe.

Gallery 121 (121 Spring St., tel. 212/925–4331). Featured are paintings, graphics, and sculpture by such artists as Erté, Salvador Dali, Haring, Joan Miró, James Rizzi, and Warhol.

Isselbacher (41 E. 78th St., tel. 212/472–1766). This gallery offers prints by late-19th- and 20th-century masters such as Henri Toulouse-Lautrec, Henri Matisse, Marc Chagall, Joan Miró, Pablo Picasso, and Edvard Munch.

Leo Castelli (420 Broadway, between Prince and Spring Sts., tel. 212/431–5160). He's the man who discovered Pop. Look for works by Jasper Johns, Roy Lichtenstein, Ed Ruscha, and Ed Rosenquist.

Mary Boone (417 Broadway, between Prince and Spring Sts., tel. 212/431–1818.) A hot '80s gallery, it's still intriguing today, with such artists as Eric Fischl and Richard Tuttle.

Multiple Impressions (128 Spring St., tel. 212/925–1313). Twentieth-century American, European, and South American paintings and prints are offered here at reasonable prices.

O. K. Harris (383 W. Broadway, tel. 212/431–3600). The oldest gallery in SoHo, opened in 1969, O. K. Harris showcases paintings, sculpture, and photography by contemporary artists.

Pace Gallery (32 E. 57th St., tel. 212/421–3292). This gallery features such well-known modern and contemporary artists as Picasso, Alexander Calder, and Julian Schnabel.

Paula Cooper (149 and 155 Wooster St., tel. 212/674–0766). Exhibits include contemporary paintings and sculpture.

SoHo Photo (15 White St., tel. 212/226–8571). In the heart of TriBeCa, this gallery exhibits various photographers' work.

Books With so many of the country's publishing houses, magazines, and writers based here, there is an abundance of bookshops, small and large. Of course, all the big national chains are here—Barnes & Noble, B. Dalton, Brentano's, Doubleday, Waldenbooks—with branches all over town.

Biography Bookshop (400 Bleecker St., tel. 212/807–8655). Diaries, letters, and other biographical and autobiographical material fill this tidy, well-organized store.

Books & Company (939 Madison Ave., between 74th and 75th Sts., tel. 212/737–1450). A comfy sofa invites lingering here.

Coliseum Books (1771 Broadway at 57th St., tel. 212/757–8381). This supermarket of a bookstore has a huge, quirky selection of remainders, best-sellers, and scholarly works.

Endicott Booksellers (450 Columbus Ave., between 81st and 82nd Sts., tel. 212/787–6300). This intelligent, wood-paneled bookstore features evening readings once or twice a week.

Gotham Book Mart (41 W. 47th St., tel. 212/719–4448). The late Frances Steloff opened this store years ago with just $200 in her pocket, half of it on loan. But she helped launch *Ulysses*, D. H. Lawrence, and Henry Miller and is now legendary among bibliophiles, as is her bookstore, an oasis for those who love to read, with nearly a quarter million books.

Irish Books (580 Broadway at Prince St., tel. 212/274–1923). Here you'll find the country's widest selection of books about Ireland, both current and out-of-print titles.

Kinokuniya Bookstore (10 W. 49th St., tel. 212/765–1461).

Come here for everything you ever wanted to read about Japan—in English and Japanese.

Librairie de France/Libraria Hispanica (610 5th Ave., in Rockefeller Ctr., tel. 212/581–8810; 115 5th Ave. at 19th St., tel. 212/673–7400). These huge collections of foreign-language books and periodicals are among the country's largest. Both sites have books in French and Spanish.

Madison Avenue Bookshop (833 Madison Ave., between 69th and 70th Sts., tel. 212/535–6130). Serious contemporary fiction and biographies are sold here in pleasant surroundings.

Revolution Books (13 E. 16th St., tel. 212/691–3345). Come here for left-wing and Third World literature.

Rizzoli (31 W. 57th St., tel. 212/759–2424; 454 West Broadway, tel. 212/674–1616; World Financial Center, tel. 212/385–1400). Uptown, an elegant marble entrance, oak paneling, chandeliers, and classical music accompany books on art, architecture, dance, design, foreign language, and travel; the downtown stores come without the fin-de-siècle frills.

Shakespeare & Company (2259 Broadway at 81st St., tel. 212/580–7800; 716 Broadway, near Astor Place, tel. 212/529–1330). The stock here represents what's happening in publishing today in just about every field. Late hours are a plus.

Tower Books (383 Lafayette St., tel. 212/228–5100). Owned by the record conglomerate, this megastore discounts thousands of titles; the magazine section alone is worth the visit.

Children's Books **Bank Street Bookstore** (2875 Broadway at 112th St., tel. 212/678–1654). Here's a mini-emporium of politically correct children's books, games, and videos.

Books of Wonder (464 Hudson St., tel. 212/645–8006; 132 7th Ave. at 18th St., tel. 212/989–3270). This store offers an excellent stock of children's books for all reading levels. Oziana is a specialty, and the 18th Street branch offers antique books as well as new publications.

Eeyore's Books for Children (2212 Broadway, between 78th and 79th Sts., tel. 212/362–0634; 25 E. 83rd St., tel. 212/988–3404). The large, shrewd selection here should delight any young reader. Weekend story hours and author appearances please the under-6 crowd.

Maps **Hagstrom Map and Travel Center** (57 W. 43rd St., tel. 212/398–1222). This may be the ultimate map store.

Rand McNally Map & Travel (150 E. 52nd St., tel. 212/758–7488). The excellent selection covers the world.

Music **Joseph Patelson Music House** (160 W. 56th St., tel. 212/582–5840). A huge collection of scores has long made this the heart of the music lover's New York.

Music Exchange (151 W. 46th St., tel. 212/354–5858). Sheet music of popular songs can be found here.

Mystery and Suspense Whodunits are the specialty at: **Foul Play** (302 W. 12th St. at 8th Ave., tel. 212/675–5115; 1465 2nd Ave., between 76th and 77th Sts., tel. 212/517–3222); **Murder Ink** (2486 Broadway, between 92nd and 93rd Sts., tel. 212/362–8905); and **Mysterious Bookshop** (129 W. 56th St., tel. 212/765–0900).

Rare and Used Books **Antiquarian Booksellers International** (Place des Antiquaires, 125 E. 57th St., tel. 212/751–5450). Nearly 30 devoted dealers reside in this posh antiques emporium.

Argosy Bookstore (116 E. 59th St., tel. 212/753–4455). This sedate nook keeps a scholarly stock of books and autographs.

Bauman Rare Books (The Waldorf-Astoria, Park Ave. at 50th St., tel. 212/759–8300). This very successful Philadelphia firm now offers New Yorkers the most impossible-to-get titles.

J. N. Bartfield Books (30 W. 57th St., 3rd floor, tel. 212/245–8890). This legend in the field offers old and antiquarian books distinguished by binding, author, edition, or content.

Pageant Print and Book Shop (109 E. 9th St., tel. 212/674–5296). Michael Caine browsed in this relic of old New York in Woody Allen's *Hannah and Her Sisters*.

Strand (828 Broadway at 12th St., tel. 212/473–1452). Eight miles of shelves house more than two million books at this biggest of Manhattan's used-book stores.

Ximenes Rare Books (19 E. 69th St., tel. 212/744–0226). This store spends much of its time searching for hard-to-find titles.

Travel Books **Complete Traveller Bookstore** (199 Madison Ave. at 35th St., tel. 212/685–9007). Old and new titles are sold here.

Traveller's Bookstore (22 W. 52nd St., tel. 212/664–0995). The stock includes essays and novels, as well as maps and guides.

Cameras and **Bi-Rite** (15 E. 30th St., tel. 212/685–2130). Once your turn
Electronics comes, this tiny discounter's Hasidic salesmen offer good service, great prices. Take model numbers; there's no showroom.

47th Street Photo (67 W. 47th St., 115 W. 45th St.; tel. 212/398–1410). Prices can be better elsewhere, but these stores manned by Hasidic Jews are a heavyweight among electronics discounters. Note Friday and Saturday closings.

Harvey Electronics (2 W. 45th St., tel. 212/575–5000). A well-informed staff offers top-of-the-line audio equipment.

Willoughby's (110 W. 32nd St., tel. 212/564–1600). Calling itself the world's largest camera store, Willoughby's rates high among amateurs and pros for selection and service.

CDs, Tapes, The city's best record stores match its music scene: diversified,
and Records esoteric, and very in-the-know. They also provide browsers with a window to New York's hipper subcultures.

Bleecker Bob's Golden Oldies (118 W. 3rd St., tel. 212/475–9677). The staff sells punk, new wave, progressive rock, reggae, and R&B until the wee hours.

Footlight Records (113 E. 12th St., tel. 212/533–1572). Stop here to browse through New York's largest selection of old and new musicals and movie soundtracks, as well as a good choice of jazz and popular recordings.

Gryphon Record Shop (251 W. 72nd St., 2nd floor, tel. 212/874–1588). *New York* magazine called this the city's best rare-record store, citing its 40,000 out-of-print and rare LPs.

HMV (2081 Broadway at 72nd St., tel. 212/721–5900; 1280 Lexington Ave. at 86th St., tel. 212/348–0800). These state-of-the-art record superstores stock 800,000 discs, tapes, and videos.

House of Oldies (35 Carmine St., tel. 212/243–0500). The specialty here is records made between 1950 and the present—45s and 78s, as well as LPs; there are more than a million titles.

Jazz Record Center (236 W. 26th St., tel. 212/675–4480). Here is the city's only jazz-record specialist.

J&R Music World (23 Park Row, tel. 212/732–8600). This store offers a huge selection with good prices on major releases. Jazz recordings are sold at 33 Park Row.

Midnight Records (263 W. 23rd St., tel. 212/675–2768). This rare-rock specialist stocks obscure artists from the '50s on.

Tower Records (692 Broadway at 4th St., tel. 212/505–1500; 1961 Broadway at 66th St., tel. 212/799–2500). The selection of

CDs and tapes can get overwhelming here. The scene is pure New York: At the Village branch, the black leather usually goes with pink, green, or tiger-striped hair in bizarre cuts; the Upper West Side outlet has good selection but less local color.

Children's Clothing **Bébé Thompson** (98 Thompson St., tel. 212/925–1122). Downtown style is evident here: plenty of black-and-white and jungle prints among the embroidered treasures. Look for sales.
Cerutti (807 Madison Ave., between 67th and 68th Sts., tel. 212/737–7540). This is where Nanny takes her Little Princess, and Yoko Ono shopped for Sean Lennon when he was a tyke.
Citykids (130 7th Ave., between 17th and 18th Sts., tel. 212/620–0906). This busy store carries colorful, fun clothing and accessories. Don't miss the hand-painted T-shirts and sweatshirts with New York themes.
Greenstones & Cie (442 Columbus Ave., between 81st and 82nd Sts., tel. 212/580–4322). Catering to junior Yuppies, this store offers some handsome clothes, particularly sweaters.
Little Eric (1331 3rd Ave. at 76th St., tel. 212/288–8987; 590 Columbus Ave. at 88th St., tel. 212/769–1610). Moms who love Eric can introduce their daughters to this happy footwear shop that's styled in an adult mode.
Space Kiddets (46 E. 21st St., tel. 212/420–9878). Casual trendsetting clothes for kids are carried here.
Wicker Garden's Baby (1327 Madison Ave., near 93rd St., tel. 212/410–7001). Top-of-the-line pretties for boys, girls, and babies are sold here.

Resale Shops **Once Upon A Time** (171 E. 92nd St., tel. 212/831–7619) and **Second Act Children's Wear** (1046 Madison Ave. at 80th St., tel. 212/988–2440) offer gently worn children's wear, sizes 0–14.

Crystal Three peerless sources are **Baccarat** (625 Madison Ave., between 58th and 59th Sts., tel. 212/826–4100); **Hoya Crystal Gallery** (450 Park Ave., between 56th and 57th Sts., tel. 212/223–6335); and **Steuben** (715 5th Ave. at 56th St., tel. 212/752–1441).

Food For food lovers, New York's gourmet specialty shops are a truly moveable feast: Much of the food can travel home with you.

Caviar **Macy's** and **Zabar's** (*see below*) feature good deals on caviars; **Caviarteria** (29 E. 60th St., tel. 212/759–7410) and **Petrossian** (182 W. 58th St., tel. 212/245–2217) are specialists.

Chocolate and **Elk Candy Company** (240 E. 86th St., tel. 212/650–1177). This
Candy is a marzipan fantasy and a chocoholic's sweet dream.
Godiva Chocolatier (793 Madison Ave. at 67th St., tel. 212/249–9444; 701 5th Ave., between 54th and 55th Sts., tel. 212/593–2845; 560 Lexington Ave. at 50th St., tel. 212/980–9810; 85 Broad St., tel. 212/514–6240). This famous maker features cleverly molded chocolates—and embossed gold boxes.
Li-Lac Chocolates (120 Christopher St., tel. 212/242–7374). This charming nook feeds the Village's sweet tooth with homemade selections in the French tradition.
Neuchatel Chocolates (2 W. 59th St., in the Plaza Hotel, tel. 212/751–7742; 55 E. 52nd St., in Park Avenue Plaza between Park and Madison, tel. 212/759–1388). Velvety chocolates come in five dozen varieties here—all made in New York to approximate the Swiss chocolates.
Teuscher Chocolates (620 5th Ave., in Rockefeller Ctr., tel. 212/246–4416; 25 E. 61st St., tel. 212/751–8482). Fabulous chocolates made in Switzerland are flown in weekly for sale in these jewel-box shops, newly decorated each season.

Coffee **Empire Coffee and Tea Company** (592 9th Ave., between 42nd and 43rd Sts., tel. 212/586–1717). The selection here numbers almost 90 different beans.

McNulty's Tea & Coffee Company (109 Christopher St., tel. 212/242–5351). Antique wood paneling says "Old New York"—indeed, this is the city's oldest coffee and tea emporium. The barrels of beans say "Timor," "Java," and "New Guinea."

Orens Daily Roast (434 3rd Ave. at 31st St., tel. 212/779–1241, and other locations). Choose from a huge selection of exotic—and prosaic—coffees, teas, and mugs.

Porto Rico Importing Company (201 Bleecker St., tel. 212/477–5421; 40½ St. Marks Pl., tel. 212/533–1982). This dark, old-fashioned, and highly aromatic store has been a local coffee source since 1907.

Sensuous Bean (66 W. 70th St., tel. 212/724–7725). Mocha meets such flavors as banana, peach, and orange.

Gourmet Markets **Balducci's** (424 6th Ave. at 9th St., tel. 212/673–2600). In this former mom-and-pop food shop, now one of the city's finest food stores, mounds of baby carrots keep company with frilly lettuce, feathery dill, and superlative meats, fish, cheeses, chocolates, baked goods, pastas, vinegars, oils, and crackers.

Dean & DeLuca (560 Broadway at Prince St., tel. 212/431–1691). This huge SoHo trendsetter, splendidly bright white, has an encyclopedic selection, from the heady array at the cheese counter to the shelves of crackers and the display cases of prepared foods.

Kam-Man (200 Canal St., tel. 212/571–0330). The city's premier Chinese market, Kam-Man is filled with exotic foods, the staccato sound of Chinese, and mysterious smells.

Zabar's (2245 Broadway at 80th St., tel. 212/787–2000). Enjoy the atmosphere of one of New York's favorite food markets. Dried herbs and spices, chocolates, and assorted bottled foods are downstairs, along with a fragrant jumble of fresh breads and the cheese, meat, and smoked-fish counters. Upstairs is one of New York's largest selections of kitchenware.

Spices **Adriana's Bazaar** (2152 Broadway at 75th St., tel. 212/877–5757). The fact that this store offers more than 25 chilis should tell you something about its vast spice inventory.

Pete's Spice & Everthing Nice (174 1st Ave. near 11th St., tel. 212/254–8773). Everything from anise to zathar can be found in this hot spot.

Wine **Acker Merrall & Condit** (160 W. 72nd St., tel. 212/787–1700). Known for its selection of red burgundies, this store has knowledgeable, helpful personnel.

Garnet Liquors (929 Lexington Ave., between 68th and 69th Sts., tel. 212/772–3211). Its fine selection includes champagne at prices that one wine writer called "almost charitable."

Morrell & Company (535 Madison Ave., near 54th St., tel. 212/688–9370). Peter Morrell is a well-regarded and very colorful figure in the wine business; his store reflects his expertise.

Sherry Lehmann (679 Madison Ave., between 61st and 62nd Sts., tel. 212/838–7500). It's a New York institution.

Sokolin (178 Madison Ave., between 33rd and 34th Sts., tel. 212/532–5893). Knowledgeable oenophiles have been shopping here for 50 years.

Fun and Games These are stores by adults, for adults, but with such humor and whimsy that kids will like them, too.

Compleat Strategist (11 E. 33rd St., tel. 212/685–3880; 320 W. 57th St., tel. 212/582–1272). All kinds of strategy games are supplied for the serious enthusiast.

Darts Unlimited (30 E. 20th St., tel. 212/533–8684). Exquisitely crafted English darts and boards are sold here.

Flosso Hornmann (45 W. 34th St., tel. 212/279–6079). This modest magic shop offers museum-class memorabilia, including a hand-painted crate used by Harry Houdini.

Game Show (474 6th Ave., between 11th and 12th Sts., tel. 212/633–6328; 1240 Lexington Ave. at 83rd St., tel. 212/472–8011). The mix here includes board games, box games, and card games.

Little Rickie (49½ 1st Ave. at 3rd St., tel. 212/505–6467). This fun spot is packed with wacky novelties and vintage treasures that baby-boomers remember from childhood.

Louis Tannen's (6 W. 32nd St., 4th floor, tel. 212/239–8383). You'll find sword chests, dove-a-matics, magic wands, and crystal balls, not to mention the all-important top hats with rabbits, at this six-decades-old magicians' supply house.

Marion & Company (147 W. 26th St., tel. 212/727–8900). Playing cards come in all shapes and sizes here.

Only Hearts (386 Columbus Ave. at 79th St., tel. 212/724–5608). Romance is the theme. Heart-shaped waffle irons, anyone?

Star Magic (743 Broadway, between 8th St. and Astor Pl., tel. 212/228–7770; 275 Amsterdam Ave. at 73rd St., tel. 212/769–2020; 1256 Lexington Ave., between 84th and 85th Sts., tel. 212/988–0300). Astronomy meets New Age in a clutter of crystals, star charts, and other celestial playthings.

Think Big! (390 West Broadway, between Broome and Spring Sts., tel. 212/925–7300). Huge replicas of various ordinary objects stock this amusing store.

Uncle Futz (408 Amsterdam Ave. at 79th St., tel. 212/799–6723). This delicious toy shop is crammed with supercool puzzles, board games, and souped-up yo-yos.

Gizmos and Whatchamacallits
Hammacher Schlemmer (147 E. 57th St., tel. 212/421–9000). The store that offered America the first pop-up toaster, the first automatic steam iron, and the first telephone answering machine and microwave oven still ferrets out the outrageous, the unusual, and the best-of-kind.

Sharper Image (Pier 17, South St. Seaport, tel. 212/693–0477; 4 W. 57th St., tel. 212/265–2550). This retail outlet of the catalogue company stocks gifts for the pampered executive who has everything.

Home Decor and Gifts
Aris Mixon & Company (381 Amsterdam Ave., between 78th and 79th Sts., tel. 212/724–6904). The intrigue here is in the mix of newly manufactured, handmade, and antique.

Avventura (463 Amsterdam Ave., between 81st and 82nd Sts., tel. 212/769–2510). Glory in Italian design in all its streamlined beauty here. Tabletop items and accessories are all stunning.

Bed, Bath & Beyond (620 6th Ave., between 19th and 20th Sts., tel. 212/255–3550). This huge Chelsea emporium has 11 sections of household items at reasonable prices.

Be Seated (66 Greenwich Ave., between 11th St. and 7th Ave., tel. 212/924–8444). Manhattan's source for the world's best basketwork is redolent of rattan and raffia.

Charlotte Moss & Company (1027 Lexington Ave., between 73rd and 74th Sts., tel. 212/772–3320). Within what looks like a vine-wrapped, chintz-cozy English country house, you'll find English country-house-style treasures.

Conran's Habitat (2–8 Astor Pl., tel. 212/505–1515; 160 E. 54th St. in Citicorp Ctr., tel. 212/371–2225; 2248 Broadway at 81st St., tel. 212/873–9250). This British Habitat outpost store stocks components of a stylish yet not-too-expensive life.

D. F. Sanders (952 Madison Ave. at 75th St., tel. 212/879–6161). The sleek, postmodern items on display at this design center are destined to be classics.

Gazebo (127 E. 57th St., tel. 212/832–7077). Quilts and wicker overflow this bastion of American style.

Jenny B. Goode (1194 Lexington Ave., between 80th and 81st Sts., tel. 212/794–2492). Charming china serving pieces and bibelots star.

Let There Be Neon City (38 White St., between Broadway and Church St., tel. 212/226–4883). Browse among the terrific collection of new and antique neon signs, clocks, and tabletop accessories. (Open Sat. by appointment only.)

Mabel's (849 Madison Ave., between 70th and 71st Sts., tel. 212/734–3263). Enchanting animal lovers is the business of this Noah's Ark of knickknacks in animal shapes.

Miya Shoji (109 W. 17th St., tel. 212/243–6774). It offers a superb selection of beautifully crafted Japanese folding screens.

The Pillowry (19 E. 69th St., tel. 212/628–3844). The selection of decorative, one-of-a-kind pillows is vast.

Pottery Barn (117 E. 59th St., tel. 212/753–5424; 2109 Broadway, between 73rd and 74th Sts., tel. 212/595–5573; 250 W. 57th St., tel. 212/315–1855; 231 10th Ave., between 23rd and 24th Sts., tel. 212/206–8118; and five other locations). The emphasis here is on setting the oh-so-chic table. Overstocks are discounted at Tenth Avenue.

Wolfman-Gold & Good Company (116 Greene St., tel. 212/431–1888). Half antique and half contemporary in spirit, this chic SoHo shop, a major New York trendsetter, is all white, with touches of blond wood and wicker. Tableware is the focus.

Zona (97 Greene St., tel. 212/925–6750). SoHo's airy, high-ceilinged bastion of the southwestern look offers Solieri bells, earthtoned textiles, and terra-cottas, all artfully displayed.

Linens   Luxurious linens enchant at **D. Porthault** (18 E. 69th St., tel. 212/688–1660), **E. Braun** (717 Madison Ave., between 63rd and 64th Sts., tel. 212/838–0650), **Frette** (799 Madison Ave., between 67th and 68th Sts., tel. 212/988–5221), and **Pratesi** (829 Madison Ave. at 69th St., tel. 212/288–2315). Chic prevails at lower prices at **Ad Hoc Softwares** (410 West Broadway at Spring St., tel. 212/925–2652), **Descamps** (723 Madison Ave., between 63rd and 64th Sts., tel. 212/355–2522), and **Sheridan** (595 Madison Ave. at 57th St., tel. 212/308–0120). Antique linens, including whimsically ruffled pillow shams, are at **Jana Starr/Jean Hoffman Antiques** (235 E. 80th St., tel. 212/861–8256). For bargains, check out the Lower East Side's dry-goods merchants (most on Grand St.) and **Century 21** (22 Cortlandt St. between Broadway and Church St., tel. 212/227–9092).

Jewelry, Watches, and Silver   Most of the world's premier jewelers have retail outlets in New York, and the nation's jewelry wholesale center is on 47th Street.

A La Vieille Russie (781 5th Ave., between 59th and 60th Sts., tel. 212/752–1727). Stop here to behold bibelots by Fabergé and others, enameled or encrusted with jewels.

Buccellati (725 5th Ave., between 56th and 57th Sts. in Trump Tower, tel. 212/308–5533). The oversize Italian jewelry here makes a statement. Silver is around the corner (46 E. 57th St., tel. 212/308–2507).

Bulgari (730 5th Ave. at 57th St., tel. 212/315–9000, and 2 E. 61st St., in the Pierre Hotel, tel. 212/486–0326). The expertly crafted jewelry here has an understated, tailored look.

Camilla Dietz Bergeron (116 E. 68th St., tel. 212/794–9100). Antique cufflinks here date back to the Roaring '20s.

Cartier (2 E. 52nd St., tel. 212/446–3400). Simple but superb pieces are displayed in the former mansion of the late yachtsman and society king Morton F. Plant.

David Webb (445 Park Ave. at 57th St., tel. 212/421–3030) features gem-studded pieces, often enameled and in animal forms.

Fortunoff (681 5th Ave., between 53rd and 54th Sts., tel. 212/758–6660). Good prices on gold and silver jewelry, flatware, and hollowware draw crowds to this large store.

Harry Winston (718 5th Ave. at 56th St., tel. 212/245–2000). The moneyed clientele here appreciates this store's oversize stones and impeccable quality.

H. Stern (645 5th Ave., between 50th and 51st Sts., tel. 212/688–0300). Colored gemstones in contemporary settings are the specialty of this Brazilian firm.

James Robinson (15 E. 57th St., tel. 212/752–6166). This family-owned business features wonderful new and antique silver, fine estate jewelry, and table accessories.

Jean Silversmiths (16 W. 45th St., tel. 212/575–0723). Where to replace the butter knife missing from your great-aunt's set? Try this dusty, crowded shop.

Tiffany & Co. (727 5th Ave. at 57th St., tel. 212/755–8000). A shiny robin's-egg-blue box from this venerable New York jeweler announces the contents as something very special. Along with the $50,000 platinum-and-diamond bracelets, there is a great deal that's affordable on a whim.

Van Cleef & Arpels (744 5th Ave. at 57th St., tel. 212/644–9500). The jewelry here is sheer perfection.

Costume Jewelry Fabulously faux wares can be found at **Ciro** (700 5th Ave., between 54th and 55th Sts., tel. 212/247–0927, and other locations); **Kenneth Jay Lane** (725 5th Ave., in Trump Tower, tel. 212/751–6166, and other locations); **Mishon Mishon** (899 Madison Ave., between 72nd and 73rd Sts., tel. 212/288–7599); and **Ylang Ylang** (806 Madison Ave., between 67th and 68th Sts., tel. 212/772–1417; 101 W. 70th St., tel. 212/496–0319; 4 W. 57th St., tel. 212/247–3580).

Luggage and Leather Goods **Altman Luggage** (135 Orchard St., between Delancey and Rivington Sts., tel. 212/254–7275). Come here for reasonably priced leather items.

Bottega Veneta (635 Madison Ave., between 59th and 60th Sts., tel. 212/319–0303). The superb goods here are for people who know real quality.

Crouch & Fitzgerald (400 Madison Ave. at 48th St., tel. 212/755–5888). Since 1839, this store has offered a terrific selection in hard- and soft-sided luggage, plus handbags.

Fine & Klein (119 Orchard St., tel. 212/674–6720). Fabulous handbags are discounted here.

Lederer Leather Goods (613 Madison Ave. at 58th St., tel. 212/355–5515). The excellent selection here includes exotic skins.

North Beach Leather (772 Madison Ave. at 66th St., tel. 212/

772–0707). High-fashion leather wear comes in many colors here.

T. Anthony (480 Park Ave. at 58th St., tel. 212/750–9797). This store's hard- and soft-sided luggage of coated fabric with leather trim has brass fasteners that look like precision machines.

Menswear Because New York is home to movie moguls, architects, writers, and international lawyers, bankers, and businessmen, its department and specialty stores offer a number of looks.

Alan Flusser Shop (14 E. 52nd St., tel. 212/888–7100; 50 Trinity Pl., tel. 212/422–3100). Fans come here for the designer's unusual take on the traditional look.

Brooks Brothers (346 Madison Ave. at 44th St., tel. 212/682–8800). The bare travertine underfoot, high ceilings overhead, and undecorated showcases on the ground floor suggest a New England spareness at this American-menswear institution, with conservative styles and fine tailoring.

Frank Stella Ltd. (440 Columbus Ave. at 81st St., tel. 212/877–5566; 1382 6th Ave., between 56th and 57th Sts., tel. 212/757–2295). Classic clothing with subtle variations is offered here.

F. R. Tripler (366 Madison Ave. at 46th St., tel. 212/922–1090). Oxxford, Hickey Freeman, and other top-notch manufacturers are represented here.

J. Press (16 E. 44th St., tel. 212/687–7642). This store emphasizes the oxford-cloth shirt, the natural-shoulder suit, the madras-patch Bermuda shorts, and the amusing club tie.

Paul Smith (108 5th Ave. at 16th St., tel. 212/627–9770). Dark mahogany Victorian cases display downtown styles.

Paul Stuart (Madison Ave. at 45th St., tel. 212/682–0320). The fabric selection is interesting, the tailoring superb, and the look traditional but not stodgy.

Saint Laurie, Ltd. (897 Broadway, between 19th and 20th Sts., tel. 212/473–0100). This family-owned business sells suits manufactured on the premises in styles ranging from the boxy to the Italianate in lovely fabrics.

Wallachs (555 5th Ave. at 46th St., tel. 212/687–0106). Here you'll find good service and reasonably priced classics.

Discounts New York men looking for bargains rely on **BFO** (149 5th Ave. at 21st St., 6th floor, tel. 212/254–0059); **Eisenberg and Eisenberg** (85 5th Ave. at 16th St., tel. 212/627–1290); **Moe Ginsburg** (162 5th Ave. at 21st St., tel. 212/242–3482); **Rothman's** (200 Park Ave. S at 17th St., tel. 212/777–7400); and **Syms** (42 Trinity Pl., tel. 212/797–1199; cash or store credit card only).

Men's Hats **Worth & Worth** (331 Madison Ave. at 43rd St., tel. 212/867–6058). Come here for elegant handmade headwear—everything from driving caps to fedoras.

Men's Shoes **Billy Martin's** (812 Madison Ave. at 68th St., tel. 212/861–3100). Quality hand-tooled and custom-made boots are carried here.

Church English Shoes (428 Madison Ave. at 49th St., tel. 212/755–4313). This store has been selling beautifully made English shoes since 1873; the fitters are especially knowledgeable.

Shoe Express (1420 2nd Ave. at 74th St., tel. 212/734–3967). The stylish selection includes rugged classics, western-style boots, and name-brand dress shoes.

Tip Top (155 W. 72nd St., tel. 212/787–4960). You'll find comfortable walking shoes and sandals here.

To Boot (256 Columbus Ave., between 71st and 72nd Sts., tel.

212/724–8249). Here you'll find stylish shoes and boots for a more fashionable business look.

Tootsie Plohound (124 Prince St., tel. 212/925–6641). This shop is tops in "downtown" shoes: fun, funky, and cool. It carries women's styles, too.

Needlecraft *Fabric* Seamstresses prize the selection and prices at shops in the upper 30s between Broadway and Eighth Avenue, such as **C&B** (250 W. 39th St., tel. 212/354–9360). Luxurious imports fill **Jerry Brown** (37 W. 57th St., tel. 212/753–3626), **Paron Fabrics** (60 W. 57th St., tel. 212/247–6451), **Paron Fabrics West** (239 W. 39th St., tel. 212/768–3266), which discounts remnants, and **Weller** (24 W. 57th St., tel. 212/247–3790).

Trimming Dingy 38th Street between Fifth and Sixth avenues is a treasure chest. Jewels include **Hyman Hendler & Sons** (67 W. 38th St., tel. 212/840–8393), the ribbon king, since 1900; and **Tinsel Trading** (47 W. 38th St., tel. 212/730–1030), for new and antique trims and tassels. Nearby **M & J Trimming** (1008 6th Ave. near 37th St., tel. 212/391–9072) stocks more than 100 styles of tassels and tiebacks. Uptown, buttons overflow the charming **Tender Buttons** (143 E. 62nd St., tel. 212/758–7004).

Yarns **Erica Wilson** (717 Madison Ave., between 63rd and 64th Sts., 2nd floor, tel. 212/832–7290). The eponymous British-born needlepoint authority is a top resource.

New York Yarn Center (1011 6th Ave., between 37th and 38th Sts., 2nd floor, tel. 212/719–5648). There's a huge selection of yarns here to suit many purposes.

Pamela Duval (833 Lexington Ave., between 63rd and 64th Sts., tel. 212/751–2126). Look for the needlepoint canvases with funny quotations.

Wallis Mayers Needlework (30 E. 68th St., tel. 212/861–5318). Have fun choosing among oodles of yarns and offbeat handpainted canvases here.

Paper, Greeting Cards, Stationery **Dempsey & Carroll** (110 E. 57th St., tel. 212/486–7526). Supplying New York's high society for a century, this firm is always correct but seldom straitlaced.

Kate's Paperie (561 Broadway, near Prince St., tel. 212/941–9816). This wonderful spot features fabulous wrapping papers, some handmade; bound blank books; and more.

Untitled (159 Prince St., tel. 212/982–2088). The stock here includes thousands of tasteful greeting cards and postcards.

Performing Arts Memorabilia **The Ballet Shop** (1887 Broadway, between 62nd and 63rd Sts., tel. 212/581–7990). This balletomane's delight near Lincoln Center showcases dance ephemera and artifacts.

Drama Book Shop (723 7th Ave., between 48th and 49th Sts., tel. 212/944–0595). The comprehensive stock here includes scripts, scores, and libretti.

Memory Shop (109 E. 12th St., tel. 212/473–2404). Movie stills and posters by the million are on sale here.

Motion Picture Arts Gallery (133 E. 58th St., 10th floor, tel. 212/223–1009). Vintage posters enchant collectors here.

Movie Star News (134 W. 18th St., tel. 212/620–8160). The film memorabilia emphasizes Hollywood glamour.

One Shubert Alley (Shubert Alley, between 44th and 45th Sts. west of Broadway, tel. 212/944–4133). Souvenirs from past and present Broadway hits reign at this Theater District shop.

Richard Stoddard (18 E. 16th St., Room 305, tel. 212/645–

9576). This veteran dealer offers out-of-print books, back issues of magazines, old programs, and other printed matter.

Theatrebooks (1600 Broadway, between 48th and 49th Sts.,
Room 1009, tel. 212/757–2834). This is a good place to schmooze
and browse.

Triton Gallery (323 W. 45th St., between 8th and 9th Aves., tel.
212/765–2472). Theatrical posters large and small can be found
here for hits and flops.

Posters   **Posteramerica** (138 W. 18th St., tel. 212/206–0499). Victorian
to 20th-century posters are displayed in this renovated carriage house, the country's oldest store of its type.

Souvenirs of   Ordinary Big Apple souvenirs can be found in and around major
New York City   tourist attractions. More-unusual items can be found at:

Accent New York (489 5th Ave., between 41st and 42nd Sts., tel.
212/599–3661). This store features every possible variation of
the New York souvenir T-shirt, mug, key chain, and so on.

Citybooks (61 Chambers St., tel. 212/669–8245). Come here for
calendars, maps, books, seals, subway-token tietacks, traffic
signs ("Don't Even Think of Parking Here"), Sanitation Department T-shirts, and teddy bears.

New York Bound Bookshop (50 Rockefeller Plaza, tel. 212/245–
8503). Old or rare New York books and prints are the specialty
in this delightfully knowledgeable store.

Think New York (875 7th Ave., between 55th and 56th Sts., tel.
212/957–8511). Here you'll find New York City stars on mugs,
aprons, and many other objects, some surprising and unusual.

Toys   Many toy companies are headquartered here, and the windows
of the Toy Center at 23rd Street and Fifth Avenue display the
latest thing, especially during February's Toy Week, when all
the out-of-town buyers come to place orders for the Christmas
season (*see also* Fun and Games, *above*).

Big City Kite Co. (1201 Lexington Ave. at 81st St., tel. 212/472–
2623). Kites of all sizes and shapes are found here.

Enchanted Forest (85 Mercer St., tel. 212/925–6677). Fancy
reigns in this shop's stock of unique handmades.

F.A.O. Schwarz (767 5th Ave. at 58th St., tel. 212/644–9400).
You will be hooked on this sprawling two-level children's store
from the minute you walk through the door and one of the costumed staff members—a donkey, a clown, a cave woman, or a
mad scientist—extends a welcome. Beyond a wonderful mechanical clock with many dials and dingbats are all the stuffed
animals in the world, dolls large and small, things to build with
(including blocks by the pound), computer games, toy cars (including a multi-thousand-dollar Ferrari), and more.

Penny Whistle Toys (132 Spring St., tel. 212/925–2088; 448 Columbus Ave., between 81st and 82nd Sts., tel. 212/873–9090;
1283 Madison Ave., between 91st and 92nd Sts., tel. 212/369–
3868). Meredith Brokaw, wife of newscaster Tom Brokaw, has
developed an intriguing selection of quality toys here.

West Side Kids (498 Amsterdam Ave. at 84th St., tel. 212/496–
7282). The shrewd selection here mixes educational toys with a
grab bag of fun little playthings.

Dolls and   **Dollhouse Antics** (1343 Madison Ave. at 94th St., tel. 212/876–
Miniatures   2288). This is a miniaturist's paradise, with infinitesimal accessories such as a small *New York Times*.

Iris Brown's Victorian Doll and Miniature Shop (253 E. 57 St., tel. 212/593–2882.) A sweet, knowledgeable owner presides over the antique dolls and dollhouses.

Toy Soldiers **The Soldier Shop** (1222 Madison Ave. at 88th St., tel. 212/535–6788). Lead soldiers old and new parade by the hundreds here.

Trains and Models Railroad aficionados will be dazzled by the vast selections at: **America's Hobby Center** (146 W. 22nd St., tel. 212/675–8922); **Red Caboose** (16 W. 45th St., 4th floor, tel. 212/575–0155); and **Train Shop** (23 W. 45th St., basement level, tel. 212/730–0409).

Umbrellas and Canes **Stanley Novak** (115 W. 30th St., Room 400, tel. 212/947–8466). The cane's the thing, and there are hundreds here.
Uncle Sam Umbrella (161 W. 57th St., tel. 212/247–7163). The city's top umbrella dealer offers both basics and oddball stuff.

Women's Clothing The department stores' collections are always good: **Saks** for its designers; **Macy's** for its breadth; **Bloomingdale's** for its extremes; **Barneys** for its trendy chic; and **Lord & Taylor** for its classicism. The following add another dimension.

Classicists **Ann Taylor** (2017 Broadway, near 69th St., tel. 212/873–7344; 25 Fulton St., tel. 212/608–5600; 805 3rd Ave. at 50th St., tel. 212/308–5333; 3 E. 57th St., tel. 212/832–2010; and other locations). These stores provide what the elegant young woman with a sense of style needs for work and play.
Burberry's (9 E. 57th St., tel. 212/371–5010). The look is classic and conservative—and nobody does a better trench coat.
Cross–Spellen (203 W. 20th St., tel. 212/675–4862). These designers offer evening gowns and dinner dresses with a hip, ladylike touch, either off-the-rack or made-to-measure.

Designer Showcases **Betsey Johnson** (130 Thompson St., tel. 212/420–0169; 248 Columbus Ave., between 71st and 72nd Sts., tel. 212/362–3364). The look here is still hip.
Chanel (5 E. 57th St., tel. 212/355–5050). The classic designs here never go out of style. Afterward, stop by **Chanel Perfume** (9 W. 57th St., tel. 212/688–5055).
Comme des Garçons (116 Wooster St., tel. 212/219–0660). This SoHo shop showcases a Japanese designer.
Emanuel Ungaro (803 Madison Ave., between 67th and 68th Sts., tel. 212/249–4090). The style here is body-conscious, but it's never flashy.
Emporio Armani (110 5th Ave., between 16th and 17th Sts., tel. 212/727–3240). The Italian designer's casual line is featured.
Geoffrey Beene (783 5th Ave. at 59th St., tel. 212/935–0470). A splendid-looking boutique houses exquisite day and evening wear by America's master designer.
Giorgio Armani (815 Madison Ave., between 67th and 68th Sts., tel. 212/988–9191). In this lofty blond-and-beige space with grand, arched windows and doors, Armani's high-end line looks oh-so-chic.
Givenchy (954 Madison Ave. at 75th St., tel. 212/772–1040). This designer is famous for timeless elegance.
Hermès (11 E. 57th St., tel. 212/751–3181). Patterned scarves and Grace Kelly bags are hallmarks.
Koos van den Akker (34 E. 67th St., tel. 212/249–5432). Collage meets couture in the home of the Dutch-born former Dior designer once known as the Rembrandt of ready-to-wear.
L. Allmeier (109 W. 24th St., tel. 212/243–7390). This shop showcases designs by the blousemaker to the stars.
Matsuda (156 5th Ave., between 20th and 21st Sts., tel. 212/

645–5151; 465 Park Ave. at 57th St., tel. 212/935–6969). Kudos go out for wonderful cuts and fine muted hues.

Missoni (836 Madison Ave. at 69th St., tel. 212/517–9339). Wonderfully textured knits, suits, and sportswear stand out.

Norma Kamali O.M.O. (11 W. 56th St., tel. 212/957–9797). The look here ranges from sweatshirts to evening gowns.

Polo/Ralph Lauren (867 Madison Ave. at 72nd St., tel. 212/606–2100). Lauren's flagship store is one of New York's most distinctive shopping experiences, in a grand, carefully renovated turn-of-the-century town house.

Sonia Rykiel (792 Madison Ave. at 67th St., tel. 212/744–0880). Signature knits for day and evening pack the racks.

Valentino (823 Madison Ave., between 68th and 69th Sts., tel. 212/744–0200). The mix here is at once audacious and beautifully cut, with the best of France and Italy on its racks.

Vera Wang (991 Madison Ave. at 77th St., tel. 212/628–3400). Sumptuous, made-to-order bridal and evening wear is shown here by appointment only.

Yohji Yamamoto (103 Grand St., tel. 212/966–9066). Severe, beautifully cut fashions come from fashion's Zen master.

Yves St. Laurent Rive Gauche (543 Madison Ave. at 53rd St., tel. 212/832–7100; 859 Madison Ave., between 70th and 71st Sts., tel. 212/517–7400). The looks range from chic to classic for day and evening.

Discount **Bolton's** (225 E. 57th St., tel. 212/755–2527; other locations). The styles won't stop traffic, but you can count on finding basics at moderate prices.

Century 21 (22 Cortlandt St., between Broadway and Church St., tel. 212/227–9092). Spiffy quarters make bargain-hunting a pleasure, and there are fabulous buys on very high fashion. Note that there are no try-ons, but items may be returned within 12 working days after purchase.

Daffy's (111 5th Ave. at 18th St., tel. 212/529–4477; 335 Madison Ave. at 44th St., tel. 212/557–4422). Cheap stuff is priced cheaper, and pricey stuff is marked way down.

Forman's (82 Orchard St., tel. 212/228–2500). This is an unexpectedly attractive longtime mainstay of the Lower East Side.

The Gap Outlet (60 W. 34th St., in Herald Sq., tel. 212/643–8960). Lower-than-sale prices prevail on Gap classics.

Loehmann's (236th St. and Broadway, the Bronx, tel. 212/543–6420). The flagship store of this premier off-price outlet is an institution among shopaholics.

Ms., Miss or Mrs./Ben Farber (462 7th Ave., between 35th and 36th Sts., 3rd floor, tel. 212/736–0557). This Garment Center fixture is known to canny shoppers for 30%–60% discounts.

S&W (165 W. 26th St., tel. 212/924–6656). Prices here are good to great on coats, furs, lingerie, handbags, and accessories.

Ethnic Looks **Putumayo** (857 Lexington Ave., between 64th and 65th Sts., tel. 212/734–3111; 341 Columbus Ave., between 76th and 77th Sts., tel. 212/595–3441; 147 Spring St., tel. 212/966–4458). There's cool cotton clothing here, much of it crinkly and easy to pack.

Hip Styles **A/E** (568 Broadway near Prince St., tel. 212/431–6000). Here's Giorgio Armani's answer to the Gap—with a sleek European touch and a higher price tag.

Canal Jean (504 Broadway, between Spring and Broome Sts., tel. 212/226–1130). Casual funk draws hip shoppers.

The Limited (691 Madison Ave. at 62nd St., tel. 212/838–8787).

Considering the address, prices are moderate for well-styled though not outrageous clothing, much of it casual.

The Limited Express (7 W. 34th St., tel. 212/629–6838; and other locations). Mass-market chic includes great leggings, sweaters, and microscopic dresses—all with a Gallic accent.

Reminiscence (74 5th Ave., between 13th and 14th Sts., tel. 212/243–2292). The theme is strictly '50s and '60s, in vintage and new clothing.

Trash and Vaudeville (4 St. Marks Pl., tel. 212/982–3590). Black, white, and electric colors are the focus here.

Women's Workout Gear (121 7th Ave. at 17th St., tel. 212/627–1117). Come here for exercise wear in all colors.

Lingerie Exquisite little things in silk and lace, both naughty and nice, are found at **Joovay** (436 West Broadway, tel. 212/431–6386); **Montenapoleone** (789 Madison Ave. at 67th St., tel. 212/535–2660); and **Victoria's Secret** (34 E. 57th St., tel. 212/758–5592).

Romantics **Laura Ashley** (21 E. 57th St., tel. 212/752–7300; 398 Columbus Ave. at 79th St., tel. 212/496–5110; 714 Madison Ave. at 64th St., tel. 212/735–5000). Old-fashioned English frocks abound here.

Salons Members of New York's charity-ball set drop more on a single dress than most of us spend on a year's wardrobe at **Sara Fredericks** (508 Park Ave., between 59th and 60th Sts., tel. 212/759–1254); **Martha** (475 Park Ave. at 58th St., tel. 212/753–1511); and **Martha International** (473 Park Ave., between 57th and 58th Sts., tel. 212/371–7400), where the look is more youthful.

Trendsetters **Agnès B.** (116 Prince St., tel. 212/925–4649). This Euro-style boutique has maintained its Soho popularity for several years. **Charivari** (2315 Broadway, between 83rd and 84th Sts., tel. 212/873–1424). Since Selma Weiser founded this store on the Upper West Side, she has made a name for herself internationally for her eagle eye on the up-and-coming and avant-garde. The branches, too, take a high-style approach: **Charivari Sport** (201 W. 79th St., tel. 212/799–8650); **Charivari Workshop** (441 Columbus Ave. at 81st St., tel. 212/496–8700); **Charivari 72** (257 Columbus Ave. at 72nd St., tel. 212/787–7272); **Charivari 57** (18 W. 57th St., tel. 212/333–4040); and **Charivari on Madison** (1001 Madison Ave. at 77th St., tel. 212/650–0078).

Patricia Field (10 E. 8th St., tel. 212/254–1699). This store collects the essence of the downtown look.

La Rue des Rêves (578 Broadway, tel. 212/226–6736). Stylish clothing for stylish women who like either an elegant, understated look or Tina Turner styles.

Vintage **Harriet Love** (126 Prince St., tel. 212/966–2280). This is the doyenne of the city's vintage clothing scene.

Screaming Mimi's (22 E. 4th St., tel. 212/677–6464). Old clothes go avant-garde here.

Women's Shoes
Designer Shoes **Charles Jourdan** (769 Madison Ave. at 66th St., tel. 212/628–0133). Shoes feature quirky heels and exuberant colors and patterns.

Manolo Blahnik (15 E. 55th St., tel. 212/582–3007). It's possibly the hautest—and costliest—footwear in town, by England's top shoe designer.

Maud Frizon (19 E. 69th St., tel. 212/249–5368). These extravagant styles come in outrageous shapes and sizzling colors.

Peter Fox (105 Thompson St., tel. 212/431–7426 and 212/431–

6359; 378 Amsterdam Ave. at 78th St., tel. 212/874–6399). Looks here are outside the fashion mainstream—really fun.

Robert Clergerie (41 E. 60 St., tel. 212/207–8600). Exquisite, high-style French footwear includes the chicest platform sandals imaginable.

Salvatore Ferragamo (717 5th Ave. at 56th St., tel. 212/759–3822). No stylistic gimmicks here, just beautiful shoemaking.

Susan Bennis Warren Edwards (22 W. 57th St., tel. 212/755–4197). Here you'll find alligator, silk, satin, suede, canvas, and buttery-soft leather exquisitely worked.

Discount and Lower-Price Shoes Discounters dot Reade Street between Church and West Broadway, including **Anbar** (93 Reade St., tel. 212/227–0253). Several Orchard Street stores discount uptown shoe styles; try **Lace-Up Shoes** (110 Orchard St., tel. 212/475–8040) for moderate discounts on very high-style shoes.

Moderately Priced Shoes The shoes at these stores tend toward the classic, in a good range of colors and styles: **Ecco** (324 Columbus Ave., between 75th and 76th Sts., tel. 212/799–5229; 94 7th Ave., between 15th and 16th Sts., tel. 212/675–5180; 111 Thompson St., tel. 212/925–8010); **Galo** (825 Lexington Ave. at 63rd St., tel. 212/832–3922; 692 Madison Ave., between 62nd and 63rd Sts., tel. 212/688–6276); **Joan & David** (816 Madison Ave. at 68th St., tel. 212/772–3970; 104 5th Ave. at 16th St., tel. 212/627–1780); **Maraolo** (782 Lexington Ave., between 60th and 61st Sts., tel. 212/832–8182); **Ritz** (14 W. 8th St., between 5th and 6th Aves., tel. 212/228–5377; 505 Park Ave. at 59th St., tel. 212/838–2556); **Shoe Express** (1420 2nd Ave. at 74th St., tel. 212/734–3967); and **Vamps** (1421 2nd Ave. at 74th St., tel. 212/744–0227).

Secondhand Shops

Resale Shops To find top-of-the-line designs at secondhand prices, try: **Encore** (1132 Madison Ave., between 84th and 85th Sts., upstairs, tel. 212/879–2850); **Exchange Unlimited** (563 2nd Ave. at 31st St., tel. 212/889–3229); **Gene London's** (897 Broadway at 19th St., tel. 212/533–4105); **Michael's Resale** (1041 Madison Ave., between 79th and 80th Sts., tel. 212/737–7273); and **Renate's** (235 E. 81st St., tel. 212/472–1698).

Thrift Shops Affluent New Yorkers donate castoffs to thrift shops run for charity. And, oh, such castoffs! Often they're supplemented by closeouts from major stores. Hours are limited, so call ahead.

Arthritis Foundation Thrift Shop (121 E. 77th St., tel. 212/772–8816).

Council Thrift Shop (767 9th Ave., between 51st and 52nd Sts., tel. 212/757–6132).

Everybody's Thrift Shop (261 Park Ave. S, between 20th and 21st Sts., tel. 212/355–9263).

Girls Club of New York Thrift Shop (202 E. 77th St., tel. 212/535–8570).

Irvington Institute for Medical Research Thrift Shop (1534 2nd Ave. at 80th St., tel. 212/879–4555).

Memorial Sloan-Kettering Cancer Center Thrift Shop (1440 3rd Ave., between 81st and 82nd Sts., tel. 212/535–1250).

New York Hospital Auxiliary Thrift Shop (439 E. 71st St., tel. 212/535–0965).

Spence-Chapin Corner Shop (1430 3rd Ave., between 80th and 81st Sts., tel. 212/737–8448).

Auctions

New York's lively auction scene means regular sales from internationally known houses. Sales are advertised in the *New York Times*, particularly in Friday's "Weekend" and Sunday's "Arts & Leisure" sections. If you note a sale of interest, attend the exhibition to inspect the wares, peruse the catalogue, discuss possible payment methods, and find out whether you'll need a paddle for bidding.

Christie's (502 Park Ave. at 59th St., tel. 212/546–1000, 212/371–5438 for recorded schedules). This London firm, more than 200 years old, has had an American presence for more than a decade. The annex is **Christie's East** (219 E. 67th St., tel. 212/606–0400).

Sotheby's (1334 York Ave. at 72nd St., tel. 212/606–7000, 212/606–7245 for recorded schedules). This is Christie's chief rival, also originally from London. On the premises is the **Arcade,** where interesting and well-priced also-rans go on the block.

William Doyle Galleries (175 E. 87th St., tel. 212/427–2730, 212/427–4885 for recorded schedules). The charismatic and amazingly energetic William Doyle has turned his instinct for accumulation into a major force on the New York auction scene.

Smaller houses include **Gotham Galleries** (80 4th Ave., between 10th and 11th Sts., tel. 212/677–3303); **Guernsey's Auction** (108 E. 73rd St., tel. 212/794–2280); **Lubin Galleries** (30 W. 26th St., tel. 212/924–3777); **Swann Galleries** (104 E. 25th St., tel. 212/254–4710); and **Tepper Galleries** (110 E. 25th St., tel. 212/677–5300).

Flea Markets

The season runs from March or April through November or December at most of these markets in school playgrounds and parking lots.

Annex Antiques Fair and Flea Market (105 W. 16th St., tel. 212/243–5343), Saturdays and Sundays.

P.S. 44 Market (Columbus Ave., between 76th and 77th Sts., tel. 212/947–6302 evenings), Sundays.

P.S. 41 (Greenwich Ave. at Charles St., tel. 212/752–8475), Saturdays.

P.S. 183 Market (67th St., between York and 1st Aves., tel. 212/737–8888), Saturdays.

Tower Market (Broadway, between W. 4th and Great Jones Sts., tel. 718/273–8702), Saturdays and Sundays.

9 Dining

By John F.
Mariani and Peter
D. Meltzer

John F. Mariani
is food and travel
correspondent for
Esquire and a
regularcontributor
to Travel
&Leisure. Peter D.
Meltzer is a
contributing
authority to Food
Arts andalso
contributes to
Gastronome.

New York retains its position as the gastronomic capital of the country no matter which way the economic index blows. The city is home to a staggering quantity of restaurants—some 16,000 in all if you count corner coffee shops and diners. More important are the variety and the quality of restaurants found within its few square miles.

The island of Manhattan spawns dozens of culinary cultures—Brazilian, Greek, Hungarian, Mexican, Japanese, even Cuban-Chinese—all enriched by a pragmatic American style and a very hip gloss. The city also offers the finest French food outside of Paris, the most authentic Italian specialties outside of Bologna, the most varied styles of Chinese cuisine outside of Hong Kong, and the spiciest Thai dishes outside of Bangkok. This is the place that gave the world lox, fettuccine primavera, negimaki, Delmonico steak, and a number of other dishes one might have thought originated in Europe or Asia. And when it comes to steak houses, New York created and defined the genre with places like the Palm, which opened in the 1920s.

The lengthy recession that has affected the restaurant community here has contributed to a substantial decline in deluxe or expense-account dining and to a rise in more casual eating habits; these changes have been a boon to consumers. Prices in many expensive restaurants have dropped or have been tempered by reduced- or fixed-price menus. What's more, many of the new "downscale" restaurants, such as Becco, Zoë, and Steak Frites, are exciting places to dine, with terrific food that will give you a real taste of New York.

It is no longer inconceivable to get a table on short notice at restaurants where it once took weeks. Yet it is worth noting that places that are deemed to represent good value (at either end of the price spectrum)—such as Jean-Georges Vongerichten's highly popular Jo Jo, Danny Meyer's Union Square Café, and Bouley—still have long waiting lists. For after all, when it comes to fine dining, New Yorkers are both a demanding and discriminating lot.

With so much to pick from, choosing where to dine in New York may be exasperating. Probably the best strategy is to select your restaurant on the basis of your budget and the neighborhood you're visiting; after that, you can decide which type of cuisine and what atmosphere you prefer. We've set this chapter up first by region and then by cost, giving choices for every price range within each neighborhood.

Prices New York may not be the most expensive city in the world when it comes to dining out (Tokyo probably takes that honor), and prices are lower in many new eateries, but by and large, New York restaurants are quite a bit more expensive than those in most other American cities. It has become increasingly difficult to find a good meal for under $20 a head. And while you might spend $100 per person in Boston, Los Angeles, or Washington, DC, you can easily spend that much in New York, even at lesser restaurants where all too often you're paying for a false sense of chic, a panorama, or a valued table. We've skirted such restaurants in favor of places we think represent true val-

All restaurant reviews in this chapter have been adapted from Passport to New York Restaurants *(Passport Press, Ltd.), a pocket guide by John F. Mariani and Peter D. Meltzer.*

ue, even for those for whom money is no object. Highly recommended restaurants in each category are indicated by a star ★.

Category	Cost*
Very Expensive	over $60
Expensive	$40–$60
Moderate	$20–$40
Inexpensive	under $20

per person, excluding drinks, service, and 8¼% sales tax

It's worth noting that lunch prices tend to be much lower than dinner prices at the better spots; you can dine regally at the most deluxe restaurants in town for $30 to $40 per person at lunch, eating the same meal that would cost you $75–$100 at dinner. Be aware, however, that most of the top-flight restaurants are not open for lunch on Saturday.

Many haute-cuisine restaurants offer three-course, fixed-price menus, which usually cost a bit less than meals ordered à la carte, but be wary of the ubiquitous supplements and surcharges on such menus. Some fixed-price meals are called "tasting menus" or, in French, *menus dégustation.* These offer a sampling of anywhere from five to 10 dishes—usually at quite a high price—and give you a very good indication of a kitchen's strengths.

Even with fixed-price meals, coffee and after-dinner beverages are almost never included, so if a waiter suggests an item, ask whether it is complimentary or additional. A waiter who asks, "Would you like a soufflé for dessert?" does not necessarily mean that it's a giveaway—it may cost you plenty on top of your bill. If a waiter says, "The owner would like to buy you a drink," however, you should not have to pay for that drink. Check your bill accordingly.

In many restaurants, your waiter may come to your table to recite a long list of the evening's specials, often without quoting prices. If you're tempted, don't be bashful about asking a dish's price—you don't want to discover when the bill arrives that you've paid for the ingredients' airfare from Alaska!

Wine Some of the best wine cellars in the country are to be found here at grand restaurants such as Le Cirque, Lutèce, and the Four Seasons. You'll find equally great wines at Felidia, Sparks, Smith & Wollensky, and the Grand Central Oyster Bar. While it's possible to spend upwards of $100 per bottle at these places, good value often lurks at the lower end of the list. As a general rule, plan on spending at least the equivalent of a dinner entrée on your bottle. Unless budget requires, don't go for the cheapest listing you find, because it's probably no bargain: A $17 bottle usually bears a much higher markup than a $28 one.

Dress Codes For men, a jacket and tie (and very often a suit) are never out of place and always welcome at New York restaurants; many specifically require them. For women, it's always safe to be dressy. There are, however, a large number of restaurants where casual dress is acceptable—as long as it's neat and carries a certain amount of taste. Blue jeans might be all right in Chinatown or a pizza parlor, but slacks and a sweater or tweed jacket will put you in better stead elsewhere. Cutoffs and shorts are worn in the heat of summer, but only at very casual restaurants.

Reservations Even though the past season has witnessed a decline in restaurant volume, that doesn't mean you can show up at any hour and expect to be seated immediately. Reservations are always a good idea and, more often than not, essential at top-rated restaurants. Weekdays are easier than weekends, and lunch easier still. You'd also be surprised how many times no-shows open up a table even on a Saturday night, so it's worth a last-minute call to find out. Another ploy to snare an otherwise booked table is to make a very early (say, 6 PM) or quite late (9:30 PM) reservation. Even the best restaurants often have tables at those hours. Sometimes you may be asked for a confirmation telephone number. Always phone when you intend to cancel, and even when you expect to be late.

Smoking New York City law now stipulates that restaurants with more than 50 seats must set aside nonsmoking sections. Make your preference known when you reserve.

Dining Hours Most New Yorkers dine out at approximately 8 PM. Pretheater dining can be a lot of fun, but expect it to be rushed: You'll want to be out by 7:45, and restaurants that cater to the theater crowd will make sure you are. If you prefer to wait until after the show to eat, you'll find that New York restaurants take good care of hungry night owls who want something more than diner food.

Seating Many people worry about the "seating game"—who gets the best tables and how to avoid being placed in what's known as Siberia—the least desirable spot in a deluxe or trendy restaurant. The best tables are customarily doled out to regulars or high-powered celebrities. Don't assume that not getting an "A" table is a deliberate slight. If you are seated at a table you find truly awful—next to the rest room, the kitchen, or service station, for instance—politely request another. If space allows, the maître d' should happily place you elsewhere—perhaps not at the window table, but at a better one. Whatever you do, *do not* "grease the palm" of the maître d': It may work, but it'll mark you as a patsy, ready to be gouged by the rest of the staff.

Tipping If you have received good service and liked where the maître d' seated you, on the way out you may want to give him a tip (anywhere from a few dollars to $10 or more if you wish to be remembered), but it is in no way mandatory. As for tipping others, remember that most service staffs pool their tips at the end of each evening (busboys and bartenders are given a share), so it is not necessary to provide a separate tip for everyone who serves you. If you do want to separate your tip in a deluxe restaurant, give 15% to the waiter and 5% to the captain. Otherwise, just leave behind 15%–20% in one lump sum.

Wine stewards are tipped only when they perform special services, such as decanting rare wines or advising you throughout a multicourse meal, in which case a tip of a few dollars is in order. Coat-check attendants usually get $1 per coat; parking valets get about the same per car. If you're just ordering drinks, a tip of $1 on a $5–$10 order is just fine.

A quick way to figure your tip is to double the tax you've been charged: That would equal 16½%, a perfectly adequate amount.

Lower Manhattan

Expensive **Fraunces Tavern.** A good, evocative American restaurant inside a historic structure (where Washington bade farewell to his troops in 1783), Fraunces Tavern is one of the last bits of Colonial New York remaining, and the museum upstairs is delightful. Downstairs there's a barroom that fills up at midday and after 5 PM with the bulls and bears of Wall Street. The main dining room is a cheery spot in antique style where you can enjoy everything from a hearty breakfast of oatmeal and eggs to lunches and dinners that focus on such classic American dishes as steak, chops, and seafood. The pies and cakes are fitting endings. *54 Pearl St. (at Broad St.), tel. 212/269-0144. Reservations required at lunch, advised at breakfast and dinner. Jacket and tie advised. AE, DC, MC, V. Closed weekends.*

Hudson River Club. The World Financial Center houses some splendid restaurants. One of the most attractive is the Hudson River Club, which looks out over the mouth of the Hudson River. This is real corporate-dining style—golden paneling, lots of brass, thick carpeting—and the ambience is civil, if not exciting. The menu, under chef Waldy Malouf, features the products and ingredients of the Hudson River valley in season; specialties include pheasant in riesling, maple-roasted chicken, and corn-crusted scallops. *4 World Financial Center, tel. 212/786-1500. Reservations advised. Jacket and tie suggested. AE, DC, MC, V. Closed Sat. lunch.*

Le Pactole. Romeo DiGobbi, former maître d' at Le Cirque, oversees this large, formal dining room with a grand panorama of the Hudson River, and it's the best restaurant of the dozen or so in the World Financial Center. The food is what is called "retro cuisine," which is an attempt to bring back classic dishes that had become clichés but that now taste new again. The menu is very large, but the kitchen does most things very well. There's even a good cheese tray. Magret of duck and confit with roasted potatoes, brandade with caviar, roasted chicken with bacon and scallion vinaigrette, and *gratin de fruits* are recommended. Le Pactole has excellent banquet facilities. *2 World Financial Center, tel. 212/945-9444. Reservations advised. Jacket and tie advised. AE, DC, MC, V.*

★ **Windows on the World.** Perched on the 107th floor of One World Trade Center, with a spectacular view of the city unfolding beneath, this restaurant is one of the country's most awesome. Remember, however, that window tables are hard to get, and you may feel disappointed if you go on a rainy or foggy night. The simpler food items—such as rack of lamb and American chocolate cake—are often the best choices. A three-course Sunset Supper ($27) is served from 5 to 6:30. The wine list at Windows is one of the most extensive in the country, with tremendous breadth of choice and very fair prices. In fact, Windows is so committed to wine that it actually offers a special dining experience for oenophiles at **Cellar in the Sky,** a compact, enclosed dining room in which a seven-course menu is served with carefully matched wines at a fixed price of $90. *1 World Trade Center, tel. 212/938-1111. Reservations required. Jacket and tie required. AE, DC, MC, V.*

Moderate **Bridge Café.** This very old, extremely amiable little café is the best bet in the South Street Seaport area—but ask for specific instructions on how to find it. The place evokes a simpler era in New York—big oak bar, red-checkered tablecloths, friendly

Downtown Manhattan Dining

Acme Bar and Grill, **11**
Alison on Dominick Street, **22**
Angelo's, **28**
Benito's II, **27**
Benny's Burritos, **5**
Boom, **25**
Bouley, **37**
Bridge Café, **43**
Capsouto Freres, **23**
Chanterelle, **35**
Ennio and Michael, **12**
Famous Ray's, **2**
Florent, **6**

Fraunces Tavern, **42**
Gotham Bar & Grill, **1**
Hudson River Club, **39**
Jerry's, **19**
Jour et Nuit, **24**
Katz's Delicatessen, **13**
Kwong and Wong, **32**
La Metairie, **9**
Le Pactole, **40**
Le Pescadou, **18**
Mandarin Court, **30**
Montrachet, **34**
Noodle Town, **31**

Nosmo King, **33**
The Odeon, **38**
The Old Homestead, **4**
Patisserie Lanciani, **7**
Peter Luger, **15**
Provence, **17**
Quatorze, **3**
The River Café, **45**
Sevilla, **8**
Soho Kitchen and Bar, **21**
South Street Seaport, **44**
Teresa's, **10**
TriBeCa Grill, **36**

Villa Mosconi, **16**
West Broadway, **26**
Windows on the World, **41**
Wong Kee, **29**
Yonah Schimmel's Knishery, **14**
Zoë, **20**

Uptown Manhattan Dining

KEY

AE American Express Office

Amerigo's, **1**
Amsterdam's Bar and Rotisserie, **10**
Arizona 206, **37**
Aureole, **35**
Bistro du Nord, **3**
Café des Artistes, **25**
Carmine's, **6**
Docks, **7**
EJ's Luncheonette, **11**
Fishin' Eddie, **13**
J.G. Melon, **12, 20**
Jackson Hole, **31**
Jo Jo, **30**

Le Cirque, **28**
Lola Belle, **32**
Lucy's, **8**
Mark's Restaurant, **18**
Mazzei, **17**
Parioli Romanissimo, **15**
Park Avenue Cafe, **33**
Poiret, **9**
Post House, **34**
Right Bank, **22**
Serendipity, **36**
Sette Mezzo, **21**
7th Regiment Mess, **23**

Sidewalkers, **14**
Sign of the Dove, **29**
Sylvia's, **2**
Table d'Hôte, **4**
Tavern on the Green, **24**
The Terrace, **5**
Vasata, **19**
Vico Ristorante, **16**
Vince & Eddie's, **26**

Al Bustan, **42**
America, **75**
American Festival Café, **57**
An American Place, **66**
Aquavit, **23**
Banana Café, **70**
Bangkok Cuisine, **16**
Barbetta, **60**
Becco, **61**
Billy's, **38**
Brasserie, **30**
Brasserie des Théâtres, **59**
Cabana Carioca, **58**
Carnegie Deli, **15**
Chefs Cuisiniers Club, **71**
Chin Chin, **45**
Coffee Shop, **72**
David K's Noodle Road, **44**
Dawat, **4**
Docks, **65**
Felidia, **3**
44, **52**
The Four Seasons, **31**
Gallagher's, **17**
Grand Central Oyster Bar & Restaurant, **50**
Hard Rock Café, **12**
Harry Cipriani, **5**
Hatsuhana, **48, 54**
Il Nido, **36**
Joe Allen, **62**
La Caravelle, **25**
La Chinita Linda, **83**
La Cité, **20**
La Colombe D'Or, **69**
La Côte Basque, **26**
La Reserve, **56**
Le Bar Bat, **11**
Le Bernardin, **19**
Le Perigord, **39**
Le Madri, **82**
Les Célébrités, **9**
Les Halles, **67**
Lespinasse, **27**
Lola, **80**
Lox Around the Clock, **81**
Lutèce, **41**
Manhattan Ocean Club, **6**
Mesa Grill, **76**
Mickey Mantle's, **7**
Nippon, **32**
Oceana, **28**
Orso, **63**
P. J. Clarke's, **34**
Palm, **46**

Midtown Manhattan Dining

waiters—and it's always warm and happy. The menu is small but changes often, and the food is basic and wholesome. Good choices include fried calamari, duck with wild rice, and fruit crumble; pasta is not the kitchen's strong point. *279 Water St. (at Dover St.), tel. 212/227–3344. Reservations advised. Dress: casual. AE, DC, MC, V. Closed Sat. lunch.*

South Street Seaport. This is not a restaurant but an impeccably restored 19th-century historic district (*see* Tour 18 in Chapter 3) stretching from Water Street to John Street. Its attractions include many restaurants that make pleasant places for lunch or dinner. A host of fast-food restaurants serve a wide variety of ethnic cooking. One good bet is **Sloppy Louie's,** a very old place (since 1874, there has been a restaurant of one sort or another on the location) specializing in seafood and antique charm, though it's a bit touristy. *92 South St., tel. 212/509–9694. Reservations advised for large groups. Dress: casual. AE, DC, MC, V.*

SoHo and TriBeCa

Very Expensive **Bouley.** This artfully restored TriBeCa structure is presently
★ the hottest ticket in town, although some may question whether it is worth making a reservation a month in advance. The price of prominence can mean a wait for a confirmed table and frustrating delays between courses, so dine early—no later than 7:30—and take your time. Gifted chef-owner David Bouley's eclectic menu is highly creative (although not every execution dazzles); recommended are the triangle of New York State goat cheese and artichoke with sun-dried-tomato dressing; panache of three salads (hot foie gras; grilled shrimp and wild mushrooms; and roast loin of veal and sweet Bermuda onions); and prime roasted sweetbreads dusted with cloves. The delectable desserts may include hot glazed chocolate with a caramelized brittle crust, hot rasberry souffle, and hazelnut dacquoise. For a complete overiew of the kitchen's range, consider the $70 fixed-price, six-course menu. There's a fine wine list, but prices are steep. Service is well intentioned and professional, but it can be cloying. *165 Duane St. (near Hudson St.), tel. 212/608–3852. Reservations required. Jacket and tie required. AE, DC, MC, V. Closed Sat. lunch and Sun.*

Chanterelle. A loyal following continues to dine at this dramatically stark but perfectly soothing restaurant, with its bare, peach-colored walls dominated by a massive floral arrangement. Chef-owner David Waltuck's menus are concise, subtle, and refined—definitely not of the knock-'em-dead-with-seasoning school. It's worth noting up front, however, that the food comes with a hefty price tag—the fixed-price menus at $70 and $89 are among the most expensive in town, and you still pay a $15 supplement to have a cheese course with the $70 menu. Recommended dishes include salad of grilled Louisiana shrimp in tomato and saffron, Pemaquid oysters in sauerkraut, grilled seafood sausage, sautéed salmon with green herbs, and rack of lamb with ratatouille juice; for dessert, try cinnamon crème brûlée or warm fig tart. *2 Harrison St. (near Hudson St.), tel. 212/966–6960. Reservations advised. Dress: casual chic. AE, DC, MC, V. Closed Sun. and Mon.*

Expensive **Alison on Dominick Street.** Now five years old, this out-of-the-
★ way SoHo eatery has become a very popular restaurant destination thanks to its indefatigable owner, Alison Price Becker,

and talented chef Tom Valenti, who has a sure hand with seasonings. The place is low-key, personable, and sophisticated without any pretense, in an attractive setting that includes cream-colored walls, blue banquettes, and striking black-and-white photos. A typical menu might include such dishes as Provençal tart, goat-cheese napoleon, asparagus flan, skate with cabbage and bacon, squab with lentils, hen, or Oregon filet mignon. You'll appreciate the cordial service. *38 Dominick St. (near Hudson St.), tel. 212/727–1188. Reservations required. Dress: casual chic. AE, DC, MC, V. Closed lunch.*

★ **Montrachet.** A convivial and pleasurable space presided over by the gifted Drew Nieporent, Montrachet remains one of the city's most consistently satisfying restaurants. Chef Debra Ponzek's flair is apparent in every dish as she demonstrates great mastery over the essential flavors of her ingredients. The wines are especially well chosen and include unique French country selections directly imported by sommelier Daniel Johnnes, along with priceless burgundies. Montrachet is priced somewhat below comparable establishments. Signature dishes include tomato saffron soup, lobster with mushrooms and pasta, sweetbreads with soy vinaigrette, roasted duckling with Swiss chard and duck confit cannelloni, beef with cepes and red wine, caramel-baked figs with pistachio crème fraîche, and banana and chocolate gratin on linzer crust. There are fixed-price menus at $25, $32, and $45, as well as à la carte offerings. *239 W. Broadway (near White St.), tel. 212/219–2777. Reservations advised. Dress: casual. AE. Closed Sun., and Mon.–Thurs. and Sat. lunch.*

Moderate **Boom.** Currently a very hot ticket, this funky, brick-walled establishment has an interior full of faux Pompeiian touches: "crumbling" walls, an oxidized copper ceiling, bizarre wall sculptures, and waiters in coolie outfits. The kitchen turns out savory and creditable East-West concoctions, and once you're seated, you'll have a lot of fun surveying the oh-so-hip crowd here (and it won't cost you much). Recommended are the spring rolls, Vietnamese quail, flat noodles with Thai yellow curry, marinated rack of lamb, plus an array of sandwiches at lunch, such as grilled shrimp and vegetables on focaccio. *152 Spring St. (between W. Broadway and Wooster St.), tel. 212/431–3663. Reservations advised. Dress: casual chic. AE.*

★ **Capsouto Frères.** Its setting in a glorious old landmark building, its view of the Hudson, and its soaring architecture of redbrick and beams make this a standout restaurant in TriBeCa, especially for its lavish brunches. The brothers Capsouto were among the first in New York to offer Provençal and Mediterranean cooking, and they do it very well indeed. The soft-shell crabs in season are sensational, the cassoulet of scallops rich and lustrous, and the roast leg of venison enormous. The wine list is solid and very decently priced. *451 Washington St. (near Watts St.), tel. 212/966–4900. Reservations advised. Dress: casual. AE, DC, MC, V. Closed Mon. lunch.*

Jour et Nuit. Once you finally get a reservation here, you might wonder what the fuss was all about. Nevertheless, this downtown bistro serving simple French fare remains a very popular destination, especially among a hip nocturnal crowd clad in black. Potato with goat cheese, hanger steak, leg of lamb, grilled salmon, and crème brûlée are popular dishes. *337 W. Broadway (at Grand St.), tel. 212/925–5971. Reservations required. Dress: casual. AE, DC, MC, V.*

★ **The Odeon.** Housed in a 1930s art-deco cafeteria, this was the first notable restaurant in the TriBeCa neighborhood. Popularized by the SoHo art set, who still make it one of their chief stomping grounds after midnight, it's a great place to plug into the "scene" in this very artsy district. Everybody seems to wear black, look slightly world-weary, and recognize each other. The food is high-quality bistro-brasserie fare with changing specials. The set-menu lunch is $14.50. *145 W. Broadway (at Thomas St.), tel. 212/233–0507. Reservations advised. Dress: casual. AE, DC, MC, V. Closed Sat. lunch.*

Provence. An authentic bistro, of the kind that dot the Riviera, this spot has become very popular for its unprepossessing decor, its decent prices, and its commendable Provençal food. The seafood dishes are especially good, from the *pissaladière* (a kind of French pizza) to the bourride. The early crowd at dinner are locals; the later crowd, artists and gallery owners from the area. The restaurant attracts a very artsy-literary bunch, as shown in the scene filmed here for the movie *Crossing Delancey*. The front room on the street is charming, but the rear is rather plain. *38 MacDougal St. (near Prince St.), tel. 212/475–7500. Reservations advised. Dress: casual chic. AE.*

★ **TriBeCa Grill.** With Robert De Niro, Mikhail Baryshnikov, Christopher Walken, and other celebs as partners, TriBeCa Grill wouldn't need more than burgers and chili to be a hit, but partner Drew Nieporent, owner of the renowned Montrachet nearby, has made sure the kitchen, under chef Don Pintabona, is first-rate and that customers are treated with real respect, even on the craziest nights. The large brick dining room, with its grand bar salvaged from Maxwell's Plum, has well separated tables and real vitality, as do dishes like lobster gazpacho, cavatelli with pecorino (pasta with sheep's milk cheese), lobster in a broth of vegetables and scallions, potato pancakes Vonnas, and lemon crème brûlée with poppyseed crust. The crowd here is very hip, but the atmosphere is comfortable. *375 Greenwich St. (near Franklin St.), tel. 212/941–3900. Reservations advised. Dress: casual. AE, DC, MC, V. Closed Sat. lunch.*

★ **West Broadway.** This lively space encompasses three dining areas: a retro-looking front room, and a two-tiered back space dominated by a massive gold mural that portrays musical instruments. Unlike at many popular spots nearby, you neither wait unduly long for a table, nor do you have to shout to be heard by your dinner companion. The menu, created by chef John Schenk, consists primarily of seafood dishes, such as fried shrimp with cucumber and seaweed salad, warm skate with red-pepper chick-pea salad and fried carrot sticks, and seared sea scallops with corn, spinach and fried leeks. The list of digestifs is more enterprising than the wine list. *349 W. Broadway (near Grand St.), tel. 212/226–5885. Reservations advised. Dress: casual. AE, DC, MC, V. Closed Sun. lunch.*

Zoë. Owners Thalia and Stephen Loffredo have created an alluring restaurant with soaring ceilings, rough-hewn pillars, sleek marble tabletops, and an open kitchen that emits wonderful aromas. The new chef, Steven Levine, shows real finesse with modern American cuisine, such as grilled foie gras with raisins, cranberries, sweet corn, and pine nuts; smoked pork loin with black-bean marinade and dried-cherry sauce; and herbed gnocchi with wild mushrooms. The menu also includes a daunting array of inventive desserts, such as blueberry *crostata* (tart). The service staff is a bit amateurish, and the owners can be particularly petulant about latecomers. The wine list is replete with critical ratings straight from *The Wine Spectator*. This is a good spot for brunch. *90 Prince St. (at Mercer St.), tel. 212/966–6722. Reservations advised. Dress: casual chic. AE, DC, MC, V. Closed Mon.*

Inexpensive **Jerry's.** The decor is cafeteria chic, and the ambience very relaxed. But the kitchen is anything but laid back in its diligentpreparation of American specialties, including duck breast and duck-sausage salad, spinach salad with Swedish bacon, grilled swordfish with cucumber-tomato *raita* (yogurt sauce), and wholesome sandwiches. Don't miss the superb *frites* (french fries). (A somewhat hipper sibling called Jerry's 103 is located farther east at 103 Second Avenue at 6th Street). *101 Prince St. (between Mercer and Greene Sts.),tel. 212/966–9464. Dinner reservations advised. Dress: casual. AE, MC, V. Closed Sun. dinner.*

★ **Le Pescadou.** This is a picturesque, brick-walled space, specializing—as the name suggests—in seafood with a Provençal accent. There are enticing daily specials, such as fried breaded oysters with spinach and salmon roe, sea scallops in cognac and cream, sautéed grouper niçoise, and standbys including calamari in a light tomato sauce and seafood ravioli in a cream sauce with asparagus. You can also count on an above-average bouillabaisse. The menu carries a few concessions to landlubbers, plus some beautifully presented desserts, including a pastry cup filled with zabaglione and fresh fruit. For an inexpensive taste, you can sample its savory appetizers at the bar. *18 King St. (corner of 6th Ave., 1 block south of Houston), tel. 212/924–3434. Reservations advised. Jacket advised. AE.*

Nosmo King. An amusing interior full of humor and flair is scene to chef Alan Harding's capable fare. The menu is southwestern in orientation, with appetizers such as grilled okra with spicy yam and peach sauce, and corn and black-bean quesadilla, but it also includes such eclectic choices as spicy Thai "fun"—noodles with green curry. Main dishes range from grilled swordfish burrito with avocado salad and refried beans to seared tuna on a bed of spinach with white beans. Typical desserts include chocolate "blackout cake" and citrus pound cake with lemon ice cream. There's a good selection of wines by the glass. (As the restaurant's name suggests, there is no smoking throughout, a condition inoffensively compensated by the fire in the food.) *54 Varick St. (½ block south of Canal St.), tel. 212/966–1239. Reservations advised. Dress: casual. AE, MC, V. Closed for lunch on weekends.*

SoHo Kitchen and Bar. This characteristic and special SoHo eatery has a great deal of spaciousness, good music, a casual but well-groomed crowd, plenty of laughter, and good, basic fare at decent prices. Soaring ceilings are a fit halo for the giant artwork here, and one of the main draws is the oversize bar offering at least 100 wines by the glass on any given night. The wines are often served in sequences of eight selections at a time. Try the crisp-edged pizzas and any of the pasta dishes. *103 Greene St. (between Prince and Spring Sts.), tel. 212/925–1866. Reservations advised for 6 or more. No reservations Sat. dinner. Dress: casual. AE, DC, MC, V.*

Chinatown, Little Italy, and the Lower East Side

Moderate **Angelo's.** An old-fashioned Italian-American spot, smack in the middle of Little Italy, this is certainly better than most of the tourist traps around it. Angelo's has a homey feel, with its simple decor and black-and-white tile floors. The pasta is very good, especially the *perciatelli* with vegetable sauce, and the chicken with garlic is as fine as you'll find in the neighborhood. Go with the whole family—this place welcomes kids. *146 Mulberry St. (near Grand St.), tel. 212/966–1277. Reservations advised weekends. Dress: casual. AE, DC, MC, V.Closed Mon.*

Benito's II. There are many restaurants in Little Italy that pack them in and turn them out, so it's nice to be able to make a reservation at Benito's II (which strangely insists it has nothing to do with Benito's across the street), enjoy a lively atmosphere complete with a strolling guitarist (he's not that good but he's fun), and some good Italian-American cooking, including garlicky chicken, manicotti, and lasagna. It may not be special, but it's a warm-hearted place. *163 Mulberry St. (near Broome St.), tel. 212/226–9012. Reservations advised. Dress: casual. No credit cards.*

★ **Kwong and Wong.** This unassuming Chinatown spot has fast become one of the most highly regarded restaurants for seafood (a fish tank is on the premises), and the big portions of dishes like geoduck (very large) clams or whole fish are meant to be shared. Skip the menu and go with the specials. *11 Division St. (near Bowery), tel. 212/431–1040. Reservations advised. Dress: casual. AE.*

Inexpensive **Katz's Delicatessen.** This is a long-standing favorite of New Yorkers who like to shop for bargains on Orchard Street, then repair to Katz's for big, fat pastrami or corned-beef sandwiches, knishes, brisket, garlicky franks, dripping pickles, terrific french fries, and cream soda. At this original Jewish deli, with a 1950s atmosphere that includes lots of schmoozing and yelling, you can buy wonderful salami and cold cuts to go; the restaurant ships anywhere in the world. Food is served cafeteria-style: You move along the line, shout your order, and then sit down. You've got to know what you want because the counter men can make sandwiches faster than you can say "pastrami on rye." *205 E. Houston St. (near Orchard St.), tel. 212/254–2246. Dress: casual. AE.*

Mandarin Court. Though the command of English here leaves something to be desired for the nonlocal, and the pace can be chaotic at times, this wildly popular dim sum parlor warrants the trip to Chinatown. (*Dim sum* is a term applied to various traditional Chinese foods served during the day in small portions, several of them consisting of steamed or fried dumplings with savory fillings.) On a Sunday you will probably have to wait for a table while you watch a parade of wonderfully steamy dim sum in all shapes pass you by. (You may wish to come here on a weekday for a shorter wait.) The food is cheap and very fresh, and everybody sits at communal tables. A meal of four kinds of dim sum with tea may total as little as $8.95. *61 Mott St. (near Canal St.), tel. 212/608–3838. Reservations accepted except on major holidays. Dress: casual. AE, DC, MC, V.*

Noodle Town. Despite the ridiculous name and premises that might charitably be called "quaint," this Chinatown noodle parlor in the Hong Kong tradition of "sit-'em-serve-'em-move-'em" offers absolutely scrumptious food at very low prices. The

American Express offers Travelers Cheques built for two.

American Express® Cheques *for Two*. The first Travelers Cheques that allow either of you to use them because both of you have signed them. And only one of you needs to be present to purchase them.

Cheques *for Two* are accepted anywhere regular American Express Travelers Cheques are, which is just about everywhere. So stop by your bank, AAA* or any American Express Travel Service Office and ask for Cheques *for Two*.

Travelers Cheques

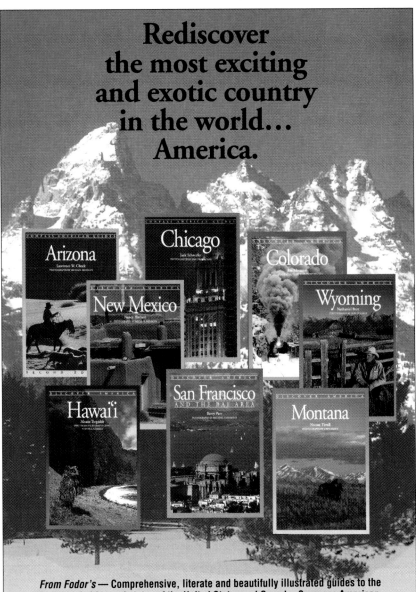

half-duck for $8.50 is the most expensive item here. Don't miss the Hong Kong noodles, the luscious brimming soups, the pan-fried noodles with black beans, or just about anything else you can point to on the enormous menu. *28½ Bowery (near Bayard St.), tel. 212/349–0923. No reservations. Dress: casual. No credit cards.*

Teresa's. One of the few remaining Polish restaurants in New York, this friendly, diner-style spot serves bountiful and rib-sticking food. Service is good and the staff very helpful with the menu, which includes borscht, stuffed veal, kielbasa (Polish smoked sausage), kishke (blood sausage), and heavy, rich desserts. You can also elect to have eggs, burgers, or sandwiches. *103 1st Ave. (near 6th St.), tel. 212/228–0604. Dress: casual. No credit cards.*

Wong Kee. Here is a clean, bright, and completely uncluttered Chinese restaurant that has the added virtue—rare in China-town—of being consistent. It's a cliché to say you should order what the Asian clientele are ordering, but here it is true: Look around and ask for whatever everybody else seems to be eating—duck with star anise, perhaps, or beef with sour cabbage. The bare-bones decor and fast service are part of the fun. There's no liquor license, so you may wish to bring your own wine or beer. *113 Mott St. (near Canal St.), tel. 212/226–9018. No reservations. Dress: casual. No credit cards.*

Yonah Schimmel's Knishery. For more than 100 years and five generations, Yonah Schimmel has been one of the preeminent examples of New York's great immigrant food culture, starting out as a pushcart across the street from its present location, where it has been since 1910. Now it's a 40-seat restaurant and take-out shop where you'll get terrific beef hot dogs, soups, and *latkes* (potato pancakes), and the real glories here are the dozen different kinds of knish—pastries stuffed with everything from potatoes to fruits and cheese. Elsewhere knishes may be heavy and deep-fried, but here they are crisp, golden, made from scratch without additives, baked, and—ready for this?—actually quite low in calories. Health-food enthusiasts order the kasha (ground buckwheat). The restaurant also serves a fabulous yogurt. *137 E. Houston St. (near 2nd Ave.), tel. 212/477–2858. Dress: casual. No credit cards.*

Greenwich Village

Expensive ★
Gotham Bar & Grill. This true Manhattan destination for gourmands is presided over by chef Alfred Portale, who is an inspiration for other chefs around town. The vast and dramatic space (complete with a Statue of Liberty) serves as a vibrant setting for serious but unpretentious eaters who are drawn here by Portale's sense of balance and textures, together with flawless technique. The tantalizing choices include caponata (chopped vegetable relish) and goat-cheese ravioli with roasted peppers; smoked-salmon pasta with chervil and ginger vinaigrette; grilled yellowfin tuna with white beans and red wine sauce; duck sausage with roasted turnips, juniper, and apricot; and grilled squab with pancetta and new potatoes. End with flourless chocolate cake or hazelnut apple tart with cinnamon ice cream. *12 E. 12th St. (between 5th Ave. and University Pl.), tel. 212/620–4020. Reservations advised. Dress: casual chic. AE, DC, MC, V. Closed for lunch on weekends.*

The Old Homestead. Claiming to be the oldest steak house in New York, the Old Homestead still has some antique charm in the barroom area, though the nonsmoking tables are situated in a dreadfully kitschy room with palette-knife paintings and ersatz brick walls. There's really only one reason to come here—for the extraordinary Japanese Kobe beef, unlike anything you'll ever taste and so rich we'd advise the sampler portion at $20.95 rather than the 16-ounce $100 entrée. The vegetable-beef soup is excellent and the prime rib is massive and beefy, but the Famous Spare Rib is only okay. The restaurant has a boring wine list and offers valet parking. *56 9th Ave. (at 15th St.), tel. 212/242-9040. Reservations adivsed. Jacket suggested. AE, DC, MC, V.*

Moderate **Ennio & Michael.** Two Abruzzese owners run this charming, sprightly place that serves robust and zesty Italian food at a fair price. This is definitely one of downtown's best Italian restaurants. Order anything with garlic; recommended dishes include zucchini fritti, *insalata di mare*, gnocchi in tomato sauce, and shrimp *fra diavolo*. *539 LaGuardia Place (near Bleecker St.), tel. 212/677-8577. Reservations advised. Dress: casual. AE, DC, MC, V.*

Florent. This is absolutely, positively one of the hippest restaurants in Lower Manhattan, not for its food—which is only passable French bistro fare (grilled flank steak, sausages, onion soup, and vegetables gratinés)—but for its retro neighborhood (the meat-market district), its decor (barely converted diner), and the late-night crowd that comes here (past visitors have included Madonna, Talking Heads, and a lot of other musicians). The waiters are friendly enough, however, so if you can get a table after 9 PM, just inhale the atmosphere and have a good time. It won't cost you much. A prix fixe dinner is $14.95 before 7:30 PM, $16.95 from 7:30 to midnight. Do take a taxi (and have one waiting outside when you exit). *69 Gansevoort St. (between Greenwich and Washington Sts.), tel. 212/989-5779. Reservations advised. Dress: casual. No credit cards. Open 24 hrs.*

★ **La Metairie.** Now that owner Sylvain Fareri has severed ties with his uptown establishment, he is devoting all his time to this informal space—and it shows. Enlivened and considerably enlarged, it still bears quaint touches of the Provence countryside, and the menu, prepared in collaboration with chef Philippe Roussel, is rich in regional influences. Specialties include carrot and mint soup; *boudin de fruits de mer* (seafood sausage); quail stuffed with foie gras and spinach in a black truffle sauce; baby squid with tomatoes; herb-roasted Cornish hen; roast rack of lamb; and crème brûlée royale. *189 W. 10th St. (corner W. 4th St., near 7th Ave.), tel. 212/989-0343. Reservations advised. Dress: casual. AE, DC, MC, V.*

★ **Quatorze.** Although the location of this attractive French bistro, loosely modeled on Paris's celebrated Brasserie Lipp, lacks the élan of Boulevard Saint-Germain, staples such as *saucisson de Lyon* (garlic sausage), *salade aux lardons* (chicory lettuce with bacon), creamy pâté, calve's liver, and *choucroute garnie* (sausages and ham on a bed of sauerkraut) are worthy of the real thing. You'll also find here one of the best apple tarts in the city, as well as a very good wine list. A fixed-price lunch is offered for $11.50. *240 W. 14th St. (off 7th Ave.), tel. 212/206-7006. Reservations advised. Dress: casual. AE, MC, V. Closed for lunch on weekends.*

Sevilla. This bustling and spirited Spanish restaurant, heavy on wood paneling and pleasantly informal in nature, caters to a somewhat youthful crowd. A traditional menu, replete with grilled chorizo, Spanish ham and olives, *mariscada* (shellfish) with green sauce, *paella Valenciana* (rice with chicken, sausage, and lobster), is both fresh and deftly prepared. What's more, most entrées fall under $16, making this an excellent spot for diners in search of good fun, good quality, and good value. *62 Charles St. (near 7th Ave.), tel. 212/243–9513. Reservations advised. Dress: casual. AE, DC, MC, V.*

Villa Mosconi. Here's a pleasant, old-fashioned Greenwich Village trattoria, the kind they don't often make anymore. Come here to eat heartily at a fair price and to be treated like an old friend by owner Peter Mosconi; you'll get a good feeling of the way the Village used to be a decade or so ago. The warm, comfortable premises have the requisite Italian landscapes and still-lifes on the walls. Among the good and gutsy food, the *tagliatelle al pesto* (flat-ribboned egg pasta in pesto sauce), *zuppa pesce* (mixed seafood in a tomato sauce), and the veal *alla giardiniera* (with vegetables) are especially recommended. *69 MacDougal St. (near Houston St.), tel. 212/673–0390. Reservations advised. Dress: casual. AE, DC, MC, V. Closed Sun.*

Inexpensive
★ **Acme Bar and Grill.** Here's an authentic, down-home Cajun joint, complete with corrugated tin ceilings, exposed beams, and every conceivable type of hot sauce ever produced, lined up along an enormous interior wall. Deep-fried oyster po' boys, Cajun shrimp, and collard greens are just a few of the regional specialties offered at this casual and ever-lively Louisiana transplant. *9 Great Jones St. (near Broadway), tel. 212/420–1934. No reservations. Dress: casual. DC, MC, V.*

Benny's Burritos. The slogan here is "Ours are bigger than yours," and it's hard to argue when you see and taste one of the massive burritos—a stuffed tortilla filled with everything from cheese to guacamole. The place is a kick—and it attracts a lively, young Greenwich Village clientele. (There's a take-out shop across the street and another Benny's over on Avenue A and 6th Street.) The selection of Mexican beers is impressive and exactly right for this kind of grub. *113 Greenwich Ave. (near Jane St.), tel. 212/633–9210. No reservations. Dress: casual. No credit cards.*

Famous Ray's. Want to create a commotion on a street corner? Yell out "The best pizza in Manhattan is at Ray's!" This will immediately cause any number of New Yorkers to argue with you about *which* Ray's you mean–Original Ray's, Ray's Pizza, Ray's Original, Ray's Famous, the One and Only Famous Ray's, Real Ray's, and others—none of them in any way related. Indeed, the various versions of Ray's have been squabbling in and out of court for years as to just who can claim to be the original, famous, real Ray's. Funny thing is, all the different Ray's pizzerias, including this one, make a similar style of pizza: puffy crust, spicy tomato and mozzarella toppings, and a generous slicing policy. *465 6th Ave. (near 11th St.), tel. 212/243–2253. No reservations. Dress: casual. No credit cards.*

Patisserie Lanciani. For a long while this has been one of the best places in Greenwich Village to enjoy a fine pastry and espresso or a sumptuously packed croissant sandwich. The French and Viennese offerings are irresistible, especially at breakfast, when this little café is jammed with people coming for espresso and cappuccino. The place is open late, so it's also a nice spot to go after a movie or a show in the area. The cakes and fruit tarts are some of the best in the city. *271 W. 4th St. (near Perry St.), tel. 212/929–0739. Dress: casual. AE.*

Chelsea, Gramercy, Murray Hill

Expensive
★

An American Place. As godfather of the new American cooking movement and heir to the mantle of James Beard, Larry Forgione has never veered from his belief that American cookery can be among the finest in the world. In his hands it is, especially at his expansive, handsome postmodern quarters. Forgione's menu includes several signature dishes, such as terrine of three smoked fish, and warm duck sausage with scallion-spoonbread griddle cakes. There are delectable appetizers, such as asparagus with country ham and cheese, peanut-barbecued Gulf shrimp, and lobster-and-wild-mushroom croquettes with spicy red-pepper sauce. Winning main courses include sautéed breast of free-range chicken, sweet-potato ravioli with pecan vinaigrette, breast of pheasant with roast peppers and wild mushrooms, and black Angus beef with potato gorgonzola galette. For dessert, be sure to try the banana Betty, the apple pan dowdy, or the peanut-butter ice cream sandwich. *2 Park Ave. (entrance on 32nd St.), tel. 212/ 684–2122. Reservations advised. Dress: casual. AE, DC, MC, V. Closed Sun.*

Le Madri. Certainly one of the most highly publicized Italian restaurants in New York and frequented by an attractive crowd of regulars from the fashion and publishing worlds, Le Madri has nevertheless succeeded not because of the hype but because of the good food. Owner Pino Luongo has hit upon the right formula: Bring regional Italian women chefs in on a rotating basis while allowing executive chef Marta Pulini to maintain day-to-day consistency. The results speak for themselves: The pizzas are terrific, the pastas authentic and true to the best in Italy, and the steak *alla fiorentina* (a thick steak) nonpareil. Don't miss the desserts either. Expect a crush, wobbly service, and too-often a wait, but this is a great spot to go after shopping at Barneys down the street. A late-supper menu is available until midnight. *168 W. 18th St. (on 7th Ave.), tel. 212/727– 8022. Reservations advised. Jacket advised. AE, MC, V.*

Moderate

Banana Café. You enter a whimsical interior, festooned, not surprisingly, with palm fronds, bananas, and monkeys. Relatively serene by day, the place is brimming at night to the tune of a loud Brazilian beat. Though the look and feel of the place are fanciful, there is nothing illusory about chef Matthew Kenney's cooking—the menu includes a spate of original pizzas; charcoal-grilled asparagus with chopped egg, Asiago and croutons; a grilled salmon "burger" with oven-dried tomato relish and spicy corn salad; and grilled prawns with beets, green beans and new potatoes. For dessert, what else? Banana split, and tropical banana trifle. *111 E. 22nd St. (near Park Ave. S), tel. 212/995–8500. Reservations advised. Dress: casual chic. AE, MC, V.*

Chefs Cuisiniers Club. "CC Club," as it's called, is a worthwhile idea well realized: Several of New York City's most notable chefs, such as Charles Palmer of Aureole, opened this pleasant little bistro as an after-service refuge where confreres can get together to eat, swap stories, and blow off steam. The public is also welcome to enjoy chef Peter Assue's restrained Mediterranean food, which is a bit underseasoned but nonetheless satisfying. Although the setting is spare, the blue jeans on the waiters slovenly, and the wine list minimal, this good neighborhood spot cannot help but intrigue those who follow the comings and goings of New York's stellar chefs. *36 E. 22nd St. (off Broadway), tel. 212/228-4399. Reservations advised. Dress: casual. AE, DC, MC, V. Closed for lunch on weekends.*

★ **La Colombe d'Or.** For years, this paragon of French bistros has been serving up good Provençal food with some modern touches under the supervision of owners George and Helen Studley. The premises are cozy, with lots of exposed brick and printed fabrics. Now that chef Naj Zougari is firmly ensconced in the kitchen, some superb dishes from his native Tangiers, such as chicken couscous, appear on the menu alongside the classics: crêpe with ratatouille, snails with white beans, grilled chicken breast and duck, and flourless chocolate cake. The wine list is very reasonably priced. *134 E. 26th St. (near Lexington Ave.), tel. 212/689-0666. Reservations advised. Dress: casual. AE, DC, MC, V. Closed for lunch on weekends.*

Les Halles. The owners of Park Bistro across the street also run this amiable, loud replication of a butcher shop–restaurant of the kind you'd once find around the former Paris food market called Les Halles. This is not a place for those who eat oat bran for breakfast. Instead, it's a carnivore's dream—hanger steak, cassoulet, french fries, and all sorts of other fat-filled, absolutely delicious bourgeois dishes, including some exemplary fruit tarts. Service is hectic, the place is always packed, and the wine list has some interesting regional bottlings. *411 Park Ave. S (near 28th St.), tel. 212/679-4111. Reservations required. Dress: casual. AE, DC, MC, V.*

★ **Lola.** After some ups and downs, Lola has emerged as one of the most exciting and innovative restaurants in the city, and certainly one of the best. The liveliness of the shadowy room, the sexy bar, the glamorous clientele, and the live jazz and gospel music are ideal accompaniments to chef Lynne Aronson's canny mix of Caribbean and Eastern flavors—so much so that it often appears necessary to take along a megaphone in order to be heard under the din of conversation and live music. The savory menu includes such choices as cayenne onion rings, shrimp and potato fritters with chipotle mayonnaise, risotto with wild mushrooms, 100-spice chicken, seared bass and sea scallops with horseradish broth, and lemon napoleon. *30 W. 22nd St. (near 5th Ave.), tel. 212/675-6700. Reservations advised. Dress: casual. AE, MC, V. Closed Sat. lunch.*

★ **Mesa Grill.** This cavernous space has been transmogrified by owners Jerry Kretchmer and Jeff Bliss and chef Bobby Flay into a southwestern extravaganza. Attractive lighting fixtures and colorful banquettes create a festive mood. (Would that the soundproofing could contain the resultant noise!) Most diners seem unperturbed by the noise as they sample Flay's largely successful menu full of spices and textures, such as salmon cakes with pineapple tomatillo salsa, swordfish with peppers and pesto, and lamb chops with jalapeño preserves. *102 5th Ave. (at 15th St.), tel. 212/807-7400. Reservations advised. Dress: casual. AE, MC, V. Closed Sun. lunch.*

★ **Park Bistro.** In look and feel, this is one of Manhattan's best approximations of a French bistro. Leather banquettes, posters, and photographs create the right ambience, and a trio of Frenchmen at the helm assures that everything will be *comme il faut* (as it should). Chef Jean-Michel Diot's Provence-inspired cooking is a delight. You might start your meal with *petatou* (warm potato salad with goat cheese). For a main course, consider the skate with cocoa beans or lamb with eggplant. *414 Park Ave. S (near 28th St.), tel. 212/689-1360. Res-*

ervations advised. Dress: casual. AE, DC, MC, V. Closed for lunch on weekends.

Periyali. This enticing Greek restaurant does some out-of-the-ordinary cooking that clearly appeals to its regular crowd. The food is nicely seasoned and amply portioned. If you're in the mood for Greek cooking—albeit not of the classic variety—Periyali (which means seashore) is the place to go. Specialties include grilled lamb chops, grilled shrimp with herbs, and charcoal-grilled octopus. Don't overlook the cinnamon ice cream. *35 W. 20th St. (near 6th Ave.), tel. 212/463-7890. Reservations advised. Dress: casual. AE, DC, MC, V. Closed Sun.*

★ **Prix Fixe.** The concept is certainly right for the times: Take over the premises of a grand café, do it up in style, put a brilliant young chef named Terry Brennan in the kitchen, and offer menus at $24 and $36 and wines in three price categories. What's amazing is the quality of food at these prices—pretty close to the pricier glories of Gotham Bar & Grill nearby—and you'll love such flavorful dishes as skate with pickled vegetables, loin of lamb with mustard broth, and fruit consommé with ginger and champagne. The noise level can be high and the service staff slow, but this is a very popular spot, and even more of a bargain for lunch. *18 W. 18th St. (between 5th and 6th Aves.), tel. 212/675-6777. Reservations advised. Dress: casual. AE, DC, MC, V. Closed Sat. lunch.*

Steak Frites. Don't be deceived by the name. There is much more to the menu than meat and potatoes (although the black Angus beef and french fries are sinfully delicious). Chef Terrance Brennan contibutes to the commendable bistro menu at near-bargain prices, with such offerings as onion soup, frisée and haricot vert salad with roquefort, terrine of vegetables with goat cheese, ravioli with eggplant ratatouille, roasted chicken, grilled salmon with fennel, and profiteroles. The cavernous, high-ceilinged space, with walls covered in fanciful murals, attracts an eclectic crowd. Service may verge on the chaotic, and noise levels are very high. *9 E. 16th St. (between 5th Ave. and Union Sq. W), tel. 212/463-7101. Reservations advised. Dress: casual. AE, DC, MC, V.*

★ **Union Square Café.** This highly popular and attractive downtown restaurant remains a thoroughly satisfying setting for animated dining. Owner Danny Meyer never rests on his laurels, and chef Michael Romano's innovative touches make this kitchen one of Manhattan's finest. Oysters Union Square remains a signature appetizer, but don't ignore the roasted vegetable and goat-cheese terrine or the *fagioli alla Toscana* (a white-bean dish). A side dish of hot-garlic potato chips is another must. You can always count on herb-roasted chicken with polenta; roasted loin of rabbit; seared salmon with corn, shiitakes and spinach; and veal medallions with mushrooms and cream. There are also nightly pasta specials worth considering. Try to leave room for the chocolate marbleized brownie. The wine list is most innovative, with a good selection by the glass. The service is among the best in town—friendly, enthusiastic, and knowledgeable. *21 E. 16th St. (near Union Sq. W), tel. 212/243-4020. Reserve well in advance. Dress: casual chic. AE, DC, MC, V. Closed Sun. lunch.*

Inexpensive **America.** This cavernous and lively spot tends to attract a youngish crowd, many of whom are content to hang out at the enormous and inviting bar and simply watch the scene. However, during the weekend and on holidays, you'll often find families here. Noise levels can be problematic. Not surprisingly, America serves up an ambitious but often inconsistent array of American favorites and specials, from po' boy sandwiches to burgers and fajitas. *9 E. 18th St. (near 5th Ave.), tel. 212/505–2110. Reservations advised. Dress: casual. AE, DC, MC, V.*

Coffee Shop. This retro hot spot has a young crowd, pretty waitresses, and a barrier at the door to keep out the overflow. The place is owned by models and looks it—all flash and glitter, but kind of fun, too. It's weathered its initial tidal wave of trendiness to settle in as a comfy spot for the likes of Brazilian cheese muffins, coconut-batter shrimp, excellent roast chicken with mashed potatoes, yummy creamed spinach, a well-made Cuban sandwich, and guava crêpes for dessert. Wear your street fashions—the tighter, the better. *29 Union Sq. (at 16th St.), tel. 212/243–7969. Reservations advised. Dress: casual chic. AE.*

La Chinita Linda. This is one of the oddities of the New York restaurant scene: A Cuban-Chinese restaurant—although it's not the only one in town. The food is an amalgam of hearty Cuban classics, such as fried bananas, avocado salad, and Cuban steak with white rice and black beans, together with Chinese dishes, such as *moo goo gai pan* (sliced chicken with mushrooms and Chinese veggies), chop suey, and sweet-and-sour pork. The place is busy at all hours with a young crowd that loves this simple, funky place and its low prices. It has far from the best Chinese food in town, but it's one of those places you really should take in if you want a unique New York experience. *166 8th Ave. (near 18th St.), tel. 212/633–1791. Dress: casual. AE, MC, V.*

Lox Around the Clock. It's a highly spirited, somewhat funky joint, heavy on decorative neon and kinetic paint. We recommend all the sandwiches named for after-hours spots, and of course, anything that contains the eponymous Jewish-American specialty, lox. It has good pizzas and matzo-ball soup, too, and is open 24 hours on weekends. *676 6th Ave. (near 21st St.), tel. 212/691–3535. Dress: casual. AE.*

Zig Zag Bar & Grill. More a bar than a grill and more a hangout than a fine restaurant, this popular Chelsea establishment hosts a cross section of New York City's artists, photographers, stylists, and other night crawlers who come here to meet their friends and to gossip about one another. You'll easily enter into the spirit of it all, for the long bar is a friendly one, and the food is actually much more than you might expect—big sandwiches of red peppers and salami, juicy hamburgers, and good, gloppy desserts. Skip the barbecued ribs. *206 W. 23rd St. (near 7th Ave.), tel. 212/645–5060. Reservations advised for 5 or more. Dress: casual. AE, MC, V.*

★ **Zip City Brewery.** This Manhattan microbrewery, replete with gleaming two-story-high copper storage vats in the center of the restaurant. Zip City is more than just another pub, despite the excellent beer made on the premises. There's a serious attempt to rise above standard fare, with ambitious dishes such as shrimp in hazelnut sauce and yellowfin tuna chili. The scene can be noisy at night. *3 W. 18th St. (near 5th Ave.), tel. 212/366–6333. Reservations accepted for 6 or more. Dress: casual. AE, DC, MC, V.*

Midtown

Very Expensive
★

The Four Seasons. No question, this is one of New York City's most important and beautiful restaurants. Its location in the Mies van der Rohe–designed Seagram Building and its Philip Johnson interior have given it unique landmark status, and indefatigable owners Tom Margittai and Paul Kovi, together with a talented management team, run the handsome Grill Room—famous for its Power-Lunch crowd—and the romantic Pool Room. The high-quality food, though no longer the trailblazing cuisine of the past, includes such fine dishes as crisped shrimp in fruit and mustard sauce, tuna carpaccio, frogs'-legs curry, fresh venison or pheasant, loin of rabbit with polenta, rack of lamb, chocolate velvet cake, and the popular spa cuisine. Prices are very high, but the $41.50 Grill Room dinner menu is an outright steal. The wine list is stellar and the service reserved but very professional. *99 E. 52nd St. (near Park Ave.), tel. 212/754–9494. Reservations required. Jacket and tie required. AE, DC, MC, V. Closed Sat. lunch and Sun.*

La Côte Basque. A Manhattan institution founded by the legendary Henri Soulé, the restaurant flourishes under chef-owner Jean-Jacques Rachou and boasts a faithful clientele. The place is quite glamorous—butter-colored walls, Riviera murals, dark beams, a glittering bar—but the greeting at the door may be indifferent to newcomers, and service abrupt. The food, however, is classic, ornate, satisfying, and well presented. Although the wine cellar here is one of New York City's finest, with many a rare claret, most white wines are listed without either a vintage or producer, making the selection process cumbersome. Recommended dishes include *saucisson chaud* (warm garlic sausage in pastry), chicken breast Gismonda, veal chop with wild mushrooms, quail and sweetbreads in puff pastry, cassoulet of seafood, *dacquoise* (French cake made of meringue and almonds) with raspberry sauce, and sky-high soufflés. The fixed-price dinner is $55, but beware the many supplements. *5 E. 55th St. (near 5th Ave.), tel. 212/688–6525. Reservations required. Jacket and tie required. AE, DC, MC, V. Closed Sun.*

★ **Lutèce.** With a reputation based on chef-owner André Soltner's 30 years of brilliant and dedicated service, Lutèce is widely regarded as the finest classic French restaurant in New York. The sprightly interior attracts a crowd of regulars who know they will find perfection in every bite, plus a bevy of curious newcomers bent on discovering what the fuss is all about. Soltner will gladly choose the meal for either client—so don't hesitate to ask. His extraordinary repertoire ranges from scallop beignets, gambas and scallops in curry cream, foie gras *en brioche*, and baked lotte Provençal to roasted guinea hen, caramelized rack of lamb, coffee praline Lutèce, chocolate mousse tart, and cold chestnut soufflé. The wine list is extensive and expensive. The fixed-price $38 lunch is well worth it. Dinner is $60. *249 E. 50th St. (near 2nd Ave.), tel. 212/752–2225. Reservations required. Jacket and tie required. AE, DC, MC, V. Closed Mon. and Sat. lunch, Sun., and Aug.*

★ **The Rainbow Room.** Towering over midtown Manhattan, this has long been the most glorious aerie for dining and dancing of any city in the world; since its $25 million renovation by master restaurateur Joe Baum, the Rainbow Room has sparkled like a jewel. The revolving dance floor, the changing bands, and the colorful decor all conspire to make this a memorable ex-

perience. The menu, under chef Andrew Wilkinson, is a safe
balance of new ideas (such as crabmeat in phyllo, and crisp red
snapper with caponata and garlic) and traditional Continental
favorites (such as tournedos Rossini and baked Alaska). During the day, the room is a private club. In the evening, the bar
becomes one of the most popular spots in town; the $38.50
pretheater dinner and à la carte after-theater supper are good
buys. *30 Rockefeller Plaza (at Rockefeller Center), tel. 212/
632–5000. Reservations required. Jacket and tie required. AE.
Closed Mon.*

The "21" Club. One of the most famous and long-lived restaurants in the world, "21" opened originally as a speakeasy during Prohibition and flourished well into the 1980s when it
entered a decline. New owners and an extensive renovation in
1987 brought about a major turnaround. Chef Michael
Lomonaco sensibly marries tradition to the finest ingredients
and keeps the menu in sync with the best American classicism
has to offer; as an added option, there are "trim menu selections." Notable dishes include grilled duck sausage with black
currants, crab cakes, wild mushroom ravioli and duck consommé, rack of lamb with Indian spices, veal chop with wild mushrooms, the "21" burger, fruit cobbler, and lemon meringue pie.
A reduced-price after-theater menu is available from 10 PM.
Sommelier William Phillips oversees a spectacular, 50,000-bottle
wine cellar that you're invited to visit. *21 W. 52nd St. (near 5th
Ave.), tel. 212/582-7200. Reservations required. Jacket and tie
required. AE, DC, MC, V. Closed Sun.*

Expensive **Aquavit.** This splendid-looking Scandinavian restaurant is set
on three levels in Nelson Rockefeller's former town house,
where soaring walls, a waterfall, a smorgasbord bar, a wonderful selection of iced aquavits, and delicious food set the mood.
At night the lighting becomes particularly dramatic, turning
the main room into a unique dining spot. By day, cool gray
tones dominate, making this a good place for a business lunch.
The menu is weighted toward seafood specialties: assorted
smoked fish, gravlax, and salmon. Don't overlook the Arctic
venison in juniper-and-apple sauce or the Swedish pancakes.
The fixed-price menu is $60, with a pretheater dinner of $19
(two courses) and $39 (three courses); an à la carte menu upstairs is good for a fast bite. *13 W. 54th St. (near 5th Ave.), tel.
212/307-7311. Reservations required downstairs. Jacket required. AE, DC, MC, V. Closed Sun.*

★ **Felidia.** Lidia and Felix Bastianich enjoy a well-deserved reputation for staying at the vanguard of all the latest developments in authentic*cucina Italiana* in New York City. They
continue to wield tremendous clout nationwide for their unbridled enthusiasm, their attention to detail, and their attentiveness to the wine list. (We have heard complaints, however, of
staff inefficiency during the crush of dinner.) The food is usually great; refined but homey, full of delicacy and flavor, and always cooked with fervor. The brick and dark-wood decor is
very cozy. Choose from a wide array of daily specials, or go
with such standbys as cold antipasti, ziti with lamb sauce,
pappardelle (wide noodles) with broccoli rape, krafi (raisin-
and ricotta-filled ravioli), salmon with mustard sauce, or
pineapple and strawberries with balsamic vinegar. Felidia's
wine cellar is one of the country's finest, and Lidia herself will
be happy to instruct you on the latest estate bottlings from Italy. *243 E. 58th St. (near 2nd. Ave.), tel. 212/758–1479. Reser-*

vations required. Jacket required. AE, DC, MC, V. Closed Sat. lunch and Sun.

★ **Grand Central Oyster Bar & Restaurant.** Opened in 1912, this granddaddy of American seafood restaurants is renowned for its extraordinary offerings of oysters and every kind of fish that swims into the Fulton Fish Market downtown. Located underneath Grand Central Terminal's Great Hall, it's an astounding space to eat in; it's always crowded at lunchtime (less so for dinner), but there's a quieter rear room, as well as that famous oyster bar. Don't try coming late for your reservation or you'll lose it. The range of offerings here—chowders, grilled and poached fish, smoked salmon—is impressive, and everything is prepared with great integrity. The white-wine list rates as one of the most interesting in the United States. *Grand Central Terminal, tel. 212/490–6650. Lunch reservations required, dinner reservations advised. Dress: casual. AE, DC, MC, V. Closed weekends.*

★ **Harry Cipriani.** When the Cipriani family returned to the Sherry-Netherlands Hotel, they were greeted by faithful customers as if they had never left (in a dispute with management five years ago), and the smart, handsome dining room rings with laughter, graying men in tight suits, and gorgeous women in tighter skirts. Like Cipriani's Bellini on Seventh Avenue, this is an outpost of Venice's legendary Harry's Bar, and the food is simple, absolutely delicious, and very expensive. Service is rushed but affable. Don't miss such legendary dishes as *tagliatelle verde gratinata* (homemade noodles in green sauce), carpaccio (invented by the Ciprianis), risotto with chicken livers, scallops with artichoke, and all the great meringue desserts. The house carafe of wine is well worth ordering, too. *781 5th Ave. (in Sherry-Netherlands Hotel), tel. 212/753–5566. Reservations required. Jacket required. AE, DC, MC, V.*

Hatsuhana. This is considered New York City's best sushi restaurant. There are two locations: The original on 48th Street is pleasant enough, but the newer Park Avenue branch (actually wedged off the avenue between the streets) is prettier, with a greenhouse dining room. At both you'll find Japanese businesspeople at the sushi bar or the tables, challenging the *itamae* (master sushi chef) to come up with something interesting. He always does—from mackerel and pickled ginger to broiled squid feet. The sashimi is perfectly fresh; the service, however, can be tired. *237 Park Ave. (on 46th St.), tel. 212/661–3400; 17 E. 48th St. (near Madison Ave.), tel. 212/355–3345. Reservations required. Jacket and tie advised. AE, DC, MC, V. Closed Sat. lunch and Sun.*

★ **Il Nido.** This is a major player in northern Italian (specifically, Tuscan) cuisine, and it's constantly jammed with expense-accounters who'll pay a hefty tab for some of the best food in New York. The dining room is sophisticated without being studied: a mix of dark-wood beams, white walls, plaid carpet, and a sea of white tablecloths. The regulars know what they like—a sampling of three pastas on one plate, massive veal chops with wild mushrooms, and the delicious *tiramisù* (mascarpone and sponge cake), which is a classic Italian dessert—but ask owner Adi Giovanetti what he'd suggest and you should be very happy. The wine list is long and impressive. *251 E. 53rd St. (near 2nd Ave.), tel. 212/753–8450. Reservations required. Jacket and tie required. AE, DC, MC, V. Closed Sun.*

★ **La Caravelle.** For 32 years, this has been a bastion of haute cuisine. Present owners Rita and André Jammet admirably assure a graceful balance of classic and modern. With its beautifully restored Jean Pagès murals and cheery peach banquettes, La Caravelle remains a quintessentially romantic spot. Chef Tadashi Ono's refreshing Oriental nuances keep this place at the top of the city's dining experiences, bolstered by pastry chef Laurent Richard—with such dishes as petite flutes (minirolls of minced duck with curry), fluke marinated in lemon and chive oil, shrimp and scallops lasagna, duck breast with green mustard and rice cake, grilled Dover sole with mustard sauce, lemon tart and melon sorbet, and chocolate surprise. Service is exemplary. Prices are very fair: à la carte at lunch, a pretheater dinner at $37, and a $54 fixed-price dinner. *33 W. 55th St. (near 5th Ave.), tel. 212/586–4252. Reservations required. Jacket and tie required. AE, DC, MC, V. Closed Sat. lunch and Sun.*

★ **La Reserve.** Catercorner to Rockefeller Center is this airy, stylish restaurant, which serves a good balance of classic, nouvelle, and regional French cuisine. The large front dining room is decorated with rural murals, the lighting is cheerful, and the staff, under owner Jean-Louis Missud, is admirably professional. The large rear room, however, lacks personality. The menu changes to suit the seasons; specialties include salmon with lentils, ravioli with scallops and beurre blanc, and apple tart. This is a very fine place—and far more friendly than many of the otherFrench deluxe establishments. The wine list is solid. Prix fixe meals are available at lunch ($31) and dinner ($40 for pretheater, otherwise $49). *4 W. 49th St. (near 5th Ave.), tel. 212/ 247–2993. Reservations advised. Jacket and tie required. AE, DC, MC, V. Closed Sat. lunch and Sun.*

★ **Le Perigord.** This deluxe French restaurant is a perfect example of how classicism can be renewed successfully and maintain its vibrancy year after year. Le Perigord, under owner Georges Briguet, has long been one of Manhattan's finest dining spots, but with the addition of chef Antoine Bouterin a few years ago, its kitchen has become truly inspired. With its soft lighting, pretty flowered accents, and superb staff, this is a very romantic place, and there is no better host than Monsieur Briguet for making a newcomer feel right at home. Your best bet is to put yourself in Bouterin's hands or go with his specials—items such as beef with truffles on a potato galette (a bed of thinly sliced potatoes) and passion-fruit mousse. His halibut in court bouillon is great. A prix fixe lunch costs $29; the set-menu dinner is $49. *405 E. 52nd St. (near 1st Ave.), tel. 212/755–6244. Reservations advised. Jacket and tie required. AE, DC, MC, V. Closed Sun.*

★ **Lespinasse.** The renovation of the grand old St. Regis Hotel has been brought off with commendable respect, including its dignified, formal dining room. Chef Gray Kunz's food has plenty of color and spark. His provocative cooking techniques bring out the best in his ingredients, and his menus are always exciting, with dishes such as fried lobster tail in a bisquelike sauce, grilled quail wrapped in light pastry, and lamb chop with eggplant tart and curry-carrot juice. Desserts are gorgeous. Fixed-price tasting menus are available at $47 and $60. *2 E. 55th St. (in St. Regis Hotel, off 5th Ave.), tel. 212/339–6719. Reservations advised. Jacket required. AE, DC, MC, V.*

★ **Manhattan Ocean Club.** A sleek and stylish interior adorned with Picasso ceramics makes this two-tiered restaurant one of the most attractive spots in the city for seafood dining. Chef Jonathan Parker has added some fine dishes to the menu while maintaining traditional favorites. Try the superb crab cakes and rosemary-crusted red snapper, plus standbys such as glistening fresh oysters, good poached salmon, grilled swordfish, blackened redfish, and the warm chocolate tart. *57 W. 58th St. (near 6th Ave.), tel. 212/371–7777. Reservations advised. Jacket and tie advised. AE, DC, MC, V. Closed weekend for lunch on weekends.*

Oceana. The Livanos family took over the former premises of a French restaurant and did little to the pastel pastoral decor, but they put a terrific young chef, James Galileo, in the kitchen. Oceana has caught on not only for its fine modern seafood and hospitable service but for its remarkably fair pricing, with no three-course dinner more than $44. For this you get very high quality, not too far from what you'd be served at Le Bernardin or the Manhattan Ocean Club, with such offerings as red snapper with farfal, cod with mashed-potatoes brandade, ravioli of tuna with mascarpone, carrot cake with sour cream, and banana strudel with coconut ice cream. *55 E. 54th St. (near Madison Ave.), tel. 212/759–5941. Reservations advised. Jacket and tie advised. AE, DC, MC, V. Closed Sat. lunch and Sun.*

Palm. Since 1926, Palm has been known as the New York steak house par excellence—though hardly for its decor: The floors are covered with sawdust, the walls with the discolored murals of favorite customers. You'll probably have to wait in the much-too-smoky, cramped bar if your reservation is any time after 6 PM. The waiters don't hold much truck with amenities, but they're not really brusque, just robotic. You come here for 16-ounce aged steaks, gargantuan lobsters, great cheesecake, and anything else on the menu (well, the spaghetti's not so good). The wine list is a joke. Palm Too, right across the street, is just as good though not as antique. *837 2nd Ave. (near 45th St.), tel. 212/687–2953. Lunch reservations required; dinner reservations for 4 or more. Dress: casual. AE, DC, MC, V. Closed Sat. lunch and Sun.*

★ **Peacock Alley.** With the arrival of talented chef Laurent Manrique, the Waldorf-Astoria is regaining the critical acclaim it enjoyed more than half a century ago under the celebrated "Oscar of the Waldorf." Never mind that Peacock Alley is a little tired looking and that the interior design smacks of haute Hilton hotel decor. Manrique's brilliant creations more than compensate. A native of southwest France, he also apprenticed at stellar Parisian restaurants. To sample his culinary range, try the $68 dégustation dinner, which may include the likes of chestnut consommé with fig-stuffed quail; fresh foie gras with porcini mushrooms and fried grapes; seared sea scallops on shredded potatoes; roasted lobster with black truffles; veal chop with sage, chestnuts, mushrooms and fennel; and caramel apple in phyllo pastry. *301 Park Avenue (at 50th St.), tel. 212/872–4895. Reservations advised. Jacket and tie advised. AE, DC, MC, V. Closed Sat. lunch, Sun. dinner.*

Restaurant Raphael. Presided over by a charming and energetic couple, Raphael and Mira Edery, Restaurant Raphael has been a long-standing favorite for its romantic setting and refined French food. Chef Jean-Michel Bergougnoux focuses on regional preparations, such as Savoy cabbage stuffed with crabmeat, fricassee of snails, grilled tuna with potato galette, risotto with lamb and star anise, and *gateau au chocolate* (chocolate cake). By day, this is also a good spot for a business lunch or a meal before or after viewing an exhibit at the nearby Museum of Modern Art. Take advantage of alfresco dining in season.

33 W. 54th St. (between 5th and 6th Aves.), tel. 212/582–8993. Reservations advised. Jacket and tie required. AE, DC, MC, V. Closed Sat. lunch and Sun.

San Pietro. Why put up with the constant commotion at Bice, when across the street, you can dine on authentic Italian fare served up by a team that is really delighted in serving you? The Bruno brothers, who also run Sistina uptown, have refashioned the room in a light, elegant, and wholly convivial way, and in good weather they place tables outside. Food here is sumptuous but simply done—the way Italian food should be. You may have to brush off a waiter who's too earnest making suggestions when he should just be describing dishes, but otherwise you'll have a wonderful time here—and at a good price. Among the gustatory delights are spaghetti with anchovies and tomatoes, ricotta-stuffed ravioli, chick-pea pasta pesto, parmigiana-crusted chicken, and veal with morels and cream. *18 E. 54th St. (near Madison Ave.), tel. 212/753–9015. Reservations advised. Jacket and tie advised. AE, DC, MC, V. Closed Sun.*

★ **Smith & Wollensky.** Here is a very large, handsome, oak-floored steak-and-seafood house; it may not have Palm's historic dowdiness, but its food can be just as good. The steaks are unassailably among the best anywhere; the breads, veal chops, lobsters, stone crabs, and apple brown Betty are all recommended; and the wine list is quite extraordinary, especially for cabernet sauvignon and vintage claret selections. Service is brisk and adequate to the job, although the place is jammed with businesspeople day and night, before theater and after work. The restaurant includes the more casual grill, which is open for lunch every day. This is a smooth operation, very much a "New York joint." *201 E. 49th St. (at 3rd Ave.), tel. 212/753–1530. Reservations advised. Dress: casual. AE, DC, MC, V. Main restaurant closed weekend lunch.*

★ **Sparks Steak House.** This mock colonial dining room is paradise for the oenophile—or even the amateur wine buff—who's curious about sampling mature vintages of French, Italian, Spanish, or Californian wine. Indeed, owner Pat Cetta can lay claim to the biggest collection of fine wines in the city. What's more, his markups are reasonable. Opt for Sparks's signature steak *au fromage* (with cheese), accompanied by one of the many rare cellar selections. (Beef is hardly de rigueur; you can choose from a wide array of fish, fowl, lamb, and veal dishes.) Cap off the evening with a late-harvest riesling or a Château d'Yquem '81 with luscious cheesecake. *210 E. 46th St. (near 3rd Ave.), tel. 212/687–4855. Reservations required. Jacket and tie advised. AE, DC, MC, V. Closed Sat. lunch and Sun.*

Moderate **Al Bustan.** Owner Elias Ghafary seems eager for patrons to experience the diversity of the refined Lebanese cuisine served in this comfortable, pleasant little dining room. If you've never had this kind of food before, the best approach is to do as the Lebanese do and order an array of appetizers, all zestily seasoned and a lot of fun to eat with pita bread. Entrées are good but not quite as enticing as the appetizers, though the lamb dishes are recommended. Desserts, except for baklava, are dull. *827 3rd Ave. (near 50th St.), tel. 212/759–5933. Reservations advised. Jacket advised. AE, DC, MC, V. Closed Sat. lunch.*

American Festival Café. If you have time for just one dining stop in New York with your family, this should be it. Set right next to the Rockefeller Center skating rink, the restaurant offers a view of the Prometheus statue, the row of flags from all nations, and majestic skyscrapers. The dining room is decorated with fine folk art in a casual, amiable way, and the food sticks to American classics, with a few modern touches. You won't go wrong with prime rib, crab cakes with cole slaw, or Sedutto's ice cream. This is a great place for pretheater dining, and the $24.95 prix fixe dinner is a bargain. At Christmastime, when the plaza's giant tree is lighted, it's the most festive spot in the city. *20 W. 50th St. (in Rockefeller Center), tel. 212/246–6699. Reservations advised. Dress: casual. AE, DC, MC, V.*

Brasserie. At any hour, 24 hours a day, you can find something warm and good to eat at the Brasserie, which can come in handy after a long evening at the opera or a brisk early morning walk. The subterranean dining room is bright and cheerful, and it serves a good rendering of French bistro classics. Try such items as the cassoulet or the roast chicken. Desserts are homey and good, too. *100 E. 53rd St. (near Park Ave.), tel. 212/ 751–4840. Dress: casual. AE, DC, MC, V.*

Chin Chin. Vintage photographs snapped in the Far East at the turn of the century, combined with bleached walls, plush banquettes, and dramatic lighting, create a sleek, stark look at this beguiling but noisy Chinese café. Happily, the kitchen's output equals the drama of the decor, making this an excellent midtown outpost for Chinese fare. It serves good pork dumplings, fried squid, three-glass chicken (a glass each of water, soy sauce, and wine are added to the sauce), orange beef, sesame noodles, and scallion pancakes. *216 E. 49th St. (near 3rd Ave.), tel. 212/888–4555. Reservations advised. Dress: casual. AE, DC, MC, V. Closed for lunch on weekends.*

David K's Noodle Road. On the main floor of a town house, veteran restaurateur David Keh has created an inviting atmosphere. The menu contains several throwbacks from Keh's earlier restaurants, such as three-glass chicken, General Tsao's chicken, and crispy orange beef. There is an appetizing collection of contemporary creations such as pork or vegetable "pan stickers" (dumplings), chicken wonton with chili sauce, Peking chicken, and pork-fried noodles. Upstairs, Keh has installed an even more glamorous night spot called Shanghai 1933, designed by the celebrated Sam Lopata. *209 E. 49th St. (between 2nd and 3rd Aves.), tel. 212/486–1800. Reservations advised. Dress: casual chic. AE, DC, MC, V. Closed for lunch on weekends.*

★ **Dawat.** Unquestionably the city's most attractive Indian restaurant, Dawat specializes in authentic and unusual regional dishes. Veteran Indian-food lovers make this their second home. The fixed-price lunches, $11.95 and $12.95, are excellent values. You won't be disappointed, whether you fancy chicken *tikka* (in curry sauce), fish or goat stew, *keema matar* (ground lamb cooked with peas and ginger), *baghari jhinga* (spiced shrimp), or such vegetable preparations as baked eggplant, green beans in coconut, or *kheer* (yogurt with shredded cucumber). Try the Taj Mahal beer. *210 E. 58th St. (near 3rd Ave.), tel. 212/355–7555. Reservations advised. Dress: casual. AE, DC, MC, V. Closed Sun. lunch.*

Mickey Mantle's. You can practically conjure up the whole scenario before setting foot in this fun midtown restaurant: Oversize television screens throughout are tuned to (what else?) baseball games past and present, and ball club paraphernalia—bats, gloves, antique uniforms—abounds. The food is hearty, and the portions, whether of burgers, fries, or salads, are very large. What's more, Mickey Mantle himself actually drops in from time to time. This place is great for kids, both little and big. *42 Central Park S (near 6th Ave.), tel. 212/688-7777. Reservations advised. Dress: casual. AE, DC, MC, V.*

★ **Nippon.** One of the first modern Japanese restaurants in the United States, Nippon has long been a pioneer in everything from offering fine decor and tatami rooms to bringing sushi and sashimi to the attention of the American public. At this large and bright place, the negimaki roll was created to satisfy Americans' taste for beef with a Japanese accent. The staff has remained cordial to all its customers. It's best to allow the chef to prepare a special dinner for you, featuring everything from imaginative sushi to exotic main courses; your meal will be unforgettable. The tatami rooms are for parties. *155 E. 52nd St. (near Lexington Ave.), tel. 212/355-9020. Reservations advised. Jacket advised. AE, DC, MC, V. Closed Sat. lunch and Sun.*

Rosa Mexicano. This is a good choice for classic regional Mexican fare, served up in attractive stucco-and-wood surroundings. Marvelous margaritas and excellent guacamole are prepared tableside to your taste; spicy sausage, beef, and chicken are cooked on an open grill. Other specialties include stuffed peppers and, for dessert, *helado* (ice cream). *1063 1st Ave. (near 58th St.), tel. 212/753-7407. Reservations advised. Dress: casual. AE, DC, MC, V. Dinner only.*

★ **Sandro's.** Nowhere will you find a more ebullient chef than in Sandro Fioriti, who bounds out of the kitchen and slaps down whatever it is that strikes his fancy that night—roast pork *alla romana* (with fennel and rosemary), roast chicken, luscious *bruschetta* (toast) with tomato, or fresh-from-the-oven lemon cookies. There is a menu, but go with Sandro's suggestions and you'll have hearty food, full of flavor. The gelati are among the best in the city. The staff is amiable, and everything is on the upswing here. The premises are effectively modern and simple, ideal for large parties or groups. *420 E. 59th St. (near 1st Ave.), tel. 212/355-5150. Reservations advised. Dress: casual. AE, DC, MC, V. Closed Sun. lunch.*

★ **Shun Lee Palace.** One of the problems with most Chinese restaurants is their lack of consistency from month to month and year to year. Shun Lee's owner, Michael Tong, however, shows what can be done when restaurateur and customer have the same standards. The result is the most reliably satisfying Chinese food in New York City, from the Peking duck and the beautifully orchestrated banquet dishes to the pork wontons and the tuna steak. The premises, though cramped, are visually exciting; the staff can be either helpful or not, depending on your captain. *155 E. 55th St. (off Lexington Ave.), tel. 212/371-8844. Reservations advised for lunch, required for dinner. Jacket advised. AE, DC, MC, V.*

Snaps. This fine new addition to this neck of the woods, just north of the Met Life Building and Grand Central, is an offshoot of the city's best (only until now) Scandinavian restaurant, Aquavit. A colorful place with tall windows and a very good lunch crowd, Snaps offers delectable Scandinavian-inspired dishes, especially the seafood, and prices are very commendable, with such choices as warm potato cake with gravlax, halibut with braised fennel in Pernod with shrimp aïoli, and sorbets. There's also a good selection of beer and Scandinavian aquavit. *230 Park Ave. (at 46th St.), tel. 212/949-*

7878. *Lunch and dinner reservations advised. Jacket and tie advised. AE, DC, MC, V. Closed Sat. lunch and Sun.*

Solera. The brightest and most convivial of a number of Spanish restaurants to open in New York recently, Solera demonstrates just how fine modern Spanish cuisine and wine can be. The chef and co-owner, Dominic Cerrone, trained at the great French seafood restaurant Le Bernardin, and his ability shows in seafood dishes such as monkfish in cream and tomato, and grilled shrimp in herbs. His vegetable paella is superb; the gazpacho, perfect. The appetizers are all very good, and the roast duck with green olives is a lovely dish. Desserts are unexpectedly fine—all at quite moderate prices. The wine list is full of the best Spain has to offer. *216 E. 53rd St. (at 3rd Ave.), tel. 212/644–1166. Reservations advised. Dress: casual. AE, DC, MC, V. Closed Sun.*

★ **Vong.** Chef Jean-Georges Vongerichten's latest creation is not another French bistro (he is owner of the popular Jo Jo) but, rather, an homage to Thailand, where he was once apprenticed. The space (which last housed a deluxe Italian ristorante) has been splendidly transformed, with a liberal use of gold leaf, creative wall treatments, specially designed lighting fixtures, and other decorative caprices. The menu includes such delicacies as crab spring roll, chicken in coconut milk, spicy bay scallops with rice noodles, lobster with Thai herbs, and rabbit curry. À la carte prices are somewhat higher than at the average Asian restaurant, but the six-course dégustation dinner at $55 actually represents good value. *200 E. 54th St. (at 3rd Ave.), tel. 212/486–9592. Reservations advised. Dress: casual chic. AE, DC, MC, V. Closed Mon.-Sat. lunch, and Sun.*

Zarela. This is one of the city's best spots for sophisticated Mexican cuisine served in comfortable surroundings. Owner Zarela Martinez (formerly of Café Marimba) continues to innovate and change her menu according to the seasonal availability of ingredients. Her trademark dishes include chicken Chilaquiles (chicken prepared with layers of fried tortillas), *calamar a la Veracruzana* (fried squid in a spicy tomato, onion, green olive, and jalapeño sauce), fajitas, whole grilled trout, and tuna with mole sauce. Sample the fried plantains, and try to leave room for the luscious desserts, especially the maple-and-spice pumpkin cheesecake. *953 2nd Ave. (near 50th St.), tel. 212/644–6740. Reservations advised. Dress: casual. AE, DC. Closed for lunch on weekends.*

Inexpensive **Billy's.** Charging a fair price for a fair meal, this neighborhood pub has been serving up seafood, steaks, chops, burgers, and corned-beef hash—a house specialty—for the better part of the century, and it numbers many a devoted regular. The old New York decor is completely apt for a relaxed meal. *948 1st Ave. (near 52nd St.), tel. 212/355–8920. Reservations advised for 3 or more. Dress: casual. AE, DC, MC, V.*

P. J. Clarke's. This throwback saloon is one of the most popular in New York. Once you wade past the crowd at the front door lined up at the bar, a thriving singles hangout (tip: enter by the side door on 55th Street and skip the throng), you'll find a pleasant dining room in the back serving burgers, chili, salads, and home fries. Convenient to Third Avenue movie theaters, this is a spot where history looms larger than the cuisine—which has declined a little of late. *915 3rd Ave. (at 55th St.), tel. 212/759–1650. Reservations advised. Dress: casual. AE, DC, MC, V.*

Royal Canadian Pancake House. Clearly not for the cholesterol- and calorie-conscious, this cramped but lively space serves up every imaginable combination on the pancake and waffle cir- cuit—more than 60 varieties in all. Portions here are so large they could accommodate both a Mountie and his horse. For a twist, try a womlet: a ham omelet served over a waffle. Then there's the Royal Canadian cracker: two fried eggs and bacon over a waffle. Leave room for the barbecued mountain sau- sages. Bring your family. Or an army. There's no liquor license. *1004 2nd Ave. (at 53rd St.), tel. 212/980–4131. No reservations. Dress: casual. MC, V. (No credit cards at another location at 145 Hudson St. between Beach and Hubert Sts.)*

Take-Sushi. This is a fast-paced and entirely worthwhile Japa- nese spot for excellent sushi at the bar or tables. Take-Sushi is very popular for lunch, and you can slip in and out without spending much money. It's convenient if you're in the Grand Central area or trying to catch a train. *71 Vanderbilt Ave. (be- tween 45th and 46th Sts.), tel. 212/867–5120. Dress: casual. AE, DC, MC, V. Closed Sat. lunch and Sun.*

Theater District

Very Expensive **Le Bernardin.** This commodious and elegant dining room has ★ dazzled the most demanding seafood lovers since its debut nearly eight years ago. With his light, flavorful sauces and tasteful creativity, Gilbert LeCoze is a true master of form and substance. Although expensive, the service is impeccable. The wine list is extremely good, with many a rarity. Creative first courses include such delights as oysters with truffle cream, black-bass tartare with caviar, marinated cod with juniper gin- ger, and shrimp and basil beignets. The fish carpaccios are ex- cellent. Poached halibut with rosemary and onion confit vies with another version prepared with capers and a warm vinai- grette. Alternatively, try the herb-crusted codfish or the trademark roasted monkfish with cabbage. Leave room for the fabulous desserts. *155 W. 51st St. (near 7th Ave.), tel. 212/489– 1515. Reservations required. Jacket and tie required. AE, DC, MC, V. Closed Sun.*

★ **Les Célébrités.** With all the downscaling in restaurants it's en- couraging to see such a posh, splendid dining room in the reno- vated Essex Hotel. The "celebrities" in question are movie and stage stars who have also exhibited their paintings here (the restaurant even owns a James Dean portrait), and the place gets its share of visiting VIPs who come to sample chef Chris- tian Delouvrier's updated French cuisine with Oriental touches. He does a "Japanese-inspired" salad of sweetbreads and wild mushrooms, and his "burger" of foie gras sandwiched on apple slices and a velvety lobster soup with fava beans are standouts. Several hearty meat dishes are prepared for two. Although many hotel dining rooms seem dull, this one has above-average charm. *160 Central Park S (in Essex Hotel, near 7th Ave.), tel. 212/484–5113. Reservations advised. Jack- et required. AE, DC, MC, V. Closed Sun., Mon., and lunch- time.*

Expensive **Barbetta.** New York's oldest family-run Italian restaurant, this ★ elegant masterpiece is presided over by Laura Maioglio. Every great musician and actor has dined here, including Toscanini. The exquisite premises actually occupy the ground floors of four entire town houses, allowing for a double-width dining room and garden. The former is decorated in superb period style. The latter provides an enchanting oasis for warm-weather dining. Upstairs are stylish private dining salons. What's more, you won't find better food in the neighborhood, with such dishes as linguine with black-olive paste, sensational risotto, penne with basil and tomato, agnolotti, and sturgeon with olives and fennel. There is a pretheater menu priced at $39, and a seven-course tasting menu at $55. A new wine list features 35 selections under $35. *321 W. 46th St. (near 8th Ave.), tel. 212/ 246–9171. Reservations advised. Jacket required. AE, DC, MC, V. Closed Sun.*

44. At this popular restaurant, you'll find without a doubt one of the most brilliant examples of contemporary decor, designed by Philippe Stark. The dining space actually lies in the open lobby (which attracts a remarkably unconventional young crowd), and the banquette tables are comfortable. After several changes of chefs, 44 is back on track, and the food's good again, though rarely terrific, revealing an excessive use of herbs. Among the specialties are polenta with wild mushrooms, skate with lentils, and profiteroles. The superior desserts are worth coming here for after seeing a play. 44 has become a big publishing hangout at lunch. *44 W. 44th St. (in Royalton Hotel, near 5th Ave.), tel. 212/944–8844. Reservations advised. Dress: casual chic. AE, DC, MC, V.*

Gallagher's. The best of the West Side steak houses, this spot has a lot of tradition and Broadway razzle-dazzle about it. The place has always been a big hangout for sports figures, and there are photos of all the great ones on the walls. The meat— unquestionably fine aged prime—hangs in the window, and the whole place buzzes with masculine guffaws. If you like that kind of environment, this is an enticing place, especially before or after the theater. Stay with the steaks, lobster, onion rings, and cheesecake and you'll be happy. *228 W. 52nd St. (off Broadway), tel. 212/245–5336. Reservations advised. Dress: casual. AE, DC, MC, V.*

Petrossian. This highly stylized deco outpost of Paris's famed caviar purveyor is no longer just an emporium for beluga, osetra, and sevruga (although $110 will snare 30 grams of each). The latest menu is much more extensive. Nevertheless, the traditionalist will delight in "teaser" appetizers—canapé-size portions of smoked sturgeon, smoked salmon filled with salmon tartare, smoked cod roe with creamer potatoes, and fillet of smoked eel with ratatouille. Other choices include excellent Russian borscht with crème fraîche and piroshki, salad of warm roasted glazed duck breast, roasted salmon with French green lentils and black-olive sauce, chocolate-raspberry terrine with espresso ice cream, and lemon tart with lemon sauce. The $29 fixed-price lunch offers good value, as does the $38 pretheater dinner. *182 W. 58th St. (at 7th Ave.), tel. 212/ 245–2214. Reservations advised. Jacket and tie advised. AE, DC, MC, V.*

★ **Russian Tea Room.** Justly famous for its longevity, its polished Imperial Palace decor, and its endless parade of celebrities (a scene from the movie *Tootsie* was filmed here), the RTR is legendary—and well it should be. Of course, if you're not Dustin Hoffman or Luciano Pavarotti, you may not get an "A" table downstairs, but upstairs is just as bright and shining, especially at holiday time. The food has improved measurably over the past year or two, since noted chef Jacques Pepin began consulting here. Enjoy the blini with caviar, the chicken Kiev, full of butter, and the delicious borscht soup. Two fixed-price dinners are offered for $39.75 each. *150 W. 57th St. (near 7th Ave.), tel. 212/265-0947. Reservations advised. Jacket required at dinner. AE, DC, MC, V.*

★ **San Domenico.** This bellwether restaurant replicates its famed namesake in Imola, Italy. Its influence on Italian cooking in the United States has been enormous, and owner Tony May is one of the most knowledgeable men in his field. Chef Theo Schoeneger has an extraordinary sense of flavor and nuance that shows in every dish, right down to desserts. The premises are stylish but not overly formal, jarred only by orange table-cloths. Enjoy foie gras à Veneto, clams with leeks on bruschetta, risotto with beef juices, pasta with squid, spaghettini with zucchini flowers, rack of lamb, lobster fricassee, and apple tart with lemon ice cream. Prix fixe menus are available at lunch ($35), pretheater ($42.50), and dinner ($55). The wine list assembled by Giorgio Lingero is one of the finest in the city. *240 Central Park S (off Columbus Circle), tel. 212/265-5959. Reservations required. Jacket required. AE, DC, MC, V. Closed for lunch on weekends.*

★ **World Yacht Cruises.** A three-hour yacht cruise around Manhattan gives you more spectacle than Windows on the World and the Rainbow Room combined. Add to this some above-average Continental cuisine, dancing to a good band, and gratuities (but not drinks)—and you'll still pay only $62–$69.50 per person ($27.50 for lunch; $39.95 for brunch). You can experience the thrill of the stars, the water, and the lights of New York over lunch, dinner, or Sunday brunch. *Pier 81, W. 42nd St. (on Hudson River), tel. 212/630-8111. Reservations required. Jacket required. AE, MC, V. Cruises Jan.–Apr., Fri.–Sun. and some weekdays; call for details.*

Moderate **Becco.** Lidia Bastianich (co-owner of Felidia) and her son, Joseph, have a winning idea, gleaned from the example of Italian countryside trattorias: They offer a set menu of antipasti and pasta for a fixed price of $16 at lunch and $19 at dinner, optionally followed by a variety of main courses and desserts for only a few dollars more. A glistening array of freshly grilled vegetables, and superb pastas (such as mushroom risotto, basil gnocchi, osso buco and pappardelle with rabbit stew) may be followed by main courses (such as osso buco, swordfish with balsamic vinegar, and spit-roasted suckling pig). Bread pudding with green apple sorbet is among the desserts priced at $5.50, including coffee. What's more, all wines are $15 a bottle. Becco is convenient for pre- and post-theater dining, and also represents great value. *355 W. 46th St. (near 9th Ave.), tel. 212/397-7597. Reservations advised. Dress: casual. AE, DC, MC, V. Closed Mon. lunch.*

Brasserie des Théâtres. Max Bernard, Jean-Michel Diot, and Philippe Lajaunie, the winning team that created Park Bistro, Les Halles, and Park Avenue Townhouse, have debuted their most ambitious undertaking yet: a full-scale brasserie, replete with a zinc bar, an antique copper serving cart, oversize banquettes, and vintage photographs of celebrated Parisian theaters. The menu is just as authentic: a broad assortment of oysters, clams and shellfish, rabbit terrine, fried calamari, choucroute royale, pot-au-feu entrecôte, and tantalizing warm chocolate tart, profiteroles, and crêpes Suzette. The brasserie serves breakfast, lunch, dinner, and late supper. *243 W. 46th*

St. (in Paramount Hotel, near 8th Ave.), tel. 212/719–5588. Reservations advised. Dress: casual chic. AE, DC, MC, V.

Le Bar Bat. Joyce Steins oversees this whimsical restaurant featuring Vietnamese food of commendable (if high-volume) quality. The decor must be seen to be believed—hanging lighted oversize bats, red satin banquettes, beaded curtains. The bar is smoky, the cocktails fanciful, there is a dance floor downstairs, and the music never lets up. The crowd is equally loud and on the make. A medley of appetizers such as Vietnamese spring rolls, sugarcane shrimp, calamari and satés is a meal in itself. Or consider such entrées as lobster in a clay pot, chicken salad, or grouper in banana leaves. *311 W. 57th St. (near 8th Ave.), tel. 212/307–7228. Reservations advised. Dress: casual. AE, DC, MC, V.*

★ **Orso.** By far, this is the most popular restaurant in the Theater District; it's tough to get a table even after the theater. The reasons are not hard to find: The atmosphere is unpretentious, the greeting at the door is warm (and apologetic if they can't fit you in), the price is extremely fair, and the rustic trattoria fare, such as pan-fried calve's liver, is very good indeed. Orso gets its fair share of celebrities, too. *322 W. 46th St. (near 8th Ave.), tel. 212/489–7212. Reservations accepted 1 wk in advance only. Dress: casual. MC, V.*

Planet Hollywood. With such celebrated co-owners as Sly Stallone and Arnold Schwarzenegger, Planet Hollywood has generated more than its fair share of publicity. Not surprisingly, the place is festooned with props, posters, and photos from famous flicks. The restaurant draws an eclectic crowd ranging from teens and families to the simply curious, all of whom wait in line for a table, hoping to catch a glimpse of a visiting celeb (who, of course, is not subjected to the line). The menu, however, is hardly a hit, featuring lots of junk food, such as nachos, Italachos (deep-fried pizza dough with barbecue sauce, guacamole, and sour cream), burgers and sandwiches, with a smattering of grown-up fare such as grilled swordfish and chicken at steep prices. *140 W. 57th St. (between 6th and 7th Aves.), tel. 212/333–7827. No reservations. Dress: casual. AE, MC, V.*

★ **Remi.** This spot has become one of New York City's finest Italian restaurants, buoyed by owner-architect Adam Tihany's spacious, grand interior (and a new outdoor patio) and chef Francesco Antonucci's bright, colorful but never extravagant cooking, which is based on Venetian traditions. From antipasti through dessert cookies and grappas, this is the kind of restaurant that defines Manhattan's genteel image. *Bigoli* (spaghetti) with wild mushrooms, goose carpaccio, gnocchi with tomato, and all desserts are superb; choose here from a creative wine list. *145 W. 53rd St. (near 7th Ave.), tel. 212/581–4242. Reservations advised. Dress: casual. AE, DC, MC, V. Closed for lunch on weekends.*

Zen Palate. Don't be put off by the name, the fact that it's a vegetarian restaurant, or by the philosophic menu lingo: This is a real find. Not only is it a smart-looking place with ocher walls, acloud-painted ceiling, and wicker café chairs, but the food is sensational. And because there are a number of fried items here, you get enough fat in your meal to satisfy your appetite, and you definitely won't leave hungry after enjoying dishes such as moo shoo basil rolls, Dream Land spinach linguine, Zen casserole, and steamed dumplings. Skip the rather insipid desserts, and be warned that reservations are not always handled with skill. It's BYOB here. *663 9th Ave. (entrance on 46th St.),* *tel. 212/582–1669. Reservations advised. Dress: casual. AE, DC, MC, V.*

Inexpensive **Bangkok Cuisine.** New York doesn't have the number of good Thai restaurants many smaller cities have, but Bangkok Cuisine is one of the oldest and best. It doesn't look like much—rather dark and bare-bones with a fish tank in the dining room—but the food is delicious and (on request) as hot as you can stand it. The pad Thai noodles and shrimp is a great dish here, as are the crispy mee krob noodles and the whole fried fish. *885 8th Ave. (near 53rd St.), tel. 212/581–6370. Reservations advised. Dress: casual. AE, MC, V. Closed Sun. lunch.*

Cabana Carioca. It may seem dingy—you follow the music up a flight of stairs to a thickly varnished, rather weird-looking dining room—but Cabana Carioca serves the best Brazilian food in New York: great platters and pots steaming with black beans, manioc flour, *feijoada* (the Brazilian national stew), and seafood. All of it is lusty and filling, and nothing is particularly expensive. *123 W. 45th St. (near 7th Ave.), tel. 212/581–8088. Reservations advised. Dress: casual. AE, DC, MC, V.*

Carnegie Deli. This stereotypical New York delicatessen is crowded and noisy, with service that is both gruff and brisk. You are seated cheek-by-jowl with your neighbor and choose from a satisfying array of humorously described entrées such as "Carnegie Haul" (triple-decker sandwich with pastrami, tongue, and salami), "Nova on a Sunday" (smoked salmon, sturgeon, and cream cheese), "Hamalot" or "Beefamania"—plus standbys such as franks, burgers, and "Egg-stravaganzas." *854 7th Ave. (at 55th St.), tel. 212/757–2245. Dress: casual. No credit cards.*

Hard Rock Cafe. People come here not so much for dinner or lunch as for a lift. Music blares from noon until the wee hours. The decor aptly consists of a collection of guitars belonging to celebrated musicians. You can count on decent hamburgers, sandwiches, and french fries. There is *always* a line to get in, even at 11:30 in the morning; they don't take reservations, so be prepared for a wait. *221 W. 57th St. (near Broadway), tel. 212/459–9320. No reservations. Dress: casual. AE, MC, V.*

Joe Allen. A longtime hangout for theater goers and actors, Joe Allen has no pretensions and serves decent, simple food. The ribs and burgers are dependable, the service is affable (often by actors between jobs), and the place buzzes with a certain theatrical history. It's a good spot for before or after the show. *326 W. 46th St. (near 8th Ave.), tel. 212/581–6464. Reservations advised. Dress: casual. MC, V.*

Upper East Side

Very Expensive **Le Cirque.** For 19 years Le Cirque has reigned as the quintes-
★ sential Manhattan restaurant with an international reputation for grand dining, glamorous clientele, and an indefatigable owner, Sirio Maccioni, who plays ringmaster to a crowd of faithful regulars. The effusive murals, the custom-designed Regis Dho porcelain, the presentation of dishes, and the flourishes of the staff make this dining spot a showplace as well as a fine restaurant. In 1993 Le Cirque acquired a new young chef, Sylvain Portay, who with his associate Sottha Khunn, turns out an astounding array of specials to augment an already lavish menu and a remarkable $29 lunch. Recent kitchen triumphs include turbot with wild mushrooms, foie gras ravioli with

black truffles, savory braised veal shank with vegetables, and Jacques Torres's spectacular desserts, including his famous crème brûlée. This is a good place for Saturday lunch, as well. *58 E. 65th St. (near Park Ave.), tel. 212/794–9292. Reservations required. Jacket and tie required. AE, DC, MC, V. Closed Sun.*

★ **Parioli Romanissimo.** The reserved beauty of Parioli, set in a town house off Fifth Avenue, makes this a very romantic spot, but it is the food that draws well-heeled customers here year after year. Owner Rubrio Rossi serves up exquisite northern Italian cooking. You may feast on *cotechino* (fresh pork sausage) with white truffles, risotto with wild mushrooms, or an enormous rack of lamb with rosemary. Leave room for a selection from the finest cheese cart in the city. Prices are very, very high, but you do get value—except on the exorbitantly priced wine list, which is not particularly extensive. *24 E. 81st St. (off 5th Ave.), tel. 212/288–2391. Reservations required. Jacket and tie required. AE, DC, MC, V. Closed for lunch, and Sun.*

Expensive **Arizona 206.** Despite its very casual atmosphere and potentially
★ piercing noise level, this remains a dynamic restaurant for its highly seasoned and imaginative southwestern cookery and its young, handsome crowd. New chef David Walzog carries on the tradition of good taste here, and portions are enormous—they should be, because prices are also quite high. Try black-bean terrine with chorizo and goat cheese, corn soup with lobster, braised rabbit tortilla, pork tamale in a chili sauce, sautéed Atlantic salmon, and chicken and green-chili pizza. Desserts include cinnamon tostado and cherry-pecan sundae. *206 E. 60th St. (near 3rd Ave.), tel. 212/838–0440. Reservations advised. Dress: casual. AE, DC, MC, V. Closed Sun. lunch.*

Aureole. From the first glimpse of its magnificent floral arrangements to the first taste of chef Charlie Palmer's innovative selections, Aureole emits its own very special glow; this is a charming restaurant for a festive lunch or dinner, with alfresco dining when weather permits. Palmer's ever-changing menu can include the likes of sea scallop "sandwiches" in a potato crust with citrus juices, or crisped sweetbreads with warm roasted eggplant and tomato vinaigrette. You can also count on what have become house staples: carpaccio of yellowfin tuna and mushroom salad, oak-smoked salmon with cucumber salad, and grilled black Angus sirloin with bourbon essence sauce. Desserts are divine, especially the warm raspberry and almond cobbler, and the bittersweet chocolate and praline timbale. There's a good wine list, an excellent selection of digestifs, and a fixed-price menu at $59. *34 E. 61st St. (near Madison Ave.), tel. 212/319–1660. Reservations required 3 weeks in advance. Jacket and tie required. AE, DC, MC, V. Closed Sat. lunch and Sun.*

★ **Mark's Restaurant.** Chef Philippe Boulot is one of Manhattan's brightest stars. His technique, acquired via Joel Robuchon and Alain Senderens, is impeccable, his ideas sound, and his food full of flavor. Boulot's wife, Susan, creates pastries that match up with his menus. At lunchtime the place is quiet but is ideal for a business meeting over a delectable Caesar salad with lobster quesadillos, paillard of chicken, or mixed seafood grill. Signature dinner dishes include lobster baked potato over a bed of spinach, napoleon of asparagus and wild-mushroom ragout, braised duck leg in game stew, and nectarine and blue-

berry crisp. Mark's is also a delightful spot for a filling afternoon tea ($14) of sandwiches, scones, sweets, and a choice of 18
varieties of tea. *77th St. at Madison Ave. (in Mark Hotel), tel.
212/879–1864. Reservations advised. Jacket and tie advised.
AE, DC, MC, V.*

★ **Sign of the Dove.** For years this place was the quintessential celebration restaurant, known for its lavish decor, its outrageous
prices, and the lineup of limos outside its door. Today the decor
is somewhat toned down but still luxurious, and the prices are
still high ($59 for the set-menu dinner)—but the food is better
than ever. Clearly owners Joe, Verge, and Henny Santo have
brought this old bird back to life, so there's good reason for romance to take hold again. Go with chef Andrew D'Amico's
grilled Muscovy duck with pumpkin pancakes, cranberry chut-
ney and poached pears, the perfect roast loin of lamb, and the
chocolate mascarpone torte. *1110 3rd Ave. (at 65th St.), tel.
212/861–8080. Reservations required. Jacket advised. AE,
DC, MC, V. Closed Mon. lunch.*

Moderate **Bistro du Nord.** A delightful sliver of a space, with a downstairs
dining room overhung with an equally cozy second-floor balco-
ny, makes this one of the cheeriest French bistros in the neighborhood. Its pale yellow walls, vintage photos by Atget,
Avedon, and Penn, and bustling atmosphere make it an inviting
spot for dinner. Chef Pascal Bonhomme has elevated the level
of cooking here quite a bit and goes well beyond the usual clichés of bistro fare. Although the place is quiet at lunch, the
noontime menu still shines with the likes of onion tart with
tapenade, or parmesan and Black Forest ham soufflé. At dinner, sample the crotin of warm chèvre in phyllo, confit of duck,
braised rabbit with pappardelle, or lamb steak with herbed
couscous. *1312 Madison Ave. (at 93rd St.), tel. 212/289–0097.
Reservations advised. Dress: casual chic. AE, DC, MC, V.*

★ **Jo Jo.** We have long thought Jean-Georges Vongerichten (formerly of the Lafayette Restaurant in the Drake Hotel) one of
New York's finest creative chefs, and now that he's got his own
bustling bistro set in a two-story town house (plus a brand-new
Franco-Vietnamese restaurant 10 blocks to the south), he is
cooking with obvious exhilaration. Jo Jo has become one of the
hottest tickets in town for marvelous cuisine at remarkably low
prices (no entrée over $21). Downstairs is loud but fun while the
upstairs bar is a bit cramped. For peace and quiet, the rear
room is intimate and sedate. Reservations could be a problem
because of its popularity, and you may have to wait in a
cramped bar area. But for dishes such as shrimp in spiced carrot juice, pork cheeks dusted with cornmeal, lobster in Sau-
ternes, grilled chicken with olives, wild-mushroom soup,
salmon in rice paper, and chocolate Valhrona cake, it's worth
the brief discomfort. *160 E. 64th St. (near Lexington Ave.), tel.
212/223–5656. Reservations required. Dress: casual. AE, MC,
V. Closed Sun.*

Lola Belle. Opened by the former co-owner of Lola's on 22nd
Street, the uptown version is slicker, more nightclubby in feel,
and mercifully, far less noisy than the original. Otherwise, the
same format prevails—predominantly Caribbean fare and live
music. While the cooking is not as fastidious as at the maiden
Lola's, the refined ambience largely compensates. Nonetheless, you'll find commendable deep-fried onion ribbons, codfish
fritters, Cajun fried chicken, and curried chicken and shrimp.
206 E. 63rd St. (between 2nd and 3rd Aves.), tel. 212/755–5652.

Reservations advised. Dress: casual chic. AE, DC, MC, V. Closed Sat. lunch.

★ **Mazzei.** Named after the 18th-century Italian who was a diplomat for the fledgling United States, Mazzei is the scene of kitchen politics that are clearly as astute as the ambassador would have expected. A concise but carefully conceived menu includes gnocchi in a wild-mushroom sauce, superb Cornish hen with peperoncini (little peppers), roast pheasant, and scallops with peas; the zabaglione (a foamy desert made with egg yolks, wine, and sugar) is spectacular. The premises are warm and comfortable—definitely the setting for some first-rate dining. *1564 2nd Ave. (near 81st St.), tel. 212/628–3131. Reservations advised. Dress: casual. AE, MC, V.*

Park Avenue Café. Seasoned restaurateur Alan Stillman (his other properties include Smith & Wollensky, the Manhattan Ocean Club, and Cité) has fashioned a crisp, originally designed eatery boasting a fanciful mix of eclectic Americana with good lighting throughout. Chef David Burke (formerly of the River Café) presides over the kitchen, devising a menu that is both creative and satisfying, with such dishes as tuna and salmon tartare, black-bean soup with shrimp quesadilla, roasted salmon, chicken pot pie, a whimsical swordfish "chop," and flourless chocolate cake. *100 E. 63rd St. (at Park Ave.), tel 212/644–1900. Dress: casual. Reservations advised. AE, DC, MC, V. Closed Sun.*

Post House. An impressive array of vintage Americana sets the backdrop for a lively business lunch or dinner. The Post House remains a perfect place to dine with guests of diverse palates; you can subsist on such standbys as Caesar salad, crab cakes, lobster cobb salad, and sirloin steak, or opt for lemon pepper chicken, poached salmon with crabmeat remoulade, Cajun rib steak, or filet tips. No matter what, don't overlook the addictive french fries and onion rings. And do take advantage of one of the city's finer wine lists. *28 E. 63rd St. (near Madison Ave.), tel. 212/935–2888. Reservations advised. Jacket and tie advised. AE, DC, MC, V. Closed for lunch on weekends.*

★ **Sette Mezzo.** In the past couple of years, this restaurant has become the Upper East Side's trattoria of record, attracting a very posh uptown crowd. The menu is similar to that at Vico, its older sibling, with such signature dishes as homemade stuffed mozzarella, fried zucchini, red snapper with balsamic vinegar, and penne with sausage and broccoli rape. The flattened, breaded veal chop is another must; alternatively, try the paillard of veal with olives and tomatoes. For dessert, sample the excellent tiramisuor *tartufo* ice cream. *969 Lexington Ave. (near 70th St.), tel. 212/472–0400. Reservations required. Dress: casual. No credit cards.*

Table d'Hôte. With a total of only nine tables, this tiny, antiques-festooned restaurant qualifies as one of the smallest eateries in New York. Yet it is an ideal spot to dine after an evening at one of the Upper East Side museums or when your travels take you to the neighborhood. Here you can count on very well prepared American Continental fare, with first courses such as snails in puff pastry, black-bean soup with jalapeño cream, or goat-cheese fritters. Entrées include grilled chicken breast with wild rice, carrots, and cabbage; lamb; and salmon. End your meal with good tarte-tatin. Nine wines are offered by the glass. The prix fixe dinner offered before 6:30 for $20 is an excellent value. *44 E. 92nd St. (near Madison Ave.), tel. 212/348–8125. Reservations advised. Dress: casual. AE, MC, V.*

Vašata. This is one of the few remaining Czech restaurants in a neighborhood that was once full of Eastern European places. Vašata is still a solid and very friendly little spot where you get good value for the dollar and you'll never leave hungry. Sample the menu—roast goose in season, dumplings, apricot crêpes—everything is wonderful and filling. The atmosphere is very Old World, and the owners are delighted you paid them a visit. *339 E. 75th St. (near 1st Ave.), tel. 212/988–7166. Reservations advised. Dress: casual. AE, MC, V. Closed Mon.*

Vico Ristorante. This intimate, white-walled sliver of a space has become a hit. Bordering on boisterous, this neighborhood trattoria more than offsets the noise level with wonderful homespun pastas and innovative creations such as wilted radicchio with grilled smoked mozzarella, expertly fried zucchini and baby artichokes, country sausage with broccoli, flattened breaded veal chop, and delicious tiramisu. *1603 2nd Ave. (near 83rd St.), tel. 212/772–2161. Reservations advised. Dress: casual. No credit cards. Closed lunch.*

Inexpensive **Jackson Hole.** It's part of a small, city-wide chain that's renowned for better-than-average fast food. This basement branch features colorful movie posters; the Columbus Avenue outpost sports a café look. Wherever you alight, expect to find generous portions and a broad selection of sandwiches and burgers. There are elaborate versions, such as the "East Sider" (hamburger with bacon, ham, grilled onions, mushrooms, and cheese) and the guacamole burger (cheese, guacamole, and tortilla chips), each weighing in at a hefty 7 ounces. *232 E. 64th St. (between 2nd and 3rd Aves.), tel. 212/371–7187. Reservations accepted for large groups. Dress: casual. AE.*

★ **J. G. Melon.** This popular neighborhood pub bristles with activity well past midnight. The casual decor is enlivened by paintings and prints of—what else?—the melon in myriad manifestations. Melon attracts a diverse uptown crowd and gives the first-time visitor an instant slice of neighborhood life. (There's also a West Side branch at 76th Street and Amsterdam Avenue. Both serve excellent bacon cheeseburgers, club sandwiches, and cottage fries, and have great bars.) *1291 3rd Ave. (at 74th St.), tel. 212/744–0585. No reservations. Dress: casual. No credit cards.*

The Right Bank. This basement-level bistro remains one of the few spots where you can catch a simple and inexpensive meal amid the glitter of Madison Avenue. It is ideal for a quick lunch or a light dinner. The menu includes good onion soup, a variety of omelets and salads, plus burgers and sandwiches—even quiche Lorraine, a pleasant throwback. *822 Madison Ave. (near 69th St.), tel. 212/737–2811. Reservations not required. Dress: casual. AE, DC, MC, V.*

Serendipity 3. Looking as bright as when it opened in the 1960s, Serendipity 3 is as good as its name—a swell little place where you'll find all sorts of surprises, from campy gifts, postcards, and paraphernalia to some very tasty food: chili, burgers, and scrumptious desserts such as frozen hot chocolate. The people who eat here range from young models to prom queens, from East Side artists to Scarsdale matrons and children of all ages. *225 E. 60th St. (near 2nd Ave.), tel. 212/838–3531. Reservations advised on weekends. Dress: casual. AE, DC, MC, V.*

7th Regiment Mess. Set in the 7th Regiment Armory, this enchanting restaurant is an antique dream, with massive dark wood, a terrific old oak bar, and some of the best down-to-earth

American fare you'll find anywhere: simple roast beef, chicken, turkey, mashed potatoes, and everything that goes with them. And the prices are amazingly cheap. It's a great place for the family, and one you won't soon forget. *643 Park Ave. (between 66th and 67th Sts.), tel. 212/744–4107. Reservations advised. Jacket advised. AE, MC, V. Closed Sun. and Mon. lunch.*

Lincoln Center

Expensive   **Café des Artistes.** The history surrounding Café des Artistes
★ dates to just after World War I, when the apartment building it's in housed many of the era's finest artists, none more famous than Howard Chandler Christy, who painted the celebrated murals of unclad nymphs romping in what looks like Central Park. Seasoned restaurateur George Lang restored this place to prominence, and his wife, Jenifer Harvey Lang, now maintains Café des Artistes with the same high standards. The enchanting dining room is made for romance, a perfect spot to go to before or after a Lincoln Center performance. You can expect to see some of the city's most notable notables dining here, appreciating such offerings as celery rémoulade, gravlax, saucisson de Lyons, steak tartare, pot-au-feu, chicken pot pie, cassoulet, and Ilona torte. An interesting array of wines by the glass is available. *1 W. 67th St. (near Central Park W), tel. 212/877-3500. Reservations required. Jacket required at dinner. AE, DC, MC, V.*

Tavern on the Green. Everyone's heard of this fanciful restaurant, and people come here to bask in the flamboyance of Warner LeRoy's Central Park fantasy of lights and antique kitsch that overwhelms and seduces. Yes, it's an "out-of-towners' restaurant," but the food in the main dining room, prepared by chef Marc Poidevin (formerly of Maxim's), is very good indeed. Standout specials include red snapper with fried leeks and shiitakes in a red-wine sauce, and quail risotto. Desserts, such as waffle with poached pears and praline ice cream, are equally winning. And still the french fries are unsurpassed; the hamburger, one of the best. The prix fixe pretheater menu ($21.50–$24.50) is an amazing bargain. *Central Park W (at 67th St.), tel. 212/873-3200. Reservations advised. Dress: casual. AE, DC, MC, V.*

Moderate   **Café Luxembourg.** Still stylish but now a lot less boisterous
★ than it was, Café Luxembourg remains one of the West Side's better bistros—and is priced accordingly (although the $28 pre- and posttheater dinner is a bargain). Its original chef has departed, but you can still expect a solid menu and satisfying specials. Go for the seafood appetizers, baby lamb, filet mignon, and crème brûlée. *200 W. 70th St. (near Amsterdam Ave.), tel. 212/873-7411. Reservations advised. Dress: casual chic. AE, DC, MC, V. Closed weekday and Sat. lunch.*

Fishin' Eddie. This newcomer to the Lincoln Center area is already popular with those who want no-frills atmsophere (the place deliberately looks like an old fish house in New England) and the freshest seafood. The owners (they also own Vince and Eddie's) run an affable eatery, and the chef is expert at all seafood techniques—frying, grilling, and steaming. The simpler dishes are best, and desserts are modest (with a lot to be modest about). But you won't fret over your budget, and you'll be amazed at how good simple seafood can be. *73 W. 71st St. (near*

Columbus Ave.), tel. 212/874–3474. Reservations advised. Dress: casual. AE, DC, MC, V.

★ **Vince & Eddie's.** Named after owners Vincent Orgera (who tends bar) and Eddie Schoenfeld, former maître d'-impresario at Auntie Yuan's and Shun Lee, this place hasn't looked back since its successful debut in 1990. The attractive, modified country look was orchestrated by Sam Lopata. The menu is devoid of gimmickry; it simply works well and costs less. Try the onion tart, fried oysters, calve's liver with apples and onion rings, lamb shank, mashed turnip with crisped shallots, red snapper with walnuts, and apple tureen. There's garden dining in season. *70 W. 68th St. (between Central Park West and Columbus Ave.), tel. 212/721–0068. Reservations advised. Dress: casual. AE, DC, MC, V.*

Upper West Side

Expensive **The Terrace.** Perched atop a Columbia University dorm (though
★ not associated with the school), this elegant dining room, with its panoramic view of Manhattan and the Hudson River, is packed most nights but unfamiliar to many New Yorkers. The food is every bit the equal of the view, with prices just about comparable to downtown deluxe. Chef Ossama Mickail presides over the kitchen and delivers the likes of quail with caramelized squash, red snapper with coriander and tomato confit, and mint-chocolate ice cream profiteroles. Service is most professional. A $48 prix fixe menu is available. *400 W. 119th St. (near Amsterdam Ave.), tel. 212/666–9490. Reservations required. Jacket and tie required for dinner. AE, DC, MC, V. Closed Sat. lunch, Sun., and Mon.*

Moderate **Amsterdam's Bar and Rotisserie.** This fast became a popular
★ Upper West Side hangout soon after it opened; jockeying for tables here was elevated to an art form. Its success is well deserved, not just because the prices are downright low and the portions enormous but because the food is very good, including such choices as roast chicken, steak, french fries, and dessert pies. Dining here, you'll have a real sense of what the West Side is all about. *428 Amsterdam Ave. (near 80th St.), tel. 212/874–1377. No reservations. Dress: casual. AE, DC, MC, V.*

Carmine's. Those who wouldn't deign to set foot in Little Italy or have never eaten in the Bronx, Brooklyn, or Queens have made Carmine's a retro-chic restaurant—a big, sprawling, loud, red-sauce, family place with old-fashioned Italian-American food served in double portions at very fair prices. Not that Carmine's is any better than dozens of other Italian-American restaurants in New York; it's just that it has caught on, and people wait an hour or more in a smoke-engulfed bar to gorge here on rubbery calamari, very good pastas, and nice garlicky chicken. Volume business means volume cooking and slow service. *2450 Broadway (near 91st St.), tel. 212/362–2200. Reservations accepted for 6 or more. Dress: casual. AE. Closed lunch.*

Docks. This highly popular spot for seafood is contemporary in look but has the charm of an old-time seafood house. You dine on two separate levels separated by stairs and a gleaming brass rail. A blackboard lists the daily oyster specials and the catch of the day (which will also be rattled off by your waiter). Such staples as broiled or fried scallops or salmon can be found on the regular menu along with grilled halibut. *2427 Broadway (near 89th St.), tel. 212/724–5588; also at 633 3rd Ave. (near 40th*

St.), tel. 212/986–8080. Reservations advised. Dress: casual. AE, DC, MC, V.

★ **Poiret.** White walls with a floral motif, candlelit tables, and a handsome flower-festooned vitrine create an airy ambience at this popular French spot. The only flaw in the design is the soundproofing, but the first-rate bistro fare more than compensates, even when you have to raise your voice a tad to be heard over the beautifully seasoned and flavorful Mediterranean soup. Try the warm shrimp mousse and frisé salad. Whether you order the filet mignon or steak bearnaise, be sure to request a side dish of pommes frites (french fries). For dessert, Poiret makes an admirable crème brûlée. *474 Columbus Ave. (between 82nd and 83rd Sts.), tel. 212/724–6880. Reservations advised. Dress: casual. AE, DC, MC, V. Closed Mon.–Sat. lunch.*

Sidewalkers. This is one of New York's few Maryland crab houses, where you drink beer while you pound and pick away at spiced blue crab claws. The huge dining room, which appears once to have been a lobby, is jammed with casually dressed West Siders. *12 W. 72nd St. (near Central Park W), tel. 212/799–6070. Reservations advised. Dress: casual. AE, DC, MC, V. Closed for lunch.*

Inexpensive **EJ's Luncheonette.** This is a popular West Side spot for a rea-
★ sonably priced breakfast, brunch, lunch, or dinner. The decor is kitsch without being contrived, and the menu, though simple, is well executed. A wide array of breakfast dishes includes flapjacks, waffles, and eggs galore. Lunch or dinner consists of a broad selection of sandwiches, burgers, and salads, some designed for the health-conscious. There are also daily specials, soups, and salads. Don't overlook the addictive french fries, milk shakes, and malteds. There's now an East Side branch at 1271 Third Avenue (at 73rd Street). *433 Amsterdam Ave. (near 80th St.), tel. 212/873–3444. No reservations. Dress: casual. No credit cards.*

Lucy's. In look and feel, this place is very much an homage to the surfing safari: a liberal use of iridescent paint, complemented by posters, photographs, even recorded music celebrating the sport of surfing. The food could best be described as Malibu Meets Mexico: primarily southwestern with a sprinkling of salads and burgers. You can count on above-average salsa, "rocamole" (guacamole with nachos), quesadillas and fajitas, plus the fancifully named "Dinner with Elvis," a combo platter of burritos, quesadillas, and tacos. *503 Columbus Ave. (at 84th St.), tel. 212/787–3009. Reservations for large parties only. Dress: casual. AE, MC, V.*

Worth a Special Trip

Brooklyn **Peter Luger.** There's no question that Peter Luger is a land-
Very Expensive mark and a bit of 19th-century New York that deserves veneration. The Teutonic look, once common in chophouses, has its antique charm, and so do the deliberately brusque waiters. You have little choice in ordering (though there is a printed menu): a nondescript tomato and onion salad, sensational porterhouse steak (prepared for two or more people), very good lamb chops, acceptable hash browns, bland creamed spinach, and the usual cheesecake. Worth a journey through some pretty rough territory? (An attendant will watch your car.) You be the judge, but this is a unique spot and dear to New Yorkers' hearts. *178*

Broadway, tel. 718/387-7400. Reservations required. Dress: casual. No credit cards.

The River Café. Even after repeated visits, the majestic view from the River Café of the Manhattan cityscape remains breathtaking, and the place itself continues to be one of the "must-go" restaurants that define the city's unique grandeur. From its inception, the Café has also been a laboratory for eclectic cooking under a series of brilliant young chefs who have gone on to their own stellar restaurants. Executive chef John Loughran works hard to impress, but there's often more razzle than dazzle in such dishes as scallops in tough, wontonlike skins and grilled tuna with green noodle cake. Eric Gouteyron's desserts here are pretty but far from thrilling climaxes to a meal. The service seems considerably friendlier than it used to be, and the wine list continues to be exemplary. The prix-fixe dinner is $59; the six-course tasting menu is $78. *1 Water St. (under Brooklyn Bridge), tel. 718/522-5200. Reservations required. Jacket required at dinner. AE, DC, MC, V.*

Harlem
Moderate

Sylvia's. If you're craving great barbecue, down-home soul food, and something uniquely New York, catch a cab to Harlem (and have one waiting outside when you exit) and stop in at Sylvia's, a marvelous and justly famous restaurant serving up huge portions of great ribs, pork chops, candied sweet potatoes, and pecan pie. Bring an appetite and expect to take something home. It's good for Sunday lunch. *328 Lenox Ave. (near 126th St.), tel. 212/996-0660. Reservations required for 10 or more. Dress: casual. No credit cards.*

The Bronx
Moderate
★

Amerigo's. In the safe Bronx neighborhood of Throgs Neck, this has been an institution for half a century; under owners Tony and Anna Cortese, it gets better every year. There are two dining rooms: one casual, the other a bit more refined, with low lighting, sculpture, and a spacious bar. The Italian-American menu offers everything from rich, lusty mozzarella with anchovy sauce and gnocchi with a verdant pesto to terrific prime steaks, chops, and fresh lobsters. The osso buco is among the best in New York City. The Italian wine list is comprehensive in all regions, and prices for enormous entrée portions are fair indeed. *3587 E. Tremont Ave., tel. 212/792-3600. Reservations required weekends. Jacket advised in main dining room. AE, DC, MC, V. Closed Mon.*

10 Lodging

By Jane Hershey

A New York–based freelance writer whose work has appeared in Good Housekeeping, US, *and* Elle, *Jane Hershey is a long-time contributor to various Fodor's guides.*

If any single element of your trip to New York City is going to cost you a lot of money, it'll be your hotel bill. European cities may offer plenty of low-priced—albeit undistinguished—lodgings, but New York doesn't. Real estate is at a premium here, and labor costs are high, so hoteliers start out with a lot of expenses to cover. And there are enough well-heeled visitors to support competition at the premium end of the spectrum, which is where the profits are. Considering the healthy occupancy rate, market forces are not likely to drive current prices down. Fleabags and flophouses aside, there's precious little here for under $100 a night. We have noted a few budget properties, but even our "Inexpensive" category includes hotels that run as high as $135 for one night's stay in a double.

Once you've accepted that you must pay the going price, though, you'll have plenty of choices. In general, Manhattan hotels don't measure up to those in other U.S. cities in terms of room size, parking, or outside landscaping. But, this being a sophisticated city, New York hotels usually compensate with fastidious service, sprucely maintained properties, and restaurants that hold their own in a city of knowledgeable diners. Where else can you sleep in Frank Lloyd Wright's former apartment, swim with a view of the Empire State Building, or eat breakfast in bed while watching sea lions at play?

Price is by no means the perfect indicator of impeccable service, pleasant surroundings, or delicious cuisine, so we've tried to indicate the shortcomings of various properties, as well as their strong points. Common sense should tell you not to anticipate the same kind of personal service from even a top-flight convention hotel, such as the New York Hilton, as you would from a smaller, sedate property like the Doral Tuscany, even though both have rooms in the same price range. Know your own taste and choose accordingly. If you like bright lights, a lively lobby, and a central location, a residential-style hotel could disappoint you, no matter how elegant it is.

Basic rules of decorum and dress are observed at the better hotels. With few exceptions, jackets (and frequently ties) are required in formal dining and bar areas after 5 or 6 PM. Bare feet or beach sandals are not allowed, and an overall sloppy appearance won't encourage good service.

Women on their own, even at upscale hotels, should be aware that they may be accosted in public areas, either by male guests trying to find companions or by hotel staff trying to chase away the hookers who transact business in hotel lobbies. Because these "working girls" often look quite respectable, any single woman may be suspect. You might want to ask the concierge to point out places where you'll feel comfortable relaxing on your own. Many female travelers find VIP floors, with their concierge-controlled lounges and complimentary beverages and snacks, a boon for avoiding such situations.

Note: Even the most exclusive hotels have security gaps. It's best to be discreet with valuables everywhere, and stay alert in public areas.

Most Manhattan hotels are in the midtown area, so we have categorized them by price range rather than location. Exact prices could be misleading: Properties change their so-called "rack rates" seasonally, and most hotels offer weekend packages that include such tempting extras as complimentary meals, drinks, or tickets to events. Your travel agent may have brochures about such packages; also look for advertisements in travel magazines or the Sunday travel sections of major newspapers such as the *New York Times*, the *Washington Post*, or the *Los Angeles Times*. Note: Many hotels offer corporate rates to regular customers if they ask.

Visitors can also take advantage of reputable discount booking services such as **Express Hotel Reservations.** This Boulder, Colorado, company offers savings of 20%–30% on superior rooms at a variety of New York hotels. There is no charge for any of the company's services (it is used frequently by major companies, such as Hallmark and the Limited). Call 800/356–1123 for further information.

Highly recommended lodgings are indicated by a star ★.

Category	Cost*
Very Expensive	over $260
Expensive	$190–$260
Moderate	$135–$190
Inexpensive	under $135

All prices are for a standard double room, excluding 21¼% city and state sales tax.

Reservations New York is constantly full of vacationers, conventioneers, and business travelers, all requiring hotel space. Try to book your room as far in advance as possible, using a major credit card to guarantee the reservation; you might even want to work through a travel agent. Because this is a tight market, overbooking can be a problem, and "lost" reservations are not unheard of. Most properties, especially those that are part of national or worldwide chains or associations (i.e., Marriott or Leading Hotels of the World), are cooperative and generous when a reservation is lost, but guaranteed reservations usually prevent any problems. When signing in, take a pleasant but firm attitude; if there is a mix-up, chances are the outcome will be an upgrade or a free night.

Hotels with famous restaurants appreciate it when guests who want to use those facilities book tables when they make their room reservations. *Note:* All chefs mentioned were in charge at press time. Call to confirm the name under the toque. It can make *all* the difference.

Services Unless otherwise noted in the individual descriptions, all the hotels listed have the following features and services: private baths, central heating, air-conditioning, private telephones, on-premises dining, valet and room service (though not necessarily 24-hour or short notice), TV (including cable and pay-per-view films), and a routine concierge staff. Larger hotels will generally have video or high-speed checkout capability.

New York City has finally allowed liquor minibars to be installed in rooms. Most hotels have added this much-anticipated amenity—at least in their more expensive units.

Pools are a rarity, but most properties have fitness centers; we note only those that are on the premises, but other hotels usually have arrangements for guests at nearby facilities. Some hotels also make nominal charges for guests' use of in-house fitness centers.

Those bringing a car to Manhattan should note the lack of hotel parking. Many properties in all price ranges *do* offer parking facilities, but they are often at independent garages that charge up to $20 or more per day.

Very Expensive

★ **The Carlyle.** Located in one of the city's finest residential areas, this beautifully appointed traditional hotel is considered one of New York's finest. The mood is English manor house; larger rooms and suites, many of them decorated by the famous interior designer Mark Hampton, have terraces, pantries, and antique furnishings. Baths, though more subdued than others in town, are marbled and chock-full of de rigueur amenities such as hair dryers, fine toiletries, and makeup mirrors. Most visitors have heard about the famous Café Carlyle, where performers such as Bobby Short entertain. But the hotel also contains the charming Bemelman's Bar, with whimsical animal murals on the walls and live piano music at night, and the formal Carlyle Restaurant, offering French cuisine and old-fashioned courtly service. There's a jewel of a fitness center that is ultraprivate and luxurious. This is one of the few grand hotels where European elegance and American friendliness really mix; you don't have to be a famous face to get a smile or good treatment. The concierge service is especially excellent. *35 E. 76th St., 10021, tel. 212/744–1600, fax 212/717–4682. 185 rooms. Facilities: restaurant, café, bar, lounge, VCRs and stereos, fax machines, kitchenettes and pantries in larger units, fitness center, meeting rooms. AE, DC, MC, V.*

★ **Essex House.** The owners, Japan's Nikko Hotels, have done wonders for this stately Central Park South property. The public interiors are an Art Deco masterpiece fit for Fred and Ginger. The hotel's informal restaurant, Café Botanica, faces Central Park and resembles a lush prewar English greenhouse. Les Célébrités (*see* Chapter 9) features the cuisine of chef Christian Delouvrier, served in an intimate setting replete with surprisingly competent celebrity artwork from folks like Billy Dee Williams and James Dean. Journey's, the hotel's wood-paneled bar, has a working fireplace. The delights continue upstairs, where guest rooms and baths resemble those in a splendid English country home. Fabrics and furnishings are elegant and inviting. Many baths feature double sinks and separate stall showers. The staff is discreet, efficient, and friendly. This is the place to take advantage of weekend rates and book that dreamed-about double on the park. *160 Central Park S (near 7th Ave.), 10019, tel. 212/247–0300, fax 212/315–1839. 593 rooms. Facilities: 3 restaurants, bar, ballroom, fitness center, meeting rooms, business center. AE, DC, MC, V.*

The Lowell. Think how nice it would be to arrive in New York and find that a rich uncle had offered you the run of his elegant pied-à-terre—that's the feeling you'll get here. There's no lobby in the true sense, just a regal front-desk area with a few chairs and newspapers. Upstairs, on the second floor, is a picture-perfect tea-and-lunch-room in the English-country-house style; adjacent is a first-rate steak restaurant, the Post House (*see* Chapter 9). The guest rooms, mostly suites, are both fashionable and homey: Furnishings are an eclectic mix of tradition-

Algonquin, **54**
Ameritania, **24**
Beekman Tower, **40**
Best Western, **30**
Best Western
Seaport Inn, **63**
Broadway American, **2**
Carlyle, **5**
Chatwal Inn, **48**
Doral Court, **59**
Doral Inn, **39**
Doral Park
Avenue, **60**
Doral Tuscany, **59**
Drake, **19**
Dumont Plaza, **62**
Embassy Suites, **49**
Essex House, **15**
Excelsior, **1**
Fitzpatrick, **33**
Gorham, **26**
Holiday Inn Crowne
Plaza, **31**
Hotel Beacon, **3**
Hotel Edison, **46**
Hotel Iroquois, **53**
Hotel Macklowe, **56**
Hotel Wentworth, **51**
Inter-Continental New
York, **42**
Journey's End, **58**
Le Parker
Meridien, **22**
Loews New York, **35**
Lowell, **10**
The Mark, **4**
Marriott Marquis, **50**
Mayfair, **8**
Michelangelo, **32**
Millenium, **65**
New York Hilton, **27**
New York Palace, **37**
NewYork Vista, **67**
Paramount, **47**
Peninsula, **21**
Pickwick Arms, **34**
Pierre, **14**
The Plaza, **17**
Plaza Athénée, **9**
Quality Inn
Midtown, **45**
Radisson Empire, **12**
Ramada Hotel, **44**
The Regency, **13**
Rihga Royal, **25**
Ritz-Carlton, **16**
Roger Smith, **43**
Royalton, **55**
St. Regis, **20**
San Carlos, **36**
Shelburne, **61**

Manhattan Lodging

KEY

AE American Express Office

0 ____ 800 yards
0 ____ 800 meters

Metropolitan
Museum of Art

E. 79th St.

Fifth Ave.
Madison Ave.
Park Ave.
Lexington Ave.
Third Ave.
Second Ave.
First Ave.
York Ave.

FDR Dr.

E. 72nd St.

Central
Park

Queensboro Br.

E. 59th St.

N,R,4,5,6

E. 57th St.

Sutton Pl.

East River

E. 52nd St.

Rockefeller
Center

E. 46th St.

Grand
Central
Terminal

42nd St.

Public
Library

E. 38th St.

(Sixth Ave.)

Empire
State
Building

E. 34th St.

Herald
Square

N

al pieces with surprisingly modern accents. Bathrooms have good lighting and generous Saks Fifth Avenue amenities. Some rooms have wood-burning fireplaces, a relative rarity in the city. There's even one super suite with its own fitness center. *28 E. 63rd St., 10021, tel. 212/838-1400 or 800/221-4444, fax 212/838-9194. 60 rooms. Facilities: restaurant, small meeting room, some kitchenettes. AE, DC, MC, V.*

The Mark. Just one block north of the Carlyle, the former Madison Avenue Hotel has been completely redone by its owner, Rafael Hotels; it provides its neighbor with some healthy competition in terms of price and amenities. Sadly, at press time some rooms were not up to previous standards. Ask to see your unit before checking in. Warm color schemes reflect the Italian neoclassical motif. Women will feel comfortable in the discreet public areas. Mark's, a cozy and elegant restaurant and lounge, features the unique French-American cuisine of chef Philippe Boulot (*see* Chapter 9). *25 E. 77th St., 10021, tel. 212/744-4300 or 800/843-6275, fax 212/744-2749. 185 rooms. Facilities: restaurant, café, lounge, meeting rooms, VIP suites with terraces. AE, DC, MC, V.*

★ **The Mayfair Baglioni.** General manager Dario Mariotti adds a cheery Italian influence to this low-key, gracious hotel. Locals know it for its traditional tea lounge and its always-white-hot restaurant, Le Cirque (*see* Chapter 9). Even the smallest of the guest rooms have marble baths and traditional-style, peach-tone decor with up-to-date extras such as dual-line telephones and outlets to accommodate portable computers and fax machines. Service is superefficient; guests are offered umbrellas, room humidifiers, customized pillow selection, and the ingenuity of longtime concierge Bruno Brunelli, who can usually conjure up impossible tickets or reservations. While its overall appearance isn't quite as glitzy as that of some other hotels in this price category, the Mayfair more than makes up for its slightly lived-in feel (which many guests, incidentally, prefer) with friendliness and an always-lively atmosphere. *610 Park Ave., 10021, tel. 212/288-0800 or 800/545-4000, fax 201/737-0538. 150 rooms. Facilities: restaurant, lounge, meeting rooms, unlimited local phone calls. AE, DC, MC, V.*

The Michelangelo. The Theater District's only true deluxe hotel, now owned by the Italian Starhotels company, provides better and friendlier service than in the past. The traditionally formal lobby is warmly lit and flower-filled. Rooms and suites are decorated in subdued colors and reflect a variety of styles, and there are some fanciful touches, such as the ingeniously concealed TVs found in some units. The marble baths feature bidets and TVs, along with the usual amenities, including robes and makeup mirrors. Bellini by Cipriani, the hotel's on-site restaurant, has established a closer relationship with the hotel by providing room service. The Michelangelo also features a complimentary Italian Continental breakfast. Besides checking out a small workout room in the hotel, guests can use the nearby Equitable Health and Swim Club for a nominal charge. The staff is helpful, with a concierge who is a cut above the usual found in New York City hotels. *152 W. 51st St., 10019, tel. 212/765-1900 or 800/237-0990, fax 212/581-7618. 178 rooms. Facilities: restaurant, lobby lounge and bar, meeting rooms, fitness center; fax machines and other business equipment available upon request. AE, DC, MC, V.*

The Peninsula. The former Gotham Hotel on Fifth Avenue, magnificently renovated as the Hotel Maxim, it is now owned and operated by the respected Peninsula Group of Hong Kong, which has wisely left the Maxim's furnishings intact, including the sumptuous (by New York or any standards) marble baths. Even the smaller rooms have graceful sculpted art nouveau headboards, desks, and armoires; some also have the same sweeping views down Fifth Avenue as the more expensive suites. Many bathrooms feature Jacuzzi tubs; all have bidets and Lanvin toiletries. The Adrienne restaurant and its less lofty café and bar serve high-style French cuisine. The rooftop health club, with state-of-the-art exercise machines, a decent-size pool, massage and facial services, and a dining area with a terrace, is a knockout. *700 5th Ave., 10019, tel. 212/247–2200 or 800/262–9467, fax 212/903–3949. 250 rooms. Facilities: restaurant, café, lounge, meeting rooms, pool, fitness center. AE, DC, MC, V.*

★ **The Pierre.** The Four Seasons, a Canadian hotel group, has made a specialty of "freshening up" classic properties, and the Pierre is one of its notable successes. One might expect haughtiness along with the creamy Oriental-carpeted halls and bright chandeliers, but you won't find that here: The staff conveys a sense of fun about working in these posh surroundings. Rooms, most of which have been recently refurbished, are traditionally decorated in soft floral patterns, with quilted bedspreads and fine wood furniture. Bathrooms have been upgraded and are generously stocked with Four Seasons amenities. The Boudoir suites, overlooking the Central Park Zoo and Wollman Rink, are worth the extra price. Café Pierre's new chef has raised the restaurant's already high standards; the Bar features low-key jazz piano in the evenings, and formal afternoon tea is served under the blue cherubim-filled dome of the Rotunda. *5th Ave. at 61st St., 10021, tel. 212/838–8000 or 800/332–3442, fax 212/940–8109. 204 rooms. Facilities: restaurant, bar, tearoom, meeting rooms, manned elevators, packing service upon request, hand-laundry service. AE, DC, MC, V.*

The Plaza. When real-estate developer and casino operator Donald Trump purchased this National Historic Landmark in 1988, locals shuddered a bit, but there is actually much to applaud. (Trump's fortunes have since waned, and by now the Plaza might be under new ownership.) This former haunt of F. Scott Fitzgerald, George M. Cohan, Frank Lloyd Wright, and the Beatles attracts a relatively demanding public. Prices have edged up, but so has the quality of even the least expensive rooms. New color schemes are in burgundy or teal blue; fresh, floral-patterned quilted spreads grace the large beds. Furnishings, though still "hotel-like" in most units, are of high quality. Bathrooms, even those not yet fully redone, have fluffy new towels and toiletries. One real advantage here is the size of guest rooms—only a handful of other classic properties can offer similar spaciousness in nearly all accommodations. The Edwardian Room and the Oak Room, always known for elegant atmosphere, now offer food to match. Even the scones at the Palm Court, that gracious, classic lobby lounge, seem fresher. However, there have been recent changes in chefs, so food quality may vary. *5th Ave. at 59th St., 10019, tel. 212/759–3000 or 800/228–3000, fax 212/546–5324. 807 rooms. Facilities: 2 restaurants, 2 bars, café, art gallery, disabled-accessible rooms, meeting rooms, packing service upon request, large concierge staff. AE, DC, MC, V.*

The Plaza Athénée. The French half of Forte Hotels' (formerly Trusthouse Forte) New York offerings used to be rather snooty to noncelebrities; however, much of that has changed. What hasn't changed, thankfully, is the quiet elegance of the guest rooms and baths. Even small rooms are well thought out, if not opulent. The red and yellow penthouses are breathtaking— and their price tags aren't, considering the space and attractiveness. The staff seems more generous with its smiles these days, even if you aren't Liz Taylor. *37 E. 64th St., tel. 212/734-9100 or 800/225-5843, fax 212/772-0958. 160 rooms. Facilities: restaurant, bar, meeting rooms. AE, DC, MC, V.*

Rihga Royal. Right behind the New York Hilton on West 54th Street is Manhattan's first all-suite luxury hotel. Japanese in ownership and largely European in staff, the Rihga suffers a bit from lack of local recognition, though film and music celebrities know it well. The hotel's Halcyon restaurant has deservedly gained a following. Suites are truly gracious, featuring subdued, modern furnishings and lavish marble baths, most with tubs and stall showers. Many units have fax machines and VCRs. While regular prices are very expensive, on weekends and during slow seasons, these generous accommodations are often deeply discounted, so ask before you book. *151 W. 54th St., 10019, tel. 212/307-5000 or 800/937-5454, fax 212/765-6530. 500 suites. Facilities: restaurant, bar, lounge, meeting rooms, business center. AE, DC, MC, V.*

★ **The Ritz-Carlton.** This property—once hot, then lukewarm— has recently been brought under genuine Ritz-Carlton management, and overall service has been raised to the company's high standards. Guest rooms have been refurbished in the R-C manner: brocade bedspreads, marble baths, and rich wood accents, and additional redecoration was in the works at press time. The rooms with Central Park views are definitely preferable, but all accommodations are identical in decor and amenities. The staff is especially friendly and helpful. Bartender Norman Bukofzer in the Jockey Club draws a coterie of convivial celebrities. *112 Central Park S, 10019, tel. 212/757-1900 or 800/241-3333, fax 212/757-9620. 210 rooms. Facilities: restaurant, bar, meeting rooms, concierge floor, small fitness center, complimentary limousine service to Wall Street. AE, DC, MC, V.*

The St. Regis. When Sheraton decided to restore this Fifth Avenue landmark, planners set a new company standard for themselves, with prices to match. Is the experience transporting enough to merit such a splurge? On the plus side is chef Gray Kunz's inspired menu in the otherwise slightly stilted restaurant, Lespinasse (*see* Chapter 9), and the delightful King Cole Bar, home to the famous Maxfield Parrish mural. Afternoon tea in the Astor Court can compete proudly with the best in town. Guest rooms are filled with Louis XV–style furnishings and expensive amenities. Marble bathrooms, with tubs, stall showers, and double sinks, are outstanding, although there are disappointments such as cheap wall-unit hair dryers and no disposable laundry bags. A fitness center is adequate. Housekeeping and butler service should be more professional, as should the concierge service: Those dealt with showed poor knowledge of restaurants and shops. In time, the St. Regis may well merit its high price tag, but not this year. *2 E. 55th St., 10022, tel. 212/753-4500 or 800/759-7550, fax 212/787-3447. 365 rooms. Facilities: restaurant, bar, lounge, banquet room, meeting rooms, business center, fitness center, unlimited local phone calls, butler service. AE, DC, MC, V.*

The Westbury. The English half of Forte Hotels' (formerly

Trusthouse Forte) New York empire combines understated British formality with genuine friendliness. Sedate and comfortable, it delivers good service. Rooms and suites are decorated in either masculine "hunt-style" Ralph Lauren fabrics or in more demure Laura Ashley fashion. Some units, though elegant, are small; all baths are less than spacious when compared to baths in other hotels in this price range—some extremely so—though all are luxurious in terms of fittings and amenities. The Polo restaurant is a pleasant place to enjoy traditional cuisine with a modern touch. There is also a new, comprehensive fitness area. *69th St. at Madison Ave., 10021, tel. 212/535–2000 or 800/321–1569, fax 212/535–5058. 235 rooms. Facilities: restaurant, lounge, meeting rooms, fitness center. AE, DC, MC, V.*

Expensive

Doral Court, Doral Park Avenue, and **Doral Tuscany.** Doral has created a cozy enclave of three hotels in the East 30s Murray Hill district. Guests at any one property can sign for meals and drinks at all three; they also have complimentary access to the Doral Saturnia Fitness Center at 90 Park Avenue. The Doral Tuscany and its adjacent neighbor, the Doral Court (which has slightly lower prices that actually put it in the "Moderate" category), have attractive, traditionally furnished guest rooms and suites; the Tuscany's baths and bedrooms are more formal and elegant, though both properties are well maintained. The Doral Park Avenue, refurbished by designer Sarah Lee, has rooms furnished in restful cream and beige tones. All three have good restaurants, the best and most acclaimed being the Tuscany's Time and Again, which features a changing menu of American nouvelle specialties. The Doral Court's Courtyard Café offers one of the city's nicer outdoor dining spaces. *Doral Court, 130 E. 39th St., 10016, tel. 212/685–1100 or 800/624–0607, fax 212/889–0287. 248 rooms. Facilities: café, meeting rooms, complimentary parking on all weekend packages. AE, DC, MC, V. Doral Park Avenue, 70 Park Ave. (at 38th St.), 10016, tel. 212/687–7050 or 800/847–4135, fax 212/808–9029. 220 rooms. Facilities: bar, café, meeting rooms, fitness center, complimentary parking on all weekend packages. AE, DC, MC, V. Doral Tuscany, 120 E. 39th St., 10016, tel. 212/686–1600 or 800/847–4078, fax 212/779–7822. 119 rooms. Facilities: restaurant, lounge, meeting rooms, complimentary parking on all weekend packages. AE, DC, MC, V.*

The Drake. This Swissôtel property is favored by many business travelers for its solid service and highly desirable location, just off Park Avenue at 56th Street. The hotel recently remodeled its public areas. Guest rooms have been refreshed with improved furnishings and a more contemporary look; the same goes for the well-stocked bathrooms. The advantage here is room size: The prewar building was originally designed as an apartment house, so the rooms have enough space for refrigerators and other homey touches. This is also the home of the acclaimed French restaurant Lafayette. (At press time, a new chef and menu were introduced.) For a good deal less money, the Café Suisse is a pleasant surprise—many locals enjoy its Swiss specialties and hard-to-find Swiss wines, and its desserts are made by the Lafayette pastry chef. There's more comfort here than spit and polish, but the prices and the quality of the food-and-beverage service more than make up for any lapses. *440 Park Ave., 10022, tel. 212/421–0900 or 800/637–9477, fax 212/371–4190. 600 rooms. Facilities: restaurant, café, bar, meeting rooms, complimentary limousine service to Wall Street, luggage check-in for Swissair passengers. AE, DC, MC, V.*

★ **Embassy Suites.** Another welcome addition to the Times Square area, this familiar name's flagship has far more flair than anticipated. The elevated lobby is done up in modern art-deco style; color schemes and furnishings are bold and contemporary. Suites have coffeemakers, small microwave ovens, refrigerators, and even complimentary sodas and snacks. Guest rooms, though hardly elegant, are cheerful and comfortable. Certain suites have been "child-proofed" with such safety features as bumpers placed over sharp edges. All rates include free full breakfast, and daily cocktails in a private lounge area. There's also a regular restaurant, the Broadway Museum Café, featuring well-priced grills and salads. A complete day-care center with trained staff is an added plus for families. The staff seems eager to please, too. Meanwhile, Embassy might improve its street-level security; the block continues to be somewhat unsavory. *1568 Broadway at 47th St., 10036, tel. 212/719–1600 or 800/EMBASSY, fax 212/921–5212. 460 suites. Facilities: restaurant, bar, meeting rooms, day-care center, complimentary use of nearby health club and pool. AE, DC, MC, V.*

★ **Holiday Inn Crowne Plaza.** The deluxe flagship of the famous commercial hotel chain, a towering roseate stone edifice, was built on the exact site of the original music publishing company of Irving Berlin—he wrote the music for the movie *Holiday Inn*, from which the chain took its name. Public areas with a rose and beige color scheme are softer and more opulent than those of its neighboring competitor, the Marriott Marquis. Upstairs, the decent-size rooms continue the rose color scheme, this time with a touch of teal blue. Guest rooms start on the 16th floor so that everyone gets an eyeful from the panoramic windows. Bathrooms are beyond basic, though the amenities found within could be more lavish. Another minor drawback is the serious lack of closet space, even in the suites. An attractive, surprisingly sophisticated lobby restaurant, Samplings, features appetizer- and full-size dishes, salads, and desserts, and there's also a larger restaurant, the Broadway Grill. The superior health club includes a shallow lap pool, run by the efficient New York Sports company. *1605 Broadway (at 49th St.), 10019, tel. 212/977–4000 or 800/HOLIDAY, fax 212/333–7393. 770 rooms. Facilities: 3 restaurants, café, lounge, concierge-level fitness center, pool, ballroom, meeting rooms, business center. AE, DC, MC, V.*

Hotel Macklowe. Real-estate magnate Harry Macklowe's answer to what savvy business travelers really want is right about on target. Though hard by Times Square, it has more elegance than other commercial hotels in the area. The lobby and dining areas are done in handsome, subdued art-deco style, with polished woods and rich carpets. There is a cozy bar and a boardroomish restaurant called Charlotte, whose new chef and manager have trimmed prices and menu excesses with positive results. Guest rooms, though not oversize, are tasteful and well appointed and keep the working traveler in mind. One unusual feature is the private dining area, which features a daily buffet and can be used by meeting groups, as can the Hudson Guild Theatre, that handles state-of-the-art presentations and events. The informed, friendly staff goes out of its way to encourage guests to enjoy a more leisurely pace and share the Big Apple with significant others and children. With competitive weekend rates, this hotel has become a popular "sleeper" for visitors who want gracious surroundings while they take in shows and shopping. *145 W. 44th St., 10036, tel. 212/768–4400 or 800/622–5569, fax 212/767–7693. 638 rooms. Facilities: restaurant, bar/lounge, meeting rooms, corporate dining and meeting suites, fitness center. AE, DC, MC, V.*

The Inter-Continental New York. The stately old Barclay was bought by this reputable worldwide company a few years ago, but, happily, not much has changed. The warmly lit traditional lobby, with its faded Persian carpets and aviary, still stands, as does the rather old-fashioned American restaurant. Rooms could use some updating, as could the charmless bathrooms. Some suites have been nicely refurnished, but even these have somewhat less panache than those of other hotels in this price category. On the plus side, the on-premises workout and massage facility is attractive and well designed, as are the redecorated banquet and meeting rooms on the same level. The restaurant's food is more up-to-date than the dull surroundings suggest. One can only hope that the Inter-Continental will get busy and spruce this place up—it has the potential to shine. *111 E. 48th St., 10017, tel. 212/755–5900 or 800/327–0200, fax 212/644–0079. 680 rooms. Facilities: restaurant, bar, meeting rooms, fitness center, complimentary parking on weekends. AE, DC, MC, V.*

Le Parker Meridien. This dramatic, modern French hotel, whose soaring blond-wood lobby links 56th and 57th streets, is near some of the city's finest stores and cultural spots. For fitness-minded visitors, there's an airy rooftop swimming pool and a state-of-the-art basement-level workout center—both complimentary to guests. A recent redecoration effort has made rooms more appealing. Baths are on a par with the rooms, and there are luscious Lanvin soaps. The hotel's service is anything but snooty. *118 W. 57th St., 10019, tel. 212/245–5000 or 800/543–4300, fax 212/307–1776. 700 rooms. Facilities: restaurant, café, bar, meeting rooms, voice mail, fitness center, pool, accompanied jogging. AE, DC, MC, V.*

The Marriott Marquis. This six-year-old giant is one of the places New Yorkers love to hate: It's obvious, brash, bright, and definitely geared to conventions and groups. Still, anything that brings life and light to the Times Square area is welcome. As at other Marriotts, the help is ultrafriendly and informative, if not terribly polished. Rooms (though Marriott claims otherwise) are *not* the largest in town, but they're large enough; their color schemes are restful and their bathrooms perfectly adequate and modern. Some rooms have dramatic urban views. There's a revolving restaurant, the View, on the 46th floor, and a second revolving lounge on the eighth-floor lobby level. Most patrons have booked here on some sort of reduced or group rate. *1535 Broadway at 45th St., 10036, tel. 212/398–1900 or 800/843–4898, fax 212/704–8930. 1,877 rooms. Facilities: 3 restaurants, café, 3 lounges, meeting rooms, fitness center, theater, VIP floor, business center. AE, DC, MC, V.*

The Millenium. This sleek black monolith is the class act of downtown, outpacing both the Marriott and Vista in terms of elegance. Rooms and suites are modern in style; they are decorated in beige tones with wood accents. A unique feature is the wide "sprawl" of window shelf space, perfect for business travelers' portable computers, fax machines, and briefcases. Higher floors have delightful views of landmark buildings and the river. The hotel's main restaurant, Taliesin, named after architect Frank Lloyd Wright's masterpiece, offers modern American cuisine with an emphasis on healthfulness. There's also a more casual Grille served by the same kitchen. Prices are reasonable for hotel fare of this caliber. The adjacent Conoisseur Bar is packed with Wall Streeters. The health club has an attractive pool with a skylight wall that looks out on St. Paul's Church. *55 Church St., 10007, tel. 212/693–2001, fax 212/571–2317. 561 rooms. Facilities: 2 restaurants, bar, meeting rooms, fitness center with pool, business center. AE, DC, M, V.*

The New York Hilton. In a sense, this is the city's premier hotel for professional meetings, large and small. It has a special conference center, a business center run by the *Wall Street Journal*, and loads of multilingual help. Hilton spends vast sums on keeping it trim, and it shows: There's a distinctive landscaped driveway, and the modern lobby sparkles with well-kept furnishings. Considering the size of this property (more than 2,000 rooms), guest areas are surprisingly well maintained, if not always spacious or terribly fashionable. Even the smaller rooms are tastefully arranged and have many modern touches, such as alarm clock–radios and remote-control TVs. Guests who pay extra for Tower Level accommodations get slightly larger rooms and use of a stylish lounge with a separate boardroom and complimentary drinks and snacks. The Grill 53 restaurant has standard but generally competent hotel fare. If you don't expect high levels of personal attention or unfaltering elegance, this well-run machine will usually satisfy, although housekeeping can lapse when the hotel is full. *1335 6th Ave., 10019, tel. 212/586–7000 or 800/HILTONS, fax 212/315–1374. 2,034 rooms. Facilities: restaurant, nightclub, 2 cafés, bar, meeting rooms, multilingual desk, VIP floor, fitness center, business center, American Express desk. AE, DC, MC, V.*

The New York Palace. This glass monolith with a landmark palazzo at its feet is many visitors' vision of the ideal New York hotel: big, slightly overwrought, and always busy. Lower prices than in the past for both rooms and dining are attracting a new clientele. Palace rooms are generous by Manhattan standards, and those on the higher floors have views of St. Patrick's Cathedral and the East Side. Furnishings are cookie-cutter plush: padded and gilded headboards, reproduction chairs and tables, and pseudo-brocade bedcovers. Smaller suites are cramped and not worth the extra money. Public rooms, many of them located in the original 100-year-old Villard Houses, contain valuable pieces of art and lovely architectural details. The hotel has a variety of bars and eating spots. The staff is friendly, and the location can't be beat for those who want to shop on Fifth Avenue or have business in midtown. *455 Madison Ave., 10022, tel. 212/888–7000 or 800/221–4982, fax 212/355–0820. 963 rooms. Facilities: restaurant, 2 lounges, tearoom, meeting rooms, kitchenettes in suites. AE, DC, MC, V.*

The New York Vista. Managed by Hilton International, this striking downtown property was the first significant hotel below 34th Street when it opened ten years ago. Now, however, there are the Marriott on West Street and the classy Millenium on Church Street. Guest rooms have nice views of nearby Battery Park City and the World Financial Center on the Hudson River. They are pleasant and decently sized. The hotel has a dramatic health club, with a swimming pool that sits in the center of a multifunction exercise area, under a running track. In addition, the hotel's dining rooms offer above-average American cuisine. The American Harvest features a seasonally changing menu of domestic meats, seafood, and produce. Windows On the World (*see* Chapter 9) is now the Vista's "official" formal restaurant. The Vista experienced considerable damage as a result of the World Trade Center bombing. It planned to reopen in October 1993, with major renovations that should improve upon the already comfortable facilities. *3 World Trade Center, 10048, tel. 212/938–9100, fax 212/321–2107. 829 rooms. Facilities: 2 restaurants, 2 lounges, meeting rooms, pool, fitness center, VIP floor, free parking with weekend packages. AE, DC, MC, V.*

★ **The Regency.** Loews's upper-echelon property is a favorite for power breakfasts and fancy press events (the working rich-and-famous enjoy its discreet and surprisingly relaxed atmosphere). The stately, chandeliered lobby is reminiscent of the kind of private apartment house that comes with a personal staff to help with every need. Guest rooms and suites feature high-quality dark-wood furniture and brocade bedspreads. Bathrooms are of marble, and some have tiny TVs. The 540 Park restaurant has an inventive lower-priced menu featuring grilled meats and seafood. Service is paramount at this property, where the King—Loews Hotel's president, Jonathan Tisch—really does stand guard (and eats breakfast every day). *540 Park Ave., 10021, tel. 212/759–4100 or 800/233–2356, fax 212/826–5674. 400 rooms. Facilities: restaurant, lounge, meeting rooms, fitness center. AE, DC, MC, V.*

The Royalton. Former Studio 54 disco kings Ian Schrager and the late Steve Rubell, in their quest for a second career as New York hotel moguls, completely rehabilitated this once-shabby property directly across from the Algonquin (*see* Moderate, *below*). The Royalton, with its witty art moderne design by French decorator Philippe Starck, has a plush but slightly spooky atmosphere: The halls are narrow and dark, as are some of the strangely shaped rooms. Still, the beds and other furnishings are quite comfy, and the bathrooms are decidedly fun—they all have either oversize slate shower stalls or giant circular tubs (a few have both). Toiletries are elegant, and so is the service. The on-premises Restaurant 44 has inventive cuisine and a full liquor license. This could be a delightful spot for a romantic theater weekend for two people with a sense of the absurd. *44 W. 44th St., 10036, tel. 212/869–4400 or 800/635–9013, fax 212/869–8965. 205 rooms. Facilities: restaurant with bar, meeting rooms, fitness center, game and library areas, VCRs, stereos. AE, DC, MC, V.*

The Tudor. Several years ago, the Tudor building fell into complete disrepair. Now the Sarova Hotel company has turned this seedy flower girl into a first-class lady faster than you can say Henry Higgins. The landmarked exterior remains, albeit with a new welcoming marquee of lights, but the interior is another story. The lobby and public areas are done in a traditional style, familiar to those who favor smaller, European-quality hotels. There is a gracious tea and lounge area, and a restaurant called Cecil's, featuring modern Continental fare and a daily carvery buffet. Rooms and suites, while not especially large, are packed with quality amenities, such as personal safes, trouser presses, and, in the marble bathrooms, bidets. Some rooms also have whirlpool baths and terraces. Business travelers can count on two-line telephones and computer outlets. The fitness center is small but comprehensive. *304 E. 42nd*

St., 10017, tel. 212/986-8800 or 800/TRY-TUDOR, fax 212/
986-1758. 303 rooms. Facilities: restaurant, lounge, meeting
rooms, fitness center, business center. AE, DC, MC, V.

★ **U.N. Plaza-Park Hyatt.** It's easy to miss the entrance to this
favorite among the business and diplomatic set—it's on a quiet
side street near (naturally) the United Nations. The small but
striking lobby gives the illusion of endless space, thanks to
clever designs in dark marble and mirrors; Japanese floral arrangements add warmth and drama. What makes this place really special, though, are the guest rooms, all with breathtaking
views of Manhattan's East Side, and the delightful rooftop
pool. The decor is modern but not overpoweringly sterile, and
the color schemes are soothing. The burgundy-hued Ambassador Grill has a new menu, featuring grilled game in season;
prices are still reasonable by hotel standards. Service throughout the hotel is first-rate. Families with young children will especially appreciate the nearby U.N. park and the hotel's safe
location. *1 United Nations Plaza, 10017, tel. 212/355-3400 or*
800/223-1234, fax 212/702-5051. 444 rooms. Facilities: restau-
rant, 2 lounges, meeting rooms, pool, fitness center, compli-
mentary limousine service to Wall Street and Theater District.
AE, DC, MC, V.

The Waldorf-Astoria. Along with the Plaza (*see* Very Expensive, *above*), this Art Deco masterpiece personifies New York
at its most lavish and powerful. Hilton, its owner, has spent a
fortune on refurbishing both public areas and guest rooms.
Original murals and mosaics, elaborate plaster ornamentation,
fine old-wood walls and doors—all look fresh and new. In the
guest rooms, some of which start at the low end of this category, there are new bedspreads, carpets, and other signs of up-
grading. Bathrooms throughout are old but beautifully kept up
and rather spacious by today's standards. A new amenities level called Astoria includes superior toiletries, complimentary
breakfast, and use of the fitness center. Of course, in the very
private Tower section, everything becomes just that much
grander than in other rooms in the hotel. There is a new French
chef at Peacock Alley, where Waldorf salad first made news.
The Plus One fitness center stresses individual training. The
hotel's richly tinted, hushed lobby serves as an interior center-
point of city life. *301 Park Ave., 10022, tel. 212/355-3000 or 800/*
HILTONS, fax 212/421-8103. 1,692 rooms. Facilities: 3 restau-
rants, coffee shop, tearoom, lounge, ballroom, fitness center,
meeting rooms. AE, DC, MC, V.

Moderate

The Algonquin. While this landmark property's English-draw-
ing-room atmosphere and burnished-wood lobby are being kept
intact, its working parts (the plumbing, for instance) are being
improved under new Westin Hotels management. This much-
beloved hotel, where the Round Table group of writers and
wits once met for lunch, still shelters celebrities, particularly
literary types visiting nearby publishing houses or the *New*
Yorker magazine offices. Late-night performances go on as usual at the Oak Room. Bathrooms and sleeping quarters retain
Victorian-style fixtures and furnishings, only now there are
larger, firmer beds, modern TVs, VCRs (upon request), computerized phones, and Caswell-Massey toiletries. Tubs, tiles,
and sinks are still too old-fashioned for these prices. Even if you
stay elsewhere, stop by the Algonquin for afternoon tea or a

drink in its cozy lobby. *59 W. 44th St., 10036, tel. 212/840–6800 or 800/548–0345, fax 212/944–1419. 165 rooms. Facilities: restaurant, 2 lounges, meeting rooms, complimentary parking on weekends, business center. AE, DC, MC, V.*

Best Western Seaport Inn. This thoroughly pleasant, restored 19th-century building is one block from the waterfront, making it convenient for South Street Seaport and lower Manhattan sightseeing, not to mention early morning forays among the ripe aromas of Fulton Street fish market. The decor is somewhere between colonial sea-captain's house and chain hotel, (with a video fire crackling in the lobby grate). The reasonably priced rooms feature dark wood, white walls and floral nylon bedcovers. There's a fine view of Brooklyn Bridge from rooms on the fifth to seventh floors facing Front Street. Ask about weekend rates. *33 Peck Slip, 10038, tel. 212/766–6600 or 800/ 468–3569, fax 212/766–6615. 65 rooms. AE, DC, MC, V.*

The Doral Inn. While this Doral is far more modest in decor and commercial in feeling than the others discussed above, it is nonetheless a good value among the many hotels along Lexington Avenue. Rooms are average in size and cheerful, if not inventive, in decor; there are some surprisingly impressive terrace suites. A small workout area is connected to a squash club, and guests can also use the Doral Park Avenue's Saturnia Fitness Center. *541 Lexington Ave., 10022, tel. 212/755–1200 or 800/223–5823, fax 212/319–8344. 700 rooms. Facilities: 2 restaurants, meeting rooms, fitness center, squash club, self-service laundry. AE, DC, MC, V.*

★ **The Fitzpatrick.** This cozy Irish "boutique" hotel is conveniently situated just south of Bloomingdale's and seconds away from anchor bus and subway routes. The first American venture for an established Irish company, it's a real winner in terms of value and charm. Nearly half of the 92 units are true suites that are priced well below the market average, even on weekdays. Amenities include trouser presses, telephones with voice mail, and subdued traditional furnishings. Though not especially large, bathrooms are modern and well equipped; most come with whirlpools. A small restaurant called Fitzers features Irish seafood in season and a lively bar, which has become popular with locals. The staff is exceptionally friendly and savvy, which may be why celebs such as Gregory Peck and Stephen Rea are checking in. *687 Lexington Ave., 10022, tel. 212/355– 0100 or 800/367–7701, fax 212/308–5166. 92 rooms. Facilities: restaurant, bar, small meeting room, fax machines and VCRs available upon request. AE, DC, MC, V.*

Gorham Hotel. This small but conveniently located lodging has modernized and redecorated guest rooms and can be recommended to the traveler who wants a location within walking distance of the best of the East and West sides of town. Renovations include pleasant fabrics and carpeting and surprisingly luxurious bathrooms in most units. There is an Italian restaurant downstairs, though one can easily find myriad other dining options nearby. The lobby is bright, and the small staff is informed, if not always overly friendly. *136 W. 55th St., 10019, tel. 212/245–1800 or 800/735–0710, fax 212/245–1800. 120 rooms. Facilities: independent on-premises restaurant, concierge. AE, DC, MC, V.*

Journey's End. This Canadian chain's first Manhattan property features no-nonsense, clean, attractive rooms and baths at one fixed price. Most accommodations come with queen-size beds; all have modern TVs and telephones with long cords. Guests can use a small lounge area for complimentary coffee and newspapers. There is an independently owned Italian restaurant on the premises. At night, this part of midtown is somewhat quiet and therefore subject to street crime. However, security at the hotel appears to be superior. Another plus—it's just a few blocks away from the airport bus departure area on Park Avenue near Grand Central Terminal. *3 E. 40th St., 10016, tel. 212/447-1500 or 800/668-4200. 189 rooms. Facilities: lounge, independent on-premises restaurant, business services on request. AE, DC, MC, V.*

★ **Loews New York Hotel.** Loews's moderate-price New York property has an impersonal style, but most of its regulars—business travelers—don't mind because the hotel generally runs quite well. Rooms, most of them refurbished, are comfortable and well designed. Deluxe units (only slightly higher in price than standard) come with goodies, such as Godiva chocolates and complimentary liquor miniatures. The Lexington Avenue Grill, with striking maroon art-deco carpeting and a wood-tone lobby, has a reliable menu of pastas, burgers, and fish entrées. Note: During low-occupancy periods, guests can actually book rooms here for the upper end of Inexpensive prices; even suites come down below the $200 range. *Lexington Ave. at 51st St., 10022, tel. 212/752-7000, fax 212/758-6311. 766 rooms. Facilities: restaurant, lounge, meeting rooms, fitness center. AE, DC, MC, V.*

★ **Manhattan Suites East.** Here's a group of good-value properties for the traveler who likes to combine full hotel service with independent pied-à-terre living. These nine midtown hotels have different characters and varying prices, though all fall within the Moderate category. The four best are the recently redone **Beekman Tower** (3 Mitchell Pl.), near the United Nations; the **Dumont Plaza** (150 E. 34th St.); the **Surrey Hotel** (20 E. 76th St.), in the neighborhood of Madison Avenue art galleries and designer boutiques; and the **Southgate Tower** (371 7th Ave.), an attractive and secure place to sleep near Madison Square Garden and Penn Station. Except for the modern style at the Dumont, all have traditional guest-room decor; the Surrey's rooms border on the truly elegant. Most accommodations have pantries, and larger units have dining areas with full-size tables. Other hotels in this group tend to be more residential, except for the full-service **Shelburne** (303 Lexington Ave.); many top corporations use them as interim lodgings for newly relocated executives. The Beekman, Surrey, Shelburne, and Dumont Plaza have restaurants (Harold's at the Dumont Plaza and the Zephyr Grill at the Beekman are trying hard, though not always succeeding), which can also be used for room service. The Dumont, Southgate, and the Shelburne have on-premises fitness centers. The older hotels in the group do have some disappointing rooms, but overall these properties are outstanding for the price, considering their convenience, location, and space. Their weekend package rates are hard to beat. *Sales office, 505 E. 75th St., 10001, tel. 212/772-2900 or 800/ME-SUITE. AE, DC, MC, V.*

Radisson Empire Hotel. This old hotel recently changed ownership, so it's a matter of time before one knows what's what, but since the new owner is media mogul John Kluge, the Empire should only gain in luster. The English country–style lobby is warm and inviting; halls are decorated in soft gray with elegant lamps. Rooms and suites are a bit like small boxes, but nicely furnished; special room features include high-tech electronics, and the small but immaculate baths have heated towel racks. There is a cozy "British" lounge for guests' exclusive use. Although this hotel's prices have gone up, it's still one of the city's better buys in terms of quality and location, right across the street from Lincoln Center. At press time there was no room service, but no matter: The neighborhood is loaded with all-hours dining options. *Broadway at 63rd St., 10023, tel. 212/265–7400, 800/221–6509, or 800/223–9868, fax 212/315–0349. 368 rooms. Facilities: restaurant, voice mail. AE, DC, MC, V.*

The Roger Smith. The lobby and public areas of this sleeper have been radically remodeled. The guest rooms upstairs are pleasant, though at press time in need of some freshening up. Special units have small but luxurious marble baths with Jacuzzis. All rooms have pantries, and there's a complimentary Continental breakfast. Guests also receive free passes (one per person) to the Museum of Modern Art. Guests may enjoy the tea lounge and the full-service restaurant, Lily's. This is a homey, attractive place to return to at the end of a busy day in midtown. *501 Lexington Ave., 10017, tel. 212/755–1400 or 800/455–0277, fax 212/319–9130. 200 rooms. Facilities: restaurant, meeting room. AE, DC, MC, V.*

The San Carlos. This small, residential-style property offers basic hotel service, clean modern rooms, and a neighborly atmosphere. Larger suites come with kitchenettes, making them a good choice for families. The small wood-paneled lobby is gracious and well lit; women travelers can feel quite secure here. *150 E. 50th St., 10022, tel. 212/755–1800 or 800/722–2012. 140 rooms. Facilities: restaurant. AE, DC, MC, V.*

The Sheraton New York Hotel & Towers, Sheraton Manhattan. The Sheraton's multimillion-dollar overhaul of the two buildings has brought vast improvement. Though rooms—even in the superior Tower section located in the Sheraton New York— are on the small side, everything is bright and cheerful. Towers guests have a private lounge and superior amenities, including private check-in and concierge. The New York's restaurant and sports-bar complex, Hudson's, is casual and attractive, as is the Manhattan's new Bistro 790, which features surprisingly tasty updated American fare. Non-Tower rooms in the New York and the Manhattan are nearly identical in decor and amenities. The Manhattan has a large renovated pool and a small fitness center, which offers swimming lessons, aquatic exercise, treadmills, and a sun deck. The public spaces of both properties are welcoming, if not elegant. *Sheraton New York: 811 7th Ave. at 53rd St., 10019, tel. 212/581–1000 or 800/325–3535, fax 212/262–4410. 1,800 rooms. Sheraton Manhattan: 790 7th Ave. at 51st St., tel. 212/581–3300 or 800/325–3535, fax 212/541–9219. 650 rooms. Combined facilities: 2 restaurants, 2 bars, pool, fitness center, upgraded Tower rooms with private lounge, ballroom, extensive meeting space. AE, DC, MC, V.*

The Wyndham. This genteel treasure sits across from the Plaza. The savvy, independent traveler who cares more about gracious rooms and a friendly atmosphere than about imposing lobbies might well choose this spot over its neighbors. Owner and general manager John Mados keeps prices down by not offering room service or fancy amenities; what he does provide are some of the prettiest and most spacious accommodations in Manhattan. Even the least expensive double room has fresh floral-print bedspreads, comfortable chairs, and decorator wall coverings. A slight drawback is the old-fashioned, white-tile bathrooms. Suites (all of which come with pantries) start as low as $160 per night; they are painted in sunny shades and fitted with antique furniture, tasteful Chinese rugs, and an eclectic mix of everything else. The small lobby is unusually secure—a doorman controls the "in" buzzer 24 hours a day. The limited staff members are pleasant. *42 W. 58th St., 10019, tel. 212/753–3500, fax 212/754–5638. 201 rooms. Facilities: restaurant. AE, DC, MC, V.*

Inexpensive

Ameritania. This converted single-room-occupancy hotel is a pleasant choice for the theater goer or business traveler with an eye on the bottom line. The lobby is modern and cheerful, as are the simple but well-designed rooms. Some units have superior baths and amenities. There is a full-service Italian restaurant on the premises. The hotel's proximity to Broadway hits and popular night spots such as the Ritz should keep the clientele on the youthful side. *1701 Broadway, 10019, tel. 212/247–5000, fax 212/247–3316. 250 rooms. Facilities: restaurant, lounge, fitness room. AE, DC, MC, V.*

Broadway American. The Upper West Side has become one of New York's hottest neighborhoods. Those wishing to be in its midst should try this small but surprisingly stylish lodging. The least expensive singles have shared baths, though most rooms come with private facilities. Decor is functional modern, with high-tech touches such as TVs with cable. The dominating color scheme is soft gray. Baths are basic but no worse than others in more expensive units around town. Everything was clean at press time. The only drawback is that some of this former single-room-occupancy hotel's oddball occupants are living in old-style rooms not yet converted for transient use. *2178 Broadway, 10024, tel. 212/362–1100 or 800/446–4556, fax 212/787–9521. 200 rooms. Facilities: independent on-premises restaurant, vending machines, laundry service, AE, DC, MC, V.*

Chatwal Inns. This hotel-group features six properties, located mostly in the Broadway-midtown area, that provide clean, attractively designed rooms at relatively unpainful prices. All guests receive a complimentary Continental breakfast and discounts to several affiliated restaurants. Some of the larger properties, such as the **Best Western** affiliate (234 W. 48th St.), have on-premises full-service restaurants as well. Rooms, though relatively small throughout all six hotels, are immaculate and have all the basic amenities travelers have come to expect, including bathroom toiletries, modern telephones, and TVs. Since many of the buildings were, until recently, rather dilapidated, don't be put off by the dingy facades of Chatwal properties like **the Quality Inn Midtown** (157 W. 47th St.) or **the Chatwal Inn** (132 W. 45th St.); their interiors are among the chain's nicest. Sant S. Chatwal, owner of Bombay Palace restaurants, is to be applauded for his restoration and pricing efforts. *Tel. 800/826–4667; in Canada: 800/621–4667. Facilities: restaurants, small meeting rooms, lounges, depending on the property. AE, DC, MC, V.*

The Excelsior. New York's Upper West Side has become a sort of "Left Bank" area. The only missing Parisian element is the wide choice of quality small hotels. The Excelsior is very much like those dependable second-class European properties. A great location (right across from the American Museum of Natural History and the Hayden Planetarium), clean, pleasant rooms, a helpful staff, and low prices make this a find. Furnishings are relatively new; baths are old but in good condition. Rooms on higher floors have lovely views of Central Park. There is frequent bus and subway service nearby. *45 W. 81st St., 10024, tel. 212/362–9200 or 800/368–4575, fax 212/721–2994. 120 rooms. Facilities: coffee shop, kitchenettes in suites. AE, DC, MC, V.*

Hotel Beacon. Here's another upper Broadway residential building that's been largely converted to a spiffy hotel that should appeal to visitors who can make their own dining and sightseeing arrangements. The decently sized rooms come with full kitchenettes—a real advantage, because some of New York's best gourmet food stores, such as Zabar's and Fairway, are in the immediate area. Furnishings are less institutional than expected, and baths are modern if not elegant. Downstairs is the well-known nightspot the China Club, and the neighborhood offers numerous delis and ethnic restaurants. The front-desk staff seems adequate when it comes to security consciousness. *2130 Broadway, 10023, tel. 212/787–1100 or 800/572–4969, fax 212/724–0839. 115 rooms. AE, DC, MC, V.*

★ **Hotel Edison.** A popular budget stop for tour groups from here and abroad, this offbeat old hotel has gotten a face-lift. A gruesome murder scene for *The Godfather* was shot in what is now Sophia's restaurant, and the pink-plaster coffee shop has become a hot place to eavesdrop on show-business gossip thanks to such celebrity regulars as Jackie Mason. Guest rooms are brighter and fresher than the dark corridors seem to hint. There's no room service, but this part of the Theater District has so many restaurants and delis that it doesn't matter much. The crowd here is perfectly wholesome, so save money on your room and spend the big bucks on better theater seats. *228 W. 47th St., 10036, tel. 212/840–5000. 1,000 rooms. Facilities: restaurant, coffee shop, bar. AE, DC, MC, V.*

Hotel Iroquois. On the same block as the Algonquin and the Royalton, this shabby but friendly hotel is becoming popular with Soviet visitors. Halls are a bit dark, with some exposed stairwells, but the rooms are presentable for the price. Suites, some with kitchens, can be real bargains during slow periods. What makes the whole scene okay is the fact that this part of 44th Street is always busy into the night. *49 W. 44th St., 10036, tel. 212/840–3080 or 800/332–7220, fax 212/827–0464. 135 rooms. Facilities: small workout area. AE, DC, MC, V.*

Hotel Wentworth. This relatively small prewar hotel is on a midtown street that's usually pulsating with South American atmosphere—some of the city's best-known Brazilian restaurants are right outside. The lobby, hallways, and many of the rooms have been modernized, making this a far more welcoming property than before. The atmosphere is similar to that of many second-class European hotels. This is a popular stop for South Americans, although one frequently sees well-dressed U.S. businessmen, too. Single women might find the area a bit eerie at night. *59 W. 46th St., 10036, tel. 212/719–2300 or 800/223–1900. 250 rooms. AE, DC, MC, V.*

★ **Paramount.** What used to be the dowdy Century Paramount is the latest transformation by the same team that owns the Royalton (*see* Expensive, *above*). In many ways, this property is both the better buy and more fun than the more expensive property. The lobby is dramatic; there's a single wide stairway leading to the mezzanine-level dining area. The public area seating groups are at once homey and high style. Even if you don't dress like Madonna, you'll feel welcome. Rooms are, as rumored, rather small, but all of the singles contain queen-size beds. Philippe Starck's furnishings, in keeping with Ian Schrager's concepts, are offbeat; the old bathrooms have been fixed up with disco touches like conical steel sinks, and storage areas take a few minutes to decipher. Larger units are out of the Inexpensive price range but can be used by up to six people at a time. There are several dining options, including a branch of Dean & DeLuca for gourmet take-out fare. The new Brasserie Des Theâtres serves moderately priced French favorites into the wee hours (*see* Chapter 9). While the Paramount is not for the old-at-heart, it's definitely a category standout. *235 W. 46th St., 10036, tel. 212/764–5500 or 800/225–7474, fax 212/354–5237. 610 rooms. Facilities: 2 restaurants, privately owned bar, take-out food shop, fitness center, children's playroom, business center, VCRs in rooms. AE, DC, MC, V.*

Pickwick Arms Hotel. This convenient East Side establishment charges $80 a night for standard renovated doubles but has older singles with shared baths for as little as $50. The marble-clad lobby is small but brightly lit, and the staff is friendly. Guest rooms have been comfortably furnished in white bamboo. Guests have access to a roof garden; although there is no restaurant, the neighborhood is loaded with places to eat, and a café on the ground floor sells sandwiches, snacks, and a great cup of coffee. This is an acceptable budget alternative in a good area. *230 E. 51st St., 10022, tel. 212/355–0300 or 800/ PICKWIK, fax 212/755–5729. 400 rooms. AE, MC, V.*

Ramada Hotel. Another of Loews's budget properties, this motel-style building has an outdoor rooftop swimming pool and lounge area with snack bar. Rooms and suites were recently upgraded. Daily garage rates are reasonable. This is a good bet for theater-bound families during the summer months. *48th St. and 8th Ave., 10019, tel. 212/581–7000 or 800/2–RAMADA, fax 212/974–0291. 366 rooms. Facilities: restaurant, lounge, pool, meeting room. AE, DC, MC, V.*

★ **Vanderbilt YMCA.** Of the various Manhattan Ys offering accommodations, this is the best as far as location and facilities are concerned. Although rooms hold up to four people, they are little more than dormitory-style cells—even with only one or two beds to a room, you may feel crowded. Each room does have a late-model TV, however. There are no private baths; communal showers and toilets are clean. Guests are provided with basics such as towels and soap. Besides the low price, this Y offers membership to its on-premises pool, gym, running track, exercise rooms, and sauna. Many of the athletic and public areas, including the pool, have been remodeled. Rooms are being refreshed, too. An informal cafeteria and a friendly hospitality desk encourage travelers to mix with one another. The Turtle Bay neighborhood is safe, convenient, and interesting (the United Nations is a few short blocks away). Other YMCAs in town include the 561-room **West Side Y** (5 W. 63rd St., 10023, tel. 212/787–4400), which may be hard to get into but is in the desirable Lincoln Center area; and the 1,490-room **Sloane House YMCA** (356 W. 34th St., 10001, tel. 212/760–5860), which is in a gritty and somewhat unsafe neighborhood. *224 E. 47th St., 10017, tel. 212/755–2410, fax 212/752–0210. 430 rooms. Facilities: cafeteria, meeting rooms, self-service laundry, gift shop, luggage storage, pool, fitness center. No credit cards.*

Washington Square Hotel. The Village has a surprising paucity of decent budget and midprice lodgings, despite its popularity as a shopping and entertainment district. This cozy hotel has a true European feel and style, from the wrought-iron and brass in the small but elegant lobby to the personal attention given by the staff. Rooms and baths are simple but pleasant and feel a bit less "cookie cutter" than those in other hotels in this price range. There is a new bistro on the premises, and within walking distance are abundant coffee shops and convenience stores. Complimentary Continental breakfast is included in the room rate. The manager has strong ties to the local jazz community and can be especially helpful to those who wish to catch top names at famous clubs such as the nearby Blue Note. *103 Waverly Pl., 10011, tel. 212/777–9515 or 800/222–0418, fax 212/ 979–8373. 160 rooms. Facilities: independent on-premises restaurant, laundry service. AE, DC, MC, V.*

Wellington Hotel. A large, old-fashioned property whose main advantages are reasonable prices and a midtown location, the Wellington attracts many budget-conscious Europeans. Rooms are small but clean and reasonably cheery; baths are serviceable. Standard hotel services are available upon request. The brightly lit lobby provides a reassuring welcome for late-night returns. *871 7th Ave. at 55th St., 10019, tel. 212/247–3900 or 800/652–1212, fax 212/768–3477. 700 rooms. Facilities: restaurant. AE, DC, MC, V.*

Bed-and-Breakfasts

Hundreds of rooms are available on a bed-and-breakfast basis in Manhattan and the outer boroughs, principally Brooklyn. B&Bs almost always cost well below $100 a night; some singles are available for under $50. New York B&Bs, however, are not the quaint old mansions you find in other localities. They fall largely into two categories: (1) *hosted apartments*, a bedroom in an apartment where the host is present; (2) *unhosted apartments*, entire apartments that are temporarily vacant. The unhosted option is scarcer and somewhat more expensive.

Along with helping you save money, B&Bs permit you to mingle with New Yorkers and stay in "real" neighborhoods rather than in tourist enclaves. The disadvantages are that accommodations, amenities, service, and privacy may fall short of what you get in hotels. Sometimes you really do get breakfast and sometimes you don't. And you usually can't pay by credit card.

Here are a few reservation agencies that book B&B accommodations in and near Manhattan. There is no fee for the service, but they advise you to make reservations as far in advance as possible. It's a good idea to find out something about the city before you contact them, and then to request accommodations in a neighborhood that you prefer.

Bed and Breakfast Network of New York (134 W. 32nd St., Suite 602, 10001, tel. 212/645–8134).

City Lights Bed and Breakfast, Ltd. (Box 20355, Cherokee Station, 10028, tel. 212/737–7049).

New World Bed and Breakfast (150 5th Ave., Suite 711, 10011, tel. 212/675–5600 or 800/443–3800).

Urban Ventures (306 W. 38th St., 10018, tel. 212/594–5650).

11 The Arts

By Susan Spano Wells

Updated by David Low

On a bad day in New York—when it's raining and a cab can't be engaged for blood or money, the subways are flooded, and the line at the cash machine seems to stretch to Poughkeepsie—many New Yorkers may feel as if they'd sell the city back to the Indians for two bits. But in the end, they put up with the urban hassles for at least one obvious reason: New York's unrivaled artistic life. Despite the immense competition and the threat of cuts in city aid to the arts, artists from all disciplines continue to come to the city to find their compatriots and to produce their work. Audiences can only benefit.

There are somewhere between 200 and 250 legitimate theaters in New York, and many more ad hoc venues—parks, churches, universities, museums, lofts, galleries, streets, and rooftops—where performances ranging from Shakespeare to sword-dancing take place. The city is, as well, a revolving door of festivals and special events: Summer jazz, one-act play marathons, international film series, and musical celebrations from the classical to the avant-garde are just a few.

In New York, the arts routinely make the headlines. Pick up a week's worth of newspapers and you'll learn of casting disputes at the Metropolitan Opera, prima ballerinas with bruised knees, big Broadway musicals whose directors are replaced hours before opening, and the constant entertaining haggles among backers, artists, and critics. It's chaos. What a town!

New York's most renowned centers for the arts are tourist attractions in themselves:

Lincoln Center (W. 62nd to 66th Sts., Columbus to Amsterdam Aves., tel. 212/875–5000) is a 14-acre complex that houses the Metropolitan Opera, the New York Philharmonic, the Juilliard School, the New York City Ballet, the American Ballet Theatre, the New York City Opera, the Film Society of Lincoln Center, the Chamber Music Society of Lincoln Center, the Lincoln Center Theater, the School of American Ballet, and the New York Public Library's Library and Museum of the Performing Arts. Tours of Lincoln Center are available (tel. 212/875–5351; *see* Tour 8 in Chapter 3).

Carnegie Hall (881 7th Ave. at 57th St., tel. 212/247–7800) is a premier hall for concerts. Music masters such as Arturo Toscanini, Leonard Bernstein, Isaac Stern, Yo-Yo Ma, Jessye Norman, Frank Sinatra, and the Beatles, along with great orchestras from around the world, have made up the Carnegie bill. Performances are held in both its main auditorium (opened in 1891 with a concert conducted by Tchaikovsky) and in Weill Recital Hall, where debuting talents often make their first New York splash. The emphasis is on classical music, but Carnegie also hosts jazz and folk music series.

Radio City Music Hall (1260 6th Ave. at 50th St., tel. 212/247–4777), an art-deco gem, opened in 1932 with 6,000 seats, a 60-foot-high foyer, two-ton chandeliers, and a powerful Wurlitzer organ. On this vast stage you'll find everything from rock and pop concerts to Christmas and Easter extravaganzas (featuring the perennial Rockettes kickline), restored movie classics, and star-studded TV specials. Tours (tel. 212/632–4041) are conducted most days (*see* Tour 1 in Chapter 3).

City Center (131 W. 55th St., tel. 212/581–7907; mailing address for ticket orders: Citytix, 130 W. 56th St., 4th floor,

10019), under its eccentric, tiled Spanish dome (built in 1923 by the Ancient and Accepted Order of the Mystic Shrine and saved from demolition in 1943 by Mayor Fiorello La Guardia) hosts dance troupes such as Alvin Ailey, Paul Taylor, and Merce Cunningham. The Manhattan Theatre Club (*see* Theater, *below*) also resides here, with its highly touted bill of innovative contemporary drama.

Madison Square Garden (W. 31st to W. 33rd St. on 7th Ave., tel. 212/465–6000), camped atop Penn Station, includes a recently renovated 20,000-seat arena, and the sleek new 5,600-seat Paramount Theater. Sports events such as basketball, ice hockey, tennis, and boxing, plus big-draw pop music concerts by stars as diverse as Barry Manilow, Paul Simon, and Santana, keep the Garden rocking. There's even room for the Knicks and the Rangers to call it home. Should your favorite rock band not be appearing at the Garden, check out its suburban sister halls: the **Nassau Coliseum** (Long Island, tel. 516/794–9300) and the **Meadowlands Arena** (New Jersey, tel. 201/935–3900).

Brooklyn Academy of Music (BAM; 30 Lafayette Ave., Brooklyn, tel. 718/636–4100) is America's oldest performing arts center (begun in 1859), but its reputation is decidedly contemporary thanks to daring and innovative dance, music, opera, and theater productions. The main hall is the Opera House, a white Renaissance Revival palace built in 1908; other spaces at BAM are the Majestic Theatre (a partly restored vaudeville house around the corner), the Helen Owen Carey Playhouse, and the Lepercq Space.

Other important arts centers include **Town Hall** (113 W. 43rd St., tel. 212/840–2824) for, among other things, concert versions of lost Broadway musicals; **Merkin Concert Hall** (129 W. 67th St., tel. 212/362–8719), which features mainly chamber music; **Symphony Space** (2537 Broadway at 95th St., tel. 212/864–5400), a cavernous converted movie theater with an eclectic offering that ranges from Irish folk music to short stories read by stars; the **92nd Street Y** (1395 Lexington Ave., tel. 212/996–1100), known for its classical music concerts, readings by famous writers, and the Lyrics and Lyricists series; and **the Kitchen** (512 W. 19th St., tel. 212/255–5793), a showcase for "downtown," avant-garde videos, music, performance art, and dance.

Getting Tickets

Much has been made of the ballooning cost of tickets, especially for Broadway shows—though major concerts and recitals don't come cheap in New York, either. *Miss Saigon* nudged top Broadway ticket prices into the $100 zone, although those seats have since been reduced somewhat with the ailing economy; top tickets for nonmusicals, too, have crept upward, hitting the $65 mark occasionally.

On the positive side, tickets for New York City's arts events aren't hard to come by—unless, of course, you're dead set on seeing the season's hottest, sold-out show. Generally, a theater or concert hall's box office is the best place to buy tickets, since in-house ticket sellers make it their business to know about their theaters and shows and don't mind pointing out (on a chart) where you'll be seated. It's always a good idea to purchase tickets in advance to avoid disappointment, especially if you're traveling a long distance. For advance purchase, send the theater or hall a certified check or money order, several alternate dates, and a self-addressed stamped envelope.

You can also pull out a credit card and call **Tele-Charge** (tel. 212/239–6200), **HIT-TIX** (tel. 212/564–8038), or **Ticketmaster** (tel. 212/307-4100 for Broadway shows, 212/307–7171 for other events) to reserve tickets—newspaper ads generally will specify which you should use for any given event. A small surcharge ($1–$3) will be added to the total, and your tickets will be waiting for you at the theater.

For those willing to pay top dollar to see that show or concert everyone's talking about but no one can get tickets for, try a ticket broker. Recently, brokers charged $100–$150 for tickets to *Phantom of the Opera;* had the same seat been available at the box office, it would have sold for $65. A few brokers to try are **N.Y. Theatre Tickets** (tel. 201/392–0999), and **Continental/Golden/Leblangs Ticket Service** (tel. 212/944–8910). Also, check the lobbies of major hotels for ticket broker outlets.

You may be tempted to buy from the ticket scalpers who frequently haunt the lobbies of hit shows. But beware: They have reportedly sold tickets to *Les Misérables* for $100–$150, when seats were still available at the box office for much less.

Off- and Off-Off-Broadway theaters have their own joint box office called **Ticket Central** (416 W. 42nd St., tel. 212/279–4200). While there are no discounts here, tickets to performances in these theaters are less expensive than Broadway tickets—Ticket Central prices average $10–$35 per person—and they cover an array of events, including legitimate theater, performance art, and dance.

Discount Tickets The best-known discount source may be the **TKTS booth** in Duffy Square (47th St. and Broadway, tel. 212/768–1818). TKTS sells day-of-performance tickets for Broadway and some Off-Broadway plays at discounts that, depending on a show's popularity, often go as low as half price (plus a $2.50 surcharge per ticket). The names of shows available on that day are posted on boards in front of the booth. If you're interested in a Wednesday or Saturday matinee, go to the booth between 10 and 2, check out what's offered, and then wait in line. For evening performances, the booth is open 3–8; for Sunday matinee and evening performances, noon–8. One caution: TKTS accepts only cash or traveler's checks—no credit cards. The wait is generally pleasant (weather permitting), as the bright lights and babble of Broadway surround you. You're likely to meet friendly theater lovers eager to review shows they've recently seen; often you'll even meet struggling actors who can give you the inside scoop. By the time you get to the booth, you may be willing to take a gamble on a show you would otherwise never have picked, and it just might be more memorable than one of the long-running hits.

So successful has TKTS proved (last year it sold nearly 1.7 million seats), that auxiliary booths operate in the Wall Street area (2 World Trade Center mezzanine) and in Brooklyn Heights (near the intersection of Court and Montague Sts.). The World Trade Center Branch is open weekdays 11–5:30, Saturday 11–3:30; for matinees and Sundays, 11–closing the day before the performance. In Brooklyn, evening-performance tickets are on sale weekdays 11–5:30, Saturday 11–3:30; tickets for matinees and Sundays are sold a day ahead; Off-Broadway tickets are sold until 1. The lines at these TKTS outstations are shorter than those at Duffy Square, though occasionally the offerings are somewhat limited.

The Ticketmaster desk on the third floor of **Bloomingdale's** department store (1000 3rd Ave. at 59th St., tel. 212/705–2000) sells tickets to certain Broadway and Off-Broadway shows at discounts of 10% to 75%. The advantages are that it opens at 10 AM, earlier than TKTS, and it accepts credit cards; the disadvantage is that a smaller selection of shows is available. The service charge ranges from $2 to $4.

A setup similar to TKTS has arisen in the **Bryant Park Music and Dance Tickets Booth,** located on 42nd Street and Sixth Avenue in Bryant Park, just west of the New York Public Library. This booth sells half-price day-of-performance tickets for several music and dance events around the city (and full-price tickets for other concerts as well). It's open Tuesday–Sunday noon–2 and 3–7. Unlike TKTS, the Bryant Park booth has a telephone information line (tel. 212/382–2323).

Discounts on big-name, long-running shows (such as *Cats* and *Les Misérables*) are often available if you can lay your hands on a couple of "twofers"—discount ticket coupons found on various cash registers around town, in line at TKTS, at the New York Visitors and Convention Bureau (at 2 Columbus Circle), and at the office of their producer, the **Hit Show Club** (630 9th Ave., 8th floor, tel. 212/581–4211; open weekdays 9–4).

The Public Theater (425 Lafayette St., tel. 212/598–7150) regularly sets aside some of its tickets for sale at a discount through its **Quiktix.** Join the Quiktix line anytime before 6 PM for evening performances, and before 1 PM for matinees. Tickets are sold on a first-come, first-served basis.

A slew of ticket clubs exist to serve repeat theatergoers, so if you plan to be in the city for a long time, they may be worth investigating. **Advance Entertainment New York** (tel. 212/239–2570) offers its members (for $119 a year) constant updates on what's hot and free ticket procurement—sometimes at a discount and with special attention paid to getting good seats. AENY can be used on a one-time, no obligation-to-join basis for a $5 fee. Other ticket groups include **Stubs Preview Club** (tel. 212/398–8370), $50 a year, specializing in preview showings; and the **Theatre Development Fund** (1501 Broadway, tel. 212/221–0885), whose TDF vouchers are available in sets of five for $20 to students, union members, teachers, performing arts professionals, and members of volunteer groups, among others. When redeemed at the box office, the vouchers reduce the cost of a ticket for dance, theater, and musical events at Off-Off-Broadway theaters. Out-of-towners must stop by the office and present identification to qualify; residents of the metropolitan tristate area are put on the TDF mailing list to receive periodical offers.

Finding Out What's On

To find out who or what's playing where, your first stop should be the newsstand. The *New York Times* isn't a prerequisite for finding out what's going on around town, but it comes in pretty handy, especially on Fridays with its "Weekend" section. On Sundays, the *Times*'s "Arts and Leisure" section features longer "think pieces" on everything from opera to TV—and a lot more ads, plus a full, detailed calendar of cultural events for the upcoming week.

If your tastes are more adventurous, try the weekly paper *The Village Voice;* its club listings are unrivaled, its "Choices" section reliable. When its club-tattler-cum-critic Michael Musto talks (in a column called "La Dolce Musto"), night prowlers and club crawlers listen. The *Voice* is published on Wednesdays.

Some of the most entertaining listings can be found in *The New Yorker* magazine. "Goings On About Town" heads off each weekly issue with ruthlessly succinct reviews of theater, dance, art, music, film, and nightlife. *New York* magazine's "Cue listings" and "Hot Line" section are useful, too. The *New York Native* and *Outweek* cover the gay scene.

The League of New York Theatres and Producers and *Playbill* magazine publish a bimonthly *Broadway Theatre Guide,* available in hotels and at the *Playbill* magazine office (52 Vanderbilt Ave., 11th fl., 212/557–5757). For information on the lower Manhattan cultural scene, write for a *Downtown Arts Activities Calendar* (Lower Manhattan Cultural Council, 1 World Trade Ctr., Suite 1717, New York, NY 10048, tel. 212/432–0900).

You can also get updated information by phone from NYC/ON STAGE, the Theatre Development Fund's 24-hour information service (tel. 212/768–1818).

Theater

Almost everyone who visits New York ends up spending several hours in a theater seat. The theater—not the Statue of Liberty or South Street Seaport—is the city's number-one tourist attraction, and uptown or downtown you can spot theater folk pursuing their work with customary passion and panache. Delicate little ladies tottering about in their pillbox hats are really theatrical grande dames, with fast answers to the flashers on Eighth Avenue; shifty-looking guys toting battered briefcases turn out to be famous directors; and the girls and boys scuttling through stage doors are chorus members rushing to exchange their Nikes for tap shoes.

Broadway Theater District To most people, New York theater means Broadway, that region bounded by 42nd and 53rd streets, between Sixth and Ninth avenues, where bright, transforming lights shine upon porn theaters and jewel-box playhouses alike (*see* Theater District map). Although the area's busy sidewalks contain more than their share of hustlers and pickpockets, visitors brave them for the playhouses' plentiful delights. Extravagant plans for redevelopment of the Times Square area continue to ricochet from marquee to marquee; amid the grunge, major hotels keep springing up in this area. With every thud of the wrecker's ball, theater devotees pray for the survival of the essential character of Broadway—as Paul Goldberger put it in the *New York Times*, "the world of memory, the magical Times Square of old, the lively, glittering district of theaters, restaurants, cabarets, hotels, and neon signs that was in many ways the city's symbolic heart."

Theater District

Historically speaking, the nation's entertainment capital was once composed of almost 50 theaters, which sprang up between 1899 and 1925 near the intersection of Broadway and 42nd Street. Many of those original showplaces have been gutted or turned into movie houses. The 38 legitimate theaters that remain are squeezed into side streets in such tight spaces that from the outside it's often hard to imagine that there's room inside for an audience, much less a stage.

Some of the old playhouses are as interesting for their history as for their current offerings: the **St. James** (246 W. 44th St.) is where Lauren Bacall served as an usherette in the '40s, and a sleeper of a musical called *Oklahoma!* woke up as a hit; the **Lyceum** (149 W. 45th St.) is New York's oldest still-functioning theater, built in 1903 with a posh apartment on top that now holds the Shubert Archive (open to scholars by appointment only); the **Shubert Theatre** (225 W. 44th St.) is where Barbra Streisand made her 1962 Broadway debut, and the long-run record-breaker, *A Chorus Line,* played for 15 years; and the **Martin Beck Theatre** (302 W. 45th St.), built in 1924 in Byzantine style, is the stage that served up premieres of Eugene O'Neill's *The Iceman Cometh*, Arthur Miller's *The Crucible*, and Tennessee Williams's *Sweet Bird of Youth*. Theater names read like a roll-call of American theater history: **Booth, Ethel Barrymore, Eugene O'Neill, Gershwin, Lunt/Fontanne, Richard Rodgers,** and **Neil Simon,** among others.

As you stroll around the theater district, you may also see: **Shubert Alley,** a shortcut between 44th and 45th streets where theater moguls used to park their limousines, today the site of a jam-packed Great White Way memorabilia store called One Shubert Alley; **Actors' Equity** (165 W. 46th St.), home of the stage actor's union, and a crashing place for auditionees between cattle calls; **Manhattan Plaza,** a largely subsidized apartment complex at Ninth Avenue and 42nd Street inhabited primarily by theater people, whose rent in hard times is assessed at 30% of their income (whatever that comes to); **Theatre Row** (42nd St. between 9th and 10th Aves.), a convivial collection of small Off-Broadway theaters; and **Restaurant Row** (46th St. between 8th and 9th Aves.), which offers plenty of choices for dining before or after a show. For a deeper drink of the district, join a **Backstage on Broadway talk** (tel. 212/575–8065), hosted by a professional actor, director, stage manager, or designer (for groups only).

In determining which Broadway show to see, first consider the long-running hits: *Cats, Crazy for You, Les Misérables, The Phantom of the Opera, Miss Saigon, The Fantasticks* (downtown), and others, which most magazine and newspaper listings helpfully point out. Then look beyond the marquees for both tomorrow's hits and today's resounding flops. Remember, there's something special about catching a show in previews or seeing a harshly reviewed play before it bites the dust. A lousy review can quickly close a show, even though discriminating audience members often disagree with the critics.

Beyond Broadway Ten years ago it was relatively simple to categorize the New York stage beyond Broadway. It was divided into Off-Broadway and Off-Off-Broadway, depending on a variety of factors that included theatrical contract type, location, and ticket price. Today such distinctions seem strained, as Off-Broadway prices have risen and the quality of some Off-Off-Broadway productions has improved markedly. Off- and Off-Off-Broadway is where Eric Bogosian, Ann Magnuson, John Leguizamo, and Laurie Anderson make their home and where *Driving Miss Daisy, Steel Magnolias,* and *Other People's Money* were first conceived. The recession seems to have hit Off-Broadway and Off-Off-Broadway theaters hard, forcing them to spend less on their productions and mount fewer shows a year, but attendance and ticket sales remain healthy, proving how vital this segment of the theater world is to New York culture. Recent long-running hits have included the irreverent *Nunsense, Tubes* by the surreal Blue Man Group, and *Forbidden Broadway,* which spoofs the Great White Way.

Name actors appear in top-flight productions at **Lincoln Center's** two theaters: the **Vivian Beaumont** and the more intimate **Mitzi E. Newhouse** (65th St. and Broadway, tel. for both 212/362–7600), which has scored some startling successes, including John Guare's *Six Degrees of Separation,* and Wendy Wasserstein's *The Sisters Rosensweig.* Downtown at the **Joseph Papp Public Theater** (425 Lafayette St., tel. 212/598–7150), renamed in 1992 to honor its late founder and long-time guiding genius, artistic director JoAnne Akalaitis continues the tradition of innovative theater, mounting new and classic plays, along with film series, dance concerts, literary readings, and musical events. In the summertime, the Public's Shakespeare Festival raises its sets in Central Park's open-air Delacorte Theater (*see* Manhattan For Free in Chapter 3).

One of the major Off-Broadway enclaves is **Theatre Row,** a collection of small houses (100 seats or less)—such as the **John Houseman Theater** (450 W. 42nd St., tel. 212/967–9077), **Douglas Fairbanks Theater** (432 W. 42nd St., tel. 212/239–4321), and **Playwrights Horizons** (416 W. 42nd St., tel. 212/279–4200)—on the downtown side of 42nd Street between Ninth and Tenth avenues. A block east of Theater Row is the **Westside Theatre** (407 W. 43rd St., tel. 212/307–4100). Another Off-Broadway neighborhood lies in Greenwich Village, around Sheridan Square. Its theaters include **Circle Rep** (99 7th Ave. S, tel. 212/924–7100), a showcase for new playwrights; **Circle in the Square Downtown** (159 Bleecker St., tel. 212/254–6330); the **Lucille Lortel Theater** (121 Christopher St., tel. 212/924–8782); the **Cherry Lane Theater** (38 Commerce St., tel. 212/989–2020); the **Perry Street Theater** (31 Perry St., tel. 212/255–7190); and the **Provincetown Playhouse** (133 MacDougal St., tel. 212/477–5048). Other estimable Off-Broadway theaters are flung across the Manhattan map: the **WPA Theatre** (519 W. 23rd St., tel. 212/206–0523), showcasing new works by American playwrights; the **Promenade Theatre** (Broadway at 76th St., tel. 212/580–1313); and the **Manhattan Theatre Club** (at City Center, 131 W. 55th St., tel. 212/581–7907).

Here are a few other Off- and Off-Off-Broadway theater groups to keep your eye on:

American Jewish Theatre (307 W. 26th St., tel. 212/633–9797) stages contemporary plays and revivals of musicals, more often than not with a Jewish theme.
The Classic Stage Company (CSC) (136 E. 13th St., tel. 212/677–4210), providing a showcase for the classics—some arcane, others European—in new translations and adaptations.
The Ensemble Studio Theatre (549 W. 52nd St., tel. 212/247–

3405), with its tried-and-true roster of players, stressing new dramatic works.

Irish Arts Center (553 W. 51st St., tel. 212/757–3318), presenting classic and contemporary Irish plays.

Jean Cocteau Repertory (Bouwerie Lane Theatre, 330 Broadway, tel. 212/677–0060), founded in 1971, with international classics, intelligently performed by its resident acting troupe.

The Jewish Repertory Theatre (Playhouse 91, 316 E. 91st St., tel. 212/831–2000), begun in 1972, producing plays about Jewish life such as *Crossing Delancey*, the basis for the hit film.

Musical Theatre Works (440 Lafayette St., tel. 212/677–0040), performing showcase productions of new musicals.

The New York Theater Workshop (79 E. 4th St., tel. 212/302–6989), producing challenging new theater by American and international artists.

The Pan Asian Repertory Theatre (Playhouse 46 in St. Clement's Church, 423 W. 46th St., tel. 212/245–2660), a center for Asian and Asian-American artists, producing new works or adapted Western plays.

Pearl Theatre Company (125 W. 22nd St., tel. 212/645–7708), with resident players focusing on a repertory of classics.

Repertorio Español (Gramercy Arts Theatre, 138 E. 27th St., tel. 212/889–2850), an Obie-award-winning Spanish arts repertory theater whose productions are in Spanish.

Second Stage (McGinn/Cazale Theatre, 2162 Broadway at W. 76th St., tel. 212/787–8302), producing new works and recent plays that may not have been given a fair shake their first time around.

The Soho Rep (46 Walker St., below Canal St. between Broadway and Church St., tel. 212/977–5955), dedicated to contemporary plays on controversial issues.

Theatre for a New Audience (St. Clement's Church, 423 W. 46th St., tel. 212/279–4200) performs both Shakespearean productions and new plays by important contemporary playwrights.

Avant-Garde Last, but not at all least, is New York's fabled theatrical avant-garde. The "experimental theater" movement's founders may no longer be the long-haired hippies they were when they first started doing mixed-media productions and promoting off-center playwrights (such as Sam Shepard) in the '60s, but they continue at the forefront. Take Ellen Stewart, also known, simply and elegantly, as "LaMama." Over the past two decades, her East Village organization has branched out to import European innovators and has grown physically as well. **La MaMa E.T.C.** (74A E. 4th St., tel. 212/475–7710) now encompasses a First Floor Theater, an Annex theater, and a club. Productions include everything from African fables to New Wave opera to reinterpretations of the Greek classics; past triumphs have included the original performances of *Godspell* and *Torch Song Trilogy.*

Another chief player in the theatrical avant-garde is **Mabou Mines** (150 1st Ave., tel. 212/473–0559), a troupe performing at different venues around the city. Mabou Mines's trademarks are its innovative use of stage technology and its collaborations with major artists from a variety of disciplines. A recently expanded four-theater cultural complex is home to the experimentalist **Theater for the New City** (155 1st Ave., tel. 212/254–1109), which devotes its productions to new playwrights. The complex also sponsors a free street-theater program, arts festivals, and Christmas and Halloween spectacles. Founded by the late Charles Ludlam in 1972, the **Ridiculous Theatrical Company** (1 Sheridan Sq., tel. 212/691–2271) still keeps audiences laughing with its unique performance style: a blend of classical acting—usually in drag—and high camp.

Performance Art At the vanishing point of the avant-garde is that curious mélange of artistic disciplines known as performance art. Intentionally difficult to categorize, it blends music and sound, dance, video and lights, words, and whatever else comes to the performance artist's mind, to produce events of erratic success—sometimes fascinating, sometimes deadening. Performance art is almost exclusively a downtown endeavor, though it is also showcased in the outer boroughs, especially Brooklyn, where the **Brooklyn Academy of Music** (30 Lafayette Ave., Brooklyn, tel. 718/636–4100) has built its considerable reputation on its annual Next Wave Festival, which features many performance works.

Other performance-art showcases are:

Dixon Place (258 Bowery, between Houston and Prince Sts., tel. 212/219–3088) presents an eccentric, eclectic schedule, including comedy acts, musicians, and readings.
Franklin Furnace (112 Franklin St., tel. 212/925–4671), since 1976 a supporter of off-center, emerging artists—this is where Eric Bogosian (seen in the movies *Funhouse* and *Talk Radio*) got his start.
The Kitchen (512 W. 19th St., tel. 212/255–5793), perhaps *the* Manhattan center for performance art, although video, dance, and music have their moments here, too.
Performance Space 122, or **P.S. 122** (150 1st Ave., tel. 212/477–5288), called by *The Village Voice* "the petri dish of downtown culture." Occupying a former public school that was comedian George Burns's alma mater, P.S. 122 presents exhibitions and productions that come and go quickly but seldom fail in freshness. Look especially for its annual marathon in February, in which scores of dazzling downtowners take part.
P.S. 1 (46–01 21st St., Queens, tel. 718/784–2084), a contemporary art museum in lively Long Island City, Queens, featuring occasional theatrical events.

Music

"Gentlemen," conductor Serge Koussevitzky once told the assembled Boston Symphony Orchestra, "maybe it's good enough for Cleveland or Cincinnati, but it's not good enough for New York." That's New York's place in the musical world, in a nutshell; quite simply, it's the top, for performers and music lovers alike.

New York possesses not only the country's oldest symphony, the New York Philharmonic, but also three renowned conservatories—The Juilliard School, The Manhattan School of Music, and Mannes College of Music—plus myriad musical performance groups. Since the turn of the century, the world's great orchestras and soloists have made Manhattan a principal stopping point. In recent years, live TV and radio broadcasts have brought the music played in New York to millions more listeners across the North American continent.

To those who visit the city for its music, New York opens like a Stradivarius case. In an average week, between 50 and 150 events—everything from zydeco to Debussy, Cole Porter, Kurt Weill, and reggae—appear in newspaper and magazine listings, and weekly concert calendars are published in all of the major newspapers. Record and music shops—such as the cavernous **Tower Records** (692 Broadway at 4th St., tel. 212/ 505–1500, and 1961 Broadway at 66th St., tel. 212/799–2500), **HMV** (2081 Broadway at 72nd St., tel. 212/721–5900; 1280 Lexington Ave. at 86th St., tel. 212/348–0800), **J & R Music World** (23 Park Row, across from City Hall, tel. 212/732–8600), the reliable **Bleecker Bob's Golden Oldies** (118 W. 3rd St., tel. 212/ 475–9677), and the classy **Patelson's** (160 W. 56th St., tel. 212/ 582–5840)—serve as music information centers, too, as do the city's radio stations. WNYC (FM 93.9 and AM 820) and WQXR (FM 96.3 and AM 1560) update listeners on current musical events, and WNCN (FM 104) does the same; WNCN's "Café 104" (Fridays, noon–1 PM) is a good source for info on weekend concerts and cultural events. The **Bryant Park Music and Dance Tickets Booth** (42nd St. just east of 6th Ave., tel. 212/382–2323) also lists music around town.

Classical Music **Lincoln Center** (W. 62nd St. and Broadway) remains the city's musical nerve center, especially when it comes to the classics. The **New York Philharmonic,** led by musical director Kurt Masur, performs at Avery Fisher Hall (tel. 212/875–5030) and will play a number of special gala concerts to celebrate its 150th anniversary season in 1992–93. In summer, the popular **Mostly Mozart** concert series presents an impressive roster of classical performers. Avery Fisher, designed by Max Abramovitz, opened in 1961 as Philharmonic Hall, but underwent drastic renovation in 1976 to improve the acoustics (at a price tag of $5 million). The result is an auditorium that follows the classic European rectangular pattern. To its stage come the world's great musicians; to its boxes, the black-tie-and-diamond-tiara set.

A note for New York Philharmonic devotees: The orchestra rehearses Thursday mornings at 9:45. In season (September–June), and when conductors and soloists are amenable, rehearsals are open to the public for $5. Call 212/875–5030 for information.

Near Avery Fisher is Alice Tully Hall (tel. 212/875–5050), an intimate "little white box," considered as acoustically perfect as concert houses get. Here the **Chamber Music Society of Lincoln Center** tunes up, along with promising Juilliard students, chamber music ensembles such as the Guarneri Quartet and Kronos Quartet, music on period instruments, choral music, famous soloists, and concert groups. Lincoln Center's outdoor Damrosch Park, and Bruno Walter Auditorium (in the Library of the Performing Arts, tel. 212/870–1630) often offer free concerts; two summer programs, **Serious Fun** and **Classical Jazz,** have been added in recent years to the Lincoln Center bill.

While Lincoln Center is only 30 years old, another famous classical music palace—**Carnegie Hall** (W. 57th St. at 7th Ave., tel. 212/247–7800)—recently celebrated its 100th birthday. This is the place where the great pianist Paderewski was attacked by ebullient crowds (who claimed kisses and locks of his hair) after a performance in 1891; where young Leonard Bernstein, standing in for New York Philharmonic conductor Bruno Walter, made his triumphant debut in 1943; where Jack Benny and Isaac Stern fiddled together and where the Beatles played one of their first U.S. concerts. When threats of the wrecker's ball loomed large in 1960, a consortium of Carnegie loyalists (headed by Isaac Stern) rose to save it; an eventual multimillion-dollar renovation in 1986 worked cosmetic wonders, but many critics believe that the face-lift damaged the Main Concert Hall's celebrated acoustics.

Other prime classical music locales are:

Aaron Davis Hall at City College (W. 133rd St. at Convent Ave., tel. 212/650–6900), uptown scene of world music events and a variety of classical concerts and dance programs.
Grace Rainey Rogers Auditorium at the Metropolitan Museum of Art (5th Ave. at 82nd St., tel. 212/570–3949), providing classical music in classic surroundings.
Merkin Concert Hall at the Abraham Goodman House (129 W. 67th St., tel. 212/362–8719), almost as prestigious as the concert halls at Lincoln Center.
Miller Theatre (Columbia University, Broadway at 116th St., 212/854–7799), featuring a varied program of classical performers, such as the New York Virtuosi Chamber Symphony.
Kaufman Concert Hall at the 92nd St. Y (1395 Lexington Ave., tel. 212/415–5440), with the New York Chamber Symphony in residence, plus star recitalists and chamber music groups.
Bargemusic at the Fulton Ferry Landing in Brooklyn (tel. 718/624–4061), with chamber music bubbling year-round from an old barge with a fabulous skyline view.
Brooklyn Academy of Music (30 Lafayette Ave., tel. 718/636–4100), ever experimenting with new and old musical styles, and still a showcase for the Brooklyn Philharmonic.

Outdoor Concerts Weather permitting, the city's great out-of-doors becomes one wide concert hall. Each August, the plaza around Lincoln Center explodes with the **Lincoln Center Out-of-Doors** series. In the summertime, both the **Metropolitan Opera** and the **New York Philharmonic** decamp to municipal parks to play free concerts, rocking the greenswards with the trills of *La Bohème* or the thunder of the *1812 Overture*. (For information call Lincoln Center, tel. 212/875–5400, or the City Parks Events Hotline, tel. 212/360–1333.) The Museum of Modern Art hosts free Friday and Saturday evening concerts of 20th-century music in their sculpture garden as part of the **Summergarden** series (tel. 212/708–9480). A **Jazzmobile** (tel. 212/866–4900) trucks jazz and Latin music to parks throughout the five boroughs, and Prospect Park comes alive with the sounds of its annual **Celebrate Brooklyn Concert Series** (tel. 718/855–7882). Starlit Saturday evenings at South Street Seaport turn Pier 16 into **Summerpier** (tel. 212/669–9400), featuring a range of musical styles.

Lunchtime Concerts During the work week, more and more lunchtime concerts provide musical midday breaks at public atriums all over the city. Events are generally free, and bag-lunching is encouraged. Check out the **World Financial Center's Winter Garden Atrium** (across the West Side Highway from the World Trade Center), the **IBM Atrium** (57th St. and Madison Ave.), and the **Citicorp Center Marketplace** (54th St. and Lexington Ave.). And, of course, everywhere—in parks, on street corners, and down under in the subway—aspiring musicians of all kinds hold forth, with their instrument cases thrown open for contributions. True, some are hacks, but others are bona fide professionals: moonlighting violinists, Broadway chorus members indulging their love of the barbershop quartet, or horn players prowling up from clubs to take in the fresh air.

Downtown, the venerable **St. Paul's Chapel** (Fulton St. and Broadway, tel. 212/602–0874) presents free lunchtime concerts of mostly classical music on Mondays and Thursdays at noon. A $2 contribution is suggested.

A midtown music break can be found at **St. Peter's Lutheran Church** (619 Lexington Ave., at the Citicorp Ctr., tel. 212/935–2200), with its Wednesday series of lunchtime jazz at 12:30.

Opera

Recent decades have sharply intensified the public's appreciation for grand opera—partly because of the charismatic personalities of such great singers as Placido Domingo and Beverly Sills, and partly because of the efforts of New York's magnetic **Metropolitan Opera.** A Met premiere draws the rich and famous, the critics, and the connoisseurs. At the Met's elegant Lincoln Center home, with its Marc Chagall murals and weighty Austrian-crystal chandeliers, the supercharged atmosphere gives audiences a sense that something special is going to happen, even before the curtain goes up. Luciano Pavarotti put it best: "When it comes to classical music, New York can truly be called a beacon of light—with that special quality that makes it *'unico in mondo,'* unique in the world."

The Metropolitan Opera (tel. 212/362–6000) performs its vaunted repertoire from October to mid-April, and though tickets can cost as much as $135 apiece, standing room is available for far less. Standing room tickets for the week's performance go on sale on Saturday.

Meanwhile, the **New York City Opera,** which performs July–November in Lincoln Center's New York State Theater (tel. 212/870–5570), has faced the departure of its famous general director, Beverly Sills. But with conductor Christopher Keene at the helm, it persists in its "tradition of taking chances on unfamiliar works, old and new" (in the words of *New York Times* critic Donal Henahan) and in nurturing young American stars-to-be. City Opera recently widened its repertoire to include several classic musical comedies, such as *Brigadoon, South Pacific,* and *A Little Night Music,* and it continues its ingenious practice of "supertitling"—electronically displaying, above the stage, line-by-line translations into English for foreign-language operas. Recent seasons have included such old favorites as *Carmen, Madama Butterfly,* and *The Magic Flute.*

Opera aficionados should also keep track of the **Carnegie Hall** schedule (tel. 212/247–7800) for debuting singers and performances by the Opera Orchestra of New York, which specializes in presenting rarely performed operas in concert form, often with star soloists. Pay close attention to provocative offerings at the **Brooklyn Academy of Music** (tel. 718/636–4100), which often premieres avant-garde works difficult to see elsewhere.

Other city opera groups include:

Amato Opera Theatre (319 Bowery, tel. 212/228–8200), a showcase for rising singers.
New York Gilbert and Sullivan Players (251 W. 91st St., Apt.

4C, tel. 212/769–1000), performing G & S classics, usually at Symphony Space (95th and Broadway).

Opera Ebony (2109 Broadway, Suite 1418, tel. 212/874–7245), a black company performing major and minor works September–June at Aaron Davis Hall, City College (W. 133rd St. and Convent Ave.).

True devotees might consider a New York opera theme tour—several days of concentrated immersion, usually conducted by an expert. Check *Opera Monthly* magazine (Box 816, Madison Square Station, 10159, tel. 212/627–2120) for the names of tour firms.

Dance

Ballet Visiting balletomanes live out their dreams in New York, where two powerhouse companies—the New York City Ballet and the American Ballet Theatre—continue to please and astonish.

The **New York City Ballet,** a hallmark troupe for over 40 years, recently presented a highly acclaimed production of *The Sleeping Beauty,* created by the company's master-in-chief, Peter Martins; his streamlined, two-act version combines the drama and beauty of the original choreography by Marius Petipa with the speed and energy for which NYCB is known. The company's vast repertory includes works by George Balanchine, Jerome Robbins, Martins, and others. NYCB performs in Lincoln Center's New York State Theater (tel. 212/879–5570). Its winter season runs from mid-November through February—with the beloved annual production of George Balanchine's *The Nutcracker* ushering in the December holiday season—while its spring season lasts from mid-April through June.

Founded by Lincoln Kirstein and Balanchine in 1948, NYCB continues to stress dance as a whole above individual ballet stars, though that hasn't stopped a number of prima ballerinas (such as Merrill Ashley, Kyra Nichols, and Darci Kistler) from standing out. The company has more than 100 dancers and performs and maintains an active repertoire of 20th-century works unmatched in the world.

Across the plaza at Lincoln Center, the Metropolitan Opera House (tel. 212/362–6000) is home to the **American Ballet Theatre,** noted especially for its brilliant renditions of story ballets and its lyrical style, as well as its world-renowned featured dancers. Its season opens in April, when the opera season closes, and runs through June.

Part of Lincoln Center's dance vitality is accounted for by the presence of the **School of American Ballet,** the focus for the dreams of young dancers across the country. Some 2,000 of them vie for spots in SAB's summer session, and a talented handful of the 200 who make it into the summer group go on to join the school. Here the Balanchine legacy lives on, and soulful-eyed baby dancers are molded into professional performers. You can see SAB students dashing across 66th and Broadway with leotard-stuffed bags slung over their shoulders, or congregating in **The Ballet Shop** (1887 Broadway, between 62nd and 63rd Sts., tel. 212/581–7990).

When the ABT and NYCB take a break from performing, Lincoln Center acts as impresario for dozens of world-renowned companies, such as the Bolshoi and Royal Danish ballets.

The varied bill at **City Center** (131 W. 55th St., tel. 212/581–7907) often includes touring ballet companies; recently the Matsuyama Ballet from Japan performed there.

Modern Dance At City Center (131 W. 55th St., tel. 212/581–7907), the moderns hold sway. In seasons past, the **Alvin Ailey Dance Company, Twyla Tharp and Dancers,** the **Martha Graham Dance Company,** the **Paul Taylor Dance Company,** the **Dance Theater of Harlem,** and the **Merce Cunningham Dance Company** have performed here. The **Brooklyn Academy of Music** (30 Lafayette Ave., tel. 718/636–4100) features both American and foreign contemporary dance troupes as part of its **Next Wave Festival** every fall.

A growing modern dance center is the **Joyce Theater** (175 8th Ave., tel. 212/242–0800), housed in a former Art Deco movie theater. The Joyce is the permanent home of **Feld Ballets/NY,** founded in 1974 by an upstart ABT dancer who went on to become a principal fixture on the dance scene. Other featured companies include the **Nikolais and Murray Louis Dance Company,** the avant-garde **ZeroMoving Company,** and the loony acrobats of **Pilobolus.** At **Symphony Space** (2537 Broadway, tel. 212/864–1414), the bill often features ethnic dance.

Here's a sampling of other, mostly experimental and avant-garde, dance forums:

Dance Theater Workshop (219 W. 19th St., tel. 212/691–6500), one of New York's most successful laboratories for new dance.
Danspace Project (at St. Mark's-in-the-Bowery Church, 10th St. and 2nd Ave., tel. 212/674–8194), with a series of avant-garde choreography that runs from September through June.
DIA Center for the Arts (155 Mercer St., tel. 212/431–9232) hosts a number of performances by interesting local dancers.
P.S. 122 (150 1st Ave., tel. 212/477–5288), where dance events border on performance art; among others, Meredith Monk occasionally cavorts here.
Repertorio Español (138 E. 27th St., tel. 212/889–2850), oft-visited by the famed Spanish stylist Pilar Rioja.
Washington Square Church (135 W. 4th St., tel. 212/777–2528), for modern dance and dance theater.

Film and Video

On any given week, New York City seems a kind of film archive featuring all the major new releases, classics renowned and arcane, unusual foreign offerings, small independent flicks, and cutting-edge experimental works. Because you don't usually need to buy tickets in advance, except on Friday and Saturday evenings, movie-going is a great spur-of-the-moment way to rest from the rigors of sightseeing. You may have to stand a while in a line that winds around the block, but even that can be entertaining—conversations overheard in such queues are generally just as good as the previews of coming attractions. Note, however, that these lines are generally for people who have already bought their tickets; be sure, as you approach the theater, to ask if there are separate lines for ticket *holders* and ticket *buyers*.

For information on first-run movie schedules and theaters, dial 212/777–FILM, the Movie Phone sponsored by WQHT 97 FM and *New York* magazine.

Festivals New York's numero uno film program remains the **New York Film Festival,** conducted by the Film Society of Lincoln Center every September and October at Alice Tully and Avery Fisher halls (tel. 212/875–5050). Its program includes 25–50 hot movies, most of them never seen before in the United States; the festival's hits usually make their way into local movie houses over the following couple of months. This festival has presented the U.S. premieres of such memorable movies as Martin Scorsese's *Mean Streets,* François Truffaut's *Day For Night,* Akira Kurosawa's *Ran,* and Neil Jordan's *The Crying Game.* In March the Film Society joins forces with the Museum of Modern Art to produce a **New Directors/New Films** series, where the best works by up-and-coming directors get their moment to flicker. This series is held at MOMA's Roy and Niuta Titus theatres (11 W. 53rd St., tel. 212/708–9480).

Museums The **American Museum of the Moving Image** (35th Ave. at 36th St., Queens, tel. 718/784–0077), housed in a building belonging to the historic Kaufman Astoria Studios, offers multiple galleries that are a movie buff's paradise, as are its 195-seat Riklis Theatre and 60-seat Warner Communications Screening Room. The museum presents changing exhibits and provocative film programs, including major artist-oriented retrospectives, Hollywood classics, experimental videos, and TV documentaries.

In midtown Manhattan, the **Museum of Television & Radio** (25 W. 52nd St., tel. 212/621–6800 for schedule of daily events or 212/621–6600 for other information) has a gigantic collection of 40,000 radio and TV shows, including everything from *The Dick Van Dyke Show* to *Soap, Cheers,* and *Taxi.* The museum's library provides 96 consoles, where you can watch or listen to whatever you wish for up to two hours at a time. The museum presents scheduled theater screenings, gallery exhibits, and series for children.

First-Run Houses New suburban-style multiscreen complexes have sprung up all over town, even in such hip urban neighborhoods as SoHo (Houston and Mercer Sts.), the East Village (2nd Ave. at 12th St. and 3rd Ave. at 11th St.), the Flatiron District (890 Broadway at 19th St.), and Hell's Kitchen (Worldwide Plaza, 320 W. 50th St.). While this increase in the number of screens seems to have eased lines at the box office somewhat, these cinemas often seem to show the same mainstream commercial movies, so long lines still snake around the corner at the few theaters that show more offbeat fare.

Only two New York theaters preserve the size and allure of the great old movie houses: The **Ziegfeld** (141 W. 54th St., west of 6th Ave., tel. 212/765–7600), with its awesome sound system, and **Radio City Music Hall** (1260 6th Ave., tel. 212/247–4777), with its 34-foot-high screen and 4,500-watt projector, only rarely used for movie screenings.

The Times Square area is still a movie mecca, though action flicks prevail on 42nd Street, and viewers should be warned to sit tight and hold on to their purses. Posh East Side first-run theaters line Third Avenue between 57th and 60th streets and continue up Second Avenue into the 60s. Other groups are clustered around East 34th Street, West 23rd Street, and Broadway between 60th and 63rd streets.

Midnight Movies At a handful of Greenwich Village theaters, midnight madness continues with late and late-late showings of eccentric classics such as *Blue Velvet,* and *The Rocky Horror Picture Show.* The **Angelika Film Center** (Houston and Mercer Sts., tel. 212/995–2000) and the **Waverly Twin** (6th Ave. at W. 3rd St., tel. 212/929–8037) are good theaters to check out for these; occasional midnight programs appear also at the **Quad Cinema** (13th St. between 5th and 6th Aves., tel. 212/255–8800).

Revival Houses One of the best places to see old films in Manhattan opened in 1991: the **Walter Reade Theater** at Lincoln Center (70 Lincoln Plaza, Broadway and 65th St., tel. 212/875–5600), operated by the Film Society of Lincoln Center. This comfortable movie house presents several fascinating series that run concurrently, devoted to specific themes or a certain director's body of work; movies for kids are featured Saturday mornings. The state-of-the-art auditorium is a little gem with excellent sight lines, and tickets can be purchased at the box office weeks in advance.

Revivals can also be found at:

American Museum of the Moving Image (35th Ave. at 36th St., Queens, tel. 718/784–0077), offering American film series, often in historical contexts.
Film Forum (209 W. Houston St., tel. 212/727–8110), with three screens showing often quirky series based on movie genres, directors, and other film artists.
Gramercy (Lexington Ave. at 23rd St., 212/475–1660), presenting imaginative double bills of American classics.
The Museum of Modern Art (11 W. 53rd St., tel. 212/708–9480), which includes rare classic films in its many series.
Theatre 80 St. Marks (80 St. Marks Pl., tel. 212/254–7400), small and shabby but convivial, specializing in double-features from the '30s and '40s.

Foreign and Independent Films Between the interest generated by the Film Festival, the city's population of foreign executives and diplomats, a resident corps of independent filmmakers, and a large contingent of cosmopolitan *cinéastes*, there's always an audience here for foreign films and for innovative new American films and videos that buck the Hollywood currents. The following cinemas more or less specialize in such films:

Angelika 57 (225 W. 57th St., tel. 212/586–1900), showing film programs similar to its downtown sister theater (*see below*).
Angelika Film Center (Houston and Mercer Sts., tel. 212/995–2000), offering several screens devoted to off-beat independent and foreign films, as well as a lively café catering to a youthful crowd.
Anthology Film Archives (32 2nd Ave. at 2nd St., tel. 212/505–5181), presenting esoteric independent fare.
Carnegie Hall Cinemas (887 7th Ave. between 56th and 57th Sts., tel. 212/265–2520), where intriguing new films find long runs.
Cinema Village 12th Street (12th St. between 5th Ave. and University Pl., tel. 212/924–3363), offering innovative independent features and occasional animation festivals.
Eastside Playhouse (Third Ave., between 55th and 56th Sts.), with an emphasis on first-run art films.

Film Forum (209 W. Houston St., tel. 212/727–8110) presenting some of the best new independent films and hard-to-see foreign movies.

The Joseph Papp Public Theater (425 Lafayette St., tel. 212/598–7171), a reliable forum for experimental and independent film.

Lincoln Plaza (Broadway between 62nd and 63rd Sts., tel. 212/757–2280), six subterranean cinemas playing long-run foreign hits.

Loews Paris Fine Arts (58th St., between 5th and 6th Aves., tel. 212/980–5656), a showcase for much-talked-about new American and foreign entries.

Millennium (66 E. 4th St., tel. 212/673–0090), with an emphasis on the avant-garde.

68th Street Playhouse (3rd Ave. at 68th St., tel. 212/734–0302), with exclusive extended runs of critically acclaimed films.

Quad Cinema (13th St. between 5th and 6th Aves., tel. 212/255–8800), with first-run Hollywood, art, and foreign films.

Village East Cinemas (2nd Ave. at 12th St., tel. 212/529–6799), presenting cutting-edge independent features alongside mainstream Hollywood productions.

Foreign and independent films and videos also run at art societies and museums around town, including:

Asia Society (725 Park Ave. at 70th St., tel. 212/288–6400).

Florence Gould Hall (55 E. 59th St., tel. 212/355–6160), the site for French films sponsored by the French Institute-Alliance Française.

Goethe House (1014 5th Ave., between 82nd and 83rd Sts., tel. 212/439–8700).

Japan Society (333 E. 47th St., tel. 212/752–3015).

The Museum of Modern Art (11 W. 53rd St., tel. 212/708–9480).

The Whitney Museum of American Art (945 Madison Ave. at 75th St., tel. 212/570–3676).

Readings and Lectures

New York is, of course, the center of the American publishing world, and as a result most writers—however reclusive—eventually find reason to come here. The Writers Guild headquarters and the U.S. offices of P.E.N. International are in Manhattan; the National Book Awards are presented here annually in the grand foyer of the New York Public Library.

If you're interested in the written word (and in stealing a look at the people who create it), a New York fiction or poetry reading is a good idea. They spring up all over the city—in bookstores, libraries, museums, bars, and legitimate theaters—drawing some of the top names in contemporary literature, writers such as E.L. Doctorow, Nadine Gordimer, Toni Morrison, Edna O'Brien, Richard Price, Philip Roth, and Amy Tan, as well as debuting talents.

The New York City Poetry Calendar (60 E. 4th St., No. 21, 10003, tel. 212/475–7110), published monthly, provides an extensive list of prose and poetry readings around the city. The calendar is available by subscription and free at several Manhattan bookstores.

A major reading and talk series held at the **Lincoln Center Library for the Performing Arts** (tel. 212/870–1630) specializes in musicians, directors, singers, and actors. In fact, the entire **New York Public Library** system (tel. 212/930–0571) is a wide-open field for reading events, as is the **Brooklyn Public Library** network (tel. 718/780–7700).

At the **Metropolitan Museum of Art** (5th Ave. at 82nd St., tel. 212/535–7710 or 570–3949), seasonal lectures regularly draw sell-out crowds. Artists such as David Hockney hold forth here, as do the world's eminent art historians.

Authors, poets, lyricists, and travelogue-spinners take the stage at the **92nd St. Y** (1395 Lexington Ave., tel. 212/996–1100), while the **West Side YMCA** (5 W. 63rd St., tel. 212/787–6557) offers readings by major novelists, poets, and humorists in a series called "The Writer's Voice." **Symphony Space** (Broadway at 95th St., tel. 212/864–5400) holds a number of readings, including the Selected Shorts series of stories read by prominent actors.

Distinguished reading series devoted primarily to poetry are sponsored by several organizations in Manhattan, including **The Academy of American Poets** (580 Broadway, Suite 1208, tel. 212/274–0343); **The Poetry Project** (St. Mark's-in-the-Bowery Church, E. 10th St. and 2nd Ave., tel. 212/674–0910); **Poetry Society of America** (15 Gramercy Park, tel. 212/254–9628); and **Poets House** (72 Spring St., tel. 212/431–7920).

More poetry readings, often with an "open-mike" policy that allows audience members to read their own stuff, have been cropping up more and more frequently in New York City clubs and bars. There may be a low ($2–$5) cover charge, and food or drink is usually available. Some reliable spots: **Cedar Tavern** (82 University Pl., tel. 212/929–9089), Sunday afternoons; **Ear Inn** (326 Spring St., tel. 212/226–9060), Saturday afternoons; **The Knitting Factory** (47 E. Houston St., tel. 212/219–3055), several evenings each week; and **Nuyorican Poets Cafe** (236 E. 3rd St., tel. 212/505–8183), with various multicultural poets scheduled weekly and a Poetry Slam competition each Friday.

Many Manhattan bookstores organize evening readings by authors of recently published books. Best bets are **Books & Co.** (939 Madison Ave. near 74th St., tel. 212/737–1450), **Brentano's** (597 5th Ave. near 48th St., tel. 212/826–2450) **Endicott Booksellers** (450 Columbus Ave. near 81st St., tel. 212/787–6300), **Three Lives and Co.** (154 W. 10th St., tel. 212/741–2069), and **Tower Books** (383 Lafayette St. at 4th St., tel. 212/228–5100).

12 Nightlife

By Susan Spano Wells

Updated by Peter Filichia

Okay, so you've taken the Staten Island Ferry, you've lunched at the Plaza, and you've visited the Met. But don't tuck yourself in just yet. Instead, get yourself truly attuned to the Big Apple's schedule, which runs more by New York nocturnal than by eastern standard time. Even if you're not a night owl by habit, it's worth staying up late at least once, for by night, Manhattan takes on a whole new identity.

Clubs and Entertainment

New York nightlife really started to swing in 1914, when a pair of ballroom dancers, Florence and Maurice Walton, took over management of the Parisian Room, in what is today's Theater District. At Chez Maurice, as the new club was called, the city's café society learned a sensual dance at "Tango Teas." Then came the Harlem Renaissance of the 1920s and '30s, and the New York jazz scene shifted north of 110th Street. In the 1950s night spots mushroomed in Greenwich Village and the East 50s. Along 52nd Street in those years, recalls columnist Pete Hamill, "you could walk down a single block and hear Art Tatum, Billie Holiday, and Charlie Parker. And you could go to the Latin Quarter and see girls running around with bananas on their heads. On the other hand, Babe Ruth doesn't play for the Yankees anymore, either."

Well, maybe not, but Patrick Ewing does play for the Knicks, and the old Copacabana Club has been reincarnated now as a discotheque. *Plus ça change* . . . In truth, the current nightclub scene is probably more varied and vital than it ever was, but in different ways. To begin with, it has moved downtown—along with just about everything else—to dead-looking East Village dives that come alive nightly, to classic jazz joints in the West Village, to sleekly decorated TriBeCa see-and-be-seen traps, and to preppy hangouts around Wall Street.

There are enough dedicated club-hoppers here to support night spots for almost every idiosyncratic taste. But keep in mind that *when* you go is just as important as where you go in clubland. Clubs vary their themes every night of the week. Depending on where you go, an appropriate costume for a night on the town could include anything from blue suede shoes to an Armani coat to a Balenciaga gown; anything from an orange fright wig to leather and chains to a vintage pink poodle skirt.

That doesn't mean that "anything goes," however, for exclusivity is the name of the game. At certain clubs, gimlet-eyed door staff zealously guard the barrier of velvet rope outside, selecting customers according to arbitrary standards. For a new crop of gypsy clubs, only those in the know can even find out where the group is meeting this week.

On Friday, the *New York Times*'s "Weekend" section carries a "Sounds Around Town" column that can give you a picture of what's in the air, as can the *Village Voice*, which probably has more nightclub ads than any other rag in the world. Or stop by Tower Records (692 Broadway, tel. 212/505–1500; 1961 Broadway, tel. 212/799–2500), where fliers about coming events and club passes are stacked outside. You may also get good tips from a suitably au courant hotel concierge. Just remember that what's hot and what's not changes almost weekly in this city, so visitors are at a distinct disadvantage. We've tried to give you a rounded sample of reliable hangouts—establishments that are likely to be still in business by the time you use this book—but clubs come and go as fast as spawning tsetse flies, so phone ahead to make sure your target night spot hasn't closed or turned into a polka hall. Most will charge a cover of at least $10 a head; some go as high as $20–$50 (nobody said catting around was going to be cheap!). Take cash because many places don't accept plastic.

Putting on the Ritz

You and your date are wearing Oscar de la Renta and Armani finery; your transport's a white stretch limo; and you've just come from dinner at Lutèce. Just remember to hide this guidebook in your tux pocket or your rhinestone clutch so people won't guess you're not regulars at:

The Ballroom (253 W. 28th St., tel. 212/244–3005). This very hip Chelsea spot has an extensive tapas bar and a nightclub where some of the great chanteuses—including Peggy Lee and Helen Schneider—rhapsodize and where Broadway's best moonlight after the shows on their nights off.

The Carlyle (35 E. 76th St., tel. 212/744–1600). The hotel's discreetly sophisticated Café Carlyle is where Bobby Short plays when he's in town; otherwise, you might find Dixie Carter honing her night-club act. Bemelmans' Bar, with murals by the author of the Madeleine books, regularly stars jazz pianist Barbara Carroll.

Nell's (246 W. 14th St., tel. 212/675–1567). Back in vogue, Nell Campbell (of *Rocky Horror* fame) reintroduced sophistication to nightlife with her club. The tone in the upstairs jazz salon is Victorian; downstairs is for tête-à-têtes and dancing. The boîte opens at 10 PM and closes at 4 AM.

The Oak Room (at the Algonquin Hotel, 59 W. 44th St., tel. 212/840–6800). You'll hear that the Algonquin has faded, but this room still offers yesteryear's charms. Just head straight for the long, narrow club-cum-watering hole; at the piano you'll find, perhaps, singer Julie Wilson, the hopelessly romantic Andrea Marcovicci, the charming Jeff Harnar, or showtune chanteuse Iris Williams.

The Rainbow Room and **Rainbow and Stars Club** (30 Rockefeller Plaza, tel. 212/632–5000). You can find two kinds of heaven high up on Rockefeller Center's 65th floor. The Rainbow Room serves dinner (*see* Chapter 9), and dancing to the strains of a live orchestra takes place on a floor right out of an Astaire-Rogers musical. At the intimate Rainbow and Stars Club, singers such as Tony Bennett and Rosemary Clooney entertain, backlit by a view of the twinkling lights of the city.

The Russian Tea Room (150 W. 57th St., tel. 212/265–0947). This latest entrant into the cabaret scene features seasoned performers such as Blossom Dearie and Margaret Whiting as well as newcomers on Sunday evenings on the second floor.

Supper Club (240 W. 47th St., tel. 212/921–1940). Note the last four digits of the telephone number. This huge, prix fixe dinner-and-dancing club specializes in cheek-to-cheek Big Band sounds, with a 10-piece orchestra, three singers, and a vast, star-covered ceiling.

Boogie and Be Seen

The city's busiest dance floors are seeing all kinds of styles revived, from "voguing" to the Twist to bebop swings and lifts. Revelers come to socialize, to find romance, to scream business deals over the music, to show off their glad rags, or to be photographed rubbing shoulders with stars.

Club USA. (218 W. 47th St., tel. 212/258–2872) This five-story wonder (the top floor is for VIPs only, thank you), housed in a former burlesque theater, offers two floors (joined by a 100-foot Plexiglass slide) for as many as 2,000 happy dancers (and frenetic ones, too).

Crane Club (408 Amsterdam Ave., tel. 212/877–3097). A plush club with a good-looking crowd (if you can stand investment bankers) offers Top-40 hits and dinner every Thursday, Friday, and Saturday.

Dukie's (in the Gold Bar, 345 E. 9th St., tel. 212/505–8270). This classic East Village neighborhood bar is transformed into a dance club on Friday nights. Interior design is not Dukie's trademark—unless you're inspired by the silver toilet seat over the bar.

Juke Box NYC (304 E. 39th St., tel. 212/685–1556). Nineteen-fifties and early '60s nostalgia—and '90s music, too—is offered here. One floor is a sports lounge where you can play air hockey or watch a game on pay-cable. The mood is that of a nonstop giddy graduation prom.

Laura Belle (120 W. 43rd St., tel. 212/819–1000). Updated '40s-style glam reigns and swing music plays for most of the night (the rock sounds come later) at this split-level club.

Le Bar Bat (311 W. 57th St., tel. 212/307–7228). The third jewel of West 57th Street's trendy clubs may follow Planet Hollywood and the Hard Rock Café in popularity, but a flashy good time can be had here.

Limelight (47 W. 20th St., tel. 212/807–7850). In this transformed Chelsea church, the stained-glass windows endure amid catwalks, spiral staircases, and energetic dancers getting down. It's a great place for garrulousness and gyration.

Private Eyes, Inc. (12 W. 21st St., tel. 212/206–7770). This quality video palace caters to a varied but generally hip Manhattan crowd. The dance floor is smallish, but the style is never cramped. Pay attention to street numbers, because there's no name on the door of this wild club.

Roseland (239 W. 52nd St., tel. 212/247–0200). This famous old ballroom-dance floor is still open Thursday and Sunday, but you should call in advance to make sure it hasn't been taken over for the evening by a concert or a private party.

Roxy (515 W. 18th St., tel. 212/645–5156). This place wins the award for the city's most cavernous club to date. The crowd is always beautiful and never modest.

Sound Factory (530 W. 27th St., tel. 212/643–0728, Saturday nights only). There's no alcohol and usually a $15 to $20 cover, but serious dancers would never miss a night at the Sound Factory—and the party lasts till noon Sunday.

Tatou (151 E. 50th St., tel. 212/753–1144). This pleasing addition to the supper-club scene offers dinner, dancing, and cabaret under one stylish roof. The contemporary American food goes down particularly well.

Webster Hall (125 E. 11th St., tel. 212/353–1600). Probably

1993's hottest ticket in town, the two dance floors and numerous lounges are always wall-to-wall with poseurs.

Jazz Notes

Jazz players always come home to Manhattan. Somehow, the city evokes their sound. Greenwich Village is still the mecca, with more than 12 jazz nightclubs, although plenty of others are strewn around town. Here are some classics:

Arthur's Tavern (57 Grove St., tel. 212/675–6879). The place starts to cook late (say 1 or 2 AM) and eschews all fancy trappings. It offers jazz on the steamy side until 3:30 AM.

Birdland (2745 Broadway, tel. 212/749–2228). Although way up on the West Side (at 105th St.), this spot is still close to the Village at heart. You'll find lots of up-and-coming groups here.

The Blue Note (131 W. 3rd St., tel. 212/475–8592). This club may be the jazz capital of the world. Just an average week could bring Irma Thomas, the Modern Jazz Quartet, and Jackie McLean. If jazz is your thing, make a beeline to the Blue Note, but expect a steep music charge.

Bradley's (70 University Pl., tel. 212/228–6440). With brighter-than-usual lighting and, generally, jazz piano (and sometimes a sax), this is a spot for serious fans of jazz.

Condon's (117 E. 15th St., tel. 212/254–0960). The jazz is top-notch, the setting cozy, and the American bistro fare downright edible at this Union Square boîte.

Dan Lynch's Blues Bar (221 2nd Ave., tel. 212/677–0911). This jazz surprise in the East Village bustles, with jam sessions on Saturday and Sunday afternoons.

Fat Tuesday's (190 3rd Ave., tel. 212/533–7902). Two sets are played here every night, but Monday is extraspecial, as legendary guitarist Les Paul plays in the intimate basement; there's a popular restaurant-bar upstairs and one downstairs.

Five Spot (4 W. 31st St., tel. 212/631–0100). This recent addition to the jazz scene features new and established musicians in a sleek restaurant setting.

Knickerbocker (33 University Pl., tel. 212/228–8490). The stylish bar-and-grill often offers a piano-bass duo.

J's (2581 Broadway at 97th St., tel. 212/666–3600). This Upper West Side haunt, one narrow flight up, serves up live jazz nightly, with a jukebox playing '60s soul and rock during the performers' breaks.

The Knitting Factory (47 E. Houston St., tel. 212/219–3055). It looks seedy on the outside, but inside there's often fine avant-gardish jazz, anything from a trio to a full orchestra.

Red Blazer Too (349 W. 46th St., tel. 212/262–3112). Roaring '20s, Dixieland, and above all swing music are on tap here. It's a hot spot for after the theater.

Sweet Basil (88 7th Ave. S, tel. 212/242–1785). A little ritzy, though reliable, this night spot presents a range that runs from swing to fusion. There are two sets each night, and three on weekends.

Tramps (45 W. 21st St., tel. 212/727–7788). The place has been on the scene for two decades now, with the likes of Albert Collins and Buster Poindexter. Come here for a little Chicago blues in the big city.

The Village Gate (Bleecker and Thompson Sts., tel. 212/475–5120). This is another of the classic Village jazz joints. Music starts at 10 PM. Upstairs there's a cabaret theater.

The Village Vanguard (178 7th Ave. S, tel. 212/255–4037). This old Thelonius Monk haunt, the prototype of the old-world jazz club, lives on in a smoky cellar.

Zinno (126 W. 13th St., tel. 212/924–5182). The food (northern Italian) is actually as good as the jazz (usually duos and trios) at this mellow village club.

Rock Around the Clock

The roots of rock may lie in America's heartland, but New York has added its own spin. Crowds at the Big Apple's rocketerias are young, enthusiastic, and hungry; the noise is often deafening, but you can catch many a rising star in this lively scene. Here's where to go:

The Bitter End (147 Bleecker St., tel. 212/673–7030). This old Village standby still serves up its share of new talent, as it once did Joan Armatrading and Warren Zevon. Check before arriving; blues, country, and jazz all make appearances here.

CBGB & OMFUG (315 Bowery, tel. 212/982–4052). Legend has it that "OMFUG" means "Other Music for Uncivilized Gourmandizers," but no one seems to know what CBGB stands for. American punk rock was born here, in this long black tunnel of a club featuring bands with inventive names: Giant Metal Insects, Angel Rot, and Utensil.

Palladium (126 E. 14th St., tel. 212/473–7171). Here you'll find the world's biggest dance floor, fashioned from the gutted hulk of a theater, along a new wave–Oriental '60s-psychedelic theme. Home to the V.I.P. Mike Todd room, and once the hotbed of Lambada fever, it is no longer the hot ticket it was a few years ago; still, this place is to clubland what Macy's is to shopping.

The Ritz (254 W. 54th St., tel. 212/541–8900). There must be something magical about the former site of Studio 54; this club is just as popular but not quite as infamous as its predecessor. Weeknight shows begin at 9 PM; the main floor is for dancing, with seating in the balcony.

The Rock 'n' Roll Café (149 Bleecker St., tel. 212/677–7630). A week's worth of band names should clue you in: the Maudlins, the Illegitimate Sons of the Blues Brothers, and of course, Kiss My Cobra.

Wetlands Preserve (161 Hudson St., tel. 212/966–4225). Billed as a "watering hole for activists," this relative newcomer specializes in psychedelic rock.

The Latin and Island Beat

Next to dependable jazz, Latin music is the sound of the moment in New York clubs. Salsa, samba, merengue—all offer an exotic counterpoint to the city's rhythms, and Big Apple musicians have found ways to integrate the Latin strain with indigenous styles. Check them out at:

The Ballroom (253 W. 28 St., tel. 212/244–3055) now includes Latin sounds at its hip nightclub.

Club Broadway (2551 Broadway, tel. 212/864–7600). This Upper West Side club is a tradition on the Latin music scene. Look for special "Salsa Nights," on which women are admitted at a discount.

S.O.B.'s (204 Varick St., tel. 212/243–4940). Since 1982, this has been the—and we mean *the*—place for reggae, Trinidadian carnival, zydeco, African, and Caribbean funk. The initials stand for Sounds of Brazil, just in case you wondered. The decor is à la Tropicana; the favored drink, a Brazilian *caipirinha*.

Down-Home Sounds

The Bottom Line (15 W. 4th St., tel. 212/228–6300). Clubs come and go, but this granddaddy has stayed around since 1974. Its reputation is for showcasing talents on their way up, as it did for both Stevie Wonder and Bruce Springsteen. There's no way to categorize the Bottom Line bill, except to say that folk has headlined consistently. The sound system is swell, but don't go for the first set and expect to stay for the next.

Eagle Tavern (355 W. 14th St., tel. 212/924–0275). Come here for Irish folk music two nights a week, bluegrass and comedy the rest.

The Lone Star Roadhouse (240 W. 52nd St., tel. 212/245–2950). In the heart of the Theater District, this offspring of a recently closed downtown landmark is an anomaly—but a welcome one. Inhabiting a heady two-story space, it has a long bar for picking up long drinks. The food runs to chili and deep-fried crayfish; the music, from doo-wop to gospel.

O'Lunney's (12 W. 44th St., tel. 212/840–6688). Green tablecloths and the smell of stale beer accompany live music—contemporary, folk, country-western—Monday–Saturday.

Rodeo Bar (375 3rd Ave., tel. 212/683–6500). This night spot lets loose jamming fiddles and accordions, as well as a comic country band called the Surreal McCoys.

Comic Relief

The *Village Voice* covers the comedy scene well, and it's worth checking its listings because lots of music clubs book comedians for periods between sets. Some cabarets and music spots that often bring in stand-ups are Eighty-eight's, Michael's Pub, the Duplex (*see* The Show's the Thing, *below*), and the Village Gate (*see* Jazz Notes, *above*). Several clubs, however, are exclusively devoted to comedy acts:

The Boston Comedy Club (82 W. 3rd St., tel. 212/477–1000). It's so named because the owner's from Beantown, but comedians come here from all over the country to test their stuff in the Big Apple.

Caroline's Comedy Club (1626 Broadway, between 49th and 50th Sts., tel. 212/757–4100). This popular club features comedians on the edge of stardom and established names.

Catch a Rising Star (1487 1st Ave., tel. 212/794–1906). Johnny Carson got his start here, and talent scouts still show up to test the comic current. This place is neither trendy nor cutting edge, but it is reliable.

Chicago City Limits (351 E. 74th St., tel. 212/772–8707). This troupe's been doing improvisational comedy for a long time, and it seldom fails to whip its audiences into a laughing frenzy. Chicago City Limits performs in an East Side church and is very strong on audience participation.

Comedy Cellar (117 MacDougal St., tel. 212/254–3630). This spot has been running for some years now beneath the Olive Tree Café, with a bill that's a good barometer of who's hot.

The Comic Strip (1568 2nd Ave., tel. 212/861–9386). The atmosphere here is strictly corner bar. The stage is brilliantly lit but minuscule (8 by 10 feet); the bill, unpredictable but worth checking out.

Dangerfield's (1118 1st Ave., tel. 212/593–1650). Since 1969, this has been an important showcase for prime comic talent. It's owned and occasionally visited by comedian Rodney Dangerfield himself.

Freestyle Repertory Company (120 W. 28th St., tel. 212/642–8202). Here's an improvisational theater group that's a step above the others. On one night, they may ask you to step on stage and quickly tell your life story, which five actors will then adapt into scenes; on other evenings, they may make a Shakespearean tragedy the funniest show in town.

The Improvisation (358 W. 44th St., tel. 212/765–8268). The Improv is to comedy what the Blue Note is to jazz. Lots of now-famous comedians got their first laughs here, among them Richard Pryor and Robin Williams. It gets crowded, especially on weekends.

Stand Up N.Y. (236 W. 78th St., tel. 212/595–0850). A 175-seat Upper West Side option for comedy devotees, this club books lots of bright faces coming off recent TV gigs.

The Show's the Thing

Cabaret takes many forms in New York City, from a lone crooner at the piano to a full-fledged song-and-dance revue. Various night spots have stages; here are some of the most consistently entertaining.

Danny's Skylight Room (346 W. 46th St., tel. 212/265–8133). Danny's is housed in the Grand Sea Palace, a fixture on Restaurant Row. It offers a little bit of everything: jazz, crooners, ivory-tinklers, and monologuists.

Don't Tell Mama (343 W. 46th St., tel. 212/757–0788). At this convivial Theater District spot, composer-lyricist hopefuls show their stuff until 4 AM. Extroverts will be tempted by the open-mike policy of the piano bar in front.

The Duplex (61 Christopher St., tel. 212/255–5438). This long-time Village favorite has moved to great new digs on the corner of Sheridan Square. Catch a singing luminary-on-the-rise in the upstairs cabaret (with the best singing waitresses in town), or join the happy crowd downstairs for a Broadway sing-along.

Eighty-eight's (228 W. 10th St., tel. 212/924–0088). Come here to hear songs by the best of Broadway's tunesmiths (among other things) and inventively assembled programs.

55 Grove Street (near Christopher St. and 7th Ave. S, tel. 212/366–5438). You may see a Judy Garland impersonator sparring with an Ann Miller impersonator, or a mother-and-daughter team that decided all anyone needs to succeed in show business is nerve—but you'll also find good entertainment, as well.

Judy's (49 W. 44th St., tel. 212/764–8930). Located in the lobby of the Hotel Iroquois, this club is known for singing pianists in the Michael Feinstein mold.

Michael's Pub (211 E. 55th St., tel. 212/758–2272). Woody Allen often moonlights on the clarinet here on Monday nights. On other evenings, other fine performers such as Mel Tormé take the stage. The crowd is very monied, very uptown.

Steve McGraw's (158 W. 72nd St., tel. 212/595–7400). This West Side supper club and bar presents sophisticated comedy revues, such as *Forever Plaid*, which originated here.

West Bank Café (407 W. 42nd St., tel. 212/695–6909). In an attractive bistro-type restaurant across from Theatre Row, moonlighting musical-comedy triple threats (actor-singer-dancers) show off; on occasion, new plays are read.

Bars

While the health-club craze may have hit New York hard, there's little danger that Manhattanites will abandon their bars. Drinking establishments thrive and multiply, particularly in TriBeCa, where it appears bar design has become a minor art. The city's liquor laws allow bars to stay open until 4 AM, so it's easy to add on a watering stop at the end of an evening's merriment.

Vintage Classics

The Algonquin Hotel Lounge (59 W. 44th St., tel. 212/840–6800). This is a venerable spot, not only because it was the site of the fabled literary Round Table, but also for its elegant tone. A fabulous grandfather clock tolls the passing hours while noted writers still come and go—despite their chagrin at the nefarious takeover by businessmen who may not tend to the place as carefully as past hoteliers did. (*See also* The Oak Room in Putting on the Ritz, *above*).

Café des Artistes (1 W. 67th St., tel. 212/877–3500). This restaurant, as well known for its glorious Beaux Art murals as for its food (*see* Chapter 9), has a small, warm bar where interesting strangers tell their life stories and the house drink is pear champagne.

Elaine's (1703 2nd Ave., tel. 212/534–8103). The food's nothing special, and you will be relegated to an inferior table, but go to crane your neck and gawk. Woody Allen's favorite table is by the cappuccino machine. It's best to visit late, when the stars rise in Elaine's firmament.

The Four Seasons (99 E. 52nd St., tel. 212/754–9494). Miró tapestries greet you as you enter this power bar through the Grill Room (*see* Chapter 9). Watch for Kissingers and Trumps.

The Jockey Club (112 Central Park S, tel. 212/757–1900). Dressy and traditional, this is a slice of upper-crust New York in the lobby of the Ritz-Carlton. It's a very double-martini sort of place.

Journeys (at the Essex House Hotel, 160 Central Park S, tel. 212/247–0300). In the exquisitely revamped art deco–style Essex House, the bar is a surprise—pure English country style with rich carved wood, sporting scenes on the walls, and a roaring fire in the enormous fireplace.

King Cole Bar (at the St. Regis Hotel, 2 E. 55th St., tel. 212/753–4500.) The famed Maxwell Parrish mural is a welcome sight at this midtown landmark, happily open again following a thorough and sensitive restoration.

The Oak Bar (at the Plaza Hotel, 5th Ave. and 59th St., tel. 212/759–3000). With its plummy, dark-wood furnishings, this old favorite continues to age well. Its great location draws sophisticates, shoppers, tourists in the know, and stars.

Pen Top Lounge (at the Peninsula Hotel, 700 5th Ave., tel. 212/247–2200). Drinks are pricey, but the Manhattan views are jaw-dropping at this spectacular, glass-lined penthouse bar.

The River Café (1 Water St., Brooklyn, tel. 718/522–5200). An eminently romantic spot, hidden at the foot of the Brooklyn

Bridge, this restaurant offers smashing views of Wall Street and the East River.

Top of the Tower (3 Mitchell Pl., near 1st Ave. at 49th St., tel. 212/355–7300). There are other, higher hotel-top lounges, but this one on the 26th floor of the Beekman Tower Hotel still feels as if it's halfway to heaven. The atmosphere is elegant and subdued, with piano arpeggios in the background.

"21" Club (21 W. 52nd St., tel. 212/582–7200). Famous for its old-time club atmosphere even before it was filmed in *All About Eve*, this isn't exactly a swinging joint, but its conservative environs evoke a sense of connections, power, and prestige. It's tough to get in unless you plan to eat here, too (*see* Chapter 9).

Windows on the World (1 World Trade Center, tel. 212/938–1111). To borrow Cole Porter's words: "You're a Botticelli, you're Keats, you're Shelley . . . you're the top." Here, you'll be 107 stories up, drinking in your favorite poison and the outstanding view (*see* Chapter 9).

Drinking Spots Around Town

South of Houston Street

The Bridge Café (279 Water St., tel. 212/227–3344). This busy little restaurant flanks the Brooklyn Bridge, a hop, skip, and a jump from South Street Seaport. The bar is abridged, but between lunch and dinner you can pass a pleasant afternoon sipping a good selection of domestic wines at a table.

Broome Street Bar (363 W. Broadway at Broome St., tel. 212/925–2086). A classic hangout, this SoHo standard attracts artsy types on weekdays, tourists on weekends.

Ear Inn (326 Spring St., tel. 212/226–9060). There's nothing fancy here, though it inhabits an 1817 Federal house. It's the artsy crowd that makes the place, along with Saturday afternoon poetry readings—they call them "lunch for the ear."

Fanelli's (94 Prince St., tel. 212/226–9412). This is a casual SoHo neighborhood bar, where many come on Sundays with the fat *New York Times* under their arms. The food's good, too.

I Tre Merli (463 W. Broadway, tel. 212/254–8699). The sound of happy drinkers spills out of the massive doors of this wide, inviting restaurant-bar. Wine by the glass is a favorite here.

NoHo Star (330 Lafayette St. at Bleecker St., tel. 212/925–0070). The mood is casual at this with-it bar and diner, popular with locals and even families.

Raoul's (180 Prince St., tel. 212/966–3518). The decor is 1950s chic; the clientele, upscale downtown.

South Street Seaport (Water and Fulton Sts.) There's no dearth of drinking opportunities at this major New York attraction: **Gianni's, Harbor Lights,** and the **Liberty Café** are among them. On warm Friday evenings, the Seaport is transformed into a gigantic college mixer, where apprentice Wall Streeters go to meet others from the Ivy League.

The Sporting Club (99 Hudson St., tel. 212/219–0900). Lots of TV monitors here stay tuned to the evening's major sports event. Aficionados come in after punching out on Wall Street.

Spring Street Bar and Restaurant (162 Spring St., tel. 212/219–0157). At the heart of trendy SoHo, this spot possesses a sleek bar and attracts an artsy clientele.

Chelsea and the Village

America (9–13 E. 18th St., tel. 212/505–2110). Outside, a lone neon star tells you you've found the place. Inside, there's a vast and stunning skylit room, with an oval bar situated beyond and above the tables. Because American cuisine is celebrated here, you can get a late-night serving of Boston baked beans, Chicago-style pizza, and even peanut butter and jelly sandwiches, along with California wines and Milwaukee beers.

Caliente Cab Company (61 7th Ave. S, tel. 212/243–8517). The party never seems to stop at this roomy Tex-Mex restaurant-bar. You'll find pleasant outside seating and plenty of tequila.

Cedar Tavern (82 University Pl., tel. 212/243–9355). Here's a very informal, warm spot for a post-double-feature beer.

Chumley's (86 Bedford St., tel. 212/675–4449). There's no sign to help you find this place—they took it down during Chumley's speakeasy days—but when you reach the corner of Barrow Street, you're very close. A fireplace warms this relaxed spot where the burgers are hearty, and the kitchen stays open past 10 PM.

Coffee Shop (29 Union Square W, tel. 212/243–7969). A hip, 23-hour-a-day hangout from Tuesday through Saturday (closed 6–7 AM), the place lures funky types, beautiful-people-in-training, and a few aging locals who frequented the place when it was a real, pre–liquor license coffeeshop. (Open 20 hours Sunday and Monday; closed 3–7 AM.)

Downtown Beirut (158 1st Ave., tel. 212/777–9011). This electrified East Village hangout attracts artists and student types. When you hear the Animals blare "We Gotta Get Outta this Place" at astronomical decibels, you may agree.

McSorley's Old Ale House (15 E. 7th St., tel. 212/473–9148). One of New York's oldest saloons (opened in 1854), this place has its own satisfying label of ale available on draft. Weekend nights are boisterous; on Sunday afternoons McSorley's offers quaint surroundings for reading the paper and munching on a plate of the house specialty, onions and cheese.

Peter MacManus Café (152 7th Ave., tel. 212/929–9691). It's known simply as MacManus's to the regulars, who like this bar's unpretentiousness. Among them are lots of actors, fresh from classes in the neighborhood.

Metropolis Café (31 Union Sq. W, tel. 212/675–2300). Soaring ceilings and lots of white marble distinguish this pretty Yuppie drink palace—it's so pretty, in fact, that it's often used as a backdrop for movies and commercials.

Mr. Fuji's Tropicana (61 5th Ave., tel. 212/243–7900). This is where the beautiful people have been seen as of late, not just for that frenetic dancing on the mezzanine but also for the Asian-Cuban menu.

Old Town Bar and Restaurant (45 E. 18th St., tel. 212/473–8874). Tawdry and proudly unpretentious, with waiters' accents as thick as slush, this bar posts signs announcing "quiche not served here," and "the coffee is only four hours old." True to its name, the Old Town has been around since 1897, long before the trendy set discovered Chelsea.

Peculier Pub (145 Bleecker St., tel. 212/353–1327). Here, in the heart of the Village, you'll find 325 brands of beer, from Aass Amber to Zyweic.

Pete's Tavern (129 E. 18th St., tel. 212/473–7676). This saloon is famous as the place where O. Henry wrote "The Gift of the Magi" (at the second booth to the right as you come in). These days, it's ever crowded with noisy, friendly souls.

The White Horse Tavern (567 Hudson St., tel. 212/243–9260). Famous among the literati, this is the place where Dylan Thomas drained his last cup to the dregs. From April through October, there's outdoor café drinking.

Midtown and the Theater District

Barrymore's (267 W. 45th St., tel. 212/391–8400). This is a pleasantly downscale Theater District spot, with the requisite show posters on the wall. Listen in on the conversations at the bar and you'll hear a few tawdry, true stories of what goes on behind Broadway stage doors.

Café Un Deux Trois (123 W. 44th St., tel. 212/354–4148). This old hotel lobby, charmingly converted, is chicly peopled. The bar itself is small, but it's a hot spot after the theater.

Century Café (132 W. 43rd St., tel. 212/398–1988). An immense vintage neon sign lights up the bar at this trendy, friendly Theater-District bistro where you *won't* find the requisite show posters.

Charley O's (on Shubert Alley, between 44th and 45th Sts., tel. 212/840–2964). Its seemingly endless bar is conveniently located for quick intermission pit stops for those theaters near Shubert Alley.

Halcyon Bar (at the Rihga Royal Hotel, 151 W. 54th St., tel. 212/307–5000). A big, airy hotel bar, with large and well-spaced tables, it's great for a private chat.

Hard Rock Café (221 W. 57th St., tel. 212/459–9230). Formerly embraced by the kids of stars—now, in fact, its clientele seems eternally prepubescent kids accompanied by muttering parents who find it big, crowded, and far too noisy for talk.

Houlihan's (49th St. and 7th Ave., tel. 212/626–7312). Of the five such-named spots in town, this one's the best of them. Great happy hours attract a congenial, postcollege crowd. This is a safe bet for before- and after-showtime fare.

Joe Allen (326 W. 46th St., tel. 212/581–6464). At this old reliable on Restaurant Row celebrated in the musical version of *All About Eve*, everybody's en route to or from a show. Its walls offer a change of pace: The posters that adorn it are from Broadway musicals that quickly bombed.

The Landmark Tavern (626 11th Ave., tel. 212/757–8595). This aged redbrick pub (opened in 1868) is blessed by the glow of warming fireplaces on each of its three floors.

P.J. Clarke's (915 3rd Ave., tel. 212/759–1650). New York's most famous Irish bar, this establishment comes complete with the requisite mirrors and polished wood. Lots of after-workers like unwinding here, in a place that recalls the days of Tammany Hall.

Planet Hollywood (140 W. 57th St., tel. 212/333–7827). It's touristy, it doesn't take reservations, and waiting lines are long. Still, the place has cachet, an undeniable star quality, and such movie memorabilia as C3PO and Dorothy's red shoes, which make up for the very compact bar.

Sardi's (234 W. 44th St., tel. 212/221–8440). "The theater is certainly not what it was," croons a cat in *Cats*—and he could be referring to this venerable spot as well. Still, if you care for the theater, don't leave New York without visiting this establishment. Yes, this recently renovated landmark has beefed up its wine list and added "light" cuisine to its menu, but it continues to serve dishes that are all but extinct, amid its caricature-covered walls.

Top of the Sixes (666 5th Ave., tel. 212/757–6662). This bar has an impressive nighttime view, whether you view St. Patrick's Cathedral to the east or Central Park to the north, from 39 stories up above Fifth Avenue.

The Whiskey (at the Paramount Hotel, 235 W. 46th St., tel. 212/764–5500). A downstairs bar graces this chic, revamped Times Square hotel that's sleek and hip, and ideal après-theater. Also fun for evening drinks is the mezzanine lounge, pure Philippe Starck-meets-the-'40s. Wear black.

East Side   **Jim McMullen's** (1341 3rd Ave., tel. 212/861–4700). A young, quintessential Upper East Side watering hole, McMullen's has a large, busy bar decked with bouquets of fresh flowers. Here you'll find lots of Gold Cards, tennis talk, and alumni fund gathering.

La Famille (2017 5th Ave., tel. 212/722–9806). The cuisine is southern at this longtime Harlem favorite, where you'll find a warm drinking lounge downstairs.

Mark's Bar (at Mark Hotel, 25 E. 77th St., tel. 212/879–1864). This sleek East Side bar in a sleek East Side hotel attracts monied Europeans and—what else?—sleek East Siders.

The Polo Lounge (at the Westbury Hotel, 15 E. 69th St., tel. 212/439–4835). This place is, in a word, classy; it's frequented by European royalty and Knickerbocker New York.

The Water Club (500 E. 30th St., tel. 212/683–3333). Right on the East River, with a pleasing outside deck (you're not on a boat, but you'll somehow feel you are), this is a special-occasion kind of place—especially for those who've already been to all the special landlocked spots in town.

The Terrace (at the Hotel Inter-Continental, 111 E. 48th St., tel. 212/421–0836). A gilded, gargantuan birdcage greets you as you enter. To your left is a spacious lounge, called Bar 111, with a pianist reinforcing the sophisticated atmosphere.

West Side   **The Conservatory** (at the Mayflower Hotel, 15 Central Park W, tel. 212/581–1293). Furnished, perhaps, out of a Bloomingdale's window, this is reputedly the haunt of Hollywood movie barons in town to cut deals. Beyond all that, it's a pleasant, quiet place in which to talk and drink.

Dublin House (225 W. 79th St., tel. 212/874–9528). Above the door glows a small neon harp; inside you'll find lots of very young professionals, Columbia students, and softball teams throwing back two-bit drafts.

J. G. Melon (340 Amsterdam Ave., tel. 212/877–2220). A quiet corner pub at the intersection of 76th Street and Amsterdam, this spot has a small but comfortable bar and additional table space in the back room. The East Side branch is at 1291 Third Avenue (tel. 212/744–0585).

Lucy's Restaurant (503 Columbus Ave., tel. 212/787–3009). This southern California–Mex hangout is a hit with young Upper West Siders, who pack themselves into the bar area and sometimes even manage to dance. The decor is playful gulf beach hut.

Museum Café (366 Columbus Ave., tel. 212/799–0150). Trendy, overdesigned joints on Columbus Avenue come and go, but this one across from the American Museum of Natural History endures thanks to nice streetside windows and high, airy ceilings. Split a homemade pizza as you drink.

O'Neal's Lincoln Center (49 W. 64th St., tel. 212/787–4663). Mike O'Neal, the owner of the beloved but now defunct Ginger Man, has moved the bar from that establishment down the street and created a series of rooms (one with a fireplace) serving good pub food.

The Saloon (1920 Broadway, tel. 212/874–1500). The menu goes on and on; the bar is large and informal; and the waitresses and waiters cruise around on roller skates. It may be gimmicky, but the spirit of fun is infectious.

Gay Bars

Cleo's 9th Avenue Saloon (656 9th Ave., tel. 212/307–1503). Near the Theater District, this small, narrow neighborhood bar draws a convivial, laid-back older crowd.

Crazy Nanny (21 7th Ave. S, tel. 212/366–6312). This women's bar is small, but that doesn't discourage the die-hard jukebox dancers.

Crowbar (339 E. 10th St., tel. 212/420–0670). Gay grungers and college students mingle happily at this East Village hot spot.

Henrietta Hudson (438 Hudson St., tel. 212/243–9879). A jukebox and video screens attract an extremely enthusiastic crowd of fun-loving women.

Julius (159 W. 10th St., tel. 212/929–9672). Warm, friendly, and low-key, Julius was one of the first bars on the gay scene. The crowd's a little older and wiser now, but the place still offers respite from more frenetic atmospheres.

Marie's Crisis (59 Grove St., tel. 212/243–9323). You've got to love it for its name, and for its ecstatic piano sing-alongs— everybody seems to know all the words to Stephen Sondheim's musical *Assassins*.

The Monster (80 Grove St., tel. 212/924–3557). Upstairs there's a piano bar, and downstairs there's a disco; both have their wildly loyal adherents.

Splash (50 W. 17th St., tel. 212/691–0073). There's no dancing—for the customers, anyway. But there's plenty to watch, what with the video monitors and the transluscent glass blocks showing scantily clad (but nevertheless clad) men taking showers while you while the night away. Yuppies are prevalant.

Stonewall (53 Christopher St., tel. 212/463–0950). Though this bar is on the actual site of the famous June 1969 birth of gay liberation (a plaque on the outside commemorates the event), it is a rebuilt and reconceived (albeit comfortable) version of the original establishment.

Uncle Charlie's Downtown (56 Greenwich Ave., tel. 212/255–8787). This extremely popular Village gay bar attracts stylish young men and distinguished-looking professionals.

The Works (428 Columbus Ave., tel. 212/799–7365). Great drink specials and a clean-cut, friendly crowd have been known to draw droves of downtown boys up to this Upper West Side institution. Its darker sister bar, **The Break** (232 8th Ave., tel. 212/627–0072) packs them in in Chelsea.

Index

Fodor's has your guide to New York!

WHEREVER YOU TRAVEL, *ℋ*ELP IS NEVER FAR AWAY.

From planning your trip to replacing
lost Cards, American Express® Travel Service
Offices* are always there to help.

American Express Tower
World Financial Center
212-640-5130

150 E. 42nd Street
212-687-3700

65 Broadway
212-493-6500

New York Hilton Hotel
212-664-7798

199 Water Street
South Street Seaport
212-943-6947

374 Park Avenue
212-421-8240

One World Trade Center
212-775-0370

Bloomingdale's
212-705-3171

Marriott Marquis Hotel
212-575-6580

822 Lexington Avenue
212-758-6510

JFK International Airport
Main Lobby, International
Arrivals Bldg. 718-656-5673

American Express Travel Service Offices are also found in
central locations throughout New York City and Suburbs.

INTRODUCING

At last, your own personalized list of what's going on in the cities you're visiting.

Keyed to the days when you're there, customized for your interests, and sent to you before you leave home.

Exclusive for purchasers of Fodor's Guides...

Fodor's
WORLDVIEW
TRAVEL UPDATE

Introducing a revolutionary way to get customized, time-sensitive travel information just before your trip.

Now you can obtain detailed information about what's going on in each city you'll be visiting <u>before</u> you leave home—up-to-the-minute, objective information about the events and activities that interest you most.

This is a special offer for purchasers of Fodor's guides – a customized Travel Update to fit your specific interests and your itinerary.

Travel Updates contain the kind of time-sensitive insider information you can get only from local contacts – or from city magazines and newspapers once you arrive. But now you can have the same information before you leave for your trip.

The choice is yours: current art exhibits, theater, music festivals and special concerts, sporting events, antiques and flower shows, shopping, fitness, and more.

The information comes from hundreds of correspondents and thousands of sources worldwide. Updated continuously, it's like having your own personal concierge or friend in the city.

You specify the cities and when you'll be there. We'll do the rest — personalizing the information for you the way no guidebook can.

It's the perfect extension to your Fodor's guide and the best way to make the most of your valuable travel time.

Your Itinerary:
Customized reports available for 160 destinations

a
tou
9902
Regent's
The ann
in this a
domain of
tion as Joe
worthwhile. I
the performanc
Tickets are usuall
venue. Alternate
mances are cancelle
given. For more infor
Open-Air Theatre, Inner
NW1 4NP Open Air Th
Tel: 935-5756. Ends: 9-11-9
International Air Tattoo
Held biennially, the world'
military air display i
d e m o s t r a -
tions, mili
band

June 1

Fodor's/Worldview presents a Travel Update for:

Mr. Gavin Lynch
201 East 50th Street
New York, New York, 10022

Fodor's
WORLDVIEW

LONDON, UK

ARRIVE 23 Jun DEPART: 21 Jul

HIGHLIGHTS—EVENTS

Wimbledon Lawn Tennis Championships

Seats for the Wimbledon championships, especiall
those for the men's and women's finals on the
Centre Court, are the hottest tickets in Lon
summer. Each winter there is a ballo
and No. 1 Court seats for the foll
nament. Through this ballot, te
ve chance of securing a ticket, te
s for top matches are included
combining hotel accommodatio
s available from the tournam
attor, NAA Events Internatio
7/04.

Open Air Theatre Season

ason of open-air theater produ
and lovely park, once the
cy dandies, is as much of an
Broadway in the Park and e
se to bring your largest unbre
often interrupted by showe
ilable for the almost 1,200-sea
s are offered when perfor-
to rain, but refunds are not
, contact Sheila Benjam
Regent's Park
Regent'

Ordering is easy.

You can order a Travel Update up to three months before you leave. Of course, the closer to your trip that you order, the more current the information.

You'll find a handy order form at the end of this eight-page section. Choose your destinations and interest categories from the lists included, fill out all sections of the order form and mail or fax it back to us.

Or if you prefer, you can call us toll-free. We'll send you a full, personalized report, similar to the samples shown here, within 48 hours of receipt of your completed order.

**Special concerts—
who's performing
what and where**

**One-of-a-kind,
one-time-only events**

**Special interest,
in-depth listings**

Children — Events
Angel Canal Festival
The festivities include a children's funfair, entertainers, a boat rally and displays on the water. Regent's Canal. Islington. N1. Tube: Angel. Tel: 267 9100. 11:30am-5:30pm. 7/04.

Blackheath Summer Kite Festival
Stunt kite displays with parachuting teddy bears and trade stands. Free admission. SE3. BR: Blackheath. 10am. 6/27.

Megabugs
Children will delight in this infestation of giant robotic insects, including a praying mantic 60 times life size. Mon-Sat 10am-6pm; Sun 11am-6pm. Admission 4.50 pounds. Natural History Museum, Cromwell Road. SW7. Tube: South Kensington. Tel: 938 9123. Ends 10/01.

Childminders
This establishment employs only women, providing nurses and qualified nannies to

Music — Jazz & Blues
Tito Puente's Golden Men of Latin Jazz
The father of mambo and Cuban rumba king comes to town. Royal Festival Hall. South Bank. SE1. Tube: Waterloo. Tel: 928 8800. 8pm. 7/15.

Georgie Fame and The New York Band
Riding a popular tide with his latest album, the smoky-voiced Fame and his keyboard are on a tour yet again. The Grand. Clapham Junction. SW11. BR: Clapham Junction. Tel: 738 9000. 7:30pm. 7/07.

Jacques Loussier Play Bach Trio
The French jazz classicist and colleagues. Kenwood Lakeside. Hampstead Lane. Kenwood. NW3. Tube: Golders Green, then bus 210. Tel: 413 1443. 7pm. 7/10.

Tony Bennett and Ronnie Scott
Royal Festival Hall. South Bank. SE1. Tube: Waterloo. Tel: 928 8800. 8pm. 7/11.

Santana
Royal Festival Hall. South Bank. SE1. Tube: Waterloo. Tel: 928 8800. 8pm. 7/12.

Count Basie Orchestra and Nancy Wilson Trio
Royal Festival Hall. South Bank. SE1. Tube: Waterloo. Tel: 928 8800. 8pm. 7/14.

King Pleasure and the Biscuit Boys
Royal Festival Hall. South Bank. SE1. Tube: Waterloo. Tel: 928 8800. 6:30 and 9pm. 7/16.

Al Green and the London Community Gospel Choir
Royal Festival Hall. South Bank. SE1. Tube: Waterloo. Tel: 928 8800. 8pm. 7/13.

BB King and Linda Hopkins
Mother of the blues and successor to Bessie Smith, Hopkins meets up with "Blues Boy" ... al Hall. South Bank. SE

Music — Classical
Marylebone Sinfonia
Kenneth Gowen conducts music by Puccini and Rossini. Queen Elizabeth Hall. South Bank. SE1. Tube: Waterloo. Tel: 928 8800. 7:45pm. 7/16.

London Philharmonic
Franz Welser-Moest and George Benjamin conduct selections by Alexander Goehr, Messiaen, and some of Benjamin's own compositions. Queen Elizabeth Hall. South Bank. SE1. Tube: Waterloo. Tel: 928 8800. 8pm.

London Pro Arte Orchestra and Forest Choir
Murray Stewart conducts selections by Rossini, Haydn and Jonathan Willcocks. Queen Elizabeth Hall. South Bank. SE Tube: Waterloo. Tel: 928 8800. 7:45pm. 7/1

Kensington Symphony Orchestra
Russell Keable conducts Dvorak's Dmit

Here's what you get . . .

Detailed information about what's going on — precisely when you'll be there.

Show openings during your visit

Reviews by local critics

Exhibitions & Shows—Antique & Flower

Westminster Antiques Fair
Over 50 stands with pre-1830 furniture and other Victorian and earlier items. Thu-Fri 11am-8pm; Sat-Sun 11am-6pm. Admission 4 pounds, children free. Old Royal Horticultural Hall. Vincent Square. SW1. Tel: 0444/48 25 14. 6-24 thru 6/27.

Royal Horticultural Society Flower Show
The show includes displays of carnations, summer fruit and vegetables. Tue 11am-7pm; Wed 10am-5pm. Admission Tue 4 pounds, Wed 2 pounds. Royal Horticultural Halls. Greycoat Street and Vincent Square. SW1. Tube: Victoria. 7/20 thru 7/21.

mpton Court Palace International Flower Show
Major international garden and flower show king place in conjunction with the British

Theater — Musical

Sunset Boulevard
In June, the four Andrew Lloyd Webber musicals which dominated London's stages in the 1980s (Cats, Starlight Express, Phantom of the Opera and Aspects of Love) are joined by the composer's latest work, a show rumored to have his best music to date. The 1950 Billy Wilder film about a helpless young writer who is drawn into the world of a possessive, aging silent screen star offers rich opportunities for Webber's evolving style. Soaring, aching melodies, lush technical effects and psychological thrills are all expected. Patti Lupone stars. Mon-Sat at 8pm; matinee Thu-Sat at 3pm. In-person sales only at the box office; credit card bookings, Tel: 344 0055. Admission 15-32.50 pounds. Adelphi Theatre. The Strand. WC2. Tube: Charing Cross. Tel: 836 7611. Starts: 6/21

Leonardo A Portrait of Love
A new musical about the great Renaissance arti and inventor comes in for a London premier tested by a brief run at Oxford's Old Fire Stati autumn. The work explores the relations Vinci and the woman '

Alberquerque • Atlanta • Atlantic City • Ne
Baltimore • Boston • Chicago • Cincinnati
Cleveland • Dallas/Ft.Worth • Denver • De
• Houston • Kansas City • Las Vegas • Los
Angeles • Memphis • Miami • Milwaukee
New Orleans • New York City • Orlando •
Springs • Philadelphia • Phoenix • Pittsburg
Portland • Salt Lake • San Antonio • San Di
• San Franc • Seattle • St. Louis • Tamp
Oslo • Wash • lu • Island
Hawaii • Kauai • Maui • Abacos • Bimini
Ber • Countryside • Hamilton • Islan
Antigua & B • Villa

Spectator Sports — Other Sports

Greyhound Racing: Wembley Stadium
This dog track offers good views of greyhound racing held on Mon, Wed and Fri. No credit cards. Stadium Way. Wembley. HA9. Tube: Wembley Park. Tel: 902 8833.

Benson & Hedges Cricket Cup Final
Lord's Cricket Ground. St. John's Wood Road. NW8. Tube: St. John's Wood. Tel: 289 1611. 11am. 7/10.

Business-Fax & Overnight Mail

Post Office, Trafalgar Square Branch
Offers a network of fax services, the Intelpost system, throughout the country and abroad. Mon-Sat 8am-8pm, Sun 9am-5pm. William IV Street. WC2. Tube: Charing Cross. Tel: 930

Gorda • Barbados • Dominica • Torto
acia • St. Vincent • Trinidad &Tobago
ymans • Puerto Plata • Santo Doming
Aruba • Bonaire • Curacao • St. Mar
ec City • Montreal • Ottawa • Toron
ancouver • Guadeloupe • Martiniqu
elemy • St. Martin • Kingston • Ixta
o Bay • Negril • Ocho Rios • Ponce
n • Grand Turk • Providenciales • S
St. John • St. Thomas • Acapulco •
& Isla Mujeres • Cozumel • Guadal
a • Los Cabos • Manzanillo • Mazatl
City • Monterrey • Oaxaca • Puerto
do • Puerto Vallarta • Veracruz • V
dam • Athens • R

Fodor's WORLDVIEW
TRAVEL UPDATE

Interest Categories

For <u>your</u> personalized Travel Update, choose the categories you're most interested in from this list. Every Travel Update automatically provides you with *Event Highlights* – the best of what's happening during the dates of your trip.

1.	**Business Services**	Fax & Overnight Mail, Computer Rentals, Photocopying, Secretarial , Messenger, Translation Services
	Dining	
2.	**All Day Dining**	Breakfast & Brunch, Cafes & Tea Rooms, Late-Night Dining
3.	**Local Cuisine**	In Every Price Range—from Budget Restaurants to the Special Splurge
4.	**European Cuisine**	Continental, French, Italian
5.	**Asian Cuisine**	Chinese, Far Eastern, Japanese, Indian
6.	**Americas Cuisine**	American, Mexican & Latin
7.	**Nightlife**	Bars, Dance Clubs, Comedy Clubs, Pubs & Beer Halls
8.	**Entertainment**	Theater—Drama, Musicals, Dance, Ticket Agencies
9.	**Music**	Classical, Traditional & Ethnic, Jazz & Blues, Pop, Rock
10.	**Children's Activities**	Events, Attractions
11.	**Tours**	Local Tours, Day Trips, Overnight Excursions, Cruises
12.	**Exhibitions, Festivals & Shows**	Antiques & Flower, History & Cultural, Art Exhibitions, Fairs & Craft Shows, Music & Art Festivals
13.	**Shopping**	Districts & Malls, Markets, Regional Specialities
14.	**Fitness**	Bicycling, Health Clubs, Hiking, Jogging
15.	**Recreational Sports**	Boating/Sailing, Fishing, Ice Skating, Skiing, Snorkeling/Scuba, Swimming
16.	**Spectator Sports**	Auto Racing, Baseball, Basketball, Football, Horse Racing, Ice Hockey, Soccer

Please note that interest category content will vary by season, destination, and length of stay.

Destinations

The Fodor's/Worldview Travel Update covers more than 160 destinations worldwide. Choose the destinations that match your itinerary from this list. (Choose bulleted destinations only.)

United States (Mainland)
- Albuquerque
- Atlanta
- Atlantic City
- Baltimore
- Boston
- Chicago
- Cincinnati
- Cleveland
- Dallas/Ft. Worth
- Denver
- Detroit
- Houston
- Kansas City
- Las Vegas
- Los Angeles
- Memphis
- Miami
- Milwaukee
- Minneapolis/ St. Paul
- New Orleans
- New York City
- Orlando
- Palm Springs
- Philadelphia
- Phoenix
- Pittsburgh
- Portland
- St. Louis
- Salt Lake City
- San Antonio
- San Diego
- San Francisco
- Seattle
- Tampa
- Washington, DC

Alaska
- Anchorage/Fair- banks/Juneau

Hawaii
- Honolulu
- Island of Hawaii
- Kauai
- Maui

Canada
- Quebec City
- Montreal
- Ottawa
- Toronto
- Vancouver

Bahamas
- Abacos
- Eleuthera/ Harbour Island
- Exumas
- Freeport
- Nassau & Paradise Island

Bermuda
- Bermuda Countryside
- Hamilton

British Leeward Islands
- Anguilla
- Antigua & Barbuda
- Montserrat
- St. Kitts & Nevis

British Virgin Islands
- Tortola & Virgin Gorda

British Windward Islands
- Barbados
- Dominica
- Grenada
- St. Lucia
- St. Vincent
- Trinidad & Tobago

Cayman Islands
- The Caymans

Dominican Republic
- Puerto Plata
- Santo Domingo

Dutch Leeward Islands
- Aruba
- Bonaire
- Curacao

Dutch Windward Islands
- St. Maarten

French West Indies
- Guadeloupe
- Martinique
- St. Barthelemy
- St. Martin

Jamaica
- Kingston
- Montego Bay
- Negril
- Ocho Rios

Puerto Rico
- Ponce
- San Juan

Turks & Caicos
- Grand Turk
- Providenciales

U.S. Virgin Islands
- St. Croix
- St. John
- St. Thomas

Mexico
- Acapulco
- Cancun & Isla Mujeres
- Cozumel
- Guadalajara
- Ixtapa & Zihuatanejo
- Los Cabos
- Manzanillo
- Mazatlan
- Mexico City
- Monterrey
- Oaxaca
- Puerto Escondido
- Puerto Vallarta
- Veracruz

Europe
- Amsterdam
- Athens
- Barcelona
- Berlin
- Brussels
- Budapest
- Copenhagen
- Dublin
- Edinburgh
- Florence
- Frankfurt
- French Riviera
- Geneva
- Glasgow
- Interlaken
- Istanbul
- Lausanne
- Lisbon
- London
- Madrid
- Milan
- Moscow
- Munich
- Oslo
- Paris
- Prague
- Provence
- Rome
- Salzburg
- St. Petersburg
- Stockholm
- Venice
- Vienna
- Zurich

Pacific Rim Australia & New Zealand
- Auckland
- Melbourne
- Sydney

China
- Beijing
- Guangzhou
- Shanghai

Japan
- Kyoto
- Nagoya
- Osaka
- Tokyo
- Yokohama

Other
- Bangkok
- Hong Kong & Macau
- Manila
- Seoul
- Singapore
- Taipei

Fodor's WORLDVIEW **Order Form**

THIS TRAVEL UPDATE IS FOR (Please print):

Name		
Address		
City	**State**	**ZIP**
Country	**Tel #** ( ) -

Title of this Fodor's guide:

Store and location where guide was purchased:

INDICATE YOUR DESTINATIONS/DATES: Write in below the destinations you want to order. Then fill in your arrival and departure dates for each destination.

		Month	Day		Month	Day
(Sample) LONDON	From:	6 /	21	To:	6 /	30
1	From:	/		To:	/	
2	From:	/		To:	/	
3	From:	/		To:	/	

You can order up to three destinations per Travel Update. Only destinations listed on the previous page are applicable. Maximum amount of time covered by a Travel Update cannot exceed 30 days.

CHOOSE YOUR INTERESTS: Select up to eight categories from the list of interest categories shown on the previous page and circle the numbers below:

1 2 3 4 5 6 7 8 9 10 11 12 13 14 15 16

CHOOSE HOW YOU WANT YOUR TRAVEL UPDATE DELIVERED (Check one):

❏ Please mail my Travel Update to the address above **OR**

❏ Fax it to me at **Fax #** ( ) -

DELIVERY CHARGE (Check one)

	Within U.S. & Canada	Outside U.S. & Canada
First Class Mail	❏ $2.50	❏ $5.00
Fax	❏ $5.00	❏ $10.00
Priority Delivery	❏ $15.00	❏ $27.00

All orders will be sent within 48 hours of receipt of a completed order form.

ADD UP YOUR ORDER HERE. *SPECIAL OFFER FOR FODOR'S PURCHASERS ONLY!*

	Suggested Retail Price	Your Price	This Order
First destination ordered	$13.95	$ 7.95	$ 7.95
Second destination (if applicable)	$ 9.95	$ 4.95	+
Third destination (if applicable)	$ 9.95	$ 4.95	+
Plus delivery charge from above			+
		TOTAL:	$

METHOD OF PAYMENT (Check one): ❏ AmEx ❏ MC ❏ Visa ❏ Discover
❏ Personal Check ❏ Money Order

Make check or money order payable to: Fodor's Worldview Travel Update

Credit Card #   **Expiration Date:**

Authorized Signature

SEND THIS COMPLETED FORM TO:
Fodor's Worldview Travel Update, 114 Sansome Street, Suite 700, San Francisco, CA 94104

OR CALL OR FAX US 24-HOURS A DAY
Telephone **1-800-799-9609** • Fax **1-800-799-9619** (From within the U.S. & Canada)
(Outside the U.S. & Canada: Telephone 415-616-9988 • Fax 415-616-9989)

(Please have this guide in front of you when you call so we can verify purchase.)

Offer valid until 12/31/94.